The Enemy in Our Hands

THE ENEMY IN OUR HANDS

America's Treatment of Enemy Prisoners of War from the Revolution to the War on Terror

ROBERT C. DOYLE

THE UNIVERSITY PRESS OF KENTUCKY

Copyright © 2010 by The University Press of Kentucky

Scholarly publisher for the Commonwealth,
serving Bellarmine University, Berea College, Centre
College of Kentucky, Eastern Kentucky University,
The Filson Historical Society, Georgetown College,
Kentucky Historical Society, Kentucky State University,
Morehead State University, Murray State University,
Northern Kentucky University, Transylvania University,
University of Kentucky, University of Louisville,
and Western Kentucky University.
All rights reserved.

Editorial and Sales Offices: The University Press of Kentucky
663 South Limestone Street, Lexington, Kentucky 40508-4008
www.kentuckypress.com

14 13 12 11 10   5 4 3 2

Library of Congress Cataloging-in-Publication Data
Doyle, Robert C.
  The enemy in our hands : America's treatment of enemy prisoners of war
from the Revolution to the War on Terror / Robert C. Doyle.
      p. cm.
  Includes bibliographical references and index.
  ISBN 978-0-8131-2589-3 (hardcover : alk. paper)
  1. Prisoners of war—United States—History. 2. Prisoners of war—
Government policy—United States—History. 3. United States—
History, Military. I. Title.
  UB803.D689 2010
  355.1'2960973—dc22
                                        2009046402

This book is printed on acid-free recycled paper meeting
the requirements of the American National Standard
for Permanence in Paper for Printed Library Materials.

Manufactured in the United States of America.

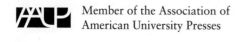   Member of the Association of
American University Presses

To Stanley and Rodelle Weintraub,
distinguished authors, scholars, friends,
mentors, and always an inspiration.

Contents

Foreword by Arnold Krammer   ix

Preface   xi

Acknowledgments   xix

Introduction: The Enemy: Imposing the Condition of Captivity   1

1. Prisoners of Independence: British and Hessian Enemy Prisoners of War   11

2. Habeas Corpus: War against Loyalists and Quakers   32

3. The Second American Revolution: Cartel and Enemy Prisoners of the War of 1812   49

4. Manifest Destiny versus Nativism: Mexico, 1846–1848   69

5. Prisoners of Politics: A Very Uncivil War   89

6. Indians as POWs in America: From Discovery to 1914   113

7. Spaniards and *Insurrectos*: Spanish-American War (1898) and War in the Philippines (1899–1905)   136

8. Over There and Over Here: Enemy Prisoners of War and Prisoners of State in the Great War   159

9. *Pensionierte Wehrmacht*: German and Italian POWs and Internees in the United States   179

10. The Reborn: Japanese Soldiers as Enemy Prisoners of War and American Nisei Internees   202

11. After the Victory: Optimism, Justice, or Vengeance?   223

12. Prisoners at War: Forced Repatriation and the Prison Revolts in Korea   247

13. Vietnam Quagmire: Enemy Prisoners of War, Phoenix, and the Vietcong Infrastructure   269

14. To Desert Storm and Beyond: Enemy Prisoners of War and the Conflict of Rules   292

Contents

15. Iraqi Freedom, Abu Ghraib, and Guantánamo: The
    Problem of the Moral High Ground   310

16. The Evolution of New Paradigms: Reflections on the
    Past, Present, and Future   334

APPENDIXES

1. Loyalist Units Organized in the American Revolution   351
2. Cartel for the Exchange of POWs in the War of 1812   351
3. Confederate and Union POW Camps   359
4. General Order 207: Instructions for the Government of
   Armies of the United States   361
5. Andersonville Deaths, 1864–1865   362
6. Hague Convention Ratified by the United States,
   3 December 1909   363
7. German Prisoners Captured by U.S. Divisions, 1917–1918   366
8. Executive Order 9066   366
9. World War II Trials of U.S. Personnel   368
10. Nuremberg Principles, 1946   368
11. Geneva Convention, 1949   369
12. U.S. Code of Conduct, 1954   360

Notes   371
Bibliography   415
Index   439

Foreword

Winston Churchill said it best: "A prisoner of war is a man who tries to kill you and fails, and then asks you not to kill him."* That is the precise situation prisoners have faced in every war: how can one survive capture when killing is the goal?

Since biblical times the fate of prisoners of war has been precarious. Ernst Jünger, a former German officer who was wounded and decorated countless times in front-line action during World War I, describes the dangers involved in the moment of capture: "The defending force, after driving their bullets into the attacking one at five paces' distance, must take the consequences. A man cannot change his feelings again during the last rush with a veil of blood before his eyes. He does not want to take prisoners but to kill. He has no scruples left; only the spell of primeval instinct remains. It is not till blood has flowed that the mist gives way to his soul."†

The first moments after capture are breathtakingly dangerous. The prisoner's life depends on a host of variables. Captives who fall into the hands of religious zealots or are the victims of ethnic cleansing have little chance of survival; indeed, the safety of a captive might hinge on such minor factors as whether the soldier who captures him recently lost buddies in the war or is short-tempered due to fighting in the rain or cold. Sometimes prisoners have been killed simply because they were too cumbersome to take along. Every conflict in recorded time has witnessed the mistreatment of prisoners of war.

Perhaps the most important determinant of the treatment of prisoners is the attitude or personality of the enemy. In short, how do the captors feel about their prisoners? Some armies, such as the Japanese, Soviets, and Germans in World War II, found them subhuman and treated them harshly; others, such as the German and British airmen

---

* Quoted in the *Observer,* 1952.

† Ernst Jünger, *The Storm of Steel: From the Diary of a German Storm-Troop Officer on the Western Front* (New York: Howard Fertig, 1975), 262–63.

in World War I, treated each other with cavalier equality. The key, of course, lies in the views of the political or military leaders of the captors, since their attitudes are translated into action at the lower levels. If a high-ranking officer or a political leader tolerates or encourages brutality toward prisoners of war, an atmosphere of intolerance can rapidly permeate the ranks, and the odds of prisoners' survival may drop precipitously.

The United States brings a particular perspective to the treatment of prisoners. According to its most elemental statements regarding the rule of law and the value of the individual, America bears a special responsibility to live up to its creed and ensure the humane treatment of captives. It has become a foundation of American values, certainly since the Geneva Convention of 1929. But it has not always been so. America's treatment of prisoners has varied widely, and the picture is often uncomfortable.

It has taken a masterful historian like Robert Doyle to evaluate the numerous forces at work and reveal, for the first time, the range of results. This study goes further. It unflinchingly examines the treatment of prisoners of war in American conflicts—a significant contribution to American military history, to the study of war, and perhaps to an understanding of national attitudes about the value of the individual.

—ARNOLD KRAMMER
Texas A&M University
College Station, Texas

Preface

Like many others before me, I spent a short time in the throes of combat and the rest of my life thinking and writing about it. Joseph Plumb Martin and Johann Conrad Döhla (Hessian) after the Revolution; Ambrose Bierce and Sidney Lanier after the Civil War, James Norman Hall and Ernest Hemingway after World War I; and James Clavell (British), Pierre Boulle (French), Alfred Andersch and Heinrich Böll (German), and David Westheimer and Kurt Vonnegut Jr. after World War II left written works that call to mind their experiences in combat. Others such as Stanley Weintraub after Korea, W. D. Ehrhart after Vietnam, and writers after more recent conflicts have followed in their footsteps. As a culture historian, I learned that war's violence has an insatiable appetite for minutiae, and the proverb "The devil lies in the details" is nowhere more applicable. There is no lack of recorded statistics for modern wars, but as Stanley Weintraub's *Last Great Victory* (1995) and *Long Day's Journey into War* (1991) show very clearly, war is human and often mysterious, and details often lie well hidden from prominent view.

Because these details form individually perceptive truths burned into the human memory, there is no lack of paradox and controversy. As I sifted through Civil War records held at the former site of Andersonville, the horrid Confederate prison camp in Georgia that set the standard for inhumanity in America during the summer of 1864, I realized why former Union prisoners of war (POWs) wanted compensation from the federal government for their injuries. In order to receive a few dollars a month (not much, really), the government asked each man to write his narrative. Many supplied photographs of themselves as visual evidence of their incarceration because they feared they would not be believed. I imagined the sound of their voices as I read their applications for compensation. Knowing that each handwritten document represented the experience of real suffering, my impartial historical sense weakened and gave way to human feelings of compassion, shock, and horror. I forgot about time; I was in Andersonville.

Not far from Andersonville, now a national historic site dedicated to the memory of all American POWs, I managed to leap more than a century forward when I sat for a day and interviewed Carl Nash (now deceased) at his home in Harlem, Georgia. Carl, a ground soldier who was captured in the Philippines in 1942, marched with thousands of others on Bataan, spent three years as a prisoner of the Imperial Japanese Army, and lived to bear witness to his experience. As Carl and I talked, my mind wandered to a bus ride I had taken as a very young, newly minted naval officer in the Philippines in 1968, one that retraced the path of the Bataan Death March. It was August then. I remembered the road signs that resembled the Stations of the Cross, and the island of Luzon was hot beyond imagination. When Carl spoke of capture and torture on Bataan, he knew what he was talking about:

We surrendered on the ninth of April and the death march began the next day. And they searched us before we took off. The Japanese were moving into Bataan as we were marching north on the main highway which was gravel. Their trucks were loaded with celebrating Japanese swinging rifle butts, hitting guys now and then. One guy in particular had his skull cracked; he laid there, and they wouldn't let us move him, and all the vehicles that were in around toward Bataan, ran over his body. The next day there were shots being fired in front of us and behind us, and one or two in our group—these were guys that fell out with malaria or dysentery, which they were getting a lot of about that time—they were either bayoneted or shot, [that is] everybody that fell out. Some guys tried to help others, hold them up and drag them along. That went on day after day it seemed. They fed us once, a mess kit of rice. We stopped at a mule barn to spend the night, and when we took a break we would sit down in the hot sun right where they had us, right where we were marching, and they'd let us do it about noon. After about five or six days of this—it must have been 700 or 800 murdered along the way, in different ways—one of them we ran across was in a little small village. There was a chinning bar with one of our boys tied by his wrists to the chinning bar, and a Jap was digging out from under his feet. His toes were allowed to touch the ground and that was all. Then the Jap dug out from under him. They let him hang there. I don't know, we kept going, I don't know whether they released him or not, I don't know what they did with him. And that's the bad part about the whole thing; no next of kin will ever know some of the circumstances that surrounded these boys' deaths.[1]

My mind wandered again, this time to the experiences of Giles Norrington, a prisoner in a different war who lived through a much longer captivity than Carl's. Giles spent five years in a North Vietnamese prison and learned to endure the perils of captivity much as Carl had:

> In my own experience as a POW for nearly five years in northern Vietnam, my personal values were put to the test. In most cases, they were adequate, although sometimes my philosophical tools were in need of sharpening. However, on rarer occasions, dearly held values had to be abandoned altogether, and new visions, ideas, and ideals had to be forged and tempered. It was in these latter circumstances that I, and those who served similarly with and before me, experienced real growth as human beings.[2]

In each of these experiences, one with written documents and two with living informants, I discovered that chronological time melted into a kind of timeless universal experience of suffering behind barbed wire. Arthur M. Schlesinger Jr. was correct: "History is to the nation as memory is to the individual"[3]

My first book, *Voices from Captivity: Interpreting the American POW Narrative* (1994), tackled the captivity experience in general through the eyes and writings of POWs themselves. Based on these recollections, combined with official documents, I discovered that there is a series of event scenarios that most prisoners suffer and write about. First, we are told of their *precapture world,* always a pleasant time bound up in their home lives, loved ones, education, and duty station, whenever and wherever it was. *Capture* is always a shock. Soldiers, it seems, are prepared for death on the battlefield, but they are seldom ready to surrender to the enemy. Then as prisoners they set out on the journey into darkness, the *long march* to some kind of POW facility—a prison camp, a jail or dungeon, sometimes a prison hulk—depending on the war, its circumstances, and what rules are in force at the time. Prisoners then become ethnologists, in that they describe the *prison landscape* with accuracy and usually with fury as their memories purge their painful existence behind the wire. As the POWs try to find some way to survive all this, various *pathways to freedom* rise to the surface. Some escape; others attempt to become anonymous; a few cooperate with their captors to varying degrees, and a mere handful turn their coats. When wars come to an end, POWs are repatriated home. Along with this joy, POWs often look back and try to make sense of what happened to them. They know instinctively that wars are won or lost in spite of them, not because of them, and in their writings they often *lament* what the experience cost them. Sometimes they analyze the experience in terms of personal gain, but more often it comes as personal loss.

No book can answer all the questions one has, and in the midst of researching and writing *Voices from Captivity,* the issues of escape, evasion, and survival captured my attention. Who were these escapers? Why did they escape? How did they go over, under, around, or through their captors' restraints? I addressed these questions in my second book, *A Prisoner's Duty: Great Escapes in U.S. Military History* (1997). I confess that the escapers became my heroes, but I soon discovered that they escaped for various reasons, not all of them heroic. I did discover a doctrine or principle of *intolerable cruelty:* that is, normal people, when they understand that death and only death faces them squarely, can and will take extraordinary measures to save their own lives. A good example is a Swiss girl who lived in Pennsylvania during the early years of the French and Indian War. Captured in 1755 and taken west to Ohio, Barbara Leininger witnessed several acts of intolerable cruelty inflicted by her Indian captors on fellow captives and committed herself to escape. She wrote in 1759:

> It is easy to imagine what an impression such fearful instances of cruelty make upon the mind of a poor captive. Does he attempt to escape from the savages [when] he knows in advance that, if retaken, he will be roasted alive. Hence he must compare two evils, namely, either to remain among them a prisoner forever, or die a cruel death. If he fully resolves to endure the latter, then he may run away with a brave heart.[4]

Along with a small party of like-minded captives, Leininger arrived in Pittsburgh on 31 March 1759 after some harrowing adventures along the way.

There are other kinds of escapers, too—those who see a flash of *opportunity* when a captor lets his guard down. One such man was twenty-year-old Robert Blakeney of Needham, Massachusetts, who was a POW in Italy during World War II:

> We enlisted men were taken to a German prison camp in Sulmona, northern Italy. When we arrived there, we saw some 3,000 to 4,000 other prisoners of war, English, French, Turks, Canadians, and oth-

ers. Some had been captured at Tobruk, Dunkirk, and other places some two, three, or four years before. Sometime in late September, we heard rumors that Italy had capitulated. We had Italian as well as German guards at the camp. We Americans had been told by the English colonel [that] we were not to try to escape without his permission. My buddy, the late John M. Hess of Uniontown, Pennsylvania, and I took walks every evening to pass the time. We thought we noticed fewer Italian guards around, especially at the gatehouses. One evening, I believe late September 1943, John and I were taking our walk when John told me that the gate didn't appear to be locked. As we walked by the gate, it appeared to be slightly open. We could not see what was on the other side of the gate, but it was definitely open. While John kept walking, I went back to our barracks, told the rest of the guys what we saw, and that John and I were going out. There was no hesitation by anyone. We casually approached the gate, opened it more, and then we all ran as fast as we could. I don't really know the number of days it took us behind the enemy lines. We estimated twenty-five days, but I believe it was shorter. We were flown back to Tunis, and then to England and thirty days' leave. I sent a telegram to my parents to let them know I was okay.[5]

Then there are the *great escapers,* POWs who reconstitute a military unit behind the wire that plans and executes a mass breakout. Though rare, this did happen in several wars, including large breakouts during the American Revolution. One took place at Millbay Naval Prison in Portsmouth, England, in 1777, when thirty-two American prisoners escaped by digging an eighteen-foot tunnel to an outside field. During the Civil War, no greater tunnel escape took place than that through the Yankee Tunnel dug at the Libby officers' prison in Richmond, where 109 Union officers escaped on the night of February 9, 1864. Forty-eight succeeded in reaching the Union lines. It was dangerous, tedious work accomplished only with discipline, dedication, and purpose. During World War I, the Villingen breakout on October 6, 1918, became the only great escape of the war planned and executed by Americans. Of the thirteen officers participating in the plan, five actually got away. Nothing tops the British great escape from Stalag Luft III in March 1944, however, when Allied officers dug three long tunnels called Tom, Dick, and Harry. The British managed to get seventy-six men out before being discovered, and of the seventy-six, the Gestapo murdered fifty in reprisal.

As a result of *A Prisoner's Duty,* I was contacted by the U.S. Air

Force's Joint Prisoner Recovery Agency at Fort Belvoir, Virginia, and joined it for one year (1998–1999) in an effort to expand its oral history archive of escapers and evaders. For that opportunity I am deeply grateful. I was also engaged as a historical consultant in several POW documentary film projects: *Return with Honor,* directed by Freida Lee Mock and Terry Sanders (American Film Foundation, Santa Monica, California, 1999); *Escape from a Living Hell,* directed by Paul Wimmer (Henninger Productions for the History Channel, 2000), winner of the 2000 Telly Award for historical/documentary programming for cable TV; and *Sworn to Secrecy: American Prisoners of War* in three parts—*The Barbed Wire Front, Battle for the Mind,* and *Code of Conduct*—directed by Deborah Blum (Documedia Productions for the History Channel, 2000). Then Hollywood knocked on my door, and I had the honor of being one of the historical consultants and technical advisors for *Hart's War,* directed by Gregory Hoblitt and starring Bruce Willis (MGM/UA, Warhart Productions, 2001). Speaking for all the directors and film personnel, I can say honestly and with passion that we did our best to tell the POW story truthfully and powerfully.

In addition, I was asked to present lectures at various prestigious institutions: the U.S. Air Force Academy's Forty-third Harmon Memorial Lecture, "Making Experience Count: American POW Narratives from the Colonial Wars to Vietnam," for the Nineteenth Military History Symposium, *The American Prisoner of War Experience,* Colorado Springs, November 2000; "Escape and Evasion in Europe," for *Celebrate Freedom* at the University of Tennessee–Knoxville Center for the Study of War and Society, November 2000; and "Behind the Wire: Libraries and Archives in the Research of the American POW Experience," for the Penn State University Library Colloquium Series, University Park, July 26, 2005. For these opportunities I will be forever grateful to Lieutenant Colonel Grant Weller of the Department of History, U.S. Air Force Academy; Dr. Kurt Piehler at the University of Tennessee; and Judith Hewes-Clark at Penn State's Pattee Library for their help and encouragement.

As *Voices from Captivity* led me to *A Prisoner's Duty,* the latter led me to complete the cycle—that is, to tell the story of how Americans have treated those men and women captured in wartime. How did we treat the "enemy" (or enemy prisoners of war [EPWs]), and in some cases, what did they say about it? The adventures presented in these pages range from glad to bad—nearly the full range of what one can endure in captivity. Some were bona fide military prisoners of war, others were prisoners of state, and some were political prisoners. As discovered by Philadelphia Quakers in 1777, political prisoners of the Union during the Civil War, and the Nisei during World War II, suspicion counts for something in war.

For the most part, I learned that Americans believe the United States has behaved reasonably well toward its wartime prisoners from other nations. Few died in captivity, and the Continental Congress and the subsequent federal governments have scrupulously obeyed international or at least traditional military provisions in place at the time. For the most part, this is the case because of the American observance of the Golden Rule: treat the enemy as one would have the enemy treat our own. In radical contrast are the circumstances when Americans have imprisoned their own citizens during wartime. For these civilians and, in the case of the Revolutionary War, for the Loyalists fighting with the British, there was no *mutatis mutandi* in place except for makeshift civil and military laws, and sometimes the altogether innocent or those merely charged with thinking wrong thoughts or saying the wrong thing to the wrong people wound up in prison or incarcerated in camps with real public enemies. Sometimes these unfortunates lost their lives; other times, they wound up enduring a state of incarceration merely for suspicion.

The objective of this work is to continue filling in some of the blanks left hazy and, in many cases, empty in the many studies of the American experience of war. My continuing ambition is to sort this out, give credit where credit is due, and show how and why behavior toward those behind barbed wire may have long-range effects that no captor can ever accurately or even adequately foresee. There are no crystal balls here, I fear to say, but at least we can take the time to distinguish between what we thought we did and what we actually did. There is a difference. I learned a personal lesson about that difference while teaching as a Fulbright professor in Germany from 1994 to 1995.

After a few months in Münster at the Wilhelms Universität, I finally found out that a real barber—as opposed to the local unisex salons— had a small shop that he ran for a few hours a week. Retired, stately, and healthy well into his eighties, this man, whose name I never learned, rode his bicycle through Münster to his shop three times a week. There I sat waiting for a haircut trying not to be noticed, until my turn came. Friendly and inquisitive, as most barbers are, he asked me the usual questions. Thankfully, my German was up to the interrogation, more or less, and then the real question came on hard: what sort of research did I conduct? By this time, the razor had appeared. I told him that I was interested in the experience of prisoners of war in general but was working on American escapers at the moment. "Oh," he said, "I was a prisoner of war of the Americans near Remagen." I asked him if he had seen the thousands of Wehrmacht POWs there. "Oh yes," he said, "and many died there, no food." The razor glided over my ears; I was completely at his mercy. I said I was sorry if he had suffered at the hands of the Americans. He smiled and told me that the Americans had let him out of the compound early. "They needed haircuts." We smiled. I returned for many haircuts during my time in Münster. To be perfectly honest, I was nothing short of humbled in his presence, and I think he knew it. We never became friends. I had the feeling that I remained the enemy in his eyes, but for him, the war was over. For me, it had just begun.

One of my German graduate students told me the story of his uncle, who had been an EPW in American hands. His uncle had been sent from Spain as a boy to "save" Germany:

> He lived with relatives and at boarding schools until he received the "honor" to serve the Reich during the final days of World War II. After a very short time he was captured and ended up at the *Rhein-wiesen* (Rhine Meadow) camps. He is a very introverted person in the first place, and he totally refuses to talk about his war experience. During the last thirty years, I heard him tell only one story from captivity. He was sitting there in the rain and put an old potato sack over most of his body to get some protection from the elements while asleep. While he was sleeping somebody ran by and stole the sack. It must really have been eat or be eaten. After his release he immediately gave up his German citizenship and became a Spaniard.[6]

For this man and the vast numbers of tired, defeated Wehrmacht soldiers who surrendered in 1945, the experience of captivity in American hands along the Rhine River was surely a nightmare. Thus, it is extremely important to define the nature of that elusive term *enemy,* what the experiences of EPWs actually were, and how we Americans have dealt with it for 300 years.

Acknowledgments

No book is written alone. I thank Dr. Stanley Weintraub, professor emeritus, Pennsylvania State University, for his constant mentoring from ideas to three books; Dr. Arnold Krammer at Texas A&M University, perhaps the most prolific and respected scholar of World War II enemy prisoners of war (EPWs) in the United States, who extended unparalleled friendship and assistance; Lieutenant Colonel Grant Weller at the U.S. Air Force Academy for his assistance in the field of prisoner of war (POW) history; Dr. Stuart Rochester, deputy historian at the Office of the Secretary of Defense, for his help with Vietnam EPWs; Markus Spiecker of Essen, Germany, my former student at the Englisches Seminar, Westfälische Wilhelms Universität, Münster, Germany, for his help with former German POWs; Dr. Michel Cieutat, my former colleague and close friend in the Département d'Etudes Anglaises et Nord-Américaines, Université Strasbourg, France, and Dr. Peter Bischoff, formerly of the Westfälische Wilhelms Universität, both of whom reminded me not to forget the POWs in American hands; and Dr. Cynthia Falk, SUNY Oneonta, for her expert help with Quaker prisoners during the American Revolution. Special gratitude is extended to several former Naval Intelligence liaison officers—Larry Serra, Tim Corcoran, and Peter Decker—and to Robert Senior, Blaise Hogan, and Barry Wallace, who served faithfully in Vietnam with the army, navy, and marines and responded to my queries about how they dealt with EPWs; my former student Kelly Hackett and Dr. Geoffrey Megargee, who told their personal stories about 9/11 in New York City and Washington, D.C.; Stephanie Adams, the Reverend Pablo Mijone, Robert Burns, Brian Moffet, Jason Miller, and Bridget Hogan for research assistance; my friend William F. Henri of Houston, Texas, for editorial help when I needed it the most; Dr. Henry Fitzpatrick for help in photo acquisition; and most important, William Jakub, Linda Franklin, Kathleen Donohue, Loretta Gossett, and all the staff of the John Paul II Library at the Franciscan University of Steubenville. I also thank my department chair, Dr. Kimberly Georgedes, and Dr. Max Bonilla, Vice President for Academic Affairs at Franciscan University of Steubenville, for granting me a sabbatical leave during the fall 2008 semester and supporting this effort from beginning to end. Allowing me to devote all my energies to research and writing for an entire semester constitutes a very special trust and confidence. I am grateful.

Last, I thank my loving wife, Beate Engel-Doyle, assistant professor and chair of Modern Languages and Literature at the Franciscan University of Steubenville. Without her remarkable patience and kindness during our years together, no book could have been written, no research done, no Fulbright professorship achieved, no years spent in Germany or France, nothing. To her, the love of my life, I owe my life's work. She has made dreams come true.

Introduction

The Enemy: Imposing the Condition of Captivity

In war, the opposing side cannot be an individual with a personal history or even a personality. The enemy is a soldier tasked to destroy the force facing him. He wears the uniform of his country, bears his country's arms legally, and is usually well trained in military arts, including the art of killing. The enemy might be a man or a woman—gender matters very little—but as a soldier, this person represents a clear and present danger and must be vigorously opposed to the death. The enemy is absolutely evil, and few students of military history could or would deny that modern war, at least in the twentieth century and possibly into the twenty-first, has evolved steadily into a struggle for national survival.

Killing the enemy is a military necessity in war, whereas in civilian life such an act is called homicide, manslaughter, or murder, depending on the circumstances. From at least the time of Caesar in Gaul, it has been clear that war is not a game; nor is it loaded with gamelike chivalry in the heat of battle. There is much hatred and loathing, anger and intemperance, impatience, and chaos. In war, countries such as the United States confer their highest awards for valor when soldiers take the lives of enemy soldiers in battle, and as J. Glen Gray points out in *The Warriors: Reflections on Men in Battle,* the act of killing in combat is an act of state rather than an act of murder or a private killing; thus it becomes an act worthy of praise rather than a crime.[1]

Soldiers kill easily and swiftly in battle because they believe the enemy is evil enough to warrant complete destruction. Even more important, soldiers are taught convincingly in basic and advanced training that a combat situation comes down to two choices: kill or be killed. Respect for the enemy's fighting skills is certainly required, but hatred for the enemy, such as existed toward the Imperial Japanese Army on Peleliu, Okinawa, and Iwo Jima during World War II, is sometimes elevated to what John Dower calls a "war without mercy," and for good reason: quarter is neither sought nor given.[2] Gray calls this phenomenon "a unified concrete universal, single in its reality as an abstract hatred

1

of a stereotype that arises from concentrating on one trait of a person or group while disregarding other features." The enemy, therefore, is a "fear-filled image of a hostile power intent on destroying our people and our lives."[3] The human response becomes total enmity for the image of evil that possesses the soldier's imagination.

There are three distinct dangers in being overwhelmed with the evil of the enemy. First is the problem of bloodlust or the pure enjoyment of killing; the second is war psychosis, the escalating hatred of the enemy usually achieved through the intake of copious amounts of propaganda; and the third is the old principle of *lex talionis,* or an-eye-for-an-eye retaliation and revenge. Individually or acting in consort, these dangers can, and often do, generate emotional trauma and possible war crimes in the field, such as those committed in My Lai (1968) in Vietnam, if not controlled by watchful officers and noncommissioned officers. The enemy kills the soldier's buddies, and the more unbearable it becomes, the greater the feeling of personal vengeance. Combat can become a vendetta.[4]

Bloodlust is, perhaps, the most dangerous psychological problem a soldier has to contend with, in that it can become overwhelmingly nonsensical and motivational at the same time. What makes bloodlust so dangerous is that the pleasure of killing the enemy becomes an overwhelming, otherworldly act of pleasure. Bloodlust, then, is difficult to contend with because it is ultimately an act of human will, barely controllable if left to its own devices. This is not to be confused with momentary snapping. A soldier can snap under pressure—and many do—causing that soldier to stop thinking and simply react in the most basic way. After such an incident is over, the soldier returns to a more normal or dispassionate way of thinking. One can think of it as the occurrence of a massive thunderstorm followed by a pleasant calm. Bloodlust never goes away and remains with many soldiers after the war, and they must live with it for the rest of their lives.

There needs to be a more positive understanding of soldiering. If one examines memoirs and diaries, personal narratives, autobiographies, and fictional accounts of battles of the Revolutionary War, soldiers like Ethan Allen in *The Narrative of Colonel Ethan Allen* (1807) and Joseph Plumb Martin in *Private Yankee Doodle* (1830) pictured themselves as heroic figures. With a clear mission, they followed a classical Roman code that emphasized martial virtue, serious regard for discipline and authority, personal integrity, guided ambition, and duty.[5] Much the same can be said of the soldiers of the War of 1812. But what of the Hessians captured at Trenton in 1776 or the thousands of British and Hessian troops captured at Saratoga in 1777 and Yorktown in 1781? What became of them? What did they have to say about battle and subsequent captivity in American hands? And what was the fate of Loyalist civilians and soldiers who fell into the hands of the Continental Army?

As we will see, there was hatred in the land, not so much against the British and German soldiers held as prisoners of war but against those Americans who sided with the king and Parliament in England, the Tories or Loyalists. At first, they believed they could be neutral, but in Boston, for example, the Sons of Liberty and later Committees of Safety in other states tarred and feathered Loyalists when they could. One could easily interpret these actions as the first American night riders attacking innocent citizens with different political identities. Then as each new state legislature established Test or Loyalty Acts, the Loyalists found themselves in a difficult if not impossible double bind: damned by their own if they took the oath to the new United States, and damned by the new American government if they refused. Thus, when Loyalists took arms on the British side against the Continentals and their neighbors, they faced serious consequences if captured (see appendix 1). So the Revolution evolved into two wars in one—international and civil—and introduced a dichotomy: prisoners of war, to whom certain rules applied, and prisoners of state, to whom they did not. As subsequent chapters show, Americans are much more violent against their own than they are against foreign soldiers in captivity.

The Mexican War (1846–1848) was different in that it was fought in a foreign country as a Manifest Destiny war of conquest. The Mexicans, of course, viewed the American action as a war of aggression aimed at annexing—stealing—what is now the American Southwest. The Americans saw it as a near completion of their providential mandate to control the North American continent (excluding Canada) from the Atlantic to the Pacific and to enforce the border with Mexico at the Rio Grande. There were no prisoner of war (POW) camps, so what happened to Mexican POWs? Not much; they were sent home on parole or recruited as scouts. Major General Zachary Taylor, "Old Rough and Ready," and Major General Winfield Scott, "Old Fuss and Feathers," did both. However, anti-immigrant nativism reared its head when it came to dealing with deserters, and the American army became drastic and draconian in its treatment and execution of the Irish and other immigrant soldiers of Saint Patrick's (*San Patricio*) Battalion. In the end, Scott put an end to the immigrant desertions harshly, but simultaneously he established his own company of deserters consisting mostly of Mexican criminals and outcasts. For their efforts in the final siege of Mexico City, these men were paid handsomely, about $16,500, and the Americans were grateful for their services.

The American Civil War presents two different sides of the captivity story—civilian and military. The accursed Union and Confederate policies inevitably led to the maiming and unnecessary deaths of many American soldiers in captivity. The numbers are simply staggering: 211,400 Union POWs in the South; 220,000 Confederate POWs in the North. Of these, 30,218 Union POWs died, as did 26,436 Confederate POWs. It is certainly true that the introduction of Francis Lieber's 1863 Rules of Land Warfare, or General Order 100 (see appendix 4), changed the way American armies obligated themselves to treat their POWs. Not only did the respective prison systems fail, but the individuals responsible for them also failed. But neglect is not the real issue; responsibility and lack of accountability are.

Wars are not won or lost because of prisoners of war; they are won or lost in spite of them. All the major players—Ulysses S. Grant, Robert E. Lee, John Henry Winder, William Hoffman, Edwin Stanton, James Seddon, and both Abraham Lincoln and Jefferson Davis—knew it too. They were all equally culpable for the deaths of so many Union and Confederate prisoners, but curiously, for different reasons. First, neither side remembered how British prisoners had been treated in the Revolution or the War of 1812 or how things had been done in the Mexican War. Had they done so, provisions would have been made for exchanges in great numbers and for humane treatment in the stockades, but Civil War politics interfered badly. Lincoln refused to acknowledge the sovereignty of the Confederacy; hence, even calling captured Confederates prisoners of war presented deep political problems. Was the Confederacy a legitimate country or not? Military necessities, of course, changed everything, and the Dix-Hill Cartel began to move prisoners to their own lines. Yet no cartel worked very well for long. By 1864 General U. S. Grant forbade formal exchanges, wanting to maintain his edge in manpower to destroy the Confederate Army, and he charged that Confederate soldiers were returned to their regiments prematurely. In addition, claiming that the Union Army had great concern for black Union POWs in Confederate hands sat well with the abolitionists, perhaps, but such concern was more propaganda than reality.

Why were there such low levels of concern for Union and Confederate prisoners' physical welfare? What role did parsimony play in the steady destruction of healthy young soldiers in enemy hands? Why was Richmond so overcrowded with Union prisoners? What was the nature of the Union and Confederate systems? Where and why did they fail? Who failed them? Perhaps the decentralization of prison systems was the problem, or perhaps it was desensitization caused by an escalating hatred for the enemy—war psychosis. Perhaps it was newspapers howling for retribution and radical Union politics hardening human feelings toward the suffering of captured enemy soldiers.

Then there was the nasty problem of civilian incarceration, the taking of political prisoners without habeas corpus simply for being neutral or sympathetic to the other side's views. Not much has been said about this phenomenon, which began with the harsh treatment of the Loyalists before and during the Revolution, yet the sad truth is that many prominent churchmen, journalists, politicians, and judges were arrested and incarcerated for political reasons under executive orders issued by Lincoln. Were Lincoln's orders constitutional in a time of civil war? Perhaps yes, perhaps no, perhaps maybe.

Nineteenth-century Americans understood their culture as one of progress and expansion that required wars of conquest to tame the land and subjugate nature. Any notion of conservation or tolerance for the native tribes eluded them completely. Manifest Destiny ruled the first fifty years of the century and created a United States that stretched from the Atlantic to the Pacific; clearing the land of hunter-gatherer Indians ruled the next fifty. Both culture and a series of shooting wars dominated the conquest of the West up to 1893, when the frontier closed. What was perceived as civilization won against what was perceived as savagery.[6] However, by the end of the Civil War in 1865, the passion for conquest subsided, but the demand for Indian lands expanded. This led to a series of wars against the Plains Indians; curiously, to subdue tribes such as the Comanches, Kiowas, and Arapahos in the 1870s and the Chiricahua Apaches in the 1880s, the U.S. Army established military commissions to establish POW status. The army removed these tribes from their traditional lands and reservations to prison facilities in Florida, Alabama, and Oklahoma, where many died of tuberculosis and other diseases. At the same time, resident Indian schools arose in places such as Carlisle, Pennsylvania, with the sole purpose of "de-Indianizing" the youth and transforming them into the nineteenth-century vision of productive, enterprising American citizens.

Both the war with Spain and the Philippine-American war were the last quests for empire wrapped in an emerging notion of American liberalism spilling over from the conquest of the West. The Cuban problem, as it was perceived in 1898, required the United States to expel more of the old world from the new, and by extension, that included the Spanish rule of the Philippine Islands. In the Treaty of Paris ending the Spanish-American War, the United States offered Spain $20 million for the archipelago, and Spain accepted. The trouble was that the Filipinos had been fighting Spanish rule for years and fully expected the Americans to defeat the Spanish and then give the islands to the Filipinos as an act of generosity. Emilio Aquinaldo and his followers were shocked when they realized that the Americans wanted the Philippines for the same reason they wanted Hawaii and Samoa—for the extension of power. Thus, the war in the Philippine Islands evolved into a guerrilla war from 1899 to 1902 and beyond. Enemy prisoners of war (EPWs) were always suspect and sometimes harshly treated, especially if the Americans believed, or had reason to believe, they might have usable field intelligence concerning the location and disposition of *insurrectos*. Despite military law, especially General Order 100, which forbade the torture of prisoners, many field commanders placed themselves in the unenviable position of being caught between the effectiveness of the "water cure" in extracting intelligence from the tough Filipino enemy and its horror and illegality.

World War I—the Great War, until World War II arrived in 1939—witnessed a world in transition. Not a war of ideologies as World War II clearly was, the Great War was a contest based on militarism, imperialism, and colonialism on one side versus humanitarianism and civilization on the other. In very stark terms, soldiers in the trenches behaved barbarically in battle, often resisting the taking of enemy prisoners for a host of reasons: sometimes out of revenge for what the other side did, and sometimes because of the war psychosis that had built up over time both at home and in the field. The Americans had General Order 100 (updated in 1914), which forbade the killing of enemy prisoners in the field, and the Hague Conventions of 1899 and 1907, which regulated the treatment of prisoners once they were behind the lines. The issue in the field was accepting prisoners and then getting them safely to a POW holding facility behind the front lines. A problem arose when French and British trainers told the Americans to avoid taking German prisoners, but after investigating what actually happened on the Western Front, the Americans ignored the French and British tendency to refuse prisoners and took them generously in most cases.

By midcentury, American soldiers fought World War II for both moral virtue and national defense. Henry R. Luce, a paramount personality of the era, set the tone in his essay "The American Century," published in February 1941: "As America enters dynamically upon the world scene, we need to seek and bring forth a unique vision of America as a world power—a vision which is authentically American."[7] Attitudes changed. New Deal antipathies against the conservative business community eased, and the American government's dependence on business to produce war goods increased, as it had in 1917. Factories worked seven days a week, twenty-four hours a day, and the government pumped $320 billion into the economy from 1941 to 1945. American ideals became the heart and soul of what the war was all about for the United States, and from 1945 to 1991, Americans became reluctant but committed warriors in the various hot flashes of the Cold War.

The treatment of EPWs during World War II marks the high point for humane and generous behavior. Americans treated POWs as well as possible, in strict observance of the 1929 Geneva Convention, with the hope that the enemy, both German and Japanese, would reciprocate. Although the Germans reacted unevenly to their Allied POWs, depending on who they were and where they were from, the Japanese were universally horrific. The Americans reacted with restraint to reports of the poor treatment of their prisoners in the Philippines and attempted to quiet any stories that seemed to be propaganda oriented, but the dam broke when escapers began to publish their narratives about the Death March on Bataan and the horrors of Japanese prison camps in general.

It has often been stated that the Pacific war was inhumane and merciless, but by 1944 the military services wanted prisoners for intelligence purposes. Even more important, planners knew that Japan was losing an entire generation. Thus, the U.S. Army created Japanese language schools to provide interpreters for interrogations and used EPWs to create leaflets and field broadcasts to urge Japanese soldiers to surrender. Although hard-line resisters existed in German and Italian EPW communities, resistance events were minimal among the Japanese held in the United States. In short, after they were "reborn" in captivity, they often became model prisoners. Still, too many died by their own hand on the battlefield due to the emperor death cult developed in Japan in the 1920s and 1930s, and nothing stopped it until Japan's surrender in 1945.

The postwar era opened with enormous optimism and hope for a shining future, but the period is confusing, in that the quest for justice partnered with a strong desire for revenge. Whether by policy, by law, or by mistake, people continued to die in prison camps, in some cases up to 1951. The issue of the great number of German deaths in Andersonville-style camps along the scenic Rhine River was addressed by Canadian novelist James Bacque in *Other Losses* (1989) and refuted by noted American and German scholars. Yet, surely too many German soldiers died in these camps from war wounds, exposure, and starvation from May to December 1945.

On the other side of the world, the Allies held numerous war crimes trials in Tokyo and other locations, prosecuting those Japanese soldiers and civilians who had murdered POWs, ordered murders, or ordered the forces of the Greater East Asian Co-Prosperity Sphere to march against Japan's neighbors. Both these trials in the East and those in Nuremberg fell under the provisions of the Nuremberg Principles, developed in 1946 to create a legal basis after the fact for new issues that arose during the war. Success and failure were both features of these war crimes trials, but British and American law assumes innocence, and therein lies the rub. Was there a presumption of guilt in these trials? If so, were they really fair?

Another issue that arose in the postwar period was the forced repatriation agreed to by the Allies at Yalta and Postdam—that is, forcing citizens to return to their home countries when such a return would mean certain death or incarceration. At first, the Americans consented (as had the British), but eventually, President Harry Truman opposed it for humanitarian reasons. If Jews of the surviving remnant feared returning to Poland, why should the Allies make them go? Should anticommunist Russians be returned to the USSR, where they would surely be murdered or incarcerated in the Gulags? This issue of forced repatriation also plagued the United Nations Command during the Korean War, especially when communist prisoners stated that they wished to either remain in South Korea or flee from the Chinese communists to Taiwan. The central EPW events were uprisings at the various UN prison facilities: how they were planned and executed, and how both the Americans and the South Koreans responded to them.

The issue of forced repatriation faded as the Vietnam War began in 1959 and evolved into a major American commitment in 1965. South Vietnam had no military prison facilities before the United States entered the scene in force. Also, because the nature of the conflict was a curious combination of insurgency and invasion from the north, categories of prisoners became important. Also important was the fact that the U.S.

Military Assistance Command Vietnam (MACV) was not the detaining power; South Vietnam was, but MACV stood behind and bankrolled all the South Vietnamese holding facilities. Treatment of EPWs was proper and humane at one level: if a prisoner was adjudicated to be a weapons-carrying soldier from North Vietnam or a Vietcong from South Vietnam, POW status and protection were granted. However, in Vietnam, civil and military prisoners were often mixed together in a chaotic and overburdened system that remained tangled until 1970. Hard field interrogations; the rules of engagement; International Committee of the Red Cross inspections of POW camps; North Vietnamese resistance to obeying the rules about POW treatment, status, and exchanges; the CIA's Phoenix Program, assaulting the heart of the communist movement; and war crime sensitivity constituted a complex mix of competing issues that prevailed until the United States abandoned South Vietnam in 1973.

Operation Desert Storm in 1991 expelled Saddam Hussein's Iraqi army from Kuwait and pursued it nearly to Baghdad. In a 100-hour war, the U.S. and Allied armies, known as the Coalition, built large EPW holding facilities in Saudi Arabia and sent advisors, mostly military police, to assist the Saudis in managing all the Iraqi EPWs. It became clear that the Iraqi army had no will to engage the Coalition forces with any vigor, and the troops surrendered in large numbers. After inflicting great losses in terms of personnel and material on the Iraqis, the Coalition agreed to an armistice and withdrew. Shortly after the armistice concluding the Persian Gulf War, I informally interviewed two U.S. Marine Corps reservists who believed that the Coalition and the marines went to extremes to render treatment strictly in accordance with the Geneva Convention on POWs. They were correct in their assessment. Saddam Hussein then focused his attention on destroying Shiites and Kurds, who opposed him politically. Tragically, the West, including the Americans, believed that the Kurdish and Shiite resistance constituted internal Iraqi problems and did nothing to rescue those groups from Saddam's wrath, which included the execution of thousands of Shiites and the use of chemical weapons against the Kurds in northern Iraq. This use of chemical weapons shocked the United States, creating fear in some circles and determination to dethrone Saddam in others.

During the 1990s and early 2000s, Saddam Hussein played into the hands of his neoconservative American enemies by practicing deception. He feigned the possession of nuclear weapons and denied UN representatives access to his weapons facilities. At the same time, in an environment of fear and a growing Islamic fundamentalist hostility toward the United States, al-Qaeda launched a momentous attack against the World Trade Center and the Pentagon on 11 September 2001. The new Republican administration of President George W. Bush, full of so-called Vulcans—the neoconservative enemies of al-Qaeda, the Afghan Taliban, and Islamic fundamentalists in general—responded by creating the global war on terror, attacking Osama bin Laden's al-Qaeda and his Taliban allies in Afghanistan. Before the attack took place, the Bush administration changed the rules of international law by denying non-nation-state, non-uniform-wearing captives in both the Afghan and Iraq wars the protection of the 1949 Geneva Convention. The United States then created prison facilities such as Bagram in Afghanistan, Camp Bucca and Abu Ghraib in Iraq, and the facility at the U.S. Naval Base at Guantánamo Bay, Cuba, to house, interrogate, and try them before military commissions. The events at Abu Ghraib, which in theory housed Iraqi detainees for interrogation, show that ill-trained, mean-spirited prison guards can impose terrible conditions on helpless prisoners; the prison at Guantánamo shows that no country can change international law without international consequences.

In the end, for some soldiers, becoming an EPW in American hands was nothing short of the horror of their lives; for others, it was good fortune; and for some, it was a miracle. Surviving the experience was another matter completely, and doing so largely depended on the cultural and legal circumstances that enveloped the war. The goal of this book is to examine how agents of the United States treated their prisoners, both military and civilian, so that we can gain a better understanding of the history and experiences of POWs in American hands from the Revolution to the wars in Southwest Asia and the Middle East. By examining their experiences and the policies, both good and evil, that guided their American captors, we have a unique opportunity to examine ourselves in a new and different way.

ONE

Prisoners of Independence

British and Hessian Enemy Prisoners of War

During this unhappy contest, there be every exercise of humanity,
which the nature of the case will possibly admit of.
—General George Washington

With the exception of spies such as British Major John André and some
others, during the Revolution the Americans treated enemy prisoners of
war (EPWs) relatively well. General George Washington made it known
in letters to British General Lord William Howe that he considered it
his duty to be humane and generous in his treatment of British and
Hessian prisoners of war (POWs), and he often complained to Howe
that Americans were not being treated with the same care. Writing to
Howe on 23 September 1776, he noted that "during this unhappy contest, there be every exercise of humanity, which the nature of the case
will possibly admit of."[1] He was right, at least to a degree: there were
instances of serious hostilities toward British POWs by American officers and civilians, most of which never came to Washington's attention.
Some did, however, as the British charges of mistreatment by Colonel
David Henley against some British officers showed.

During the Revolution, captures and exchanges large and small took
place from the beginning to the end of the war. At first, status became
a serious issue. As far as the British were concerned, from 1775 to 1776
the American war in Massachusetts consisted of rebellious individuals and local militias organized to defend the colonies against Indian
attacks, and any rebels captured were considered to be civil prisoners
guilty of treason against the Crown. The British, however, were more
concerned about subduing the rebellious Massachusetts colony than
conducting public war. Hence, those soldiers who came into captivity
were not executed but held in jails. After the Declaration of Independence was signed and announced during the summer of 1776, everything changed. This act presented the British with a wholly new set of
problems—specifically, how to treat those Americans who surrendered

and became actual prisoners of war: hang them as traitors or, perhaps, use them as bargaining chips to get their own soldiers back. As usual, privates, corporals, and sergeants counted for little. Writing to Howe, Washington stated, "The exchange of privates, I shall take the earliest opportunity in my power to carry into execution; but their being greatly dispersed through New England Governments, in order to their better accommodation, will prevent it for some time."[2] Officers, however, became increasingly more important in potential exchanges.

As the war progressed, important Continental officers were captured and then exchanged. For example, Colonel Benedict Arnold surrendered after his defeat in Canada in 1775 and was subsequently exchanged. British General Prescott was exchanged for American Brigadier General Lord Stirling in 1776. Writing to the president of Congress on 25 September 1776, Washington expressed his humane philosophy, one that he held for the war's duration, that Congress must pay attention to its support of Americans in British captivity. After the Battle of Long Island in August 1776, Washington reported, "As to those taken on the 15th, they greatly exceed the number that I supposed fell into their hands in the retreat from the City." Stressing that Congress must appoint officers, called commissaries of prisoners, to tend to American prisoners, he reminded Congress, "I took the liberty of urging more than once that the prisoners might be treated with humanity and have their wants particularly attended to."[3] Washington's rationale was simple: if Congress supported American prisoners in British hands, if and when they were released or exchanged, they would be fit for further duty. Washington also made certain that the British could support their POWs in American hands.

The American Continental Army, various state militias, and naval forces captured more than 14,000 enemy soldiers and sailors. Their status never became a problem for the Americans as it did for the British; where to put them did. Because the American Revolution rose in intensity from a localized New England rebellion to a world war for the British and a total war for the Americans, housing and feeding vast numbers of enemy military prisoners became a major concern, particularly for the Americans. In the eighteenth century, belligerents were expected to supply and pay their own prisoners in enemy hands and appoint commissaries of prisoners to tend to their needs. In Philadelphia, American Tory Joshua Loring became the commissary of prisoners for the British, whereas the Americans appointed Elias Boudinot at first and several others from 1776 to 1783.

Small group captures took place throughout the war on both sides. British soldiers captured in the Revolution and again in the War of 1812 were held in dungeons, makeshift jails, and barracks and were exchanged much the way Americans were.[4] Senior officers were usually exchanged by direct correspondence and agreements between General Washington and British General Howe and later Sir Henry Clinton. There were three large group captures of British and Hessian troops: 919 Hessian troops under the command of Colonel Johann Gottlieb Rall (killed in action) at the Battle of Trenton in 1776 (General Washington commanding the Americans); 2,600 British (commanded by Major General John Burgoyne), 2,400 Hessian (commanded by Major General Friedrich Adolph, Baron von Riedesel), and 800 Canadian EPWs at the Battle of Saratoga in 1777 (General Horatio Gates commanding the Americans); and 7,241 EPWs at the Battle of Yorktown in 1781 under the command of General Charles Lord Cornwallis (Washington and French General Rochambeau commanding the Americans). A smaller engagement, the Battle of King's Mountain in South Carolina's backwoods in 1780, yielded over 500 Loyalist EPWs and ended most armed Loyalist activities in the Revolution.

Christmas Day 1776 was an important day for General George Washington and the Continental Army. In his biography of Washington, Douglas Southall Freeman asks how the Hessians could have allowed themselves to be surprised by the ragtag Continentals at Trenton. Perhaps it was the horrid weather; after all, it was late December in central New Jersey. Perhaps it was the German propensity to celebrate Christmas heartily. Washington's army was in terrible condition after the beatings it had taken: 1,500 dead at the Battle of Long Island, White Plains, and Fort Washington, where the Americans lost 2,000 POWs to the Hessians, and at Fort Lee, where the British caught General Nathanael Greene off guard and captured the bulk of Greene's materials. If anyone was frustrated with the fall campaign of 1776, it was General George Washington. He needed a victory, any victory, to sustain his army.[5]

It was clearly good fortune for the Americans that the Hessians failed to spot Washington's attacking columns after they recrossed the partially frozen Delaware River. The battle was a complete surprise, and it took only two hours, from 8 to 10 AM on Christmas morning, for the Americans to neutralize the large Hessian force.[6] Colonel Rall died of his wounds after speaking briefly to General Washington on his death bed, one of the twenty-five to thirty Hessians killed in action at

Trenton. In addition to the EPWs, Washington captured six pieces of brass artillery and 900 to 1,000 stands of arms.[7] It was an impressive morning's work and something that would take place again, though on a much larger scale, at Saratoga, New York, in October 1777 when Major General Horatio Gates defeated Lieutenant General John Burgoyne.

John Burgoyne, or "Gentleman Johnny," had a bold plan: he wanted to march a large British force south from Canada to Albany, New York, to cut the colonies in two. If this were accomplished, he, along with General Sir William Howe in New York City and General Sir Guy Carleton in Canada, believed the distasteful American war might conclude in their favor. On paper the plan looked good, but Burgoyne had little notion of New York's difficult terrain along the invasion route, and when he attempted to march south from friendly Canada, he permitted huge supply columns consisting of cooks, hospital attendants, servants, smiths, carpenters, officers' wives, ammunition wagons, and drovers with herds of cattle to follow close by.[8] It was surely a recipe for failure.

Slowly, the Americans cut down Burgoyne's force in a series of engagements. At Sword's Farm at dawn on 17 September 1777, a party of British soldiers (disobeying orders not to forage) was attempting to dig up a potato patch when they were surprised by a group of Daniel "Big Dan" Morgan's expert Virginia riflemen, who killed, wounded, and captured about thirty men.[9] Fighting continued with attacks and counterattacks on both sides and great loss of life on the British side, with about a third of Burgoyne's main force lost. The Americans continued their relentless pursuit using sharpshooters or snipers with special homemade rifles that were deadly accurate, especially against British officers.

In retreat, the British soldiers suffered not only from exhaustion but also from a lack of supplies and fits of rainy, cool autumn weather. It was becoming evident to Burgoyne that he needed help from Clinton and Howe if he were to get his army past General Gates and safely to Albany. One attempt was Clinton's expedition up the Hudson River. It had limited success, but he could not relieve Burgoyne. Daniel Taylor, a Loyalist dispatch rider, attempted to take a secret message to Burgoyne on 8 October, but the Americans captured him and read the message: "Nothing now between us but Gates. I sincerely hope this *little* success of ours may facilitate your operations. I heartily wish you success."[10] For his efforts, Taylor was tried, convicted of being a spy, and hanged.

After more fighting and the loss of more officers, including the distinguished Brigadier General Simon Fraser, and facing the ferocity of American troops under Benedict Arnold, who was nothing short of mad in battle, Burgoyne found himself outflanked and was forced to retreat to Saratoga in a soaking rain. The British were wet, hungry, tired, and nearly completely surrounded. With American cannonades constantly falling into his own troops' positions, Burgoyne realized he had to discuss terms with Gates. He sent his adjutant general, Major Kingston, to see if the Americans might be interested in a deal. Gates was thrilled; capturing Burgoyne and his army in the field was the mark of true generalship. According to Sergeant Roger Lamb of the Royal Welsh Fusileers, Burgoyne wrote to Gates: "He [Burgoyne] is apprised of the superiority of your numbers, and the disposition of your troops, to impede his supplies, and render his retreat a scene of carnage on both sides. In this situation he is compelled by humanity, and thinks himself justified by established principles, and precedents of state, and of war, to spare the lives of brave men upon honorable terms." Gates took this as an offer to surrender and wrote back: "General Burgoyne's army being exceedingly reduced by repeated defeats, by desertions, sickness, &c. their provisions exhausted, their military horses, tents and baggage taken or destroyed, their retreat cut off, and their camp invested, they can only be allowed to surrender prisoners of war."[11]

After some bargaining, especially about the fate of the Loyalist soldiers in Burgoyne's command, Gates permitted Burgoyne to create a unique surrender document. Instead of calling it a surrender or a capitulation, it became known as the Convention. Before signing it, however, Burgoyne advised his Loyalists not to surrender but to make their way back north to Canada. According to Susan Burnham Greeley, those who were able to escape did so, saying, "Canada, you see, has always been a refuge for the oppressed."[12] Gates and Burgoyne agreed to the following major provisions: the prisoners were to be marched to Boston and transported to Great Britain, with the understanding that they could never again return to fight in America. It all seemed so simple and gentlemanly, especially when Gates, Burgoyne, and their staff officers sat down together for dinner and drinks. General von Riedesel's wife Friederike, following her husband and having suffered considerably during the battle's cannonades, was aghast at the cordial hospitality the opposing generals extended to each other.

What became known as the Convention Army consisted of 2,600

British soldiers, 2,400 Hessians, and 800 Canadians, but the agreement between these two generals carried little weight in Congress, which jealously guarded its own prerogatives. In other words, a jurisdictional dispute erupted between General Gates and Congress over all these EPWs. Congress refused to honor the Convention of Saratoga and released only General Burgoyne and several staff officers. In separate groups, the remainder marched from state to state and from camp to camp. British Major General William Phillips, acting as senior British officer, kept order and discipline in this captive army, which remained in America until 1783.[13] Virginians set up the first American POW camp in 1779 to house British and Germans, just a year after the military police were created as the Marechaussee Corps.

Battles count as the currency of war. The British surrender at Saratoga in 1777 brought the French into a treaty with the Americans against the British, their traditional enemy, and elevated the American Revolution into an important segment of a world war. Though the British won the world war, it cost them the American colonies. The French played no small part, especially at the concluding battle at Yorktown, Virginia, in October 1781, which was actually the culmination of the British southern campaign that had begun in 1780 with the successful siege of Charleston, South Carolina. It was the fifth year of the war, and times were not good. The Continental dollar had become a worthless currency and was often not accepted by merchants. To say that the country was war weary would be an understatement, and the British knew it. Sir Henry Clinton in New York decided that the time was ripe to take the American South.

Clinton amassed a 100-ship flotilla with 8,500 men for the nineteen-day siege against Charleston, commanded by American General Benjamin Lincoln. After constant bombardments, Lincoln surrendered, and the British took 5,466 American POWs. This was the worst day for American arms until General William Hull's 1812 surrender to the British in Detroit and later the surrender of American forces to the Imperial Japanese Army at Bataan in 1942. The British put most of these men into their prison ship system, where many died. The Americans operated prison hulks too. Connecticut, New York, Virginia, and Massachusetts all operated hulks for British EPWs during the war, complete with stinking dungeons, bad water, skimpy provisions, and overcrowding.[14] Perhaps it would be fair to call it vengeance, but the use of prison hulks was common at the time. Not common were the many deaths in

16

them. In all, the British took well over 18,000 American POWs, but the actual number who died is not clear.[15]

Aside from General Lincoln's surrendered regulars in Charleston, there were only ill-trained, part-time militias in the South. This sad fact led Clinton to return to New York and leave General Charles Lord Cornwallis in charge, with the idea that he need only mop up the South by enlisting the many Loyalists, who would fight aggressively against their neighbors. In May 1780 Cornwallis sent the dashing Lieutenant Colonel Banastre Tarleton and his mounted British Legion of Loyalists into the backcountry to establish outposts. Tarleton knew that a force of Virginia regulars, the Seventh Virginia Regiment, two companies of the Second Virginia Regiment, and an artillery detachment with two guns, Colonel Abraham Buford commanding, were in the area, and he thought that John Rutledge, rebel governor of South Carolina, rode with them. Tarleton's intelligence was incorrect; Rutledge was already in North Carolina at the time. When Tarleton caught Buford, he offered surrender as an option, but Buford refused: "Sir, I reject your proposals, and shall defend myself to the last extremity."[16] Tarleton broke the Continental line in short order. Buford managed to escape, but Tarleton's soldiers began killing as many Continentals as they could, even after they knelt in surrender. Whether Tarleton ordered it or not is irrelevant; his men went mad in the field. Fortunately, the madness ended thanks to British discipline, and the survivors were taken to nearby plantations for medical aid and subsequently paroled home. The effect of this rather small engagement was staggering, however. It raised American determination in the South to oppose British forces and led directly to the Battle of King's Mountain.

Although it is not one of the three major captures of EPWs during the Revolution, King's Mountain in western South Carolina's Blue Ridge Mountains and eastern Tennessee was considered the frontier. Many of the locals were friendly to the Crown—it was Loyalist country in the mountainous Scots-Irish frontier regions—but this section of South Carolina was rebel to the core. Instead of being able to recruit young Tories, British Lieutenant Colonel Patrick Ferguson ran into a force of 3,000 rebel mountain militiamen spoiling for a fight. Armed with individually manufactured muskets with rifled bores, these soldiers were excellent shots and usually hit what they aimed at. Ferguson, realizing that his position was perilous, sent one dispatch rider after another back to the Loyalist command in Charlotte hoping for relief, but every one of them was killed en route by the American sharpshooters. Knowing that he faced a major rebel force, he took up a defensive position on King's Mountain, a logical place at the crest of a steep hill—the classic high ground. The frontier rebel force, broken into four groups under the command of Colonel William Campbell of the Virginia Militia, initiated the climb up the thickly wooded slope. Ferguson turned his men to face them. According to Captain Alexander Chesney, a Loyalist officer from South Carolina:

> King's Mountain from its height would have enabled us to oppose a superior force with advantage had it not been covered with wood which sheltered the Americans and enabled them to fight in their favorite manner. In fact, after driving in our pickets, they were enabled to advance to the crest of the hill in perfect safety, until they took post and opened an irregular but destructive fire from behind trees and other cover. In this manner the engagement was maintained for near an hour.[17]

Thinking the battle was going his way, Ferguson shouted, "Hurrah brave boys, the day is ours." Met with blasts of accurate rebel bullets, Ferguson fell dead in his saddle; his horse collapsed, and both dead man and horse rolled over a hill.[18] White flags went up everywhere on the battlefield, but the rebels wanted some backwoods justice against those Loyalists of the British Legion commanded by the infamous Colonel Banastre Tarleton, who had roamed the region conducting war against civilians. Shouting the popular "Tarleton's Quarter," meaning no prisoners, the militia went on a rampage, attacking, shooting, and bayoneting Loyalists until King's Mountain ran red with Loyalist blood.

On that day, 7 October 1780, more than 700 EPWs, all Loyalists, were taken. By the time they arrived at Bethabara, South Carolina, 300 remained. By early December the number dropped to 130, and by 6 January there were only 6 left.[19] What accounts for such a depletion in EPWs? Many must have been wounded and left behind before the march; others may have escaped, because security in militia units was often lax; nine Loyalist officers were tried and hanged, and some were paroled. In general, these EPWs received very rough treatment at the hands of their American captors. The Continental generals were not pleased, however, because they wanted to use this wonderful boon to the EPW population as exchange fodder for the Continentals captured at Charleston, South Carolina, in 1780. General Horatio Gates, known as "Granny" Gates to the troops because of his age and gruff temperament, was especially angry and blamed the state government for incompetence in handling prisoners of war. George Washington weighed in as well:

> All the prisoners taken by Colonel Campbell [at King's Mountain] have been dismissed, paroled and enlisted in the Militia Service for three months except 130. Thus we have lost by the folly, not to say anything worse, of those who had them in charge upwards of 600 men. I am told Lord Cornwallis has lately made a proposition to General Smallwood for exchanging all the prisoners in North and South Carolina. If it is upon terms that are just and equal, I shall avail myself of it for a great number of prisoners is a heavy weight upon our hands.[20]

Such an exchange was not to be. The Americans had lost their chance, but important upcoming events changed the nation's fate completely.

In July 1780 a new American army marched south under General Horatio Gates, the hero of Saratoga, with the intention of aggressively attacking and defeating Cornwallis and recovering the South for Congress. The trouble was that supplies simply did not exist, and the soldiers suffered terribly from the lack of food. In August, Gates fought Cornwallis at Camden, South Carolina, with militia units that ran from the field at the sight of bayonets. Gates did have a strong force of Maryland and Delaware Continentals who held their ground until the British overran them with bayonets and hand-to-hand combat. In the end, even these units fled after losing their heroic Bavarian commander Johann DeKalb, bayoneted to death by British attackers. Tarleton then pursued the Americans for about twenty-five miles, killing many along the way. In disgrace, Gates left his army in defeat and rode 180 miles north to safety.

Between the major defeats at Charleston and Camden, there was no American army left in the South. Taking over the battleground, limited as it was, were the partisan groups led by amateur soldiers such as "Carolina Gamecock" Thomas Sumter, William Davie, and "Swamp Fox" Francis Marion, all of whom attempted to bleed the British rear service units white. Like any insurgency-counterinsurgency war, the landscape got bloody, especially with the hit-and-run tactics each independent partisan unit employed against the British and their Loyalist allies. Although one must give credit where appropriate, the partisan units accomplished little other than making the American Revolution in the South a very ugly war full of revenge and personal vendetta.

In the North the war in 1780 went no better. General Benedict Arnold, the hero of Saratoga and other fights, turned his coat and joined the British after negotiations with the handsome and dashing Major John André, Clinton's intelligence chief. Arnold summoned André to his command at West Point along the Hudson River, a new fort that defended the valuable Hudson Valley. The British dearly wanted to seize it, and Arnold gave André the plans, which he put in his boot for safekeeping on the ride back to New York. Some militiamen, who probably had in mind robbing a stranger rather than capturing a spy, seized André on 23 September 1780, frisked him for valuables, and instead found the maps of West Point in his boot. They also found his pass signed by Arnold. André confessed his identity immediately. The militiamen took André to Lieutenant Colonel Jameson at North Castle, who sent a report to his commanding officer, Arnold, to find out what was going on. Meanwhile, George Washington arrived to inspect West Point, but Arnold was already gone, aboard the British warship *Vulture* making way down the Hudson River. Washington could not have been surprised; he was the master of intelligence.

Washington used espionage skillfully. One spy was a Yale graduate and schoolteacher, the American patron saint of espionage, Captain Nathan Hale. Captured while conducting reconnaissance against the British on Long Island in his civilian clothes, he was quickly condemned to execution by hanging and died on 22 September 1776. Before the British hanged Hale, they asked him whether he had any last words or regrets. He responded by saying, "I regret that I have only one life to lose for my country." It is small wonder why his statue stands in CIA headquarters today. Another practitioner was Major Benjamin Tallmadge, whom Washington sent to spy on Clinton in New York City. Leader of the Culper Spy Ring, Tallmadge, who used tradecraft such as pseudonyms and invisible inks, detected Arnold's treachery at West Point.[21]

Outraged by the whole affair, Washington did not hesitate in dealing with Arnold's perfidy. Hale's execution in 1776 had not been forgotten by Washington, and after a brief trial, the military tribunal ordered André hanged as a spy in 1780. There is little doubt that Washington would have delighted in executing Arnold as well, and he even offered Clinton a trade: André for Arnold. But as far as Washington was concerned, André would do. Clinton himself faced a dilemma: he had offered Arnold the Crown's protection for his treachery and the plans for West Point, so an exchange was impossible. Though admired for his

Major John André asked to be executed by firing
squad, but General George Washington insisted that
he be hanged as a spy in retribution for Captain
Nathan Hale's execution by the British. Library of
Congress.

charm and honesty, and though he asked to be executed as a soldier by
musketry, André faced the gallows with dignity on 2 October 1780 in a
full dress uniform provided by Washington himself. The army, however,
focused its hatred squarely on Benedict Arnold. Joseph Plumb Martin,
a Continental soldier who knew Arnold from childhood, met him on a

road near Dobbs Ferry, New York, a few days before he deserted and noted, "He looked guilty, and well he might, for Satan was in as full possession of him at that instant as ever he was of Judas; it only wanted a musket ball to have driven him out."[22]

In 1781, in the middle of a stalemate in New York, Washington assigned Nathanael Greene of Rhode Island as commander of the southern army. Greene, a former Quaker excommunicated for joining the Continental Army, found the army in terrible shape in Charlotte, North Carolina. In a bold move, he split his army and sent Colonel "Big Dan" Morgan with 600 men to attack the British at Cowpens near the Broad River in northwest South Carolina, where Morgan faced Tarleton with his Loyalists and British regulars. Morgan's genius was simple: he never asked any of his soldiers to do anything more than they actually could. Thus, he developed a "shoot and scoot" approach for the militia: fire two shots and leave the battlefield to the Continentals who waited in the rear for the British to chase the militia. It worked a miracle for Morgan; 90 percent of Tarleton's force fell to American shot. Cornwallis was outraged.

Cornwallis tried to catch Morgan but failed. After burning everything his soldiers could not carry, he began a footrace with Greene and Morgan, who marched 200 miles in midwinter to the Dan River in northern North Carolina. Greene got his army across just as the British approached the riverbank on 14 February 1781. On 24 February, Greene returned to the Dan River, recrossed, and, with reinforcements that arrived on 14 March, met Cornwallis on 15 March 1781 at Guilford Courthouse. It was a Pyrrhic victory for Cornwallis, who lost about 500 soldiers—a quarter of his army. He realized that he had to abandon North Carolina and moved the army to Virginia.

In the spring of 1781 the French entered the final scene of the American Revolution. Washington deceived the British with false dispatches saying that he intended to attack New York City.[23] The intention was to keep the British from interfering with his planned march with the French General Rochambeau to Virginia to confront and ultimately defeat the British holed up at Yorktown. On 19 August 1781 the Continental and French armies left New York on the 400-mile march south to Yorktown, Virginia.

With the Chesapeake Bay blocked by a French naval force of thirty warships under Comte de Grasse and the land route blocked by the newly arrived Continental and French armies, Cornwallis was trapped. The siege began on 6 October 1791; the first cannonade began on 9

October. By 15 October Cornwallis informed Clinton that the situation was dire, and on 17 October Cornwallis asked for a twenty-four-hour cease-fire. Washington, in turn, demanded an unconditional surrender and got it on 19 October 1781. As the Marquis de Lafayette said, "The play, sir, is over."[24] But it was far from over for the British EPWs in American hands.

In terms of classifying EPWs of the Revolution, British soldiers and sailors presented no real legal, ethical, or moral problems. The same was true for the Hessians, who either were exchanged or deserted to become Americans. Tories or Loyalists presented a particular set of problems that is the subject of the next chapter. Canadian prisoners taken before the Declaration of Independence were exchanged, as were some but not many of General Burgoyne's Convention prisoners.[25]

The status and treatment of the British and Hessian EPWs during the Revolutionary War were respectable, in that the Americans conformed to common practice when and where they could. After the Battle of Trenton, Washington ordered the wounded Hessians paroled and left in Trenton. General Lord Stirling's brigade was ordered to guard all the prisoners and secure their safety.[26] The Americans then marched their prisoners to a safe crossing of the nearly frozen Delaware River and, with great difficulty, managed to get them across. The officers were confined in a ferry house at the landing at Johnson's Ferry, but the enlisted men were immediately marched to Newtown, five miles west of the Delaware, where they spent the night in the Presbyterian church and the Bucks County jail.[27] Stirling then took three Hessian EPWs to visit with Washington, who promptly invited them to stay for dinner while other officers dined with Stirling. The Hessian commander in chief, General von Heister, had done the same thing for Stirling when he became a POW after the Battle of Long Island. It was Washington's nature to be generous with captured officers, and he allowed one German, a Lieutenant Wiederhold, to return to Trenton to get his personal effects, including his underwear and uniform. At a minimum, the Germans were impressed with Washington's courtesy, demeanor, and consideration.

At Newtown, Pennsylvania, the Hessian officers signed a parole of honor. On 30 December 1776 the Hessian enlisted men marched from Newtown south into Philadelphia through Frankford and Kensington. From Philadelphia they marched west on 2 January 1777 toward Lancaster and were afterward scattered in different places in western Pennsylvania and Virginia. The Hessian band, consisting of nine expert musicians, remained in Philadelphia and gained a reputation for

Hessian prisoners marched to Philadelphia after their surrender at Trenton. Library of Congress.

outstanding musicianship for the rest of the war. Hardly a party or a patriotic event took place without the popular Hessian band. The other men went to work on regional farms, and by war's end, many Hessians captured at Trenton had simply meshed into the numerous German-speaking portions of Pennsylvania. Many of them married German

American women and started families, but they gathered again at the war's end for a formal release, with the option of staying in America or returning home.

The EPWs captured at Saratoga had a wholly different set of problems. As Convention prisoners, the British, Canadian, and German EPWs began an extended POW experience that lasted for many soldiers until 1783, the longest captivity of the Revolution. It began at Saratoga with the agreement between Gates and Burgoyne. According to British Sergeant Roger Lamb, the Americans ordered "the troops to march out of their camp with the honors of war, and the artillery of the entrenchments, to the verge of the river, where their arms and artillery must be left. The arms to be piled by word of command from their own officers."[28] While these formalities and customs of war were taking place, Gates ordered the American fifers and drummers to play "Yankee Doodle" to honor the occasion. Another British EPW, Lieutenant Thomas Anburey, lauded Burgoyne:

> General Burgoyne has done everything in this convention for the good of the troops, consistent with the service of his King and country: all that wisdom, valor, and a strict sense of honor could suggest. Confident, no doubt, of having exerted himself with indefatigable spirit in their service, he will despise popular clamor, truly sensible that no perfect and unbiased judge of actual service can condemn him.[29]

Burgoyne and a few of his staff officers were the only members of that army allowed to go home early; everyone else stayed to be exchanged for captured Americans whenever and wherever possible in this long war.

For British and Hessian officers, the captivity experience included paroles for up to ten miles, so they could roam around freely; housing in inns or private residences; pay from British paymasters in hard British currency; and hospitality when and where it might be given from what Anburey called "friends of government," that is, Loyalists. The British did not suffer much yet complained bitterly about their American captors. Anburey, for example, despised New England Congregationalists, radical Presbyterians who seemed terribly oppressive: "The inhabitants [of Massachusetts] will not suffer any other religion but the Congregationalist; they were happy to seize the opportunity of suppressing the Church of England, as it was gaining ground very fast, and therefore objected to it on the ground of praying for the King and Royal Family. Toleration is no part of their creed."[30]

Anburey was also upset when an American officer, Colonel David Henley, insulted, threatened, and assaulted several British officers. General Burgoyne himself brought charges against Henley and even argued the case.[31] Writing letters from his EPW encampment in Cambridge, Massachusetts, in 1778, Anburey noted Burgoyne's elegance in presenting the case but lamented the decision of the court:

> Colonel David Henley, late Commanding Officer of the post at Cambridge, tried at the Special General Court Martial, whereof Brigadier General Glover was President, accused by Lieutenant General Burgoyne, of a general tenor of language and conduct heinously criminal as an officer, and unbecoming as a man, of the most indecent, violent, vindictive severity against unarmed men, and of an intentional murder. The court, after mature consideration, are of the opinion, that the charge against Colonel Henley is not supported, and that he be discharged from his arrest.[32]

It was all a sham. Hensley was guilty as charged, but the American officers could not bring themselves to convict one of their own of such a serious crime against British EPWs. Immediately after he returned to command, the Americans quietly replaced Henley.

Soon the Convention prisoners were on the move to winter in Virginia. The South looked good, much better than New England. En route, they passed through upstate New York, then Valley Forge in Pennsylvania in the autumn of 1778, and finally to Virginia. Anburey finally admitted that exchange did not seem likely: "We shall remain prisoners the remainder of the war. The British officers have contributed to render their situation as comfortable as the nature of the country will possibly allow."[33] The troops, however, lived in wooden shacks and suffered rather badly in Winchester. Anburey wrote: "The soldiers have been so indifferently supplied with provisions, the barracks swarm with rats of an enormous size continually destroying the men's cloaths and bedding during the night; it is no very uncommon thing to see them running six or seven, one after the other, in the interstices of the logs with which the huts are constructed."[34] They were actually housed in a makeshift POW camp complete with guards placed around a fort.

On the march again in April 1781, Anburey's group recrossed the Blue Ridge and stayed a while in Frederick, Maryland, and later moved to Lancaster, Pennsylvania, where the Americans ordered the officers separated from the men. According to Anburey:

It was such a scene as must leave an everlasting impression on the mind. To behold so many men, who had bravely fought by our side—who in all their sufferings looked up to us for protection, forced from us into a prison, where, experiencing every severity, perhaps famishing for want of food, and ready to perish with cold, they had no one to look up to for redress, and little to expect from the humanity of Americans.[35]

Little did Anburey know that he and his fellow Convention prisoners were on their way to King's Bridge near New York, where in late 1781 they crossed into British lines. Paroled, they soon boarded transports home.

The Yorktown prisoners, unlike their fellow soldiers of Burgoyne's army, did not languish in captivity for long. According to Article 5 of the Articles of Capitulation, "The Soldiers [were] to be kept in Virginia, Maryland, or Pennsylvania & as much by Regiments as possible, and supplied with the same Rations or Provisions as are Allowed to Soldiers in the Service of America."[36] They were quickly taken to New York and paroled, and the American War of Independence was nearly over for them.

Captured Hessian soldiers serving with the British army fared a little better in American hands than the British did. Although many Hessians were tough professional soldiers, the Americans believed that many private soldiers had been conscripted against their will and that chances were good to neutralize them as a force. They were either exchanged or, if they decided to remain with the Americans, paroled. According to Lucy Leigh Bowie, the British paid 30 marks for each German recruit. If they were killed, wounded, or captured, the German rulers received another 30 marks. If they deserted, they got nothing.[37]

According to historian Edward J. Lovell, more than 18,000 German soldiers sailed to America in 1776 alone. One folksong full of gallows humor but sung with gusto by Hessian soldiers at the time was "Juchheiße nach Amerika":

Juchheiße nach Amerika,
  dir Deutschland gute Nacht!
Ihr Hessen, präsentiert's Gewehr,
  der Landgraf kommt zur Wacht.

Ade, Herr Landgraf Friederich,
  du zahlts uns Schnapps und Bier!

Schießst Arme man und Bein uns ab,
so zahlt sie England nach.[38]

The translation:

Yippee off to America,
Dear Germany, good night!
You Hessians present your rifles,
The count inspects his troops.

Farewell, Lord Count Frederick,
You pay for our booze and beer!
Should they shoot off our arms and legs,
Then England will pay you.

Yippee off to America,
Dear Germany, good night!
You Hessians present your rifles,
The count inspects his troops.[39]

According to ethnomusicologists Ludwig Erk and Franz Magnus Böhme writing in 1895, "The soldiers sang this song with military good humor in front of Her Excellency as the troops departed Kassel in 1775. The gallows humor in these verses probably did not register with their contemporaries."[40] Of the nearly 30,000 German soldiers sent to British America, 12,562 never returned; approximately 5,000 defected.[41]

When they were interned in German-speaking Pennsylvania villages and towns loyal to the Continental Congress, such as Reading and York, the locals did not welcome the Hessians, and although they were not held in close confinement like the British POWs, life was often very hard. Local Pennsylvania Germans were simply aghast when Hessian prisoners were placed near their homes in America. After all, German institutional militarism had been one of their principal reasons for leaving Germany in the first place.[42]

The term *Hessian* in America became derogatory and signified an aggressive, professional soldier full of disdain and contempt for Americans; more important, he was a soldier who killed only for money. In short, in the popular view, he was a mercenary. Truth, however, can be subsumed by propaganda in wartime. Keeping in mind that Germany was not a nation-state until 1871, these German soldiers were nothing of the sort. They were serving the German states of Brunswick, Hesse-

Cassel, Hesse-Hanau, Anspach-Bayreuth, Waldeck, and Anhalt-Zerbst, each of which had signed treaties with the king of England, and certainly not all of them were actually Hessian.

In a late-nineteenth-century defense of these soldiers, Joseph G. Rosengarten argued that Hesse, as a stronghold of the Protestants of north Germany, had been a close ally of England in wars before the American Revolution. For a century and a half, Hessian soldiers had fought shoulder to shoulder with the British, mainly against France.[43] In 1775 England approached the Hessian states for help in America, and the German aristocracy, always fearful of breakaway republics, was enthusiastic. True, an enormous amount of money exchanged hands between the British government and the Hessian nobility. Wilhelm IX, who received around £12,000 a year for his troops, built a new castle called Wilhelmshohe outside the city of Kassel with funds received from the British. The duke of Brunswick, who sent only 4,300 soldiers to America, cashed in £160,000 before the end of the war.[44] Though impressive, the soldiers never considered themselves mercenaries; they were just doing their duty.[45]

One problem for the Americans was the Hessian custom of taking booty from civilians as partial pay in the war zone. The Americans saw such actions as theft and propagandized the German soldiers as foreign mercenary evil-doers. In any event, the Hessians never wanted for pay, supplies, and amenities in the field while in America. Discipline was rigid in the German units, with a fair share of honesty, courage, and kindness, and whether in the field or in captivity, they often obtained respect from the Americans they fought. At least the Americans showed far less animosity toward them than toward the British. One sees that puzzling phenomenon in their personal narratives.[46]

For the Hessians, like the British, the surrender at Yorktown determined the fate of the Revolutionary War in October 1781. In 1782 both Sir Henry Clinton and General Wilhelm von Knyphausen returned home, but the German troops remained in captivity on the outskirts of towns such as Lancaster, Lebanon, York, and Reading in Pennsylvania and Frederick, Maryland. In June 1782 the Hessians of Burgoyne's Convention Army, some of whom had settled and married, were sought out and jailed. This became the first signal that repatriation might be on the horizon. According to Johann Conrad Döhla, a private in the Fourth Company of the Bayreuth Regiment from Ansbach-Bayreuth, in September 1782 Congress ordered all the German prisoners from Cornwallis's and Burgoyne's army to return to their regiments and enter the barracks, but times were changing. The Americans offered any soldier married to an American release for a fixed sum. Congress also gave permission for the German soldiers to swear allegiance, or "for thirty pounds, that is, eighty Spanish dollars, it was possible to buy freedom out of captivity, or to allow an inhabitant to buy freedom, and we could work off the indebtedness."[47] They could also join the Continental Army, and American recruiters made special efforts to sign them up. The Americans made no such offers to their British prisoners.

In 1783 Hessian prisoners received an offer of citizenship. Döhla recorded the event in his diary on 11 May: "Here in Frederick, a notice was posted that every captive had the choice of remaining in the country if he wished, and could work, trade, and farm without hindrance and, in all respects, be treated as a native-born citizen of America and enjoy all the customary freedoms. Because of this, the four regiments lost many men who stayed behind."[48] Döhla noted that on the day his two regiments marched out of Frederick, most of the city's inhabitants wished them luck, but he especially noted that they had left more than half their survivors to seek their lives and fortunes in America. From Frederick, they marched to Philadelphia and then all the way to New York, leaving for Germany on British ships.

General Sir Guy Carleton assumed command in New York and took on the unpleasant task of removing all British, Germans, former slaves who had cast their lot with the British, and Loyalists from the United States. They left for Canada and Great Britain in 1783 and observed as they began their trip home that American flags were raised in New York, something they had not seen during their stay. Those who remained became Americans.[49]

In retrospect, George Washington and Congress ordered decent treatment for British and Hessian soldiers captured by American forces. For the most part, treatment corresponded to the political climate, the culture and temper of the population, the season, the geographic features, and even the temperature of the regions where the war was fought. British officer EPWs often received paroles of honor within a designated area and, at their own expense, found quarters in private homes or inns while they awaited exchange. Enlisted prisoners resided in special encampments consisting of barracks surrounded by barricades; no real standards existed, and many escapes took place.[50] The Continental Congress allowed them $2 per week for support, although the Continental dollar was almost worthless. Exchanges took place on a local basis between commanders in the field because the British re-fused to acknowledge the sovereignty of the United States. Neither side ever solved accounting problems for EPW support, and when American prisoners did return, they were often too sick for further service. The British and Hessians returned home healthy for the most part, but the treatment of Loyalists was a wholly different matter.

Two

Habeas Corpus

War against Loyalists and Quakers

Should one of them [Loyalists] be captured by the rebels, however, he is hanged without mercy, and they neither give nor take quarter.
—Johann Conrad Döhla

The treatment of Loyalists and some Quakers was much harsher than that accorded to the British and Hessians who became EPWs of the Continental Army or state militias, in part because both groups were Americans. In terms of precedents, the Revolution set the stage for what would take place repeatedly in American military history: the United States treats foreign enemy prisoners of war humanely and in accordance with the rules of war that exist at the time; however, internal prisoners, especially Americans perceived as disloyal to cause and country, face a host of troubles. To understand the level of hatred between Loyalists and Patriots, it is useful to examine its roots.

Prior to the signing of the Declaration of Independence in July 1776, Americans were universally unhappy with England, the mother country. Starting in 1763, the year that marked the successful end of the French and Indian War, the British complained that it was too expensive to keep an army in the colonies and demanded that the American colonists, wealthy and untaxed as they were, help pay for their own defense. Additionally, to keep the eastern tribal allies content, the British attempted to block westward movement by the American colonists past an arbitrary Indian demarcation line that ran northeast to southwest from western New York through Pennsylvania and south through the Allegheny Mountains. From time to time the British actually attempted to enforce this prohibition, but they failed to do so effectively. To the colonists, the Indians represented a distinct impediment to progress and were untrustworthy allies in war. Thus, the British commitment to the Indians meant very little and actually lowered the esteem for England held by many American colonists.

In England, as in America, two political groups took shape in the middle of the eighteenth century: Tories or conservatives, and Whigs or liberals. As Enlightenment ideas of political freedom, separation of powers, religious tolerance and deism, upward mobility through striving, scientific inquiry, and education migrated from France into the English-speaking world, British and American Whigs embraced them, while the Tories held firmly to the traditional position of Crown and top-down aristocratic power in government.

In America, the Tory approach made sense if one considers how diverse the colonies really were. The American colonies conducted their affairs as separate little countries and hired men such as Benjamin Franklin to lobby for their best interests in Parliament. That the colonies enjoyed no direct representation might have been unfortunate but not lethal to most subjects in the colonies. What bound them together was not religion—though most colonies had indeed been founded as religious utopias, that notion collapsed in 1693 in Salem, Massachusetts—and certainly not any sort of uniformity in institutions. What provided commonality was the fact that they were Englishmen, ruled by local oligarchies in accordance with the British Constitution as they perceived it, English common law, British currency and economic principles, and basic British social hierarchies. King George III was certainly revered, but absent were the lords and ladies of England. Present were the ministers, lawyers, farmers, and merchants who wielded the real power in America. The difference between Tories and Whigs in the American colonies had less to do with philosophy than with practicality, especially in determining the kind of institutions that were growing in the colonies and how they functioned. America, after all, was a rough-and-tumble place, and the Crown represented a real security blanket, but not enough of one to make a difference in the end. "The basic weakness of the Tories," writes William H. Nelson, "was not their attachment to Britain, for this was a consequence of their weakness; rather their weakness lay in the fact that they held social or political opinions which could prevail in America only with British assistance."[1]

Both Whigs and Tories grew increasingly distraught over British attitudes toward the colonies starting in 1763, when Parliament decided to reorganize the British empire and tax the colonies. The Currency Act of 1764 stopped the colonies from printing paper money. One result was that it drove many merchants out of business; the other was anger. The same year the Sugar Act taxed sugar smuggled from the islands in the Caribbean, with the same effect. In 1765 Parliament emphatically bypassed the colonial assemblies and, with the Stamp Act, attempted to show the colonials who controlled the taxing authority in the British

Empire: Parliament. The radical Sons of Liberty, led by Samuel Adams in Boston, responded with controlled violence: they tore up the agents' homes and offices and then marched to the royal governor's house and destroyed it. Royal Governor Thomas Hutchinson was aghast at this political misbehavior. How could men who supported the notion of liberty burn down a governor's home? There was no obvious answer other than the radical notion of a total break from England. Nevertheless, the American Tories maintained that any opposition to parliamentary taxation was a challenge to British sovereignty in America.

In London the Chancellor of the Exchequer introduced the first measures to tax America in the House of Commons in 1767—the Townsend Acts, which resorted to port duties on wine, oil, fruits, glass, paper, lead colors, and tea. The idea was to raise money internally to pay fixed salaries to royal governors and civil servants and to raise money to supply the army.[2] According to Nelson, the Tories were as "indignant as the Whigs at what seemed an unjust and arbitrary exercise of British authority."[3] Tories such as Thomas Hutchinson of Massachusetts attacked the Stamp Act; Whigs such as John Adams not only petitioned the king but also circulated a letter to the colonial legislatures urging them to allow no taxes except those levied by themselves. Successful? Absolutely! The radical Sons of Liberty, mostly wealthy merchants in Boston, agreed not to import any taxed goods, and the Daughters of Liberty promised to wear homespun clothing and not drink any English tea.[4] The divisions between colonies and Crown may well have begun here, but events escalated the discord.

Positions hardened. In 1766 the Declaratory Act held that Parliament had the right to tax the American colonies, and the Quartering Act said that British troops could be barracked in private homes. It now seemed that an army of protection devolved into an army of occupation, and in 1768 British troops arrived in Boston on armed patrol. Community relations descended into a cauldron of political intrigue and seething hatred. On 5 March 1770 a riot broke out on the Boston docks. The British troops, fully understanding that they were in severe trouble and hearing a shot fired, presumed it had been aimed at them and returned fire, killing five men and wounding eight. Successfully defending the British troops in an American court of law was none other than John Adams. But the damage had been done.

In 1772 the Sons of Liberty expanded their activities and established Committees of Correspondence designed to report on British activities. Of particular interest was the issue of tea and the Tea Act of 1773. The

Americans preferred untaxed smuggled tea from the Dutch and refused to pay any taxes on British tea imported by the East India Tea Company. The Sons of Liberty took direct action; they dressed up in Indian costumes and threw all the British tea into Boston Harbor—an act known as the Boston Tea Party. The British overreacted and passed four acts, what the Americans called the Intolerable Acts, in 1774: the Port Act, which closed Boston to trade until the citizens paid the East India Company for the dumped tea; the Massachusetts Government Act, which transferred power from the assembly to the royal governor; the Justice Act, which provided for royal officials accused of capital crimes to be tried only in England; and the Quartering Act, similar to the prior one, but putting Boston under martial law under General Thomas Gage. The idea of paying for the tea was ridiculed. One Bostonian quipped, "If a man draws his sword on me to deprive me of life or liberty and I break his sword, ought I pay for the sword?"[5]

To make things worse in 1774, Parliament passed the Quebec Act, which recognized Catholicism in Canada and allowed Catholics to hold office. Article V read:

And, for the more perfect Security and Ease of the Minds of the Inhabitants of the said Province, it is hereby declared: That his Majesty's Subjects, professing the Religion of the Church of Rome of and in the said Province of Quebec, may have, hold, and enjoy, the free Exercise of the Religion of the Church of Rome and that the Clergy of the said Church may hold, receive, and enjoy, their accustomed Dues and Rights, with respect to such Persons only as shall profess the said Religion.[6]

Nothing infuriated New England Congregationalists more.

The Quebec Act challenged all the antipapal rhetoric that dominated New England's pulpits and meeting houses. According to historian Francis D. Cogliano, the Continental Congress resolved not to submit to this act because George III must be a secret Catholic and thus the "Pope of Canada."[7] The Quebec Act also extended Canada south to the Ohio River, which blocked off what was beginning to be called the Northwest Territory, and declared it to be Indian land forever. To Massachusetts, Pennsylvania, Connecticut, and Virginia, this was completely unacceptable.[8]

The year 1774 culminated with the First Continental Congress, which had no official standing or sanction from Parliament and was, in British eyes, an illegal gathering. Present were three basic groups: the radicals, consisting of all the Massachusetts Whigs who demanded a boycott of and ultimately independence from Britain; the conservatives, consisting of Tories who advocated a capitulation to the will of Crown and Parliament; and the compromisers, who advocated a denouement. From all the talk came some action. The Continental Association agreed to boycott all English goods; John Adams wrote a Declaration of Rights and Grievances; and, most important, the Congress passed the Suffolk County Resolves on 6 September 1774, a provision to strengthen armories in and around Boston so that local and regional militias could defend themselves against British armed oppression. After all, General Thomas Gage had threatened to arrest any rebels he found, and the Sons of Liberty were just as determined to stop him.

By 1775 the lines had been clearly drawn. Many Loyalists became officeholders whose incomes depended totally on the existing regime. Anglicans with close connections to the English-established church were mostly Loyalists, or what the Patriot Congregationalists called "king worshippers." Loyalists who believed that Parliament possessed the right to tax the American colonies were known as "legality Tories." As one can imagine, these events and documents created a complete polarization between Tories and Whigs, mainly in New England. Tories became Loyalists; Whigs became Rebels or Patriots.

In mid-April 1775 General Gage ordered units of the British army to arrest rebel leaders and seize the stores in the armories. The "Red Coats"—or "Lobster back Sons-a-Bitches," as the Americans rudely called them—marched west from Boston to Lexington and found themselves facing the town's militia, mostly blooded veterans of the last war against the French and Indians who were not backing down. Like the Boston Massacre, a shot was fired by someone (neither the militia nor the British troops), and the British opened fire—the first shots of the American Revolution, which would last eight years. Before the smoke cleared, the British marched off to Concord, where the Americans sat waiting for them in a *rage militaire* that put hundreds of farmers in the position of carrying out what they believed to be a legal and moral defense of their homes and families. According to historians James Kirby Martin and Mark Edward Lender, "With the advantage of historical hindsight, it makes more sense to conclude that both sides drifted toward a state of civil war because they could not comprehend the intention of the other."[9] Then came the Battle of Bunker (Breed's) Hill near Boston shortly thereafter, and it was clear that real war had begun in North America.

The Second Continental Congress was called in 1775 to develop an "Olive Branch Petition" to present to Crown and Parliament before things got worse. The Americans would stop fighting if the British army went home and Parliament revoked the Intolerable Acts. Congress also realized that the Massachusetts militia needed a general and chose George Washington of Virginia, who happened to attend in his Continental colonel's uniform. As a result, this militia evolved into the Continental Army. The Olive Branch Petition was too little too late. On 23 August 1775 King George III declared war against the rebellious American colonies in a "Proclamation by the King for Suppressing Rebellion and Sedition." It read:

Whereas many of our subjects in divers parts of our Colonies and Plantations in North America, misled by dangerous and ill designing men and forgetting the allegiance which they owe to the power that has protected and supported them; after various disorderly acts committed in disturbance of the public peace, to the obstruction of lawful commerce, and to the oppression of our loyal subjects carrying on the same; have at length proceeded to open and avowed rebellion, by arraying themselves in a hostile manner, to withstand the execution of the law, and traitorously preparing, ordering and levying war against us: and whereas there is reason to apprehend that such rebellion hath been much promoted and encouraged by traitorous correspondence, counsels and comfort of divers wicked and desperate persons within this realm: To the end therefore, that none of our subjects may neglect their duty through ignorance thereof, or through any doubt of the protection of the law will afford to their loyalty and zeal, we have thought fit by and with the advice of our Privy Council, to issue our Royal Proclamation, hereby declaring, that not only all our officers, civil and military, are obliged to exert their utmost endeavors to suppress such rebellion, and to bring the traitors to justice, but that all our subjects of this realm, and the dominions thereunto belonging, are bound by law to be aiding and assisting in the suppression of such rebellion, and to disclose and make known all traitorous conspiracies and attempts against us, our crown and dignity; and we do accordingly strictly charge and command all our Officers, as well civil as military, and all others our obedient and loyal subjects, to use their utmost endeavors to withstand and suppress such rebellion, and to disclose and make known all treasons and traitorous conspiracies which they shall know to be against us, our crown and dignity; and for that purpose, that they transmit to one of our principal Secretaries of State, or other proper officer, due and full information of all persons who shall be found carrying on correspondence with, or in any manner or degree aiding or abetting the persons now in open arms and rebellion against our Government, within any of our Colonies and Plantations in North America, in order to bring to consign punishment the authors, perpetrators, and abetters of such traitorous designs.[10]

This proclamation was clearly a declaration of war against the New England and other Whigs who began to bear arms against the British army in the colonies. George III followed it up with the American Prohibitory Act, which declared that all manner of trade and commerce was prohibited and certainly ended any chance for reconciliation.[11] There was only one piece left to complete the puzzle.

Thomas Paine's pamphlet *Common Sense,* published anonymously in 1776, called for the total rejection of absolute rule by any king anywhere. Radical perhaps, but this unsigned document poured oil on an already lighted fire and inflamed the colonies into action. Richard Henry Lee of Virginia declared the colonies to be "free and independent states" in June 1776, but Congress postponed the vote until July for want of a formal legal document. So Congress did what it did best: it appointed a committee consisting of John Adams of Massachusetts, Roger Sherman of Connecticut, Benjamin Franklin of Pennsylvania, Robert Livingston of New York, and Thomas Jefferson of Virginia. Jefferson, the youngest member, wrote the initial drafts in three distinct parts: a statement of its Enlightenment philosophy and intent, a long list of grievances against the Crown, and a statement of resolve and intention. After changes initiated by Franklin, Adams, and the others, the Declaration of Independence, reading like a divorce decree, transformed the colonies into states and the states into a sovereign country. It was clearly treason against the Crown; it clearly forced Americans to take sides, regardless of any individual desire to do so; and it clearly meant war. The Loyalist community stood in shock. From 1774 to 1776 Loyalists attempted to respond to Patriot propaganda by appealing to Americans' sense of duty to the Crown and their "Englishness"; most important, they offered alternative solutions to revolution and war. Try as they might, the Loyalists paled in comparison to the powerful Patriot propaganda, and as the war dragged on, they began to lose all their battles.[12]

American Patriots despised the Loyalists. In 1776 and 1777 the new states required Association Test Acts, early loyalty oaths designed to uphold the sovereignty and reject the validity of King George III's rule over the new American states. Massachusetts passed its first Test Act in 1776, requiring every male person older than sixteen years of age to swear loyalty, with the following penalties: disarmament, surrender of the ability to hold public office, and loss of salaries for ministers, school masters, and the governors of Harvard College. In January 1778 Massachusetts raised the stakes. Persons who joined the enemy after 19 April 1775 and were captured could be committed to jail and then sent to British lines. If they returned, the death penalty could be imposed. Connecticut did much the same. In October 1776 its Test Act required members of the general assembly, civil and military officers, and all freemen to take the oath. Anyone who refused was deprived of office or disenfranchised. New York went for the money. In June 1778 New York required an oath from all persons of neutral and equivocal character (Loyalists) who had sufficient influence to do harm. Anyone who refused could be removed to anyplace within the enemy's lines, and names would be recorded. Anyone who failed to appear in court on summons would be guilty of treason, and his lands would be double taxed. New Jersey went for the land. In June 1777 an oath was required for reconciliation. Failure to take the oath meant the forfeiture of one's personal estate; worse, no transfer of real estate was permitted.

Pennsylvania was similarly heavy-handed. In June 1777 it required oaths from all male inhabitants over eighteen years old. Anyone who refused would be unable to hold office; serve on a jury; sue for debts; vote or be elected to anything; buy, sell, or transfer lands; or carry arms. In October 1777, as a supplement to the June Test Act, Pennsylvania threatened jail without bail for any male older than sixteen years traveling outside Philadelphia or persons suspected of being unfriendly, with costs levied on any goods he owned. Delaware threatened to confiscate estates in its Test Acts; Maryland exempted Quakers, Mennonites, and Dunkers from swearing an oath, but they had to "affirm" instead. Anyone who refused had to pay three times the tax in all public and county assessments for life, could not sue in court, was subject to fines, and was forbidden to practice law or medicine, preach, teach, hold office, or vote.

In the South the Test Acts were a little less severe. Virginia threatened prosecution but not death, and North Carolina initiated land restrictions. South Carolina, however, in 1778 required anyone refusing to take the oath to sell his land and leave; if he refused to leave or came back—death. Georgia, a heavily Loyalist region, required its Test Act oath in 1781 and banished anyone who refused it.[13]

Thus, one can see how the Patriots in power separated the Loyalists from their midst: denial of property rights, double or triple taxation, disenfranchisement, banishment, and even death. The process did not end there: states passed a host of other anti-Loyalist statutes that made life miserable for them.

In 1778 the stakes for Loyalists rose when several states passed exile laws, and the Continental Congress ordered the seizure, burning, and destruction of their properties. States heavily populated by Loyalists, such as Maryland and New York, earned millions of dollars from the sale of these confiscated properties, and five states disenfranchised Loyalists completely. States passed statutes against counterfeiting currency and tickets for the U.S. lottery, and most states forbade anyone to trade with the British, despite the fact that American Continental currency had depreciated to nearly no value at all. It is not difficult to see how the Loyalists quickly became refugees in their own country.

Forming military units, surprisingly, did not come easy for Loyalists, but in time they formed many known as Rangers (see appendix 1). Yet the Loyalists failed to form military organizations like the Continental Army, with its disciplined training at Valley Forge under Baron Friedrich von Steuben in 1777. At first, the Loyalists became raiders, going into the countryside to prey on their neighbors, driving off horses, kidnapping landowners, killing livestock, and in some cases leaving whole villages in ruin. According to historians Robert A. East and Jacob Judd, certain groups of armed Loyalists were notorious for engaging in the ugliest kinds of violence. Andrew Elliott, the eventual lieutenant governor of British-controlled New York, warned that such a destructive war would be totally counterproductive; yet day by day, the Loyalists conducted raids, ambushes, and atrocities.[14] In short, these men believed they had a license to kill anyone in the New York countryside they perceived as an enemy. On 30 December 1777 Congress insisted that those Loyalists captured while serving voluntarily be returned to their home states for punishment.[15]

In New York, Loyalists joined Iroquois allies under Chief Joseph Brant in 1777 and spread brutality and murder over the Wyoming Valley in north-central Pennsylvania. With a force of 110 Loyalists and 450 Iroquois, they struck hard. The American militia consisted of only 360 men, who left the protection of the local stockade and ran into a deadly fight. All were lost; those captured were killed by fire or beheaded, and for the people of the Wyoming Valley, the event was a holocaust.[16] As a

Along with Loyalist troops, Chief Joseph Brant spread brutality and murder over the Wyoming Valley in north-central Pennsylvania in 1777. National Archives of Canada.

result, Congress ordered Washington to do something about the troubles in the backcountry. In 1779 enough was enough, and Washington sent General John Sullivan to check Loyalist-Indian activity in New York. With a force of nearly 3,000 Continental soldiers, Sullivan defeated the Iroquois and Butler's Rangers at the Battle of Newtown (present-day Elmira) near the Pennsylvania–New York border. Sullivan did not stop there. His forces continued deep into New York's Indian country, destroying villages and crops wherever they could find them. In all, forty-one towns were ransacked, burned, and leveled.[17] Both sides acted savagely; quarter was out of the question, and the Iroquois retreated from the war. It is no wonder that this sort of warfare generated a great deal of hatred in the land, especially in the backcountry. Farmers lived in abject fear of Loyalist and Indian raids, often leaving crops in the fields rather than risking their lives to bring them in.

In New York much of the Revolution devolved into a guerrilla war. The colorful James DeLancey led a group of Westchester Refugees (Loyalists) known as DeLancey's Cowboys, a unit of about 500 men who surpassed the bounds of conventional warfare and were simply conducting self-interested freebooting.[18] Despite the local farmers' desire to be left alone, DeLancey's unit ravaged the land and inflicted terrible suffering on the innocent people in the county. Some may have been honorable men fighting for homes and rights taken away from them by Test Acts and other statutes, but most were simply thugs in search of plunder, despite the fact that most had been properly enrolled in the British army before they joined DeLancey's Cowboys. At sea, Loyalists became privateers against private American shipping and exchanged their prisoners only for other Loyalists. All this was done to emancipate the country from "Republican tyranny," and retaliations and reprisals became the norm—tit for tat, *lex talionis,* an eye for an eye. The danger in this civil war was that no one could be neutral; everyone became the enemy of someone.

Loyalists joined the British army in significant numbers. According to historian Claude Halstead Van Tyne, New York alone furnished about 15,000 men to the British army and Royal Navy, and more than 8,000 joined the Loyalist militia. In all, the British enlisted about 50,000 men from American sympathizers.[19] Yet the British never unleashed Loyalist troops in an all-out counterinsurgency war, except perhaps in the Carolinas in 1780 and 1781. In 1779 seventy Loyalists were captured in North Carolina while slaughtering cattle for food. They were convicted of high treason and condemned to death: five of the most active prisoners were hanged, and the others were pardoned.[20] Loyalists joined British Lieutenant Colonel Banastre Tarleton to conduct a reign of terror against civilians and attempt to chase partisans such as Francis Marion, William Davie, and Thomas Sumter. America was not Ireland, however, and the British had no desire to turn it into one.

Those Loyalists captured while actively under arms at nearly every engagement during the Revolution were not exchanged as the British and Hessians were; instead, they were returned in close confinement to their state of origin for disposition.[21] Many of the officers were tried and executed out of hand, but the Americans made some effort to recruit captured troops into their own militias if possible. In his diary entry of 1 February 1779, Johann Conrad Döhla, a private in the Fourth Company of the Hessian Bayreuth Regiment, described what Americans did to other Americans: "These Countrymen are inhabitants who have sworn allegiance to the King of England and receive English pay and provisions, and in the war perform valuable service. What they capture, however, they keep for themselves. Should one of them be captured by the rebels, however, he is hanged without mercy, and they neither give nor take quarter."[22] An escalated level of hatred gripped the land.

James Moody was one of those New Jersey Loyalist officers who got very close to the hangman. In 1783 Moody published his story, *Lieut. James Moody's Narrative of His Exertions and Sufferings in the Cause of Government, since the Year 1776*. At its conclusion, one finds a series of certificates of authenticity written by an interesting cast of characters: William Franklin,[23] Loyalist governor of New Jersey before the Americans captured and imprisoned him at the Newgate Prison–Simsbury Mines in Connecticut; British Major General James Pattison; and Major George Beckwith, aide-de-camp to Hessian General Wilhelm von Knyphausen. Moody was an idealist. He believed that however real the Americans' grievances were, they were no excuse for war. "Rebellion," wrote Moody, "was not the way to redress them. It required moreover but little skill to know, that rebellion is the foulest of all crimes, and that what was begun in wickedness must end in ruin."[24]

For the most part, Moody went on spying missions against Washington's army. Once he conceived of a plan to kidnap the Patriot governor of New Jersey; another plan involved blowing up a magazine not far from Morristown. Neither plan came to fruition. He did, however, manage to rescue a British POW sentenced to death for robbing a Patriot house. Captured in July 1780 by troops of General Anthony Wayne, Moody was removed to West Point under Benedict Arnold's command and petitioned him for relief. After Washington arrived and the turncoat Arnold left, Washington ordered Moody removed to his own camp on 11 September 1780. There, Moody received quite a surprise: a trial for his life. The verdict was harsh: "You are so obnoxious; you have been, and are likely to be, so mischievous to us, that, be assured, we are resolved to get rid of you at any rate. Besides, you cannot deny, and it can be proved by incontestable evidence, that you have enlisted men in this State for the King's service, and this, by our laws, is *death*."[25] Moody understood that death was inevitable unless he did something about it, so he escaped and returned to British headquarters in New York.

His next mission took him into rebel country in the hope of intercepting General Washington's dispatches. After failing the first time, Moody managed to accomplish his mission, brought the dispatches back to headquarters, and even received a promotion from ensign to lieutenant for his valor. Moody continued his spying activities until the end of the war and, like so many landless and poverty-stricken Loyalists, left America in 1783 for England.

There are two other categories of Loyalists that need to be addressed: blacks and Quakers. In 1775 the last royal governor of Virginia, John Murray, the fourth Lord Dunmore, called on the slaves of rebel owners to flee their plantations and join the army loyal to King George III. Approximately 800 black Loyalists formed a unit called the Ethiopian Regiment; they lost one battle and died in large numbers from disease in the British camps. At war's end, slaveholding Loyalists took their slaves with them, some 75,000 to 100,000 people, to Nova Scotia and New Brunswick in Canada and to England. Some freed slaves eventually wound up in Sierra Leone in Africa after 1787.

The Society of Friends, or Quakers, became embroiled in a truly odd captivity. For them, even suspicions of Loyalism caused problems. The Continental Congress took some prominent pacifist Philadelphia Quakers as political prisoners and ordered them into temporary exile in Virginia for fear of their suspected loyalties to the Crown.[26] Pennsylvania was the only colony where Quakers had any real importance or any real problems with Congress. Politically, despite their close connections to Quakers in England, many expressed solid sympathy with the complaints about taxation imposed by Parliament and later with the independence movement, but under no circumstances could they abide the violence associated with it. Thus, the Friends dissuaded their membership from any participation in military or wartime activities and turned their attention to the relief of those distressed, regardless of denomination.[27]

Quakers are forbidden to take oaths, and although other states were flexible with their Quaker citizens in terms of their Test Acts, Pennsylvania was not. Knowing or suspecting that the British were going to occupy Philadelphia soon, the Continental Congress (meeting in Philadelphia and getting ready to evacuate westward to York) recommended to the Supreme Executive Council that a number of prominent Quakers be arrested and sent to the backcountry, "there to be confined or enlarged upon parole as their characters and behavior may require."[28] The Quakers were horrified and claimed they had no notion why orders for their exile had been issued. What crime had they committed? Why was there no trial or hearing? Were the basic assumptions of English common law, habeas corpus, and corpus delicti discarded because of hostilities in Pennsylvania and the colonies in general?

How we understand the law—that is, how we interpret the idea of the law—forms the structure underlying the rationale for individual and institutional responses to conflicts. This is especially true relative to personal freedom. Colonial Americans subscribed to English common law, especially in the domain of personal freedom. Habeas corpus has often been called "the great writ of English liberty." It reflects Roman and English law prior to the Norman conquest of Britain in 1066 and predates the Magna Carta (1215). In English common law, invoking the writ of habeas corpus (literally, "give us" or "let us have the body") means that a person indicted on any crime can offer bail and be released until trial. The writ also provides that the prosecution must bring an accused person into public court to face his or her accusers. In 1679 the "great writ" of personal freedom was codified as the Habeas Corpus Act; however, it excluded bail for treason or for unreasonable or outrageous crimes.

In American law, the writ of habeas corpus acts as the basis for the legal proceeding that determines whether one person must remain in the custody of another. In short, custody or freedom depends on the legal adequacy of the custodian's explanation of why a particular captive ought to be held. It appears in the U.S. Constitution (1787) in Article I, Section 9, Clause 2: "The Privilege of the Writ of Habeas Corpus shall not be suspended unless when in Cases of Rebellion, or Invasion the public safety may require it." In addition to the writ of habeas corpus, the rule of corpus delicti ("the body of the crime") plays a role in defining what we accept as the substance of the crime. In other words, corpus delicti defines not only the crime's existence but also a criminal agency as its cause. Linked together, habeas corpus and corpus delicti form a very powerful, two-pronged legal basis for Americans to act when they believe they have been wronged, regardless of the arena. Although these principles do not apply pro forma to the international arena, they constitute part of our common fund of traditional legal ideas that serve as guidelines for specific actions and socially constructed activities.

The Continental Congress simply bypassed both habeas corpus and corpus delicti for fear that the Quakers might do business, cooperate, or be friendly with the British on their way to Philadelphia in 1777. When Major General John Sullivan supposedly discovered a document from the Quakers' Spanktown Yearly Meeting, he wrote a letter to Congress on 25 August 1777: "Among baggage taken on Staten Island, the 22d instant, I find a number of important papers. A copy of three I enclose for the perusal of Congress. The one of the Yearly Meeting of Spanktown, held the 19th instant, I think worthy of attention of Congress."[29]

Information from Jersey, 19th August 1777

It is said General Howe landed near the head of Chesapeake Bay, but cannot learn the particular spot, or when.

Washington lays in Pennsylvania, about twelve miles from Coryell's Ferry.

Sullivan lays about six miles north of Morristown, with about two thousand men.

Spanktown Yearly Meeting

It was clearly a fake document—there was never a meeting of Quakers in Spanktown, New Jersey—but it was very damning nevertheless.

With all these misunderstandings, and perhaps intentional forgeries under foot, the twenty Quakers under suspicion of Loyalism drew no sympathy. Henry Laurens, then president of Congress, complained of wasting hours debating the "silly point" of whether the prisoners even deserved a hearing in their defense. James Lovell, another member of Congress, considered the arrest of the group justified for the safety of the union. According to historian Robert F. Oaks, with attitudes like these, further petitions were useless.[30] The twenty arrested were James Pemberton, Miers Fisher, John Pemberton, Samuel Pleasants, Thomas Gilpin, Samuel Fisher, Owen Jones Jr., Edward Pennington, William Drewet Smith, Charles Eddy, Israel Pemberton, John Hunt, Thomas Pike, Thomas Fisher, Henry Drinker, Elijah Brown, William Smith, Charles Jervis, Thomas Affleck, and Thomas Wharton Sr.

On 10 September 1777 the Pennsylvania Supreme Council directed the officers of the Philadelphia Troop of Light Horse to escort the Quakers first to Reading, where they remained for a week. During this time, two Quakers attempted to convince the British to rescue them. After Congress discovered the plot, John Roberts and Abraham Carlisle were accused of high treason, tried, convicted, and executed by hanging in June 1778. Winding up in Winchester, Virginia, along with Hessian EPWs from the Battle of Trenton and British EPWs, the Quakers were housed in private homes. They wrote letters and petitions to family and politicians, held religious meetings, and tried to contain their boredom and indignation as best they could. Virginia Quakers attempted to offer some assistance by calling on General Washington himself, but the commander in chief stayed out of the fray. Besides, Washington may have held a grudge against the Pennsylvania Quakers because he had difficulties obtaining food from Quaker farmers for his soldiers at Valley Forge.

One Quaker escaped. Dr. William Drewet Smith, a man who had actually taken the required oath, simply got on his horse one morning and left Winchester. The other prisoners were annoyed by Dr. Smith's escape and feared reprisals, for good reason: threats were made to remove them even farther from home, this time to Staunton, but that never happened; they remained in Winchester. Another prisoner learned that a British officer was living in his home in Philadelphia. Henry Drinker learned through letters from his wife that his family's "new guest behaves unexceptionally, and much like a gentleman."[31] No one in the Drinker household was happy about having a British officer as a forced houseguest, but there was little anyone could do about it as long as the British occupied Philadelphia that winter.

As 1778 opened, Congress gave the prisoners another chance to pledge their allegiance, this time to Pennsylvania, but this was unacceptable to the Quakers. By March 1778 illness struck Winchester, and two prisoners died—John Hunt and Thomas Gilpin. The wives back in Philadelphia began to take action. First they sent medical supplies to their husbands in Winchester; then they rode to Valley Forge to see General Washington himself. Washington told them that because their husbands were prisoners of state, he had neither control nor influence over their fate.

The process of freeing these political prisoners began in March 1778, when the Pennsylvania Council asked Congress to return them from Virginia and place them under its authority in Lancaster, Pennsylvania. Virginia complied, and all the remaining exiles arrived in Lancaster on 27 April 1778 and at once petitioned for their release. Rather than responding positively, the Supreme Executive Council of Pennsylvania simply gave them safe passage to Philadelphia. By the time the British abandoned Philadelphia in favor of establishing headquarters in New York, the entire Quaker issue began to be an embarrassment. The Quaker imprisonment problem came to an end by the summer of 1778, but the feelings of hostility remained for anyone accused of siding with the Crown. According to Arthur J. Mekeel, the American Revolution caused the Quakers' final separation from any participation in political life, whereas once they had been very active. A distinct kind of Quakerism developed in the United States, one quite different from its British cousin.[32]

Were these men Loyalists? For the most part, no. Did they question the colonies' right to rebel against the authority of Crown and Parliament? In part, yes. Was their imprisonment by Congress in Virginia legal? In part, yes, because there were no statutes prohibiting such action in wartime. More important, each state passed rigid Test Acts that required oaths the Quakers refused to take. Although the infringement on the rights of these Quakers was an early violation of the civil liberties that Americans enjoy today, one cannot indulge in presentism and judge the past with the today's sensibilities. One thing is certain, though: the Quakers paid dearly for the luxury of conscience.[33]

By the end of the war, approximately 100,000 Loyalists left the United States for Britain or Canada, and as part of the peace process from 1783 until 1790, the British government established a claims commission that examined 4,118 claims and paid £3,292,452 in compensation. That the American Revolution was in part a vicious and unforgiving civil war cannot go unnoticed. The sons of the American Loyalists—the United Empire Loyalists—would meet the sons of the United States nineteen years later in another war.

THREE

The Second American Revolution

Cartel and Enemy Prisoners of the War of 1812

To secure a sufficient number of hostages, to answer in their persons
for the proper treatment of a certain number of American officers
now in possession of the enemy.
—James Madison

When the Revolution ended in 1783, Americans believed the rest of the
world would leave them alone. Issues such as banking and fiscal management of the American government commanded center stage; foreign
trade and diplomacy fell a long way down the ladder of priorities. America needed a constitution, an army, a navy, taxation, and banking rules.
There were other vital issues left on the table when the Revolution came
to an end in 1783. Internally, how was the nation going to expand and
grow into the Northwest Territories that several colonies had claimed?
How was it going to deal with the native Indian populations that lived
in the interior and had fought both for and against the Americans in the
Revolution?

Externally, the international arena was full too. In an effort to
resolve differences with France that had been accumulating since the
Treaty of Alliance of 1778, President John Adams dispatched a commission of three men to meet with French Minister of Foreign Affairs
Charles-Maurice de Talleyrand-Périgord in 1797. After many delays,
three Talleyrand intermediaries approached the anonymous American
commissioners and demanded apologies for Adams's allusions that were
critical of France plus the payment of a bribe of several million dollars before official negotiations could proceed. Convinced that further
negotiations were hopeless, the three commissioners returned to the
United States, and President Adams released their dispatches to Congress, substituting X, Y, and Z for the names of Talleyrand's agents.
"I will never send another minister to France without assurances that
he will be received, respected, and honored, as the representative of a
great, free, powerful, and independent nation," Adams declared. The
American public was outraged at the publication of the dispatches, and

Congress enacted a series of measures to raise an army and authorize a Navy Department. It also unilaterally abrogated treaties with France, authorizing privateers and public vessels to attack French ships found competing with American commerce. Between 1798 and 1800 the U.S. Navy captured more than eighty French ships, although neither country officially declared war.[1]

The British delighted in the anti-French uproar in America and moved to assist the United States against a common foe: revolutionary France. President Adams wanted to avoid a major war and was confident that if France had wanted war, it would have responded to American attacks against French ships. Talleyrand feared that limited hostilities with the United States might escalate into a full-scale war and let it be known that he would accept a new American diplomatic representative. In the midst of public and Federalist disappointment that there would be no war, Adams conceded to Federalist demands and expanded the single representative into a commission of three. Although the Franco-American negotiations were initially deadlocked, France finally agreed to cancel the Treaty of Alliance of 1778 if the United States dropped financial claims involving the recent seizure of American merchant shipping. The resulting Convention of 1800 terminated the only formal alliance the United States ever made until it joined the North Atlantic Treaty Organization (NATO) nearly a century and a half later.

The so-called quasi-war with France was a brief contest that took place in the West Indies and witnessed the rebirth of the U.S. Navy as a force to be reckoned with. Notably, Captain Thomas "Terrible Tom" Truxton in the thirty-eight-gun frigate USS *Constellation* defeated and captured the French forty-gun frigate *l'Insurgente* in 1799.[2] This small mismatch of a great power with a smaller one stands as the only one in which the United States and France ever came close to formally exchanging gunfire. However, there were other troubles brewing in the world—namely, in the Mediterranean with the Barbary powers Algiers, Morocco, Tripoli, and Tunis.

During the Barbary Wars, skilled American merchant and naval sailors who were captured were sold as chattel slaves. Those without special skills remained the property of the bashaw, or Turkish governor. Life became a drudgery of endless work and constant danger, and the prisoners enjoyed only those privileges granted them by their jailers. Confined to a slave prison, called a bagnio, a slave was expected to fulfill two requirements: to be productive in his work and to give no trouble to his masters. According to H. M. Barnby, Christian slaves in

Algiers were accepted as part of Algerian society because their slavery was considered the will of Allah rather than some kind of curse or the result of a heroic military victory. Discipline was rigorous but arbitrary. If a Christian overseer reported an infraction of the rules to a Muslim captor, the prisoner would receive the bastinado, or whipping of the feet, weeks in chains, or beheading if the infraction was serious enough. The slaves had their own hospital staffed by Catholic priests, taverns owned by successful slaves, chapels, and brothels. Every morning the slaves marched to their work; every night they came back to the bagnio. To the Barbary powers, prisoners represented cash—either cheap labor or ransom. Few died in captivity.[3]

Confident that the United States needed a major fleet, the Adams administration responded by ordering several powerful frigates built, but when Thomas Jefferson became president in 1800, he canceled the orders. Jefferson's idea was to have militias, an army, and a navy, which would form the backbone of national defense. Small gunboats replaced big, powerful frigates, but Jefferson learned a difficult lesson: the United States lived in a dangerous world, and many countries wished it ill or, worse, planned deadly mischief.

The purchase of French Louisiana in 1803 is perhaps the crown jewel of Jefferson's presidency. France acquired the territory in 1800 from Spain and abrogated the existing Spanish-American trade agreements in place concerning New Orleans and use of the Mississippi River. Napoleon needed money for his land wars in Europe and had trouble with rebellions in Santo Domingo (now Haiti) and needed to withdraw French troops from the Caribbean. In 1803 the United States' purchase of Louisiana at 6 cents an acre sent gold to Napoleon and doubled the tiny American nation's size.

The Barbary Wars finally ended in 1815 with treaties, but before that time a great deal of cash and booty changed hands. The United States concluded a treaty with the sultan of Morocco in 1786, ending American tribute and Moroccan piracy. In 1793 the United States paid Algeria $40,000 for the relief of its prisoners and nearly $1 million for a treaty in 1796. In 1798 the United States paid Tunis $107,000 in cash, jewels, small arms, and other presents for the dey of Algiers. From 1787 on, Tripoli wanted $100,000 a year, but that sum was never paid. In all, the United States paid the Barbary powers more than $2 million in ransom and tribute. President Jefferson, a pacifist at heart, realized the country was going broke paying blackmail to the leaders of three of the four Barbary states and finally decided that it would be cheaper to build a new navy and marine corps to put force behind American diplomacy. The United States signed an agreement with Tripoli on 4 June 1805 stipulating that if war broke out between them, the POWs captured by either party would not be made slaves but would be exchanged rank for rank. It further stipulated that if there was a deficiency on either side, it would be made up by the payment of 500 Spanish dollars for each seaman. Most important, this treaty put a time cap on the period of incarceration—twelve months after capture.[4]

The freedom of the seas, always a concern for American seafarers, took a serious and deadly turn for the worse between the United States and Great Britain. The War of 1812 took place between Great Britain and the United States from 18 February 1812 to 24 December 1814 over serious challenges to American sovereignty at its borders and at sea. The British refused to recognize the principle of naturalization after the Revolution. As far as they were concerned, once a British subject, always a British subject, especially when the Royal Navy needed men in its warships to fight the French. Between 1803 and 1812 the British took more than 8,000 sailors, mostly merchantmen, from American ships and impressed them into the Royal Navy. In 1807 the game changed when the HMS *Leopard* stopped the USS *Chesapeake,* boarded it, and removed naturalized American sailors, all of whom claimed American citizenship and in most (but not all) cases had the papers to prove it. President Jefferson was outraged and demanded the sailors returned. The British did not budge in their position, so Jefferson declared an embargo against all of Europe. This proved too much for merchants in New England, who enjoyed good trading relationships with their European partners; when they nearly rebelled, Jefferson rescinded his order.

The situation in the northwestern frontier complicated the issue even more. Following their defeat at the Battle of Fallen Timbers (1794) and the 1795 Treaty of Greenville, the Shawnees, under the leadership of Tecumseh and his brother Tenskwatawa, attempted to unite all the tribes against the encroaching Americans by joining with the British in Canada to reclaim their lost lands. The Americans boiled with the realities of British usurpations at sea and interference with the frontier. On 11 February 1811 President James Madison cut off trade relations with England; on 16 February 1812 the British Cabinet decided to back off, but it was too late. Madison asked Congress to declare war, which it did on 18 February 1812. The War Hawks, those who advocated hostilities against England, were divided in their approach: those in the North wanted to invade and conquer Canada; those in the South wanted to an-

President James Madison oversaw the War of 1812. Library of Congress.

nex Florida. According to historian Leland D. Baldwin, "Each was willing and anxious to thwart each other. Already both were thinking of the rivalry between farmers and planters, between free labor and slavery."[5]

Americans were unprepared to pursue all their war aims on land. It was nearly impossible to defeat the Indians when they allied with the British, and it was also impossible to acquire Canada for the American Union. The British land forces in North America totaled 8,125 early in 1812. Of this number, 2,100 were Canadian auxiliaries.[6] The British had stationed few troops in the region before the war because there had been no need. Fighting the Americans were sons of American Loyalists of the Revolution who were now loyal Canadians, the United Empire Loyalists, and they had a grudge. The armies met at Montreal, where the Americans were defeated soundly. The Americans who crossed into Canada at Niagara met the Canadians at Queenston and were defeated again. Tecumseh's Indians forced the surrender of Fort Dearborn in Chicago, and the Indians massacred the prisoners. American General William Hull attempted a halfhearted invasion of Canada, retreated to Detroit, and surrendered his entire command to the British. In all four areas of operation in the North—Detroit, Niagara, the upper Saint

General Zebulon Pike's death at the Battle of York. Courtesy of the
Canadian Military History Gateway.

Lawrence, and Lake Champlain—the Americans lost their battles, with
the exception of Lake Champlain and Lake Erie. In addition, the entire
Northwest Territory was open to Indian attack, and the Ohio Valley
discovered that its desire for war and expansion had been thwarted
completely.[7]

The battle at York (now Toronto), the Canadian capital, was another
matter. On 27 April 1813 American troops descended on the city and
opened fire with cannon. British General Sheaffe ordered the ammunition magazine to be blown up, and American General Zebulon Pike was
killed in the explosion, temporarily throwing his army into disarray.
The British regulars abandoned York; only the Canadian militiamen
remained, and they were immediately taken prisoner by the Americans.
Stephen Jarvis, the Canadian adjutant general in York, commented with
disgust, "To the everlasting disgrace of the Country, they were hourly
coming in and giving themselves to Major General Dearborn as prisoners."[8] After burning the city, the Americans withdrew.

At sea, the Americans showed grit and aggressive fighting abilities,
despite the navy's small size. In the spring of 1812 there were 4,010 en-

listed sailors and 1,523 marines, most of whom were native born. The officer corps numbered 234, with nearly half coming from the southern states.[9] The American warships were superbly built, and the sailors were well drilled in seamanship and gunnery. The core of the U.S. Navy consisted of seven of the best frigates in the world plus nine oceangoing brigs, sloops, and corvettes, all rebuilt schooners.[10]

The British deployed about eighty-five men-of-war to the American coast. Unlike the British, the American navy had no admirals; rather, the rank of commodore was awarded to the senior officer of a squadron of ships at sea, and all captains wrote after-action reports directly to the secretary of the navy. Historian John K. Mahon notes in *The War of 1812* that the *London Times* described the U.S. Navy as a "few fir built frigates with strips of bunting, manned by sons of bitches and outlaws."[11] One must suppose that a compliment of that magnitude was more than welcome.

Naval vessels engaged other men-of-war, but the American navy depended heavily on privateers, as it had during the Revolution, to wage war against British merchantmen. As a result, American maritime forces captured a huge amount of British shipping, about 450 ships, causing the British nothing but economic horror. Being captured by a privateer was not a pleasant experience. On 21 November 1813, within one day of reaching Barbados, the Post Office packet ship *Lapwing*, commanded by John Furze, met the American privateer *Fox*, and the battle began. At first, the *Lapwing* attempted to outrun the *Fox*. H. H. Brinkley, writing in 1930 about the loss of the *Lapwing*, quotes Colonel Henry Senior of the British army, who was aboard the *Lapwing* as a passenger:

> We were now about two miles from the nearest point of land. It was about two o'clock, the privateer rapidly came up, and in true Yankee ostentation, all the crew mounted on the rigging, stood on the ship's side and managed to show us her superiority of numbers (just four to one), gave three most insulting cheers, and called on us to surrender. Our brave little crew gave three cheers and fired a broadside into her as answer, the privateer returned it instantly.[12]

The fight was particularly bloody. According to Colonel Senior, "The deck now presented a horrid scene, from more than half of our crew being stretched there killed or wounded, and the quantity of blood spilt on so small a space made it almost a continued slop, and so slippery that I frequently fell."[13] Later, the captain of the *Fox* stated that had he known the *Lapwing* was only a mail ship, he would have left it alone. After a lengthy voyage and some other adventures, Colonel Senior and the remaining sailors of the *Lapwing* were finally freed in Jamaica.

American frigates such as the *Constitution, United States, Wasp, Hornet, Essex,* and *Constellation* patrolled the seas, defeated British warships, and took large numbers of merchant prizes as well. Captains Stephen Decatur, Oliver Hazard Perry, James Lawrence, and Isaac Hull achieved nearly hero status. On 19 August 1812 the USS *Constitution* met the frigate HMS *Guerriere* in battle, and in his report to Vice Admiral Herbert Sawyer, Royal Navy, concerning his defeat, the *Guerriere*'s captain, James R. Dacres, reflected the common courtesies at sea:

> The *Guerriere* was so cut up, that all attempts to get her in would have been useless. As soon as the wounded were got out of her, they set her on fire, and I feel it my duty to state that the conduct of Captain Hull and his Officers to our Men has been that of a brave enemy, the greatest care being taken to prevent our Men losing the smallest trifle, and the greatest attention being paid to the wounded who through the attention and skill of Mr. [John] Irvine, Surgeon, I hope will do well.[14]

Dacres wrote this report to his commanding officer from Boston, where he was a prisoner of war until exchanged.

Another American captain made extraordinary efforts to save British sailors from death after a major engagement at sea. On 19 March 1813, writing from his ship the USS *Hornet,* Captain James Lawrence reported to the secretary of the navy his defeat of the brig of war HMS *Peacock,* noting that "a number of her crew were killed including Captain Peake and wounded and that she was sinking fast, she having then six feet of water in her hold."[15] Lawrence sent a boarding party to the stricken ship, now full of holes, to attempt to save the *Peacock* and its surviving crew members. Lawrence was only partially successful. He managed to save the master (navigator), one midshipman, a carpenter, a captain's clerk, and twenty-nine wounded men, most of them severely injured. Sadly, three British sailors died of their wounds in captivity, and nine men drowned.[16] Badly overcrowded, the *Hornet* then sailed for the United States, arriving at Martha's Vineyard on 19 March 1813.[17] Nevertheless, Captain Lawrence did everything he could to save the lives of his enemy, and that act constitutes the unwritten law of the sea to this

The USS *Constitution* engaged the frigate HMS *Guerriere* in battle. U.S. Navy painting.

day. Concerning Captain Lawrence's treatment of his British prisoners, one *Peacock* crewman recorded in a notebook that five British officers wrote a letter of thanks to Lawrence for his kind treatment. The letter read in part, "We ceased to consider ourselves prisoners."[18]

On Lake Erie, Commodore Oliver Hazard Perry made history by building his own fleet and defeating the British. Perry's 1813 report, "We have met the enemy and they are ours," made naval history and became the stuff of legend. But as Baldwin points out, the American navy became a minor force at war's end, when it was completely blockaded and bound to its piers.[19] Lack of naval activity thus bore major consequences on land and sea alike. In 1813 President Madison ordered that all American merchant ships remain in port, and again, New England bore the brunt. Business was devastated at first, and the New Englanders nearly seceded because of it. However, New England continued to trade illegally with England and Canada and, despite the antiwar rhetoric, grew wealthy.

William Henry Harrison lost 900 Americans to the British and Indians at the Battle of River Raisin, and again, the Indians massacred the prisoners. The only bright light on land was Harrison's victory on 5 October 1813 at the Battle of the Thames in Canada over British General Henry Proctor. With Perry's victory at Put-in-Bay on Lake Erie, Proctor abandoned Detroit and marched overland until Harrison caught him. Tecumseh was killed, and the Indians lost the greatest leader they ever had, changing their fate completely.

By 1814 prospects became a little brighter for the Americans, although they were $35 million in debt. The Battle of Lake Champlain on 11 September found Lieutenant Thomas MacDonough victorious over the British fleet, and the planned British invasion turned back for Canada. On land, British General Sir George Prevost gave up his attack on Plattsburgh, New York, and was ultimately defeated by the state militia there. In Europe, however, where the British fielded their best troops, the allies defeated Napoleon at Leipzig, Lord Wellington defeated him in Spain, and the allies entered Paris on 31 March 1814. As a result, the British could field better troops in America to finish up the war.[20]

Three battles changed the landscape of the War of 1812. Horseshoe Bend was fought in Alabama on 27 March 1814, where Major General Andrew Jackson and his Tennessee Volunteers attacked and defeated the Red Stick Creeks allied with the British. Jackson, a furious fighter, took no prisoners and killed about 800 Indians, establishing his presence at Horseshoe Bend much as Hull, Perry, Lawrence, and Decatur had at sea. Jackson's stock rose considerably at New Orleans in 1815 and even more so three years later, when he defeated the Spanish in Florida. His military prowess contributed in large part to his overall reputation, and he became president of the United States, holding office from 1829 to 1837.[21]

The British, infuriated at their upstart American enemies, brought their finest troops to the American war after they defeated Napoleon in 1814 and exiled him to Elba. As historian Donald R. Hickey commented, "For the first time in more than a decade, Europe was at peace."[22] After landing at Alexandria, Virginia, they defeated the American militia under General William H. Winder at Bladensburg and then attacked Washington, D.C., on 24 August 1814, burning most of the government buildings, including the White House. Fortunately, President Madison had been informed of the landing by a French spy and saved the Declaration of Independence and Constitution from the British fires while First Lady Dolley Madison saved the Gilbert Stewart portrait of George Washington. After burning Washington the British marched to Baltimore, where they lost a vicious fight, and reboarded their ships, which then bombarded Fort McHenry in Baltimore Harbor. Fortunately for the Americans, Francis Scott Key sat aboard one of the British ships trying to free a prisoner and scribbled his famous "Star-Spangled Banner" as a huge American flag flew defiantly after the bombardment. Following a considerable amount of raiding and burning at will, the British force sailed from the Maryland coast south to the Gulf of Mexico.

Both sides now knew that winning the war was impossible. Peace negotiations took place at Ghent in Belgium, and in 1814 the British and Americans addressed their differences more in terms of an armistice than a surrender. Both sides were indeed war weary, and Lord Wellington, the hero of Waterloo, advised the British to settle with the Americans. The issues that arose on the frontier, such as British forts in Michigan and British influence with the hostile Indians, were settled in favor of American sovereignty. The regional Indians knew in 1813 that trouble would continue, especially after the Battle of the Thames when Tecumseh died, but the British left the Americans to deal with them. The Royal Navy's impressment of American sailors at sea, one of the primary issues in the war, was given up by the British, and naturalization was recognized. Last, the British acknowledged the legitimacy of American expansion west. All was well, there was peace without victory, and everyone signed the treaty on 24 December 1814. The war was over—or at least it should have been—but in 1814 news traveled slowly.

In August 1814 the British landed at Pensacola, in Spanish Florida, and Jackson's Americans counterattacked in force. Pensacola, however, was never the real target, and the British retreated quickly. When Jackson realized that New Orleans was the actual target, he sped to this magnificent French city on the Gulf of Mexico. After some skirmishing while the Americans fortified their positions with cotton bales, the grand assault took place on 8 January 1815. American forces under Major General Andrew Jackson met the elite Gordon Highlanders under General Edward M. Packingham outside New Orleans. The British simply marched into a hail of accurate fire and lost 300 dead on the field and 1,700 wounded; American losses were light, with 13 dead and 58 wounded.[23] The Treaty of Ghent arrived shortly after the battle, and the country was relieved that the war was over and the deadly and mighty British army had been humiliated. The War of 1812's true significance was lost in the jubilation over the victory at New Orleans.

During "Mr. Madison's" War of 1812, British treatment of American prisoners of war improved considerably. In all, approximately 20,000 Americans were taken as POWs by the British, including soldiers both regular and militia, sailors, and privateers. The militiamen were largely considered untrained, nearly harmless citizen-soldiers, and the British often released them home on parole shortly after capture. Those regulars, including naval personnel and privateers, held by the British were kept in prisons in England, in Halifax and Quebec in Canada, and in Jamaica in the Caribbean. The Americans kept British and Canadian prisoners at Salem, Pittsfield, and Worcester in Massachusetts; Albany, New York; Savannah, Georgia; and Chillicothe, Ohio. In these facilities, the British prisoners and their representatives often complained about inadequate food and clothing, unsuitable quarters, and being housed in a common jail.[24]

Unlike the status difficulties during the Revolution, the British no longer considered American military prisoners to be criminals; the North Act of 1777 that had declared them pirates and rebels had been repealed. The British Transport Board kept intact the prison hulk system it had used during the American Revolution, but there were so many French and Spanish sailors captured in the Napoleonic Wars in Europe that the British housed them in large prison facilities. In 1813 many Americans were moved from the hulks to the gruesome military prison at Dartmoor. Chosen for its location near the sea and the consequent inclement weather, Dartmoor prison was constructed in 1806–1809 to hold 5,000 men. Thirty-six acres were enclosed by stone walls, with the outer wall rising twelve to sixteen feet high. There were also barracks for 400 soldiers and officers. Located about seventeen miles from Plymouth in rural eastern England, Dartmoor became known as Britain's national dungeon. The Americans had no equivalent.

Beginning in 1812, British and American representatives met in Halifax, Nova Scotia, to establish a cartel (see appendix 2). The British representative, Thomas Barclay, had served as consul general in the United States for fourteen years prior to the war and knew the country well. His American counterpart, John Mason, lived near Washington on an opulent island plantation in the Potomac River. The idea was to create an equitable system so that each side could get its soldiers and sailors back well enough to return to duty. If one side became deceitful, however, the whole system would collapse. Article 1 stated the case very well: "The Prisoners taken at sea or on land on both sides shall be treated with humanity conformable to the usage and practice of the most civilized nations during war; and such prisoners shall without delay, and as speedily as circumstances will admit, be exchanged."[25] Exchange rates were also established in Article 1:

> An Admiral or a General commanding in chief shall be exchanged for officers of equal rank or for sixty men each: a vice admiral or a Lieutenant General for officers of equal rank or for forty men each, a Rear Admiral or a Major General, for officers of equal rank, or for thirty men each; a Commodore with a broad pendant and a Captain under him or a Brigadier General for officers of equal rank or for twenty men each; a Captain of a line of Battle ship or a Colonel for officers of equal rank or for fifteen men each; a Captain of a frigate, or Lieutenant Colonel for officers of equal rank or for ten men each; Commanders of sloops of war, Bomb Catches, fire ships, and Packets or a Major for officers of equal rank, or for eight men each; Lieutenants or masters in the navy, or Captains in the army, for officers of equal rank, or for six men each; Masters-Mates, or Lieutenants in the army for officers of equal rank, or for four men each; Midshipmen, warrant officers, Masters of merchant vessels, and Captains of private armed vessels, or sub Lieutenants and Ensigns for officers of equal rank, or for three Men each; Lieutenants and mates of private armed vessels, Mates of merchant vessels and all petty officers of ships of war, or all non commissioned officers of the army, for officers of equal rank, or for two men each; seamen and private soldiers one for the other.

In addition, efforts were made to grant freedom to all noncombatants. Article 2 stated:

> All non combatants that is to say, surgeons and surgeons mates, pursers, secretaries, chaplains and schoolmasters, belonging to the army or men of war; surgeons and surgeons mates of merchant vessels, or privateers; passengers, and all other men who are not engaged in the naval or military service of the enemy, not being sea faring persons; all women and girls, and all Boys under twelve years of age; every person of the foregoing description, or of whatever description exempt from capture by the usage and practice of the most civilized nations when at war—if taken shall be immediately released without exchange and shall take their departure at their own charge, agreeably to passports to be granted them, or otherwise shall be put on board the next cartel which sails; persons found on board recaptured ships, whatever situation they may have held in the capturing ship, shall not be considered

as noncombatants—noncombatants are not to be imprisoned except for improper conduct, and if poor or unprovided with means to support themselves, the government of each nation will allow them a reasonable subsistence, having respect to their rank and situation in life.

Article 3 created the commissary officers responsible for the prisoners' well-being, pay, and clothing. They would be stationed at major receiving points and were also responsible for creating cartel shipments. Article 4 covered agreements for paroles of honor and created specific forms and responsibilities, such as behaving decently with respect to the laws of the holding power. Article 5 defined the kinds of internment facilities that could be used. Article 6 demanded that prisoners honor paroles; if broken, each side was responsible to the other for the "surrender and restoration of any prisoner who shall violate his parole." Article 7 addressed treatment. Prisoners would not be struck by a whip or anything else, and their complaints would be attended to rapidly. Article 7 also covered rations, implying that prisoners of war were to receive the same or similar rations as the soldiers of the other belligerent. Article 8 maintained the integrity of exchange and the respective commissaries of prisoners. Article 9 provided guidelines for actual exchanges, including the kind and size of ships involved. Article 10 covered temporary or ad hoc cartels, and Article 11 discussed the possibility of captains of public ships at war being able to send flags of truce into any station for the purpose of exchanging prisoners. Article 12 permitted the use of ships of neutral nations for exchange purposes, and Article 13 addressed lists and receipts for exchanged prisoners. Article 14 could be deadly if one side attempted to deceive the other. It provided that "if either nation at anytime have delivered more prisoners than it has received, it is optional with such a nation to stop sending any more prisoners on credit, until a return shall be made equal in number to the balance so in advance." Last, Article 15 required ratification from the governments of both Great Britain and the United States. The agreement was prepared and signed by both sides on 12 May 1813.[26]

All this worked very well for those prisoners who could prove they were actually citizens of the United States. According to legal scholar Ralph Robinson, the policies of the two countries with respect to allegiance stood in diametric opposition and framed one of the major issues of the War of 1812.[27] The issue first arose at sea when the British impressed American sailors from merchantmen and then from warships.

It was compounded when the war broke out and the British continued taking American prisoners, claiming that naturalization meant nothing. The British intended to send those men back to England to stand trial for treason, which at the time meant carrying arms against the king. Prior to the outbreak of the war, American merchant and some naval vessels did indeed carry a sizable number of former British sailors who had deserted the British in favor of the higher pay offered by the Americans. With the large number of naval and merchant ships at sea at the time, the British were desperate for sailors, making the use of the press gang at least understandable, albeit distasteful. Thomas Barclay, the resident British agent of POWs, wrote in a confidential letter to Robert Stewart (Lord Castlereagh), the British foreign secretary:

In the American Navy, at least one half are British seamen. The remainder are subjects of Sweden, Denmark, Prussia &c., &c., and few Americans. From the great influx of seamen, the commanders of American Ships of War have it in their power to select young well-made prime seamen. Those who are subjects of His Majesty fight with desperation, most of them being deserters. It is a lamentable truth that our seamen are tired and dissatisfied with their success, and long confinement on board ship in consequence of twenty years' war, and I fear capture by the Americans is not disagreeable to many of them.[28]

After the conclusion of the Napoleonic Wars, the Royal Navy contracted significantly, lessening the acute need for sailors and the press gangs. However, the British never gave up their right to impress sailors on the high seas, even after the Treaty of Ghent in 1814.

On 13 October 1812 the British and Canadians defeated the American force at the Battle of Queenston in Canada, and among the prisoners were twenty-three soldiers that the British claimed were British subjects. Questioning this claim was their fellow POW, Lieutenant Colonel Winfield Scott, who vigorously objected, but to no avail. The men were put in irons and sent to England. The prisoners themselves wrote to the American secretary of war begging for action, stating that they were naturalized Americans and had homes and wives in the United States.[29]

Scott was paroled quickly and traveled directly to Washington to confer with John Armstrong, the secretary of war. By May 1813 President Madison took action. Reprisals were in order. Armstrong ordered

Major General John Dearborn, in command of the American forces near the Canadian border at Niagara, New York, to put twenty-three British soldiers in close confinement, similar to what the British had done. Once this sort of policy of reprisal was put into action, events took their own course and quickly spun out of control, endangering the spirit, if not the letter, of the cartel.

The next step in the escalation came on the British side. The British commanding officer in Canada, Sir George Prevost, was infuriated and informed Lord Bathurst, the British minister for the colonies, that the twenty-three prisoners had been "sent home to be disposed of according to the pleasure of His Royal Highness, the Prince Regent."[30] Bathurst then directed Prevost to lock up forty-six Americans as hostages for the twenty-three British and ordered that Dearborn be informed that if the British were harmed or executed, the same would be done to the Americans at double the rate. Against the spirit of the cartel, Bathurst directed Prevost not to worry overly about the problem because the British forces were ready to raise the level of hostilities against American cities and towns.

Dearborn left his command for health reasons and was replaced by Major General James Wilkinson, famed in the army for his stormy and difficult ways. He sent the Prevost letter to President Madison, who in turn directed John Mason, the American commissary of prisoners, to confine all British commissioned officers of every rank in the states of Massachusetts, Kentucky, and Ohio.[31] It should be noted that these states, as well as others such as Pennsylvania, were tasked with holding British prisoners in their state prison facilities. Public Law 79, No. 50, of the Commonwealth of Pennsylvania, passed on 3 March 1814, stated:

> Keepers of prisons to receive prisoners of war. All sheriffs, jailers, prison keepers, and . . . each and every [one] of their deputies within this Commonwealth, to whom any person or persons shall be sent or committed, by any order from the Government of the United States, as hostages or prisoners of war, shall be required to receive such person or persons into custody, and to keep them safely until they shall be discharged by the President of the United States.[32]

Madison was angry, and knowing that he had access to British prisoners in these states, issued his order "to secure a sufficient number of hostages, to answer in their persons for the proper treatment of a certain number of American officers now in possession of the enemy, on whom

the British authorities have recently threatened to exercise a severity unknown to civilized warfare, and outraging humanity."[33] If ever military
and civilian officers were playing high-stakes poker with one another,
Dearborn, Prevost, Bathurst, Madison, and Wilkinson were.

Making the situation even worse, in June 1813 the British captured
fifty-nine more naturalized Americans at Beaver Dams. Like the prior
group, they received deportation orders and, as British subjects, were
bound for England and trial for treason. About the same time, General William Henry Harrison captured fifty-nine British soldiers at the
Battle of the Thames. So the ante went up again. There were charges
and countercharges of abuse and hardship suffered by those in captivity
on both sides. It looked as if neither side would budge an inch from its
hardened position.

The impasse broke when Prevost granted a sixty-day parole to Brigadier General William H. Winder, captured at the Battle of Stoney Creek
in 1813. Prevost believed that Winder could go to Washington and calm
the dogs of war, at least on the reprisal issue. Winder, a hostage himself,
believed that the United States was in no position to make its threats a
reality, but he failed to convince anyone in Washington and returned
to Quebec on 22 March 1814. Before he reached Quebec, however, he
learned that the storm had broken in Washington. The president had
granted him authority to propose an immediate exchange, followed up
by a letter from Secretary of State James Monroe to Prevost that sub-
stantially brought both sides back to the spirit of the cartel.

The efforts were successful this time, and on 16 April 1814 the two
sides agreed to a "convention" much like the one established between
Generals Gates and Burgoyne at Saratoga in 1777. Plans to put anyone
on trial for treason ended with a whimper, but the original twenty-three
men sent to England for trial remained there until 1815, after the signing
and ratification of the Treaty of Ghent. Winder so impressed Madison
and Monroe that after his exchange they gave him command of a new
military district that included Washington, Baltimore, and Annapolis.
His success was short-lived, however. It was Winder's militia units that
met the British army at the Battle of Bladensburg—the American defeat
known as the Bladensburg Races that permitted the British to avenge
the American burning of York by doing the same to Washington in
1814.

Reporting on that event was British Major General Robert Ross,
writing to the secretary of state for war and the colonies on 30 August
1814:

I have the honour to Communicate to your Lordship that on the night of the 24th Instant after Defeating the Army of the United States on that day the Troops under my command entered and took possession of the City of Washington. An attack upon an Enemy so strongly posted could not be effected without Loss. I have to lament that the wounds received by Colonel Thornton and the other Officers and Soldiers left at Bladensburg were such as prevented their removal. As many of the wounded as could be brought off were removed, the others being left with medical care and attendants. The arrangements made by Staff Surgeon Baxter for their Accommodation have been as satisfactory as circumstances would admit of. The Agent for British Prisoners of War very fortunately residing at Bladensburg, I have recommended the wounded Officers and Men to his particular attention and trust to his being able to effect their exchange when sufficiently recovered.[34]

Ross never mentioned that he and his soldiers enjoyed President Madison's dinner and stole some presidential china before burning the White House.

After the Battle of New Orleans and the conclusion of the Treaty of Ghent, the frictions, passions, and disappointments of war gave way to jubilation on the part of the Americans: not being defeated was a victory. Although the war actually ended as a stalemate, as far as the Americans were concerned, it was a "second American Revolution" (the third American Revolution would arrive in midcentury, when the Americans would fight one another in the bloodiest war the nation ever fought). Without a doubt, the War of 1812 left an enduring legacy of Anglophobia in the United States, particularly concerning Indian atrocities in the West, the burning of Washington, and British raids in the Chesapeake region.[35] Yet the United States was able to develop a firmer foreign policy. In 1823 President James Monroe, secretary of state during the war, informed Europe that the United States had no intention of interfering in European affairs; conversely, the Monroe Doctrine insisted that European nations stay out of the American continent, North and South. By this action, Monroe closed the American continent to European colonization, but that was not the case for Americans, who were looking west to consolidate the country from the Atlantic to the Pacific.

Internally, the War of 1812 nearly broke the United States into two sections: New England and everywhere else. At the Hartford Convention, held in Connecticut from 15 December 1814 to 4 January 1815, New England Federalists, who advocated a separate peace with Great Britain, discussed but ultimately rejected secession from the Union if the war continued indefinitely. Rancor developed between North and South over the convention, and the Americans were lucky to avoid a civil war, at least for a while. The Federalists, however, lost political clout and disintegrated, but the notion of states' sovereignty remained strong, especially in the South.

Canada developed a new nationalist spirit called the "militia myth," based on the belief that Canadian militia units rather than British regulars had defeated the Americans. Like the Americans, the Canadians developed a strong national identity, whereas before the war, Canadians had considered themselves only a weak sister in the British Empire. In this sense, the Canadians were winners. The British government viewed the peace as a status quo ante and looked to other parts of the empire—namely, India and Africa—to enrich its coffers, yet it took little time to reestablish trade relationships with the United States. There was money to be made.

The big losers were the native tribes of the South and the Northwest Territories, which began to see the end of their power and influence, much as the eastern tribes had experienced similar losses after the Revolution. Article IX of the Treaty of Ghent stipulated that the United States would guarantee the tribes the same status and territory they had in 1811, but it was hardly the Americans' intention to do that in good faith, especially after the major battles and land cessions in both the North and the South. The Indians watched with great dismay as the British withdrew from their forts, knowing full well that the Americans were coming in great numbers.[36]

The War of 1812 evolved into a brutal affair on both sides. Exact figures are elusive, but the British held far more POWs—around 20,000, all told—than the Americans held. Although the cartel guaranteed a humane form of exchange and the commissaries of prisoners cared for POWs on both sides, there was outright vandalism in all the theaters of the war. Both national capitals, American and Canadian, were burned, and POWs suffered on both sides, although few died in captivity from anything other than war wounds. Some Americans remained in the British Dartmoor prison after the war's end when no ships came to take them home. On 6 April 1815 they rioted, and the guards killed five and wounded thirty-four. The survivors returned home shortly thereafter.

The war cost the United States about $105 million. In Canada, after starting the war with just over 8,000 troops, the British raised the level to 25,975 troops by the war's end.[37] According to Gerard T. Altoff, had the war continued, the United States would have continued to fight; commanders got better as they received on-the-job training in the art of war, and recruiting expanded as revenge filled the air for the burning of Washington.[38] In the end, the war may have ended in a status quo antebellum, and perhaps it should never have been fought, but it strengthened both the American and Canadian nations internally and brought an emerging Canada closer to Britain. Sadly, distrust and ill will between Canada and the United States continued well into the twentieth century. It some ways, the wounds of the War of 1812 never really healed.

Four

Manifest Destiny versus Nativism

Mexico, 1846–1848

Let all our soldiers professing the Catholic religion remember the
fate of the deserters taken at Churubusco.
—General Winfield Scott

When the War of 1812 ended, Americans felt relatively secure from attacks by foreign countries. The militia system had been discredited, and
states created their own volunteer regiments—what we know today as
the National Guard—that could be federalized very quickly in case of a
national emergency. The standing army grew as well and evolved into a
frontier army of tough soldiers who were invisible in the sophisticated
East, which enjoyed industrial expansion unparalleled in American history up to that point. The issue was expansion of the American nation
west, and the disputes rested on how and where that expansion would
take place and whether the new United States would be slaveholding or
free.

On 12 April 1844 Texas nearly became a territory of the United
States; however, the agreement was rejected by the Senate, which was em-
broiled in arguments over expansion and slavery. A year later the United
States annexed Texas, and to Sam Houston's joy, Texas became a state
on 29 December 1845, an event that changed the nature of Mexican-
American relations permanently. A month earlier, President James K.
Polk had offered Mexico $5 million to purchase New Mexico and $25
million for California. Both offers had been refused as an assault on
Mexican sovereignty. Alarmed at a clear manifestation of American
expansionism, the Mexicans broke diplomatic relations but stopped
short of declaring war on the United States. The president was clearly
responding to the popular cry of *Manifest Destiny,* a term coined by
journalist and editor John L. O'Sullivan in 1845 in the *United States
Democratic Review.*[1] Polk was also responding to what he perceived
to be a military threat to the border area of the newly acquired state.
A solid Jacksonian Democrat from Tennessee and a friend of Sam

General Zachary Taylor, "Old Rough and Ready," commanded the American army during the first part of the Mexican-American War and established the policy of paroling enemy prisoners of war. Library of Congress.

Houston in Texas, he sent American army troops, mostly southerners sympathetic to Texas in the first place, to occupy the disputed border territory along the Rio Grande.

American and Mexican patrols clashed on the morning of 25 April 1846 when a large detachment of Mexican troops crossed the Rio Grande and battled a U.S. Army scouting party. Sixteen American soldiers died, and the survivors were taken prisoner. American troops under the command of General Zachary Taylor, "Old Rough and Ready," had taken up a position on the north bank of the Rio Grande in the spring of 1846, after Mexican President Mariano Paredes refused to negotiate with the United States and threatened an invasion of Texas, claiming that the Nueces River deep in Texas, rather than the Rio Grande, was the border. To President Polk, this was unacceptable, and he declared in 1846 that American blood spilled on U.S. territory demanded satisfaction. In his message to Congress on 11 May 1846 he said, "She [Mexico] has proclaimed that hostilities have commenced, and that the two nations are now at war. We are called upon by every consideration of duty and patriotism to vindicate with decision the honor, the rights, and the interests of our country."[2] Congress declared war on 9 May 1846 and authorized the president to call for 50,000 volunteers.

EPW policy quickly fixed on a new precedent. Because of the expense of holding and supplying captured enemy soldiers behind friendly lines, or even sending them back to the United States for internment, General Taylor advocated release on parole for as many as possible, allowing them to return to their homes and not reengage the American army. Mexican soldiers who refused their parole under these circumstances would be held as prisoners of war. President Polk approved this policy, and Secretary of War William L. Marcy wrote to Taylor: "The President has seen, with much satisfaction, the civility and kindness with which you have treated your prisoners, and all the inhabitants with whom you have come in contact. He wishes the course of conduct continued, and all opportunities taken to conciliate the inhabitants, and to let them see that peace is within their reach the moment their rulers will consent to do us justice."[3]

There were ten battles in this two-year war—some large, most relatively small. Palo Alto was the first on 8 May 1846. General Taylor claimed victory over General Mariano Arista after an artillery duel that showed the Mexicans to be weak and indecisive. Writing to Roger Jones, adjutant general of the army, from his camp near Matamoros, Mexico, on 16 May 1846, Taylor reported:

Our loss this day was nine killed, forty-four wounded, and two missing. Among the wounded were Major Ringgold, who has since died, and Captain Page, dangerously wounded; Lieut. Luther slightly so. I annex a tabular statement of the casualties of the day.

Our own force engaged is shown by the field report (herewith) to have been 177 officers and 2,111 men; aggregate 2,288. The Mexican force, according to the statements of their own officers taken prisoner in the affair of the 9th, was not less than 6,000 regular troops, with ten pieces of artillery, and probably exceeded that number; the irregular force not known. Their loss was not less than 200 killed and 400 wounded—probably greater. This estimate is very moderate, and formed upon the number actually counted upon the field, and upon the reports of their own officers.

As already reported in my first brief dispatch, the conduct of our officers and men was everything that could be desired. Exposed for hours to the severest trial, a cannonade of artillery, our troops displayed a coolness and constancy which gave me, throughout, the assurance of victory.[4]

On the American side, Brevet Major Samuel Ringgold, an artillery officer, had developed what was called the "Flying Artillery" into a razor-sharp weapon. Essentially, Ringgold trained his men to "shoot and scoot"—that is, stop, set up, fire, and move rapidly to keep continuous support for the infantry as it advanced. Although Ringgold died at Palo Alto, his memory became epic, and his method of the Flying Artillery remained intact for the entire war.

The next day saw the second battle, Resaca de la Palma, as Taylor pursued Arista. As John S. D. Eisenhower observes in *So Far from God,* "The Battle of Resaca de la Palma degenerated into a rout. Taylor's army followed the panic stricken enemy as closely as possible to the Rio Grande."[5] Casualties were light: Palo Alto cost 4 American dead and 10 wounded, whereas the Mexicans lost 200 dead and about 300 wounded. Resaca de la Palma was more expensive. Thirty-five American soldiers died and 98 were wounded in action, whereas the Mexicans lost about 200 dead and 400 wounded. In his after-action report dated 17 May 1846, Taylor wrote, "Our victory has been decisive. A small force has overcome immense odds of the best troops that Mexico can furnish—veteran regiments, perfectly equipped and appointed. Eight pieces of artillery, several colors and standards, a great number of prisoners (including fourteen officers) and a large amount of baggage and public property, have fallen into our hands."[6] Mexican losses in killed, wounded, and captured became increasingly extreme as the war headed into its blackest period.

The third battle was much larger and took place at Monterrey from 19 to 24 September 1846. The man of the hour in this battle was Brigadier General William J. Worth. Like many of the other senior officers, Worth had seen combat service in the War of 1812, distinguishing himself as a captain at the Battle of Niagara (also known as Lundy's Lane) and earning a promotion to major for valor on the field. After the peace Worth went to West Point and served as an instructor. In 1842 Worth deployed to Florida for the Seminole War, but it was with Taylor at Monterrey that his abilities shined. Also at Monterrey was a young militia officer commanding the Mississippi Volunteers, Colonel Jefferson Davis. Commanding the Mexican forces was General Pedro de Ampudia, a capable officer of personal distinction who nearly defeated the attacking Americans on 21 September, but two days later the Americans assaulted the town and fought hand to hand, house to house, wiping out the Mexican defenders slowly and deliberately. By the last day of the battle, General Ampudia became fearful that the Americans would destroy the cathedral. The solution was a truce.

General Ampudia offered conditions to Taylor, but Taylor demanded unconditional surrender. Ampudia vacillated and tried again. After more back-and-forth discussions, Ampudia and Taylor signed a surrender document. On 25 September 1846 Taylor reported:

> It will be seen that the terms granted the Mexican garrison are less rigorous than those first imposed. The gallant defense of the town, and the fact of a recent change of government in Mexico, believed to be favorable to the interests of peace, induced me to concur with the commission in these terms, which will, I trust, receive the approval of the government. The latter consideration also prompted the convention for a temporary cessation of hostilities.[7]

Ampudia's army marched out of Monterrey with a battery of field artillery; the cavalry kept its horses, and officers kept their sidearms. It was anything but a defeated army.[8] Taylor installed Worth as the governor-general of Monterrey, and the army rested. At Monterrey, Americans lost 120 dead in action, 368 wounded; Mexican losses were large, with 700 killed in action and a huge but unknown number of wounded. Similar to the Gates-Burgoyne Convention at Saratoga in 1777, the American government was not pleased with the agreement. President Polk winced at the terms of the surrender and believed that Taylor had failed to carry out his orders properly. Polk wanted Ampudia's army destroyed and disarmed, the survivors put on parole and sent home. He certainly did not want the Mexicans to leave the battlefield with honor, flags flying, and ready to fight another day.

General Antonio Lopez de Santa Anna, living in exile in Cuba, accepted the Americans' offer to return him to Mexico for the purpose of trying to settle the issues between the United States and Mexico. Upon his arrival at the port of Vera Cruz, any promise to the Americans disappeared. Santa Anna realized in short order that the Mexican people were united in their opposition to the American invasion of their country, and he also realized that he could exploit the Mexican resistance to serve his own best interests. Rebuilding the army became his first objective, confronting the Americans with this new army was the second, and paying for it the third. Who had money in Mexico? Certainly not the government or the people, but the Catholic Church was wealthy

General Antonio Lopez de
Santa Anna led Mexican
forces against the Americans.

and patriotic, and Santa Anna obtained a loan of 10 million pesos. By January 1847 Santa Anna had used the church's loan to create a powerful army of over 20,000 men, trained them well, and transformed these defeated ragtag amateurs into a substantial force, probably the best the Mexicans would field for the entire war.[9]

Next came the battle at Tampico. This was a naval operation. The American ships had approached the harbor ready for action, but the townspeople arrived to say that there were no Mexican soldiers in the area and to plead for a peaceful occupation. There was no shooting, and the occupation proceeded without incident. However, the president took that opportunity to order Taylor to resume operations beginning on 15 November 1846. By the beginning of 1847, Polk changed the war's strategy: instead of being a limited war that failed to achieve its desired end—a quick victory and border settlement—it became a war of conquest with Mexico City as the final target. The issue of who would command the army arose: Taylor was too old school; Polk needed a more aggressive field commander, someone with a firm grasp of diplomacy and strategy. Major General Winfield Scott, then in Washington, became the man of the hour.

December 1846 marked the imposition of the new strategy in

Mexico when Scott departed Washington for his new assignment to defeat the Mexican army completely. He wrote to Taylor, "I am not coming, my dear general, to supersede you in the immediate command on the line of operations. My proposed theatre is different."[10] Scott then informed Taylor that he would rob Peter to pay Paul, in that he had to take most of Taylor's officers and troops to build his own army, hoping that reinforcements would be forthcoming in the spring. And in a subsequent letter, Scott noted, "Providence may defeat me, but I do not believe the Mexicans can."[11]

When Taylor became aware of the shift in troop strength to Scott, his anger rose. Feeling demeaned and embarrassed after achieving nothing but victory, Taylor considered resignation; instead he remained in Mexico. Santa Anna, having gained possession of copies of Scott's instructions to Taylor, set out to engage "Old Rough and Ready." He marched his army, 20,000 strong, across a desert between San Luis Potosi and Saltillo, losing about 5,000 soldiers to thirst, hunger, and fatigue. The Battle of Buena Vista, the fourth in this war, was about to begin.

Taylor's army sat at quiet Monterrey while Santa Anna's army marched through the desert. Taylor's officers, after learning of the enemy's movements, urged Taylor to retreat to a better defensive position. Retreat was not in Taylor's vocabulary at the time, and he resisted. In the end, however, he realized that his officers were correct and moved his army to La Angostura; the Battle of Buena Vista was fought only six miles away. Generals Taylor and John E. Wool put their heads together and came up with a good defensive position that covered Santa Anna's three possible avenues of approach. Beginning on 22 February 1847 Santa Anna offered Taylor surrender terms, but Taylor declined. Skirmishing began around 3 PM and concluded at nightfall. Not much happened, but the next day became a hell on earth.

Santa Anna's men broke several American units of the Arkansas and Kentucky Cavalry as well as the Second Indiana Infantry. The survivors withdrew, chased by the Mexicans. Unfortunately, the Mexicans placed themselves in the sights of American artillery, and as the grapeshot decimated their ranks, victory left Santa Anna's grasp very quickly. The Mississippi Rifles, the Third Indiana Infantry, and Braxton Bragg's artillery intercepted a Mexican division on a ridge and ambushed it with rifles and hand-to-hand combat. Only a rainstorm saved the Mexicans from total disaster at Buena Vista. By evening, both armies were exhausted from the day's work, but they prepared for the next day. Taylor commented, "Our loss has been especially severe in officers,

Major General Winfield Scott, "Old Fuss and Feathers," was in command of the American army by the end of the Mexican War and issued orders for the trial and execution of the San Patricios. Library of Congress.

twenty-eight having been killed upon the field."[12] Forty wagons of food and ammunition arrived and saved Taylor's army from defeat. Santa Anna, however, made a stunning decision to retreat and save his army from further bloodletting. He had suffered more than 2,100 casualties, with approximately 300 captured. There was little doubt that Santa Anna needed time to regroup. For Zachary Taylor, now a major general, Buena Vista became his last battle. It was now Winfield Scott's turn at the general's helm.

The next battle of note, the fifth of the war, took place at Sacramento, about fifteen miles from Chihuahua. Not a battle of great generals, it was fought on 28 February 1848 by the Missouri militia under the command of a frontier-type leader, Alexander W. Doniphan, and Brigadier General Garcia Condé, who had arrived to take command of Chihuahua. Condé, the former minister of war for the Republic of Mexico, had a considerable force under his command, about 1,500 infantry, 1,200 cavalry, and 119 artillerymen manning cannon and musketoons.[13] Doniphan had only one regiment, the First Missouri Mounted Infantry, 924 of the most unmilitary-looking men in the Mexican-American War. Condé positioned his force to intercept the rough-looking Americans on a road, but Doniphan knew better than to keep his small force in such a vulnerable position. Instead, he deployed his men across a field and attacked the Mexicans with a fury that became legendary. In hand-to-hand combat, the First Missouri Mounted Infantry killed approximately 300 Mexican soldiers and wounded approximately 300, while losing 1 killed and 8 wounded itself. Doniphan wrote:

> The field was literally covered with the dead and wounded from our artillery and the unerring fire of our riflemen. Night put a stop to the carnage, the battle having commenced about three o'clock. Our loss was one killed, one mortally wounded, and seven so wounded as to recover without any loss of limbs. I cannot speak too highly of the coolness, gallantry, and bravery of the officers and men under my command.[14]

The objective of this battle was the town and state of Chihuahua. Doniphan wanted to neutralize them, but the Mexicans continued to resist. After the battle, Doniphan's men occupied Chihuahua, making fine homes into stables and quartering themselves in slovenly fashion in the nicest haciendas. Informal arrangements of peace took place between the Americans and Mexicans concerning Chihuahua, and Doniphan's First Missouri Mounted Infantry left town and presented itself to Zachary Taylor in Monterrey. Enlistments were nearing an end, so Taylor immediately sent the men for discharge, payment, and a huge welcome back home.[15]

Enter Major General Winfield Scott into the fray. The sixth battle of the war took place at Vera Cruz, a siege lasting from November 1846 to March 1847. Coordinated with the navy, the landing at Vera Cruz was the largest amphibious operation in American history to date. Blockading Vera Cruz was Commodore David E. Connor, who wanted to help Scott any way he could. Scott commanded 12,000 men, and on 2 March 1847 he issued orders to move. On 7 March, Scott decided to visit the landing area under fire in a small ship before ordering the entire army to hit the beach. Among his staff on that rather dangerous reconnaissance trip were George Meade, Robert E. Lee, and Joseph E. Johnston, each of whom became a prominent officer in the Civil War. Had that little ship been hit and destroyed, the Civil War's list of generals would have read somewhat differently.

The landing of 12,000 American troops took place on 9 March 1847 outside of Vera Cruz at the beach of Collada. The U.S. Navy moved the army from transports to warships, then from warships to shore. With the troops, animals, artillery, and ammunition safely ashore, Scott began to deploy his artillery for the siege of Vera Cruz. Commodore Matthew G. Perry replaced Connor and offered Scott a host of heavy naval guns to pound the city into submission. Scott accepted the offer, and Captain Robert E. Lee placed them behind protective sand dunes. Meanwhile, Scott sent an ultimatum to General Juan Morales, commander of the fort and the city of Vera Cruz.[16] Morales paid little attention to Scott's demands, and Scott opened fire during the evening of 24 March 1847.

The bombardment destroyed Vera Cruz. Nothing was spared; even the beautiful cathedral of San Augustin suffered considerable damage. Vera Cruz was a trading port city that contained a sizable number of international diplomats, all of whom pleaded with Scott to stop firing and allow neutrals to leave the city. Scott refused, pointing out that Morales had been given a chance to do that earlier. The diplomats then demanded surrender from Morales, who deferred to his second in command, General J. J. Landero. Landero arranged a convention with Scott, much like the one Taylor had arranged with Ampudia at Monterrey. After haggling and Scott's belligerent response, the Mexicans signed the document on 27 March 1847. Five thousand Mexican soldiers were taken as prisoners of war, but because Scott had no place to put them, he continued the new precedent: they were all paroled in the field until they could be exchanged. Their war was over; they all went home or someplace to await exchange.

The occupation of Vera Cruz created unique problems for Scott. First, many American soldiers took out their frustrations on the populace and vandalized property. Scott issued General Order 20 proclaiming martial law, more to control his own troops than to subjugate the Mexican civilians. Second, Scott had to come to terms with the Catholic Church in Mexico, not by ignoring or denigrating it but by showing respect. Scott asked for Mexican Catholic clergy to say mass for his Catholic troops, and he even attended mass himself at the cathedral, much to the unhappiness of nativists both in the army and back home. Lastly, Scott needed to saddle up and get on with the war: on to Mexico City and battle with Santa Anna's army.

In a month, Santa Anna lost about 10,500 men in battles and marches, but he knew that his future depended on defeating Scott in battle. Returning paroled prisoners of war illegally to the ranks was certainly not beyond Santa Anna, and the Americans could do nothing about it. Leaving Mexico City after shoring up his political position, Santa Anna met Scott's army at the town of Cerro Gordo (Fat Mountain), the seventh battle of the war. Santa Anna set his troops up in a defensive position and waited for the Americans to approach.

Marching up the Mexican National Road were Brigadier General David E. Twiggs and his 2,600 infantry, artillery, and mounted dragoons. On 11 April 1847 Twiggs learned that the Mexican army stood nearby, so he halted his march and deployed his men in defensive positions, waiting for reinforcements. They arrived the next day, and Twiggs began to reconnoiter the Mexican positions. Scott then arrived and sent Captain Robert E. Lee to further reconnoiter the enemy positions. Scott had far fewer troops that Santa Anna—about 12,000 against 18,000 Mexicans. These were not good odds, but Scott was aggressive and determined to bring the war home to the Mexican army in the field.

In charges and counterattacks, Santa Anna believed he won the day because of heavy American losses, but the Americans kept coming and showed their skills in hand-to-hand fighting. The Mexicans broke their lines one after another, fell apart at the seams, and believed there were many more American soldiers in the field than there actually were.[17] Concerning 3,000 EPWs, Scott wrote:

> I have determined to parole the prisoners—officers and men—as I have not the means of feeding them here, beyond to-day, and cannot afford to detach a body of horse and foot, with wagons, to accompany them to Vera Cruz. Our baggage train, though increasing, is not half large enough to give an assured progress to this army.
>
> Besides, a greater number of prisoners would, probably, escape from the escort in the long and deep sandy road, without subsistence—ten to one—than we shall find again, out of the same body of men, in the ranks opposed to us. Not one of the Vera Cruz prisoners is believed to have been in the lines of Cerro Gordo. Some six of the officers, highest in rank, refuse to give their paroles, except to go to Vera Cruz, and thence, perhaps, to the United States.[18]

Command had broken down in Santa Anna's army. Cerro Gordo evolved into a victory more complete than Scott could have dreamed of and opened the way to Mexico City. However, Scott's generous EPW policy was challenged by Washington:

> Your course hitherto, in relations to prisoners of war, both men and officers, in discharging them on parole, has been liberal and kind; but whether it ought to be still longer continued, or in some respects changed, has been under the consideration of the President, and so far

as relates to the officers, he thinks they should be detained until duly exchanged. In that case, it will probably be found expedient to send them, or most of them, to the United States. You will not, therefore, except for special reasons in particular cases, discharge the officers, who may be taken prisoners, but detain them with you, or send them to the United States, as you shall deem most expedient.[19]

Scott certainly obeyed orders. In the assault against Mexico City, the Americans took and kept 800 Mexican officers and men. But his attention was not on prisoners of war; he was focused on ending the war.[20]

Before assaulting Mexico City itself, Scott needed some intelligence on the disposition of Santa Anna's forces along the way. Two officers, both engineers, received the assignment: Major William Turnbull and Captain Robert E. Lee. Together they gathered and presented what information they had to Scott, but the general needed more direct observation, so he assigned that task to Lee. Lee discovered that the Mexicans had powerful defenses on the direct route, but the Acapulco Road to the south looked good because it skirted Lake Chalco and ended just south of Mexico City. General Worth sent his own scouts, and everyone concurred that the Acapulco Road made sense. Scott ordered his army on a twenty-five-mile march to begin the attack on Mexico City.

Santa Anna's scouts had reported the American movement to the south, and knowing that he needed to set up defenses, he chose a line along the Churubusco River. His confidence was reinforced in knowing that he had about 20,000 troops to the American 10,000. A two-to-one numerical advantage represented a considerable amount of firepower in 1847. First to move on 18 August 1847 was Worth's division, but he ran headlong into heavy cannon fire and was forced to stop. Meanwhile, a new Mexican army arrived on the scene, one commanded by the fiery political General Gabriel Valencia, an avowed enemy of Santa Anna who thought nothing of disobeying Santa Anna's orders to leave the scene.

According to Eisenhower, the battles of Contreras and Churubusco, both fought on Friday, 20 August 1847, were actually two parts of one battle.[21] The two towns were only a few miles apart, and a good number of troops who fought in one place fought in the other as well. Scott found his army in serious difficulty as it attempted to continue on the road: a lava field called the Pedregal formed a barrier to all except the infantry. Lee supervised the makeshift road building across the Pedregal, and a force of 3,500 Americans finally arrived at the empty town of San Geronimo. General Valencia, meanwhile, focused his attention not on the Americans on his flank but on an artillery duel to his front. He thought he had won it and chose to celebrate his victory instead of gathering intelligence on the Americans, who were getting closer. The Americans in San Geronimo saw Santa Anna's main force entering the scene. Fortunately for the Americans, Santa Anna took too much time to deploy his force and sealed his doom.

Valencia's 7,000 troops expected to be reinforced by Santa Anna sometime during the night, but instead of Santa Anna, they met 4,500 very angry Americans the next morning. Tired and cold, the Mexicans broke at Contreras in a quarter hour, while Santa Anna retired to Churubusco. Santa Anna and Valencia hated each other, and after watching the rout from a distance, Santa Anna ordered Valencia shot. That never happened, but phase two, the fight at Churubusco, did.

Beginning around noon on Friday, 20 August 1847, the battle for Churubusco cost Santa Anna an estimated 4,000 killed or wounded and 3,000 captured, including eight generals. The Americans lost 1,053 officers and men that day, 139 killed in action.[22] In the end, Scott could have easily taken Mexico City that day, but he decided against it. In his 28 August 1847 dispatch to Secretary of War Marcy, he reported:

> After so many victories, we might, with but little additional loss, have occupied the capital the same evening. But Mr. Trist, commissioner, &c., as well as myself, had been admonished by the best friends of peace—intelligent neutrals and some American residents—against precipitation; lest, by wantonly driving away the government and others—dishonored—we might scatter the elements of peace, excite a spirit of national desperation, and thus, indefinitely postpone the hope of accommodation. Deeply impressed with this danger, and remembering our mission—to conquer a peace—the army very cheerfully sacrificed to patriotism—to the great wish and want of our country—the eclat that would have followed an entrance—sword in hand—into a great capital. I halted our victorious corps at the gates of the city (at least for a time), and have them now cantoned in the neighboring villages, where they are still sheltered and supplied with all necessaries.[23]

The eighth battle concluded with Scott's complete victory over Santa Anna; the ninth and last battles would begin soon. In the interim, Scott offered Santa Anna a truce, thinking that, in the best interests of his army, country, and future, Santa Anna would agree to start negotiations to end the war. Santa Anna leaped at the chance of a truce, bogus or not, because it gave him the chance to rebuild, redeploy, and prepare to meet Scott's Americans on his own terms. While the Americans observed all the specifications of the truce, including prisoner exchange—the Mexicans held about forty-seven American POWs in Mexico City at the time—Santa Anna did not. Peace negotiations were a sham. Nicholas Trist and the Mexican commissioners were officially negotiating while Santa Anna refortified the city. Enough was enough, and Scott told Santa Anna to stop fortifying the city or face the consequences. The truce was off. The peace would soon be welded in place by two battles days apart, Molino del Rey and Chapultepec Castle.

The ninth battle of the Mexican-American War took place outside Mexico City on the morning of 8 September 1847. Based on command intelligence, Worth's 3,500 men believed that Molino del Rey contained a foundry for casting cannons and was a worthy target for assault. In Scott's report to Marcy on 11 September 1847, he noted:

> The same afternoon a large body of the enemy was discovered hovering about the Molino del Rey, within a mile and a third of this village, where I am quartered with the general staff of Worth's division.
>
> It might have been supposed that an attack upon us was intended; but knowing the great value to the enemy of those mills (Molino del Rey) containing a cannon foundry, with a large deposit of powder in Casa Mata near them; and having heard, two days before, that many church bells had been sent out to be cast into guns, the enemy's movement was easily understood, and I resolved, at once, to drive him early the next morning, to seize the powder, and to destroy the foundry.[24]

To assault Molino, Worth called for a special assault force, similar to the specialized German storm troops of World War I, consisting of about 500 specially selected soldiers from various units under the command of Major George Wright. In the assault, Wright died, as did most of his officers, and the Americans withdrew when the Mexicans realized how small this special assault force really was. However, the survivors were rescued and returned to their units. The battle continued for two hours. Although it was indeed an American victory, it cost 116 dead on the field, and to make matters worse, there was no foundry in Molino del Rey.

The tenth and last battle took place at Chapultepec Castle. Scott called a council of war with his officers, and after listening to several possibilities, including one from Robert E. Lee and an important one from P. T. G. Beauregard, Scott decided on the simplest plan—his own and Beauregard's: storm the castle and take it directly. The attack on the castle began with a full day's bombardment, punching holes in the buildings and walls. The next day more special assault parties, including forty marines, were created to scale the walls. Inside the castle were only 260 Mexican troops, the rest being outside. The assault began at 7:30 AM. In the battle's chaos, troops of various American units mixed together, and when the scaling ladders arrived, enough Americans reached the top to force the Mexicans back. The real killing at Chapultepec began with the hand-to-hand combat as the maddened Americans took revenge against the Mexican defenders for killing their wounded at Molino del Rey.

Chapultepec was expensive. Santa Anna lost 1,800 men, Mexico City, and the war. Scott wrote to Marcy on 18 September 1847:

This small force has beaten on the same occasions in view of their capital, the whole Mexican army, of (at the beginning) thirty-odd thousand men—posted, always, in chosen positions, behind entrenchments, or more formidable defenses of nature and art; killed or wounded, of that number, more than seven thousand officers and men; taken 3,730 prisoners, one-seventh officers, including thirteen generals, of whom three have been presidents of this republic; captured more than twenty colours and standards, seventy-five pieces of ordnance, besides fifty-seven wall-pieces, twenty-thousand small-arms, an immense quantity of shot, shells, powder, &c. &c.

Of that enemy, once so formidable in numbers, appointments, artillery, &c., twenty-odd thousand have disbanded themselves in despair, leaving, as is known, not more than three fragments—the largest about 2,500—now wandering in different directions, without magazines or a military chest, and living at free quarters upon their own people.

General Santa Anna, himself a fugitive, is believed to be on the point of resigning the chief-magistracy, and escaping to neutral Guatemala. A new President, no doubt, will soon be declared, and the federal Congress is expected to reassemble at Queretaro, a hundred and twenty-five miles north of this, on the Zacatecas road, some time in October. I have seen and given safe-conduct through this city, to several of its members. The government will find itself without resources; no army, no arsenals, no magazines, and but little revenue, internal or external. Still, such is the obstinacy, or rather infatuation, of this people, that it is very doubtful whether the new authorities will dare to sue for peace on the terms which, in the recent negotiations, were made known by our minister.[25]

Scott never mentioned the execution of the San Patricio deserters. When the American flag rose on Chapultepec Castle, thirty members of the San Patricio Battalion—deserters from the American army, most of them Irish immigrants—were hanged. Rarely had any large number of Americans defected to an enemy, yet there were more than 200 American deserters during the Mexican War. Who were they? Why did so many desert from the U.S. Army in wartime? How did Scott deal with religion and the prevailing nativism of the era?

The Mexicans realized that a considerable amount of friction existed among the American troops revolving around two major issues: slavery and the regional sectionalism between North and South, and religious conflict between the native-born Protestants and the immigrant Catholics. There were about 3,000 Catholics in General Winfield Scott's army, mostly Irish and German immigrants who suffered terribly from anti-Catholic feelings among the native-born, largely southern troops. The Mexicans seized the initiative and attempted to recruit these men, hoping that they might be unhappy enough to join the Catholic Mexicans. General Santa Anna issued a proclamation in which he offered $10 and 200 acres of land to any American deserter, plus bonuses for weapons. Concerning religion, General Santa Anna wrote: "Can you fight by the side of those who put fire to your temples in Boston and Philadelphia? Come over to us! May Mexicans and Irishmen, united by the sacred ties of religion and benevolence, form only one people."[26]

Not to be outmaneuvered by Santa Anna or any of his generals, General Scott, a Queenston prisoner in the War of 1812, did some recruiting of his own. When he reached the town of Puebla in July 1847, he decided to muster the inmates of the town jail, mostly murderers and cutthroats, promising freedom to all those who would ride with a group called Dominguez's Scouts, led by Manuel Dominguez, a condemned murderer. For their efforts in the final siege of Mexico City, the men were paid handsomely, about $16,500, and the Americans were grateful for their services. After the war, Dominguez moved to New Orleans with his family. There the American government abandoned him and left him to his own devices, despite his loyalty.[27]

A closer look at the Irish problem is necessary to understand why these people left their homes for an uncertain future in America. The year 1845 was catastrophic for the people of Ireland. The blight *Phytophthora infestans,* unknown in Europe before 1840, struck the potato crop throughout the continent, but because the Irish were so dependent on the potato for food, the failed crop created the greatest famine in its history. In Ireland, between 1.1 and 1.5 million people died of starvation and famine-related diseases out of a population of about 8.5 million.[28] Amid all the dying, about 1.5 million survivors left Ireland, unwilling immigrants to America.[29] Facing these pennyless, rough-living, mostly illiterate Catholic immigrants were nativist forces so hostile to them and their Catholicism that the Irish quickly learned that in America, one had to work or die, hang tough and together, and defend one's life and faith, in that order. It was their pugnacity and clannishness, however, that caused bitter denunciation, suspicion, and distrust by the nativists, who feared a Vatican conspiracy to catholicize Protestant America. The Irish also learned that they had to become Americans as quickly as possible. One route for men was to join the American army.

According to Kevin Kenny, about half the troops recruited to fight for the Americans in the Mexican War were born outside the United States, and one-quarter of this number came from Ireland.[30] The story began when General Zachary Taylor moved his small army from Corpus Christi, Texas, to a point on the Rio Grande across from Matamoros, Mexico. The Mexicans had told President Polk that such a move meant war, and they turned to a propaganda attack in an attempt to lure Taylor's foreign-born Catholic troops to desert.[31] Among the first Irish American soldiers to desert was Sergeant John Reilly (aka Riley, O'Riley) of Company K, Fifth U.S. Infantry, who had served earlier in the British army in Canada and was an expert artilleryman. With permission granted to cross the river to attend mass, Reilly was heartily received into the Mexican army and commissioned a lieutenant.[32] Soon, Reilly formed the Battalion of Saint Patrick (called *San Patricios* by the Mexicans), composed of other foreign-born American soldiers—mostly Irish, but also some Germans, British, and Poles. As a fighting unit, the San Patricios accounted very well for themselves against their former comrades. They began their work in the defense of Monterrey and showed their artillery prowess at Saltillo. Then they marched to Mexico City, where their ranks grew from more foreign deserters from the American army.

Of the 200 American soldiers who crossed to the Mexican side, not all were active deserters. A few men were captured while drunk and impressed into the battalion; these soldiers later received pardons by General Scott.[33] The Battalion of Saint Patrick, called the "Irish Deserters" by the Americans, consisted of two companies of infantry and artillery. After a desperate battle against American forces at Churubusco, about eighty members of the San Patricios were captured in the convent of San Angel. After trial by court-martial, fifty men were condemned to death by hanging. The rest, who, like Reilly, had deserted before war was declared, received severe whippings, branding, and dishonorable dismissal from the American army at war's end. On 12 November 1847 General Winfield Scott issued General Order 340 in the *American Star:* the lucky ones whose death sentences were commuted would receive "fifty lashes on the bare back well laid on, have the letter 'D' (for Deserter) indelibly branded on the cheek with a red-hot iron, to be confined at hard labor, wearing about the neck an iron collar having three prongs each six inches long, the whole weighing eight pounds, for six months, and at the expiration of that time have the head shaved and be drummed out of the service."[34]

Sixteen men were hanged on a common gallows beginning on 10 September 1847. Thirty San Patricios were executed in a most bizarre way at Mixcoac on 13 September 1847. They were kept standing on an elevated gallows while Chapultepec Castle was assaulted by American troops. Told that the trap would be released when the American flag flew victoriously over the castle, the condemned men stood rigidly for hours in the heat while the battle raged. Finally, when the Mexican flag came down and the American flag was raised, the thirty men cheered and then dropped to their deaths. Others were hanged on a tree the next day.

What angered Scott and the American command was the Mexicans' reasonably effective pro-Catholic, anti-American propaganda. To put a halt to it, Scott not only showed respect for the Catholic Church in Mexico but also used the executed deserters from Churubusco as an example. He issued General Order 296, published in the English and Spanish newspaper the *American Star* on 23 September 1847:

The conspirators have also the services of several false priests who dishonor the religion which they only profess for the special occasion. Their plan is to . . . entice our Roman Catholic soldiers, who have done honor to our colors, to desert, under the promise of lands in

California which our armies have already acquired and which are and forever will remain a part of the United States. Let all our soldiers professing the Catholic religion remember the fate of the deserters taken at Churubusco.[35]

Thus ended the Battalion of Saint Patrick incident. True, most immigrant soldiers remained loyal to their adopted country and showed little pathos toward the San Patricios.

It was a stern lesson to immigrant Catholics in the American army that deserters and renegades would be treated as capital offenders. Although anti-Catholic nativism was regrettable during that era, it was no reason to turn one's coat. The price was just too high, much as it had been for the many Loyalists who were summarily executed for treason during the Revolution. Another valuable lesson comes from Lance Hool's feature film *One Man's Hero* (1999): the right kind of critical, issue-oriented propaganda can be a very useful weapon in war, especially in the hands of an enemy whose ideology has a powerful appeal to a small, sometimes zealously oppressed segment of the opposing army.[36]

The Mexican-American War finally ended with the signing of the Treaty of Guadalupe-Hidalgo on 2 February 1848. According to Article 4 of the treaty, "all prisoners of war taken on either side, on land or on sea, shall be restored as soon as practicable, after the exchange of the ratifications of this treaty."[37] The United States also promised to obtain the release of any Mexicans taken prisoner by Indian tribes in the region. The terms also included Mexican recognition of Texas as part of the United States, with the Rio Grande as the border between the two countries. Territorial cessions by Mexico were huge: more than 500,000 square miles, perhaps a quarter of the present-day United States, including California, Nevada, Utah, most of New Mexico, Arizona, and parts of Colorado and Wyoming. The United States paid Mexico $15 million. The butcher's bill came to 1,721 American dead and 4,102 wounded; an additional 11,000 died of war-related disease.[38]

The Mexican-American War continued the practice of permitting generals to establish terms of surrender and release as events warranted, such as Taylor's agreement with Ampudia at Monterrey, which permitted the defeated Mexicans to march out of the city under arms and with flags flying. Taylor also established a unique precedent, albeit a practical one: to be civil and kind to EPWs. He even went so far as to grant all EPWs who promised not to engage in hostilities a parole home until they could be properly exchanged. Had this been remembered in the American Civil War, far fewer soldiers would have died in the large prison camps of both the Union and Confederate armies. Winfield Scott's successor, General William O. Butler, issued General Order 116 on 1 June 1848, releasing all prisoners.[39] The American army left Mexico City on 12 June 1848, and in 1950, as a gesture of friendship between the two nations, the United States returned to Mexico all the battle flags captured during the war.[40]

FIVE

Prisoners of Politics

A Very Uncivil War

The increase in sickness, the horrors of the prison, the oily atmosphere, the ignominious carnage of the dead, the useless flight of time, the fear of being incarcerated for years, which so affected my spirits that I felt a few more days of these scenes would drive me mad.
—Sir Henry Morton Stanley

The Civil War (1861–1865) initially continued the tradition of paroles in the field established during the Revolution, the War of 1812, and the Mexican War, but in time, each side realized that the parole system was a failure. Honor meant very little, especially to troop-hungry armies; they wanted their soldiers returned to their units as quickly as possible. Most certainly, the Union possessed all the advantages: a large population, an established navy, most of the industrial power of the nation, and the political will expressed by President Abraham Lincoln to hold the Union together. The Confederacy had believed strongly, albeit naively, that it could leave the Union if forced into the untenable position of being oppressed by the northern states in terms of culture, traditions, and politics.

Beginning in 1860, when South Carolina seceded after Lincoln's election to the presidency, the unthinkable became a reality: the Union split in two. The old theories of states' rights, nullification, and interposition prevailed throughout the agrarian South, and eleven states formed a confederacy much like the American confederacy that had been formed in 1777 under the Articles of Confederation. In response, Lincoln called up 75,000 ninety-day volunteers to secure federal forts and armories in the South; the Confederates considered the move to be a call for invasion. The war was on.

Depending on whose version of events and experiences one accepts, the war veterans on both sides believed that their captivities became scandalous exercises in prisoner mistreatment. Both Union and Confederate veterans wrote extensively about their experiences in Northern and Southern prison camps, and their narratives are universally negative. Both Yankees and Rebels truly believed that the other side intended to destroy them in their respective prison camps, murder them out of hand by starvation, debilitation, or diseases such as dysentery, pneumonia, and smallpox (see appendix 3).

The number of prisoners of war taken by the Union and Confederacy was enormous. According to William Best Hesseltine, the following numbers are relatively accurate.[1]

	Participants	Total Deaths	POWs	Paroled	Died in captivity
Union	2,203,000	364,000	211,400	16,668	30,218
Confederate	1,000,000	133,821	220,000	unknown	26,436

In 1876 Alexander H. Stephens, former vice president of the Confederacy, stated that of the 270,000 Union prisoners in Confederate hands (higher than Hesseltine's numbers), only 22,576 died. The Union held approximately 220,000 Confederates, of whom 26,436 died in captivity. According to Stephens, the mortality figures show conclusively that Union treatment of Confederate prisoners was far worse than Confederate treatment of Union prisoners.[2] However, exact numbers are always difficult to ascertain for the Civil War. Noted historian Drew Gilpin Faust commented on the problem in 2006: "Just as Americans had neglected to identify the slain, so too they had failed accurately to count them, to compile reliable and comprehensive numbers of those killed either in particular battles, in larger campaigns, or in the war as a whole."[3]

The POW issue lasted well into the twentieth century, at least for the veterans who wrote prolifically about their experiences. In their memoirs, Union POWs such as Allen O. Abbott, Chester D. Berry, Frederick Fernandez Cavada, Bernhard Domschcke, Willard W. Glazier, Robert H. Kellogg, John McElroy, John L. Ransom, and John W. Urban, and Confederate POWs such as Joe Barbiere, Berry Benson, Griffin Frost, Isaac W. K. Handy, Anthony M. Keiley, John R. King, Buehring H. Jones, and Beckwith West, could not resist polemics, charging that their captors tried to kill them all. Modern Civil War scholarship on prisoners of war has questioned what these veterans had to say, choosing to analyze Union and Confederate policies to debunk what is now perceived as pure vindictive propaganda from both sides.[4]

In his analysis of the Union prison at Fort Delaware (one of the many large star forts, which also included Fort Sumter in Charleston, South Carolina, and Fort Warren in Boston, Massachusetts), Brian

Alexander H. Stephens, former vice president of the Confederacy, stated that only 22,576 Union prisoners died in Confederate hands, contributing to the POW controversy that lasted for decades. Library of Congress.

Temple asserts that the fort presented a perfect opportunity for the Union Army to house large numbers of Confederate POWs and political prisoners.[5] Using postwar narratives, local newspapers, and numerous official reports found in government sources, Temple points out that Union prison authorities created administrative and management problems that essentially caused the premature death of many POWs. Although Union authorities considered Fort Delaware an ideal POW facility, poor housing, food, medical attention, sanitation, and staff all made prison life nearly unbearable, evidenced by the 2,436 Confederate dead buried nearby at Finn's Point, New Jersey. The real problem, this author notes, was the Union cessation of POW exchanges in 1864. POW numbers mounted on both sides; too many died needlessly. But there were more factors at work.

Charles W. Sanders criticizes both Union and Confederate policies that led to the maiming and unnecessary deaths of so many American soldiers in captivity.[6] Not only did the respective prison systems fail, but the individuals responsible for them also failed. Neglect was not the issue for Sanders; responsibility and lack of accountability were. Wars are not won or lost because of POWs; they are won or lost in spite of them. All the major players—Ulysses S. Grant, Robert E. Lee, John Henry Winder, William Hoffman, Edwin M. Stanton, James Seddon, Abraham Lincoln, and Jefferson Davis—knew that. In Sanders's view, they were all equally evil, but for different reasons. First, neither side remembered how prisoners had been treated in the Revolution, the War of 1812, or the Mexican War. Had they done so, provisions would have been made for exchanges in great numbers, and humane treatment would have prevailed in the stockades, but Civil War politics interfered badly. Lincoln refused to acknowledge the sovereignty of the Confederacy, so even calling captured Confederates prisoners of war presented problems—similar to the issue between the British and Americans during the Revolution. Military necessities changed everything, and the Dix-Hill Cartel began to move prisoners to their own lines. Yet no cartel worked very well for long.

By 1863 the rules changed for prisoners of war. Through Adjutant General Henry W. Halleck, Lincoln asked Francis Lieber, a professor of international law at Columbia College in New York City, to use his training and experience to devise a practical set of rules that both the Union and Confederacy could agree on and adhere to. Lieber, who had sons fighting on both sides, understood war and soldiering. He was a Prussian immigrant who had soldiered under Prussian rules and European military traditions with von Blücher at Liegnitz, Waterloo, and Namur. He produced the first comprehensive codification of the rules of war used internally by any government anywhere, as well as the first published legal code pertaining to the treatment of POWs. He delivered the finished document to General Halleck. President Lincoln called it General Order 207: Instructions for the Government of Armies of the United States

Andersonville prison camp, Georgia, 1864. Print from John McElroy, *Andersonville* (1869).

and issued it on 3 July 1863 through the War Department. Additionally, Lincoln ordered the document delivered to every field commander in the Union and Confederate armies. At first, some Confederates thought it was a trick. Many Confederate field commanders, General Robert E. Lee not included, believed the instructions were merely propaganda from a hostile, advantage-seeking federal government.

With Lieber's document and Lincoln's vision came a new era in the protection of American POWs. The most important precept in General Order 207, later known as General Order 100: The Rules of Land Warfare, was the actual status of a POW: he was the prisoner of the government, not of the captor in the field (see appendix 4). Fundamental to Lieber's thinking was the moral precept formulated by Hugo Grotius that recognized an enemy as a fellow human being with lawful rights. If these rights were violated, the offender could be brought to trial. After hostilities ceased in April 1865, Captain Henry Wirtz, Confederate States of America (CSA), the interior commandant of the Andersonville prison (Camp Sumter) in south-central Georgia, was arrested and charged with murdering Union prisoners. Exempted from the general amnesty for Confederate soldiers in 1865, Wirtz was brought to Washington for trial. After a military trial with questionable procedures and even more questionable witnesses, Wirtz was found guilty and executed in the courtyard of the Old Capitol Prison in Washington. He was the first person tried, convicted, and executed in America for the mistreatment of POWs.[7]

By 1864 Ulysses S. Grant, in league with Secretary of War Edwin M. Stanton, forbade formal exchanges, knowing full well that he had to maintain his edge in manpower to destroy the Confederate Army. As far as paroled prisoners were concerned, Grant charged that Confederate soldiers were being returned to their regiments prematurely—that is, while on parole, before they were formally exchanged. Grant also demanded that the Confederate government treat black Union POWs in accordance with the instructions issued by Lincoln. Showing concern for black POWs in Confederate hands sat well with the abolitionists, perhaps, but such concern was likely more propaganda than reality. Stopping the exchanges was not propaganda, however.

Sanders poses several fascinating questions: Were there low levels of concern for Union and Confederate prisoners' physical welfare? What role did parsimony play in the steady destruction of healthy young soldiers in enemy hands? His answer is complex, in that decentralization of the prison systems, personalities affected by an escalating war psychosis, newspapers howling for retribution, and radical Union politics that hardened human feelings toward the suffering of the enemy on both sides all came together to create a catastrophe for POWs.[8] The fight continued in the literature.

In 2008 James M. Gillispie published *Andersonvilles of the North*, which debunks the Southern postwar Lost Cause myth found in most Civil War captivity narratives. This myth claims that the 26,436 Confederate deaths in federal prison camps were due to a deliberate policy of ill treatment perpetrated by policy makers, including Stanton, Grant, and even Lincoln, which caused misery, disease, starvation, and death throughout the Northern prison system. According to Gillispie, researchers in the past have leaned heavily on this theory, bypassing the accurate reportage in the *Official Records of the War of the Rebellion* (1899) and *The Medical and Surgical History of the War of the Rebellion* (1875) in favor of what the former POWs had to say. This, according to the author, was a mistake.[9]

The most prominent theme in Yankee captivity narratives was negative commentary about the Andersonville experience. The former prisoners charged that all Confederate jailers, especially Andersonville's commandant, Captain Henry Wirtz, were cruel, barbaric monsters acting on orders from Jefferson Davis himself to murder them. In both the

Confederate cemetery at Camp Chase in Columbus, Ohio. It holds the graves of more than 2,350, most of whom died from disease. Author's collection.

North and the South, the postwar readership accepted these chilling but mostly exaggerated and sometimes totally inaccurate accounts as gospel, even up to the present era. What makes Gillispie's approach unique is that he follows up on Hesseltine's 1930 study and counters the Lost Cause accounts with inspection reports ordered by Union Colonel William Hoffman, the commissary general of prisoners. He concludes that Hoffman, who had the reputation of being overly parsimonious, responded to the problems in the camps as positively as he could.

There is no shortage of commentary about each of the following camps—Alton and Douglas in Illinois, Morton and Rock Island in Indiana, Johnson's Island and Chase in Ohio, Point Lookout in Maryland, Fort Delaware in Delaware Bay, and Elmira in New York—being a "hell-hole" (see appendix 3). Of these camps, only Elmira, called "Hellmira" by the prisoners, fell below an acceptable level, in part because of its bad location, frigid weather, large prison population, and passivity of Colonel Hoffman. None of these facilities was a hotel, but when comparing the death rate in each with that at the Chimborazzo Hospital in Richmond, one can only conclude that sick Confederates had a better chance of survival in a Yankee prison camp (with the exception of Elmira) than in a major Confederate military medical facility.

The Union decision to halt exchanges through the Dix-Hill Cartel in mid-1863 had a significant impact on the POW problem on both sides. Denying the Confederacy the use of manpower is often cited as the reason for doing so (especially by Sanders), but Gillispie concludes that the Davis administration's decision to reenslave captured black troops and execute the white officers who led them was the real reason. Most certainly, it was not a mere act of propaganda. Confederate Secretary of War James A. Seddon made it very clear that the Confederacy would not consider black Union troops to be prisoners of war.[10] In the field, no white officers of the U.S. Colored Troops were ever executed out of hand by the Confederates, but the Lincoln administration wanted to force the Confederate government to change its POW policy toward black Union troops, whom the federal government felt a responsibility to protect. It was not until 1 February 1865, when Grant was sure of a Union victory, that he reinstated the formal exchange system.

Starvation, always a major charge against both prison systems, did not take place in federal prison camps, even when rations were cut back in 1864. On Saturday, 31 December 1864, the *Portsmouth (NH) Morning Chronicle* reported: "A letter from Hilton Head states that an order has been received to place rebel prisoners at that point on reduced fare, in retaliation for the brutality shown to our soldiers in the prison pens of Georgia and South Carolina. On the day the letter was written, hard bread and water were dealt out to the two hundred and fifty or more rebel officers held at that point, in compliance with this order." In the major prison facilities, the Confederates received exactly what the Union troops received—about 4,000 to 4,500 calories a day—but the problem was the diet: meat and bread without fruits or vegetables. Scurvy often resulted. The Confederates also received food and clothing from friends by mail, and they could buy a few luxury items from camp sutlers if they had any money.

The real problem in Northern and Southern prisons was disease. Often the Union and Confederate troops arrived in camp with wounds that festered and killed them quickly. Diseases contracted in camp or on the battlefield spread in prison, and the dirt, fleas, and lice exacerbated the health problems, which included diarrhea or dysentery, smallpox, scurvy, and typhoid fever, all of which appeared regularly in the camps, battlefields, and prison pens in North and South alike. Modern concepts of hygiene and the science of communicable diseases were simply unknown. In the end, the hard living conditions in all prison camps took their ugly toll on the captured soldiers. Primitive medical treatment and mortality were the norms. Such were the horrors and misfortunes of the American Civil War.

Changing sides was not common among POWs in the Civil War, but it occurred regularly on a small scale. As in the Revolution, political policies toward POWs wavered on both sides. In 1862, after New Orleans fell to Union forces, General Benjamin "Beast" Butler began to urge Confederate prisoners to change sides and fight with the Union. He referred to them as "repentant rebels"; they were later referred to as "whitewashed" rebels. As former soldiers of the Confederacy, they took an oath of allegiance to the United States, and between September 1864 and November 1866, volunteer units of "galvanized" or converted Confederate prisoners were sent to the western frontier as Union soldiers to fight Indians and keep the peace. As the frontier corps of the U.S. Volunteers, they risked their lives in battle for the Union, but never against their former comrades.[11]

Not all of them went west. One notable galvanized Yankee who stayed in the East was Henry Morton Stanley. Born in England and an immigrant to the United States before the Civil War, Stanley was captured by Union troops at Shiloh and suffered a terrifying experience in Camp Douglas. He decided that switching sides was a better idea than remaining loyal to a doubtful cause. He stated in his autobiography that his resolve to be a Confederate POW was undermined for several reasons:

> These were the increase in sickness, the horrors of the prison, the oily atmosphere, the ignominious carnage of the dead, the useless flight of time, the fear of being incarcerated for years, which so affected my spirits that I felt a few more days of these scenes would drive me mad. Finally, I was persuaded to accept with several other prisoners the terms of release, and enrolled myself in the U.S. Artillery Service, and, on the 4th June, was once more free to inhale the fresh air.[12]

Once he took the oath of allegiance, Stanley was released from prison on 4 June 1862, but shortly thereafter he came down with dysentery and fever and was discharged from the Union Army on 22 June. Out of work, Stanley joined the U.S. Navy, where he learned the journalist's trade. Stanley subsequently became a newspaperman and explorer—he was the man who found Dr. Livingston in Africa. Stanley eventually left the United States in disgust and gave up his American citizenship for British knighthood. He died Sir Henry Morton Stanley, an immigrant in a foreign land, former Confederate soldier, galvanized Yankee, journalist, explorer, celebrity, and, finally, American expatriate.[13]

Becoming a galvanized Yankee was not an easy task for native sons of the South. Angry, betrayed comrades and mess mates would often harass them in camp before they left their midst. Colonel Buehring H. Jones, CSA, described an experience that took place while he was a prisoner at the prison camp for Confederate officers at Johnson's Island, Ohio. One officer decided to take the oath of allegiance rather than remain a POW, but when his mess mates discovered his treachery, they began to "kick him out" of their compound, physically kicking him until the Union guards forced them to stop. Then, as a result of his decision to change sides, the young man was shunned. Jones wrote:

His former friends will not speak to him, nor allow him to speak to them. Every hand will be against him; every tongue will hiss at him; every heart will loathe him. Even the Federals, whom he seeks to propitiate, will regard him with ill concealed scorn and contempt. Because they believed, he had not the manhood to endure imprisonment, with its privations and suffering, for a cause, that, in his heart, he believes is just; but chose rather to take a solemn oath—an oath that he is too cowardly to perform—to support a cause that he believes is wrong.[14]

Regardless of the ill treatment in camp by former comrades in arms, the galvanized Yankees freed Union troops for the battlefields of the Southeast to confront the Confederate legions. At first, these men were received with skepticism, suspicion, and even dislike, because few Union field commanders believed the Confederates would make good soldiers. The skeptics were wrong. When the former Confederate troops confronted the fury and military skill of the Native American tribes on Great Plains, the galvanized Yankees fought with distinction, discipline, and a sense of duty admired by their Union commanders and feared by their enemies.

The first star in the intelligence system during the Civil War was the detective Allan Pinkerton, who had discovered a plot to assassinate President-elect Lincoln in Baltimore in 1860. As a result, Lincoln changed his route to Washington, D.C., and arrived undetected. As the war marched on month by month, Lincoln worried more and more about a Confederate fifth column in the North consisting of antiwar Democrats (mostly in Indiana and Ohio) who called themselves "Copperheads." He took unprecedented actions, such as suspending writs of habeas corpus, declaring martial law in areas not in the combat zone, and trying civilians in military courts.[15] Union POW camps held more than Confederate soldiers; they also held political prisoners jailed for antiwar or Confederate sympathies. Where insurrection existed or was suspected to exist, sometimes the innocent as well as the guilty went to jail as political prisoners (prisoners of state), sometimes for extended periods. None of this could take place today in American society, but from the Revolution onward, catastrophic civil war has had a way of changing the rules.

Despite Chief Justice Roger Taney's opposition in *Ex parte Merryman* (1861), Lincoln ordered his regional commanders to imprison anyone expressing even a hint of sedition against the government of the United States. In Lincoln's view, he held the legal high ground on the strength of Article I, Section 9 of the Constitution, which gives the president extraordinary powers as commander in chief of the armed forces and the mandate to stop rebellion and invasion and maintain public safety. Lincoln issued the first such proclamation on 10 May 1861, granting the commander of Union forces in Florida the power, "if he shall find it necessary, to suspend the writ of *habeas corpus* and to remove all dangerous or suspected persons."[16] Executive Order 1, relating to political prisoners, was issued on 14 February 1862; however, as the war progressed beyond a police problem to a war of conquest, both armed Confederate and Union troops became traditional prisoners of war.[17] By the summer of 1863, soldiers on both sides were protected by Lieber's laws, but civilians were not.

On 27 April 1862 Lincoln suspended the writ of habeas corpus along the rail line from Philadelphia to Washington. By the middle of July the order was extended to New York City, and military authorities could arrest anyone thought to be aiding the Confederacy directly or the Confederate cause indirectly by giving a speech or making a public statement against Union policy. This order bothered few people in the North, who were fearful of Confederate fifth columns, until the arrest of John Merryman, a lieutenant of a secessionist drill company in Maryland, who was imprisoned in Fort McHenry. Chief Justice Roger Taney, a Maryland Democrat remembered for his infamous *Dred Scott* decision in 1857, issued a writ of habeas corpus for Merryman and ruled Lincoln's arrest order unconstitutional, claiming that only Congress could suspend habeas corpus. Taney also charged that Lincoln had acted unlawfully and reminded him to "take care that the laws be faithfully executed," warning that if such actions continued, "the people of the United States are no longer living under a government of laws."[18] Lincoln ignored Taney's order.

On 24 September 1862 Lincoln suspended habeas corpus throughout the Union for all cases of disloyalty and ordered the arbitrary arrest of anyone guilty of disloyalty in speech or in practice. As one can only imagine, this had a chilling effect on newspapers opposed to the president's war or political policies. Editors rightly feared not only the power of the presidency but also the possibility of imprisonment at Old Capitol Prison in downtown Washington or at Fort Lafayette in New York. Lincoln told Congress, "These measures, whether strictly legal or not, were ventured upon under what appeared to be a popular demand and a public necessity, trusting, then as now, that Congress would readily ratify them."[19]

The November 1862 elections brought a raft of Democrats into Congress with three variations: the War Democrats, who backed the war and Lincoln's policies; the mainstream Democrats, who backed the war for the preservation of the Union but opposed Lincoln's ideas about emancipation and civil rights, and the Peace Democrats or Copperheads, who favored a negotiated end to the war and recognition of the Confederacy. Many members of Congress and Democratic military officers revolted against Lincoln's emancipation policies in particular, claiming that the president was using the idea of preserving the Union as a pretext for freeing the slaves and saying that if the Republicans would not end the war, they "were making money out of it."[20]

Over the next three years many Democratic opponents were arrested and held in confinement as political prisoners, much as the Quakers had been held during the Revolution. One such prisoner was J. W. Packard, born in Bridgewater, Massachusetts, in 1833. He had moved to Richmond to sell sewing machine needles but wanted to return north in 1862 and received permission to do so. On his way, Confederate forces stopped and arrested him, but he later won release from the Confederate governor of Virginia. Finally reaching Philadelphia, Packard was again arrested, this time by a Union detective who stripped him of his suitcases, money, and clothes before throwing him into jail. A member of the Philadelphia Bar Association met with Packard and assured him that he would be released because he was a good Republican and not a threat to the war effort. Unfortunately for Packard, the detective informed him that he was going to be transferred to Fort Lafayette, where the following prison rules were posted on the casemates on 3 August 1861:

Regulations for the Guidance of Citizen Prisoners
Confined at This Post

1. The rooms of all prisoners will be ready for inspection at 9 o'clock AM. All cleaning will be done by the prisoners themselves unless otherwise directed. All washing will be done in the yard.
2. No conversation will be allowed with any member of this garrison, and all communications in regard to their wants will be made to the Sergeant of the Guard.
3. No prisoner will leave his room without the permission of the Sergeant of the Guard.
4. Prisoners will avoid all conversations on the political affairs of this country, within the hearing of any member of this garrison.
5. Light will be allowed in the prisoners' rooms until 9:15 PM. After this hour, all talking, or noise of any kind, will cease.
6. The prisoners will obey implicitly the directions of any member of the guard.
7. Cases of sickness will be reported at 7 AM.
8. Any transgressions of the foregoing rules will be corrected by solitary imprisonment, or such other restrictions as may be required to the strict enforcement thereof.

Additional orders were posted from time to time, such as the following:

No prisoner will be allowed to recognize or have any communication with any persons visiting this Fort, excepting when the visitor brings an order from the proper authority, permitting an interview, which interview will be held in the presence of an officer, and not to exceed one hour; the conversation during the interview will be carried on in a tone of voice low enough to be distinctly heard by the officer in whose presence the interview is held.[21]

After ten days at the fort, Packard was released, but he had to pay $300 for his room and board while in prison.[22]

Another citizen accused of sedition was Joseph Kugler, born in New Jersey in 1805. Kugler, a prosperous farmer, often found himself in political arguments and, unfortunately, tended to voice his opinions loudly. S. B. Hudnut reported in an affidavit that Kugler had said, "Lincoln had no right to call out seventy-five thousand troops without first convening Congress; and that, if the South had been given her just dues, there would never have been a rebellion."[23] The affidavit also claimed that Kugler discouraged enlistments. That was more than enough for Kugler to be arrested. After he spent six days in the Burlington County Jail in Mount Holley, New Jersey, Secretary of War Stanton ordered him to the Old Capitol Prison in Washington, D.C., where he remained for eight days. He was released after a considerable effort was made by his friends to show that Kugler never said such things in public.

The most prominent of the political prisoners (there were hundreds, according to postwar writer John A. Marshall in his vitriolic, anti-Lincoln *American Bastile*) was Lamdin P. Milligan, a citizen of Indiana who was arrested at his home on 5 October 1864. As a known opponent of Republican war policies, he was brought before a military commission in Indianapolis and charged with conspiracy against the government of the United States; affording aid and comfort to rebels against the authority of the United States; and inciting insurrection, disloyal practices, and violation of the laws of war. Each charge had additional specifications, but the general claim was that, through his association with pro-Southern groups such as the Order of American Knights or the Sons of Liberty, Milligan had aided the Confederacy. The prosecution believed that he had plotted to overthrow the government, communicated with the enemy, plotted to free Confederate prisoners of war (probably at Camp Morton in Indiana), resisted the military draft, and conspired to steal war materials stored in local arsenals. All this, true or not, was taken seriously, and Milligan was in deep trouble.

During his trial Milligan raised the issue of jurisdiction, objecting to being a civilian tried by a military tribunal, but that bore no weight at all, in part because he was considered a local nuisance and a Confederate sympathizer. Witnesses were paraded into court and harassed or even threatened to get them to testify as they had been coached. Then the unthinkable took place: actor John Wilkes Booth assassinated Abraham Lincoln at Ford's Theater in Washington, D.C., and the public wanted revenge. Milligan was a convenient target in April 1865 and was found guilty as charged. The court set his execution date for 19 May 1865, but on 10 May, Milligan filed a petition with the Circuit Court of the United States that delayed his execution until 2 June 1865. Curiously, the military commandant of the region ordered a subordinate to take Milligan to the local penitentiary, where he was forced to perform hard labor. Being stubborn but sickly, Milligan landed in the prison hospital, awaiting his fate. In 1866 the Supreme Court heard his case, found him not subject to military legal procedure, and let him go free. Justice David Davis wrote in his decision:

> A petition for a writ of *habeas corpus,* duly presented, is the institution of a cause on behalf of the petitioner, and an allowance or refusal of the process, as well as the subsequent disposition of the prisoner is matter of law, and not of digression.
>
> Military commissions organized during the late civil war, in a State not yet invaded and not engaged in rebellion, in which the Federal courts were open, and in the proper and unobstructed exercise of their judicial functions, had no jurisdiction to try, convict, or sentence for any criminal offense, a citizen who was neither a resident of a rebellious State not a prisoner of war, nor a person in the military or naval service. And Congress could not invest them with such power.[24]

This famous decision is known today as *Ex parte Milligan.* In it, Justice Davis made it clear that civilians could not be held as prisoners of war and that neither president nor Congress, nor even a judiciary, could disturb any civil liberties incorporated in the Constitution. According to former Chief Justice William Rehnquist, "The Milligan decision is justly celebrated for its rejection of the government's position that the Bill of Rights has no application in wartime."[25] Thus a serious precedent was established, one that would be flaunted in the twentieth century in two wars.

One other civilian prisoner who caused trouble for the Lincoln administration was an Ohio Copperhead, Clement L. Vallandigham of Toledo. Over and over, Vallandigham criticized Lincoln's use of war powers without congressional approval, and by 1861 the executive branch viewed Vallandigham more as a traitor than as the political opposition. The Ohio legislature tired of him too and gerrymandered him out of a job, making sure he lost the election in 1862. Undaunted in his opposition to the war and the Lincoln administration, Vallandigham ran for governor in 1863, but the Ohio Democrats refused to let him represent them on the ticket. It seemed that the game was up for Vallandigham, but not quite.

General Ambrose Burnside, who managed to make a fool of himself at the Battle of Antietam in 1862, issued General Order 38 on 13 April 1863 from his headquarters in Cincinnati. It stated that no one was permitted to speak ill of the president or the government. Delighted, Vallandigham screamed against emancipation, conscription, and Lincoln's assault on civil rights. An outraged Burnside ordered his immediate arrest. On 5 June 1863 the arresting officers dragged Vallandigham from his bed, stood him before a military tribunal for two days, convicted him, and sentenced him to two years in prison. But Vallandigham avoided prison and went to the Supreme Court.

Naturally, as a lawyer, Vallandigham understood exactly what the writ of habeas corpus meant, despite Burnside's refusal to consider it. In December 1863 the Supreme Court heard his case. To Vallandigham's horror, the Court agreed that Burnside had every right to arrest him under the circumstances of civil war and that Burnside had no obligation to grant habeas corpus during a military tribunal. In short, Vallandigham lost his case.[26] Prior to his imprisonment, Vallandigham became a media spectacle, and the president had had enough of this man. At an 18 June 1863 cabinet meeting, Lincoln announced his decision to deport Vallandigham to the Confederacy. He was first deposited with the Confederates at Murfreesboro, Tennessee, but Jefferson Davis refused to welcome or keep him, so he was sent to North Carolina, then to Bermuda, and finally to Canada. Was this the end for Clement L. Vallandigham? Lincoln enjoyed no such luck.

The Copperhead Democrats in Ohio nominated Vallandigham for governor in the November 1863 election. Lincoln was horrified at first, but Vallandigham lost the election by 100,000 votes. With Vallandigham defanged, Lincoln had no objection to his returning to the United States; the president had an election of his own to worry about. Opposing Lincoln in 1864 was General George McClellan of New Jersey, a Democrat and former commanding officer of the Army of the Potomac who, known affectionately as "Little Mac," was extremely popular with his troops. Unfortunately for McClellan, the Democratic Party hired Vallandigham to be the chief plank writer of its 1864 platform, and naturally, Vallandigham created a peace plank that ultimately lost the election for McClellan.[27] Vallandigham's political career came to end after the war with his failed run for a senatorial seat. He returned to the bar in Toledo and died in court of an accidental, self-inflicted gunshot wound in 1871.

The next category of prisoner held during the Civil War was that of spy. One of the most famous episodes of pure stubbornness was the capture and execution of Sam Davis of Tennessee. Davis, a Confederate scout for General Braxton Bragg, CSA, was sent on a dangerous mission to gather information concerning General Grant's troop strength around Chattanooga. After scouting Grant's lines and learning that the entire Sixth Army Corps under the command of General G. M. Dodge, USA, was poised to attack Confederate lines, Davis tried to make his way back to deliver this valuable information to General Bragg, but he was captured by Federal forces.

In a replay of the John André affair during the Revolution, Davis had concealed a map of Federal fortifications in Nashville in his saddle, and his boot hid a letter written by his commanding officer addressed to General Bragg that contained information about Federal troop movements. Although he was captured in uniform (André had worn civilian clothes), Union officers charged Davis with espionage. He was found guilty and sentenced to die. At his execution, while the trap was being adjusted, one of Dodge's officers renewed an offer made earlier—information for his life—but Davis refused, saying, "If I had a thousand lives, I would lose them all here before I would betray my friend or the confidence of my informer." Without any help from his executioners, Davis stepped on the trap himself and died a few moments later.[28] In retaliation for Davis's execution, the Confederates executed two Union soldiers in Richmond. Like Major André for the British and Nathan Hale for the Americans in the Revolution, Davis would become a symbol of selfless duty, resistance to a captor, and soldierly determination not to give in regardless of the consequences. As a classic captivity defeat hero, Sam Davis, like Nathan Hale before him, attracted a following. Hale's statue stands in the CIA's rotunda in Langley, Virginia; Davis's memory has attained nearly cult status among those interested in the Civil War's Southern cause.[29]

Women spies were not executed during the Civil War; instead, the Union Army incarcerated them in the Old Capitol Prison in Washington. Such was the fate of three women: Antonia Ford, Belle Boyd, and Rose O'Neal Greenhow. Antonia Ford came from a Southern-sympathizing family in Fairfax, Virginia, and her brother served with J. E. B. Stuart. Stuart would visit the family when he operated in the region, and the young, attractive Antonia became his eyes and ears in town. After frequently reporting Union movements to Stuart, she was arrested and imprisoned in the Old Capitol in 1862. Union Major Joseph Willard, heir to the Willard Hotel in Washington and Ford's escort officer to the prison, interceded on her behalf. After her release from Old Capitol, Willard left the army and married her.

Eighteen-year-old Belle Boyd, known as "la belle Rebele," "Cleopatra of the Secession," the "Rebel Joan of Arc," and the "Siren of the

Old Capitol Prison in Washington, D.C., which housed Confederate spies during the Civil War. Library of Congress.

Shenandoah," operated out of her father's hotel in Front Royal, Virginia. Her primary contact was General Thomas "Stonewall" Jackson, CSA, and she provided intelligence support for his operations in the Shenandoah Valley. Boyd was a woman with lovers, one of whom informed the Union Army about her espionage activities. At age nineteen she was sent to Old Capitol Prison for one month, where she contracted typhoid fever. Released on 1 December 1863, Boyd traveled to Europe to recover. On the way back to America her blockade runner was captured, but she fell in love with the prize captain, Ensign Samuel Hardinge, who later married her. It was a short marriage. Boyd's husband, who had been court-martialed for assisting a Southern spy, was dismissed from the navy and traveled to England, but Belle convinced him to return to the United States to work for the Confederacy. Caught and imprisoned, he died after being detained by Union forces late in the war. Boyd returned to Britain, pursued a stage career, and, after coming home to the United States, wrote her memoir, *Belle Boyd, Confederate Spy.* She traveled around the country talking about her spying activities during the Civil War until her death in 1900.[30]

The queen of captured Confederate spies was Rose O'Neal Greenhow of Montgomery County, Maryland. Called "Wild Rose" from the time of her youth, she certainly lived up to that tag throughout her life.[31] As a passionate Southern sympathizer in 1861, Greenhow contacted General P. T. G. Beauregard, CSA, with a ten-word message concerning Union troop deployments at Manassas (Bull Run). After the Confederate victory, Jefferson Davis credited her with the win. Notoriety finally caught up with Wild Rose, and like the other female spies, she wound up in Old Capitol Prison, where she continued sending messages. Her tradecraft was, perhaps, more sophisticated than that of the other spies in Confederate service. Rather than execution, the Union Army exiled Greenhow from Maryland to the Confederacy, and Jefferson Davis sent her to Britain and France as a propagandist. Shortly after her arrival in London in 1863 she published her memoir, *My Imprisonment and the First Year of Abolition Rule at Washington,* and became quite a celebrity, meeting major European personalities such as Queen Victoria, Napoleon III, Thomas Carlyle, and others.

The fast life came to an end soon, however. After a year flitting around Europe as Jefferson Davis's unofficial social ambassador, Greenhow boarded the *Condor,* a British blockade runner, for home. Around her waist she carried a large money belt full of gold she had received as royalties on her book. Just before arriving at Wilmington, North Carolina, in October 1864, while being pursued by a Union gunboat, the *Condor*'s captain ran the ship aground. With absolutely no desire to be recaptured by Union forces with that much gold in her possession, Greenhow took one of the ship's boats and tried to reach shore. The sea swelled, her little boat capsized, and Greenhow went to the bottom, along with all her gold. After the Confederates recovered her body (without the gold), they buried her with full military honors in Wilmington.[32]

The last prisoners of the Union Army during the Civil War were the war criminals: Henry Wirtz, Jefferson Davis, and the Lincoln conspirators. Without a doubt, Union wrath concerning the 12,711 deaths at Andersonville warranted retribution, and the Union Army delivered it in Wirtz's trial and execution (see appendix 5).[33] According to Andersonville historian Ovid L. Futch, to justify Wirtz's legal lynching, Northerners called him the "demon of Andersonville," "fiend incarnate," and "human monster," charging that he had murdered helpless prisoners in cold blood.[34] Profane he might have been, but he was no murderer. The Confederate prison system simply broke down under the strain of Union military pressure. The prisoners suffered, and Wirtz was hanged for it.

Before his execution, Wirtz wrote a petition to President Andrew Johnson from his prison cell at Old Capitol, upholding his belief in his innocence and his resolve to die like a soldier. The president did not respond. For the execution the government printed 250 spectator tickets, and Secretary of War Stanton commissioned Alexander Gardner to photograph the event. Wirtz died on the morning of 10 November 1865, at that point the only EPW to die for war crimes committed in a POW camp.[35] Curiously, there is a monument to his memory in the village of Andersonville, Georgia, built by the United Daughters of the Confederacy in 1909. One side eulogizes Wirtz, another side quotes Grant, and the third side cites Jefferson Davis's words written in 1888: "When time shall have softened passion and prejudice, when reason shall have stripped the mask of misinterpretation, then justice holding even her scales, will require of past censure and praise to change sides."[36]

After the war, the Andersonville prison site was confiscated by the federal government, and the cemetery was administered by the U.S. Army. As the wooden grave markers wore away, they were replaced by marble markers, thanks to the research and devotion of Clara Barton, who used Union POW Dorrance Atwater's secret list to mark the Andersonville dead. Andersonville today is an active national cemetery. With a large monument from the state of Georgia to all American POWs, the old Confederate Camp Sumter, now administered by the National Park Service, serves as the site of the National Prisoner of War Memorial. Johnson's Island is in private hands, except for the Confederate cemetery. Fort Delaware—part bird sanctuary, part museum—belongs to the state of Delaware and is open for visitors; Point Lookout, now a park, belongs to the state of Maryland. The others are gone, their memories preserved only by cemeteries and regional historical associations.

The Lincoln conspirators—George Atzerodt, David Herold, Lewis Powell, and Mary Surratt—were also held, tried by a military commission, and executed by hanging on 7 July 1865 at the Washington Arsenal. Dr. Samuel Mudd, who treated Lincoln's assassin for his leg injury, was imprisoned at Fort Jefferson in the Dry Tortugas. Mudd remained a model prisoner until his pardon on 8 February 1869 for assisting the medical personnel during an outbreak of yellow fever. The very last prisoner of the Civil War, Jefferson Davis, was captured in Irwinville,

Georgia, along with what remained of the gold in the Confederate treasury after he had abandoned Richmond in 1865.

After his capture Davis was taken to Savannah, and he was very lucky not to have been assassinated during the journey. Feelings against him were extreme; it was natural that Americans, both Northern and Southern, blamed him for the Civil War. At Savannah, Davis was imprisoned with Alexander Stephens, his former vice president, but the army moved Stephens to Fort Warren in Boston Harbor, where he stayed for only five months before being released.[37] On 22 May 1865 Davis arrived at Fort Monroe in Virginia and was treated more like a demon than a prisoner of state. His jailer, General Nelson A. Miles, ordered Davis to be put into a small, damp cell, shackled with leg irons, and treated like a common criminal.[38] After five days, Secretary of War Stanton ordered Miles to remove the shackles.

In prison, the army held Davis in close confinement. With little exercise, a lamp burning twenty-four hours a day, constant harassment from the guards, cell inspections every fifteen minutes or so, and, worst of all, silence, there is little doubt that his captors intentionally treated Davis very badly. As a result, Davis's health failed, and he was holding on by a slim psychological rope as well. His family suffered harassment in Savannah, especially when they had to listen to people singing, "Let's Hang Jeff Davis from a Sour Apple Tree." They nearly did. But Davis had had absolutely nothing to do with the Lincoln assassination. He was being held for treason only, and for a year he received no support at all from his fellow Southerners and, of course, no trial date.

After a year of suffering terribly, both physically and psychologically, Jefferson Davis saw the first signs of dawn in 1866. Andrew Johnson removed General Miles from his post at Fort Monroe and replaced him with Colonel H. S. Burton, a kinder and more understanding officer. Burton allowed Davis daily exercise, gave him a drier cell, and allowed Varina Davis to visit her husband regularly. He eventually allowed her to live with her husband in the fort.[39] Dawn finally broke into morning for Jefferson Davis.

A movement arose to free Davis from prison. His prison doctor, Dr. John Craven, and writer Charles Halpine published *The Prison Life of Jefferson Davis* in 1866. As the Davis controversy rose to nearly the boiling point, President Johnson tried to make it go away by offering Davis a pardon—but only if he applied for one. Davis, stubborn and defiant as always, demanded a trial.[40] The federal government wanted nothing to do with Davis by this point and decided to turn him over to the state of Virginia for action. Finally, the U.S. Circuit Court for the District of Virginia issued a writ of habeas corpus for Davis on 1 May 1867, and under instructions from the War Department, General Burton obeyed the writ and set Davis free on 13 May.[41]

Davis never stood trial. In 1868 Chief Justice Salmon P. Chase dismissed the indictment, and the president issued a general amnesty and a pardon.[42] Davis's troubles continued, however: he failed to find work in Canada and England; failed as head of the Carolina Life Insurance Company in Memphis, Tennessee; and failed to revive his plantation in Mississippi. And all the while, he lost friends like Robert E. Lee and family members to death. At this stage of his life, he sat down and wrote his two-volume *Rise and Fall of the Confederate Government,* and only two months before his death in New Orleans in 1889, he completed *A Short History of the Confederate States of America.* To this day, the South is full of memorials to him, although his experience as an American prisoner of state has faded away with time.

There is little historical doubt that the Civil War started small in 1861, but there is also little doubt that it evolved into the most catastrophic war the United States ever experienced. Except for medicine and the understanding of diet and bacterial diseases, it was the first really modern war, especially in terms of EPWs. In earlier wars, there had been no real POW camps of any size, and officers were usually paroled either home or to a defined region until they were exchanged. Appendix 3 lists the POW camps on each side, and after the Union ceased exchanging prisoners, the men languished in these camps, which grew exponentially as men poured into them during the battles of 1864. Too many men sat in horribly dirty enclosures with inadequate rations, leading to medical disaster for thousands of Union and Confederate prisoners. Disease has no mercy, no parole, no exchange, and looking at the 12,711 deaths at Andersonville prison in Georgia, this truth bore its ugly fruit.

Just as the War of 1812 had established a very successful cartel, the officers of the Civil War attempted to replicate it with the Dix-Hill Cartel, concluded on 22 July 1862. Prior to that agreement, field commanders often exchanged their prisoners on an informal basis for humanitarian reasons, as had been done in Mexico, for the most part. The Civil War grew to huge proportions, and what had been successful in the past faced an impasse in 1862. Secretary of War Edwin M. Stanton appointed Major General John A. Dix to negotiate for the Union;

General Robert E. Lee appointed Major General D. H. Hill to assume negotiation duties for the Confederacy. By and large, the exchanges went relatively smoothly, but by 1863 the cartel broke down, mainly due to the lack of good faith on both sides and especially because of the Confederates' refusal to exchange black Union soldiers. Numbers can only be approximated, but it is safe to say that the Union paroled or exchanged about 329,000 Confederates, while the Confederates did the same for about 152,000 Union soldiers.[43] By June 1863 the Dix-Hill Cartel ended; the prisoners on both sides were stranded.

The month of April 1863 not only changed the Civil War but also gave the international community of great military powers a new set of rules to follow—real rules that had real consequences if one broke them. Francis Lieber wrote a magnificent document, and it is fair to conclude that it created wholly new precedents for the treatment of POWs worldwide. Following the American lead, Europeans began to think seriously about international rules of war and the protection of warriors in captivity. Henri Dunant's important 1862 book *Un Souvenir de Solferino* described the inhumane fate of victims of battle in Europe. Its popularity contributed to the formation of the International Red Cross in 1864. Meetings were called in Geneva in 1864, 1868, and 1906 to address relief for wounded combatants, regardless of flag. The Brussels meeting, called by the Imperial Russian government in 1874, was the first European conference to consider POWs as a humanitarian as well as a military issue. At Brussels, the representatives incorporated many of Lieber's suggestions into the parameters of modern European warfare and developed something very new in European culture—the Brussels Code for the treatment of prisoners of war.[44]

The Civil War also witnessed another phase of hostility against those citizens who opposed it: political prisoners who were denied habeas corpus, often tried by military commissions, and sometimes executed (or, as in the case of Lamdin Milligan, condemned but not executed). In a way, Lincoln's use of executive orders to his military commandants in regions not invaded by Southern forces approximated the Continental Congress's orders to arrest Philadelphia Quakers and state legislatures' orders to arrest Loyalists during the Revolution. If a precedent was set here, the evidence shows that at this point in American history, the United States continued its basic humanitarian treatment of EPWs, but when those prisoners were Americans, especially political prisoners perceived as disloyal or traitorous, then decent, humane treatment might be in doubt.

Spies are usually treated harshly in wartime, and they were normally executed in the field during the Civil War. Women, however, were not. As seen with Antonia Ford, Belle Boyd, and Rose O'Neal Greenhow, when female spies were caught, they were not executed, as the men were, but were put in Old Capitol Prison in Washington and often deported. The Lincoln conspirators directly involved with John Wilkes Booth's assassination of the president, except for Dr. Samuel A. Mudd and two others who had nothing to do with it, were executed. The interior commandant of Andersonville prison was also executed. Jefferson Davis was nearly executed. The rancor and regional hatred between North and South did not abate until World War II, but the country began to look west in the postwar period, and the U.S. Army faced a new problem—the tribes of the Great Plains and beyond. They too became EPWs in American hands.

Six

Indians as POWs in America

From Discovery to 1914

For nearly two years we were kept at hard labor in this place, and
we did not see our families until May 1887. This treatment was in
direct violation of our treaty made at Skeleton Cañon.
—Geronimo

In 1561 a Spanish ship landed in Virginia and took one Indian captive
to Spain, where he was baptized Don Luis de Velasco. During his Spanish sojourn, he was educated and granted Spanish citizenship. In 1570
Velasco returned to the New World, along with several Spanish Jesuit
missionaries he knew very well. On shore, Velasco quickly returned to
his native ways and led a raid that killed all. One wonders why the level
of violence was so high, and why the act of getting even, if Velasco's
calculated murders are any indication, must have been so sweet. A look
back to the early part of the sixteenth century in New Spain might
prove useful.

The Spaniards were fascinated with the people they found in the
New World. Columbus relished their beauty and simplicity, seized a
few, and took them back to Spain as a spectacle for everyone to look at.
Amerigo Vespucci, another Italian working for the Spanish, was fascinated too, and in a 1504 letter to Piero Soderini, gonfaloniere, he noted
that the American natives were so friendly that they could not refrain
from loving him and his crew. He wrote, "They showed themselves very
desirous of copulating with us Christians." He continued by noting,
when "they give you their wives and daughters, they esteem themselves
highly honored; and in this way they practice the full extreme of hospitality."[1] Hospitality, however, usually gave way to hostility in short
order.

The discovery of a new world with unknown and unidentifiable inhabitants presented a crisis for Europeans: who were these people, and
how should they be treated? The Dominican friar Bartolomé de las Casas declared in *Devastation of the Indies* (1552) that "God had crowded
into these lands the great majority of mankind."[2] In order to rule this

vast population, the Spanish created the *encomienda* system, basically a remake of the feudal state in which the conquistador was given land to harvest, while the inhabitants owed him manual labor. Without doubt, the Spaniards sought to enslave the Indians they found in the New World and worked them to death in gold mines and plantations. Like the aboriginal peoples who encountered Europeans in North America later, they died in great numbers of diseases against which they had no natural immunity or committed suicide rather than suffer enslavement.

In 1511 the Dominicans gathered on the island of Hispaniola (present-day Haiti and the Dominican Republic) to proclaim their belief that the Indians should be released from the oppressive *encomienda* system because they were capable of embracing Christianity. In 1514 de las Casas described the Indians as a peaceful and innocent people in his *Very Brief Relation of the Destruction of the Indies*. In 1537 Pope Paul III published his encyclical *Sublimus Dei*, in which he recognized that the Indians were truly men and could not be deprived of either their liberty or their property. In effect, de las Casas won his battle with the Spanish conquistadors. By 1540 the Spanish Crown eradicated the *encomienda* system, and in 1551 it formally ended Indian slavery in its colonies. African slavery, already established in Portugal and Spain, quickly replaced it.

The Spaniards created an empire in America that incorporated the native peoples they found and eventually ruled them as subjects. The British in their colonies in North America formed a society only for themselves, without any concern for the native inhabitants, except when they formed military alliances with or fought wars against them. In older scholarship, the numerous colonial wars against the eastern tribes were known collectively as the Forest Wars, due mainly to the densely forested East Coast of the United States at that time. The settlers in Jamestown fought the Powhatan Feedfights (1610–1614) in Virginia over their seizure of Indian fields. The Virginia or First Tidewater War was fought between 1622 and 1632 when the tribes attacked Virginia settlements in the Tidewater region. In this engagement, known as the Virginia Massacre, the settlers counterattacked successfully; more importantly, this is remembered as the first full-scale Indian war in British North America.

The Pequot War, fought along the Mystic River in Connecticut in 1637, marked the first Puritan war against the New England tribes, which by 1637 fully realized that the British settlers intended to take their land for themselves. In New York, Keift's War, fought between

Dutch settlers and the local tribes in 1643–1645, also decided who owned the land. They fought again in the Esopus War (1655–1664), over the same issues. The Second Tidewater War (1644–1646) finished up the previous war in Virginia and drove the Virginia tribes from their traditional lands. The last major Forest War fought in New England was King Philip's War in 1677. The Wampanoag tribe resisted Puritan expansion and attacked settlements in Massachusetts, where the settlers lost one-sixth of the male population and twenty-five towns in combat with the tribe. Metacom (aka King Philip) was captured and executed. His wife, Wootonokanuske, had been captured earlier that year, along with their nine-year old son, and sold into slavery.[3] The Tuscarora War (1711–1713) was fought in North Carolina; the Yamasee War (1715–1728) took place in South Carolina; and Dummer's War (1722–1726) occurred in Maine, where English settlers fought against the Abenaki tribe and the French in Canada.

The largest Forest War by far was the French and Indian War (1754–1763), fought in Canada, New England, Pennsylvania, and New York. Known as the Seven Years' War in Europe, in America it was a frontier trading war. The French attempted to contain the British trading and expansion efforts in Pennsylvania's western frontier. They built a chain of forts along the major rivers from Lake Erie to Ohio and enlisted the Hurons to help them. After a series of battles and skirmishes, the French and their Indian allies were ultimately defeated by the British and their Iroquois allies and surrendered all of Canada to the British in 1763. The British formulated an end-of-war agreement with their tribal allies to establish a demarcation line that protected tribal lands and forbade the Americans from founding any settlements west of it. Although the British attempted to enforce the agreement, the westward-moving Americans ignored it.

In the southern colony of North Carolina, British colonists fought the Cherokees from 1759 to 1761, over control of the land, and again from 1763 to 1764. Chief Pontiac realized that the Americans wanted all the traditional lands. The Ottawa tribes were desperate to retain their traditional hunting and living areas from Erie to Detroit, and they resisted. The last Forest War before the Revolution was fought in western Virginia in 1774. In Lord Dunmore's War, named after the last colonial governor of Virginia, the Shawnees attempted to assert control over their traditional hunting grounds along the Ohio River. Defeated by units of the British army and Royal American Militia, the Shawnees assimilated into other tribes.

In America's international wars, including the Revolution, the War of 1812, the Mexican War, and the Civil War, enemy soldiers taken prisoner were treated relatively well, or at least they were treated fairly, in accordance with the rules governing nations and the American army's internal rules at the time. There were exceptions, most of which took place during hostilities against the native tribes. After the 1637 Pequot War in New England, the tribe's surviving remnant sued for peace and received harsh terms from the British Puritans. The Treaty of Hartford, signed on 21 September 1638, stipulated that most of the Pequots became the property of the settlers' Indian allies: the Mohegans, Narragansetts, and Niantics. The name of the tribe was erased, and a few members were sent into slavery in the Caribbean.[4] Curiously, it took centuries for some justice to be done: the remaining Pequots have returned to Connecticut and now operate a successful gambling casino.[5]

The American Revolution (1775–1783) was also a Forest War of sorts. The eastern and southern tribes allied themselves with the British against the land-hungry Americans. The Iroquois Six Nation Confederation in New York and Pennsylvania allied with the British at first, then attempted to remain neutral. Neutrality aside, the Iroquois always sympathized with the British, who promised them peace and land after the American defeat. Following the Revolution, the victorious Americans established retributive policies of westward expansion, preemption, and removal from traditional lands when possible. Taking prisoners never seemed to be a consideration; the issue with the tribes was always one of ownership of the land.

Following the Revolution, the Americans established the Northwest Ordinances, which gave the new nation a way to colonize itself. To do that, the Americans established the doctrine of preemption, which denied unlimited Indian title to the land: the tribes would be ready to sell when the government was ready to buy. Known as "expansion with honor," this program was based on a land-for-peace and civilization deal formulated by Henry Knox, the first secretary of war and a former general in the Continental Army. Each state retained the right of preemption of all lands within it limits, but the federal government retained the power to make all treaties with the Indians, which determined the status of peace or war. The federal government also recognized the "nation" status of all the tribes within its boundaries.

Americans of the nation's first generation believed that the tribes possessed more land than they could ever use. They also believed that the tribes would cede the land because they could migrate west and resume their migratory ways, despite the fact that the eastern tribes were sedentary farmers. Also, the new Americans believed with some validity that Indians would die of disease when whites approached. If they became "civilized," they would surely disappear as Indians and assimilate into the general population. Henry Knox and the Washington administration believed that whatever was good for whites was good for Indians; thus the government assumed a *stewardship* for Indian interests.

The native tribes, of course, never accepted these beliefs or assumptions. They resisted the federal encroachment on their lands furiously, beginning with the Ohio Invasions of 1789–1794. In a punitive expedition, Josiah Harmar was defeated by Indians in 1790, as was Arthur St. Clair shortly thereafter. General Anthony Wayne defeated the Indians at the Battle of Fallen Timbers in 1794, and in the Treaty of Greenville, the tribes surrendered southern Ohio to the United States. In Jay's Treaty of 1794, the British agreed to abandon their outposts in the United States, and the Ohio Invasions ended the formal alliance between the eastern tribes and the British in America.

In the south, Kentucky became a state in 1792 after a war against the Creeks in 1791. As we have already seen, the British again attempted to secure Indian allies in the West in 1812. Tecumseh, a Shawnee chief, attempted to unite all the eastern tribes against the Americans and nearly succeeded. Tecumseh was defeated by William Henry Harrison at the Battle of Tippecanoe (1811), and he died during the Battle of the Thames (1813) against the Americans in Canada. British and Americans established peace in 1814; the Indians were defeated and dispersed, and Indiana and Illinois were opened up for settlement.

The wars of expansion continued unabated. In 1825 the Creeks were forced from their lands in Alabama, removed, and relocated to Indian Territory—today, Oklahoma. The next target was Florida and the Seminoles. Between 1832 and 1841 the Florida Seminoles under Chief Osceola resisted removal, and although Osceola was captured, imprisoned, and died as an enemy prisoner of war in 1838, the Seminoles were successful against the army until 1841. This series of wars cost the United States $20 million, engaged 30,000 soldiers, and left 1,500 of them dead.[6]

Black Hawk's War was fought in 1832. Beginning in 1825, U.S. government policy dictated the removal of tribes from the Old Northwest. Regional tribes were forced from their traditional lands by preemption, forced to surrender their hunting grounds, and given either annuities or reservations beyond the Mississippi in Indian Territory. Sauk (Sac) and Fox under Black Hawk resisted, fought, and surrendered, but they were massacred by 1,300 army volunteers. Taking prisoners was never a consideration in this kind of warfare. Future president Abraham Lincoln was part of the militia but claimed he saw no combat.

Problems then arose in northern Georgia, where a large number of Cherokees lived in peace on their plantations. Thinking they were secure from American encroachment, they became literate, shed their traditional garb, and believed they lived in their own nation. But the state of Georgia claimed their lands and declared that a nation cannot exist within a nation, to say nothing of the state of Georgia. Rather than fighting another war with the Americans—1812 had been more than enough—the Cherokees took the issue to the Supreme Court in 1831 and asked for an injunction against the state's decision to seize their lands. Denied by Chief Justice John Marshall, the Cherokees as well as all the other tribes were defined as *domestic dependent nations* in a state of *pupilage* to the federal government only. The Cherokee problem then became a state's rights versus federal supremacy issue in a hurry. The tribal newspaper, the *Cherokee Phoenix,* expressed outrage that the state of Georgia and the federal government were acting together against them.

In 1834 Congress created the Bureau of Indian Affairs under the War Department—transferred to the Department of the Interior in 1849—with three functions: to carry out federal programs authorized by Congress, to act as trustee for Indian lands and resources, and to create a climate in which the Indian groups could operate by themselves. Congress also established the Indian Territory west of the Mississippi River in present-day Oklahoma.

The stage was set for a huge removal. It happened when General Winfield Scott issued a proclamation on 10 May 1838 that every Indian man, woman, and child must leave within a month. The Cherokees refused to leave of their own accord, and the army was ordered to round them up. During the capture and removal of the Cherokees and four other tribes—the Choctaw, Chickasaw, Creek, and Seminole—from their homelands in Georgia and other states to Oklahoma in 1838–1839, the 800-mile forced march known as the Trail of Tears killed more than 4,000 innocent persons. The Oregon Campaigns (1855–1858) forced the tribes of the Pacific Northwest to cede their lands and live on reservations due to a new policy established in 1848: concentration, which stated that Indian tribes must be separated and concentrated on reservations. It was precisely this policy that plagued the army, the country, and the tribes of the West and the Great Plains for the rest of the nineteenth and early twentieth centuries.

Prior to the Civil War, the U.S. Army expanded in the West and used the tactic of a large force to track and contest smaller, more mobile Indian forces. But when the Confederates bombarded Fort Sumter in Charleston Harbor, needs changed radically. The regular army split itself up—some officers and men going North, others going South. The Indian wars had to wait for new troops, and as mentioned in the last chapter, "galvanized Yankees"—former Confederate POWs who took an oath of allegiance to the Union—filled the ranks. Ranks were also filled by state volunteer units, such as the Third Colorado Cavalry. In what was known as the Great Plains Wars (1861–1867), the Cheyenne and Arapaho tribes fought farmers and attacked stagecoach stations. At the conclusion of hostilities, white prisoners were returned, and the Indians thought they were at peace. The Colorado militia, known as the Blood Thirsters, under the command of Colonel John M. Chivington (more an aspiring politician than a soldier), attacked and massacred most of the remaining Cheyenne under Black Kettle at Sand Creek on 29 November 1864. The murder of these innocent people resulted in mass Indian distrust of American intentions, yet the U.S. government continued the policy of enforced concentration on the reservations.

What took place in Minnesota became one of the greatest tragedies of the Civil War era. The Sioux, or Lakota, people living in southwestern Minnesota, known as the Santee Sioux, had sold their lands to the federal government in treaties during the 1850s for $3,075,000 to be paid in annuities over several years.[7] The Sioux then moved to reservations along the Minnesota River, subjecting themselves to government oversight, while the Sioux land opened the region for settlement and statehood in 1858. Pressure from settlers for more Sioux land led the tribe to cede more reservation land north of the Minnesota River. Cultural pressures also affected tribal members, forcing many to abandon traditional dress and their hunter-gatherer lifeways. According to Dee Brown, Chief Big Eagle lamented all this: "The whites were always trying to make the Indians give up their life and live like white men—farming, work hard and do as they did—and the Indians did not know how to do that, and did not want to anyway. If the Indians had tried to make the whites live like them, the whites would have resisted, and it was the same way with many Indians."[8] Trouble brewed in Minnesota as the Civil War approached in the north country.

Dependent on the federal government for their annuities, the Minnesota Sioux watched as 24,000 men joined the Union Army and marched south. They also observed Union recruiters coming to the reservation and successfully creating the Renville Rangers, consisting mostly of half-breed soldiers.[9] Minnesota now had virtually no troops in the state. Simultaneously, crop failures created starving conditions during a brutally cold winter heading into the fateful year of 1862.[10] The annuities failed to arrive in the spring; the Indians were told to be patient, but in August the situation came to a boiling point. The Lower Sioux Agency's storekeeper, Andrew Myrick, refused to extend credit to the Sioux, saying, "If they are hungry, let them eat grass." At that point, enough was enough, even though the annuities arrived in gold coin on 16 August 1862.[11]

Despite the futility of a war, the Santee Sioux attacked the Lower Sioux Agency on 18 August, looting and burning it to the ground. Myrick was found among the dead with grass shoved down his throat. The survivors, about forty-seven whites and some Indians, made their way to Fort Ridgely, the only outpost in southeastern Minnesota, where they discovered that $71,000 in annuities had indeed arrived. The garrison commander had been taking the money to the Sioux Agency for distribution when he and his men were attacked near the Minnesota River; thirteen men were lost in moments, including the only experienced officer among them. The Sioux attacked the Upper Agency too, and news of the uprising spread very quickly.

The attacks across the region were swift and deadly, especially against the isolated homesteads that had no idea what was happening to the Sioux. Panic spread through the land. On 6 September 1862 the *St. Paul Press* reported, "Fort Abercrombie Besieged. Burning of Hutchinson. Burning at Forest City. Indians on the Minnesota River. Indians on the Red River. Indians on the Cow River. Indians Everywhere!" The newspaper was correct: hundreds of settlers attempting to flee the fighting were killed in Little Crow's attacks, and he set his sights on the weak but attractive Fort Ridgely, defended by only forty U.S. soldiers. His men decided to attack the town of New Ulm instead, with 900 German immigrants living there; this allowed the government to reinforce Fort Ridgely quickly. The New Ulm Germans repulsed the Sioux, but more attacks were coming soon.

On 20 August 1862 the Sioux attacked Fort Ridgely. Repulsed by cannon, they attacked again in force on 22 August with 800 warriors and were again repulsed by the cannon's canister rounds. According to historian Robert H. Jones, Little Crow's attack on Fort Ridgely was one of the few direct assaults on a U.S. fort by Indians.[12] On 23 August the Sioux attacked New Ulm again, this time with a far more coordinated force led by three chiefs: Mankato, Wabasha, and Big Eagle. After charge and countercharge, the Americans finally forced the Sioux from New Ulm, now a total shambles, and the people were evacuated to the city of Mankato.[13]

Henry H. Sibley, colonel of the Minnesota Volunteers, eventually reached the area with about 1,500 untested, relatively green troops. Soon the largest and bloodiest battle of this war took place at Birch Coulee, where the Sioux quietly surrounded Sibley's force and surprised his men nearly in the open. The battle lasted thirty-one hours and ended only when reinforcements arrived from Fort Ridgely.[14] Minnesota was in trouble and needed help from the federal government. On 6 September 1862 the War Department appointed General John Pope, loser of the Second Battle of Bull Run in Virginia, to command the newly formed Military Department of the Northwest. But the region needed experienced soldiers, not greenhorns to fight the Sioux, so Secretary of War Edwin M. Stanton turned to the galvanized Yankees to confront the Santee uprising. Meanwhile, Little Crow continued his attacks against forts and small towns in the region, but with little success. Sibley's first orders from Pope were to destroy the Indians; his response was, "It is my purpose utterly to exterminate the Sioux. They are to be treated as maniacs or wild beasts, and by no means as people with whom treaties or compromises can be made."[15] None of this boded well for future relations with Minnesota's Sioux tribes, and especially for Little Crow and his Santee warriors.

The next battle became the last one of the Santee war. Sibley encamped near Battle Lake on 22 September, and the Santee set a massive ambush during the night. By pure luck, a few soldiers wandered from camp against orders and discovered the Sioux's hiding places, tripping the ambush early.[16] Little Crow rushed the soldiers, but the arrival of the Renville Rangers drove Little Crow's force into confusion and retreat. Some retreated far enough west to tell the Lakota and other tribes in the Dakota Territory about the perceived double dealing perpetrated by the whites in Minnesota. Others remained in the region to continue the fight. Colonel Sibley called for Little Crow's surrender, but the defiant Sioux fled to Canada, saying, "The long merchant Sibley would like to put a rope around my neck, but he won't get a chance."[17] Sibley, however, rounded up 1,200 Santee Sioux and released all their white prisoners. The time for retribution had arrived.

On 28 September 1862 a military commission was appointed to try those Santee Sioux warriors engaged in the hostilities. With so much war in Minnesota, the inhabitants' blood was up; hatred and the law of retribution ruled, and the press cried for blood. The trials were quick: in just one day, the military commission tried forty Santees, with some trials lasting only five minutes.[18] When the proceedings concluded on 5 December 1862, the commission had sentenced 300 of the 392 men on trial to death by hanging.[19] The people of Minnesota may have felt vindicated, but President Abraham Lincoln believed the sentences were excessive. On 6 December he insisted that only those convicted of rape or murder should be executed; the rest should receive jail sentences.[20] As a result, thirty-eight Santee warriors received the death sentence.

In December 1862 the largest mass execution in American history took place in Mankato, Minnesota, when thirty-eight men on a gallows dropped to their death at once. What had been a just war for one side became a huge war crime for the other. Approximately 500 settlers, traders, and soldiers died in the uprising, making it one of the bloodiest wars between Indians and whites in the nineteenth century. Consequences were extreme not only for those Sioux directly involved; the long-range effects set the tone for all future relationships between the U.S. government and America's Indian peoples for the rest of the century. On 16 February 1863 the government abrogated and annulled all the treaties it had ever made with the Minnesota Sioux tribes and rescinded all the annuities owed to them. As far as the Americans were concerned, the Indians had initiated an unjust, unprovoked, and savage war against the United States, and the United States owed them nothing.[21]

The punishment did not end there. On 3 March 1863 Congress ordered the four Minnesota Sioux tribes, about 2,000 people, removed from the state to a reservation on Crow Creek near the Missouri River. If not for a civil war taking place in the East, more incursions against the Sioux tribes would have taken place, but they would not have to wait very long. Any accommodation with the native tribes was gone. The wars of removal were over; the wars of annihilation would begin soon. A series of small wars was fought between the United States and the Sioux between 1865 and 1868. After the Fetterman Massacre, the Teton Sioux under Red Cloud's leadership forced the army to retreat from Sioux lands. In return, Red Cloud later accepted President Ulysses

S. Grant's peace policy and remained on assigned reservations. This was the only conflict the Indians ever clearly won.

The year 1866 brought disaster to Indian country. According to historian William Brandon, the Railroad Enabling Act of 1866 sliced some choice cuts from a number of reservations. This act gave railroad builders alternate sections of public lands forty miles deep on either side of a projected right-of-way as an inducement to railroad building. The forty-mile depth was later extended to fifty miles to offset losses from prior claims of white settlers. For purposes of the act, reservations were considered public lands, and unlucky Indian communities found themselves being evicted from railroad property.[22]

The Medicine Lodge Treaty of 1867 established two large reservations in Indian Territory (Oklahoma)—one for the Cheyenne and Arapaho, the other for the Kiowa, Comanche, and Kiowa-Apache. The Indians received clothing and tools and were expected to support themselves through agriculture. Plains Indians resisted agriculture, however; they preferred horticulture and hunting buffalo. When Civil War General William T. Sherman became the chief of the army, the western tribes—Cheyenne, Arapaho, Comanche, Kiowa, and Apache—living off the reservations were declared "hostile" and were hunted down and destroyed by Generals Sheridan, Custer, Crook, Miles, and others. Custer conducted the Washita Massacre of peaceful Cheyenne families on Sheridan's orders, and Black Kettle and his wife, who had survived Chivington's Sand Creek Massacre in 1864, were killed on 26 November 1868.

The bad times for the Cheyenne began on 11 September 1874. John and Lydia German, along with their seven children, were camped along the Smokey Hill River in western Kansas, making their way from postwar, Reconstruction-era Georgia to Colorado to build a new life in a new land.[23] A party of nineteen Cheyenne dog soldiers shadowed them and attacked viciously, killing John immediately and then working their way through the rest of the German family. Only four daughters survived; two remained captives, and the other two were traded away. The dog soldiers knew exactly what they were doing and headed for Texas quickly. Across the country, newspapers called for swift and total retribution.

Some Kiowas were also at war, attacking U.S. Army supply wagons in Oklahoma. As usual, the army pursued them, and on 28 September 1874 soldiers attacked a Kiowa village. Although the Kiowa warriors had maneuvered away from the village, the soldiers found hidden camps of women and children at Palo Duro Canyon. Rather than attacking the people, the soldiers burned the village and killed over a thousand horses.[24] During the winter of 1874 General Pope, who had moved from Minnesota to Fort Leavenworth, Kansas, ordered the Sixth Cavalry and Fifth Infantry to police the Cheyenne and Arapaho reservations. While on patrol, they discovered Julia and Adelaide German in an abandoned lodge, and the region exploded yet again.

The question was what to do with the warriors and their families taken prisoner in these engagements on the Great Plains. One solution was to replicate what had happened in Minnesota in 1862—quick trials and mass executions. Lieutenant General Philip Sheridan telegraphed President Grant and recommended that those who committed murder or stole cattle should be tried by a military commission and face justice.[25] Sheridan was determined to remove the ringleaders to a secure American facility such as Fort Snelling, Minnesota, for trial. He also had Indian prisoners at Fort Sill, Oklahoma, and at the Cheyenne agency as well. Citing a previous legal opinion of the Justice Department in 1873, Sheridan argued for military commissioners to adjudicate the cases of murder, depredation, and theft. On 9 December he proposed banishing all the guilty to the coast of Florida. Adjutant General E. D. Townsend agreed and suggested the use of an empty fort at St. Augustine.[26] The Quaker agent of the Kiowa and Comanche tribes, James M. Harworth, suggested that the army remove these tribes (or at least part of them) from their native lands because if they remained, trouble would continue without end. He even suggested that the army provide a teacher so that when their time in prison ended, the Kiowas and Comanches would have the necessary skills to be of service to their tribes back home. As far as the Indians were concerned, this was a scheme to separate the leaders from their people, and at its worst, the new policy represented a form of ethnic cleansing. Army leadership agreed: the Arapaho, Comanche, Kiowa, and Cheyenne tribes were about to become prisoners of the U.S. Army.

Richard Henry Pratt was an enlisted soldier and then an officer during the Civil War. After the war, Lieutenant Pratt served as an officer with the Buffalo Soldiers, the black Tenth Cavalry Regiment, in the southern plains of the United States. One of Pratt's jobs was to command the enlisted Indian scouts for the Tenth Cavalry. In March 1875 at Fort Sill, he met Major C. D. Emory, the judge advocate for the army's Department of Texas. Emory had orders to indict the Indians captured by the army, and he told the fort's commander, Colonel Ranald Mack-

Richard Henry Pratt advocated educating rather than exterminating the Indian peoples and started the Indian school at Carlisle, Pennsylvania, in 1879. Library of Congress.

enzie, that he was not sure the warriors could be held as prisoners of war or be indicted for anything at all. Emory asked Pratt to seek out more non-Indian testimony to seal the indictments.[27] Everyone from the president on down understood that a state of war had to be legally in place before the army could try any non–service member for anything. Yet the cries for vengeance never ceased in the press, and something had to be done. President Grant finally decided that those ringleaders of hostile bands could be selected for confinement in Florida. The order finally fell to Pratt to select which prisoners would be banished to Florida. He did his work well. Seventy-five members of the Comanche, Arapaho, Kiowa, and southern Cheyenne tribes were rounded up for imprisonment without trial and without the rights of prisoners of war, the rationale being that if the major warlike personalities were removed, things would settle down on the reservations.

Their long train trip began at Fort Leavenworth with Pratt, his daughter, and his army guards aboard for security. When they arrived at Indianapolis, Indiana, on 18 May 1875, the Union Depot overflowed with locals hoping to see the prisoners. It must have been quite a spectacle for civilians in the East who had never seen a Native American in person before. Instead of being morose, the prisoners were friendly and sociable to their visitors. From Indianapolis they traveled to Louisville, where another circus of onlookers appeared. Nashville was next, and another frenzy broke out. Shortly after the train pulled out of Nashville, Lean Bear, a Cheyenne, attempted suicide, and after struggling with the guards he played opossum. Thinking he was dead, the guards took him off the train, and the "dead" man jumped up and tried to escape. After a second escape attempt, Lean Bear calmed down for the rest of the trip.[28] Moving into the South, they passed through Chattanooga and Atlanta and paused in Macon, Georgia, briefly.

On 25 May 1875 the train entered Florida and another Cheyenne, Gray Beard, jumped out and ran for the woods. Pratt could not find him before the train had to leave, so he left a small detachment in place. When the soldiers found Gray Beard he refused to halt, and they shot him at close quarters. Before he died, Gray Beard said that he would rather die than live in captivity. Later that day the train arrived at St. Augustine, Florida, and the prisoners walked to their place of imprisonment, Fort Marion, where Chief Osceola had died as a prisoner in the Second Seminole War.

During the Civil War the Union used the numerous star forts built after the War of 1812 as POW camps for Confederates. Fort Marion was no star fort; rather, it was an old Spanish fortress built in 1672. When the Americans acquired Florida in 1821, the Castillo de San Marcos became Fort Marion in honor the South Carolina Revolutionary War hero Francis Marion, known as the "Swamp Fox." One can only imagine what the newest prisoners thought of such a structure. After twenty-four days as guarded passengers on a train, the army's most recent EPWs were now imprisoned in their new home.

Pratt controlled every aspect of the Fort Marion prisoners' lives. Shortly after their arrival he removed the prisoners' shackles, cut their hair, and issued them military uniforms. The prisoners were expected to polish their buttons and shoes and clean and press their trousers. After a time, they were organized into companies and given instruction in military drill. Eventually, their army guards were dismissed, and several of the most trusted prisoners were chosen to serve as guards. In short, they guarded themselves.

Pratt was also an innovator and an important contributor to the

Fort Marion, St. Augustine, Florida. This old Spanish fortress, built in 1672, housed members of the Kiowa, Comanche, Arapaho, southern Cheyenne, and Chiricahua tribes as prisoners of war. National Park Service photograph.

Indian reform movement at the time. His idea about educating rather than exterminating Indian peoples began to take shape at Fort Marion. He agreed with other reformers that educating his prisoners would turn them into God-fearing, agrarian countrymen. By the end of the prisoners' term of incarceration in 1878, Pratt had turned the prison's casemates into classrooms and convinced seventeen prisoners to further their education by enrolling in the Hampton Institute in Virginia. When these prisoners were released, they went home and enjoyed a reasonable amount of success in a world full of new realities for the tribes of the Great Plains.

Hampton Institute was founded in 1868 by Samuel Chapman Armstrong as a government boarding school for ex-slaves and their children, designed to educate by training "the head, the hand, and the heart." Its goal was to train ex-slaves and return them to their communities to become leaders and professionals among their people. One of Armstrong's students was Booker T. Washington, who took the Armstrong philosophy to heart and founded Tuskegee Institute in Alabama. Tuskegee became a huge success in the post-Reconstruction South, and Pratt believed that a similar effort could work well for the

Indians. Pratt's developing philosophy about Indian assimilation, much like Armstrong's and Washington's relative to freedmen, led him to formulate a model similar to Hampton Institute. In 1879, while still in the army, Pratt became superintendent of the new Carlisle Indian School at the army's Carlisle Barracks in southern Pennsylvania. Pratt and his associates then traveled to the various Indian agencies to recruit students. Not surprisingly, his former Fort Marion prisoners fully supported the effort, with eleven arriving at Carlisle to help out. On 1 November 1879 the Carlisle Indian School opened and soon enrolled 158 students from twelve different tribes.[29] By 1903 Pratt was a brigadier general, and enrollment reached 1,200 Indian boys and girls from seventy-seven tribes. He retired a year later.

For the Kiowa, Comanche, Arapaho, and southern Cheyenne prisoners, Fort Marion became a pivot point in their ultimate survival. Pratt's experiment was successful, and they returned home with honor. One wonders why, in these times of vicious wars of concentration between the U.S. Army and various tribes in the Great Plains and the West, Chief Joseph and the Nez Perce were not declared prisoners of war in 1877 and imprisoned like the others. Perhaps it was the respect everyone had for Chief Joseph; perhaps it was his noble speech of surrender on 5 October: "I am tired. My heart is sick and sad. From where the sun stands, I will fight no more for ever."[30] At the end of the Nez Perce war, the army moved the tribe to Kansas and then to Oklahoma until 1884, when the Bureau of Indian Affairs placed them on the Colville Reservation in the state of Washington, far from their homeland in the Wallowa Valley in northeastern Oregon. For the rest of his life Chief Joseph longed to go home, but he died on the Colville Reservation in 1904.

The Chiricahua Apaches, however, have a far more tragic history. Apaches were the last tribe to recognize that the reservation system, as bad as it was, represented their only possible means of survival. In 1876, after Cochise's death in 1874, the government ordered the Apaches to the San Carlos Reservation, but they refused or resisted removal. Geronimo became the last resister. Trouble began at San Carlos in August 1881 when Geronimo, a Chiricahua, killed the police chief and forced many people to go to Mexico with him. In response, General George Crook, a Civil War hero with an impressive war record, imposed martial law on San Carlos and recruited five companies of Apache scouts under young officers such as Lieutenant Charles Gatewood.[31] Crook required mobility and decided to use mules rather than wagons. Geronimo went to the Sierra Madre mountain region in Mexico, where he eventually surrendered to Crook and returned to San Carlos. Unhappy with reservation life, Geronimo began drinking heavily at San Carlos and decided to break out. On 25 March 1886 he left for Canyon de los Embudos in Mexico. Crook followed him. When they met, Crook said, "I'll keep after you and kill the last one, if it takes fifty years." Geronimo agreed to return to the reservation, but he and his band returned to the Sierra Madre instead. This action cost General Crook his command.

General Philip Sheridan replaced General William T. Sherman as head of the army. He had never approved of Crook's use of Apache scouts and generally considered Crook too trusting of the Indians. Sheridan told Crook to break his word to the Apaches who had refused to follow Geronimo back to Mexico, but Crook refused and asked to be replaced. Sheridan then assigned Brigadier General Nelson A. Miles to the command and ordered him to bring Geronimo in. In the meantime, all the Apaches on the San Carlos Reservation were sent to Fort Marion at St. Augustine, Florida, including all the Apache scouts who had helped Crook. Like the first group of Kiowa and Comanche prisoners of war before them, the first group of Chiricahua Apaches boarded trains for the odyssey east to Fort Marion. Historian H. Henrietta Stockel wrote that, unknown to any of them, that trip began nearly thirty years of captivity; even worse, imprisonment meant a death sentence due to disease, especially tuberculosis, for many.[32] Knowledge of contagious diseases had advanced little since the Civil War, when many POWs in Northern and Southern camps had succumbed. Despite all the disease, the army reported that the Apaches were doing just fine at Fort Marion, but officials quickly became concerned about the steady deaths. Colonel Loomis L. Langdon, optimistic at first about his prisoners in Fort Marion, became worried. When the acting secretary of war telegraphed Loomis, asking how many Apaches his prison could hold, he responded that he could take only seventy-five more and recommended that no more be sent. General Sheridan, however, decided that 502 Chiricahuas needed to be sent east.

What is unique here is that the army ordered all the Chiricahua Apaches to leave the San Carlos Reservation, even those Indian scouts who had served the army so well under General Crook. One of these scouts was Chatto, one of the most warlike Chiricahuas in the band. Along with a delegation of twelve others, Chatto actually went to Washington, D.C., to speak with Secretary of War William C. Endicott, who told the Chiricahuas they should move to a different reservation east of the Mississippi. Chatto told Secretary of Interior L. Q. C. Lamar that the tribe had thrived as farmers in Arizona and had no desire to move. After receiving a medal and thanks, Chatto and his delegation headed home to Arizona, but their train was stopped and diverted to Fort Leavenworth, Kansas, where they were imprisoned for two months. On 12 September 1886 Chatto and his friends left Fort Leavenworth as prisoners, headed for Fort Marion.[33]

General Miles followed Geronimo into Mexico, then sent Lieutenant Charles Gatewood to talk to him. When Geronimo asked to go back to San Carlos, Gatewood told him that all the Apaches had been sent to Florida. Stunned, Geronimo said he would surrender only to Miles personally, and he did so in Skeleton Canyon on 4 September 1886.[34] According to Geronimo, "General Miles drew a line on the ground and said, 'This represents the ocean,' and putting a small rock beside the line, he said, 'This represents the place where Chiricahua is with his band.' He then picked up another stone and placed it a short distance from the first, and said, 'This represents you, Geronimo. . . . That is what the President wants to do, get all of you together.' "[35] There were nineteen men and twenty-eight women and children with Geronimo. Six of the Apaches, three men and three women, refused to accept the surrender and fled to Mexico, where death at the hands of the Mexican border guards awaited them.

Along with other Apaches who had hunted him for the army, Geronimo was sent east and held in lifelong POW status. On the morning of 8 September 1886 General Miles sent the Apaches east on a train under heavy guard. Thus began years of captivity as prisoners of war in a strange land, and with their departure, the Indian wars of the Southwest came to an end. For the more than 500 Chiricahua Apache prisoners who arrived at Fort Marion in the 1880s, failure and tragedy lurked close by. At least twenty-four died during thirteen months inside Fort Marion, after which time they continued their POW status in different detention facilities.

Fort Pickens near Pensacola served as another prison for the Chiricahua Apaches. Larger than Fort Marion, it could hold more prisoners with relative safety. According to Geronimo, "In forty days they took me there to Fort Pickens, Florida. Here they put me to sawing up large logs. There were several other Apache warriors with me, and all of us had to work every day. For nearly two years we were kept at hard labor in this place, and we did not see our families until May 1887. This treatment was in direct violation of our treaty made at Skeleton Cañon." He

Fort Pickens near Pensacola served as a prison for Geronimo and other Chiricahua Apaches in 1886. Library of Congress.

observed, "We were not healthy in this place, for the climate disagreed with us. So many of our people died."[36]

The last band of Apaches landed at Fort Pickens on 6 November 1886. Word spread in St. Augustine and Pensacola that the feared Apaches were close by, and the local civilians could not resist seeing for themselves. In effect, the Apaches became tourist attractions in both Florida prisons. Today, one would think that visiting a prison as one would visit a zoo is tasteless at best, demeaning of human dignity at worst, but sensibilities in the nineteenth century were much different from those in the twenty-first. During the Civil War, for example, the people of Elmira, New York, liked to take Sunday afternoon promenades on a boardwalk around the prison compound to see the starving Confederates. The Confederates were not amused, but at Fort Pickens the Apaches liked it. Geronimo became a celebrity, and he played that role very well, selling trinkets he carved from driftwood and buttons from his clothing as souvenirs.[37] In modern parlance, Geronimo learned how to "work the system" in Pensacola and became better at it in time, especially when he and the other Apaches were transferred to Fort Sill, Oklahoma.

In the meantime, the army decided to rejoin split families. Some were are at Fort Marion, some at Fort Pickens, and it was a relatively easy matter to bring them together. When wives and husbands reunited, family life began to return. However, the Chiricahuas were still dying of disease in both places, and the army decided that a new place was needed to hold them. Mount Vernon, a town about thirty miles north of Mobile, Alabama, was opened for twenty women and eleven children on 27 April 1887.[38] One former prisoner remembered:

> We had thought that anything would be better than Fort Marion with its rain, mosquitoes, and malaria, but we were to find out that it was good in comparison with Mt. Vernon Barracks. We didn't know what misery was until they dumped us in those swamps. It rained nearly all the time. The mosquitoes almost ate us alive. Babies died from their bites our people got the shaking sickness. We burned one minute and froze the next. We chilled and shook.[39]

Although it is not generally swampy in this region, it is not difficult to understand this description, given that the Chiricahuas' real home was Arizona.

At Mount Vernon, much like in their former Fort Marion and Fort Pickens prisons, the Apaches became tourist attractions, and they responded accordingly. More important, a new personality entered the scene, Dr. Walter Reed, an excellent physician for his time and deeply concerned about his Apache patients at Mount Vernon. He pleaded with the government to increase the amount and quality of rations, and when the War Department responded, the Apaches' health improved significantly. Nevertheless, by the end of 1887, the once feared Chiricahua nation had been reduced to 348 prisoners at Mount Vernon and 48 at Fort Pickens. Approximately 100 student prisoners, some sick and 6 already dead, were at Carlisle Indian School in Pennsylvania. Of the entire group—70 men, 165 women, and 100 children—at Mount Vernon, only 30 men were considered healthy after eight months' incarceration.[40] Yet it was Reed who kept these prisoners alive—he befriended them, and they befriended him. Soon the time came for the next removal, this time west to Fort Sill, Oklahoma, the last depot for the Chiricahua as prisoners of war.

On 4 October 1894, 346 Chiricahua men, women, and children arrived at Fort Sill as POWs. Geronimo noted, "When we first came to Fort Sill, houses [were] built for us by the Government. We were also given from the Government, cattle, hogs, turkeys and chickens. With

Geronimo (Goyathlay), leader of the last Native American fighting force to formally capitulate to the United States, photographed by Ben Wittick in 1887. Courtesy of the National Archives and Records Administration.

the cattle we have done very well indeed, and we like to raise them."[41] At Fort Sill they lived outside in tents for the first year, but in time parcels of land were issued, funds for cattle were provided, and the Chiricahua settled down for the long haul—as it turned out, until 1914. Most assuredly, they were better off at Fort Sill than anywhere else.

In 1912 the U.S. Army, realizing that it needed to upgrade its artillery capabilities, opened its artillery school at Fort Sill. However, rounds from the firing ranges landed right on the Apaches' land parcels. What to do? Remain in Oklahoma or move in with their cousins, the Mescalero Apaches? The ordeal of captivity came to an end for 187 Chiricahua Apaches on 2 April 1914 when they moved to the Mescalero Apache reservation in New Mexico.[42] Acreage was granted to them, between 23 and 158 acres per family; seventy-seven Chiricahuas who remained in Oklahoma remained in a kind of legal limbo.

Geronimo was the leader of the last Native American fighting force to formally capitulate to the United States. Because he fought against such daunting odds and held out the longest, he became the most famous Apache of all. To the Apaches, Geronimo embodied the very essence of Apache values—aggressiveness and courage in the face of difficulty.[43] Geronimo's life in captivity took some odd turns. After becoming a devout Christian, he toured with a Wild West show, was an attraction at the Omaha and Buffalo expositions, and was exhibited at the St. Louis World's Fair in 1904. Always the prisoner of war, Geronimo commented, "There were many strange things in these shows. The Government send guards with me when I went to exhibits, and I was not allowed to go anywhere without them."[44] He died at Fort Sill in 1909, still a prisoner of war.

The 1880s marked a real change in the way Americans, at least in the East, viewed the native tribes. In October 1883 the Indian reform establishment met at a Lake Mohonk resort in the Catskills. Attending the Lake Mohonk Conference of the Friends of the Indian were representatives of the Indian Rights Association, Women's National Indian Association, Boston Indian Citizenship Committee, Ladies National Indian League, and Board of Indian Commissioners. The purpose of the gathering was to set the agenda for government-Indian relations after Grant's peace policy failed; create a political organization with influence, wealth, and power; further the 1867 idea of "conquest by kindness"; combine the emerging political platform and the pulpit; and express outrage over government iniquity and the continued barbarism of the frontier whites. Behind the agenda was the popular philosophy of Americanism, which proposed to Americanize and civilize the Indian of the late nineteenth century to live a Christian life in terms of the Protestant work ethic—that is, work is holy—and to support one's self and one's family through agricultural labor.[45] Richard Henry Pratt's vision of a vocational school fit hand in glove with this vision, regardless of what his students and their parents may have felt about it.

Population and casualty statistics bring the overall problem of dealing with the Native Americans into better focus. According to Robert M. Utley, in 1850 there were about 559,000 Indians in the United States: 75,000 lived on the Great Plains; 84,000 were immigrant tribes in Oklahoma in the former Permanent Indian Frontier; 200,000 lived in U.S. territories; 25,000 lived in Texas, although Texas never granted Indians title to any lands; 150,000 lived in the Mexican cession of 1848 (California and New Mexico); and 25,000 lived in the Oregon Territory, which included the present states of Oregon and Washington. The enormous population shift east to west in the mid-nineteenth century shows that of about 20 million Americans, 1.4 million lived in the West in 1860 and 8.5 million in 1890.[46] Casualties in the plains wars reveal the uneven nature of warfare from 1861 to 1891: Sixty-nine American officers were killed in action; sixty-eight were wounded. Approximately 870 enlisted soldiers died on the various battlefields; 990 were wounded. Approximately 4,371 Indians were killed in action; 1,279 were wounded. All told, a little over 10,300 were captured.[47] To conclude that the last wars against the plains and western tribes were lopsided is nothing short of a gross understatement. They never had a chance.

Indian prisoners in the Great Plains Wars suffered terribly confused captivities from 1868 until the turn of the twentieth century at the hands of military commissions, as had Confederate sympathizers, real or imaginary, during the Civil War. Native Americans living on the reservations were not even citizens of the United States until 1924. In prison, many died from mistreatment, but most died of diseases such as tuberculosis; some were executed or remained, like Geronimo, prisoners of war, confined to reservations for the rest of their lives.[48] More to the point, although the past is clouded with a succession of serious misdeeds of nearly unbelievable proportion—many dripping with a continuation of fairy tales, sanguinary racism, ethnocentric separatism, and, in the long run, the overwhelming passion to get even for deeds of the past—such thinking harmed everyone. Although their numbers were not great, the Great Plains tribes and the Chiricahua Apaches endured the longest captivity as enemy prisoners of war in American history. Their endurance was remarkable. That they have maintained their pride and culture despite the adversity remains nothing short of a miracle. Then again, miracles do happen.[49]

Seven

Spaniards and *Insurrectos*

Spanish-American War (1898) and War in the Philippines (1899–1905)

The courteous and sympathetic welcome given to all of us by the distinguished families living in the Academy is one more title to our gratitude, and Your Excellency may rest assured that it will never be effaced from our memories.
—Rear Admiral Pascual Cervera

I proclaim solemnly that I have not recognized the sovereignty of America over this beloved soil.
—Emilio Aguinaldo

According to Frederick Jackson Turner, the American continental frontier came to an end in 1893; the mid-nineteenth-century notion of Manifest Destiny was fulfilled; the native tribes all lived on reservations and were wards of the federal government, and the United States had no clear national mission. The "Lower Forty-eight," as the remote Alaskan territorials called them, were soon to become forty-eight states, and it seemed that a powerful lobby advocated more movement to the west and south, even if it was outside the continental boundaries. To personalities such as Theodore Roosevelt, unless a country, like a physical organism, grew, it withered and died.

There is no doubt that the United States wanted colonies by the end of the nineteenth century. After all, the Europeans had colonized nearly all of Africa and the southern Pacific islands by 1890. If the Americans wanted to become a great power, they needed colonies too, if for no other reason than to provide military and naval bases around the world. Hawaii became an American colony in 1898 after its contentious annexation, certainly not because of the pineapple or sugar business but because of the vast naval reach that Pearl Harbor provided in the Pacific Ocean.[1] Policy makers worldwide read Alfred Thayer Mahan's *The Influence of Sea Power upon History, 1660–1783* (1890) with awe. Mahan argued that great powers needed colonies and large navies to defend them. England, France, and Imperial Germany understood that real power demanded the extension of their reach and influence well beyond their own borders. Thus, colonialism and imperialism went hand in hand and dominated the international political and military landscape until the outbreak of World War I in 1914.

Hawaii was just not enough for the United States. The Germans and Americans divided the Samoan chain between them in 1889, with the eastern islands becoming an American colony in 1900. Although the new president, William McKinley of Ohio (the last Civil War veteran who became president), had no stomach for the overt takeover of colonies, others did. The Americans knew from experience in the Mexican-American War that they could not walk into another country and claim territory with impunity. A war was necessary to do that. Looking west of Hawaii at territories controlled by once powerful Spain in the Pacific region, U.S. expansionists found both Guam and the Philippine Islands highly desirable. The British held Hong Kong, Singapore, and Malaya; the French held several Pacific islands and Indochina; the Germans colonized several island chains; and the Dutch colonized the East Indies, what is now Indonesia.

In the Caribbean were Spain's last two royal colonies in the Americas—Puerto Rico and Cuba. Cuba was already in rebellion, and both seemed ripe for American intervention to Americanize and civilize those regional inhabitants then under Spain's thumb.[2] Although there were plenty of boosters for this expansionist philosophy in Congress, the American press could hardly be controlled. What came to be called "yellow journalism" sprang to life, and publishers such as William Randolph Hearst and Joseph Pulitzer excelled in calling for war against Spain. Sensation piled upon sensation in the yellow press from 1895 onward. Reporters in Cuba kept the supply of phony Spanish outrages and American heroics steadily flowing north. For example, correspondent Frederick Lawrence reported that he had single-handedly captured the city of Pinar del Rio using a nonexistent battery of Gatling guns manned by a crew of imaginary American volunteers. Names and events were nearly always fictitious.[3] All this and more found its way to American readers at home who were eager for more of this wild reporting devoid of any conceivable truth. Why did anyone believe it? Why did no one bother to check the details? How could the American people be misled so badly? Because a martial spirit began to dominate the United States in the middle to late 1890s. This was not new to the United States, but nothing so strong, so intense, or so utterly fictitious had ever happened before. War against Spain became a national obsession.

Cubans had rebelled steadily against Spain during the latter part of the nineteenth century, but José Julián Marti, nationalist Cuban political poet and intellectual, influenced the Cuban émigrés dispersed in the Americas to come together to resist the Spanish with violence. From 1881 to 1895 Marti lived and worked in New York City and commented on American life in a broad selection of Latin American newspapers. He formed the Cuban Revolutionary Party in 1892, and his efforts, central to the Cuban movement toward liberty, were ignored by Americans.[4] In 1895 Marti returned to an embattled Cuba and was killed in a firefight against Spanish soldiers. In death he became the martyr for the cause.

Grover Cleveland was president, and he had no interest in Cuba. Spain kept about 50,000 soldiers in Cuba in 1895, but the independence movement was so strong they could not defeat the 600 to 800 rebels who opposed them. In a sense, for the Spanish, the Cuban insurrection was nothing short of an insurgency, and Spain increased its troop strength to about 150,000 in 1897. The Spanish commander in Cuba, General Valeriano Weyler, resorted to the creation of concentration camps for Cuban civilians (what were called strategic hamlets in Vietnam), the assumption being that those inside were friendly, while those outside were the enemy. Not since General Sherman destroyed central Georgia during the Civil War had an army waged war against civilians as Weyler did in Cuba. As one can imagine, these camps became dangerous places to live; filth and poor diets bred rampant diseases that killed Cubans and Spaniards alike, but the effect escalated the hatred and alienation between the Cubans and the Spaniards.

By 1897 the Spanish government had had enough of Wyler's misdeeds in Cuba and removed him from command and granted a general amnesty for all Cuban political prisoners. In November 1897 Spain granted universal suffrage in Cuba and Puerto Rico and granted autonomy to Cuba. As far as Spain was concerned, the war was over in January 1898, but in reality, a much larger war was about to begin. In North America citizens became very sympathetic toward the Cuban *insurrectos,* and the press thrived on romantic stories of Cuban and American bravery and determination. By early 1898 Spain could no longer guarantee safety for the multitude of foreign nationals who lived and worked in Cuba, and the United States made the decision to send the USS *Maine* to show the flag and give support to American nationals.[5] The *Maine* was one of newest ships in the American fleet and carried the most advanced weapons. It was a beautiful ship in every way—sleek, noble, and modern. The mission was simple: go to Havana

Harbor, anchor, show the flag, and just sit there as a representative of American naval and diplomatic power. The ship arrived on 25 January 1898. The crew looked forward to sailing to New Orleans to celebrate Mardi Gras in February, but Captain Charles D. Sigsbee had to tell his officers and men that the New Orleans trip was canceled. On the evening of 15 February the crew heard "Taps" and "Lights out, quiet on the ship"—typical calls from the boatswain's mate of the watch—and then the ship exploded, lifting the bow nearly out of the water and throwing sailors' bodies overboard. The ship changed in a moment from a mighty American warship to a twisted, smoking mess and began to settle to the bottom. Captain Sigsbee, unharmed by the blast, lowered the boats and began collecting survivors as well as the dead. Of the 350-man crew, 265 men died; only 85 survived.

The Spanish authorities in Havana were horrified at the sight and sound of the *Maine*'s death and sent boats to assist in the rescue. The U.S. Navy began to investigate the sinking as early as 21 February and came to the conclusion that a mine had sunk the ship, and with the help of the press, the nation believed it had been a Spanish mine. The nation demanded satisfaction.[6] Meanwhile, Spanish Ambassador Enrique Dupuy de Lôme criticized President McKinley in a private letter to a Madrid newspaper editor. The press in the United States received and published a copy. All this incensed the American public, and although he apologized, de Lôme resigned and returned to Spain. On 19 February 1898, four days after the *Maine*'s sinking, the United States issued four resolutions to Spain: Cuba should be independent; Spain must withdraw at once; Congress would use force to ensure Spain's withdrawal; and, in what became known as the Teller Amendment, the United States had no intention of annexing Cuba and would leave as soon as possible following hostilities. In response, although Spain conceded to most of the American demands, it declared war on 23 April 1898, knowing full well that it had little or no chance to defeat the United States at sea or on the field of battle in Cuba.

In 1898 the American army was small, with only about 28,000 regulars, former Indian fighters in the West, ready for deployment. But it was relatively easy to raise a large volunteer force of federalized state units. By August the United States raised more than 300,000 soldiers and sailors for the war.[7] Logistics, however, became a nightmare. The War Department was unable to supply modern weapons to the volunteer units, and some carried leftovers from the Indian wars. Food was also a problem, and the medical community had little or no idea that the great filth in the training camps would kill more soldiers than died on any battlefield or at sea. The figures cite 362 killed in action, 1,637 wounded, and 2,621 dead of disease.[8]

After gathering the troops in Tampa, Florida, for training, the U.S. Army landed at Daiquiri and Siboney, about eighteen miles east of Santiago de Cuba in Oriente Province, on 20 June 1898. The first battles were fought a few days later at Las Guasimas and El Caney, where the Americans prevailed and took eighty-four EPWs. Fighting continued unabated from day to day, and finally troops under General Jacob Kent and former Confederate Joe Wheeler stormed San Juan and Kettle Hills on 1 July. The way was now open to Santiago de Cuba. On 4 July the United States and Spain drew up a truce to allow all the foreigners to leave Santiago before the siege, and on 10 July the Americans began a terrible bombardment of the city. Ten days later, amid the town's rubble, the Spanish garrison surrendered to the Americans, and on 26 July Spain asked the French to serve as mediators in the search for peace. On 11 August 1898 the Spanish Council of Ministers accepted the American conditions for peace: Spain must renounce its sovereignty over Cuba, Puerto Rico, and other islands of the West Indies; Spain must cede Puerto Rico to the United States and evacuate both Cuba and Puerto Rico immediately; and the United States would hold Manila until a peace treaty was signed and a government formed.[9]

The slogan "Remember the *Maine*" was sounded by every sailor in the fleet after war was declared, and the U.S. Navy sailed for Cuba, aggressively seeking battle. Unlike the army, the navy had a fleet of newly constructed ships with experienced, highly motivated, well-trained crews. Spain kept a large army in Cuba and the Philippines, but it had allowed its navy to age badly. Rear Admiral Pascual Cervera knew that his fleet could not stand up to the Americans at sea; the U.S. Navy was three times larger than Spain's. In his preparations, Assistant Secretary of the Navy Theodore Roosevelt used the Office of Naval Intelligence as a planning tool for naval operations against Spain. Together, they developed the Kimball Plan, which called for blockades of both Cuba and Manila.[10]

In the actual preparation for operations in the Pacific, the U.S. Asiatic Squadron under Commodore George Dewey aboard the USS *Olympia* received orders from Roosevelt to proceed to the Philippines and prepare for an attack. On 1 May 1898 Dewey attacked and wiped out the decrepit Spanish fleet under Admiral Patricio Montojo at Cavite near Manila. The real problem, however, was locating the main Span-

Commodore George Dewey aboard the USS *Olympia*
attacked and wiped out the Spanish fleet at Cavite near
Manila. Library of Congress.

ish fleet that had sailed from Cadiz in April and threatened the entire American East Coast. No one knew where it was or where it was
headed. The Americans were nearly in a panic at the time, but some
Cuban telegraph operators working as agents for the Office of Naval
Intelligence discovered the Spanish plans and sailing orders for Cuba
and reported them to the Americans. In response, the North Atlantic
Squadron under Admiral William Sampson sailed to Cuba and put the

Cuban coast under blockade, awaiting the arrival of the Spanish fleet under Rear Admiral Cervera. On 1 May Cervera's ships entered Santiago Harbor, despite the American blockade, but the Americans closed the door on 28 May.[11] Cervera was trapped, and he knew it.

On 3 July 1898 Rear Admiral Cervera sailed from Santiago to engage the U.S. Navy. With four cruisers and two destroyers he engaged the Americans under Admiral Schley—Admiral Sampson was visiting the land commander, General William "Pecos Bill" Shafter—and the American gunners destroyed all the ships one by one except the *Cristóbal Colon,* which finally beached. The battle brought an end to Spanish naval power in the Atlantic; it also brought an end to that "Splendid Little War," as John Hay termed it.

Nearly 26,000 Spaniards were taken as EPWs in Cuba during military engagements in the Spanish-American War, and the United States paid for their transportation home. After the peace treaty and ceding of the Philippines to the United States, 13,000 Spanish soldiers were sent home promptly.[12] After the sea battle of Santiago Bay off the Cuban coast on 3 July 1898, the American navy took 1,774 Spanish sailors and officers. The United States had no facility large enough to house all these EPWs; instead, the navy dispersed them to different locations. For example, 1,661 enlisted sailors and some soldiers captured in skirmishes at Santiago Bay were housed at Seaveys Island, Portsmouth, New Hampshire; sixteen went to American military facilities such as Fort McPherson, four miles south of Atlanta, Georgia.[13] Writing in the "Life and Letters" section of *Harper's Weekly* in 1898, reporter W. D. Howells commented about the treatment of the Spanish prisoners at Portsmouth:

> The whole thing was very American in the perfect decorum and the utter absence of ceremony. Our officer ironically professed his intention of messing with the Spanish officers. But there was no grudge, and not a shadow of ill will, or of that stupid and atrocious hate toward the public enemy which abominable newspapers and politicians have tried to breed in the popular mind. There was nothing manifest but a sort of cheerful purpose to live up to that military ideal of duty which is so much nobler than the civil ideal of self-interest. Perhaps duty will yet become the civil ideal, when the peoples shall have learned to live for the common good, and are united for the operation of the industries as they now are for the hostilities.[14]

Only thirty-one prisoners died at Portsmouth, mostly from wounds received in battle and from diseases they had contracted before being captured.

Governing American treatment of EPWs was the Geneva Convention of 1864, which mandated the protection of prisoners from both Cuban and Filipino civilians. Most of the Spanish army EPWs remained in protected status in Cuba until their repatriation, but the Naval Academy at Annapolis, Maryland, played the genteel host to Rear Admiral Cervera, his son, his officers, and their servants from 16 July to 5 September 1898. In what was probably the most unusual captivity experience of the nineteenth century, Cervera was given every comfort and pleasure, including a verbal parole to visit the city of Annapolis as he pleased. Upon arrival, the navy had demanded that Cervera and the others sign a parole agreement, which read:

> I do pledge my word of honor that during the period of my retention at the United States Naval Academy as a prisoner of war, I will not go beyond such limits as may be prescribed by the superintendent and freely agree to abide by such regulations as said superintendent may from time to time establish. The limits now established will be the grounds of the Naval Academy and the City of Annapolis from eight o'clock until sundown.[15]

Cervera refused to sign it, and so did Captain Antonio Eulate. Cervera made it known that his word was his bond, and Spanish law forbade him to sign such a document. The Americans accepted his word but forced the others to sign the parole before allowing them off the Naval Academy's grounds. The Spanish officers were polite, and according to eyewitnesses, the people of Annapolis treated them with courtesy and respect.[16]

What became known as the *Harvard* Incident caused grave concern to Admiral Cervera and his officers at Annapolis. Prisoners aboard the *Harvard* were guarded by the Ninth Massachusetts Regiment, a volunteer unit, and at about 11:30 PM on the night of 4 July 1898, one of the Spanish prisoners stepped over a kind of deadline established to keep them segregated from the rest of the ship. The American guard ordered him to return, but the Spanish sailor paid no attention, causing the guard to fire his weapon. The noise woke everyone, and the ship's watch, also armed, ordered the Spaniards to return to their assigned places. The Spanish sailors refused to obey the Americans, who then fired a volley into the group, killing six and wounding others. Terrified that the Americans were executing them on the spot, many jumped overboard and had to be rescued by the ship's boats. The remaining *Harvard* prisoners, thirty-four men, were landed at Annapolis on 20 July. Admiral Cervera was outraged and complained to the secretary of the navy, who assured him that he would launch an investigation. No charges were ever made.[17]

On 31 August 1898 President William McKinley ordered the superintendent of the Naval Academy, Admiral McNair, to release all the Spanish prisoners to the custody of the Navy Department. Admiral Cervera and his staff left Annapolis on 8 September for Portsmouth, New Hampshire, where they boarded the *City of Rome* for the trip home on 12 September. Before leaving Annapolis, Cervera wrote to McNair: "The courteous and sympathetic welcome given to all of us by the distinguished families living in the Academy is one more title to our gratitude, and Your Excellency may rest assured that it will never be effaced from our memories."[18]

On 10 October 1898 the peace conference convened in Paris, and the final treaty was signed on 10 December. Article I gave the United States the right to occupy Cuba temporarily; Article II required Spain to cede Puerto Rico and Guam in the Mariana Island chain in the Pacific to the United States; Article III forced Spain to cede the Philippine Islands to the United States for the price of $20 million; Article IV resumed Spanish commerce with the Philippines on the same terms as with the United States; Article V restored all Spanish EPWs taken in the Philippines, as well as their arms and other property belonging to Spain; Article VI returned all POWs from both sides to their home countries; Article VII relinquished all indemnity claims of citizens against either country; Article VIII ceded all public property to the United States, retained private property rights, and required all archives to remain accessible; Article IX allowed Spanish subjects to remain in Cuba and the Philippines but gave the U.S. Congress authority to determine both the civil rights and the political status of the native populations; Article X guaranteed the free exercise of religion in the new territories; Article XI made certain that Spaniards in U.S. territories had access to American courts; Article XII regulated civil suits and criminal trials; and Articles XIII through XVIII enabled both countries to put the treaty into force.[19] As of 1 January 1899 Cuba belonged to the United States for five years under the provisions of the Platt Amendment of 1901.[20] On 18 October 1899, after the Spanish evacuation, the United States annexed Puerto Rico. The annexation and occupation of the Philippine Islands would evolve into an American problem of major proportions.

The Philippine-American War began on 4 February 1899, a month and a half after the Spanish-American War ended. It was a conflict local to the Philippines, fought between the United States and the Filipinos in the archipelago. The war lasted officially until 1902, although fighting occurred as late as 1906. Most certainly, the war was longer and bloodier than the one against Spain, but it was not a global conflict. Spain was not involved, although Spanish forces remained in the Philippines when the Americans arrived. Although it was closely related, the Philippine annexation was a separate and different conflict from the Spanish-American War.[21]

After Admiral George Dewey destroyed the Spanish fleet in the Philippines, he stayed in Manila attempting to nurture the relationship between the Filipinos and the U.S. government. On 12 June 1898 the leader of the Filipino resistance against Spanish rule, Emilio Aguinaldo, declared Philippine independence and attempted to establish a republic with a written constitution.[22] Then on 21 December, unexpectedly for the Filipinos, President William McKinley issued what was known as the Benevolent Assimilation Proclamation:

The military commander of the United States is enjoined to make known to the inhabitants of the Philippine Islands that in succeeding to the sovereignty of Spain, in severing the former political relations, and in establishing a new political power, the authority of the United States is to be exerted for the securing of the persons and property of the people of the Islands and for the confirmation of all private rights and relations by proving to them that the mission of the United States is one of benevolent assimilation, substituting the mild sway of justice and right for arbitrary rule. For the greatest good of the governed, there must be sedulously maintained the strong arm of authority, to repress disturbance and to overcome all obstacles to the bestowal of the blessings of good and stable government upon the people of the Philippine Islands under the flag of the United States.[23]

On 4 January 1899 the military governor of the Philippines, General Elwell S. Otis, U.S. Army, issued his own proclamation, extending the hand of friendship while protecting American sovereignty:

The United States came here to give the blessings of peace and individual freedom to the Philippine people, that we are here as friends of the Filipinos, to protect them in their homes, their employments, their individual and religious liberty; that all persons, who either by active aid or honest endeavor cooperate with the government of the United States to give effect to these beneficent purposes, will receive the reward of its support and protection.[24]

General Otis truly understood what this contest was all about—politics—and he always stressed reform rather than military action, especially before he acquired an adequate force to deal with a war.[25] Unfortunately for Otis, the Filipinos had other ideas.

Fighting against Spanish rule as allies of the Americans and expecting the United States to support the Filipino cause of liberty and independence, Aguinaldo and his loyalists were surprised by the McKinley proclamation. The next day, Aguinaldo issued his own stinging manifesto:

I proclaim solemnly that I have not recognized the sovereignty of America over this beloved soil. I say that I returned to these Islands on an American warship on the 19th of May last for the express purpose of making war on the Spaniards to regain our liberty and independence. All this was confirmed by the American General Merritt himself, predecessor of General Otis, in his Manifesto to the Philippine people. In that Manifesto it is distinctly stated that the naval and field forces of the United States had come to give us our liberty, and I hereby protest against this unexpected act of the United States claiming sovereignty over these Islands.[26]

There was no doubt that General Otis and his command understood Aguinaldo's manifesto as a declaration of war.

What was called the Philippine Insurrection by historians for most of the twentieth century and the Bamboo War by its veterans began in February 1899 when the Americans drove Aguinaldo's Filipino forces out of Manila. Between 1899 and the war's partial end in 1902, more than 70,000 Americans fought in the Philippine Islands, with 4,200 killed in action and 2,800 wounded, and at a stunning cost of $400 million—much more than the cost of defeating Spain.[27] Over the course of the war, the Filipinos fared much worse than the Americans. According to historian Richard E. Welch Jr., battlefield casualties reached somewhere between 16,000 and 20,000, but civilian casualties were extreme: between famine and disease, approximately 200,000 Filipinos died.[28] Yet John M. Gates reminds readers not to jump to the conclusion that the Americans acted as butchers, committing genocide in the name of "benevolent assimilation." "One must be wary," he writes, "of attributing all the war-related casualties to action by the Americans. One cannot absolve the Filipino revolutionaries from all responsibility for a portion of the wartime casualties."[29]

In this war, escalation and brutality simply got out of hand, and although ethnicity and race played a significant role, a lack of humane rules of engagement did as well. Some soldiers probably felt they were fighting another frontier Indian war. They called the Filipinos "niggers" in their letters home and "Goo Goos" in the field. Recalling that race structured societies in both the North and the South following the Civil War, none of this was very surprising at the turn of the twentieth century. In an insurgent or small war, taking prisoners was inconvenient for soldiers on the move because there were no holding facilities, and it is probable that those soldiers who lived past capture were the lucky ones. Many did, but exactly how many is impossible to ascertain. One soldier, H. C. Thompson of Company C, Second Oregon Volunteer Infantry, remembered, "We met a collection of wounded Filipinos under guard. I offered a groaning fellow a drink from my canteen, but he asked for a cigarillo. All wanted cigarillos. So I gave them my pack, and they seemed quite content."[30] Thompson's unit left the Philippines early in the war, before the counterinsurgency raised the level of hatred for the guerrillas.

Reminiscent of the San Patricios' fate during the Mexican War, some American soldiers changed sides for causes they believed to be just. The Twenty-fourth Infantry Regiment, an all-black unit of Buffalo Soldiers, fought the Filipino insurgents and suffered high casualties. In *Smoked Yankees and the Struggle for Empire,* historian Willard B. Gatewood Jr. describes the activities of the renegade David Fagan, who deserted his regiment on 17 November 1899 to accept a commission in the insurgent army. Fagan, angry about the overt racism in the U.S. Army at the time, wreaked havoc on American forces for two years before being killed.[31] Other historians point out that although the American command believed he was a "butcher," Fagan treated captured American soldiers kindly.[32] Concerning Fagan's mysterious death, Michael C. Robinson and Frank N. Schubert point out that a Filipino, Anastasio Bartoloméo, actually killed Fagan with a bolo knife and brought his head back to the Americans as confirmation.[33]

The army in the Philippines used General Order 100 as its principal guideline for action against enemy soldiers captured in battle. As the war evolved from a conventional to a guerrilla war, the Rules of Land Warfare made it clear who was and was not to be accorded POW status. Partisans, according to Section III, Article 81, were considered soldiers, provided they wore and received the protection of their uniform. If captured, they enjoyed the privileges of being prisoners of war. Article 82, however, denied POW status to nonuniformed enemy fighters who conducted hostilities:

> Without being part and portion of the organized hostile army, and without sharing continuously in the war, but who do so with intermitting returns to their homes and avocations, or with the occasional assumption of the semblance of peaceful pursuits, divesting themselves of the character or appearance of soldiers—such men, or squads of men, are not public enemies, and, therefore, if captured, are not entitled to the privileges of prisoners of war, but shall be treated summarily as highway robbers or pirates.

Section IV, Article 83 is even more specific about guerrillas: "Scouts, or single soldiers, if disguised in the dress of the country or in the uniform of the army hostile to their own, employed in obtaining information, if found within or lurking about the lines of the captor, are treated as spies, and suffer death." Article 85 finally puts the guerrilla, or "war rebel," outside the protection of American military law:

> War-rebels are persons within an occupied territory who rise in arms against the occupying or conquering army, or against the authorities established by the same. If captured, they may suffer death, whether they rise singly, in small or large bands, and whether called upon to do so by their own, but expelled, government or not. They are not prisoners of war; nor are they if discovered and secured before their conspiracy has matured to an actual rising or armed violence.[34]

Thus, the Filipino guerrillas who became EPWs of the Americans did not enjoy POW status, especially after Aguinaldo abandoned conventional warfare on 13 November 1899 in favor of a guerrilla effort with approximately 40,000 troops under General Vincente Lukban. Individual fates were often determined by military commissions, the same practice as in the Civil War and the Indian wars in the late nineteenth century. Writing in 1902, Captain D. H. Boughton of the Third U.S. Cavalry noted that these commissions enforced the laws of war and explained how they functioned in the Philippines:

> In our service these tribunals are known as the military commission. In the Philippine Islands these tribunals have tried many hundreds of cases and have inflicted punishments varying from small fines, or a few days' imprisonment, to forfeitures of many thousands of dollars and the infliction of the death penalty.
>
> While these tribunals have been necessary instruments in the suppression of crime at a time when crime was common, they have also been powerful adjuncts, especially the provost court, in putting an end to the insurrection, and making the establishment of civil government possible.[35]

During the long, dirty war in the new "heart of darkness," the Philippines, the American force used counterinsurgent tactics—what the marines called the "small war"—against the Filipinos throughout the islands. Soldiers coined a phrase for the Filipino outback—the *boondocks*—which may be an Americanization of the Tagalog word *bundok*, meaning "mountain." Jungle trails were often laced with booby traps, and some of the remote tribes were traditional head hunters.[36] In all, the two sides fought 2,811 engagements from 1899 to 1902. Fortunately for the Americans, they were better shots and more disciplined soldiers than the Filipinos, who usually suffered more casualties per engagement than the Americans did.[37]

A few examples might be useful. On Panay, for example, Filipino guerrillas attacked a small American patrol on 6 June 1900 at a town called Damangus. The Filipinos drove the Americans into a church and then burned it down, forcing the Americans to run for their lives. Attacks like this one took place by the hundreds. Patrols and wagon trains were ambushed everywhere by Filipino guerrillas, who usually outnumbered their American enemies because, in the counterinsurgency phase, the Americans usually operated in small groups stationed at outposts. In another incident on the island of Samar, a band of guerrillas posing as friendlies under the command of General Lukban turned on seventy-four soldiers of Company C, Ninth Infantry Regiment, on 28 September 1901 at Balangiga. In a surprise attack while the unarmed Americans ate their breakfast, forty-four were killed, their bodies terribly mutilated.[38] At a signal given by the police chief and the local priest, a band of guerrillas who had infiltrated the town earlier opened fire.[39] The Americans, who believed the war was all but over, were outraged, and "Hell Roaring" Jake Smith received orders to take revenge. Samar was known to the Americans as the "dark and bloody ground," and en route, the marines lost eleven men from pure exhaustion and starvation, but the real problem was the treachery of the Filipino guides. As one can imagine, the troops were hard to control in this frame of mind, and Marine Corps Major Littleton W. T. Waller was later charged with the unlawful execution of eleven Filipino guides. Waller claimed that his actions were completely justified because the guides had withheld knowledge of food on the trail. Other officers, such as Major C. J. Crane, wrote that there was no doubt in his mind that "the service of a guide in the face of the enemy is deemed so important that a false guide may even be put to death, under the authority contained in Paragraph 97 (of General Order 100)."[40] Repercussions over this event were felt by veterans for years after their return.[41]

Some letters written home reported positive events. Colonel Cornelius Gardner of the Thirty-first Michigan Volunteers wrote to his friend, Michigan Governor H. S. Pingree, on 21 February 1900, "We released three Spanish prisoners held by the insurgents, captured five rifles, but got no insurgents. The insurgents are generally very kind to our prisoners."[42] He told the governor that the insurgents had captured one of his men but returned him when he became sick. Gardner was indeed impressed with the behavior of the Filipinos. "The Filipinos are not ignorant," he wrote, "they have read our history and our race antipathy to any person of dark skin."[43] He was also dismayed by the behavior of some American soldiers. In the same letter he informed the governor:

> Then came the soldiers. I do not know that the American is worse than other soldiers, but surely he was bad enough, and after a month's campaigning is very demoralizing and bad for discipline. They destroyed for the fun of it. Every church and some graveyards were thoroughly gone through. However, where my regiment came only, no church has been entered or looting done, for I placed guards immediately to prevent it. A man at home who would not take a pin, will here steal anything he can lay his hands on, and under some plea or other make himself, and try to make others believe that this is alright here.[44]

Apparently, in Gardner's view, the Ten Commandments did not exist in the Philippine campaign for those American soldiers intent on plunder. His officers were distressed as well, thinking that they should not remain in the Philippine Islands "a day longer that it took to reestablish order and rebuild a government that we destroyed."[45]

The home front suffered considerably when letters written by soldiers to friends and family members were widely reported in the press. Privates and corporals often used soldier slang, possibly to impress the folks back home with their fighting prowess. One soldier in a California unit wrote that if the natives refused to return to their huts, they shot them, claiming that he saw his unit murder 300 civilians in one night. Another soldier wrote home about going on "GooGoo hunts."[46] One has to accept the fact that some soldiers embellish their "war stories" about their adventures in the field. They may hold a grain of truth, but only a grain. Unfortunately, all this fed the anti-imperialist press with all sorts of grist for the antiwar mill, and in most instances, truth was never an issue. In the ranks of this movement, according to Glenn A. May, were many distinguished politicians, businessmen, and intellectuals of the day.[47] Mark Twain was one of them.

Mark Twain became a fervent anti-imperialist and joined the Anti-Imperialist League; his sentiments were published nationwide. Writing in the *New York Herald* on 15 October 1900, Twain noted, "I have read carefully the Treaty of Paris, and I have seen that we do not intend to free, but to subjugate the people of the Philippines. We have gone there to conquer, not to redeem."[48] But despite the opposition to the war in newspapers and intellectual circles, more Americans supported it at home than opposed it.[49] Correspondents such as Frederick Palmer writing for *Scribner's Magazine* reported that the "natives only destroyed the churches." Elaborating on the destruction in the Philippines, Palmer wrote: "They [the *insurrectos*] tortured the Chinese shopkeepers to ascertain where the money was hidden, robbed the houses of the well-to-do, and played the part of brigands who impress whatever they need for their purposes. If there was any burning on our side, it was usually the result of carelessness or of the viciousness of a bad volunteer soldier who took advantage of easy discipline."[50] This is not to say that soldiers in any war wear halos, but in the heat of battle, one's ability to make rational decisions may become radically impaired. As Palmer stated quite correctly, "No soldier thinks much of abstract justice after a bullet from the bushes has killed a comrade."[51] Commenting in 1902, General Oliver O. Howard, whose experience in the Civil and Indian wars gives him credibility, wrote:

We shall always be subjected to the charge of cruelties and methods of warfare which every true American abominates; but I think when we have rising up against our flag and country organized mobs and robbers who bury their enemies alive, subject them not only to horrible deaths, but to preliminary tortures, and when so called "enemies" are worthy people, hurting nobody, but looking to our army for protection, that we ought to be very careful not to condemn the army for severe measures which appear to be necessary.[52]

Facing guerrilla tactics is not an easy task for any uniformed soldier, especially an American soldier imbued with a sense of moral order and discipline by his upbringing and his training. When he witnesses or even hears about an enemy violating the code of conduct, there might be hell to pay. Violating a flag of truce, attacking by surprise in civilian clothes, killing cooperative civilians, and especially torturing and mutilating American prisoners violate his sense of right and wrong. Todd D. Wagoner, who fought as a private with Company F, Twentieth Kansas Volunteer Infantry, early in the war, noted, "They fired on our flag of truce. They placed their women and children in front of their ranks and attempted an assault, presuming on the tenderheartedness of the American if they did not care any more for their own families than that, we didn't."[53] Retribution in the form of execution was not unthinkable, and many such incidents actually took place.

According to historian Brian McAllister Linn, most incidents of torture took place at the hands of sergeants, corporals, and junior officers who needed operational intelligence in the field at that moment.[54] The most notorious method was the "water cure." If the prisoner refused to cooperate, he was laid on his back and held down by his torturers, who then inserted a bamboo tube in his mouth and poured dirty water down the tube into his stomach until his midsection extended nearly to the point of explosion. Then the victim would be rolled over until he vomited all the water out, at which time the process started over again.[55] The modern "water board," cousin to the medieval water cure, is a little different. Usually, the interrogator slaps a large, wet towel over the victim's face, hindering the ability to breathe. If the towel is applied too long, the victim will die, but a skilled interrogator can usually get the answers he wants in about thirty seconds. Moral? No. Lawful? No. Effective? Absolutely. In the Philippine war, senior officers preferred to look the other way when told about these interrogation methods, while at the same time they issued general orders against the physical abuse of prisoners. Brigadier General Clarence H. Bowers, who served with the Eighteenth U.S. Infantry during the war, wrote after his retirement that he was positive no American officer had knowingly permitted the water cure to be used; if it was used, it must have been done by Filipino scouts attached to the American units in the field. "Personally," he wrote, "I have never permitted its use, knowingly, and I have always cautioned my men never to resort to it."[56]

Captain J. A. Ryan of the Fifteenth U.S. Cavalry was court-martialed for sticking prisoners' heads into a barrel of water—a far cry from the full extent of the water cure—to extract information. In his defense, published in 1902, Ryan wrote, "Did my sticking the heads of these treacherous, lying, native office-holders into a pail of water, thereby washing away an impediment in their speech, constitute a greater crime than treason against the flag and the soldiers who defend it? Could I have done anything else than to arrest these guilty officials?" Finally, Ryan stated what was perhaps the true feeling of many American officers and enlisted men in the Philippines: "To say that under such circumstances as these, ducking of the heads into a pail of water was unlawful is to my mind crying out 'Law' where there is no law."[57] From 1900 to 1902 it was understood that in a guerrilla war, conditions in the field, rather than strict adherence to the laws of war, sometimes dictated the methods used. Thus, a serious conundrum arose: American soldiers were damned by the law if they used unconventional methods, and damned by the failure to obtain hard field intelligence if they refrained.

One Filipino EPW who made the headlines around the world was Emilio Aguinaldo himself. How he became a prisoner of the Americans became the stuff of legend. Brigadier General "Fight'n' Fred" Funston, born in Ohio but really a Kansan, became one of the most celebrated counterinsurgency officers in the U.S. Army in the Philippines. Funston was one of those adventurers who is always searching for odd, even bizarre things to do in life. By the time he turned thirty years old, he had been a teacher, university student, newspaper reporter, railroad conductor, and lecturer. He roamed Alaska and one time paddled 1,500 miles down the Yukon River. In 1896 he trundled off to Cuba and joined the Cuban revolutionaries against Spain. Wounded several times, he returned to the United States to publicize his adventures and the Cuban cause.[58] His celebrity for his Cuban service and his political connections at home combined to get him appointed a colonel in the Twentieth Kan-

Emilio Aguinaldo led the
guerrilla war against the
U.S. Army in the Philippines.
Library of Congress.

sas Infantry. After a trip home with his Kansas unit, Funston became a
brigadier general in the fall of 1899, a remarkable promotion for someone with nearly no formal military experience or training.[59]

After Aguinaldo's command collapsed as a formal organized army
and he took up guerrilla operations against the Americans, General Otis
divided the Philippines into military districts with their own troops.
Generals Arthur MacArthur and Adna Chaffee never changed that
organization significantly during the entire war.[60] General Otis had an
array of faults, but selecting officers like Funston was not one of them.
In December 1899 Funston received command of the Fourth District
in the Department of Northern Luzon.[61] After learning that with care,
excellent intelligence, and a good plan he could actually launch a covert
mission to capture the president of the Philippine republic, Funston,
along with four officers and a group of seventy-eight loyal Filipinos
called the Philippine Cavalry or Macabebe Scouts, devised an ingenious
and innovative operation to capture Aguinaldo alive.[62]

Combining duplicity with an enormous amount of courage, luck, and
permission from his commanding officer, General Arthur MacArthur,

Funston decided to take a gunboat to within sixty miles of Aguinaldo's camp at Palinan on the northeast coast of Luzon and then hike the rest of the way. In rough mountainous terrain, the march was extremely difficult. As they approached the target, the scouts told the insurgents that they had American prisoners, but the Filipinos refused to allow captured Americans in the camp. So the scouts hid the prisoners while they were led into the camp. As Aguinaldo's guard rendered them a salute, the scouts surrounded them. Moments later the insurgents were all dead; Aguinaldo was taken prisoner in his bedroom and informed on 23 March 1901 that he was a prisoner of the U.S. Army.[63] On 1 April 1901 Emilio Aguinaldo took an oath of allegiance to the United States, and on 19 April he signed a manifesto calling on his countrymen to give up the fight. It read in part:

> The country has declared unmistakably in favor of peace; so be it. Enough of blood; enough of tears and desolation. This wish cannot be ignored by the men still in arms if they are animated by no other desire than to serve this noble people which has clearly manifested its will.
>
> By acknowledging and accepting the sovereignty of the United States throughout the entire archipelago, as I now do without any reservations whatsoever, I believe that I am serving thee, my beloved country. May happiness be thine![64]

Aguinaldo's surrender and manifesto may well have been a turning point—Vice President Theodore Roosevelt called Funston a "perfect corker"—but the war continued.[65] Other guerrilla commands remained in the field. William Howard Taft took charge in Manila as the civil governor on 4 July 1901, and General Adna Chaffee replaced General Arthur MacArthur as the commanding general of military forces.

The war, known first as the Philippine Insurrection to contemporaries, the Bamboo War to veterans, and the Philippine-American War now, ground to an end as Filipino leaders realized that the people of the archipelago no longer supported Aguinaldo's independence movement. In Funston's case in northern Luzon, he used his former adversaries to aid the pacification of the districts. Those *insurrectos* who surrendered were, according to Linn, expected to bring in their men and arms, but after surrendering they were often given positions within the American civil governments.[66] This is not to say that Funston never inflicted capital punishment on his enemy. On 27 March 1900 he ordered the execution of two Filipino officers he had caught red-handed attempting to execute two Macabebe Scouts. Funston claimed that he killed these men in accordance with General Order 100, and few, if any, batted an eyelash, in part because he made a full report of the event.[67] Funston, as Linn points out, was without a doubt one of the bright lights of the war. His evaluation of Funston sparkles:

> He showed himself a capable, practical, and efficient civil-military leader with considerable political and military skills. For over a year he fought a long and frustrating guerrilla war with very limited resources. He demonstrated a marked talent for developing and implementing pragmatic pacification policies. In this respect, Funston is symbolic of successful U.S. Army counterinsurgency policies in the Philippines.[68]

By the end of 1901, in part because of men like Funston, the fighting in Luzon had all but ended, yet it continued in Samar and in Muslim Mindanao well into 1902 and beyond. In July 1901 units of 150 Filipinos led by Americans took the field as the counterinsurgency-oriented Philippine Constabulary, and within six months this police force grew to 3,000 men.

The official end of this war took place on 4 July 1902 when President Theodore Roosevelt announced not only an end to hostilities but also a general pardon and amnesty to those Filipinos (but not to the Moro tribes in Mindanao) who had fought for independence against the U.S. Army. He wrote:

> Whereas, it is deemed to be wise and humane, in accordance with the beneficent purposes of the Government of the United States toward the Filipino people, and conducive to peace, order, and loyalty among them, that the doers of such acts who have not already suffered punishment shall not be held criminally responsible, but shall be relieved from punishment for participation in these insurrections, and for unlawful acts committed during the course thereof, by general amnesty and pardon.[69]

But part of this document required that any Filipino who raised arms against the United States had to take an oath of allegiance:

> I, _____, solemnly swear (or affirm) that I recognize and accept the supreme authority of the United States of America in the

Philippine Islands and will maintain true faith and allegiance thereto; that I impose upon myself this obligation voluntarily, without mental reservation or purpose of evasion. So help me God.[70]

The long arm of judgment affected the veterans of this war in ways they never came to terms with. The war had become so unpopular at home by 1902 that the United States decided to withdraw its main forces, especially from Islamic Mindanao, and left a relatively small police force in its wake. Although antiwar feelings and the Anti-Imperialist League never amounted to much in terms of political influence, when the veterans finally arrived in San Francisco they were not well received, in spite of Roosevelt's official thanks for their courage and fortitude. One soldier remembered, "Instead of glad hands, people stared at a khaki-clad man as though he had escaped from a zoo. People shied away as though you were an Apache with the small pox."[71] Another veteran noted sadly, "There weren't any bands to welcome us home. For the most part, people back home had pretty much forgotten about us."[72]

Although America experienced easy victory against Spain in Cuba, conquering the Philippines was a far more difficult affair.[73] Fighting in Cuba was short, and the rules of General Order 100 remained intact. The Americans were humane, even generous, toward their Spanish EPWs. Every rule of warfare was observed in Cuba and later in the United States during the short incarceration of Spanish officers and men in 1898. To many soldiers, fighting the Filipino guerrillas fell outside General Order 100, and they resented being called to task for the mistreatment of enemy prisoners and civilians who helped them. Fighting an unseen, nonuniformed enemy was then and remains today anathema to the American soldier in the field, and not until Vietnam would rules be developed that partially solved this dilemma.

The American veterans of the war organized very quickly and started several organizations exclusive to themselves. They were angry that the War Department had not granted them combat pay because it claimed the Philippine war was not a war but merely an insurrection. No campaign medal, something very important to war veterans, was issued until 1905, and not until 1922 did the veterans receive the same benefits as World War I veterans received. William W. Grayson, after receiving a small pension, wrote a simple letter to the Veterans' Administration in 1934, stating, "I fired the First Shot that opened the Philippine Insurrection, February 4, 1899." He died in 1941 from malaria and myriad complications contracted while soldiering in the Philippines.[74]

By 1907 the United States passed internal control of the Philippines to those Filipinos striving for independence, and the Jones Act of 1916 pledged independence for the islands. Colonialism had run its course, although the United States retains Guam and Puerto Rico today and purchased the American Virgin Islands in 1917 from Denmark. In 1934 the United States approved the Tydings-McDuffie Act, promising Philippine independence in 1946, and the transition to independence began. In 1935 the Filipino people approved a constitution creating the Commonwealth of the Philippines, with Manuel Quezon as president. World War II saw an invasion of the Philippines by the Imperial Japanese Army and an attempt to bring it into the Greater East Asia Co-Prosperity Sphere. Filipinos rejected this effort and fought the Japanese in a successful guerrilla war alongside the few Americans who escaped or evaded Japanese captivity. In 1946 the Philippines became an independent nation, and Manuel Roxas became the first elected president. Only the bloodshed and terrors of World War II brought the Filipino and American peoples together in lasting friendship and mutual trust. This time they fought together against a common enemy, not against each other.

EIGHT

Over There and Over Here

Enemy Prisoners of War and Prisoners of State in the Great War

> It was everywhere noticeable that whether in prison or at work, the German soldier always retained his military bearing and his excellent discipline.
> —General John J. Pershing

By the end of the nineteenth century, Americans began to worry more about populist threats to their democratic institutions and economic opportunities and less about the frontier.[1] By the twentieth century, Americans saw themselves as noble and moral crusaders for liberal democratic traditions that included the rule of law, progress, freedom, and individual rights. With this kind of liberalism firmly in control of the American vision of itself, President Woodrow Wilson took pride in keeping the United States out of the Great War until 1917. To the deep chagrin of the British and former president Theodore Roosevelt, who advocated military readiness, the Wilson administration kept up its resistance to engagement by saying it was too proud to fight, while at the same time providing millions of dollars worth of military supplies to the Allies. America grew wealthy during the Great War, capitalizing on Europe's pain. The American economy lifted from the recession of 1913–1914, factories hummed at nearly full production, and corporate profits soared.[2] After all, to Americans from 1914 to 1917, much like the Federalists of the 1812–1814 era, business was business, even in wartime, as long as the war took place somewhere else.

In 1917, when the United States went to war against Imperial Germany, the use of prison hulks was long past; international rules for the treatment of POWs were in place; the Red Cross had come to the aid of American POWs in German hands; and, during hostilities, aside from the usual complaints about the food, there were virtually no serious problems to contend with, at least on the surface. In Room 40 at Naval Headquarters in London, the home of British cryptanalysts, the American and German diplomatic codes were broken easily. On 17 January

1917 Room 40 intercepted and broke a diplomatic message to Mexico that said, in essence, if Mexico joined the German war effort and invaded the United States, Germany would return Texas, Arizona, and New Mexico to the Mexicans after the victory. The author, German Foreign Minister Arthur Zimmermann, actually confirmed the message later, but it was too late. Woodrow Wilson, outraged by this German affront to American sovereignty, asked Congress to declare war against Germany to "make the world safe for democracy."

Slogans aside, the Americans did indeed set their sights on creating a 4 million–man force, the American Expeditionary Force (AEF), to fight in France, and General John J. Pershing set his sights on marching a victorious army into Berlin itself by 1920. The Americans did manage to send more than 2 million troops to Europe, and it is fair to say that this force tipped the balance of victory in 1918.[3] The American army trained for months before entering the fight, and French and British trainers advised the young Americans to avoid taking prisoners if possible. This must have sounded strange coming from French and British battle veterans; both countries were signatories of the Hague Convention, and the armed forces of the United States had long upheld the tradition of taking prisoners in battle. The rules of the Hague Convention (1899, 1907) were clear to all (see appendix 6). From June 1918 to the end of March 1919, according to Pershing's final report, the AEF held 48,280 German soldiers as prisoners of war in France, of whom 93 died and 73 escaped without recapture.[4] The actual number taken, however, was larger.

It may seem odd, but during World War I the Americans feared domestic subversion in the form of disloyalty among foreign-born citizens and soldiers more than the presence of real German agents engaged in sabotage. The Americans also feared efforts toward a social and economic revolution from socialist subversion more than anything the Germans were doing. In response, Congress reacted strongly and passed the Espionage Act in 1917 and its supplement, the Sedition Act, in 1918. Working together, these pieces of social legislation allowed federal law enforcement to rampage the immigrant communities in what is now called the Red Scare. According to historian Thomas Fleming, the big targets included the Industrial Workers of the World (IWW, or Wobblies), the Socialist Party led by Eugene V. Debs, any antiwar or pro-German group or club, pacifists, and private citizens who had any good words to say about Imperial Germany.[5] People from each group experienced time in prison during the war years.

About 8 million men surrendered and were held in POW camps until the war ended. With the exceptions of Serbia and Montenegro, all nations pledged to follow the Hague rules on the fair treatment of prisoners of war, and in general, the POWs had a much higher survival rate than their peers who were not captured. Individual surrenders were uncommon; usually, for safety's sake, a large unit surrendered all its men. At Tannenberg, 92,000 Russians surrendered during the battle. When the besieged garrison of Kaunas surrendered in 1915, 20,000 Russians became prisoners. More than half the Russian losses were prisoners (as a proportion of those captured, wounded, or killed); for other countries, the proportions were as follows: Austria 32 percent, Italy 26 percent, France 12 percent, Germany 9 percent, and Britain 7 percent. Prisoners from the Allied armies totaled about 1.4 million, not including Russia, which lost between 2.5 and 3.5 million men as prisoners. From the Central Powers, about 3.3 million men became prisoners.[6] Germany held 2.5 million prisoners, Russia held 2.9 million, and Britain and France held about 720,000, most of them gained in the period just before the armistice in 1918.

The most dangerous moment was the act of surrender, when helpless soldiers were sometimes gunned down. Niall Ferguson offers a strong explanation: "Surrender on the Western Front was dangerous," he writes, "indeed, for much of the war most soldiers felt that the risks a man ran by surrendering were greater than the risks he ran by fighting on." Ferguson notes that on many occasions, soldiers on both sides killed enemy soldiers not only in the act of surrender but also after it. He concludes that this fact created desperate battlefield environments and possibly lengthened the war.[7] Tim Cook, a historian at the Canadian War Museum, agrees in part but makes the point that murdering prisoners made no sense, although Canadian troops did their share of it on the Western Front. From 1915 to 1918 these murders sometimes occurred during mindless rampages of vengeance, sometimes with the tacit understanding and approval of senior officers, and they made surrendering after vicious close combat an unknown outcome at best.[8] Part of this problem rested in the heat of battle and the fog of war. Every soldier knew that killing an enemy on the battlefield was no crime, but without a doubt, American soldiers on the Western Front had to make life-or-death decisions about taking enemy prisoners when the bullets were flying. Once prisoners reached a camp, conditions were satisfactory.[9]

Another component of the problem came from training—not in the United States, where rudimentary training lasted six months, but in France, where General John J. Pershing, the American supreme commander of the AEF, had established two-month schools for all newly arriving soldiers of all ranks. After establishing his headquarters at Chaumont, Pershing knew that his army fell short on real-world battlefield training, and to the dismay of the impatient Allies, he demanded that the AEF receive specific instruction in trench warfare and what to expect from the German army in the field.

All the British and French instructors were veterans who found the young Americans' enthusiasm refreshing, even startling at times. Yet these veterans brought a considerable amount of skepticism into their instruction sessions. One instructor told this war story:

> We made an attack one day. As our first wave carried the enemy trench, they heard shouts from a dugout: "Kamerad!" The Germans surrendered. The first wave rushed on, leaving it to the second wave to take the prisoners. As soon as the first wave passed, the Germans emerged from their dugout with a hidden machine gun and broke it out on the backs of the men who had been white enough not to give them the cold steel. So now, men, when we hear "Kamerad" coming from the depths of a dugout in a captured trench we call down: "How many?" If the answer comes back "Six," we decide that one hand grenade ought to be enough to take care of six and toss it in.[10]

Whether the young Americans took the British and French infantry instructors seriously is hard to say, but it seems likely that this sort of battlefield behavior was very distant from the American way of war.

By the fall of 1918 the German army was war weary, and many German soldiers, convinced that the war was lost, were glad to surrender to the Americans, although it seems the Americans were as harsh in the field as the British and French. One marine, Elton E. Mackin, reported one occasion when no prisoners were taken except for one wounded German soldier.[11] In one dugout, troops of the Forty-second Division found an officer sitting at a table with a bottle of schnapps, waiting to welcome his captors. One of the Austrians taken prisoner was a reservist who had lived in the United States in 1914. He asked if he could return to Sharon, Pennsylvania.[12] In Mackin's remarkable narrative, *Suddenly We Didn't Want to Die,* he notes that his marines had a clear choice about taking prisoners. "Lone fellows," he writes, "gave resistance, taking a toll, and tried too late for mercy, screaming 'Kamerad.' Some cowered in foxholes peacefully; arising only when the victors called them up. It's safer done that way. The fellow with the bayonet gets time to think. He's not apt to kill a kneeling man." Mackin goes on to say with considerable insight:

> Might it be a trap? Odd things happen on a battlefield. Wounded fanatics have been known to exact a price for dying. Never beaten, many Germans didn't know enough to quit until they died—or took long chances, risking any gamble in attempting to rejoin their kind. There are such men in every uniform.
>
> Fighting men respect the enemy. They never trust them. Staunch foe, the Boche. Only a fool doubts his courage. Men who know him marvel at his willingness to fight, at any odds. Trusting Heinie is another matter. Men who trust too much do not come back alive.[13]

In his book *How to Live at the Front,* written for newly minted American doughboys in 1917, British artillery officer Hector Macquarrie advises: "Don't trust the enemy an inch, but remember that when you feel like paying him back in his own coin that you are an American, not a Hun. The greatest victory you can ever win is the victory over hatred—generous treatment to a fallen foe, but don't be a fool with them—take no chances. They can be unbelievably dirty in their methods." Macquarrie goes on to say that if one hears, "Kammerad pardon," it does not mean the German soldiers are giving up. If an American decides to take prisoners, he warns, "Keep them covered. Don't let those hands come down till you are sure they are unarmed. . . . When sure that they are harmless," he writes, "then your chance comes to be generous, and you will be." But he reminds his young readers, "They hate the British most at present—the day will come when they may hate you more."[14]

Illustrating the potential danger of taking prisoners is the story of Sergeant Harry J. Adams. When Adams saw a German soldier run into a large dugout, he ran in after him, firing his two remaining rounds through the door and yelling to the German soldier to surrender. Solemnly, more than 300 Germans filed out of the dugout. Somewhat distressed that he had no ammunition in his pistol, Adams marched his prisoners back to his platoon.[15]

By the autumn of 1918 most of the elite German infantry units had perished in the five Ludendorff offensives during the spring and summer. The American battles in these offensives have become nearly legendary in the annals of American arms. Cantigny took place in April 1918, when the First Division under the command of Major General Robert

Lee Bullard fought to straighten out the line, albeit at great cost.[16] The Americans took about 200 German soldiers as their first prisoners of war. Belleau Wood was fought by the Second Division under the command of James Harbord in June and July 1918. Both these divisions were regulars and contained marine units. With heavy coverage by the press, Belleau Wood became part of the Marine Corps' heroic lore. One gunnery sergeant roused his pinned-down troops by asking, "Come on, you sons of bitches, do you want to live forever?" For this and other actions during the battle, Gunnery Sergeant Dan Daly was awarded the Navy Cross.[17] That battle was the bloodiest of the U.S. Marine Corps' history to that point, and the Fifth and Sixth Regiments were awarded the French Fourragère and Croix de Guerre. Approximately 1,600 enemy troops were taken prisoner. Following the war, the French government renamed the forest Wood of the Marine Brigade, and one of the many "Iron Mike" statues was dedicated there in 1923.[18] The marines loved the thought of being called *Teufelhunde* ("Devil Dogs") respectfully by the German troops, and statues of the mythic "Iron Mike" character at the marine training bases in Parris Island, South Carolina, and Quantico, Virginia, were dedicated to the marines who died in World War I.

The battle at Vaux, fought by the Third Brigade, Second Division, on 1 July 1918 stopped the German advance toward Paris and cost the Americans 9,000 casualties. Better known as Chateau-Thierry,[19] it was a battle that stopped General Erich Ludendorff's last offensive, and the Third Infantry Division became known as the "Rock of the Marne Division" in its history. Also in July, a huge battle at Soissons that turned the tide of the war in favor of the Allies involved a large number of American divisions, including the Twenty-eighth Infantry Division of the Pennsylvania National Guard, whose red Keystone arm patch became known as the "bucket of blood." According to *New York Times* war reporter Edwin L. James, captured German soldiers began to tell Americans that they did not believe they could win the war.[20] By July 1918 the AEF consisted of 1.2 million soldiers in forty-three infantry divisions and increased at a rate of 250,000 a month.[21] It is no wonder that the German soldiers were war weary; the numerical odds were overwhelming.

The battle at Saint-Mihiel, fought from 12 to 14 September 1918, was a great success for the Americans. After taking approximately 15,000 German EPWs, the rear areas were beginning to fill up with prisoners.[22] The Meuse-Argonne campaign was the last for the Ameri-

Alvin C. York of Tennessee won the Medal of Honor for capturing 132 German soldiers. Left to right: Representative Hull of Tennessee, York, and Senators McKellar and Chamberlain of Tennessee. Library of Congress.

cans. At Montfauçon, taken in just one day, the Americans were later forced to retreat in the face of stiff German resistance, but they took another 15,000 EPWs in the Argonne offensive in October 1918. While serving as a corporal in Company G, 328th Infantry, Eighty-second Division (also known as the All-American Division) near Chatel-Chehery, France, on 8 October 1918, Alvin C. York of Tennessee won the Medal of Honor. His citation reads:

> After his platoon had suffered heavy casualties and three other noncommissioned officers had become casualties, Corporal York assumed command. Fearlessly leading seven men, he charged with great daring a machine gun nest which was pouring deadly and incessant fire upon his platoon. In this heroic feat, the machine gun nest was taken, together with four officers and 128 men and several guns.[23]

General Julian R. Lindsey, the division commander, sent for him and said, "Well York, I hear you have captured the whole damn German army." "No sir," he replied, "I got only 132."[24] The German unit was the First Battalion, 120th Regiment, of the Second Würtemberg Land-wehr Division, a reserve unit—certainly not one of the German army's first-rate infantry divisions. Demoralized by this time, German soldiers began to surrender eagerly and in larger and larger numbers as the Western Front collapsed.

The Americans under Pershing's leadership were determined to push the Germans out of France completely. The shooting stopped on 11 November 1918, and in France, the Americans held 48,280 Germans in makeshift prison facilities, although the official divisional records reported 63,079. Like the British, the Americans used German prison-ers in labor battalions in the rear, and according to Colonel Leonard P. Ayres, "The figures for the numbers taken are from the official records of the different divisions. The total is somewhat higher than the rolls of American prisoner stockades have shown, but the difference is probably in prisoners turned over to the French or British.[25] There is no reason to doubt Ayres's numbers (see appendix 7). Pershing had no qualms cooperating with the Allies when it worked to his advantage.

Describing how the British Expeditionary Force (BEF) utilized EPWs, Craig Tibbitts of the Australian War Memorial cites an article in *Army Quarterly and Defence Journal* written by Peter T. Scott. In many ways, the AEF mirrored the BEF. Scott notes:

Each Division had its own cage, pushed as far forward as circum-stances would permit, to which prisoners were brought under Bri-gade arrangements. Here prisoners were taken over and the Provost Marshal's branch became responsible for their safe custody. From Divisional cages prisoners were sent in batches to the Corps cage where they were interrogated and dispatched to the Army cage. There they were searched and given a medical check before being sorted into those fit for work and those not. Up until 1916, all were sent for internment in Great Britain. After the losses on the Somme, with the drain on manpower and shipping, they decided to keep most of them in France to work on felling trees, quarrying stone or labouring on the docks. They were assigned to POW (labour) Companies, about 450 men apiece. During the last few months of the war, the number of camps in France and Belgium rose to over 300, with around 180,000 prisoners. They accounted for 44% of the BEF's labour force. A mid 1917 agreement between Britain, Germany and France stipulated that no prisoners could be kept closer than 30 km from the front. The armistice included a clause whereby the Allies would keep German prisoners until the peace treaty was finalised. Therefore the prisoners worked clearing the old battlefields for nearly a year, returning to their homeland in August–September 1919.[26]

Curiously, the Americans held nearly no animosity toward their German prisoners in Europe. General Pershing notes in his memoirs, "There was an officers' prison camp at Fort Penfold, nearby, which we found in satisfactory condition. Incidentally, it was everywhere noticeable that whether in prison or at work, the German soldier always retained his military bearing and his excellent discipline."[27] Perhaps the Americans had not been engaged long enough for hatred to set in. More likely, the Americans now had the Hague Convention in addition to their own General Order 100 to guide the treatment of their German prisoners. Perhaps cultural factors played a role too. From colonial times onward, the United States was home to huge numbers of German immigrants, from the Lutherans in New Sweden (New Jersey) in the late seventeenth century to the Forty-eighters fleeing Germany after their failed revolution against the powerful Prussians in 1848. German units fought in the Union Army in the Civil War. German Americans took pride in a strong German press, had strong German religious faiths, and excelled in business and civic pursuits in states such as Pennsylvania, Wisconsin, Illinois, Missouri, and Minnesota.

Americans and Germans had not been enemies on the field of battle since the Revolution. Politically, Americans had enjoyed a peaceful relationship with Germany since 1785, when Prussia and the United States signed their first agreement, the Treaty of Amity, which contained provisions against using prison hulks such as those employed by the British during the Revolution. After the signing and ratification of the treaty, no state of war came to pass between the United States and Prussia until 1917, when Prussia evolved into Imperial Germany. Nonetheless, the Treaty of Amity theoretically remained in force, regardless of the chaotic state of international politics. The real benefit was that both nations' POWs had solid protection in the form of an old and enduring treaty, General Order 100 from 1863, and a new one, the Hague Convention of 1899 and 1907, rather than depending solely on the whim of the captor or on the usual customs and traditions of war.[28]

Following the American lead in 1863, the Europeans took a very close look at Francis Lieber's General Order 100 and concluded that it could form the basis of an attempt to humanize warfare and protect their battlefield soldiers. Henri Dunant's important book *Un Souvenir de Solferino* (1862) described the inhumane fate of victims of battle in Europe. Its popularity contributed to the formation of the International Red Cross in 1864. The American Red Cross was organized in 1881 by Clara Barton and received its first federal charter in 1900. In 1905 it was brought into a closer relationship with the government when a new congressional charter was granted. When World War I broke out in 1914 the International Committee of the Red Cross (ICRC) opened the International POW Agency, which collected lists of POWs from each belligerent and transmitted them through intermediaries who functioned as protective powers for several countries. Keeping this information on cross-listed cards, the ICRC could respond to inquiries from relatives and friends. The ICRC also handled mail, money, and parcel delivery, about 1.8 million pieces, to all POWs. This work, perhaps Switzerland's greatest contribution to a world at war, continued until the office closed in 1923. It was reactivated in 1939 for the next war.[29]

Meetings were called in Geneva in 1864, 1868, and 1906 to address relief for wounded combatants, regardless of flag. The Brussels meeting, called by the Imperial Russian government in 1874, was the first European conference to consider POWs as a humanitarian as well as a military issue. At Brussels the representatives incorporated many of Lieber's suggestions from General Order 100 into the parameters of modern European warfare and developed something very new in European culture—the Brussels Code for the treatment of POWs. The Hague Conference of 1899 was called by Russian Czar Nicholas II to address disarmament, war at sea, and the establishment of a World Court to adjudicate international disputes in lieu of war. The POW provisions reflected the basic Brussels Code, and these were amended and reaffirmed in 1907 and ratified by the United States on 3 December 1909. The most significant POW provisions are reproduced in appendix 6.

Another conference was called in 1914, but the Great War interfered. At first the United States took the position that the Hague Convention was not germane because it stated that all belligerents needed to be signatories for it to be in force. Serbia and Montenegro were belligerents but not signatories; therefore, the applicability of the Hague Convention was immediately in question. Nonetheless, the United States decided to comply with its provisions and hoped that the other nations would do the same. To ensure international compliance, the United States, France, and England concluded separate treaties with the Germans in 1917 and 1918 concerning the treatment of POWs. Germany and the United States convened their conference on 23 September 1918 and signed their POW treaty on 9 November 1918, only two days before the armistice.[30] By so doing, the treatment of EPWs on all sides—5 million Allied prisoners held by the Central Powers and 3.5 million held by the Allies—was perhaps the most benevolent of the entire twentieth century. Although there were interrogations to gain military information, there were no prison hulks, no hellholes like Andersonville or Elmira, and no tortures like the water cure. Exchanges of sick and wounded POWs and diplomats took place throughout the war, and because of the ICRC's POW Agency, few prisoners starved over here or over there.

On 5 June 1918 General Peyton C. March, chief of staff in Washington, instructed General Pershing at his headquarters in Chaumont to send all German POWs to the United States. Pershing objected in part because he felt obligated to provide critical POW labor to the British and French, but before any plans could be formulated, the war came to an end.[31] In the United States, the War Department's General Order 54, issued 17 May 1917, established POW camps mostly for the 1,356 German naval personnel and 1,800 German merchant seamen who happened to be in port at the time of the declaration of war in April 1917. Another 500 German merchant crewmen came from Panama and the Philippines to the United States for internment. By war's end, 2,300 enemy alien internees added to the overall number.[32]

Under the supervision of the Office of the Adjutant General of the Army, Fort Oglethorpe opened near the Georgia-Tennessee border, just south of Chattanooga, for these sailors in 1917; another camp opened at Fort McPherson near Atlanta, Georgia, and one at Fort Douglas, Utah. The Labor Department opened a camp at Hot Springs, North Carolina, a former resort, that held approximately 4,000 EPWs and enemy aliens during the war. After 28 March 1918 Fort McPherson held all the German military and merchant marine EPWs.[33]

When the sailors at Oglethorpe and Hot Springs moved to Fort McPherson, that left Oglethorpe with mostly internees, many of whom were German intellectual elite living in the United States at the time. In most cases the EPWs ran their own camps and could work outside in road construction and other jobs.[34] Fort McPherson provided a secure environment for prisoners in both the Spanish-American War, when a small number of Spaniards were housed there, and World War I, when it held 1,300 German soldiers and sailors. Many of the German prisoners joined a number of local civilians to build Camp Jessup, another installation adjacent to Fort McPherson that served as a vehicle maintenance and supply facility.[35]

At Fort Douglas, Utah, the officers were housed in cabins consisting of three rooms: a dining-living room, a bedroom, and a kitchen (never used, because their food was brought to them from the general mess). The enlisted men were housed in 100-man barracks, slept in two-tiered bunks, and ate in the mess hall, which could seat only 100 men at a time. Great care was taken to feed these prisoners exactly what American soldiers ate, although the rations were prepared to suit their own tastes by their own German cooks. In their inspection of Fort Douglas on 20–21 November 1917, Dr. Karl Huebecher of the Swiss Commission for the Inspection of War Prison Camps in the United States and Charles Vuillenmeier, the Swiss consul, concluded that the "food and service is very good and the German cooks understand the preparation of the materials at hand in sufficient quantities."[36] Unlike the World War II camps for Germans in the United States, there was no canteen; no sales of sundries such as beer, tobacco, or chocolates; and no clothes with the letters "PW" printed on them.[37] Instead, these prisoners dressed almost like civilians.

It must have been difficult to dislike Utah. Recreation included an eighteen-piece orchestra, movies provided by the YMCA, a theater group, a brass band, choral groups, and sports. Catholic EPWs heard mass each morning; Protestant services were conducted by a local Lutheran minister every other Sunday.[38] Local civilians were kept at a distance and not allowed to mix with the prisoners, although from time to time some attempted to do that unsuccessfully. Even behind the wire, for wartime captivity, life was good. Officers received $83.35 to $95.25 per month; enlisted men received a maximum pay of $31.[39] Yet the German EPWs complained about several things. The enlisted men often complained about receiving no pay, thus preventing them from purchasing items they considered important. They also complained about a lack of clothing, shoes, socks, and work schedules. The officers complained about the lack of a canteen to buy sundries and the lack of opportunities to visit Salt Lake City and other areas of interest; oddly, although many of their wives accompanied them into internship, visits were prohibited.[40] Some prisoners escaped; only one made it to Mexico. In the end, most German military prisoners of war happily left the United States for home in September 1919. One wonders whether any EPW thought that a much larger repeat performance of years behind barbed wire would take place in their lifetime. Ferguson comments with insight that, "though weary of war, men seem not to have been weary of violence."[41] The Nazis in Germany, Fascists in Italy, and Communists in Russia proved Ferguson right without a doubt.

In addition to military prisoners of war, another important category of World War I prisoner was the enemy alien.[42] Enemy aliens—those German and Austro-Hungarian citizens living in the United States—became vulnerable to arrest after President Woodrow Wilson issued Proclamation 1364 on 6 April 1917. Without a doubt, Wilson shocked this large community when he wrote: "All natives, citizens, denizens, or subjects of a hostile nation or government, being males of the age of fourteen years and upwards, who shall be within the United States, and not actually naturalized, shall be liable to be apprehended, restrained, secured, and removed as alien enemies." Wilson ordered all alien enemies to preserve the peace toward the United States; to refrain from violating the laws of the United States and of the states and territories; to refrain from actual hostility or giving information, aid, or comfort to the enemies of the United States; and to comply strictly with the regulations promulgated by the president. Then came Article 12, the proclamation's provision for arrest:

> An alien enemy whom there may be reasonable cause to believe to be aiding or about to aid the enemy, or who may be at large to the danger of the public peace or safety, or who violates or attempts to violate, or of whom there is reasonable ground to believe that he is about to violate, any regulation duly promulgated by the President, or any criminal law of the United States, or of the States or Territories thereof, will be subject to summary arrest by the United States Marshal, or his deputy, or such other officer as the President shall designate, and to confinement in such penitentiary, prison, jail, military camp, or other place of detention as may be directed by the President.[43]

There is little doubt what Wilson meant to do with these people. German-born males older than fourteen years were also prohibited from owning guns, radios, or explosives and from making their homes within a half mile of munitions factories, aircraft stations, forts, arsenals, or naval installations. After 16 November 1917 male enemy aliens had to register at U.S. Post Offices, and it became illegal for them not to carry their registrations cards. On 18 April 1918 the restrictions extended to women as well. Germans changed their surnames; hamburgers became "liberty steaks," sauerkraut became "liberty cabbage," and frankfurters became "hot dogs"; and the German Lutheran Church switched from German to English in its religious services.[44] Mitchel Yockelson addressed this issue directly in a paper presented to the Society for Military History in April 1998. He notes critically that "scrutiny against the aliens actually commenced in August 1914."[45] By the time the United States joined the war, the Justice Department had already collected approximately 480,000 names of possible enemies living in the United States, but by the war's end, only 6,300 aliens had been arrested; those arrested by civilian authorities eventually reached the War Department for incarceration.[46] The concept of free speech in wartime, established by *Ex parte Milligan* in 1866, simply evaporated in 1917 and 1918. Included were American political prisoners arrested in the 1917 dragnet against members of the IWW, who claimed conscientious objector status but were imprisoned as radical socialists intent on destroying the U.S. government.

Enemy aliens, especially wealthy ones, enjoyed a separate barracks in their camps and often hired other prisoners to serve their personal needs.[47] Discipline was tolerable, as were their daily activities. Although 11 November 1918 marked the end of the shooting war in Europe, it did not constitute an end of the Great War. The Versailles Treaty in May 1919 did that, and the enemy aliens had to wait until the treaty was signed to begin the release process. Some were repatriated to Germany; others who wished to remain in the United States were forced to apply for residence. Several died in camp, mostly from the Spanish flu epidemic and pneumonia, as did soldiers on the Western Front and countless citizens worldwide. One alien, in a letter written to the camp commandant after his release from Fort Oglethorpe, expressed his "deep felt thanks for the excellent, fair, and just treatment, that has been accorded to me by you and those under you during my stay at the Camp. I shall never look back upon those days with regret, they have been a wonderful lesson for me, and have in many ways developed that democratic idea, that is so truly American."[48] Yet this is only one voice; one can imagine that others were far less thankful for their time spent behind barbed wire, losing their positions, homes, families, or wealth—to say nothing of personal dignity—as an enemy alien in the United States during the Great War.

The British initiated government control of public discourse in 1914. The government wanted to make certain that the country stood behind the defense of British civilization and law, and in 1914 it enacted the Defense of the Realm Act (DORA), intended, at first glance, to protect the country from treasonous acts. However, the wording was loose, and it permitted the government to control all the instruments of communication and transmission of information. The United States had a different problem. After being a neutral country for three years, the United States not surprisingly encountered problems when it abandoned isolationism and entered the war with the Allies.

The American nation was a melting pot of different ethnic groups, with the Germans being the second most populous after the Irish. Sentiments against Irish immigrants never really quieted during the nineteenth century, as evidenced by the anti-Catholic nativist movement and the Know-Nothings before the Civil War and the American Protective League at the turn of the twentieth century. The question remained, as the United States drifted toward a European war in 1917, whether these "hyphenated" Americans would fight for their native land or their adopted country. In addition, most but not all Americans supported the United States' decision to enter the war. As a result, after the declaration of war in April 1917, Wilson appointed journalist George Creel to spearhead the Committee on Public Information (CPI), which was charged "with portraying the absolute justice of America's cause and the absolute selflessness of America's aims."[49] Tasked with disseminating its own propaganda and coordinating the propaganda activities of other federal agencies, the CPI recruited approximately 78,000 "Four-Minute Men" to speak at movie theaters, carnivals, state fairs, and any other place where people gathered on topics of a wartime interest—namely, draft registration and American war aims. With these short speeches, the government secured the support of millions of Americans who believed that war was "terrible" but were "glad" to do their part to stop it.[50]

Still, there were many immigrant Germans, mainly living in the American heartland, who felt some deference for the kaiser and the fatherland, and the predominantly Catholic Irish Americans in the eastern cities remained infuriated at the British for everything. Anarchists and socialists opposed America's support of the British and French causes for economic and political reasons, and antiwar conscientious objectors opposed American entry into World War I for religious reasons or due to an Anglophobic abhorrence of becoming an ally of the British. President Wilson, a true Anglophile, had a real problem on his hands: if the United States went to war against Imperial Germany, how would the government deal with dissenters? Did anyone remember what the Supreme Court had said in *Ex parte Milligan?* How Wilson dealt with First Amendment rights in wartime became a serious issue.

Woodrow Wilson was considered to be a liberal thinker before the war, but he changed and urged Congress to develop and pass the Espionage Act. Passed on 15 June 1917, the act criminalized any action that conveyed information intended to interfere with successful military operations or promoted the success of America's enemies. Stunningly, a twenty-year prison sentence awaited those found guilty of this provision. Other provisions were added later: causing or attempting to cause insubordination, disloyalty, mutiny, refusal of duty in the military or naval forces of the United States, or willfully obstructing the recruiting or enlistment service of the United States. Awaiting anyone found guilty was a $10,000 fine and twenty years behind barbed wire. The law was later extended by the Sedition Act of 1918, which made it illegal to speak out against the government.[51]

Precedent for this legislation stretches back to the John Adams administration. Adams faced the embarrassment of the XYZ Affair and an undeclared war with France. There is no doubt that he agonized over signing a sedition act. Facing what he believed to be a challenge to American freedom, Adams chose containing antigovernment rhetoric for the good of the country over the rights of free speech of individual citizens. Passed on 14 July 1798, the Sedition Act of 1798 attempted to quiet subversion and dissent and punished persons conspiring to oppose, obstruct, or even publish writings critical of the government.

Together, the Espionage and Sedition Acts of 1917 and 1918 were stronger than the 1798 laws. They were repealed in 1921. Today, no one would find these provisions acceptable, but looking backward at the Test Acts against the Loyalists during the Revolution and the presidential executive orders against the Copperheads and other Confederate sympathizers during the Civil War, and looking forward to the government infiltration of antiwar organizations during the Vietnam era, the tradition of hard political oversight against dissent was not unthinkable as the twentieth century began. For many, these laws reinstated the category of political prisoner, along with prisoner of state and prisoner of war.

Perhaps the case of socialist labor leader Eugene V. Debs serves as the most prominent example of the era. Debs was born in Terre Haute, Indiana, on 5 November 1855 and left home at age fourteen to work on the railroad. He soon became interested in union activity, eventually becoming the president of the American Railway Union and leading a successful strike against the Great Northern Railroad in 1894. Two months later he found himself in jail for his role in a strike against the

Socialist Eugene V. Debs opposed America's entry
into World War I and was convicted of obstructing
the war program under the Espionage and Sedition
acts of 1917 and 1918. Library of Congress.

Chicago Pullman Palace Car Company. While in jail, Debs declared
himself a socialist and set the course for his lifelong political activities.
In 1901 he formed the Social Democratic Party, akin to the party of
the same name in Germany, and represented the Far Left in American
politics. He became a perennial presidential candidate and ran on the
Socialist ticket in 1904, 1908, 1912, and 1920; he received his greatest popular support—about 915,000 votes—in 1920 while he was in
jail. Opposed to America's entry into World War I, and believing the
socialist stratagem that the war was being fought by the poor to benefit
the rich, Debs was arrested for obstructing the war program under the

Espionage and Sedition acts of 1917 and 1918.[52] At trial, Debs defended himself eloquently. Recorded by leftist journalist Max Eastman for the *Liberator* in 1918, Debs addressed the jury:

> For the first time in my life I appear before a jury in a court of law to answer to an indictment for crime. I am not a lawyer. I know little about court procedure, about the rules of evidence or legal practice. I know only that you gentlemen are to hear the evidence brought against me, that the Court is to instruct you in the law, and that you are then to determine by your verdict whether I shall be branded with criminal guilt and be consigned, perhaps, to the end of my life in a felon's cell.[53]

After being found guilty, Debs responded to the judge: "Your Honor, I ask no mercy and I plead for no immunity. I realize that finally the right must prevail. I never so clearly comprehended as now the great struggle between the powers of greed and exploitation on the one hand and upon the other the rising hosts of industrial freedom and social justice."[54] Debs was released in 1921 and died in Elmhurst, Illinois, on 20 October 1926.

Debs may have been the most visible of the socialists, aliens, and Wobblies put behind barbed wire during World War I, but there were many others who were not so prominent in history. One group of seventy-eight people from Montana received a posthumous pardon in 2006 after a book written by law professor Clemens P. Work, *Darkest before Dawn,* shed light on civilian and governmental misdeeds in that era. Law students at the University of Montana's Law School brought these cases to Governor Brian Sweitzer for review.[55]

In the end, World War I saw a mixture of the old and the new relative to enemy prisoners of war, political prisoners, prisoners of state, and conscientious objectors. The army on Europe's Western Front had two rule books to guide its behavior: General Order 100 and the Hague Convention. Despite these strong documents, soldiers on the front sometimes killed the enemy wounded, declared an unofficial "no prisoner" policy before a battle, or shot EPWs on the way to the rear. But once German soldiers arrived safely behind the lines and were put into the hands of the military police, the Hague rules forced the detaining army to obey international law. Over here, as Allan Kent Powell reveals in *Splinters of a Nation,* German EPWs—mostly naval officers, naval crews, and merchant sailors taken in 1917 in American ports—enjoyed a relatively benign captivity in the American West and South. The same is true for most of the enemy aliens, especially the intellectual elites.

Political prisoners, especially the committed communist members of the Industrial Workers of the World and the Social Democratic Party, ring a less delicate bell. The war, they declared, had been contrived by industrialists in search of armament orders and vast new markets. Military discipline, in their view, was imposed on the American population as a means of social repression.[56] By 1915 these people took their stand and expelled any party member who supported the war in any way. In April 1917, during the debate in Congress over whether the United States should declare war, Republican Senator George Norris of Nebraska shouted, "I feel that we are committing sin against humanity and against our countrymen. I would like to say to this war god: You shall not coin into gold the lifeblood of my brethren. I feel that we are about to put the dollar sign upon the American flag."[57] Senator Norris was immune from any statutes concerning espionage or sedition; nongovernmental civilians such as Debs and the others were not. For this, they suffered imprisonment by the federal government, much as antiwar dissenters in wars past had suffered.

To say that Americans became disillusioned toward the entire war experience is indeed an understatement; the people of the United States saw little need for a large military, diplomatic, or intelligence establishment.[58] It is no wonder that after General John J. Pershing's army defeated the Germans on the Western Front in 1918, Wilson left Versailles in 1919 with nothing he had hoped for in a treaty Congress ultimately refused to ratify. The armistice of 11 November 1918 demanded immediate repatriation of all Allied prisoners of war under German control; however, the armistice upheld the victor's prerogative by making certain that the "return of German prisoners of war shall be settled at the conclusion of peace preliminaries."[59] Thus, these men continued to bear the burdens and hardships of being a massive workforce in Allied hands until May 1919.

To the credit of both the Allied and German sides during World War I, no harm was perpetrated by questioning prisoners of war regarding military matters.[60] Article 25 of the German-American agreement of 1918 stated the general rule: "Forcible means of any kind to compel prisoners of war to give information about their army or their country are strictly forbidden. Prisoners of war who refuse to give information may neither be threatened nor insulted nor subjected to any other treatment which puts them in a less favorable position than other prisoners."[61] Nor was anyone repatriated forcibly.

The veterans on both sides refused to forget the Great War. In Paris the AEF veterans formed the American Legion under the guidance of Colonel Theodore Roosevelt Jr., and it became the most powerful organization of its kind since the Grand Army of the Republic formed by Union veterans after the Civil War. It was anything but a social club or a lobbying organization for veterans' benefits.[62] It immediately went to work at home to promote Americanism and destroy anarchism, bolshevism, and socialism wherever and whenever possible. Red-baiting seemed to be one of its organizing principles. Its anti-IWW activism became the material of legend beginning in 1919.

In Germany, the Communist Party was rising, the kaiser had abdicated, and the weak Weimar Republic strained to hold the country together. Formed to fight the Bolsheviks in the streets, the *Freikorps* consisted of radicalized war veterans who had no hope of continuing their military careers under the limitations of the Versailles Treaty. The *Freikorps* evolved into the *Sturmabteilung* (SA) and the *Schutzstaffel* (SS) when a new movement rose from the political ashes left by the Great War. By 1933 Adolf Hitler and the National Socialist German Workers Party, or Nazis, controlled a country hungry for bread, work, stability, and national pride. More important, the Nazis sought revenge for the Allied-imposed war guilt, which the Germans never accepted. In 1929 the nations of the world gathered in Geneva, Switzerland, to rewrite the rules of war. The Great War's dead rested silently in their graves; war with its appetite for violence, death, and horror would come again soon.

NINE

Pensionierte Wehrmacht

German and Italian POWs and Internees in the United States

Vexed and quarrelsome because of hunger and thirst, we are tormented spiritually because of the uncertainty and chaos that threaten to break out at any moment.
—Helmut Hörner

Never in the history of warfare were so many human beings held behind barbed wire as during World War II (1939–1945). Categories abound: prisoners of war, internees, political prisoners, Holocaust prisoners from various countries, war criminals, disarmed enemy personnel, and prisoners of state. More than 10 million German soldiers were held as prisoners in twenty countries during and after World War II. Between 1942 and 1946 the U.S. Army held over 425,000 German, 50,000 Italian, and 5,000 Japanese prisoners in some 500 prison camps throughout the United States.[1] Beginning in 1943 with the surrender of the Afrika Korps to the British and Americans in Tunisia and then thousands of German soldiers to the Allies in France after the invasion of Normandy in June 1944, the numbers escalated until the entire Wehrmacht surrendered in May 1945.

As Helmut Hörner describes in his memoir *A German Odyssey*, the Americans created prison pens in France in 1944 but failed to feed their prisoners properly. Hunger, not the American guards, became the enemy. He recalled, "Like stupid, sick animals we squat or lie with sunken cheeks in our places. No reasonable word passes from our lips. Vexed and quarrelsome because of hunger and thirst, we are tormented spiritually because of the uncertainty and chaos that threaten to break out at any moment." In his tent, a paratrooper screamed, "Dear God in heaven, have mercy on us!"[2] In colonial times, it had been known as the "starving time"; in the European prison pens, a similar experience was imposed on recent captures. American field rations eventually reached the Germans, and although they suffered a great deal from hunger, the situation slowly stabilized, and in time they were shipped to the

United States. Naturally, like all soldiers and marines in troopships for the first time, the German soldiers suffered dreaded seasickness aboard the American Liberty ships and were delighted to reach anything that resembled land.

Once they reached the United States, few Germans failed to be impressed with cities such as New York, Boston, or Norfolk, all ports of entry for EPWs during World War II. Hörner wrote, "Our amazed focus is on the mighty monuments of stone. The skyscrapers of Manhattan, weathered, gray, cold, and foreign, completely impersonal, towering in the American sky."[3] Then they boarded trains that took them across the country. One sergeant commented to Hörner, "It is clear to me that even in this land there is much that we will have to face." Another German soldier saw through the difficulties and stated, "By comparison with Russia, the difference is like Heaven and Hell."[4] On the way, some Americans showed them kindness during their cross-country train trips, especially when they stopped in railroad stations. Hörner commented, "The Americans conduct themselves properly toward us in all places. Not one false statement or threat can be registered. Although it is easy to see the surprise in their faces when they see us, quickly they fall back into indifference, and in part sympathy for us. But visible hate is not there."[5]

When the often war-weary Germans captured in France in 1944 met EPWs from the Afrika Korps, the two groups kept their distance. The Afrikaners, captured in Tunisia shortly after the Stalingrad disaster in February 1943, remained believers in the final German victory, in the strength of Adolf Hitler and the Nazi Party, and in themselves. Commenting on the Afrika Korps prisoners, Hans Werner Richter wrote in his autobiographical novel *Die Geschlagenen* (The Defeated), "For them, since the beginning of their captivity in '43, nothing has changed in Germany; all they have heard is Nazi propaganda. In camp, they try to keep everything under their control and even try to prevent the Americans from giving information to the soldiers."[6] The Afrikaners found the new prisoners, the *Franzozen,* demoralized defeatists with little sense of pride and showing little solid resistance to their American captors. Those captured in France often arrived in the American prison camp system near the war's end and had to deal with the labor system established in 1943. Writing a letter from Camp Joseph T. Robinson in New York to his sister Viktoria in Berlin, Private Leo Korcz told her exactly what would pass an American German-speaking censor:

Dear Sister,

   You must have worried that I haven't written for a long time. Yes, the trip over here took a long time. I am well and I hope that all of you are enjoying good health. Now that you have my address, you can finally answer me. Our work consists of picking cotton. The food is good, and I have the chance to play the accordion. Please give Suzanna my hearty greetings and say to her that I will write to her although I miss that fact that she no longer lives in Berlin. From now on according to the rules, I can write, and everyone will hear from me more often.

With heartfelt greetings,

Leo[7]

   Whereas the Hague Convention attempted to first regulate the means of war and then protect the victims of war, the Geneva Convention of 1925 regulated the use of gas as a weapon of war and then in 1929 focused on the responsibilities of the belligerents toward prisoners taken on the battlefield. Its ninety-seven articles required signatories to treat EPWs much as they treated their own garrison troops, especially in terms of food, work, housing, punishment, and repatriation. Historian S. P. MacKenzie notes that "the impulse toward openly disrespecting the more onerous elements of the Geneva Convention was canceled out by the fear of what this might mean for those already in enemy hands."[8] He notes too that ten separate exchanges of seriously disabled prisoners and medical personnel took place between 1942 and 1944 through neutral ports, and the International Red Cross reported that more than 6,000 Italian and 14,000 German prisoners were exchanged for 12,400 British and other Allied POWs.[9]

   Most important, the Geneva Convention of 1929 required prisoners to give only their name, rank, and service number, nothing more. Prisoners could not be coerced into providing military information, although interrogators on both sides achieved intelligence-gathering objectives in more subtle ways. It should be noted too that more than forty nations signed the Geneva Convention. Sadly, and with great consequences to their own prisoners in German hands numbering in the millions, the Soviet government refused.[10] The Japanese government signed in Geneva but refused to ratify it at home. Thus, Soviet prisoners in German hands, and any prisoner of war in Russian or Japanese hands, enjoyed no protection whatsoever.[11]

Arnold Krammer notes that the most significant problem for American camp authorities was distinguishing among four kinds of Axis prisoners: political opportunists who used the POW experience for their own benefit; German nationalists who fought for the greater glory of the Reich; nonpolitical soldiers (the largest category), most of whom were draftees who wanted only to be left alone by both Americans and other prisoners and go home to their respective prewar professions; and dedicated Nazi Party members, sometimes SS or Gestapo, who hid among the other groups.[12] In Krammer's view, there was no such thing as a typical experience for Axis prisoners in America. They shared experiences, but the specifics differed greatly.[13] In accordance with the provisions of the 1929 Geneva Convention, officers and senior sergeants were not required to work, but some did so simply to remedy the boredom. According to historians Jake W. Spidle and Arnold Krammer, treatment was proper, just, firm, humane, and generally consistent with the 1929 Geneva Convention requirements.[14]

More than 2,000 German prisoners escaped, but for the most part they had nowhere to go and no outside help, and they were apprehended quickly by the local police, American military police, or Federal Bureau of Investigation (FBI). A considerable number of these escapees had no serious intention of escaping at all; many on them were on work details and just missed their buses and found themselves stranded in the American countryside. For committed escapees, however, being loose in the vastness of the United States became a problem.[15] After realizing that escape was a futile act, many returned of their own volition. No German escapee committed any act of sabotage, and they indulged in only minor crimes such as the theft of food, clothes, or even cars from time to time.[16] Saboteurs did arrive in the United States, however.

Near midnight on 13 June 1942 a group of four specially trained German saboteurs landed on a beach at Amagansett, Long Island, from a U-202 sailing very close to the coast. Another group of four landed at Ponte Verde, Florida. Both groups, part of the German Military Intelligence Service's Operation Pastorius, consisted of English speakers who had spent years working and living in the United States before World War II broke out. In the German spy school at Quentz Lake, about forty miles west of Berlin, they had received weapons and explosives training, but their orders were vague: blend into American society and then take whatever opportunity presented itself to commit sabotage against metal production, transportation facilities, and power stations. In the end, they proved ineffective—unlike the German saboteurs in World War I

German prisoners of war with "PW" clearly marked on their clothing. The German soldiers jokingly claimed that this stood for *Pensionierte Wehrmacht*, or military retiree. NARA, courtesy of Arnold Krammer.

who blew up the Kingsland arsenal and the Black Tom munitions plant in New Jersey. Curiously, one man, Georg Dasch, considered himself an anti-Nazi and a hero when he called the FBI and told Agent Dean F. McWhorter that he wanted to talk to J. Edgar Hoover. On 19 June 1942 Dasch called again and talked to Agent Duane L. Traynor, telling him exactly who he was and what he had been ordered to accomplish in the United States. Hoover never spoke to any of these saboteurs, but to the FBI agents, Dasch and his comrades seemed like characters in a bad movie script. Nevertheless, they told Dasch to remain in place and arrested him promptly.

With help from Dasch and another saboteur, Ernest Peter Berger, the FBI arrested the other six saboteurs in 1942 and turned them over to a military commission for adjudication. President Franklin D. Roosevelt believed that these men, including two naturalized American citizens, were traitors and spies worthy of the death penalty. On 2 July 1942

Roosevelt announced that all eight men would stand trial, but the entire event remained top secret and was never disseminated to the American press. The trial opened on 8 July, and each saboteur claimed the "under orders" defense. The case came to a temporary halt when defense attorneys attempted to use the *Ex Parte Milligan* (1866) argument, sending the case to the Supreme Court for review. On 31 July 1942 the Court flatly refused to apply the *Milligan* defense and allowed the military commission to continue the trial.[17] The verdict was no surprise: Dasch and Berger went to prison, having been spared the death sentence for their help in the capture and prosecution of the other spies. Six suffered death in the electric chair on 8 August 1942, one after the other. In 1948 Dasch and Berger were returned to Germany, where they suffered constant harassment from their neighbors.[18]

Noted POW historians such as Arnold Krammer in the United States and Erich Maschte, Günter Bischof, Hermann Jung, and Kurt Böhme in Germany, as well as former German EPWs Alfred Andersch, Helmut Hörner, and Hans Werner Richter, agree that the Germans' American, British, and Canadian POW experiences were relatively benign. For example, German soldiers jokingly called the "PW" stamped on the backs of their shirts and trousers *Pensionierte Wehrmacht,* or "military retiree," meaning they considered themselves put out to pasture. There were indeed instances of German prisoners harassing and killing one another in ideological disputes; however, most German POWs spent their years uneventfully and in many cases enjoyably. They worked on farms; studied literature, history, and politics; played endless soccer matches and card games; developed their own theater; and attended church services performed by their own captured chaplains or German-speaking local clergy.

Following the provisions of Article 21 of the 1929 Geneva Convention to the end, the American government paid all the former German POWs held in the United States both their salaries (concurrent with their respective ranks) and the monies they earned for their work during incarceration. Officers received monthly salaries of $20 for lieutenants, $30 for captains and $40 for majors and officers of higher rank.[19] For work outside the camp (known as class II labor), including supervisory work, German prisoners, including the officers who volunteered to work, received 80 cents a day, which they could use as canteen coupons or have credited to a trust fund account that would be paid to them, according to Article 34, at the end of their captivity.[20] Upon repatriation, nearly all the German prisoners stuffed their duffel bags full of

German POWs performed agricultural work throughout the United States until their repatriation in 1946. NARA, courtesy of Arnold Krammer.

canteen articles they knew their families would need in the postwar occupation.

What happened to the German generals? After all, these senior officers were a special class of prisoner, at least to the British. Krammer notes that the German armed forces contained 3,363 generals, compared with just over 1,500 in the American army.[21] The treatment varied considerably between the British and the Americans. The British, much like the Germans, still linked class to rank and bestowed an array of comforts on their captured German generals. Reminiscent of the cordial relationship between Generals Horatio Gates and John Burgoyne after the surrender at Saratoga in 1777, General Bernard Montgomery invited Lieutenant General Ritter von Thoma (after his capture at Tel el Mamspra) to a sumptuous dinner where the two men spent the evening discussing the battle.[22] In Britain, the generals of the Afrika Korps, including the commanding general Jürgen von Arnim, made their home in a barbed wire enclosure at nicely manicured Wilton Park.

British intelligence exploited these senior officers for information of all kinds during their long conversations, but because the British Isles were so full of German and Italian EPWs, the British offered the Americans a "parcel" of five German generals in the spirit of diplomacy and Allied cooperation. The War Department was delighted to get them and, after their arrival and in-processing at Fort George Meade in Maryland, shipped them off to posh Byron Hot Springs, California, for a two-month interrogation program. The problem was that the Americans had little experience in exploiting senior officers, and the interrogations simply ran out of steam. What to do? On 28 August 1943 the War Department transferred the generals first to Camp Mexia, Texas, and then to the newly operational Camp Clinton, not far from Jackson, Mississippi. Already there were thousands of Afrika Korps EPWs, who turned out to welcome their generals on 22 September 1943. They lived well; their quarters were neat, clean, and so ornate that the prisoners themselves called it the "Ritz."[23]

Unlike the British, the Americans saw no real need to treat these senior officers with any more deference than was minimally required by regulations. Krammer points out that "the generals complained about being 'razzed' from sentry towers, and mimicked by goose-stepping guards along the fence. Once in a while their gardens were trampled at night."[24] They complained, but Colonel James McIlhenny, a hard-bitten former sergeant and the camp commandant, did little on their behalf. After an inspection and deep criticism of the camp's leadership, the Americans changed command, and Major General Preston Brown took over. Brown's war record dated back to World War I, which delighted the German generals, and life at Camp Clinton became more bearable.[25]

The only real exploitation exercised by the Americans came in the form of debriefs or "lessons learned," which the generals gladly wrote in great detail for the American Historical Division when they got back to Germany after the war. Unlike the British, the Americans saw these generals as relics of a despised class-based system that they had defeated completely. They believed that the American military services had little to learn and thus had little reason to pamper them. The age of chivalry was fast coming to an end.

Each camp in the United States had a canteen where prisoners could buy personal sundries and a library full of books, including the twenty-four-volume Libraries of the New World collection published in Stockholm by Bermann-Fischer, with titles such as Erich Marie Remarque's

All Quiet on the Western Front, Thomas Mann's *Zauberberg,* Franz Werfel's *Song of Bernadette,* and other literary classics the Nazis had forbidden in Germany for over a decade. In a short commentary in the intercamp journal *Der Ruf* (The Calling), German prisoner Curt Vinz wrote, "Had we only had the opportunity to read these books before, our introduction to life and to war, the expanse of politics would have been different."[26] After the war, Bermann-Fischer returned to Germany as Fischer Verlag, specializing in publishing inexpensive volumes of classic literature, and *Der Ruf,* which achieved moderate popularity among the more literary prisoners, continued as an important literary journal in the western zone of occupied Germany until 1947, when American occupation authorities banned it under the pretext that paper was scarce.[27] Once they started in the prison camps in the United States, German literary efforts could not be stopped, and one long-range, positive effect of American captivity was the new beginning of German letters following the mass repatriations and discharges from 1945 to 1947.

Even better conditions existed in Canada, where German POWs enjoyed better than adequate treatment; it was so good, in fact, that many ex-prisoners returned to settle there after the war. Much like Australia's lenient policy, in Canada the guards were not stern military police, as they often were in the United States; rather, the force consisted mainly of kind old veterans of the Great War who patriotically volunteered for POW camp guard duty.[28]

Paradoxically, it was from law-abiding Canada that the most famous German escapee, twenty-six-year-old Luftwaffe Oberleutnant Franz von Werra, slipped his bonds and fled to the United States in 1941, before the Americans entered the war. In a biographical thriller, Kendal Burt and James Leasor lionize von Werra's winter escape from Canada across the frozen St. Lawrence River in *The One that Got Away.* Once in the United States, the American popular media pounced on von Werra's story so tenaciously that the German authorities secretly sent him to Mexico, where the German embassy arranged a passport under an assumed name and secured his passage back to Germany in April 1941 via Rio de Janeiro and Rome. At home, after one of the most daring exploits in the war up to that point, von Werra received a promotion and the Knight's Cross for valor, but the Nazi press remained silent.[29]

Von Werra's next assignment took him to Luftwaffe intelligence, where his experiences had some long-range effects on Allied airmen for the next four years of hostilities in Europe. Shortly after being shot down over England in 1940 during the Battle of Britain, his first experiences with skilled British interrogators had been deceptively positive. As a young man, he found them unexpectedly cordial, sometimes elderly, and always curious about trivialities. In time, however, von Werra discovered that these skilled intelligence officers could piece together entire dossiers from the most minute and seemingly trivial details provided by their prisoners. In captivity, von Werra began collecting stories from other German pilots in British hands and discovered that his treatment had been anything but unique. They had all been subjected to an extremely successful technique to develop military intelligence significant to the British war effort. As a result, German military intelligence expanded von Werra's after-action report into a small booklet issued to all Luftwaffe pilots engaging the western Allies. Further, von Werra participated in formulating the interrogation procedures used in the Durchgangslager Luftwaffe, the German air force's transient camp near Wetzlar that existed solely to collect intelligence from captured Allied airmen.[30] He also toured POW camps and urged good treatment in order to secure intelligence from Allied POWs. However, the Nazi Propaganda Ministry banned the publication of his book manuscript, *Mein Flucht aus England* (My Escape from England), in part because it believed the book was far too pro-British, and in part because von Werra never actually escaped from England. On 25 October 1941 Franz von Werra died on a routine patrol off the coast of Holland after his ME-109 developed engine trouble and crashed into the sea. Without a doubt, he was one of the most colorful characters of World War II. After Burt and Leasor's heroic biography told his story in print, it found its way to the silver screen in both German and English.[31]

As the Allies pressed the war toward Germany and took more prisoners on land, the Royal and American navies captured more submarine crews at sea. Otto Kretschmer, the German navy's ace U-boat captain, surrendered to the Royal Navy's HMS *Walker* after the British sank his U-99. After being sent to Canada's Bowmansville prison camp, he organized a tunnel escape based on coded letters sent from naval headquarters in Berlin. Only one officer managed to leave the camp, but he was picked up by shore patrols.[32] Kretschmer, never a member of the Nazi Party, retained his sense of honor and enjoyed a renewed career in the Federal Republic of Germany's Bundesmarine later.

Captain Wolfgang Hermann Hellfritsch escaped from the POW camp at Crossville, Tennessee, on 23 October 1943. He spoke fluent English, found work as a farmhand, and was free for seven months before his recapture. Three German sailors escaped from Crossville into the high mountains nearby, but when they stopped at a cabin for water, an old woman shot one man with birdshot and told the others to "Git." When told that she had shot at German POWs, the granny sobbed and replied, "I thought they wuz Yankees."[33]

Arizona was the site of perhaps the only mass escape of German EPWs in the United States. German officers understood the Geneva Convention's rules as well as the British and the Americans. and they knew there could be no reprisals because of escape attempts. For all military prisoners, escape was their duty. Led by frigate Captain Jürgen Wattenberg, a group of twenty-five navy men, including officers Hans Werner Kraus, Friedrich Guggenberger, August Maus, and Jürgen Quaet-Faslem, masterminded, built, and escaped through the 178-foot "Faustball Tunnel" from Camp Papago Park near Phoenix on 24 December 1944.[34] Their objective was to cross into Mexico, but Mexico stood with the Allies during World War II. Free for only a short time, with no reliable maps, no plans, and no outside help, nearly all the Faustball escapees were recaptured quickly. Only one prisoner, Walter Kozur, spent weeks in the Arizona mountains. There were, however, other German escapees, 2,222 in all. For some, recapture came shortly after leaving the camps; for others, recapture came years after the war's end, and one man held out in the United States into his middle age.[35]

After Allied armies liberated Nazi death camps such as Dachau, Buchenwald, Bergen Belsen, Flossenberg, and Auschwitz in 1945, calls for retribution against German EPWs in the United States began to raise the temperature in the national media. Inside the camps, the Americans required all German prisoners to attend documentary films of the Holocaust concentration camps, called *Knockenfilmen,* or "bone films." Many German soldiers and sailors refused to believe what they saw. When Helmut Hörner and his friends saw the films, he lamented:

> The newspapers have poisoned the whole atmosphere with their reports of the German concentration camps about whose existence we had no idea. We knew that Hitler locked up those who spoke against him, but the gassing and complete destruction of the Jewish people in the lands controlled by the Third Reich was not known to anyone among us. But now we have to bear the consequences of the inhumane crimes, even though it surpasses our understanding to believe these atrocities happened.[36]

But in all cases, the German EPWs were ordered to sit and discuss what they saw. Some prisoners maintained that the dead were actually Germans killed by Allied air raids on Hamburg, Münster, or Dresden. From time to time, a German prisoner confessed quietly to his peers that he had known about this or that camp, or that he might have known about the *Einsatzgruppen* (Special Operations Groups) in Poland and Russia that rounded up and murdered Jews and other innocents in the conquered lands. For these men, it was a sobering experience.

Cries of "coddling" began to appear in the press, and rumors began to spread about something the German prisoners really feared—transfer to French or, worse, Russian prison camps in Europe. Conditions worsened rapidly for the German EPWs in the American camps following the Nazi surrender on 8 May 1945, and as historians and popular writers such as Kurt Böhme and James Bacque point out, conditions became catastrophic in Europe.[37] In the United States, the provost marshal changed the German EPWs' status from prisoner of war to "disarmed enemy personnel." By so doing, American authorities could reduce food and tobacco rations, and they closed canteens or reduced the items sold, leaving the Germans with canteen coupons earned from working but no place to spend them. With a grim future in Europe, with knowledge of the Holocaust, and with conditions deteriorating in the American camps, the German EPWs faced an uncertain future.

Any attempt to propagandize prisoners of war was clearly against the Geneva Convention. With some exceptions—such as the efforts of Mildred "Axis Sally" Gillers and Iva "Tokyo Rose" Toguri, broadcasting shows on the radio—neither the Germans nor the Japanese made substantial attempts to convert their American prisoners to their respective national or cultural philosophies. The Office of Strategic Services (OSS) ran Operation Sauerkraut to entice German soldiers to quit the fight and surrender in Italy. Between July 1944 and May 1945, thirteen Sauerkraut missions distributed more than 15,000 leaflets, and the German EPWs, now OSS "spies," brought in a considerable number of prisoners.[38] However, the Russians worked feverously to convince their German prisoners, especially after the fall of Stalingrad in 1943, that communism was not only viable but also essential to revitalize Germany in the postwar period. The prisoners called the pseudo-communist camp organization AntiFa, short for anti fascism; the officer version was called the League of German Officers, and both became the roots of the Communist Party of Germany in the postwar period and the political foundation of the German Democratic Republic in communist East

Germany. Historian Frank Biess estimates that approximately 70,000 German POWs participated in three- or six-month courses at 120 camp schools, 50 regional schools, and 2 central schools. The courses offered doctrinaire Marxism in a way that highlighted the advantages of "scientific socialism," the history of the Soviet Union, and the history of the Communist Party.[39] Upon the repatriation of 1,125,352 German Wehrmacht soldiers held by the Red Army and later the NKVD (People's Commissariat of Internal Affairs), most rejected communist reeducation and fled to the West.[40]

By late 1943 the American War Department knew about the Soviet efforts, became concerned, and began to look into doing something similar but less offensive. The American idea was to send Germans home as democrats, with the grand hope that American-style democracy and federalism might take hold among the true anti-Nazis in their midst. Writing in January 1944, Dr. Curt Bondy of the College of William and Mary stated that the German soldiers "must experience what freedom of speech means in this country, by reading periodicals, newspapers, listening to the radio, and by having discussions." He suggested too that "a special study would be necessary to determine how far methods of mass and group education could be applied with these prisoners."[41]

Publisher Henry R. Luce writing in 1941 encapsulated the dream of American influence in the twentieth century:

> America as the dynamic center of ever-widening spheres of enterprise, America as the training center of the skillful servants of mankind, America as the Good Samaritan, really believing again that it is more blessed to give than to receive, and America as the powerhouse of the ideals of Freedom and Justice—out of these four elements can be fashioned a vision of the 20th century to which we can devote ourselves in gladness and enthusiasm. It is in this spirit that all of us are called, each to his own measure of capacity, and each in the widest horizon of his vision, to create the first great American century.[42]

This context functioned as the organizing principle for reeducating the Germans; however, American authorities failed to undermine the cohesion of the German EPW subculture.[43] To fix this problem, the U.S. Army created the Special Projects Division (SPD) under Edward Davison, a former professor at the University of Colorado, as a new branch of the Office of the Provost Marshal. Called the Factory, its first major product was the EPW journal *Der Ruf*, more an intellectual than an entertainment instrument, but effective nonetheless in reaching those strong anti-Nazi prisoners who would become prominent personalities in postwar German letters.[44] Composed by anti-Nazi prisoners under American supervision, the first nonpolitical edition appeared on 1 March 1945 and increased publication to two editions per month by May at a price of 5 cents per copy. Then *Der Ruf* changed radically. The German editors took strong political positions concerning what postwar Germany would look like. Socialists such as Hans Werner Richter rejected anything like collective guilt and suggested that a new socialist Germany should stand as a buffer between capitalist America and communist Russia.

For average EPWs, the heavily politicized, academic *Der Ruf* played virtually no role in their lives behind the wire. Historian Ron Robin comments, "*Der Ruf* failed to accomplish its goals because its editors and mentors maintained their studious detachment from the concerns of ordinary POWs. As such, *Der Ruf* introduced nothing new into the lives of the cross section of the German nation incarcerated in the camps."[45] German POW Helmut Hörner agreed and commented, "Do you seriously believe that this newspaper was produced by German prisoners of war?"[46] Skepticism of the validity of *Der Ruf* remained strong, especially among the nonpolitical EPWs. The SPD understood that *Der Ruf* enjoyed a limited and skeptical audience but decided that the imperative remained to reach the thousands of Germans getting ready for repatriation. The answer rested not only in the continuation of *Der Ruf* but also in the creation of an undergraduate crash course in American democracy for moderate anti-Nazis at Fort Kearney, Rhode Island. Ambitious in its approach, the program featured classes in history and political science, stressing that the guiding hands of the future welfare of a new Germany belonged to these men. As with most inmates in any prison, education is understood to be a pathway to early release, and in the spring of 1946 German EPWs were more than ready to go home. For departing prisoners, the SPD created a two-week course in the American way of life, politics, and other topics at Camp Upton in New York. Some prisoners were indeed genuinely interested; for others, it was just another hoop the Americans forced them to jump through. They sat, listened, responded, and thought only of going home.

The last shipload of German former prisoners of war sailed for Europe and final repatriation in July 1946, but few went home directly. Instead, the healthy, well-fed, often suntanned former prisoners of the Americans were shipped to Le Havre, France, or Portsmouth, England, where they were used as forced labor, some for two years before being allowed to go home with a discharge in hand. The French were particularly bitter toward the German prisoners returning from the United States and held them the longest of the western European countries, until 1948.[47] However, in 1946 war erupted in Indochina as the communist Vietminh attempted to wrest independence from France. France needed soldiers and offered many former German soldiers the opportunity to fight the communists in the jungles of Vietnam, Cambodia, and Laos rather than dig up land mines in France. Hundreds of Germans, all anticommunist professional soldiers, joined the French Foreign Legion at this time and were shipped out to another war.[48]

Remaining behind in the United States were forty-three men who were missing in action—twenty-eight German and fifteen Italian escapees known to be at large somewhere in the country. In 1947 the FBI apprehended a few; in 1953 the Bureau finally recaptured one of the most elusive and successful of all the German escapees, Sergeant Reinhold Pabel. Captured in Sicily during the fighting in 1943, by 1944 Pabel sat in Camp Ellis near Washington, Illinois. Having learned English, he eagerly read American newspapers and magazines, one of which was an article written by J. Edgar Hoover titled "Enemies at Large" published in the April 1944 edition of *American Magazine*.[49] To escape-minded Pabel, Hoover's warnings became his guidelines: do it alone and tell no one about your plans, have some ready cash on hand, talk to no one unless it becomes absolutely necessary, and go as far and as fast as possible.[50]

After the war's end in May 1945, Pabel suffered from tensions caused by continuous hunger, the accelerated American reeducation program, and camp rumors about the proposed Morgenthau Plan that promised Germany a postwar future without industry, growth, or virtually any recovery at all. By August 1945 Pabel knew enough English to mingle freely with Americans and decided that he had had enough of being behind barbed wire. He called his plan Operation Vapor—the idea being to disappear into mainstream, war-weary, but optimistic America and fend for himself. Taking Hoover's advice, he saved up $15 in contraband cash and managed to obtain some roadmaps to his target, busy Chicago, where he could easily blend into the congestion of a large city full of a century's worth of European immigrants. His obtained his first job washing dishes by identifying himself as a Dutch refugee and taking an alias: Phil Brick. As Brick, Pabel married an American woman and opened a small bookstore in Chicago. In 1953 the FBI appeared and arrested him as an escaped POW and an illegal resident. After one trip back to the United States and a television interview with the popular journalist Dave Garroway, Pabel settled down in Hamburg, where he continued his book business until he retired. Pabel died in 1995.

After the Pabel case, the FBI arrested two more German escapees—Harry Girth, a house painter in Atlantic City, New Jersey, in 1953, and Kurt Rossmeisl in 1959. The last German POW in America was Georg Gaertner, who escaped from the prison camp at Alamogordo Army Air Field in 1945. Why did he escape? He said:

> I was a product of Discipline and Order. And after three years in the *Wehrmacht* and another two in American POW camps, I decided that I had had enough! No one was going to tell me what to do again. I was twenty-four, after all, and wanted to travel, meet girls, play sports, and meet girls. And where better to find that independence than in America? We'd been lectured to death about the virtues of democracy; it was time to see for myself.[51]

He escaped on 22 September 1945 and remained a fugitive until the early 1980s. Although he created a home and family in the United States, Gaertner realized that evading the law for the rest of his life was unacceptable. He first contacted Professor Arnold Krammer at Texas A&M University and then surrendered to the FBI of his own free will. Krammer helped Gaertner tell his story in *Hitler's Last Soldier in America.* Krammer notes that between 1948 and 1960, 30,000 immigrants came from Germany each year, and there is no way to know exactly how many were former POWs. Krammer estimates approximately 5,000 men.[52]

The first Italians were taken prisoner of war in the 1941–1942 British campaign in North Africa and were sent to England, to British-held locations in the Middle East, Kenya, and South Africa, and to Australia.[53] By May 1943 the British and Americans closed in on Tunisia, and all Axis forces surrendered. Whereas the German members of the Afrika Korps remained faithful to the belief in a German victory for most of their time in American captivity, most Italians held no such beliefs. They were weary early in the war and were, for the most part, delighted to surrender. In northern Italy the Germans captured 640,000 Italian officers and men in 1943 when Italy changed sides and held them in German prison camps, where some 30,000 died.[54] In the United States nearly 50,000 Italian prisoners sat behind barbed wire in twenty-three states. According to historian Louis Keefer, the first weeks in America consisted of "good food, hot showers, and clean beds," things the Italians had not enjoyed in years of hard fighting in North Africa. "Glad to be safely out of the war," writes Keefer, "they had not yet begun to worry about the long years they would have to endure before going home."[55] Although the Italians arrived in the United States with the Afrika Korps, the two groups of EPWs mixed very little.

The American media painted the Germans and Japanese as monsters, but not the Italians. They seemed to be cooperative, and as Keefer notes, there "emerged a stereotype Italian prisoner: easy-going, humble, not too disciplined, sometimes sloppy in his appearance, anything but dangerous, a happy-go-lucky fellow with a laugh and a smile, unlikely to escape, and just happy to be in America."[56] Like all stereotypes, such composite images may have bits of truth in the telling and lots of falsehoods in the application. Nevertheless, both Germans and Italians worked inside and outside their camps, filling a huge need for labor in the United States. After all, crops needed to be harvested, roads built, trees felled, and fruit picked.[57] They did it all, for the most part happily, but the status of the Italians changed after General Pietro Badoglio took over the Italian government and negotiated an armistice with the British and Americans, signed at the Fairfield Camp, Sicily, on 3 September 1943, which began Italy's future as an Ally. Article 3 of the armistice required the Italians to turn over all POWs and internees to the Allies and not permit the Germans to transport them to Germany. However, after a two- or three-day lull, Italian guards left their posts, and German guards arrived. Although there were hundreds of Allied escapes, most of the Allied POWs remained where they were, as ordered by the British "stay-in-place" order. In 1943 they became POWs of the Nazis and were sent north by train to German prison camps.[58] Thus, the Allies decided to keep the Italians as EPWs rather than repatriating them, but toying with their status was imminent.[59]

It is an odd happenstance in modern times when an enemy changes sides during wartime. Especially difficult to devise was some kind of new or different status for the Italian EPWs, which the U.S. Army had used as a labor force in North Africa in 1943. As of 26 January 1944 the Italians in captivity in the United States numbered 3,642 officers, 7,115 noncommissioned officers, and 39,068 enlisted men, and the plan to establish a labor force was approved on 12 February 1944 in secrecy, with John B. Eager designated commandant.[60] On 13 March 1944 the U.S. Army's adjutant general established Italian Service Units (ISUs), a unique kind of volunteer military unit consisting of unarmed Italian

Many Italian EPWs were members of Italian Service Units, volunteer military units led by Italian officers but supervised by senior Allied officers. U.S. Army Signal Corps photograph, courtesy of the Special Collections Department, Stewart Library, Weber State University.

EPWs led by their own officers but supervised by Allied senior officers. With this new status, the Italians remained prisoners of war, but in practice, a heavy burden was certainly lifted from their shoulders.

To join an ISU, an Italian EPW signed a promise that, because of the armistice between Italy and the United States, he would "work on the behalf of the United States of America at any place, on any task except in actual combat, and that he will assist the United States to the best of his ability in the prosecution of its cause against the common enemy, Germany."[61] Most men, the antifascists at least, were delighted to sign. According to John Hammond Moore, each enlisted man was given a standard GI uniform with a distinctive green shoulder patch bearing the word "Italy"; $24 a month, one-third in cash and two-thirds in post exchange scrip; freedom to use most of the camp facilities open to American soldiers; and, in time, passes to visit nearby towns and cities.[62]

The ISU was a good deal for the Italians, but it was neither complete freedom nor utopia. POW status remained intact despite their freedoms, and as 1944 turned into 1945, social problems crept into the scene. First, many Italians were country boys and lacked a technical education; thus they worked well in agriculture and general labor, but complex machines were often difficult for them to master. A second problem involved race relations between black soldiers and members of the ISUs. On 14 August 1944 a riot erupted at Camp George Johnson near Fort Lawton in Seattle, Washington, between the Italians and black soldiers when Private Guglielmo Olivotto was found hanged on the base.[63] Third, the men of the ISUs sought female companionship, and some women obliged at dances and other social occasions. With some predictability, the Pentagon banned marriages for ISU members on 14 December 1944 and kept the ban in place until repatriation. Some men married before the ban went into place, however, and the government could not prohibit engagements. After VE Day on 8 May 1945, it became even more difficult to restrict ISU men from visiting the private homes of Italian Americans, who welcomed them. As the War Department learned, "Love conquers all" is not a proverb to be tampered with.

The ISUs disbanded in September 1945, and the Italians were quickly repatriated to war-torn Italy. American fiancées followed and often married in Italy before bringing their new husbands back to the United States. Yet the idea of creating and maintaining an ISU of enemy prisoners of war was one of the more fuzzy inconsistencies of American policy during World War II. No one, certainly not the War Department or anyone directly involved, was completely satisfied. Charges of "coddling" these men rose often to a fever pitch in regional newspapers comparing their treatment to the treatment of Americans in German prison camps. However, one thing is certain in terms of both the German and Italian EPWs: if one had to be captured in war, being captured by the Americans might ensure survival.

As in World War I, foreign enemy aliens also found themselves interned by the United States as prisoners of state. Approximately 600,000 Italian citizens, legal immigrants who had not yet received American citizenship, were classified as enemy aliens in the United States during World War II. Along with merchant marine sailors, visitors, and some diplomats, about 1,600 Italian aliens faced arrest by the FBI, and approximately 300 were considered supporters of Italy's fascist regime and subsequently interned at Fort Missoula in western Montana, called Bella Vista by the inmates. On the West Coast, about 10,000 Italians were forced to move from their longtime homes inland and lost their livelihoods in the process. In 1942 the movements of other people not interned were restricted to five miles from their homes.

On the positive side, anti-Italian feelings in the United States lasted for a relatively short time, about a year. President Franklin D. Roosevelt sought Italian American support for the war effort in general and especially for the invasion of Italy after the Allied successes in North Africa in 1943.[64] In 1999, as a result of lobbying by the Italian American community, Congress addressed the treatment of Italian Americans during World War II. House Resolution 2442 acknowledged that the United States had violated the civil rights of Italian Americans during World War II. The bill was passed in the House of Representatives in 1999 and the Senate in 2000; it was signed by President Clinton in 2000.[65]

The situation with German aliens was quite different. As in the past, expediency and principles came into conflict. During the Revolution, the Patriots wreaked havoc on their Loyalist neighbors. The Alien Enemies Act of 1792 targeted the French who were making trouble in the United States, and part of the Alien and Sedition Act was never repealed. During the Mexican War, nativists created enormous amounts of trouble for Catholic immigrants in and outside the army. Regardless of the principle of wartime civil rights expressed in *Ex parte Milligan* in 1866, Woodrow Wilson lowered the governmental hammer on immigrants and foreigners during World War I. Thus, what took place during World War II was neither surprising nor unique. As Krammer notes in *Undue Process,* his brilliant study of German enemy alien internees, "Foreigners in any country have always been viewed with some suspicion, especially during times of international tension."[66]

The first problem in the German American community was the German American Bund, a solidly Nazi organization of about 10,000 members headed by Fritz Kuhn in 1934. The Bund held pro-Nazi rallies up to the declaration of war in December 1941, and eventually Kuhn was interned with other enemy aliens and deported to Germany after the war, where he died in Munich in 1951.[67] If the government's anti-German activities during World War I serve as a yardstick for what it could do, legally or illegally, this sort of activity put German American citizens and German immigrants in peril, especially those who had not yet been granted American citizenship.

When the Hobbs bill became law on 5 May 1939, foreigners suddenly became a very suspicious group. Similar to what Woodrow Wilson had done in 1917, Franklin D. Roosevelt created the Emergency Detention Program. which, in the event of war, could incarcerate anyone the

Justice Department considered dangerous. J. Edgar Hoover, suspicious by nature of just about everyone and everything, illegally created the super-secret Custodial Detention Index, which contained thousands of names to be investigated in case war broke out. When that happened, the FBI was more than ready to take on the perceived enemy within America's borders.

The first enemy alien internment camp was Fort Stanton in rural New Mexico. It held about 400 German sailors from the German luxury liner SS *Columbus,* scuttled by its captain, Wilhelm Daehne, on 19 December 1939 to prevent British capture. At first the crew were "guests"; then, after war broke out, they became interned enemy aliens, as did many thousands of Germans living in the United States. On 27 August 1940 Congress passed the Alien Registration Act, which required all noncitizen immigrants to register at their local post offices.[68] Although such a procedure is foreign to Americans, in Europe all citizens and foreigners are required to register their names and addresses with the local police to this day. There, it is simply a matter of custom, in one sense. However, introduced by Napoleon in the nineteenth century in every conquered land, registration makes it easy for the police to arrest anyone under suspicion of a crime of any sort, civil or political.

Diplomats were arrested immediately after war was declared. Instead of being sent to bleak internment camps, these people went to luxury hotels like the Greenbrier in West Virginia's hill country and others in Asheville, North Carolina, Cincinnati, Ohio, and New Orleans, Louisiana. By April 1942 all the diplomats left for home aboard neutral ships. Next, civilian enemy aliens were brought before rather hostile boards for hearings. These boards, first established on 2 February 1942, consisted of representatives from the FBI, the Immigration and Naturalization Service (INS), and the Justice Department. The aliens were often asked leading questions simply to establish their guilt or guilt by association with Nazi organizations. Many enemy aliens on the East Coast wound up imprisoned on Ellis Island, New York. Aside from the belief that these aliens were connected to the Nazi movement at home, Krammer concludes that they were also being used as bargaining chips for Americans held by the three Axis countries.[69]

Whereas the U.S. Army operated all the prisoner of war camps, the INS operated most of the internment camps. Border patrolmen rather than soldiers guarded them. Inside these camps, one found not only enemy aliens who lived in the United States but also many Germans, known as "detainees," who had been sent to the United States from

Latin America, where prewar German populations had grown along with opportunities for European companies to expand. Additionally, there were Jewish refugees from the Nazis living in Latin America; despite being oppressed by the Nazis in Europe, they were considered German citizens in their respective host countries. It took the efforts of the American Jewish Joint Distribution Committee, the National Refugee Service, Catholic groups, the American Civil Liberties Union, and many other organizations to untangle the complexities and force the State Department to permit them to resettle in the United States after finding sponsors.

Life in the internment camps was boring, much like life in POW camps, but these Americanized Germans found ways to integrate American and German lifeways. Food was adequate for the most part; no one starved, and no guards shot anyone. Escapes were few and unsuccessful. By war's end, 4,450 Germans and their families were exchanged through the good offices of the Swiss Legation and Swedish ships, most aboard the SS *Gripsholm* and *Drottningholm*. Most of the others returned to their old professions when and where possible. Yet, as Krammer concludes from his interviews, many former interned enemy aliens lamented their time behind the wire in terms of their personal losses: wealth, reputation in their communities, and personal honor.[70] In the end, of the more than 300,000 Germans living in the United States with or without American citizenship, the FBI arrested 10,905, a rather small percentage. A total of 31,275 enemy aliens from Germany, Italy, Hungary, Bulgaria, Romania, Japan, and other countries were interned in fifty-four camps and holding facilities during World War II.[71]

There is little doubt that American policies toward EPWs brought to the United States were fair, humane, and even generous. Properly housed and fed, German and Italian EPWs left in much better condition than they arrived, and the 1942–1946 era marked perhaps America's finest hour. By strict adherence to the Geneva Convention, the moral high ground was most certainly achieved. Problems, however, arose in postwar Europe when the Americans were forced to address the unexpected: the surrender of an entire army and how to feed and house it.

As was true during the war years 1917–1918, the war years of 1941–1945 were not good times to be an immigrant in the United States, especially if one came from an enemy country. After arrest and incarceration in one of the many camps, these people lost everything they possessed: homes, businesses, personal assets, friendships, status in their communities, and even families. It is true that any country can legally rid itself of enemy aliens in time of war; however, one must wonder why the United States was so heavy-handed about it. Then again, with guardians like J. Edgar Hoover and the FBI of that era, could one expect anything else?

In 1995 Germany celebrated the fiftieth anniversary of the end of World War II. Many young Germans believe that the Allies liberated them too. During the summer of 1994 the Russians and Americans decommissioned their respective commands in Berlin, but forty years earlier, on 24 October each year from 1950 to 1954, the German police stopped all street traffic, buses, and highway movement to remember in silence the "Day of German Prisoners of War" who still remained in the Soviet Union. All this was done to keep the issue before the public eye. Chancellor Konrad Adenauer and the German Red Cross were directly responsible for the return of over 10,000 German POWs from Russia in 1954, and although they came home in their tattered ten-year-old Wehrmacht uniforms, the men were generally well received. Like all POWs, escapees, or full-term prisoners, they were glad to be home.[72] In an act of supreme irony, the Germans returned to Holoman Air Force Base near Alamogordo, New Mexico, in 1996, where the new German Luftwaffe shared part of the base to train its jet pilots.[73] Instead of coming as enemy prisoners of war, this time the Germans came as friends and allies.

TEN

The Reborn

Japanese Soldiers as Enemy Prisoners of War and American Nisei Internees

Our capture is equal to our rebirth. We are born again. It is our solemn obligation to live this renewed life as men.
—Kazuo Sakamaki

The Japanese did not begin the twentieth century as draconian captors or suicidal maniacs. The radical change in Japanese military attitudes and behavior toward prisoners of war in World War II and their collective decision against surrender were formed in part as a result of cultural retribution for European double-dealing in the early part of the twentieth century and the development of militant Bushido. Originally issued as *Japanese Army Regulations for Handling Prisoners of War* in February 1904, Army Instruction 22, Article 2 of the General Rules, stated, "Prisoners of war shall be treated with a spirit of goodwill and shall never be subjected to cruelties or humiliation."[1] From 1904 until 1945, a down-spiraling series of events proved fateful.

After stunning victories during the Russo-Japanese War in 1904 and 1905, the Japanese took considerable numbers of Russian prisoners and treated them very well. At Port Arthur several Russian medical officers were astonished at how kind the Japanese were to the Russian sick in the naval barracks. The Russian Red Cross confirmed these reports: "Since the surrender, the whole attitude of the Japanese Army toward us has been exactly the same as if it were dictated by the fundamental values of European civilization[;] there has been nothing lacking on any point in the treatment by the Japanese medical staff of our sick and wounded."[2] What astounded the Russian doctors and the British observers was that the Japanese army was indeed a full participant in the Hague Conventions and acted accordingly in good faith. The Russians, in contrast, had trouble keeping up their end of the agreement.

It became apparent that the Russians had wildly inflated views of their own prowess and suffered their losses badly. In Japanese captivity, Russian officers complained bitterly about trivial matters instead of supporting the general welfare of their men, and the Russian commander in chief, General Kuropatkin, admitted openly that he had difficulty restraining his troops from killing their prisoners or any wounded Japanese they found.[3] In effect, the Russian army set the traditional Golden Rule aside in favor of mistreating Japanese wounded, sick, and healthy POWs while foolishly expecting the Japanese army to be one-sided humanitarians. How inconsistent it must have appeared during the Russo-Japanese War to discover Russians killing Japanese prisoners, including the sick and wounded, when the czar of Russia himself led the movement to establish rules of war for the entire international community. What Europeans created for the world on paper was one thing; what they did in battle and after it was another.

Japan had signed and ratified the Hague Conventions, the international standards that regulated combatants' behavior in World War I, and the Imperial Japanese Army had treated German prisoners taken in the Pacific during World War I very well.[4] Following the Great War, however, culture changed in Japan. The country was seized by men consumed with the idea that they had to militarize the entire nation to eliminate political, economic, and social dependence on European values. Beginning with children in elementary school, they set a goal of creating a society that thought in terms of conformity, collateral value assessment, and hierarchical decision making.[5] As historian Philip A. Towle points out, the Japanese military elite no longer felt the need to satisfy Western standards.[6] The traditional Bushido warrior code, incorporated in the *Imperial Rescript to Soldiers and Sailors* (1882), spoke of dedication to the emperor, personal courtesy and health, truthfulness, obedience, frugality, and honor, which regulated traditional Japanese knights, or samurai.[7] Twentieth-century militant Bushido hardened the traditional code steeped in Buddhist culture into a distinctly nationalistic ethos and began to filter it into nonmilitary culture.

Radically different from the cultural trends in nineteenth-century Europe, Japan's drive toward conformity in a military society contrasted significantly with Europe's liberal notions of regulating individual—and, by extension, national—behavior through the power of law. Whereas Europeans who gathered at the Hague in the Netherlands in 1899 thought in terms of mitigating the horrors of war for individuals and possibly outlawing war in general, the militant Japanese officer corps began to see war as a means to achieve a new kind of cultural destiny. By the 1920s Japan and Europe were going in different directions. Japan evolved into a quasi-military state, whereas most of Europe had tired of war and sought ways to end it. In the 1930s the forces of national socialism in Germany and fascism in Italy followed Japan's example and led the world into the most devastating total war in human history.

The pivotal period for Japan was the Meiji era from 1868 to 1912. Named after the emperor who assumed the throne in 1868, this period witnessed an end to Japan's unique form of feudalism and the partial Westernization of its culture in only forty years. The emperor introduced a constitution in 1868, and then the government divided the country into new political subdivisions rather than the traditional confederation of small kingdoms. With a strong central government in place in 1872, Meiji introduced universal conscription and deprived the influential professional military of its power and class status. Although most samurai accepted the emperor's orders, some conceived the notion that he was ill advised. Led by Saigo, one of the staunchest supporters of imperial restoration in 1887, a group of samurai revolted. Saigo failed. By 1905, after a solid victory over Imperial Russia on the eve of World War I, Japan had modernized, industrialized, and evolved into a world military power to be reckoned with.[8]

Events that followed World War I showed conclusively that the European colonial powers were not ready to deal with Japan as an equal. After the Allies stripped Germany of its colonies in the Pacific following the Versailles Treaty in 1919, militarily powerful Western nations, encumbered with a false sense of cultural superiority over Asia and its peoples, created an expansive colonial system in Japan's backyard. During the Versailles meetings, the Japanese delegation asked the Western nations to insert a racial equality clause in the Covenant of the League of Nations. The Western nations ignored the request, causing a strain of bitterness to arise among those Japanese officers who had lived through Meiji, defeated the Russians, and fought on the side of the Allies against the European Central Powers.[9]

To these men, Westernization meant something. Japan's postwar imperial gains at Versailles were substantial, including some important German colonies and trading concessions in the Pacific region; however, something at least as important was missing: full equality with the nations of the West.[10] When the colonizing nations refused to take the Japanese request seriously, the prominent political luminaries in the Imperial Japanese Army and Navy took offense. Military leaders began to oust civilians from government, and by the 1930s a decidedly militant Japanese officer corps controlled most governmental decision making.

Bitter feelings toward European and American political snobbishness and blatant racism regenerated feelings of political xenophobia among the Japanese, which in turn lockstepped in a unique form of Japanese cultural isolation and dramatically exalted notions of sociocultural superiority. Meiji acted first to transform Japan's government from a feudal system to a constitutional monarchy, and the spirit of traditional Bushido, once the distinctive mark of honor and the knightly code of the samurai, evolved into the radicalized warrior code of World War II. Instead of a code of honor, it stressed absolute obedience, brutal discipline, and a vastly increased hatred for the enemy.[11] As an emperor-obedience cult, complete with an overwhelming sense of moral and racial superiority, militant Bushido developed a very real spirit of regional destiny to lead Asia in the creation of a distinctly Asian empire.[12] Death was likened to the cherry blossom; its fall was as beautiful as it was inevitable. In the name of the emperor, the stage was set for aggression, war, and ultimately war crimes.

The Japanese called their new empire the Greater East Asia Co-Prosperity Sphere, and war became the means to achieve it. With Korea firmly in place as a Japanese colony by 1910, Manchuria to Korea's north became the second seizure in 1931 as Imperial Japanese militarists began flexing their muscles. China, Britain, Canada, Australia, New Zealand, Burma, French Indochina, Dutch East Indies, Thailand, the Philippines, and the United States discovered that when Japan acted as a world military power, it became imperialistic, belligerent, and dangerous. Saburo Ienaga notes that the Japanese military "insisted upon the widest latitude for command prerogatives but refused to take any responsibility for mistakes or the undesirable consequences of their actions. They were utterly irresponsible and arrogant."[13] To outsiders, especially to those men and women who became prisoners of war and internees, militant Bushido took a terrible toll in lives. Rather than showing justice, sincerity, self-control, and honor—all values that formed the basis of the traditional *Rescript to Soldiers and Sailors* (1882) and the benign *Japanese Army Regulations for Handling Prisoners of War* (1904)—the Imperial Japanese Army adopted the prescriptive *Military Field Code* in 1941. It read in part, "Those who know shame are weak. Always think of preserving the honor of your community and be a credit to yourself and your family. Never live to experience shame as a prisoner. By dying you will avoid leaving behind the crime of a stain on your honor."[14] This unbending document required absolute obedience to superiors, from generals to privates; total conformity in all military and personal matters; an understanding and complete acceptance of Japan's military and moral superiority; and suicide in place of an honorable surrender.[15]

Because they believed that surrender was an act of shame and disgrace to all soldiers of all nations, the white flag of surrender meant little to the Japanese. Regardless of how deceitful it may have seemed, Japanese soldiers often lured their enemies into open death traps where, instead of surrendering honorably, they waited in ambush. Wounded men kept hand grenades for use against unsuspecting enemy soldiers who attempted to help them.[16] It is no wonder that Allied soldiers became leery of accepting Japanese surrenders when they did come sporadically or even accidentally, and it had nothing to do with racial hatred. From the earliest encounters, the war in the Pacific was inhumane and merciless.

The Imperial Japanese Army inflicted numerous forms of cruelty on hundreds of thousands of Allied POWs and innocent Asian civilians in the name of cultural superiority and empire building.[17] "In these circumstances," writes S. P. MacKenzie, "the Western origin and nature of the principles and laws governing the treatment of POWs became grounds for suspicion and, in practice, repudiation rather than emulation."[18] Beginning with the murder of approximately 200,000 people in Nanking, China, in 1937, the Imperial Japanese Army committed atrocity after atrocity in the name of victory. Tamura Yoshio, an operative at Unit 731, the bacteriological research unit responsible for vivisections of Chinese and Western POWs near the town of Harbin, Manchuria, explained the behavior in terms of racial superiority. "I had already gotten to where I lacked pity. After all, we were already implanted with a narrow racism, in the form of a belief in the superiority of the so-called 'Yamato Race.' We disparaged all other races. If we didn't have a feeling of racial superiority, we couldn't have done it."[19] In Ienaga's view, Unit 731 did the devil's work, and the U.S. occupation authorities were extremely lenient.[20]

When British and Australian prisoners were put to work on the Burma-Thailand or "Death" Railway, the Japanese literally worked thousands of them to death with impunity. Systematically, prisoners of war and internees were murdered, beaten, and starved everywhere in the Pacific region. In a personal letter written in 1993, novelist James Clavell, a former prisoner of war, discussed his brilliant POW novel *King Rat,* set in Changi prison in Singapore: "The happenings in the novel happened. At least as I remember them after bottling them from

More than 600 Americans and perhaps thousands of Filipinos died during the Bataan Death March from Mariveles to San Fernando. NARA photograph, courtesy of the American Ex-POW Association.

'45 until '61 when they flooded—for the first time. Not all of them occurred in Changi, some in Java and elsewhere, most I saw, the rest came from eye witnesses, the living and the dead. Living on the edge of death for so long is a curious experience, to go there and come back."[21]

Americans lived on the edge of death not in Changi but in the Philippines. After the American capitulation in April 1942, the Bataan Death March killed over 600 Americans and possibly thousands of Filipinos on the trek from Mariveles to San Fernando.[22] During the capture of Singapore, the Japanese behaved atrociously by bayoneting British doctors, nurses, and patients at the Alexandra Hospital.[23] Later in the war, when American B-29s began to bomb Japan heavily, crews were routinely beheaded shortly after capture and, in some cases, were subjected to murder by vivisection.[24] About 24.8 percent of the British and 41.6 percent of the Americans died in Japanese captivity.[25] Never in the history of warfare, since the Romans marched with a singular ferocity against their enemies, had systematic brutality been inflicted on so many people for so long. It is no wonder that American and Allied soldiers sought revenge on the battlefield and justice after the war's conclusion.

The Japanese soldier knew that his government did not acknowledge that prisoners of war existed; therefore, in his eyes, if he ever became a prisoner, he would simply be a nonperson at home. In air battles, no airmen ever crash-landed and gave themselves up. During the attack on Pearl Harbor, every plane unable to make it back but still flyable was deliberately crashed into a target if one could be reached, making this the first kamikaze mission, before the term existed. Japanese soldiers, airmen, and sailors simply disappeared, were erased from the rolls, and vanished if captured alive. Such was the case with the first Japanese EPW of World War II, Ensign Kazuo Sakamaki, who served as one of the five captains of midget, two-man submarines that attacked the American fleet at Pearl Harbor on 7 December 1941.[26] Of this group, Sakamaki was the sole survivor, taken prisoner by the Hawaii Territorial Guard after he swam 500 yards to shore. In Japan the government received official notice that Ensign Sakamaki had been taken prisoner and then wiped his name from the list of the dead submariners. The propaganda effort then focused on the "nine heroic warriors," the "nine gods of war," and the Japanese government never notified Sakamaki's parents about their son's capture.[27] The Imperial Japanese Navy was embarrassed and wiped Sakamaki off the books. When he became an EPW of the Americans, he became a nonperson in Japan.

As one might expect of a Japanese naval officer at the time, Sakamaki believed he was a failure not simply because his mission had failed but because he was a prisoner of war. Overcome with shame, guilt, and thoughts of suicide, he responded slowly to his interrogators in Hawaii and begged two Japanese-speaking Nisei sergeants to kill him. When they refused, Sakamaki became very angry. After his transfer to Camp McCoy in Wisconsin his bizarre behavior continued, but he slowly recovered from his emotional distress when he was joined by other Japanese EPWs. At Camp McCoy, Sakamaki became the camp spokesman and constantly complained to Spanish representatives—Spain acted as the protecting power under the Geneva Convention—about relatively petty issues.[28] By 1944 Ensign Sakamaki had learned English and decided to become a model prisoner, actively working to forestall violence fomented by the more hard-line resisters among the Japanese prisoners. In an address to fellow EPWs in camp, he said, "A person's true mettle shows itself in crisis. How you handle yourself when you have a serious failure is what is all important. Instead of letting your past torture you, build your future upon your failure. Often a misery has a way of turning into a blessing."[29] For this, his American captors learned to respect him, and when he returned to Japan after the war's end, he found work with Toyota Motor Corporation. He also testified at the Tokyo war crimes trials that he had been treated well by his American captors and wrote the first narrative of captivity by a former Japanese prisoner of war in American hands, entitled *I Attacked Pearl Harbor*. In it, Sakamaki traces the nature of his transformation from warrior to individual: "My steps were these: all-out attack, failure, capture, a sense of dilemma, mental struggle, attempts at suicide, failure again, self-contempt, deep disillusionment, despair and melancholy, reflections, desire to learn and yearning for truth, meditation, rediscovering myself, self-encouragement, discovery of a new duty, freedom through love, a desire for reconstruction."[30] He died on 29 November 1999, still known to the Japanese press as "Prisoner No. 1."

The paucity of Japanese prisoners taken during World War II, voluntarily or involuntarily, is staggering. When Japan surrendered on 15 August 1945, the Allies—the United States, Australia, New Zealand, and the United Kingdom—held a total of 38,666 Japanese prisoners in the Pacific theater: 26,304 army and 12,362 navy.[31] In comparison, there were 1,140,000 army and 410,000 navy dead. How many died by suicide rather than being killed in action can never be known; however, one can see by these numbers the sad truth that nearly an entire generation of young Japanese men died during World War II.

Yamauchi Takeo, who served on Saipan when the Americans attacked in 1944, recalled the choice he had to make:

In those days, Japanese soldiers really accepted the idea that they must die. If you were taken alive as a prisoner you could never face your own family. Those unable to move were told to die by a hand grenade or by taking cyanide. The women and children had cyanide. Those who didn't, jumped off cliffs. Ones like me, who from the beginning were thinking about how to become prisoners, were real exceptions.[32]

Takeo surrendered on 14 July 1944. He was taken to Angel Island near San Francisco for interrogation and then to Camp McCoy, where he became, like many others, a model prisoner. He remarked, "The nation didn't matter to me any more. It was the best time I ever experienced, one I look on fondly, even now."[33] On Okinawa, Japanese civilians mixed with the soldiery and believed that the Americans were devils and murderers. One student nurse, Miyagi Kikuko, found herself on a cliff ready to jump to her death when an American boat approached the coast. In Japanese, a voice cried out, "'Those who can swim, swim out! We'll save you. Those who can't swim, walk toward Minatogawa (a nearby town). Walk by day. Don't travel by night! We have food! We will rescue you!' They actually did. We never dreamt the enemy would rescue us."[34]

The battles for the Philippines in 1944 and 1945 were particularly disastrous for the Japanese. According to Japanese data, there were 127,200 troops on duty on 15 August 1945, the last day of the war. Prior to that date, however, 486,600 Japanese had died fighting the Americans and Filipinos. On 25 January 1945 American soldiers took Ooka Shohei prisoner on the island of Mindoro. After being drafted in 1944, Shohei had served as a communications private before the American invasion. He rejected the suicide ethic commonly found in the Imperial Japanese Army, and in his powerfully reflective narrative *Taken Captive: A Japanese POW's Story,* he recalls that while on the march in the mountains he made the decision to live:

> Yet, once we had lost our only route of escape and my brothers in arms began dying one after the other, a peculiar transformation came over me: I suddenly believed in the possibility of my survival. The 99 percent certainty of death was abruptly swept aside in my mind. I found myself imagining instead of a medley of ways by which I might actually ensure my survival, and I determined to pursue them.[35]

He did attempt suicide but failed, probably because he was terribly debilitated by malaria. Like most Japanese soldiers taken prisoner, he thought the Americans intended to execute him immediately: "I do not know how I got it into my head that they were taking me to my execution, but that is what I thought."[36] Instead, the Americans gave him water and a cigarette, followed by a cursory interrogation conducted by Nisei American soldiers. As an English speaker, Shohei was able to communicate with his captors and commented extensively on their kindness. "Not one American soldier I encountered during my captivity," he notes, "treated me with anything but the greatest courtesy."[37] Shohei remained in the Philippines until his repatriation in November 1945.

On 13 August 1945, two days before the end of the war, Japanese naval officer Kojima Kiofumi decided to surrender himself and his small group of men to the Americans on Luzon because he knew the Filipino native defense forces would never take them alive. He commented, "They really did kill Japanese men by poking out their eyes and cutting off their noses. So we couldn't afford to give up our arms until we were approaching the American forces." He continued, "Our hands weren't up. But I honestly didn't know what to do. I'd never surrendered before."[38] Instead of shooting them, the Americans offered food and Lucky Strike cigarettes, both very welcome. Kiofumi got along very well with his American captors and was shipped to a prison camp in Hawaii, where he helped prepare leaflets to be dropped over Japan describing the demands of the Potsdam Declaration for immediate surrender. Repatriated in October 1946, Kojima Kiofumi became a newspaperman in rural Japan without any stigma about being a prisoner of war.

Each Japanese prisoner was interrogated by Japanese-speaking Americans, mostly Nisei assigned to field intelligence billets. Their voluminous reports from the New Guinea region became the tedious work of the Allied Translator and Intelligence Section of the Southwest Pacific Area.[39] Some EPWs said they had surrendered because they believed the leaflets and decided to live. The fact that they had no food and no hope of getting any helped too. Others had been captured while they were too sick to move or too dazed from hunger and illness to resist, but most Japanese expressed a fear of going home because of the strong perception of family shame. Private Naoshige Kumagi, captured on Aitape, New Guinea, was unconscious with malaria and could not resist. Another EPW said that at the time of his capture he thought he would be killed and wished for death. Later, however, he felt less desperate and hoped to make the best of his situation. In true Japanese military thinking, he believed he had given his maximum effort in service to the emperor, yet it remained a disgrace to have been captured.[40]

Capture and internment turned into a positive experience for most if not all of the Japanese soldiers and sailors in American hands after their fears had been allayed. Instead of being killed, they received food, medical care, and proper housing. Those who spoke English, like Shohei and others, often became representatives of their men to the American authorities or interpreters for their own camp leadership. However, the Americans had some problems of their own to address. Too many Japanese were killing themselves and their comrades on the battlefields of the Pacific. How could the Americans bring that to an end?

Stoic Japanese prisoners ready themselves for American captivity in the Pacific. NARA, courtesy of Arnold Krammer.

The answer was psychological warfare, which included the creation of propaganda to urge the Japanese soldiers to put down their arms, stop fighting, stop resorting to suicide, and preserve their lives for their families and to rebuild Japan after hostilities ceased. In Allison B. Gilmore's study of Japanese prisoners in the Pacific, she reminds readers that the Japanese soldiers were steeped in Buddhism, which mandates the belief in rebirth after death. The Japanese soldier or sailor who had died for the emperor could be reborn as a prisoner and become as loyal to the Americans as he had been to the emperor.[41] Thus, once convinced that rebirth had taken place, Japanese prisoners became wonderfully useful in the creation of propaganda that told the truth—the best propaganda is always true—to Japanese soldiers and civilians. This included the creation of leaflets and culturally sensitive loudspeaker broadcasts on the battlefields asking the Japanese to cease resistance—honorable—rather than simply to surrender—dishonorable.[42] The secret to this operation was being able to communicate sensibly. That is where the Nisei played a significant role.

In the fall of 1941 the U.S. Army launched an intensive Japanese language program at the Presidio in San Francisco with sixty students. Once the war began, white and Nisei were separated by race, with the Nisei staying at Camp Savage, a former Civilian Conservation Corps camp, and the white soldiers moving to Fort Snelling in Minnesota. By war's end, the Military Intelligence Service Language School had trained 5,700 Nisei and 780 white soldiers in the Japanese language.[43] Only Nisei and white soldiers who already knew some Japanese gained admittance to the program; the instructors were all Nisei recruited from the internment camps. When the first Japanese-speaking graduates arrived in the Pacific theater, their primary work was translating captured documents until 1944, when the volume of EPWs increased dramatically. Then they worked as interrogators until the end of the war.

The navy also launched a language program at the University of Colorado in Boulder. One student, Paul F. Boller Jr., graduated in 1943 and became an intelligence officer at the Joint Intelligence Center, Pacific Ocean Area (JOICPOA), in the Z or translation section. Most of the documents Boller's office translated were routine captured Japanese military materials that were forwarded from JOICPOA in Hawaii to the Washington Document Center. By 1944 the documents took on a more crucial aspect, especially thirty-nine volumes of prisoner of war interviews and volumes of special translations that his commanding officer believed to be strategically important to the overall war effort.[44] One day, a psychological warfare officer approached Boller with an idea: why not explore the possibility of getting Japanese EPWs in a nearby POW camp to rephrase leaflets for the B-29s to drop before a major raid? It worked, and millions of leaflets were dropped, including reprints in Japanese of the Potsdam Declaration demanding unconditional surrender in 1945.[45] Although the leaflets seemed to work reasonably well, it took the atomic bombs on Hiroshima and Nagasaki in August 1945 to convince Emperor Hirohito to order an end to hostilities.

Creating permanent prison camp facilities led to another set of problems for the Allies. In the continental United States, 5,424 Japanese EPWs were held at Camp McCoy in Wisconsin; smaller numbers were housed in camps at Huntsville, Hearne, and Kenedy in Texas, Camp Clarinda in Iowa, and Camp Livingston in Louisiana.[46] Most Japanese taken prisoner toward the end of the war were held in place near the battlefields.[47] Inside the Japanese compounds three factions developed: cooperators, mostly educated draftees who had bonded with their captors and provided intelligence during their interrogations; hard-liners, mostly professional career officers and noncommissioned officers who resisted their captors and insisted on mass breakouts; and neutrals, who just wanted to survive and were committed to no one.[48] Arnold Krammer notes that in the United States only fourteen Japanese escaped, all from McCoy. The first, Terumasa Kibata, left camp on 3 July 1944 with no knowledge that the FBI, local police, and military authorities in the area were frantically searching for him. He returned to camp the next day. Other escapes followed, but as Krammer points out, none were successful or spectacular.[49] After hostilities ended, tensions existed in the Pacific compounds between soldiers who surrendered before and after the emperor's edict of surrender. The latter EPWs refused to accept that they had surrendered; rather, they believed they had just obeyed the emperor's command.

EPW docility may have shown itself in the United States, where the Japanese prisoners remained quiet and cooperative, but not in New Zealand and Australia. Two major uprisings took place: the first in Camp Featherston in New Zealand; the second at Cowra in Australia. Opened in September 1942 for Japanese prisoners captured in Guadalcanal, by 1943 Featherston housed more than 800 prisoners, a significant number of them crewmen of the sunken Japanese heavy cruiser *Furutaka*. The naval noncommissioned officers were tough resisters and pushed the New Zealanders to their limits. In a melee over building an athletic area for the guards, approximately 240 prisoners revolted and charged the gates and guard towers. Guns were lowered and fired. Forty-eight prisoners died; seventy-four suffered wounds. It took camp reforms and more interactions between the Japanese EPWs and their New Zealand captors to calm Camp Featherston, which by war's end had become relatively quiet.[50] The uprising at the Australian camp at Cowra, about 150 miles west of Sydney, was much more serious.

Cowra began life as Number 12 Prison Camp for German and Italian prisoners captured in North Africa, but by 1943 Japanese prisoners began to arrive in sizable numbers. By August 1944 approximately 1,100 Japanese prisoners in Camp B burst Cowra's seams. The Australians believed that international law required the prisoners to have more space, so they decided to transfer all lower-ranked Japanese prisoners to another camp. The Australians refused to allow their Japanese prisoners to dictate camp policy and refused to consider any appeals against the removal. As a result, the prisoners in Cowra Camp B revolted.[51] At first, it appeared to be a mass escape attempt. Two parts of the compound fence were breached, and eight Australians were killed. In all, 309 Japanese actually left the camp, but the Australians recaptured them within nine days; however, 231 prisoners died in the revolt, 183 from gunshot wounds and 48 by suicide. If the uprising at Cowra was an escape attempt, it was a failure. If it was an attempt at mass suicide as the prisoners stormed the barbed-wire perimeter and threw themselves at the guns, it was a success.[52]

The end of the captivity experience for the Japanese came at the end of 1945 and in early 1946. At that time, the army emptied the camps in the eastern United States, moving the Japanese repatriates west to holding camps in California until maritime transport to Japan could be arranged from Los Angeles or San Francisco. Most had enjoyed their first experience of democracy and faced an uncertain future in Japan. In an interview with author John Toland in 1960, Kazuo Sakamaki noted that during his captivity he had learned to admire and respect the Americans he met. For him, "It was a rebirth of reason."[53] Without a doubt, he, like many others, became one of the reborn.

As in wars past, internal inconsistencies arose between the government and citizens perceived to be sympathetic with the enemy—in this case, the Japanese living in the western regions of the United States. Whereas German Americans managed to avoid a dragnet of mass roundups and were interned on an individual basis, depending on their sympathies toward the Nazi movement, Japanese Americans were not so lucky. After the Imperial Japanese Navy bombed Pearl Harbor on 7 December 1941 and attacked the Philippine Islands, Guam, Wake Island, Singapore, and other targets in the "Go South" campaign, FBI agents rounded up Japanese Americans and other aliens they believed to be a direct threat to American security. On 29 January 1942 the Attorney General's Office established the first restricted zones along the West Coast, regulating the movement of alien enemies within these zones.[54] President Roosevelt's eventual response to growing discontent in the western United States came on 19 February 1942, when he issued Executive Order 9066 that created military zones where persons considered a threat could be prohibited or removed (see appendix 8).

With a strong presence on the Pacific coast, the Japanese were best known for their industry and frugality in fishing and farming. Despite their contributions to society, there had been a pervasive tendency toward racism aimed against them since their earliest arrival in the United

States in the late nineteenth century. With Japan's attack on Pearl Harbor, American sentiment toward the Japanese immigrants became violent.[55] Many Japanese did not leave their homes, or fled their homes altogether, due to the fear of violent attacks by angry Americans.[56] The war-generated aggression against a suspect immigrant population caught the attention of government officials, who thought it might be safer to collectively round up those Japanese who were being persecuted and put them someplace they would be safe. The idea was a novel one.

Spearheading the effort to round up the entire Japanese American population in the West was the military commander for the Western Command, General John L. DeWitt.[57] DeWitt believed that the Japanese Americans were conspiring to create an armed uprising and, worse, constituted a perfect fifth column to serve the Imperial Japanese forces when they invaded the West Coast. How small children could possibly be conspirators is beyond the imagination; however, California Attorney General Earl Warren apparently believed it. He testified to Congress that Japanese Americans' silence about Pearl Harbor was proof enough that they were preparing to act against the United States in the future.[58] Executive Order 9066 in essence created the War Relocation Administration (WRA) and rounded up 120,000 alien Japanese nationals, the Issei, and their children, the Nisei (all American citizens). They were distributed among ten internment camps or "relocation centers," where many of them remained for the next two years.[59] As explained by the WRA:

> The relocation centers, however, are NOT and never were intended to be internment camps or places of confinement. They were established for two primary purposes: (1) To provide communities where evacuees might live and contribute, through their work, to their own support pending their gradual reabsorption into private employment and normal American life; and (2) to serve as wartime homes for those evacuees who might be unable or unfit to relocate in ordinary American communities.[60]

They may have been communities, but they had barbed wire around them and towers with armed guards.

Historically, the mass imprisonment of the Nisei and Issei is the only one ever based solely on ethnicity, and it sparked a great deal of criticism against the government. Some Americans, such as Attorney General Francis Biddle and FBI Director J. Edgar Hoover, believed

Manzanar relocation camp, California. Library of Congress.

it was an act of pure racism against American citizens who posed no threat to national security. Others conceded that the government was acting on classified intelligence and was taking measures to ensure the safety and well-being of *all* American citizens. However, edicts ordering incarceration with no habeas corpus were not new to the United States. During the Revolution, hatred toward the Loyalists rose to such a high pitch that Congress simply forced them out of the country and confiscated their property in the Test Acts; President John Adams's Alien and Sedition Acts prohibited anti-American speech and publishing; President Andrew Jackson defied the Supreme Court and ordered the Cherokees removed from northern Georgia; Abraham Lincoln's executive orders locked up Confederate sympathizers. Such was the case here, but on a much grander scale.[61]

Then there was Hawaii. The American territory of Hawaii was viewed as the biggest threat; more than 40 percent of its population consisted of Japanese Americans.[62] It was simply impossible to incarcerate such a high percentage of the population. The very fact that the economy would plummet without their presence convinced President Franklin D. Roosevelt to declare martial law in the territory follow-

Residents of Japanese ancestry awaiting the bus at the Wartime Civil Control station, San Francisco, April 1942. Library of Congress.

ing the declaration of war until its end in 1945.[63] Although this move worked for Hawaii, Roosevelt decided not to place the rest of the West Coast under such an order; instead, government officials began to gather classified intelligence in an effort to determine which measures would best ensure the safety of America's western citizens.

By mid-1942 the states of Washington, Oregon, and California, as well as sections of Arizona and Nevada, were designated military zones. The WRA established ten camps in which the entire Japanese population of Alaska, Washington, Oregon, California, and southwestern Arizona was interned. These camps were Manzanar and Tule Lake in California, Poston and Gila River in Arizona, Minidokia in Idaho, Topaz in Utah, Heart Mountain in Wyoming, Amache in Colorado, and Jerome and Rohwer in Arkansas.[64] Of these, Tule Lake was designated a segregation center, or internment camp. Persons incarcerated there were those who requested repatriation or expatriation from Japan;

citizens who refused, during registration, to state unqualified allegiance to the United States and aliens who refused to agree to abide by U.S. laws; those with intelligence records or other records indicating that they might endanger the national security or interfere with the war effort; and close relatives of persons in the preceding three groups who expressed a preference to remain with the segregates rather than disrupt family ties.[65] Altogether, Tule Lake had a total of 18,000 inhabitants, while the other WRA centers averaged between 10,000 and 15,000 people. The U.S. government was intent on ensuring that all people of Japanese origin living on the West Coast were put into these centers. DeWitt even ordered 250 orphans from Alaska to be transported into the United States for internment.[66]

As the Japanese were rounded up, most were forced to sell their valued homes, businesses, and possessions; they could not bring anything to the assembly centers that they could not carry by hand. Peddlers and scavengers took advantage of the suddenness of the situation, and many Japanese Americans were forced to auction off their belongings at a fraction of what they were worth. When they arrived most of the camps were unfinished, and the internees were forced to build them themselves. Jeanne Wakatsuki Houston recalls arriving at the camp at Manzanar:

> The shacks were built of one thickness of pine planking covered with tar paper. They sat on concrete footings, with about two feet of open space between the floorboards and the ground. Gaps showed between the planks. Each barracks was divided into six units, sixteen by twenty feet, about the size of a living room, with one bare bulb hanging from the ceiling and an oil stove for heat. We were assigned two of these for the twelve people in our family group. We were issued steel army cots, two brown army blankets each, and some mattress covers, which my brothers stuffed with straw.[67]

One can only imagine the shock these people endured.

Japanese American troops fought for America in large numbers. Initially, after the attack on Pearl Harbor, many Nisei soldiers who were already enlisted were either discharged or given noncombatant posts. Japanese American men were not enlisted during the draft of June 1942.[68] The Army Intelligence Service, however, recognized that Nisei soldiers could be put to valuable use doing antiespionage work as interpreters, translators, and especially EPW interrogators. After putting the soldiers through rigorous language and military training, they employed about 6,000 Nisei soldiers both in the Pacific combat areas and on the home front.[69]

Although the U.S. Army recognized the value of using the Nisei as interpreters, convincing officials that the Nisei could also be effective fighters was not as easy. Increased pressure from the Japanese-American Citizens' League (JACL), as well as the increasing demand for soldiers, finally convinced the government of the need for Japanese American troops.[70] The army decided to appeal to Assistant Secretary of War John McCloy for the use of Japanese American troops. Finally, on 1 February 1943, President Roosevelt approved a plan to organize a combat unit composed entirely of Nisei. Because the majority of eligible males were residing in internment camps, army recruiters were forced to go into the camps to sign up the young Nisei. Most were eager; some were not. Fortunately, the recruiters were successful, and from the soldiers they gathered arose one of the most successful regiments in the history of American arms: the all-Japanese 442nd Regimental Combat Team (442nd RCT). From the time they began training together, this group of soldiers determined that they would stand above the rest. Its motto, "Go for Broke," was borrowed from gamblers in Hawaii. This regiment became noted for its battlefield ferocity in Italy and France, with the highest percentage of Purple Hearts ever won by a U.S. Army unit and a 300 percent casualty turnover. Altogether, more than 33,000 Japanese Americans—known as "Our Japs" in American newspapers at home—fought in the U.S. Army while their parents and siblings sat in internment camps.[71]

In July 1946 President Harry S. Truman presented the heroic 442nd RCT the Presidential Unit Citation. The Nisei American soldiers stood rigidly as the president fixed the award to their regimental colors. It was a good day. It was a long way from March 1942, when they had been classified "4C, Enemy Aliens," by the Selective Service Board.[72] In 1943 the 442nd RCT acquainted themselves with the German army in Italy. Stories of their aggressive battlefield behavior abound. Probably the most notable was their rescue of the First Battalion, 141st Infantry, Thirty-sixth Division (the Texas National Guard). Surrounded by the Waffen SS in the Vosges Mountains in Alsace, this 279-man unit became known as the "Lost Battalion" of World War II. After calling for help, the 442nd marched to the rescue, defeated the Waffen SS troops, and rescued the Lost Battalion of weary Texans. No greater respect was ever shown to the 442nd RCT than that given by the soldiers of the Lost

Battalion: they made all the members of the 442nd honorary Texans and invited them to attend their reunions into old age. In twenty months of combat, this unusual unit earned more than 18,000 individual awards, including a Medal of Honor, more than 9,400 Purple Hearts, 52 Distinguished Service Crosses, and 588 Silver Stars. The Presidential Unit Citation given by President Truman was only one of twenty.[73]

The Supreme Court played a significant role in the government's relationship with the Nisei. The first case that challenged Executive Order 9066 involved Mary Asaba Ventura, whose lawyers petitioned the court for a writ of habeas corpus in April 1942. The federal district court judge who heard the case felt that if Mrs. Ventura were a loyal citizen, as she claimed, she would not question the order.[74] The second case involved Gordon Hirabayashi, a senior at Washington State University who refused to submit to a curfew for Japanese Americans in 1942. In his view, such an order had to apply to all Americans, not just the Nisei. In *Hirabayashi v. United States,* the Supreme Court upheld the restriction because the Japanese may have had "ethnic affiliations."[75] Further, his conviction for curfew violations and failing to report for evacuation were upheld, and in 1943 he received a sentence of three months for each violation (served concurrently).[76]

The third case involved another Nisei who resisted reporting for evacuation. Fred Korematsu, a welder by trade, attempted to join the navy but was denied enlistment because of his ethnicity. He actually questioned the legality of the evacuation order itself and refused to report as ordered. Arguing for Korematsu, the American Civil Liberties Union filed an amicus curiae brief asking the Court whether an American citizen could be incarcerated in a concentration camp. Unfortunately for Korematsu, the Supreme Court upheld the order and refused to call the internment camps "concentration camps." Justice Hugo Black noted that it was not race but military necessity that brought the Nisei and Issei to the detention centers.[77] With no relief, Mitsuye Endo, a California civil servant, sued in the fourth major case. After she arrived at Camp Topaz, she maintained that innocent people were being held against their will without due process of law and filed for habeas corpus. The WRA fought the writ and won a unanimous decision from the Supreme Court that the evacuation was legal. In *Ex parte Endo* (1944) the Court decided that Mitsuye Endo could go free, but not back to the restricted areas on the West Coast. Although it was not a complete nullification of the internment program, *Ex parte Endo* represented the beginning of the end of the internment experience.

None of these cases gave relief to the thousands of Japanese Americans in the internment camps. Only the end of the war in the Pacific provided that. By 1946 the camps closed and the prisoners went home, where they were forced to start from scratch at farming, store ownership, and other successful professional pursuits. But on 2 July 1948 the JACL took the Japanese internment issue to Congress, and the Japanese-American Evacuation Claims Act was passed, giving the internees the right to claim compensation from the government for the loss of real or personal property as a consequence of the evacuation.[78] The claimants, however, had trouble proving their losses because of the lack of personal papers. In 1970 the JACL came up with another plan: $25,000 should be awarded to every surviving internee. On 7 August 1979 Senate Bill 1647 was introduced; President Jimmy Carter signed it as Public Law 96–317, which established a committee to investigate the problem. In 1983 the committee reported that along with an apology, the government should pay a one-time tax-free settlement of $20,000 given to each survivor.[79]

On 6 October 1983 a bill was introduced in the House of Representatives to support the committee's recommendations. After years of contentious argument, President Ronald Reagan finally signed the Civil Liberties Act into law. It took forty-five years for some Japanese Americans to receive justice under American law. The government acknowledged the fundamental injustice of the relocation and internment, apologized, and provided public funds to inform the public about what had happened and prevent any replay of the event in the future. Last, it authorized restitution to those former internees still living. On 9 October 1990 the funds began to flow, but the money was the least important part of the program. As so many former internees have said in memoirs, articles, poems, and oral histories, the apology and the acknowledgment of Japanese American innocence were far more important. For the people of Japan, the postwar period shook the roots of its twentieth-century militarism, especially when the Allies began the Tokyo trials, but Japanese stoicism endured. The Americans inherited the Imperial Japanese Empire, and the new era of the Cold War ensued.

ELEVEN

After the Victory

Optimism, Justice, or Vengeance?

We also enjoyed the benevolence of guards who now and then
allowed us a rummage through their garbage-cans in search of
eatables. This saved us from starvation.
—Walter F. Greiner

No war in modern history took more military and civilian lives than
World War II. The United States lost 293,121 killed in action on all
fronts and 115,185 nonhostile deaths. In general terms, about 11 million civilians and 4.5 million soldiers perished on all sides in the Pacific
theater of operations. In Europe, approximately 28 million civilians and
14 million soldiers perished. In the Holocaust, approximately 12 million people died, including 5.7 million Jews intentionally murdered by
the Nazis from 1939 to 1945.[1] Amid the joy of victory and optimism for
the future that certainly existed in 1945, some semblance of justice had
to be brought to bear on those individuals who inflicted so much death
on the world. The question was how.

A second question was what to do with all the German soldiers who
surrendered at the end of the war. Keeping bona fide enemy prisoners of
war was a requirement of all belligerent signatories to the 1929 Geneva
Convention, but handling so many soldiers in 1945, many of them boys
and old men, strained Allied assets in Europe to the breaking point until
the U.S. Army and the other Allies devised a plan of action to deal with
them. The third question in Europe was what to do with the "surviving
remnant" of the Holocaust, and under what military or civilian statutes
could the perpetrators of this horror be brought to justice? The fourth
question was similar to the third but had to do with the Japanese perpetrators of the Greater East Asian Co-Prosperity Sphere that terrorized
millions of people.

Before dealing with postwar problems, the U.S. Army dealt with
some old business: what to do with fifteen German EPWs convicted by
courts-martial in 1944 of murdering fellow prisoners and held for ex-

ecution at the U.S. Disciplinary Barracks at Fort Leavenworth, Kansas.[2] The largest group consisted of seven German U-boat sailors at the POW camp at Papago Park, Arizona. On 12 March 1944, for reasons they believed justified, the Germans administered what the prisoners called the "Holy Ghost"—a severe beating—and then hanged their victim, Werner Dreschler, for helping the Americans develop intelligence about them while they had been imprisoned together at Fort Meade, Maryland. American naval personnel were outraged at the army for sending Dreschler to Papago Park knowing full well the danger he faced from the other German naval prisoners there. According to Richard Whittingham, who studied this killing closely in *Martial Justice,* the navy believed the army sent Werner Dreschler to his death.[3]

No prisoners of war appreciate traitors in their midst. However, although the German sailors at Papago Park may have believed they were morally justified in executing Dreschler, the 1929 Geneva Convention put this behavior out of their hands and into the captor's. They could have petitioned the American authorities to remove Dreschler from the camp, but they chose a more violent alternative. All the German sailors stood trial together under the American Articles of War and were condemned to death by hanging on 16 August 1945.

Before the war's end on 8 May 1945, the possibility existed for an exchange with Nazi Germany for an equal number of American POWs who had supposedly been convicted of capital crimes under German military law. However, negotiations between the Americans and the Germans had to go through the Swiss legation in the United States, the State Department in Washington, D.C., and the Foreign Ministry in Switzerland. All this took time, and most German diplomatic communications broke down in April 1945.[4] By this time, fifteen German EPWs had been convicted of murder and sentenced to death by hanging. After 8 May 1945 there was no German government, and the Allies had little pity. One condemned prisoner, Edgar Menschner, received a reprieve from President Harry S. Truman on 6 July 1945; the other fourteen faced the hangman. The first group of five died on 9 July 1945; two more died on 14 July; and the last group of seven, Dreschler's murderers, died on 25 August 1945. The *Fort Leavenworth News,* an army newspaper, reported, "The trap was sprung on the first man at 12:10, and the last man went to his death at 2:48 A.M. A new system for mass hangings has been devised at the institution which saved more than an hour in the procedure."[5] Their graves remain at Fort Leavenworth today.

Werner Dreschler (on the left) helped the Americans develop intelligence about other German U-boat sailors during their imprisonment at Fort Meade, Maryland. This led to his murder by fellow EPWs at Papago Park in 1944. NARA, courtesy Captain Jerry Mason, U.S. Navy (Ret.).

As in all armies in wartime, there were occasions when the American army had to try and execute its own soldiers. Every army has its share of criminals: during World War II, ninety-five Americans were hanged as war criminals for crimes of violence, mostly rape and murder, against unarmed civilians. Unlike the Wehrmacht, which executed thousands of its own soldiers for military and political reasons, the Americans executed only one of their own for cowardice. On 31 January 1945 Private Eddie Slovik, on orders signed by General Dwight D. Eisenhower, supreme commander of the Allied Expeditionary Force, died by firing squad in the Alsatian town of Sainte-Marie-au-Mines (see appendix 9). This quiet little town was, curiously, the place where the pacifist Amish sect formed in the early 1700s. Although only one American soldier was executed for cowardice during World War II, approximately 40,000 were charged with desertion before the enemy, and 2,864 were tried by general courts-martial. Forty-nine were found guilty and received death sentences, but all the executions were commuted except for Slovik's.[6]

The end of World War II in Europe was a confusing, chaotic time for everyone anywhere near the war zone. Approximately 7 million civilians were on the move, in addition to 7.8 million German soldiers held by the Allies.[7] Mark Wyman notes that in 1945 the Supreme Headquarters, Allied Expeditionary Force (SHAEF) awarded the legal status of displaced person (DP) to evacuees, war or political refugees, political prisoners, forced or voluntary workers, German labor organization (Todt) workers, former members of forces under German command, deportees, intruded persons, extruded persons, civilian internees, ex–prisoners of war, and stateless persons.[8] When the DPs became too much for Allied occupation soldiers to manage, the military turned to the United Nations Relief and Rehabilitation Administration (UNRRA), first established in 1943 and in service in Europe until 1947, to tend to these suffering millions. In December 1944 UNRRA was ordered to create 200 teams of thirteen members to help control the massive flood of refugees as Allied armies fought their way to a Nazi surrender.[9]

After 8 May 1945 UNRRA took responsibility for all the DP camps in the American, British, and French Zones of Occupation. By the end of the year it ran 227 centers in the Western Zones in Germany and 25 in Austria; by late 1947 the workload increased to 8 in Italy, 21 in Austria, 416 in the American Zone, 272 in the British Zone, and 45 in the French Zone.[10] UNRRA personnel operated mainly in the noncommunist regions, but early in the occupation they also delivered much-needed supplies inside the Red Army's communist areas.[11] The major problem, aside from feeding, clothing, and delousing all these refugees, was getting them home. In 1945 and 1946 this would evolve into a problem so serious that it became a major contributor to the descent of the Iron Curtain in 1947 and the existence of the Cold War until 1991.

The repatriation problem began at the Yalta Conference in February 1945, where Joseph Stalin, Winston Churchill, and Franklin Roosevelt agreed to forever prevent Germany from becoming a world power; agreed to create the United Nations; created zones of occupation in Germany and Austria; changed Germany's borders, giving large swaths of Germany to Poland; and provided for the protection of liberated countries. But there was a secret portion of the Yalta agreement that surfaced shortly after the German surrender: American and Soviet citizens would be returned to their respective home countries as soon as possible. On 23 May 1945 the Soviets met the British and Americans at the German city of Halle and agreed that all former prisoners of war would be delivered to their home countries without regard for their personal desires.[12] In other words, repatriation was not a choice but a requirement. Often, noncommunist Ukrainians and noncommunist Russians had little desire to return to life under the yoke of the Soviet Union, especially those who had fought the Russians in the German armed forces. Both those Russians who had joined Wehrmacht efforts against Stalinist communism and those who had simply surrendered and survived the POW experience in German hands knew the Soviet dictum against becoming a POW in the first place: Decree 270 of 1942 stated, "a prisoner captured alive by the enemy ipso facto is a traitor."[13] Hence, forced repatriation evolved into a major issue. Political asylum, so valuable to Americans, evaporated for the 5.5 million Soviet citizens living outside the USSR in 1945.

The Americans were naive at first. They wanted to recover their own POWs liberated by Soviets from the eastern POW camps quickly, and it was important throughout the war years to show solidarity with their Soviet wartime ally. As a result, the American army cooperated with the Soviets and turned over thousands of unwilling former Soviet soldiers and civilian DPs in what was called Operation Keelhaul.[14] However, when 134 noncommunist Russians committed suicide near Leinz, Austria, on 1–2 June 1945 and 154 Russians killed themselves at Fort Dix, New Jersey, on 29 June 1945, it became clear that something was far from normal or even acceptable.[15] In Europe, eyewitnesses began to report that Soviet troops murdered many returnees or that some returnees committed suicide rather than returning home. Regardless of these reports and American soldiers' distaste for turning these people over to the Soviets in the field, policy trumped human feelings in 1945 and 1946, and orders were obeyed. Complaints arrived at SHAEF that the policy needed to be rethought, and the Americans finally changed it in 1947.[16] Forced repatriation was no longer acceptable. In defiance of the Soviet policy, Poles, Ukrainians, Czechoslovaks, Serbs, Slovenians, and Croats in American care were granted political asylum.

DP camp inmates from eastern Europe feared and hated the Soviets and the communist governments they had installed in their homelands. Russian representatives came into the DP camps and attempted to convince these people to return home, but repeatedly the DPs revolted against the effort, often subjecting the Russian officers to violence. Soviet officers often resorted to kidnapping when all else failed until the Cold War broke out between the communist East, the Soviet region of influence, and the West, where the Americans dominated the political thinking. The issue of forced repatriation was never solved during the postwar period and reared its ugly head again in Korea.

As Allied armies invaded from the west and the Soviets advanced from the east, they discovered about 500 concentration camps and satellite work camps. Estimates of the number that died in these camps vary from 6.6 to 12 million, but despite this disparity, little doubt exists that the camps disgusted the American, British, French, and Russian troops who liberated them. No veteran relates his stories about liberating Belsen, Natzweiler, Flossenburg, Mauthausen, Dachau, Buchenwald, or Auschwitz with anything short of horror at the shocking scenes around them. If soldiers reached into their pockets for cameras, intelligence officers confiscated the film.[17] Some men fainted. Soldiers who had believed that the German soldiers were worthy adversaries suddenly lost their generosity, seeking revenge or perhaps justice for the victims of these atrocities. Many considered all the German people guilty of these acts of inhumanity. The war had changed, and the Americans had little patience for Germans living around these camps who claimed no knowledge of what had happened. As a result, American commanders and military police ordered German mayors and citizens to see for themselves what the SS had actually done to their victims.

Of the 12 million people murdered, almost 6 million Jews, or 72 percent of Europe's Jewish population, died in the Holocaust; those who survived called themselves the "spared" or the "surviving remnant."[18] Unlike some DPs who decided to return home, wherever it was, European Jews had little intention of imperiling themselves yet again if other alternatives existed. The plight of these Jews became a cause célèbre for some journalists and Jewish spokesmen, and as early as 21 July 1945 the World Jewish Congress appealed to Allied leaders meeting in Potsdam to release all the former concentration camp inmates, citing inhumane conditions and the bizarre circumstance of former Nazis being put in charge of their former prisoners in some cases. When President Harry Truman heard about this, he contacted Earl G. Harrison, dean of the Law School at the University of Pennsylvania in Philadelphia, to look into the matter. What Harrison witnessed in Europe galled him, and his report to Truman called for dramatic changes in treatment, including better food, decent clothing, and adequate housing in the DP camps.[19] In response to Harrison's report, General Eisenhower ordered the U.S. Army to create separate facilities for Jews and increase their diets to 2,500 calories a day. Improvements came even quicker in Austria under the leadership of General Mark Clark, who believed the Jews should receive first consideration in any Allied relief efforts. As life improved, the Jewish dream of a homeland grew. In a movement called Zionism, Jews rejected their presence among Christians in Europe, claiming that in return for their labors, all they got was death. The British protectorate of Palestine, now Israel, became home in the thoughts and dreams of the surviving remnant, despite any religious, social, or economic differences between them.

Of all the countries in eastern Europe, Poland had the largest Jewish population, and in 1945, when many Jews attempted to return or join their surviving relatives, they found it extremely inhospitable. Anti-Semitism pervaded the Polish atmosphere; murders of Jews took place in Krakow, Lublin, and Kielce. Jews who had returned home left Poland by the thousands, heading to the American Zone of Occupation as rapidly as possible. DP camps filled with Jews whose objective was to link up with the Bricha organization that smuggled Jews from Europe to Palestine under the noses of the British. Bricha specialized in creating false documents all along the escape line from Poland to the Middle East. It became a true exodus from 1945 to 1947. On 1 September 1947 the United Nations Special Committee on Palestine called for the end of the British mandate first established in 1919 at Versailles, and on 15 May 1948 the state of Israel was born. Jews finally had a homeland.

On 28 June 1948 President Truman signed the first Displaced Person Act and then another one on 16 June 1950. Together, these two acts brought approximately 400,000 DPs from Europe to the United States. The elaborate system of actually clearing DPs for entry came under the auspices of the U.S. Displaced Persons Commission, nicknamed the "pipeline."[20] The idea was to expedite visas to those DPs who had "assurances" of support in the United States, real, anonymous, or imaginary. The mountains of paperwork seemed staggering at the time, but for most Europeans, the effort was worth it. America remained the land of opportunity, and the DPs believed the United States offered a chance to better themselves and give their children a future—something that seemed unlikely in war-torn Europe.

General Eisenhower had more than Europe's displaced Jews to worry about. According to German historian Kurt Böhme, 7,614,794 German soldiers surrendered to the American army in 1945, and the Americans discharged 1,660,138 shortly after hostilities ended on 8 May.[21] Because the war was over, the remaining Wehrmacht troops could no longer be classified as prisoners of war. The problem of status was solved when the German ex-soldiers became "disarmed enemy forces" (DEFs), but with that status change, the protection of the Geneva Convention disappeared, as did the rations for POWs coming from the Red Cross and camp inspections by the International Committee of the Red Cross. The German DEFs went hungry when SHAEF declared that the Allies were no longer responsible for providing them with equal rations to the American army. Some writers, such as James Bacque, claim that Eisenhower deliberately caused the death of more than a million German soldiers held in the Rhine Meadow Camps along the scenic Rhine River. Major historians, both German and American, dispute Bacque's figures, saying that no more than 50,000 died in these camps. The bitter academic fight between Bacque on one side and Günter Bischof and Stephen E. Ambrose on the other illustrates the problem. Arguing that Bacque's analysis is incorrect, the Bischof-Ambrose collaboration follows the numbers in the historically sound Maschke Commission volumes published in Germany between 1962 and 1974.[22] Erich Maschke, a highly respected German historian, was himself a POW in Russia. The Maschke series, produced after extensive archival and interview research, initially drew criticism because it was censored to a limited degree by the German Foreign Office to avoid any facts that might be distressing to the policy of détente at the time. Yet even today the subject of POWs is not popular in Germany. Guilt remains the preferred feeling, and if someone observes that Germans also suffered injustice, cruelty, and revenge, even Germans declare that German deeds were worse, and they got what they deserved.[23]

How could even 50,000 men deserve death as DEFs after the hostilities had ended? Part of the answer refers to the American efforts to rescue and feed the millions of DPs spreading out all over Europe and especially in the American Zone of Occupation. Rations went to them instead of the German DEFs, and none went to the German civilian population in 1945 and 1946. American sympathy for the DPs was strong up to 1947, when the tide began to turn against them in favor of the Germans. Perhaps one reason for this change was the new set of soldiers who arrived for occupation duty, replacing the combat soldiers who had returned home. They found the Germans to be industrious workers, friendly, and socially appealing, which improved German-American relations significantly, especially as the Cold War descended on a recovering Europe and Marshall Plan money began to flow into the rubble.

In the chaos of surrender in 1944 and 1945, the German soldiers were put into Andersonville-like enclosures with barbed wire and tents, similar to the setup in France for surrendering German prisoners after the Normandy invasion. At first, stripped of their possessions and personal items, the Germans captured in France suffered terribly, according to Helmut Hörner's memoir, in part because the Americans possessed few extra rations to feed the prisoners properly, but in a relatively short time the Americans upgraded conditions before sending these men to the United States. In the Rhine camps, rations were set at 1,000 calories in the beginning. It took a little longer to upgrade the food, build shelters, and discharge the Germans into civilian life. In the meantime, without tents or outbuildings, huge numbers of soldiers dug holes to sleep in, and the camps resembled molehills rather than places for human beings. Without adequate food or water, some resorted to eating grass and drinking their own urine. The conditions resembled those in the Japanese camps for Allied POWs, and many Germans died of dysentery, pneumonia, exhaustion, and war wounds, all exacerbated by the cruelty of these camps.[24] One former German prisoner in American hands in Bavaria commented in a letter to the *Times Literary Supplement*:

> I was only fifteen when I was forced to vegetate as a POW in an American compound in Bavaria where 12,000 captured soldiers were "left to themselves" for a good while! It was the exceptionally good weather in 1945 that made survival possible—when it rained and through thunderstorms we got up from the mud and could wait for the sun to dry our emaciated bodies that lived "unhoused" in the muck. We also enjoyed the benevolence of guards who now and then allowed us a rummage through their garbage-cans in search of eatables. This saved us from starvation.[25]

Rhine Meadow Camp Bad Kreuznach, with enclosures of
barbed wire and tents. Many German prisoners died of dysentery, pneumonia, exhaustion, and war wounds, all exacerbated
by the harsh camp environment. U.S. Army photograph.

At only fifteen years of age, this German boy soldier could not have seen
much of the war and even less of the death camps liberated by the Americans, British, and Russians a short time earlier. But he certainly felt the
result: a great deal of Allied contempt for soldiers of the German army.

The Rhine camp most remembered by the Germans was Bad
Kreuznach. Food was days in coming, and when it finally arrived the
prisoners received only one loaf of white bread—a food unknown and
disliked by Germans even today—for twenty-five men; then for a long
time they got one loaf for ten men.[26] Pretty soon men started dying in
camp. Water was not plentiful either. The Americans rolled a water
wagon up to the wire daily, but often it had only one faucet and emptied
swiftly. The prisoners had nearly no tools, few tents, and no comforts at
all. They slept in the mud and had no latrines. Like Andersonville, the
camp was a cesspool, and dysentery became the major killer instead of
bullets or bombs. In 1946 one unreconstructed German told American
war correspondent W. L. White:

I have a comrade who was in your camp at Kreuznach an Rhein, where the death rate among our boys from cold, exhaustion and starvation [was] between 130 and 150 per day. Not as many died here as died at our concentration camps. But your treatment of our prisoners was in no way better, and surely it could have been worse. It can be said that only 130 corpses daily is not much, but if Goebbels could have photographed them, the pictures would have been quite as impressive as those you took at Belsen. The point is, however, that you filled our papers with what had been done at Belsen, with not one word of what had gone on at Kreuznach am Rhein, although just at that time our boys were coming back to tell us of this.[27]

To be sure, the men became numb; they stopped helping one another, and the spirit of comradeship so dominant in the German army declined as conditions worsened.

In time, as the Americans slowly issued discharges to most of their prisoners, they also searched for SS men by examining their underarms for tattooed blood groups. These men, if and when discovered, were held and investigated for war crimes. The others, if cleared of any suspicion, received their discharges and left the camps for home. By 8 September 1945 the Americans had discharged approximately 2.2 million German prisoners in the American Zone only.[28] Officers received 60 marks, enlisted men received 30 marks, and both received a set of civilian clothes for the trip home. They also received their impounded personal possessions, which they had presumed were gone forever as American souvenirs.

One war may have been over, but another type was just beginning in the form of war crimes trials in both Europe and Asia. Prior to Nuremberg, jurisdiction over war crimes was limited to each country's military courts. After World War I, when the victors accused the Germans of serious war crimes and demanded their surrender to the Allied military courts, the Germans insisted on trying the accused themselves in the 1920 Leipzig trials. Of the 896 Germans facing charges, the courts accepted a mere twelve cases. Three defendants never even appeared, charges against another three were dropped, and the remaining six received trivial sentences.[29] Determined to avoid a reoccurrence of this mockery of the justice system, the Allies decided that the Nazis could not be tried by their own countries but would be punished by the joint decision of the Allied governments.[30]

The idea of an International Military Tribunal (IMT), a four-power

All the class A prisoners at Nuremberg pleaded not guilty. NARA, courtesy of U.S. Holocaust Memorial Museum.

judiciary consisting of Britain, France, the United States, and the Soviet Union roughly patterned after a military court, arose in a series of meetings among the Allies in January 1942, when reports of Nazi brutality were proliferating.[31] The IMT was officially established on 8 August 1945, along with a charter dictating the procedures for the hearings against the Nazis.[32] By October 1945 the IMT ordered notices of the impending trials of persons and organizations to be circulated in the press throughout occupied Germany, as well as inside the internment, DP, and POW camps. Based on the Nuremberg Principles (see appendix 10), the IMT classified war crimes into three major categories: crimes against the peace, conventional war crimes, and crimes against humanity. Individuals were then grouped into classes A, B, and C. Class A criminals were those charged with planning, preparing, initiating, and waging an aggressive war or a war in violation of international law; class B covered those charged with ordering and directing atrocities; and class C consisted of those charged with execution of the atrocities.[33]

In Nuremberg, the following class A criminals were on the docket: Hermann Goering, Rudolf Hess, Joachim von Ribbontrop, Wilhelm Keitel, Alfred Rosenberg, Hans Frank, Wilhelm Frick, Julius Streicher, Walther Funk, Hjalmar Schacht, Karl Doenitz, Erich Raeder, Baldur von Schirach, Fritz Saukel, Alfred Jodl, Franz von Papen, Arthur Seyss-Inquart, Albert Speer, Konstantin von Neurath, Hans Fritche, and Ernst Kaltenbrunner. They all pleaded not guilty; however, most were charged not as individuals but as members or heads of Nazi organizations.[34] The thinking was that if an organization was guilty, then everyone in it was likewise guilty. At Nuremberg, the American and British presumption of innocence required the prosecution to present mountains of evidence. Additionally, the prosecution cross-examined witnesses for the defense while the judge remained silent. None of this was common practice in the German, French, or Russian legal systems; in European courts, judges rather than attorneys direct the flow of the proceedings.

The death sentences of Hans Frank, Wilhelm Frick, Alfred Jodl, Ernst Kaltenbrunner, Joachim von Ribbontrop, Alfred Rosenberg, Arthur Seyss-Inquart, and Julius Streicher were carried out 16 October 1946 by hanging; the executioner was John C. Woods. Hermann Goering committed suicide by poison and avoided the hangman. The rest were either acquitted or received jail sentences. Most were free by 1954; only Rudolf Hess remained in Berlin's Spandau prison until his death in 1987. After Hess died, the Allies closed Spandau forever.

Another series of trials took place from 1945 to 1948 and was conducted exclusively by the American army at the Dachau concentration camp. These trials focused on crimes committed in various concentration camps, including Buchenwald, Dachau, Flossenburg, Mauthausen, and Nordhausen; the murders of American POWs by the SS at Malmédy during the Battle of the Bulge; and other murders.[35] Juries were not impaneled for these trials; rather, a seven-man military commission and a "law member," a senior officer with extensive experience in military law, were the fact finders. In each of the trials prosecuted at Dachau, only offenses against Allied nationals were tried, leaving to the German court system the prosecution of crimes committed by Germans against other Germans. By the time the American military court had permanently adjourned in December 1947, it had tried 1,200 defendants for war crimes committed during World War II, achieving a conviction rate of approximately 73 percent.[36]

The Nuremberg trials were revolutionary for several reasons. It was the first time in legal history that the charge of crimes against peace was recognized. It was also the first time a declaration of aggressive war was considered an international crime. In a letter to President Truman, prosecutor Robert H. Jackson reiterated the importance of the trials:

> By the Agreement and this trial we have put International Law squarely on the side of peace against aggressive warfare, and on the side of humanity against persecution. In the present depressing world outlook it is possible that the Nuremberg trial may constitute the most important moral advance to grow out of this war. The trial and decision by which the four nations have forfeited the lives of some of the most powerful political and military leaders of Germany because they have violated fundamental International Law, does more than anything in our time to give to International Law what Woodrow Wilson described as "the kind of vitality it can only have if it is a real expression of our moral judgment."[37]

Also developed at the Nuremberg trials was the idea that an entire nation could not be held responsible for the actions of individuals, which was certainly a different approach from that taken in the 1919 Treaty of Versailles.[38] Although the trials served as a warning that the civilized world would not tolerate such barbarity, they were also seen as an attempt to achieve justice without vengeance, because the Allies had every reason to destroy the vanquished without pity.[39] In contrast, the issue of conspiracy to wage aggressive war acted as the guiding theme with the class A criminals. In retrospect, it may have been wrong that the accused were not permitted to use the argument that the Allies had done the same thing, that is, the tu quoque argument that the Allies had shot prisoners, bombed civilian targets, and planned an offensive war. In fact, one wonders whether any completely just resolution was even possible.

Following World War II twelve Americans were indicted for treason. Most were well-known broadcasters such as Robert H. Best, Max Otto Koischwitz, Douglas Chandler, and Frederick W. Kaltenbach, who served the Nazi Propaganda Ministry. The Americans wanted Kaltenbach, but the Russians had captured him and refused to swap him for some SS men the Americans had captured.[40] He died in a Soviet labor camp in October 1945, cause unknown. Best and Chandler both faced American justice and served considerable time in prison for their on-air treason. Faced with a life sentence, Best died in prison in 1951; Chandler was released in 1961.

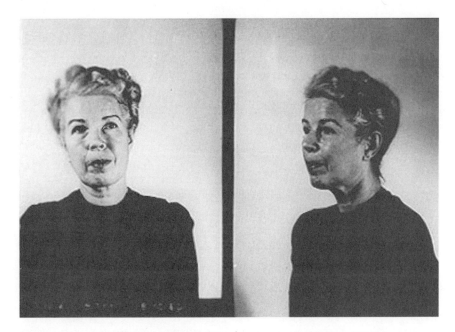

Mildred Gillers, called "Axis Sally" by American soldiers, aired her propaganda program "Home Sweet Home" from occupied Paris until July 1944. Bureau of Prisons photograph.

The stars of the postwar treason trials were two women: Mildred Gillers, known as "Axis Sally" by American soldiers, who broadcast her radio shows from Berlin, and Iva Toguri, known as "Tokyo Rose," whose voice became standard fare in the Pacific. Both were arrested and returned to the United States for trial. These two civilian women found themselves caught up in the rush of the war's events: one was clearly guilty; the other became a victim of popular culture. Both suffered jail time for what they did.

Mildred Gillers was born Mildred Elizabeth Sisk in Portland, Maine, in 1900. She was raised in Ohio and studied speech from 1918 to 1922 at Ohio Wesleyan University, then dropped out to pursue an acting career in New York City. When her acting career failed, she left the United States for a romantic fling in Algiers, landing in Germany in 1934. In poverty and desperation, Gillers finally landed a job as an announcer with German radio in 1940, and the U.S. vice-consul in Berlin confiscated her passport. Gradually she slid into a true commitment to both Nazi Germany and Max Otto Koischwitz.[41] Koischwitz, a literature professor at Hunter College in New York City, became a Nazi propagandist in professorial disguise. The unconventional Koischwitz became a naturalized American citizen in 1935 and maintained a high profile with the undergraduate students. As war came closer in 1939, Koischwitz specialized in criticizing American literature as a vehicle for Allied propaganda with ever-increasing vehemence. Hunter College responded by denying him any promotion beyond assistant professor. The Board of Higher Education at Hunter granted Koischwitz an unpaid leave of absence beginning on 1 September 1939, and he left for Nazi Germany. After securing his place in the Ministry of Propaganda and renouncing his American citizenship, he broadcast programs from Paris under the pseudonyms "Dr. Anders" and "Mr. O.K." Although married to Emma Koischwitz, who was pregnant in 1943 with their fourth child, he fell in love with Mildred Gillers.[42]

Her propaganda program, on the air from occupied Paris until July 1944, was known as "Home Sweet Home." Cohosted with Koischwitz, it aired daily and was heard all over Europe, the Mediterranean, North Africa, and the United States. She referred to herself as "Midge at the Mike"; however, GIs dubbed her "Axis Sally," in part because she teased and taunted the American military about their wives and sweethearts back in the States. Soldiers were more amused than horrified by the broadcasts and relished the American music she played. For the first and last time, Midge Gillers was a star. The Koischwitz-Gillers team visited numerous German POW camps, where she tried to convince American POWs to talk to her, sometimes under the guise of being with the Red Cross. On the air, both Koischwitz and Gillers attempted to portray the Nazi POW camps as pleasant, comfortable summer camps.[43] But as the American army approached Paris, first Koischwitz and then Gillers left France in a hurry for Berlin. The press reported that Koischwitz died by his own hand, but he actually died of tuberculosis and heart failure on 31 August 1944. Gillers, who had arrived in Berlin by then, attended his funeral on 4 September 1944.[44]

After Germany's defeat Gillers became just another refugee among the Germans in Berlin. In December 1945, nearly starved to death, she spent a few weeks in an American hospital facility, after which she was moved to an internment camp. She received amnesty in 1946 and moved to the French Zone of Occupation in Berlin, but eventually she was arrested and kept in detention for a year in Frankfurt until the army returned her for trial in the United States. After her return in custody, the FBI incarcerated Gillers in the Washington, D.C., district jail without bond. She was charged with ten counts of treason in a trial that began on 25 January 1949 in the district court in Washington and lasted until 8 March.

The prosecution had an easy time presenting the case against her. The defense argued that Gillers was naive and had little idea of what she was doing. Finally, the jury found her guilty of one count of treason based on her broadcast of Koischwitz's play *Vision of an Invasion,* and she received a sentence of ten to thirty years in prison and a $10,000 fine. Mildred Gillers, alias "Axis Sally," was transported to the Federal Women's Reformatory in Alderson, West Virginia.[45] Eligible for parole after ten years, she won parole after twelve years at Alderson and then taught German, French, and music at a Catholic convent school in Columbus, Ohio. Gillers returned to Ohio Wesleyan University to complete her bachelor's degree in speech in 1973 and died quietly at age eighty-seven in 1988.

There was no pity forthcoming in Asia in the postwar period. The Potsdam Declaration stated clearly on 26 July 1945: "We do not intend that the Japanese shall be enslaved as a race or destroyed as a nation, but stern justice shall be meted out to all war criminals including those who have visited cruelties upon our prisoners."[46] In January 1946 the Allies created the IMT for the Far East, with representatives of eleven countries—United States, China, Great Britain, Soviet Union, Australia, Canada, France, Holland, New Zealand, India, and Philippines—sitting to implement the prisoner clause of the Potsdam Declaration. Proceedings began on 29 April 1946 when twenty-eight Japanese defendants were formally indicted.[47]

The class A criminals in Asia were taken to and held in Sugamo prison and subsequently tried by the Tokyo War Crimes Tribunal; the class B and C criminals were tried in Yokohama or where they had been stationed by tribunals appointed by the Allied powers. In all, approximately 4,000 Japanese officers, enlisted men, and civilians were arrested as war criminals, with only fourteen listed as class A; the rest were class B and C. Of this number, 1,068 were executed or died of disease, accident, or suicide in prison between 1946 and 1951, the year the Allies and Japan signed the final peace treaty in San Francisco. At that time, authority and responsibility for the convicted war criminals shifted to Japan, which was then ruled by General Douglas MacArthur, whose only duty was to "pass on the final judgments of the tribunal and to enforce the sentences."[48] The United States hanged 167 Japanese war criminals; China executed 175, Britain 254, the Netherlands 273, the Philippines 17, France 33, and Australia 135. Among this group only seven class A criminals were hanged in succession on 23 December 1948; seven died before or after conviction of disease, and none committed suicide.[49]

Like at the Nuremberg and Dachau trials, the presumption of guilt seemed to guide the proceedings, and no tu quoque defense was offered. Owen Cunningham, one of the more controversial defense attorneys in Tokyo, delivered a paper entitled "The Major Evils of the Tokyo Trial" to the American Bar Association in 1948, stating that the cases against all the class A defendants should have been dismissed. He believed that the object of the trials was vengeance, vindication, and propaganda; that the accused did not receive fair trials; and that the prosecuting nations had done much the same thing as the Japanese during the war.[50] Such a charge outraged survivors of the Bataan Death March, the Death Railway, the rape of Nanking, and the rape of Manila, all of whom yearned for justice. Whatever the case, at 4:12 PM on 12 November 1948, two years and ninety days after they convened, the war crimes trials in Tokyo ended.[51] In Washington the U.S. Supreme Court, in an appeal from the defense team, held that it had no authority to "review, to affirm, set aside, or annul the judgment or sentences."[52]

In his indictment of the Tokyo trials as morality plays, Richard H. Minear notes, "Gross injustice was committed at Tokyo. The leaders of the defeated nation, and they alone, were offered as a sacrifice to a better world."[53] Thus, for the Japanese and the Germans on trial, the indictments appeared to be based more on revenge than on a sense of justice. Yet Douglas MacArthur found himself "pleasantly surprised at the attitude of the Japanese people during the period of the trial. They seemed to be impressed both by the fairness of the procedures and by the lack of vindictiveness on the part of the prosecutors."[54] Many Japanese intellectuals believed the opposite was true. For instance, according to Saburo Ienaga, "The executed prisoners included many who had no chance to defend themselves properly and many cases of mistaken identity where the wrong man was put to death. The executions were more expedient revenge than careful justice."[55]

Often, the condemned class B and C prisoners wrote letters. One Japanese navy lieutenant wrote: "I deeply regret that I am going to be executed because of a false accusation. However, if Japan, after her acceptance of unconditional surrender, is to preserve her national polity, retain her territory, and save her people from annihilation, reparation by blood is necessary. Carrying this deep in my mind, I am willing to sacrifice myself as a part of that reparation."[56] Another naval prisoner wrote in the same vein: "Although I am not guilty, I am going to die with serenity, taking upon myself all the sins of others, as the commander responsible for my company and for the rebirth of the Japanese nation. I am happy to sacrifice myself to neutralize the evil feelings of the allied powers toward my country." According to Kazuko Tsurumi, when these junior officers used phrases such as "blood reparation" and "human sacrifice," they were responding to ancient Japanese customs of clan warfare, in that one death must atone for another.[57] Tsurumi also suspected that because most of the major newspapers in Japan supported the war crimes trials and the outcomes, this absolved the rest of the Japanese people from any sort of self-examination. In their remarkable book *Japan at War: An Oral History,* Haruko Taya Cook and Theodore F. Cook note that for the average Japanese citizen in the postwar period, the question of guilt or innocence fell to the Americans who had conquered them. "Sorting out the experience," they write, "found little place in rebuilding and starting again."[58]

History certainly won a great victory, though. Both in Germany and in Japan, the horrors inflicted on everyone began to make sense in the recounting. The shades were pulled from the secretive world of dictatorships, and justice was applied, however imperfectly. One thing is certain: despite all the indictments and the testimony given in the Far East war crimes trials, to this day, the Japanese people see themselves more as victims than as perpetrators of World War II.

No American-born Nisei Japanese remained in federal custody after the conclusion of World War II except for one: Iva Toguri, more commonly known as the elusive Tokyo Rose. In Japanese American society prior to the war, it was common for families to send sons and daughters to Japan to acquaint them with relatives, learn proper Japanese, and get a solid feel for Japanese culture. Rarely, if ever, was there any political intent, and certainly no Japanese American got caught up in the militant Bushido culture that ravaged Japan in the 1920s and 1930s. Iva Toguri was born Ikuko Toguri in Los Angeles, California, on 4 July 1916. Her mother and father were both Issei, having immigrated at the turn of the twentieth century. She was well schooled and earned a bachelor of science degree in zoology from UCLA in 1940. Ready for life as a young Japanese American woman, she pleased her family by agreeing to go to Japan for a while. It was at this point that Toguri began to experience some problems.

Perhaps out of naivete or a lack of political sophistication, on 5 July 1940 Toguri sailed from San Petro for Japan without a passport.

She presented herself to the American vice-consul in Tokyo to obtain one, saying that she wanted to return to the United States. The problem was one of procedure: the vice-consul had to forward her application to the Department of State in Washington for consideration. Before the process could be completed, the Japanese initiated the "Go South" campaign and attacked Pearl Harbor on 7 December 1941. Toguri and several other Nisei women found themselves marooned in Japan for the duration of the war and in desperate need of work. In 1942 Toguri worked mostly as a typist, first for the Domei News Agency and in August 1943 for Radio Tokyo. In November 1943 Toguri was forced to become a broadcaster for the "Zero Hour" program, part of a Japanese psychological warfare campaign developed by Major Tsuneishi and designed to lower the morale of the American armed forces in the Pacific. Featured were reports of major accidents, fires, floods, and other bad news from the United States.[59] "Zero Hour" was broadcast every day except Sunday from 6 to 7:15 PM., Tokyo time. Toguri participated in most weekday broadcasts, but other marooned Nisei women handled the weekend duties.

Never was the name "Tokyo Rose" used on "Zero Hour"—only the Americans called her that. Her on-air name was "Orphan Ann" or "Orphan Annie," and for about twenty minutes each day she made propaganda statements developed by the staff at Radio Tokyo. By late 1944 Toguri was writing some of her own material for the program, helped by a Japanese American POW, Sergeant Frank Fugita, and an Australian POW, Major Charles W. Cousens. According to Fugita, the propaganda programs began in 1942 when the Japanese forced POWs with some radio or entertainment experience to read false statements about Japanese victories in the Pacific. Fugita notes, "A few cooperated willingly, but most attempted, by the manner in which they read their scripts, to discredit the Japanese message, and otherwise render their presentations unbelievable."[60] As far as its propaganda value was concerned, U.S. Army analyses suggested that the program had no negative effect on troop morale and might have even raised it a bit. The sole concern about the broadcasts was that "Annie" appeared to have good intelligence on American ship and troop movements.

On 19 April 1945, before the war ended, Iva Toguri married Felipe d'Aquino, a Portuguese citizen of Japanese ancestry. The marriage was registered with the Portuguese consulate in Tokyo; however, d'Aquino did not renounce her American citizenship and continued her "Zero

Iva Toguri d'Aquino, known as "Tokyo Rose," participated in the "Zero Hour" program in Tokyo. The U.S. Army in Japan cleared her of any treachery, but she was persecuted by American civilians at home. NARA, U.S. Army photograph.

Hour" broadcast until the war was over. Two scoop-seeking reporters, Henry Brundidge of *Cosmopolitan* magazine and Clark Lee, a correspondent for the International News Service, sought Tokyo Rose in postwar Japan as part of the search for war criminals. In their minds, they were looking for a 1945 version of "Dragon Lady," but they found anything but the infamous fictional character from the popular "yellow peril" fiction. Brundidge and Lee offered her the significant sum of $2,000, which they later reneged on paying, for the exclusive right to interview her. Hiding d'Aquino and her husband in the Imperial Hotel, they obtained her confession that she was the "one and only Tokyo Rose."[61] The problem was that she lied; she was not the "one and only," since other Nisei women had participated in the broadcasts. For that reason, Brundidge and Lee refused to pay her the promised $2,000. When the story broke that Tokyo Rose had been found, General Douglas MacArthur's headquarters announced that warrants were being issued for suspected war criminals. The military police arrested her on 16 October 1945 and took her to Yokohama prison until 16 November, then transferred her to Sugamo prison near Tokyo, the jail that housed all the major war criminals.

The FBI and the Army Counterintelligence Corps conducted an extensive investigation to determine whether Iva Toguri d'Aquino had committed crimes against the United States. By the following October, authorities decided that the evidence did not merit prosecution, and she was released.[62] When her case was forwarded to Assistant Attorney General Theron L. Caudle in the Criminal Division, he sent it to Nathan T. Elliff of the Chief Internal Security Section for evaluation and recommendation, who determined that prosecution for treason was not warranted. After d'Aquino applied for a passport to return to the United States in 1947, word leaked out that Tokyo Rose wanted to come home, and the national commander of the American Legion and the Native Sons of the Golden West Americanism Committee demanded a treason trial by contacting J. Edgar Hoover and George C. Marshall, among others.[63] Had the Justice Department put an end to the case at this point, the Tokyo Rose issue would have died right there, but another voice entered the arena: broadcaster and gossip columnist Walter Winchell.

During the late 1940s and throughout the 1950s, Walter Winchell was perhaps the most popular voice on the radio and early television. Although he started out as a Rooseveltian New Dealer, in the postwar years, like some of his colleagues, he turned to the Right. Winchell's problem was not his on-air persona—his was indeed the voice of doom—but his overblown ego and vanity. In the d'Aquino case, he believed the Justice Department had denied him a scoop, that is, a first and exclusive shot at reporting a treason case—something he believed he deserved as the dean of reportage in New York.

Thomas DeWolfe had served the Justice Department since 1927 and had participated in the treason trials of other broadcasters. He had no illusions that he could prosecute Iva d'Aquino successfully, but when his bosses instructed him to proceed vigorously, he had no choice. Iva d'Aquino returned under guard to the United States in the transport ship *General H. F. Hodges,* which left Yokohama on 15 September 1948 and arrived in San Francisco on 25 September. Defending her was Wayne Collins, one of the most important defense lawyers in San Francisco at the time. The trial began on 5 July 1949 with an all-white, middle-class jury and lasted for fifty-two days of testimony. The jury finally received the case on 26 September 1949 and found her guilty of one count of treason. Judge Michael J. Roche sentenced Iva Toguri d'Aquino to ten years in prison and a $10,000 fine. She joined Mildred Gillers at the Federal Women's Reformatory at Alderson, West Virginia. Initially, her attorneys appealed to the Ninth Circuit Court of Appeals and then to the U.S. Supreme Court but failed to gain even a hearing.

After her release from Alderson in January 1956, d'Aquino moved to Chicago, where her father had opened a Japanese import retail store after his release from the Gila River relocation center in September 1943. She never reunited with nor saw her husband again. After her trial he had been deported to Japan, and she divorced him in 1980; he died in 1996. According to historian Stanley I. Kutler, the Justice Department continued to hound d'Aquino for full payment of the $10,000 up to 1971. Finally in 1977, in the closing days of Gerald R. Ford's administration, the president pardoned Iva Toguri d'Aquino.[64] She lived quietly and worked at her father's store until her death in 2006.[65]

Each war brings an end to one era and begins another. This was certainly true of World War II. Not since 1945 has the world been at war to the degree it was between 1939 and 1945, but the war did not really end in 1945. German soldiers in Europe died in American prison camps from neglect; German war criminals, including those who murdered their own comrades in American POW camps, died by the hangman. There were no Rhine Meadow Camps in Japan, but the number of Japanese convicted of and executed for war crimes was high. The trials in Nuremberg, Dachau, and Tokyo reminded the world that evil deeds in defiance of international law, including the murder of prisoners of war, deportation, slave labor, and raw genocide, constitute capital crimes against the peace and crimes against humanity, as outlined in the Nuremberg Principles of 1946. The "only obeying orders" defense counted for nothing anymore. With the conviction that men and women are rational, moral beings responsible for their actions at all times, the Nuremberg Principles had teeth. One problem that faced the international community was international law itself. The 1929 Geneva Convention had no provisions for these crimes, and in response, the nations of the world met in Geneva to formulate a new convention in 1949 (see appendix 11), resulting in the provisions of international law that the world lives by today.

Every modern war has to deal with refugees uprooted from their homes on the battlefield. With Europe having fought as much a race war as a political or ideological war, and with Europe split into zones of occupation and spheres of influence, some of its DPs died at the hands of their former countrymen if they tried to return home. Zionism on the one hand and communism on the other prevented the Jewish surviving remnant, former POWs, slave laborers, and innocents caught up in the war's dislocations from returning to their homes in the Soviet Zone of Occupation, which was all of eastern Europe. Zionist Jews, having rejected the prospect of living among European Christians, immigrated to British Palestine, which became the Jewish state of Israel in 1948; others immigrated to North and South America, Canada, England, Australia, and New Zealand, all realizing a bit late that deadly political mistakes about immigration had been made prior to 1939.

Traitors were dealt with harshly following World War II. The British hanged two of their traitors—William "Lord Haw Haw" Joyce on 2 January 1946 and John Amery on 29 December. Both traitors received trials and faced the hangman, Albert Pierrepoint. Commenting on the Amery execution, Pierrepoint called him the bravest man he ever hanged.[66] Other British renegades, most of them members of the British Free Corps in the German army, received jail sentences. The Americans executed no one for treason after World War II but did imprison traitors. The Soviets considered all their POWs held by the Germans enemies of the state and shipped many off to Siberian work camps upon their return home. Those anticommunist Russians who had fought for the Germans, after being forcibly repatriated from camps in the West, often faced execution when they arrived in the waiting arms of the NKVD, the Soviet secret police. Today, few thoughtful people would deny that the Yalta agreement inflicted a severe injustice on those former Soviet citizens who returned but in no way assisted the Nazis or the Nazi cause.[67] The issue of forced repatriation haunted the communist and noncommunist worlds not only in the ensuing Cold War but also when the next clash of arms erupted in Korea in 1950.

TWELVE

Prisoners at War

*Forced Repatriation and the
Prison Revolts in Korea*

To force those people to go back to a life of terror and persecution
is something that would violate every moral standard by which
America lives.
—Dwight D. Eisenhower

The American military services recognized that political conscience was
more important in the Cold War than it had been during World War
II. A middle ground was essential because a political act or statement
in a prison camp is radically different from an individual political act
at home. Prisoners do not represent themselves; they act as direct representatives of their government and the military services engaged in
public war. After the Korean War, the American government decided
that something had to be done so that its free-thinking soldiers, accustomed to the rule of law, could better understand what was expected
of them (see appendix 12). The lessons gained from Korean captivity
in general implied that future hostilities in the Cold War would involve
strong political issues for soldiers to come to terms with, from capture
to repatriation.

International law changed slightly when the 1949 Geneva Convention replaced the 1929 version, but more significantly for the time, political captivity replaced traditional notions of military captivity. As Allied
POWs discovered in Asia during World War II, international law meant
very little when captors developed other agendas. They never needed a
code before; they had the 1929 Geneva Convention, which required all
prisoners of war to give only their name, rank, and serial number. There
was a second, unwritten code as well, one built into their individual
and collective personalities. The American soldier-escapees of the Civil
War had called this code "pure cussedness," which required POWs to
cause as much trouble for their captors as possible.[1] The United Nations
Command in Korea learned that the quality of "pure cussedness" was
present not only in American and Allied armies but also among the
enemy—in this case, the North Korean and Chinese communist armies.

Forced repatriation was the key issue in the Korean War's UN prison camps, but it is necessary to examine its roots in the Soviet Union before returning to Korea. Fear about conspiracies within its military services began in 1935, when Marshal Joseph Stalin, probably the arch-paranoid of the twentieth century, believed his army officers were plotting to overthrow his rule of the Soviet Union. Allegedly, Marshal M. N. Tukachevsky, the highest-ranking officer of the Red Army, along with many of his officers, was collaborating with the British to overthrow Hitler and then Stalin. When Stalin learned about this treachery, he ordered approximately 30,000 officers arrested.[2] Of the high command, 3 of the 5 marshals were executed, as were 14 of 16 army commanders, all 8 admirals, 60 of 67 corps commanders, 136 of 199 divisional commanders, and 221 of 397 brigade commanders.[3] This action constituted nothing short of a catastrophe for the Red Army, because when the Germans invaded in June 1941, they found the Red Army weakly led by incapable but politically stable Soviet officers. The other effect was that Stalin held his army in contempt, distrusted its loyalty, and was ready to punish anyone he declared to be an enemy of the state.

The Soviets focused considerable attention on recovering two large groups of Russians after the end of World War II: prisoners of war, whom Stalin considered traitors, and those Soviet citizens who had joined the German cause either willfully or against their will as forced laborers. On 11 February 1945 Franklin Roosevelt, Winston Churchill, and Joseph Stalin met at Yalta in Soviet Crimea to discuss the fate of those Slavic national groups held in German captivity. The predominant belief, held by Churchill and Roosevelt, was that all captives wished to return to their native countries and that their home countries would welcome them. Yet, according to Nikolai Tolstoy, "The Yalta Agreement on Prisoners of War contained no provisions regarding the return of unwilling citizens to the USSR."[4] All the prominent members of the Yalta group knew that traitors existed in Germany who meant the Allies harm; these included Mildred Gillers and other broadcasters for the Americans, and John Amery, William "Lord Haw Haw" Joyce, and members of the Nazi British Free Corps for the British. The Soviets focused their attention on those thousands of persons who had been citizens of the Soviet Union on 1 September 1939 and had been captured in German uniform, especially if they had been members of the Red Army on 22 June 1941 or had collaborated with the enemy.[5] Diplomat George Kennan, present at Yalta, summarized the decision: "Knowing as we did, that the entire responsibility for the handling of the repatriations, and the punishment of those repatriated, was in the hands of the NKVD [Soviet political police], and being under no illusion as to the fate that awaited these people on arrival in the Soviet Union, I was in full horror and mortification over what the Western governments were doing."[6] The decision to force expatriate noncommunist Russians back into the arms of their most hated enemies, the communists, became a death warrant for many.

Returning Russians who were subject to the forced repatriation rules came in several categories: those who had served in German uniform; members of the Committee for the Liberation of the Peoples of Russia, led by General Andrei Vlasov, who had been captured by the British and Americans mostly in Austria and Czechoslovakia; those Russians who had served the Germans as forced laborers and been detained as displaced persons in the Western Zones of Occupation; and finally those members of the Red Army who had been taken captive and somehow survived German POW camps. That Stalin considered all POWs held by the Germans to be traitors and enemies of the state became an anomaly; no other nation in 1945 considered its POWs in that light unless there was strong evidence of individual collaboration. It was bizarre and nonsensical that returning Russian POWs who had suffered so terribly—millions had died in German hands—would be condemned and shipped to Siberian work camps or Gulags upon their return home.[7] The Gulags (an acronym for the "main administration of camps") consisted of a vast system of prisons, camps, psychiatric hospitals, and special laboratories, all operated under the Soviet Ministry of the Interior, that housed millions of prisoners, or *zeks*.[8]

Those anticommunist Russians who had fought for the Germans often suffered execution in Austria when they were returned forcibly to the NKVD. Although the British continued to participate in the repatriation policy faithfully, President Harry S. Truman ordered the American European command to cease forced Soviet repatriations of any persons against their will. In part, this act went hand in hand with the deterioration of Soviet-American relations on account of the Cold War, the Marshall Plan, the creation of the Iron Curtain, and the Berlin Airlift. In Korea, the issue of forced repatriation not only surfaced but also forced the war to continue until 1953 instead of ending in 1951.

In June 1950, with Stalin's permission, the Korean People's Army (KPA) of the People's Republic of Korea crossed the thirty-eighth parallel and invaded the Republic of Korea (ROK) with full force. Beginning in 1950 the United States ordered 1,319,000 service personnel to participate in what evolved from a so-called police action into the Korean War. Forces of the United Nations, including South Koreans, Americans, British, Canadians, Australians, New Zealanders, South Africans, Greeks, French, and Turks, fought against the military and political forces of North Korea and China over nearly the full length of the Korean peninsula. The war cost the United States approximately $70 billion, and American military forces lost nearly 37,000 dead from combat and other reasons.[9] For a country recovering from World War II's price tag of more than $560 billion and 350,000 dead, the action in Korea was expensive not only in monetary but also in human terms, especially for POWs. Communist and South Korean atrocities were commonplace, and the number of prisoners mounted as the fighting intensified: 7,140 American servicemen were known to have been captured; 2,701 prisoners died in captivity, and 4,418 were returned to UN control at the end of hostilities in 1953.

Memories of the cruel fates of anticommunist Russians forcibly returned to the NKVD in 1945 to 1947 conditioned American policies during the Korean War relative to EPWs. Forced repatriation was simply out of the question, regardless of the cost. From 1950 to 1951, even before the first armistice talks took place, UN forces took more than 130,000 North Korean and Chinese prisoners of war. The Inchon landing on 15 September 1950 and the Pusan breakout three days later netted more than 20,000 North Korean EPWs by the end of September. When the South Korean (ROK) army crossed the thirty-eighth parallel in October 1950, it took 6,765 prisoners initially and 14,028 from 4 to 6 October. According to Hyo-Soon Song, deputy provost marshal of the ROK army, his troops simply "collected" surrenderers.[10] By a ratio of four to one, they refused repatriation, and most historians agree that this issue alone caused the war's prolongation for two more years.[11]

Unlike the Japanese soldiers in World War II, the Koreans and Chinese never bound themselves to any sort of suicidal death cult. They surrendered in droves, especially when the weather turned wintry or their military situation stalled. At Inchon after the American landings from 6 to 16 September 1950, one soldier recalled that while urinating in the field, "out jumped a North Korean who began bowing and scraping and chin-chinning to me. Talk about getting scared out of your wits. I damn near jumped out of my shoes."[12] Keyes Beech, one of the premier reporters in Korea, recalled some incidents with EPWs and his close friend and competitor, the scoop-oriented reporter Marguerite "Maggie" Higgins.

"The only obstacle that ever blocked Higgins from a story," according to Beech, "was naked men."[13] Beech recalls amusingly:

> On the north bank of the Han River during the battle for Seoul we passed a drove of North Korean prisoners who were being marched to the rear in the buff for security reasons. Higgins primly fixed her gaze directly on the road ahead. Out of the corners of their eyes, the mortified prisoners spotted the passing American woman and hastily covered their loins with their hands. It was a noble but inadequate gesture and entirely lost on the marine guards, who promptly ordered the prisoners to raise their hands again.[14]

Then Higgins and Beech learned of a North Korean army captain being interrogated at the Combat Information Center (CIC). While Higgins watched all the naked EPWs in the river, Beech went to the CIC, where he learned that the prisoner was a deserter and had told the marines that "the Peoples Army had shot its wad, that it had nothing between its front and its rear," and recommended that the Americans make a landing at Inchon.[15]

In a sense, Korea saw its share of problems related to taking prisoners in the heat of battle. In a study of the Twenty-fourth Infantry Regiment in Korea, the U.S. Army's Center of Military History noted that the enemy deliberately tried to intimidate its opponents at all times. Rumors flowed through the ranks that the North Koreans tortured and killed black Americans. One soldier noted that a captured American had been tied between a truck and a tree and then torn in two when the vehicle drove off. Another soldier reported that two American captives had been burned alive in a bonfire within full view of American patrols. In response, many Americans in front-line units established their own unofficial policy of no quarter and brought back captives only when ordered to do so.[16]

The UN Command's counteroffensive ground operations came to a halt in June 1951. They had some startling results in stopping the Chinese forces from reuniting the Korean peninsula. Communist casualties sustained from 15 to 31 May were estimated by the Eighth Army at 105,000, including 17,000 known dead and an unprecedented 11,526 prisoners, mostly Chinese soldiers trying unsuccessfully to avoid surrender and captivity.[17] In March, April, and May 1951 the U.S. Air Force hired the Research and Development (RAND) Corporation to interview Chinese EPWs during their in-processing at Camp 5 near Pusan. Alexander L. George was the interviewer and worked with eighty-six prisoners who agreed to talk and fill in questionnaires concerning their motivations. Although it was a nonscientific study in the strictest sense, George learned why these men fought. He also learned that despite warnings by Chinese communist political officers that the Americans would torture or kill them, the men had decided to seek safety as EPWs. They did not necessarily experience a radical change in their political thinking, however.

The Allied intelligence community began to think about using EPWs in a wholly new kind of operation. Why not select and train cadres of noncommunist EPW volunteers to return to their home regions to gather intelligence and, if possible, form insurgent units of like-minded comrades to fight the communists? First, anticommunist EPW officers and men were recruited for Operation Aviary, a covert mission to conduct long-range reconnaissance patrols into enemy territory, often to retrieve agents.[18] Other intelligence operations took place in Korea; those codenamed Turncoat and Bobcat both used former EPWs as agents. Turncoat recruited captured North Korean and Chinese soldiers from the Koje-do POW camp to return to North Korea by airdrop as spies and covert operatives. Bobcat was similar, except that it targeted partisan-held islands on the Yellow Sea side of Korea. None of these efforts paid major dividends, but they did succeed in rescuing some downed pilots and gathering some intelligence concerning how badly the North Koreans and Chinese were treating UN POWs.[19]

Inside the POW camps on both sides, issues arose that stressed the POW populations to the limit. In the communist camps along the Yalu River, the communist Chinese focused their attention on developing propaganda targeted against the UN prisoners' loyalty to their respective countries and causes. The Chinese were much better at this than their allies the North Koreans. They administered supposed Red Cross surveys to determine a POW's background, and if that failed to elicit the desired information—as it usually did, once the POW realized the deception—starvation became the tool of choice until the POW caved in to self-criticism sessions.[20] The communists based their actions on four main motives: to gain military information, to use informers to control the other POWs in camp, to convert POWs from capitalism to communism, and to undermine POWs' faith in their own countries and institutions.[21] Rarely, if ever, was military information obtained from POWs of any value; it was too old for a fast-moving war like Korea.

But forcing a man to reveal what he thought was valuable information became a huge step in breaking a POW's resistance. General William F. Dean, the highest-ranking American POW in Korea, initially thought the North Koreans wanted military information, but he discovered they wanted propaganda more. He wrote:

> Pressure on me was greatest to agree to perfectly obvious falsities: that the United States was an aggressor; that we had exploited the people of South Korea or wished to do so; that General Douglas MacArthur had ordered Syngman Rhee to start the war. On questions of real significance—our defense plans for Japan, commitment of troops, infantry strategy or organization—they gave up when met with boldfaced lies or a simple refusal to answer. There was also an almost pathological insistence on getting something signed.[22]

This desire for propaganda over substance carried over to the enlisted ranks as well. Lloyd Pate, a tough sergeant from Georgia who found himself a prisoner of the Chinese, wrote, "I didn't like a guy to stand over me and preach things I knew were a pack of lies."[23] Perhaps oral historian Lewis H. Carlson explained it best in *Remembered Prisoners of a Forgotten War:* "Although only a small minority of the prisoners ever took the Chinese propaganda and indoctrination techniques seriously, the people back home certainly did. . . . For the American public, caught in the throes of Cold War and McCarthy paranoia, the massive effort to indoctrinate and 'brainwash' their captives became the indelible legacy of the Korean War POWs."[24]

Twenty-one Americans and one British soldier actually refused repatriation after the armistice and opted for China.[25] All but one ultimately returned home. While they were in China, the twenty-one Americans received dishonorable discharges, and when they returned to the United States, the U.S. Army was powerless to charge them with treason. The FBI likewise could not charge them with anything because their treasonous acts had taken place while they were in the army. So, in an odd turnabout, they returned to the United States as civilians free to reintegrate into American life.

On the United Nations' side of the lines, there were zealous activities in the EPW compounds as well. In 1951 the UN Command reported:

> In accordance with Article 38 of the Geneva convention (1949) intellectual, educational, and recreational pursuits of North Korean and

Chinese Communist Force prisoners of war have been actively encouraged. Instructional centres have been erected in each compound, and four hours per week of classroom instruction are provided for all prisoners on a voluntary basis. Attendance for the weekly reporting period was 68.9 percent. All persons had the opportunity of seeing at least one motion picture programme each week. Radio broadcasts, including news, music, and POW-produced entertainment programmes were available to a majority of the prisoners. Athletics, vocational training, hobbies, and handicrafts are becoming increasingly popular. Daily and weekly news sheets are provided for the use of all literate prisoners and reading groups are encouraged for the benefit of the illiterate.[26]

Many of the North Korean and communist Chinese EPWs had no intention of participating in such activities, or if they did, it was merely a ruse. For example, some vocational activities involved manufacturing harmless items; they made knives and spears instead. It became clear that the committed communist EPWs were still at war and meant it.

Under no circumstances were the Americans or the UN Command willing to hand back anyone who wanted to remain in noncommunist hands. This policy was backed by British Prime Minister Anthony Eden, who told the House of Commons on 7 May 1952, "I am sure the House will feel that the United Nations Command has had no alternative but to resist the forcible repatriation of communist prisoners-of-war who have shown such a strong determination to remain in the free world."[27] Korea was America's first coalition war under the United Nations flag, and South Korea became the detaining power, retaining sovereignty on its own soil; the South Koreans participated, along with the Americans, in the operation of all the UN POW camps. The UN Command had to make certain that the enemy prisoners exercised their right to choose freely. Camp authorities formulated a massive plan to individually screen the North Korean prisoners. Loudspeakers were installed in all the camp compounds and broadcast an amnesty declaration for two days in April 1952:

All prisoners of war will be individually interviewed in the next few days. This interview is being conducted for the purpose of determining which prisoners of war desire to be repatriated to the Korean People's Army or to the Chinese People's Volunteers, and which ones have compelling reasons which they feel would make it impossible for them to return to their own side.

North Korean tuberculosis compound, a ward of the Sixty-fourth Field Hospital at the Koje-do prison camp in South Korea. Courtesy of Joseph Roberts.

At this time I must caution you that the decision you make is a most important one, possibly the most vital one you will ever be called upon to make. You must most carefully consider each aspect of the matter. You must make your own decision, and for your own safety it is essential that you do not discuss this matter with others, and above all that you let no other person, even your best friend, know what your decision will be.[28]

The loudspeakers went on to point out that the prisoners had to consider their families and reminded them that the communists often took hostile action against the families of those soldiers they considered to be traitors. Finally, the loudspeakers announced to every compound, "Depending upon each individual's decision, he will remain in his present compound or be moved immediately."[29] The plan was to move prisoners who chose amnesty away from their communist comrades to the safety of being with like-minded people.

One of the largest prison facilities for North Korean and Chinese EPWs was constructed on the island of Koje-do, south of the mainland. At first, the UN Command considered Cheju-do, a large island with more than 250,000 inhabitants, but Koje-do, less populated, was chosen despite its mountainous terrain.[30] General Matthew B. Ridgway commented, "This was merely a choice between evils, for Koje-do was itself hardly the ground a sane man would have chosen to erect camp sites." He also knew that he had serious problems with the guard force, lamenting in his memoir, "The personnel we could spare to take charge of the camps was not of the quality to insure the alertness needed to detect these plots or to identify and isolate the ringleaders."[31] The EPW population grew astoundingly in 1952, so much so that Ridgway opened two more island prison camps, one on Cheju-do and the other on Pongam-do.

The actual screenings at Koje began on 8 April 1952 in the largest Chinese compound of approximately 8,100 EPWs. Seven questions were posed to each man:

1. Will you voluntarily be repatriated to communist China?
2. Will you forcibly resist repatriation?
3. Have you carefully considered the impact of such actions on your family?
4. Do you realize that you may remain here at Koje-do long after those electing repatriation have returned?
5. Do you realize that the United Nations cannot promise that you will be sent to any certain place?
6. Are you still determined that you would violently resist repatriation?
7. What would you do if you are repatriated in spite of this decision?

The questions were posed one at a time, but as soon as a prisoner expressed the desire to be repatriated, the questions stopped immediately.[32]

The results stunned the Americans and infuriated the communist Chinese and North Koreans. Among the Chinese, 6,900 EPWs, roughly 85 percent, chose an eventual move to Taiwan; among the North Koreans, it was more difficult to tally the results because several communist compounds resisted screening completely. What the UN Command learned later was that the communists had developed an ingenious program of sending trained agents provocateur into the camps to implement their political policies.[33] One such agent was KPA Colonel Pak Sang-hyon, one of the original group of thirty-six Soviet Koreans brought to North Korea in 1945 to help create the communist regime. Pak used the alias Joen Moon Il for his prison records, and he called himself a private. Neither Ridgway nor anyone else in the UN Command had any knowledge of Pak and other high-ranking communist officers infiltrating the UN EPW compounds. In Ridgway's words, "In the person of Nam Il [the North Koreans' chief communist negotiator], he contrived to stage a whole series of incidents that were intended to damage the United Nations in the eyes of the people of Asia."[34] Biographer and historian Stanley Weintraub, himself a Korean War veteran, remembered Colonel Pak:

> We knew of such special agents as Lt. Col. Pak, and on occasion the mask slipped, as when ordinary POWs were seen acting very deferential to someone who was self-identified as a mere private like themselves. We recognized that names given us meant nothing (there are only about six common surnames anyway!), and we identified POWs from capture through incarceration by fingerprints accompanying serial numbers.[35]

Pak obeyed orders by organizing and controlling all the communist compounds in Koje and became the leader of the resistance. He issued instructions, directives, and propaganda, and it was he who sentenced to death many of the prisoners who dared to defy Communist Party directions.[36]

At two compounds that did agree to the screening, repatriation proved to be unpopular. At one compound, known as the "Anti-Communist Youth League," 82 percent chose amnesty; at the second, the "Christian Compound," the total was 50 percent.[37] Although it is impossible to assert with certainty, perhaps the Chinese numbers were so high because many members of the Chinese People's Volunteers were not volunteers at all; rather, they were members of the former Chinese Nationalist army forced to fight in Korea against their will. No one can know for sure. After the screenings in April 1952, UN delegates to the armistice talks in Panmunjom told the North Koreans and the Chinese that of the 150,000 communist prisoners of war in UN hands, only 70,000 wished to return home willingly. As far as the communists were concerned, this flew in the face of the 1949 Geneva Convention, which required all POWs to be released and repatriated without delay after the cessation of hostilities. The Americans' policy of granting political asylum became a huge success for the UN Command and an embarrassment for the North Korean and Chinese communists.

Before the screening program began, much violence took place on

Koje-do between the communist and noncommunist EPWs. As early as June 1951 communist prisoners attacked a UN Command work detail, leaving three dead and eight wounded. Demonstrations in August left eight noncommunists dead, and in September fifteen noncommunist EPWs died at the hands of a communist "people's court." Three more EPWs died in riots in Compound 78, and UN troops rushed to save 200 noncommunist prisoners deemed to be in mortal danger. The Americans felt helpless, and on 18 September 1951 Colonel Albert C. Morgan, chief of staff of the Second Logistical Command, in charge of all the Korean POW camps, wrote to General James Van Fleet, commander of the Eighth Army, requesting an increase in the guard staff.[38]

The first screenings, intended to establish the status of 38,000 South Koreans dragooned into the communist KPA, took place on Koje in November 1951. The idea was to clear these men from the compounds by classifying them as civilian internees and then turning them loose.[39] Although General Ridgway believed the program was successful, by December huge fights broke out, followed by riots and demonstrations that left fourteen noncommunist prisoners dead and others injured and wounded. Screenings continued, and the fighting escalated.

During the 1952 screenings the prison camps on Koje-do and Cheju-do and the First POW Field Hospital on the mainland exploded in violence. At Koje-do in May and June 1952, communist POW resisters in the camps staged one of the most brutal camp uprisings in POW history. On 8 May 1952, after arming themselves with makeshift weapons, the prisoners seized the American camp commandant, Brigadier General Francis Dodd, and held him as ransom for political concessions. Actually, Colonel Pak had been planning Dodd's apprehension for quite a while. The EPWs knew that Dodd had ordered the compound gates left open to facilitate camp chores and general housekeeping, and the prisoners took advantage of that. To say that camp discipline was lax is a broad understatement, but part of the discipline problem rested on General James Van Fleet's belief that an armistice was at hand, requiring the Americans to impose as few restrictions as possible on the prisoners. At 2 PM Dodd and his assistant, Lieutenant Colonel Wilbur R. Raven, the commanding officer of the Ninety-fourth Military Police Battalion on Koje-do, went to the gate of Compound 76 to talk to the North Korean prisoners about concerns they supposedly had. They invited Dodd and Raven in, but both officers refused to enter. The prisoners then ran up to Dodd and Raven and attempted to pull them into the compound. Raven

Generals of the Korean War, November 1951 (left to right): General James Van Fleet, General Matthew Ridgway, and General Omar Bradley. They are standing in front of the only prewar building of the mainland UN POW hospital. Courtesy of Stanley Weintraub.

got loose and freed himself; Dodd became a prisoner of his prisoners. The North Koreans then posted a large sign saying, "We Capture Dodd. As long as our demands will be solved, his safety is secured. If there happens brutal act such as shooting, his life is danger."[40] It is possible that Dodd had little idea who or what he was dealing with at the time.

General Mark W. Clark, who was in the process of replacing Ridgway as overall commander of the Far East Command, commented with ire that the Americans ought to "let them keep that dumb son of a bitch Dodd, and then go in and level the place."[41] Still in charge, General Ridgway ordered Van Fleet to beef up a force to retake Koje Compound 76, and Van Fleet instructed Brigadier General Paul F. Yount, commander of the Second Logistical Command and Dodd's boss, to appoint Brigadier General Charles F. Colson to replace Dodd immediately. Colson was ordered to send an official demand to Compound 76 for Dodd's release and state that Dodd no longer had any authority to deal with the prisoners. If Dodd was not released, Colson would hold the prisoners responsible for his safety. Yount also made it clear that Colson should fight his way into the compound, free Dodd, and gain control.[42] As a result, plans were made to assault Compound 76.

The EPWs could plainly see that the Americans planned to act soon. Troops and tanks were arriving on Koje-do Island, and the prisoners began to show some fear. Wisely, Colson extended the deadline to 10 May, allowing the prisoners and himself some latitude. Meanwhile, the North Koreans decided to conduct a trial, charging General Dodd with nineteen counts of death or injury to inmates. The North Koreans then invited Colson to join them for discussions inside the compound. Colson declined. By then, the Americans had massed approximately 11,000 troops outside the compound, and Colson talked to Dodd inside the wire. On day four, 10 May 1952, twenty M-46 Patton tanks stood ready to level the compound, with Dodd still in it. Colson sent another demand: free Dodd or else. No one was injured or dead yet, but the hour was quickly approaching for a showdown, and the Americans were ready.

Then came another twist in events: the Compound 76 communist EPWs sent out another set of demands, the most important being to cease screenings. Colson also learned that the other communist compounds planned uprisings as soon as the assault got under way. This was indeed a serious problem for Colson. Looking for some kind of compromise to save lives, including Dodd's, Colson extended the deadline for several hours on his own authority. In back-and-forth messages, Dodd assisted the communist prisoners in formulating their demands in language the Americans could understand. The trouble was that Dodd and Colson were giving the communists too many concessions to suit Van Fleet at headquarters. After producing what appeared to be a confession of sorts, at 9:30 PM on 10 May 1952, Brigadier General Dodd came out of Compound 76, but the damage had been done. The communist EPWs had scored a huge propaganda victory over their American captors.

General Clark reneged on all the promises made under duress. Two days later, on 12 May 1952, command headquarters in Pusan launched an investigation of Dodd's and Colson's actions. Both officers had sought to avoid bloodshed, knowing that the 6,500 communist prisoners in Compound 76 were well armed and very dangerous. But Colson had clearly disobeyed Van Fleet's orders stating that 10 AM was the unbreakable deadline. General Clark, always a tiger about officers' decisions, stated in his memoirs: "You don't negotiate with prisoners of war, particularly fanatical Communist PWs who consider themselves combatants despite capture."[43] Ridgway wrote: "In wartime, a general's life is no more precious than the life of a common soldier. Each is asked to risk his life every day to protect the safety, the freedom, and the honor of his country. If, in order to save an officer's life, we abandoned the cause for which enlisted men had died, we would be guilty of betraying the men whose lives had been placed in our care."[44] Both Dodd and Colson were reduced in rank from brigadier general to colonel and retired from the service.

The Koje-do uprising continued. A new general arrived, and the real fight began. General Haydon L. "Bull" Boatner relieved Colson immediately after Dodd's release and prepared for the onslaught to come. The idea now was to reduce the huge prison population on Koje-do to more manageable numbers. Boatner began with the bullies of Compound 76.[45] At 5:45 AM on 10 June 1952, a month to the day after Dodd's release, Boatner used loudspeakers to announce his intentions to the prisoners. The North Koreans armed themselves with tent poles, knives, spears, and rocks; the Americans used tear gas grenades, throwing them into the prisoners' ranks. After the battle, about 5,000 prisoners surrendered to the 187th Airborne Regimental Combat Team and allowed the evacuation to proceed without any real difficulties. About 1,500 prisoners ganged up for a last stand. By 8:45 AM, the assault was over. Boatner used more tear gas and concussion grenades for mob control. He won, although the Americans lost one man dead and fourteen wounded. Among the prisoners, 31 were killed and 139 wounded.[46] Boatner also discovered the bodies of sixteen murdered prisoners and a stash of homemade weapons, including 3,000 spears, 1,000 gasoline grenades, and 4,500 knives.[47] Colonel Lee Hak-koo, one of the leaders of the communists, was captured, and Compound 77, just as tough as 76, submitted easily.

Boatner executed his orders from Van Fleet faithfully in three phases throughout Koje-do. The first phase demanded that, as commandant, he restore a captor-prisoner relationship—that is, the basic discipline that structures a POW camp and permits a captor to obey the Geneva Convention (1949) and international law. Without this discipline, chaos rules a prison camp, and the ever-present dangers can easily escalate into bloodshed. Phase two required Boatner to build new, smaller compounds to house his prisoners, which took a month, from 10 May to 10 June 1952, to accomplish. Phase three was the actual assault on Compound 76. What shocked Boatner and his colleagues was the intelligence they garnered. American soldiers discovered communist plans for a mass breakout from all the Koje compounds on 20 June 1952.[48] Luckily, Boatner preempted the plan buried in Compound 76 and possibly prevented a slaughter on Koje-do. The Americans learned that, under the protection of the 1949 Geneva Convention, the North Korean and Chinese communist prisoners had seized the opportunity not only to resist their captors individually but also to develop new organizational structures to conduct mass operations. Were it not for the airborne soldiers' assault, the Koje uprising might well have evolved into the largest revolt and breakout in military history.

The troubles with prisoners in Korea did not end with the Koje-do uprising in 1952. Serious trouble broke out on 14 December 1952 at the camp for civilian communists at Pongam-do, another coastal island near Koje-do. It was reminiscent of the Japanese rioting at the Australian and New Zealand camps of Cowra and Featherston during World War II. UN troops moved in, and the subsequent fighting resulted in 85 prisoners killed and 113 wounded and hospitalized.[49] The UN Command issued a press release on 28 January 1953 and quoted the communist side:

> The Communist concept of prisoner of war "fighters" continuing the war within UNC camps is well illustrated by a handwritten communist summary of the result of the mass breakout at Pongam-do on December 14, 1952. The summary recognized that heavy casualties had been expected but that "our fighting comrades were determined to die a glorious death. Although the task imposed on us by the party and the fatherland—which was to break out—could not be fulfilled, the main purpose was to develop a class fight to give the enemy a crushing defeat."[50]

It is clear that the war on the battlefield extended into the POW camps in South Korea. More to the point, the communist Koreans and Chinese changed the long-standing POW paradigm of docility, including reasonable obedience to the captor's rules and directives, waiting out the war, and ultimately going home, to one that involved a continuation of war inside the wire. Commenting in his war memoir *From the Danube to the Yalu,* General Mark W. Clark notes, "During the war they ordered prisoners to riot in our camps in South Korea so that we would lose prestige in the eyes of the world, lose bargaining power at the armistice talks, and be forced to drain off combat troops from the front to guard the POWs."[51] Clark discovered that the communist high command regarded the EPWs in American hands as still having combat status and used them in planned military operations.[52] This change was seminal: prisoners *of* war evolved into prisoners *at* war.

One answer to the resistance and insurrection problems in the South Korean camps was to separate communist and noncommunist prisoners on arrival; another involved some clever paper-shuffling by the American intelligence community. Beginning in 1952, many defecting communist POWs were killed on paper and reported dead so that armistice negotiations could proceed in Panmunjom.[53] Some of this was accomplished at the First POW Field Hospital across from Koje-do on the mainland. Stanley Weintraub, then a first lieutenant and one of the hospital's administrative officers, understood how organized the communists were:

> The main POW hospital for which I was admissions officer was their message center to and from Koje via feigned illnesses, and more communications came from radios and hand-messages smuggled in by bribed or otherwise untrustworthy ROK prison guards who were easy marks because of their low status and even lower pay. They were able to access local villagers outside who were communist in sympathy or merely paid for services rendered. Some messages from the North even came in through honey-wagon ox-cart drivers, who were never searched because their fecal odor was as overwhelming as their conveyances and cargo. There were always ways. One of my own interpreters, a POW also surnamed Pak, was loyal, but many "trustees" were actually spies, employed naively by us because they could cope with English.[54]

Weintraub also railed at the communist assertions that the hospital was a death camp where "many American doctors and scientists have come on the pretext of rendering medical aid, but as eyewitnesses testify, they secretly experiment on living persons with the latest vaccines and chemical preparations, prepared for the murder of people." Outraged, Weintraub comments, "This accusation was the amazing example of twisting virtue into sin."[55]

The same sort of battle over screening that took place on Koje-do took place inside every POW camp in South Korea, including the First POW Field Hospital, despite its humane mission. Simply stated, the communist EPWs took over the hospital wards, including the women's compound. Weintraub notes that there was the usual screaming, sing-

Delousing North Korean EPWs in Compound 4 of
the Combined Third and Fourteenth Hospitals on the
Korean mainland. Courtesy of Stanley Weintraub.

ing, flag waving, and rock throwing as in the men's compounds, but
inside the women's compound were many children. Instead of giving the
little ones prison records, the Americans decided to ignore them in the
head counts but treat them for diseases anyway, another profound act
of humanity. Like the actions at Koje and the other camps in rebellion,
infantry units came to the First POW Field Hospital, and in May 1952,
one by one, they pacified the wards and screened the inmate patients.

Joseph Stalin died on 5 March 1953, a welcome event to the noncommunist world. On 28 March 1953 the communist command, including
both the Chinese and the North Koreans, sent a message to General
Clark in Tokyo informing him that they sought an exchange of sick and

wounded prisoners and a resumption of peace negotiations, which had been suspended for six months. In part, the communiqué read:

> Since your side now expresses readiness to apply the provisions of the Geneva Convention to sick and injured prisoners of war in the custody of both sides, our side, as an expression of a similar intent, fully agrees to your side's proposal to exchange sick and injured prisoners of war of both sides during the period of hostilities. This proposal should be dealt with in accordance with the provisions of Article 109 of the Geneva Convention.[56]

Despite the communist effort to shift blame for the suspension of negotiations to the UN Command, and despite his fear that the communists sought yet another propaganda coup, Clark responded:

> Accordingly, I will be prepared to instruct my Liaison Group as a second order of business to meet with your Liaison Group to arrange for a resumption of Armistice Negotiations by our respective delegations. We take it as implicit in your suggestion in the respect that you would be prepared to accept United Nations command proposals or make some comparable constructive proposal of your own which would constitute a vital basis for resumption of delegation meetings.[57]

This time, speaking for the communist side was Premier and Foreign Minister Chou En-lai, one of the true pragmatic geniuses of the post–World War II and Cold War era. It was Chou, not Mao Zedong or Kim Il Sung or any of the warring generals, who engineered the end of the Korean War.

Finally in 1953 the communist Chinese and North Koreans accepted a compromise on prisoner return. Both sides agreed that all prisoners of war who sought repatriation would be returned home. Anyone who refused repatriation on either side would be taken to an area between the two sides, known as the Demilitarized Zone, in the custody of a Neutral Nations Repatriation Commission; India directed this effort. There, the prisoners would talk to representatives of their home country, who would attempt to convince them to return home. If that effort failed, the United Nations would discharge them as free civilians and help them settle in homelands of their choice.[58] On 28 March 1953 the communist commanders agreed to an exchange and suggested that this might be a

South Korean President Syngman Rhee with General Douglas MacArthur before the Korean War. NARA, U.S. Army photograph

wider window of opportunity for a general armistice. On 11 April 1953 representatives from both sides signed an initial agreement establishing an exchange of sick and wounded prisoners of war. Operation Little Switch, begun on 20 April and lasting until 3 May 1953, exchanged 6,670 North Koreans and Chinese communists for 684 UN prisoners, including 149 Americans. Caught off guard, the UN Command learned that many of the exchanged Americans were "progressives," POWs who had cooperated with the communists in camp. Yet again, the communists won a propaganda victory.

South Korean President Syngman Rhee did not agree with any of this. His three-fold plan was to "go north alone," if necessary, to unify the Korean peninsula under his control; withdraw the ROK forces from the UN Command; and release all anticommunist prisoners without involving the Americans or anyone else.[59] The first two elements never came to fruition; however, Rhee formed a plan with his generals to release all the noncommunist Korean prisoners of war himself in what he called "D-Day." In June 1953 there were a total of nine POW camps throughout South Korea detaining approximately 36,000 EPWs. In a bid to snub the armistice talks at Panmunjom, Rhee concocted a masterful plan to neutralize American efforts to deal with the communists. When the Americans learned of the plan after the fact, they were aghast but incapable of stopping it. At camp after camp, the South Koreans immobilized or bypassed the Americans and released all the noncommunist North Koreans into the general population. Calling them "escapers," the local police often welcomed them and even provided them with new civilian clothes. In effect, they were free men, to the embarrassment of the Americans. Clark expressed his anger to Rhee in a letter: "I am profoundly shocked by this unilateral abrogation of your personal commitment. On several occasions in recent weeks you have personally assured both Ambassador Briggs and me that you would not take unilateral action with reference to ROK forces under my command until after full and frank discussion with me. Your actions today have clearly abrogated these assurances."[60] The cat was out of the bag, the deed was done, and American hopes to recapture these "escaped" prisoners were dashed.

The trouble continued. Beginning with Little Switch, part of the communist mission involved embarrassing the UN Command as much as possible. On Koje-do the communist EPWs chanted, shouted, and attacked the UN guards until dispersed with tear gas. When the EPWs involved in Little Switch arrived at a collecting point in Pusan, they started fights, ripped and tore their newly issued UN clothing from their backs, and discarded soap and other toiletries. Some Chinese returnees staged a sit-down strike aboard an American landing ship that brought them from Cheju-do to Pusan; the American sailors cheerfully used the ship's fire hoses to disembark them.

After the general armistice was signed on 27 July 1953, both sides established Operation Big Switch and exchanged a total of 88,596 prisoners.[61] In a cumbersome operation, UN POWs were put into cattle cars without any food for a train ride from their camps in North Korea to Keasong, where they sat for days awaiting a truck ride to "Freedom Village"—the last step in their journey. Under the terms of the agreement, POWs who refused repatriation were placed in the custody of the Neutral Nations Repatriation Commission, which had agreed to furnish troops to guard them. When the commission took custody, the names of twenty-three UN POWs were announced; in addition, 325 South Koreans had cast their lot with the communists. Efforts to convince these men to return to their own side met with little success.

The Korean War ended only after a face-saving compromise permitted the communist side to free its UN POWs for repatriation. More important, the North Koreans and communist Chinese acquiesced in allowing their own people who refused to return to stay in South Korea or Taiwan. Of the more than 171,000 EPWs taken by all the forces of the UN Command, about half decided to repatriate home, and the other half chose to remain in noncommunist lands. This indeed represented a victory in this limited but vicious war. The other victory was for the communists, who changed the POW tradition of docility in quarantine and kept EPWs in a combat environment inside enemy POW camps. Only General Haydon "Bull" Boatner's assertive command at Koje-do controlled the compounds.[62]

The Korean War ended with an armistice at the thirty-eighth parallel, where it had begun in 1950, but technically, the war continues today. The border between North and South Korea remains armed beyond anyone's wildest imagination. Today, North Korea, armed to the teeth, is always prepared for an American invasion that in all probability will never come. Although considerably rebuilt from the horrors of war, North Korea remains a pauper on the world stage. Yet neither communist China nor communist North Korea was defeated. It was indeed a "peace without victory," to borrow the phrase used by Pope Benedict XV and Woodrow Wilson from World War I. If prisoners of war are supposed to be disruptive and make life miserable for their captors, as was the general thinking during World War II, then the Korean and Chinese communist prisoners outdid themselves in their resistance to screening in the South Korean POW camps. If, however, one concludes that forced repatriation was an inhumane act, then it seems clear that the American affirmation of the right of political asylum was both moral and humane, despite the human cost. The communist demand for forced repatriation of unwilling EPWs, in a replay of the dizzying events perpetrated by Joseph Stalin after World War II, ended in Korea. The moral high ground of humane and proper treatment for all enemy prisoners of war and political asylum for those EPWs who desired it prevailed in Korea and remains in place today.

THIRTEEN

Vietnam Quagmire

Enemy Prisoners of War, Phoenix, and the Vietcong Infrastructure

The courage and skill of our men in battle will be matched by their magnanimity when the battle ends. And all American military action in Vietnam will stop as soon as aggression by others is stopped.
—Lyndon B. Johnson

During the Vietnam War, especially from 1965 to 1971, when American combat units took prisoners in the field, thousands of Vietcong and North Vietnamese soldiers fell into American hands. If enemy soldiers were captured in uniform, the process was relatively simple and standard. In accordance with the Rules of Engagement and the 1949 Geneva Convention, they were sent to one of the prison camps in South Vietnam to wait out the war in POW quarantine. The 1949 Geneva Convention and the 1964 agreement between the United States and South Vietnam protected North Vietnamese military prisoners and confirmed that North Vietnamese EPWs were to be treated fairly and humanely, with oversight by the International Red Cross. The Americans and the South Vietnamese agreed to respect the enemy's uniform. The Vietcong, both military and civilian, constituted completely different and far more complicated problems.

The first problem involved sovereignty. North Vietnam, or the Democratic Republic of Vietnam (DRV), was established in 1954 after the French left Indochina and signed the 1954 Geneva Accords. Vietnam was split into North and South, but the DRV claimed sovereignty over all of Vietnam. Analogous to the problem with North Korea before the Korean War, the United States refused to recognize North Vietnam's sovereignty diplomatically, although it did recognize its agreement to honor the Geneva Convention of 1949. Along with eighty-seven nations, the United States recognized South Vietnam, or the Government of Vietnam (GVN), although the Soviet Union vetoed its admission to the United Nations in 1957. As far as the North Vietnamese communists were concerned, the South was merely a puppet or surrogate of the United States, and they considered themselves the true patriots of a united homeland. Thus the Vietnam War, which lasted from 1959 to 1975, was a civil war from 1959 to 1964, an international war from 1964 to 1973, and a fight between North and South Vietnam from 1973 to 1975, when Saigon fell to the communist People's Army of Vietnam.

From 1959 to 1964 the contest between the DRV and the GVN consisted of a relatively low-level insurgency war between the communists in the South, directed by the Politburo in Hanoi, against the noncommunists in the South, who were also fighting one another for power in Saigon. During this period the communists proved to be successful not only as a guerrilla fighting force but also as masterful political operatives, showing by word and deed that they were the true patriots. That they committed outrageous atrocities against the noncommunist southerners seemed to play a very small role in their successful recruiting. Thus, the old Vietminh, or Vietnam Independence League, victors over the French at the Battle of Dien Bien Phu in 1954, evolved into the National Liberation Front (NLF) and grew in substantial numbers in the forty-four provinces of South Vietnam. The president of South Vietnam, Ngo Dinh Diem, a northern Catholic from Hue, knew well that the Vietminh retained the respect of the predominantly Buddhist Vietnamese people for defeating the French colonialists, and he issued a directive that called them the Vietcong (VC) or Vietnamese communists. The Americans simplified all this and called them "Charlie," named after their use of the phonetic alphabet, "Victor Charlie," for VC on the field phones.

Prior to the large American commitment to South Vietnam in 1965, the South Vietnamese considered captured Vietcong soldiers as criminals and sought to try them publicly. According to military legal historian George S. Prugh, from 1965 onward both North and South Vietnam fielded regular army divisions. The GVN formed the Army of Vietnam (ARVN) and also fielded Regional and Popular forces, whereas the Vietcong fielded Main Force and Local Force units, all with numerical designations. The South also fielded its secretive Civilian Irregular Defense Forces, while the communists likewise engaged their own secret self-defense groups of Vietcong. Prugh notes that "the battlefield was everywhere and nowhere, with no identifiable front lines, and no safe rear areas."[1]

As far as EPWs were concerned, some agreement had to be established relative to their status and treatment. Prior to 1965 the South Vietnamese had declared that all Vietcong (that is, South Vietnamese communist fighters) captured with or without arms were criminals.

With this status, the Vietcong enjoyed none of the protections of the Geneva Convention; however, the American command became sensitive to the treatment accorded its own prisoners in enemy hands and convinced the South Vietnamese to confer POW status to Vietcong captured bearing arms. In his autobiography *A Soldier Reports,* Military Assistance Command Vietnam (MACV) commander General William C. Westmoreland explains the problem:

> The South Vietnamese have greater tolerance for cruelty than most Americans. Having long experienced the calculated cruelty and terrorism of the Viet Cong—parading the severed head of an official through a village was commonplace—some South Vietnamese saw little point in observing niceties with prisoners of war. Yet responsible officials recognized—and I constantly stressed—that aside from humanitarian reasons, there were advantages in taking prisoners and treating them decently. Live prisoners can talk, establishing a basic source of intelligence, and word that prisoners and returnees under the *Chieu Hoi* program were well cared for would spread, prompting more to give up. There was also hope, however vain, that the VC and the North Vietnamese would follow the example and treat their prisoners well.[2]

General Westmoreland believed that the Americans retained responsibility not only for those prisoners taken by the Americans but also for those kept by the South Vietnamese.[3] Something had to be done.

On 27 November 1965 the joint Military Committee at MACV proposed a workable plan to apply the Geneva Convention to American, Vietnamese, and Free World forces. The plan called for the construction of five POW camps, one in each tactical zone and one in the Saigon region. The initial plan, similar to the one used in Korea, called for each camp to house 1,000 EPWs with a South Vietnamese guard force and American military police advisors.[4] The temporary military prison camp at Bien Hoa in III Corps near Saigon opened in May 1966; the Pleiku camp opened in II Corps in August 1966; the Da Nang camp in the I Corps area opened in November 1966; the Can Tho camp in the IV Corps Mekong Delta area opened in December 1966; the Qui Nhon camp for female EPWs opened in March 1968; and the largest camp, on Phu Quoc Island off the coast of Cambodia, opened in 1967.

From 1965 to the end of the war, both North Vietnamese and Vietcong fighters lived together in South Vietnam's POW camps, and for

Phu Quoc Island, South Vietnam. The POW camp is located in the upper part of the photograph. Courtesy of C. Timothy Corcoran.

the first time some central planning went into a repatriation program, EPW accountability, identification, and record keeping. Some efforts were made to provide EPW education and labor programs, mail from home, Red Cross visits, and medical attention. Both MACV and the GVN developed an overall sensitivity to the requirements of the Geneva Convention, and by the end of 1967 POW camp capacity increased from 3,000 to 13,000. By the end of 1968 the camps could house 21,000 EPWs. At the end of the Tet Offensive in March 1968, Phu Quoc alone held approximately 28,000 EPWs.[5] By the end of 1971 the South Vietnamese government held 35,665 EPWs in six camps. Of these, American forces had captured 13,365.[6] There still remained the question of communist cadre, unarmed members of the Communist Party who fell into American or GVN hands.

In 1965 Nguyen Kao Ky's government publicly executed Nguyen Van Troi, a committed Vietcong political cadre and sapper, in Saigon's busy downtown marketplace.[7] The National Liberation Front announced that it had killed U.S. Army Sergeant Harold C. Bennett as a reprisal for Troi's execution. Seemingly, the NLF made no differentiation between its

American and South Vietnamese POWs, and on Sunday, 26 September 1965, the NLF announced over Liberation Radio that it had executed army Captain Humbert "Rocky" Versace and Sergeant Kenneth Roraback, both innocent POWs, as further acts of retaliation and reprisal.[8] The Vietcong rejected the 1949 Geneva Convention for the Protection of Prisoners of War in 1964 and held the power of life and death over its POWs, with no international supervision whatsoever. There was no Geneva Convention in the jungle, and the Americans discovered that they were on their own in a war seemingly without rules.

In August 1966, with sentiment in the United States still supporting the war, two North Vietnamese officials called press conferences in Prague and Beijing to announce that captured American airmen were war criminals who had forfeited all claims to protection. Hanoi's legal position was based on its decision to invoke its exception to the American-sponsored Article 85 of the 1949 Geneva Convention, and it promised large-scale, public international trials.[9] As a response to actions in Hanoi, President Lyndon Johnson tried to maneuver the United States and North Vietnam into a negotiating position by calling on the neutral International Committee of the Red Cross (ICRC) for help. The ICRC was powerless to intercede, however, because as early as 1964 Hanoi refused to allow its representatives to enter North Vietnam for the traditional purpose of protecting POWs and inspecting the prison camps. The result was tragic. Although in 1968 the ICRC complimented U.S. efforts to establish the Geneva Convention as the international rulebook for prisoners of war, the American POWs in both North and South Vietnam were alone from beginning to end, left to the whims of their captors and the shifting fortunes of a very long war, whereas the communist soldiers in the South Vietnamese camps were held under the rules of the Geneva Convention. Samuel A. Gonard, president of the ICRC wrote, "We are convinced that in the context of the war in Vietnam the U.S. Forces are devoting a major effort to the spread of knowledge of the Geneva Conventions."[10]

Lyndon Johnson tried another approach to persuade Ho Chi Minh to begin negotiations. Johnson and Pope Paul VI met for the first time on 4 October 1965 at the Waldorf-Astoria in New York City. At this brief and cordial meeting, the pope congratulated Johnson for his focus on educating children and his concern for the poor.[11] Paul VI had traveled to New York to address the United Nations, where he distanced himself from the ever-growing polarization the Cold War was causing in the world. He wished to defend world peace and social justice without advocating one particular side. His unwillingness to identify with one particular faction and his determination to seek peace independently explain his ability to maintain diplomatic relations with communist nations, including North Vietnam, praise American intentions to save Vietnam from a communist takeover, and openly criticize the ever-expanding American bombing operations against North Vietnam.[12]

In his effort to bring about world peace, Paul VI attempted to bring Hanoi to the bargaining table in 1966. The pope used an Italian communist delegation to Vietnam to contact Ho Chi Minh on 29 November 1966. The Vatican requested Ho Chi Minh to allow relief teams and supplies to enter North Vietnam and offered him the Vatican as a location for peace talks with the United States. Ho's response was initially positive, but he dismissed the possibility of talking when the United States began bombing Hanoi on 13 December. A frustrated Pope Paul VI continued the dialogue in vain with North Vietnam. He maintained this peace-seeking dialogue despite the lack of an American diplomat in the Vatican to explain Johnson's intentions and plans in Vietnam.[13] First, the president wished Paul VI to address the South Vietnamese directly or indirectly to ensure the defeat of the communist National Liberation Front at the polls and maintain a communist-free South Vietnam. Second, he petitioned the pope to send a delegation to inspect POW camps in both North and South Vietnam to report on the condition of the prisoners. Johnson was worried about the possible inhumane treatment of American prisoners in North Vietnam.

To the end, Americans hoped that the Vietnamese might embrace the Golden Rule, but accusations of war crimes from both sides got in the way, culminating in a major public humiliation of American POWs on 6 July 1966, when the North Vietnamese paraded them through downtown Hanoi in handcuffs amid angry crowds of civilians. Individually and as a group, the Americans looked gaunt and dejected, and some American media reported that they resembled the American POWs during the Korean War.[14] There was something wrong in Hanoi. At home, the Vietnam War posed a strategic dilemma. South Vietnam's strength was based not on its own determination for victory or political stability but on military commitments made by the United States and a few other Southeast Asia Treaty Organization (SEATO) allies. The United States had little or no will to win but an inordinate fear of losing, which generated significant discrepancies between what the American military said it did and what actually occurred in the field. Journalists called this inconsistency the "credibility gap."

Lyndon Johnson, a masterful press manipulator with regard to domestic politics, abhorred negative press concerning the war. His successor, Richard Nixon, who hated the press most of the time, commented that the negative images of soldiers' behavior in the field actually helped change the course of the war. By the 1970s television, newspapers, and magazines had brought so much of the Vietnam War into American homes that people tired of its reality. Film and literature historian Peter C. Rollins rightly notes that those who captured images of the Vietnam War and screened them were never fully aware of the impact of their work, which led directly to image manipulation. Simply put, the images were real; the conclusions were not.[15] "For many," writes Rollins, "Vietnam was the antithesis of the promise of American life."[16] In negative form, it showed itself not only in newspaper accounts but also, and more importantly, in a celluloid war of movies and slanted documentaries and in personal narratives and novels, newsletters, and journals. After the press broke the My Lai story in 1969 and told the American people and the world that members of C Company, First Platoon, First Battalion, Twentieth Infantry Regiment of the Americal Division had committed a serious war crime in 1968, President Nixon declared that the media were more friendly to the enemy than to the allies.

There was no doubt that a serious war crime had taken place in My Lai, but there was some truth in Nixon's statement too. From the start of open hostilities in 1961 through 1964, the American press hardly reported the political murders of South Vietnamese citizens committed by the North Vietnamese or the Vietcong. According to Roger Hilsman, from 1961 to 1964 the Vietcong kidnapped 28,504 and assassinated 6,587 Vietnamese civilians. Later, some reporting focused on the discovery of thousands of South Vietnamese civilians murdered in the city of Hue, their hands tied behind their backs, by communist cadres during the Tet Offensive of 1968. Nevertheless, the American war crime at My Lai in 1968 became an icon for the war; North Vietnamese and Vietcong war crimes went virtually unnoticed, except by the South Vietnamese.[17]

Contact with EPWs was a daily occurrence, but it went virtually unreported in Vietnam. There was just no news value in it. But years later soldiers' recollections often reveal fascinating experiences. One veteran wrote:

I was in the 9th Infantry Division, 15th Battalion of Engineers, Headquarters Company, Flame Platoon. One day when I was sitting in my truck whose cab sat well above the LCM's [landing craft, medium] hull, some American soldiers offloaded a young Vietnamese female peasant. She had her hands tied and was blindfolded. Apparently, she was caught making a map of our position, and these guys apprehended her. They brought her to the pontoon to await orders from higher up. In the meantime, one of the captors began harassing this young woman by grabbing her and pushing her around. I could tell she was petrified because she was trembling, and her face was ashen. I felt sorry for her but didn't have the courage to say anything. The longer these soldiers harassed her, the more they laughed, and the more they escalated the torment. Then one of them produced a bayonet, grabbed the woman from behind, and slid the back side of the knife across her throat. At that point a shout came from the deck of the LST [landing ship, tank] asking the soldiers "what the hell they thought they were doing." The tough guy with the knife answered, "interrogating the prisoner," not fully comprehending and thus not caring whom he was talking to. Sometimes an enlisted man can be under the illusion his different branch of service makes him immune to others' authority. Who this miscreant was talking to was a small-in-stature navy officer, captain of the ship and the surrounding pontoons. In no uncertain terms, this "little man" told this miscreant and his buddies to cease and desist, and if they didn't, he'd "have their asses."[18]

The soldiers obeyed the navy officer, and a small boat arrived to remove the woman to a local interrogation center, where intelligence personnel could determine her status and deal with her in a more professional way.

Hospitals and medical care were important, and the Americans brought injured EPWs into field hospitals regularly, just as they had done in Korea. MACV policy and the Geneva Convention dictated that EPWs receive the same medical treatment as American wounded. Mobile surgical units and evacuation hospitals had EPW wards, and the American army made certain that wounded North Vietnamese and Vietcong soldiers received the best care possible. This is not to say that things went smoothly in these wards. Anne Simon Auger, an army nurse, noted that she took out a lot of frustrations on the EPWs. Once she made an EPW chew his aspirin for pain because she did not think he had any right to complain while so many Americans lay wounded and injured in the next ward. She recalled too that "one of the POWs attacked me once—tried to choke me—and I hit back at him. Two MPs were all over him. I never saw him again."[19] Yet her strongest and most traumatic experience on the POW ward occurred when a North Vietnamese Army (NVA) soldier was admitted with gunshot wounds he received on an ambush against American soldiers.[20] She believed he was personally responsible for the death of six American soldiers—word travels fast on a hospital ward—and she just snapped with hatred and rage. She recalled, "I couldn't go near this guy because I knew I would kill him. I was shaking from trying to keep my hands off his neck. This scared me to death, and for twelve years after I was scared of experiencing it again."[21] Another nurse, Grace Barolet O'Brien, noted that after returning from an R&R (rest and recreation) trip to Hong Kong in the fall of 1966 she learned that her ward contained ten Vietcong EPWs, one a woman. She became incensed and thought, "God, I didn't come here to take care of POWs; I want to take care of our guys."[22]

Whether they liked it or not, the American nurses and navy corpsmen obeyed General Order 100, the Rules of Engagement, and the Geneva Convention, each of which mandated care for the prisoners in American hands. Recalling his time in the field, one navy corpsman who served with the U.S. Marine Corps in Vietnam in 1967 wrote in 1990:

> Our Lt. Colonel was really into civic action. I never saw prisoners mistreated. Approximately 2 December 1967, the battalion became part of the special landing team operating along the Cua Viet River, Cam Lo, Camp Carroll, the Rock Pile, Highway II, Route 9, and aiding Khe Sanh with operations adjacent to its base. Lt. Colonel McGowan was adamant about taking prisoners and not abusing them. During the Battalion Landing Team operations, I didn't see any prisoners abused. Anyone who did abuse them had to personally explain why to the Colonel.[23]

Stories like this abound among Vietnam combat veterans, but so do stories of accidents and atrocities. W. D. Ehrhart, a marine corporal fighting in the Battle of Hue in 1968, wrote about his encounter with North Vietnamese prisoners in *Vietnam-Perkesie:*

> As we got close to the MACV compound, we could hear shouts of "Fire! Fire!" Even I could hear it, and I could see men running toward a flickering glow. We hurried up, coming out between two buildings into the open courtyard in the center of the compound. In one corner of the courtyard, the small shed that housed about a dozen NVA prisoners was burning. The fire was already beyond control, the entire shed engulfed in flames. We could hear screams, and through the

open door of the shed, we could see bodies covered from head to toe in fire. Some of them were still moving frantically. There was no way to reach them. The courtyard was filled with people watching the North Vietnamese burn.[24]

Ehrhart never mentions whether the fire was started intentionally by the marines, by the EPWs themselves, or by the enemy in battle. Those men in the courtyard had no idea or concern. As combat personnel, they saw only one side of the EPW issue. Intelligence officers, however, saw another side and valued EPWs the most.[25]

Dealing with North Vietnamese regulars may have been difficult in terms of personal interaction with them; there is no doubt that some were tough, well-trained, and highly motivated soldiers. Michael Lee Lanning and Dan Cragg note in their study of the NVA that training before deployment to South Vietnam included a significant amount of indoctrination. NVA soldiers were told that the Americans were cruel captors who often put their captives in bags and threw them into the sea. More deviously, the soldiers were told that if they were captured, the Americans would send them to Korea as slave laborers.[26] There was no limit to American cruelty according to North Vietnamese political officers, and communist propagandists maintained that American military personnel, like the French before them, were true barbarians.[27]

Eric M. Smith, a former member of several military intelligence detachments in Vietnam, recalled that his interrogation unit had a list of vital information, and they used it when they questioned EPWs near Chu Lai. Essential, for example, were several kinds of data, such as accurate personal information on the prisoner; his unit; infiltration route from North Vietnam; names of officers in his unit; types of weapons used; any knowledge of the unit's plans, intentions, and travel routes; hospital locations, and locations of weapons caches.[28] Smith noted that his units seldom encountered North Vietnamese officers, but when they did, it became a major event, and information gained from them could be useful. Avoided was any sort of force or intimidation, because it proved useless. According to Smith, the best kind of information is given willingly: "If you use force on a prisoner, he's going to try to tell you things he thinks you want to hear."[29] The big problem for American captors was the short time available for rigorous, in-depth interrogations. Forty-eight hours—the maximum amount of time the Americans had to interrogate their prisoners—was just not enough time to accomplish very much before turning their EPWs over to the South Vietnamese.

Other Americans who faced NVA EPWs dealt with similar problems, especially when they witnessed how some South Vietnamese soldiers treated them. One naval officer wrote:

We took two handcuffed NVA prisoners from Chau Doc to Tan Chau or somewhere, wherever the PIC [province interrogation center] was located. The ARVN guy with us was sitting in the Jeep with a loaded M-16 pointed at the two NVA kids (about 16 or 17 years old) in the back, with the Jeep bouncing over potholes. He was also threatening and intimidating them, and they were already scared shitless. The guy was an asshole and pissed me off, so I stopped the Jeep, took his M-16 away from him, unloaded it, and put it in the front passenger well. I think we also stopped by a roadside palapa stand which made fruit drinks with Star Brand sugared condensed milk, ice and fresh fruit, which she [the proprietor] mixed with a Waring Blender that she ran off a 12 volt car battery! We all had fruit drinks, and the ride was otherwise uneventful.[30]

The kindness and the cold drink probably accomplished more to break down the EPWs' resistance than the M-16. At least they learned that this American was no barbarian.

Another naval officer interested in VC riverine operations agreed that force never worked on prisoners, but there were other alternatives. "We wanted to know what worked, what did not work, and if it did not, why not, along with likely crossing areas, particularly new ones, as well as the periodicity of the runs and if that schedule was affected by our efforts. The interrogation tactics, techniques and procedures employed were more the standard police practices and we concluded independently that force did NOT work. Alternatively, fear was very effective."[31] To put that theory to work, this officer and his colleague developed an interesting *Playboy* technique:

My U.S. Air Force counterpart (a full blooded Sioux who stood 6' 5"—I was 6' 4" so we towered over all Vietnamese) and I worked out a routine that bore fruit more often than not. John got someone at Ton Son Nhut to phony up a Vietnamese newspaper with a *Chu Hoi* story in it. The fresh caught (nailed the night before) Vietnamese, having been isolated in a connex box since capture, was brought to one of three provincial interrogation rooms. This was a dirt floored eight by ten by twelve feet high room with no windows. (Nine inch screened vents cut high on the wall at roof level was the source of all light and fresh air.) Each room had one table and three chairs and nothing else. We left the prisoner shackled to a chair for ten minutes or so; no doubt it seemed longer to him. John and I would then march into the darkened interrogation room in our camouflage fatigues, he in his dark blue beret and I in my black one, and both wearing aviator sunglasses to unshackle the subject.

We had the EPW's complete and undivided attention and usually could get his name and determine from his accent if he was local or from the north. John (who was fluent in Vietnamese) would then ask several canned questions, at least one which we already knew the correct answer to. If the EPW talked, we would continue. If he was cooperating, normally, I would leave for a moment and John would take out a *Playboy* with a fold-out of an oriental gal. If John could get the guy to assure him that all the gals from his village had shapes like that then we would treat everything he said with a healthy degree of skepticism. If not, we would storm out of the room yelling at each other; we found yelling "watermelon" with different inflections to be particularly effective. We would wait two or three minutes and then storm back into the room and drag the hapless EPW out into the bright, sun lit, courtyard where a Spec. 4, who worked for the Province G-2 (Intelligence section), was waiting with a camera. With the EPW held firmly between us—we were both smiling like idiots of course—the camera would come up, the flash-bulb would go off, and then we would drag the EPW back into the interrogation room. Once seated the phony paper was presented to him, often it had to be read to him, and we waited for real panic to set in. The story was one of those PAO (Public Affairs Office) blurbs about "Lucky So-and So" having seen the light and voluntarily come over to the government side and been accorded all the blessings of freedom along with a nice chunk of change. Particularly if the guy was NVA, or if his village was firmly under VC control, publishing such a story would result in his family being summarily shot and he knew it. Again the *Playboy* came out, and we would see what we could get. I think the gal's name was China Lee and she had a green and white sweater strategically unbuttoned to show all her assets. She was a great validity check.[32]

Even if the *Playboy* technique worked from time to time, usually the committed communist NVA and VC prisoners refused to cooperate.

Vietnam was as much a political war as a military one, and there was another prison system in place in the South, a civilian system operated by the South Vietnamese government. There were four major civilian prisons in South Vietnam—Chi Hoa National Prison in Saigon, Tam Hiep National Prison, Thu Duc National Prison, and Con Son National Prison—plus forty-two provincial jails. None of the POW camps nor any of the prisons in South Vietnam were administrated, guarded, or actually run by American civilian or military personnel; rather, the ARVN operated the POW camps and the Ministry of the Interior, Department of Corrections, ran the civilian prisons and jails. In 1961 the Americans provided one advisor for all the civilian prisons, and he was appalled that there were no prison standards to speak of. As the war escalated, a small army of civilian prison advisors appeared in Vietnam, but rarely could they penetrate the long-standing prison system established by the French more than a century earlier.

The civilian prisons were designed to detain criminals, nothing more. In these prisons one found five different kinds of prisoners. In his personal memoir *Tiger Cage: An Untold Story,* police advisor Donald E. Bordenkircher categorizes them as common criminals, military offenders, and category A, B, and C communist criminals. Common criminal is perhaps the easiest to define: a civil law breaker having nothing to do with politics. Military offenders, according to Bordenkircher, were "members of the South Vietnamese military convicted of committing a civil crime or deserting their units."[33] The communist criminals, all captured unarmed, were divided as follows: category A prisoners held political leadership positions in the Communist Party of South Vietnam, what was called the Vietcong infrastructure (VCI), and served as an illegal shadow government; category B prisoners were also VCI but at a lower support level, such as propaganda teams, tax collectors, or transportation personnel; category C prisoners, perhaps the most common in the civilian prisons, consisted of the lowest-level support personnel. According to Bordenkircher, not all the category Cs were actual members of the Communist Party; most were simple peasants caught up in the war and apprehended while completing menial tasks for the Vietcong.[34] It should be noted, as Bordenkircher does, that all the communist criminals "were held under warrant of the Police Special Branch, advised only by covert CIA personnel, called OSA or "Office of the Special Ambassador."[35] In terms of the war effort, probably the most serious shortcoming of the prisons was that the common criminals, Vietcong suspects, prisoners of war, and even juvenile delinquents were all mixed together.[36] Untangling them became one of the Americans' nightmares.

Like the United States during the Civil War and World War I, South Vietnam kept its share of political prisoners. Like Lamdin P. Milligan and Clement Vallandigham during the Civil War and Eugene V. Debs during World War I, the South Vietnamese considered a few noncommunist members of society dangerous, such as the radical Buddhist religious sects the Cao Dai and Hoa Hao, which challenged both the war and the government. According to Bordenkircher, in late 1967 the entire population of the Vietnamese penal system rose to approximately 32,000, with about 70 percent being communist criminals.[37]

The Vietcong viewed itself as a force of national liberators and freedom fighters. Although the National Liberation Front was allied to the communist apparatus in the North, it saw itself as an independent force. The South Vietnamese government considered the Vietcong a collection of loosely organized indigenous guerrillas, more akin to the partisans in World War II than to soldiers defined in the 1949 Geneva Convention. As far as the Saigon authorities were concerned, "Charlie" was a criminal and deserved nothing more than treatment as one. Hatred between the two sides escalated considerably, and as a result, the Vietcong focused on the South Vietnamese civilian prison system. Beginning in 1967 units of Vietcong began to attack the civilian prisons, freeing more than 2,603 communist prisoners. By mid-1968 additional attacks freed 2,223 more. These operations were not just intended to clear the civilian prisons and get their operatives back; the Vietcong specialized in executing jailers, wives, and children in the most gruesome ways for all to see.[38]

Most American and other allied soldiers knew better and treated the captured Vietcong as soldiers. They were shocked that the South Vietnamese authorities felt differently. Few American soldiers or sailors had any idea that their prisoners were heading for something other than POW camps. They had little idea that the South Vietnamese held hearings on prisoners' status and only if adjudicated a "rebel fighter" would the Vietcong be sent to a POW camp. How long that process took varied from case to case, but there were a considerable number of Vietcong soldiers in limbo in the civilian prisons waiting for their day in court. In 1966 prison facilities in South Vietnam were full, and many prisoners were simply freed to make room for more.[39]

What concerned the American intelligence community was neither forced repatriation nor administering aid to refugees, as had been the case after World War II and Korea. Hostilities in Vietnam included the not-so-covert Central Intelligence Agency (CIA) mission of destroying the Communist Party.[40] By the time Vietnam appeared on the map as a real war in 1964, President Lyndon B. Johnson directed the CIA to

Lyndon B. Johnson and Robert Komer discussing intelligence programs in
Vietnam. LBJ Library.

play a larger role than it had in Korea. Combining the CIA, the military services, and the State Department, the Vietnam war from 1964 to
1973 became the largest intelligence effort since World War II. Literally
everything was connected to one intelligence program or another. The
historical question is whether the intelligence community was successful. Or did it become so unwieldy as to work against itself in the effort
to save South Vietnam from being overrun by the North Vietnamese
communists?

   In 1965 CIA Director Richard Helms ordered Robert W. Komer
(whose nickname in the agency was "Blowtorch"), then head of the Civilian Operations Revolutionary Development Staff in Saigon, to create
counterterror teams with navy SEAL (sea, air, land) advisors to root out
and destroy the VCI.[41] Known initially as the Intelligence Coordination
and Exploitation of the Enemy (ICEX) group, it had three subsections:
the Intelligence Unit evaluated attacks; the Plans and Programs Unit
was responsible for intelligence collection, coordination, and reaction
operations, as well as the screening, detention, and judicial processing
of civilian detainees; and a third unit handled the interrogation of prisoners and defectors.[42] The idea was to beat the communist insurgents

at their own game by developing and using Vietcong techniques of terror to attack and destroy the VCI. The Komer ICEX plan received endorsements from Ambassador Elsworth Bunker and General William C. Westmoreland in Vietnam and eventually made its way to the White House, where it was immediately approved.[43]

William E. Colby took over the program in 1968, renamed it Phoenix, implemented some reforms, and made its mission objectives nearly public knowledge: to kill, capture, or rally members of the Communist Party.[44] Did it work? There is little consensus in this regard, but the North Vietnamese knew that it was the greatest threat to their objective of unifying the communist North with the noncommunist South.[45] Each province had a Phoenix officer who attempted to coordinate the military activities, but in effect, the Phoenix program extended well beyond the military realm. Colby was essentially antimilitary in outlook. He understood the war as a political campaign on the village level rather than merely a military struggle between the North and South Vietnamese. One ingredient in the formula became the *Chieu Hoi* (Open Arms) program. The Americans and South Vietnamese invited any member of the Communist Party—that is, any level of political cadre, main force, local force, or guerrilla soldier—to change sides. Called "rallying" in Vietnam, this program was similar to the Union Army's creation of "galvanized Yankees" during the Civil War. Captured enemy soldiers, especially skilled sappers and other highly trained personnel, were especially welcome and became known as *Hoi Chanh,* or ralliers. With no end to the war in sight, thousands of former prisoners, many of whom were willing or unwilling professional soldiers with no other training or skill, knew that a life sentence awaited them as POWs and decided to become ralliers. After an initial resettlement period of about six months, they often joined special units such as the Kit Carson Scouts, which worked for the American army directly, or the Province Reconnaissance Units, the old counterterror teams that worked for the CIA at the provincial level in the Phoenix program's combat arm.[46] Both were political forces designed to destroy the South Vietnamese Communist Party, often conducting highly secretive operations with the goal of killing or capturing their prey.

Enemy soldiers and cadres (male and female) who rallied to the allied side were interviewed regularly because they were excellent sources of current information about what was planned or being considered in the Communist Party, the community, or the enemy's military organization. This was especially true if the interviewer—interrogator is an

The Kit Carson Scouts, former North Vietnamese soldiers who worked for the American army. Author's collection.

inappropriate term here—persisted in his efforts over extended periods and was patient. For the most part, the *Hoi Chanh* looked and acted like "country bumpkins," but once an interrogator realized that he was talking to the enemy, or perhaps even a respected member of the local or regional Communist Party, each *Hoi Chanh* took on specific importance, in that each person could provide a small but important piece of the puzzle. No *Hoi Chanh* seemed to know very much about very much, but each bit of information contributed something.[47]

The Provincial Reconnaissance Units, South Vietnamese National Police Field Force, and sometimes the Kit Carson Scouts worked as paramilitary units, arresting and jailing civilians they knew or suspected to be party members, without habeas corpus. With procedures styled after the British counterinsurgency activities in Malaya from 1948 to 1960, the political prisoners were first classified as "detainees"—captives with no defined status; then they were often jailed in the provincial jails and interviewed in the province interrogation centers. If they were uncooperative or overtly resisted, they were often treated harshly and sent into squalid conditions such as those found on Con Son Island, South Vietnam's equivalent to the French Devil's Island. This was the brutal and unforgiving side of the Vietnam War, with brutal and unforgiving tactics on both sides.

Political prisoners and communist cadres held by the South Vietnamese, often with the silent consent of the American intelligence personnel and advisors on the scene, received treatment similar to that given to their counterparts in North Vietnam. Neither state granted POW status to its political prisoners, nor did they enjoy oversight by the International Red Cross, a situation that cast a shadow over American POW activities in South Vietnam. On 21 August 1965 President Lyndon B. Johnson addressed the EPW issue directly: "The courage and skill of our men in battle will be matched by their magnanimity when the battle ends. And all American military action in Vietnam will stop as soon as aggression by others is stopped." In the field, at the direction of the president, MACV issued a three- by five-inch card to all American troops containing instructions titled "The Enemy in Your Hands." It not only ordered them to obey the Geneva Convention but also provided positive directions about how to do it. For example, it stated clearly that EPWs should be disarmed, searched, segregated from other prisoners under guard, and removed from the battlefield. Soldiers were under orders not to mistreat their prisoners or humiliate them. Nonmilitary personal effects remained in the prisoners' possession, and medical services could not be denied.[48] The soldiers were also reminded that mistreatment of any captive constituted a criminal offense and instructed to leave any punishment to the courts and judges.

The problem in the field centered on misunderstandings between ARVN troops and their American military advisors. The South Vietnamese soldiers, often serving as interpreters for the Americans, treated their enemy very harshly. Some Americans were shocked by what they saw but could do virtually nothing about it. When tactical information was needed in a hurry, the ARVN rarely constrained itself. Certainly acting well beyond the prohibitions of the Geneva Convention of 1949, many ARVN interrogators were absolutely merciless, kicking, slapping, and using knives on their prisoners; dunking their head into barrels of water; inflicting electric shock by attaching field phones to prisoners' bodies during questioning; and using other tortures designed to force prisoners to reveal military information quickly.[49] Accusations that ARVN and American soldiers threw prisoners from helicopters also arose in Vietnam and alarmed the home front considerably. How many phony war stories evolved into news by a hostile American media is difficult to assert, but abuse certainly took place.

Although little doubt exists that individual American soldiers treated prisoners cruelly, on 18 May 1968 MACV issued a clear directive against such actions. Directive 20-41 noted, "A grave breach of the Geneva Conventions is the most serious type of war crime." It went on to delineate prohibited acts: the use of forbidden arms or ammunition, treacherous requests for quarter, maltreatment of dead bodies, firing on localities that were undefended and without military significance, abuse of or firing on the flag of truce, misuse of the Red Cross emblem, use of civilian clothing by troops to conceal their military character during battle (called "indigenous" operations in Vietnam), poisoning of wells or streams, pillage or purposeless destruction, and the killing of spies or other hostiles without trial. More important, the directive ordered anyone with knowledge of these war crimes to report them to his commanding officer as soon as possible.[50] MACV was serious about punishing war crimes and directed the staff judge advocate to prosecute them vigorously. From 1965 to 1973, 201 army personnel and 77 marines were tried by general and special courts-martial for crimes against Vietnamese civilians.[51] Vietnam was not a lawless theater of operations; nor did any sort of "Wild West" attitude pervade the MACV command structure. The number of general courts-martial totaled 1,926; special courts-martial totaled 31,579.[52] Soldiers in Vietnam called Long Binh Jail, the American prison for American soldiers, "LBJ," with obvious humorous intent. "All the way with LBJ" meant something other than the president's 1964 campaign slogan.

MACV and the Republic of Vietnam made serious efforts to establish reciprocal repatriation of EPWs on both sides. This effort created a problem for the Americans in Hanoi. Section 3 of the U.S. Code of Conduct (see appendix 12) states: "I will not accept parole nor special favors from the enemy." This meant not accepting repatriation without permission from the senior ranking officer in the camp or possibly orders arriving secretly from outside the camp. Yet on 3 February 1967 twenty-eight North Vietnamese EPWs crossed the Ba Hai River and returned home through the Demilitarized Zone (DMZ) separating North and South Vietnam. On 11 March 1967 the Vietcong released two American POWs in the South; the Americans responded by releasing two Vietcong EPWs. On 20 March 1967 the U.S. Navy repatriated two North Vietnamese PT-boat crewmen through Cambodia. On 22 March 1967 the South Vietnamese released twenty-two Vietcong prisoners, and on 23 June 1967 three Vietcong captured by the Americans were released at a jungle rendezvous in exchange for two Americans and a Filipino.[53] In April 1967 MACV began looking into a screening program for sick and wounded EPWs who could be repatriated under Articles 109 and 110 of the Geneva Convention. As a result, forty communist prisoners passed through the DMZ and went home. It is fair to say that 1967 evolved into a reasonably good year for repatriations during hostilities: in all, a total of 139 EPWs were either released in South Vietnam or repatriated to North Vietnam, but 1968 proved to be much more difficult.

Offers made by South Vietnam via the ICRC or directly in peace talks received cold or no responses from the communists in the North. In 1968 the GVN attempted to repatriate forty sick and wounded EPWs and twenty-four civilians to the DRV, with no response. In 1969 these efforts continued with no response. At the Paris Peace Talks on 13 November 1969, the South Vietnamese proposed returning sixty-two sick and wounded. The offer was declined.[54] Finally, after more offers and rejections, the North Vietnamese accepted 570 sick and wounded EPWs, but only a small number wanted to return to the North. Like the policy followed in Korea, no forced repatriation could be imposed on any EPW in Vietnam. When the South Vietnamese attempted to return thirteen EPWs who requested repatriation, the DRV canceled the agreement and ended any efforts at repatriation. In the South the Vietnamese began releasing their EPWs, especially indigenous Vietcong, into the *Chieu Hoi* program and enjoyed considerable success. Writing in the *Connecticut Sunday Herald* in 1972, Edith K. Roosevelt noted naively that MACV had reason to be proud of its compliance with the Geneva Convention, but like prisoners of war everywhere, the EPWs were "unhappy about their confinement."[55] By 1 March 1972 only 188 of 5,960 EPWs had been repatriated to North Vietnam, and 3,084 rallied and became *Hoi Chanh*. In contrast, by the beginning of 1972 the communists had released only fifty-three American POWs and had refused any inspections of their camps in Hanoi and surrounding areas by the ICRC. Even worse, they had made no effort to return any sick and wounded, had refused to supply lists of POWs to the Red Cross, and imposed severe conditions on the Americans and other prisoners of war in their hands.[56]

Most North Vietnamese EPWs were repatriated in 1973 after the Paris Peace Accords were enacted. Like the North Koreans at Panmunjom in 1953, as they crossed the Ba Hai River in boats into the DRV, they tore off the clothes issued to them in South Vietnam to show defiance against their captors and solidarity with their communist brothers.

After the NVA's victory in 1975, the surviving political detainees were freed from their prisons, and any remaining North Vietnamese soldiers were repatriated. Tragedy enveloped the *Hoi Chanh* ralliers in the South when they became victims of retributive wrath yet again. Often returned to their original combat units, they were usually charged and often executed as deserters. Abandoned by their American protectors in a lost war, they had no place to go and suffered the consequences.[57]

The 1973 Paris Peace Accords among the United States, the Democratic Republic of Vietnam, the National Liberation Front, and South Vietnam brought a temporary halt to the war and returned 566 American POWs from the region. In April 1975 the NVA invaded and defeated South Vietnam. By 1976 Vietnam became one country; the NLF was dissolved, and the communists established the Socialist Republic of Vietnam. The United States responded by imposing a trade embargo and demanded a resolution of the lingering and complicated issue of the 2,453 missing Americans. That embargo came to an end in 1994 when President Bill Clinton granted the Socialist Republic of Vietnam full diplomatic and trade status. Relations between the United States and the Socialist Republic of Vietnam have improved to the point that thousands of American veterans revisit their old battlefields and even their old prisons, while their tour guides often misrepresent the history of the war and its aftermath.

Only one American remained in Vietnam after hostilities ended—Private Robert Garwood, who left Vietnam after a long custody from 1965 to 1979.[58] In 1978 Garwood managed to make several trips to the Victory Hotel in Hanoi, where he posed as a foreign worker buying cigarettes and liquor. One night he saw a group of middle-aged Westerners sitting in a corner speaking English. After so many years of speaking only Vietnamese, Garwood's English had faded. He wrote, "I am an American in Vietnam. Are you interested."[59] He then rolled the note as small as he could and asked one of the Westerners for a cigarette. After a short conversation, he put the note in the man's lap. The man was indeed interested and began the process of facilitating Garwood's release. Asked by a Vietnamese colonel what was important, Garwood responded, "Only my freedom."[60] The Marine Corps felt terribly blemished by the Garwood situation, so it prosecuted him and found him guilty of collaboration with the enemy and physical mistreatment of other prisoners. He lost all his back pay, about $140,000, and left the Marine Corps in disgrace and without a cent.[61]

When the war in Vietnam began, it became painfully obvious that international law was inadequate to deal with an insurgency of this kind.[62] The need for a declaration of war disappeared at the onset of the Korean War in 1950, and no such declaration was ever issued for the war in Vietnam. President Lyndon B. Johnson used the Tonkin Gulf Declaration (1964) as his mandate for unlimited military activities, yet he sought grounds for peace from the beginning. Johnson's dealings with Pope Paul VI in an attempt to bring Hanoi to the peace table serves as convincing evidence. But do countries always revert to fighting the last war? In a way, yes. The Nuremberg Principles in 1946 and the 1949 rewrite of the Geneva Convention attempted to upgrade international law based on unforeseen circumstances encountered during World War II. Korea also bore bitter lessons for the Americans who fought there, especially in the prison camps on both sides. On the American side, the armed services issued a Code of Conduct in 1954 for their uniformed members that provided guidelines and expectations for behavior in captivity. The communists saw nearly half their captured soldiers defect to noncommunist countries.

To their credit, the Americans and South Vietnamese expanded the provisions of the Geneva Convention of 1949 to include nonuniformed Vietcong instead of simply declaring them partisans or guerrillas without any protections. This was done despite South Vietnamese objections and their reluctance to extend even minimum humanitarian treatment because of their belief that doing so would mean recognizing the legitimacy of the DRV. The solution was the establishment of a joint U.S.-GVN interrogation system from the national to the provincial level, while the United States maintained all the individual EPW records.[63]

The United States recognized South Vietnam as the detaining power despite the fact that American field forces took large numbers of prisoners during the fighting from 1965 to 1972. From the beginning MACV wanted to establish the principle of the Golden Rule with the DRV and the NLF. It failed because none of the belligerents except the United States agreed to follow the provisions of the Geneva Convention. Hanoi even refused to allow the ICRC to inspect any of its POW camps. In retrospect, perhaps the United States should have retained custody of enemy prisoners of war, but rightly or wrongly, General Westmoreland held Americans responsible for the misbehavior of the South Vietnamese and constantly urged the South Vietnamese to conform to the rules.[64] That alone caused morale problems and at times the breakdown of discipline among the Americans.

The repatriation program was nearly one-sided, with many more opportunities offered to the communists than were offered to the Americans or the South Vietnamese. In Hanoi the North Vietnamese claimed the Americans they held in captivity were criminals and deserved to be tried for war crimes. In the South the GVN created a cumbersome administrative network to deal with EPWs, which included the American Phoenix program, designed to destroy the Communist Party. One wonders why some Vietnamese officials routinely accepted bribes to destroy Vietcong dossiers or release key Vietcong cadres or take no action against them.[65] Perhaps these officials had premonitions about their future. That the People's Army of Vietnam and not the Vietcong defeated the ARVN in 1975 left all EPW issues in limbo. Administrative and legal problems disappear when governments fall. Closely following that victory came Hanoi's call for all South Vietnamese civilian and military officers to report to school. For some, this became years of imprisonment in a brutal reeducation program run by their enemy. In Vietnam, the war was over, but the age of the Gulag continued.

FOURTEEN

To Desert Storm and Beyond

Enemy Prisoners of War and the Conflict of Rules

We have before us the opportunity to forge for ourselves and for future generations a new world order, a world where the rule of law, not the law of the jungle, governs the conduct of nations.
—President George H. W. Bush

On 23 October 1983 a truck loaded with thousands of pounds of explosives slammed into the headquarters of the American and French contingent of a multinational force in Beirut, Lebanon. The people of the United States, the president, and the Marine Corps were horrified as they began to understand the nature and danger of Islamic fundamentalism.[1] The American military services, with the possible exceptions of the garrison forces in Korea, in Germany during the Cold War, and in Bosnia, had never been exceptional international peacekeepers in the contemporary sense. Neither the U.S. Army nor the Marine Corps was a trained police force. With nineteenth-century-like naivete, the Reagan administration wrongly believed that the mere presence of marines on the ground and a battleship at sea could generate enough fear and respect to force opposing sides to negotiate a settlement within the framework of a reasonable compromise. Instead, the American peacekeepers became easy targets, and on 23 October 1983 the terrorist group Hezbollah killed more than 200 marines in one fanatical suicide bombing attack. The survivors showed bitter faces as they dug dead marines from the wreckage, and the news services reported that Americans had not witnessed that number of dead soldiers at one time and place since the Vietnam War.

Two days later the United States engaged its forces in Granada, an island about 100 miles north of Venezuela. In launching Operation Urgent Fury, the United States accepted a call to action to stop a Cuban and Grenadian communist takeover of the government. On 25 October 1983 Urgent Fury targeted the airport, which was being constructed with Cuban assistance and was perceived as a danger to the United States. The U.S. force, consisting of about 7,000 American troops and a few hundred from Jamaica and other small Caribbean countries, encountered about 1,500 hostile Grenadian soldiers and about 700 Cubans. They also found military advisors from the Soviet Union, North Korea, East Germany, Bulgaria, and Libya; took them all prisoner; and quickly repatriated them. President Ronald Reagan commented, "Granada, we were told, was a friendly island paradise for tourism. Well, it wasn't. It was a Soviet-Cuban colony, being readied as a major military bastion to export terror and undermine democracy. We got there just in time."[2]

Serving as deputy commander of the invasion force, Major General Norman Schwartzkopf realized that the American military services had to solve some serious problems before going into any future battle. Nearly everyone involved with Urgent Fury learned that they had little intelligence about Grenada. Accurate maps were nonexistent, radio communications were inadequate among the different services, and there were several incidents of friendly fire killing American troops. According to Ronald H. Cole's comprehensive study of the operation, American forces lost 19 killed in action, the Cubans lost 25 killed and 638 captured, and the Granadians lost 45 killed.[3]

One major result of Urgent Fury in Granada was an overhaul of military doctrine, organization, and operating procedures in the Defense Reorganization Act of 1986, also known as the Goldwater-Nichols Act. Among other reforms, it created effective joint commands and the Special Operations Command, both of which would play important organizational roles in the wars to come.[4] No longer would each military service tend only to its own area of expertise, as they had in Vietnam; instead, each would integrate its strengths with the other services in a truly unified command both in the planning stages of an operation and in the field. The reformers made certain that those operations after 1986 looked very different from those that took place earlier. This new type of military engagement, linked closely with expanded political goals, shaped the context of modern warfare. It began in Panama but extended to Afghanistan and Iraq as well.

In 1989's Operation Just Cause, American forces, now reformed and upgraded, were deployed to capture one man: Manuel Antonio Noriega, the president of Panama. Noriega had been indicted for drug trafficking in 1988 by a federal grand jury, and as far as the Bush administration was concerned, it was protecting American lives in Panama as well as upholding democracy and human rights. Panama had become a center for the drug trade, and the United States believed it had to protect the strategic integrity of the Panama Canal. According to the *New York*

Times, administration officials claimed that the military maintained 12,000 troops, mostly combat forces, in Panama. Additional units were flown into the country to assist in the operation.[5] At first, the Americans wanted Noriega to resign, but when he failed to respond and harassed American citizens in Panama, President Bush ordered the American military to capture him and bring him to justice, not as an EPW but as a high-profile criminal. For the first time since its opening in 1914, the Panama Canal closed to traffic while the fighting took place. In house-to-house urban warfare, the marines hunted for Noriega, who had taken refuge in the Vatican embassy in Panama City. Noriega was finally located, surrendered by the embassy, and captured in January 1990. Brought to the United States for trial, he was convicted of drug trafficking in Miami, Florida, on 10 April 1992. The Noriega affair constitutes a true anomaly in American military history: the first time the United States captured, indicted, tried, convicted, and jailed a head of state for civil crimes. In all, 324 Panamanian soldiers died in battle, and 5,313 were taken prisoner; 19 American soldiers lost their lives as well. Noriega received a forty-year sentence.[6]

The main event of the 1990s took place in the Middle East. The Persian Gulf War, called Operation Desert Shield and then Desert Storm, became one of the most highly planned, well-organized confrontations in the twentieth century. On 2 August 1990 Saddam Hussein's Iraqi army invaded the kingdom of Kuwait, a neighbor and competitor of long standing. After numerous diplomatic attempts between Secretary of State James Baker and Iraqi Foreign Minister Tariq Aziz to urge Hussein to withdraw his forces from Kuwait and voluntarily abide by the United Nations Security Council resolutions, the United States and its allies formed what became known as the Coalition on 7 August 1990 to liberate Kuwait. When Aziz confirmed Iraq's plan to attack Israel with rockets, frustrations rose to a fever pitch. Also, there were great fears that Saddam Hussein would invade Saudi Arabia, the United States' major oil source. President George H. W. Bush believed he had little choice but to go to war, and he began to amass a huge invasion force while simultaneously continuing a highly public diplomatic frenzy to avoid it. Little did the United States realize that dealing with Saddam Hussein and the Baath Party in Iraq would be more akin to dealing with Adolf Hitler's Nazis than with rational men. Journalist David Brooks commented, "The Baath Party bears stronger resemblance to the Nazi party because it is based ultimately on a burning faith in racial superiority." Brooks noted, "in Saddam's terms, [revolution] is not just a political event, as the Russian or French revolution was a political event; it is a mystical, never-ending process of struggle, ascent, and salvation."[7] If Brooks was correct, trying to avoid a war with Saddam's Iraq would be an impossibility.

The first hostile act involved money. The United States froze Iraqi assets in American banks and cut off trade.[8] Then the Coalition established a naval blockade while the U.S. Air Force began a buildup at Saudi Arabia's air bases. By 9 August 1990 U.S. Army units began to arrive in Saudi Arabia as well, and by the end of October, army and marine troop strength totaled 210,000, in addition to 65,000 troops from other Coalition nations.[9] On 29 November the United States set 15 January 1991 as the deadline for Iraq to abandon Kuwait, and as that date approached, the Coalition force approached 450,000 troops. On 16 January 1991 President Bush announced that the United States and its allies "have no choice but to force Saddam from Kuwait by force. We will not fail."[10] Saddam quipped that Bush was a hypocritical criminal and vowed to crush the satanic intentions of the White House. Bush responded that the goal was not the conquest of Iraq—that came later, in 2003—but the liberation of Kuwait. The Coalition knew it faced more than 100,000 Iraqi soldiers under arms, and Saddam Hussein's bluster about the "mother of all battles" added a generous amount of scary propaganda to the mix. Fear of a Vietnam-like defeat dominated American strategic and tactical thinking, but with more than 170 warships, including 6 aircraft carriers and 2 battleships, and a total air component of 2,200 aircraft prepared for war, Saddam Hussein's forces had no chance against the Coalition.

The massive air campaign, approximately 88,000 missions, began on 16 January 1991 and lasted for thirty-eight days. There were constant air assaults, mostly against command and control targets. President Bush addressed the nation on the television, saying:

> Tonight, twenty-eight nations, countries from five continents—Europe and Asia, Africa, and the Arab League—have forces in the Gulf area standing shoulder-to-shoulder against Saddam Hussein. These countries had hoped the use of force could be avoided. This is an historic moment. We have in this past year made great progress in ending the long era of conflict and Cold War. We have before us the opportunity to forge for ourselves and for future generations a new world order, a world where the rule of law, not the law of the jungle, governs the conduct of nations.[11]

The Iraqi air force never showed itself in any strength. For the most part, it hid its aircraft in concealed bunkers or flew its combat aircraft to Iran for safekeeping. The Iraqis did launch old Soviet Scud surface-to-air missiles at targets in both Israel and Saudi Arabia. At the behest of the United States, the Israelis, never hesitant to defend themselves, did not respond to Saddam's provocations. Although there is little agreement on exact numbers, the Coalition destroyed approximately 80 percent of the Scuds launched against Saudi Arabia and 50 percent of those launched against Israel.[12]

At precisely 4 AM on 24 February 1991, after thirty-eight days of constant bombing, Operation Desert Storm began in earnest. With most of the Iraqi command and control facilities damaged or wiped out completely, the Iraqis lost both effective communications and any ground initiatives they may have launched against the Coalition. The Coalition forces initiated the ground war to cut Iraqi forces off from Kuwait and were successful nearly beyond belief. According to the report *United States Army Reserve in Operation Desert Storm,* "The Iraqis were stunned. Never had they imagined the extent of the Coalition triumph, the most visible results of which were the liberation of Kuwait and one of the largest mass capitulations in history."[13] After 100 hours of combat, Coalition losses amounted to 95 killed, 368 wounded, and 20 missing. A cease-fire was negotiated that ended hostilities on 28 February 1991, with Iraq agreeing to all American terms.

A large number of Iraqis deserted their units and surrendered, in part because of leaflet drops assuring them that they would receive good treatment by the Coalition, and in part because of the savage nature of the air and ground attacks. Despite the leaflets, some Iraqi soldiers were terribly concerned about the treatment they would receive from the Americans. According to a study conducted at the U.S. Army War College in 1992, Lieutenant Colonel Jon Bilbo found that "throughout Desert Shield, the Iraqi government and its military leadership conducted an aggressive propaganda campaign designed to discourage desertions, retreats, and surrenders."[14] Like the Japanese during World War II and the communists in Korea, the Iraqi propagandists tried to convince their soldiers that they would be mistreated, if not tortured or killed outright. None of this was true.

Although Saddam Hussein remained in power, Iraqi casualties were enormous: approximately 50,000 killed in action; 50,000 wounded in action; 3,700 tanks destroyed; 2,600 assorted artillery pieces destroyed, captured, or taken out of action; 2,400 armored vehicles destroyed; and more than 69,822 Iraqi EPWs taken.[15] No nation's combat forces had been as successful on the battlefield or as successful in taking EPWs since World War II, and with the changes in U.S. Army organization, dealing with the unexpectedly large numbers of EPWs became the mission of the army's reserve military police units.

In Operation Desert Storm, agreements were concluded to formalize EPW procedures among the separate services and Coalition partners, including the British, French, and Arab allies. There was also a great deal of international interest and concern shown toward EPW treatment and accountability. As in Vietnam, the prisoners were turned over to an allied detaining power—in this case, Saudi Arabia—to ensure that Arab prisoners were treated in accordance with Arab culture and Islamic religious and dietary practices.[16] If any doubt existed as to status, the Americans resorted to military commissions to separate EPWs from civilians, and if the civilians were determined to be displaced and unwilling to be repatriated to Iraq, they became refugees eligible for resettlement somewhere else.

The Americans agreed to perform all EPW registrations in accordance with the Geneva Convention of 1949. All this was accomplished by the military police force consisting of 76 percent reservists and National Guard called up for wartime service.[17] Occasionally the Americans came in contact with elitist Iraqi officers, usually members of the Republican Guard. On one occasion an English-speaking, highly educated, senior field-grade medical officer was captured and complained of a minor illness. An American medical team at the Al Khanjar EPW collection point gave him some tea and asked him to help them treat other EPWs at the complex. He flatly refused and referred to officers of the regular Iraqi army as "scum" and "underlings." He then demanded other amenities, but the Americans found his obnoxious behavior terribly off-putting and highly arrogant. Instead of helping the Americans treat other Iraqis, this officer showed his true colors: he was a bad-tempered, goldbricking malingerer who warranted nothing more than being sent to an officers' EPW camp in Saudi Arabia as quickly as possible.[18] Another Republican Guard officer brought to the same medical unit for treatment turned out to be a petty thief; after being caught stealing cigarettes, he was removed to Saudi Arabia immediately.

Saudi Arabia played a vital role in dealing with EPWs in Desert Storm. Similar to what MACV had done in South Vietnam, the Americans provided liaison teams for management, logistics, and administrative assistance; however, unlike the South Vietnamese, the Saudis cooperated fully with the Americans. Two large EPW complexes were built: two large camps called "Bronx" designed to support U.S. Marine Corps and allied captures; and two camps designated "Brooklyn" to house EPWs taken by the rest of the Coalition.[19] Additionally, there were theater camps, or temporary holding facilities, behind the fighting lines. That the United States, British, and French took more than 69,000 EPWs was spectacular; add another 25,000 EPWs taken by the Arab allies, and one has to conclude that the Iraqi soldiers had no desire to fight for Saddam Hussein. The effort to treat EPWs properly was so successful that a member of the International Committee of the Red Cross (ICRC) stationed in Riyadh, Saudi Arabia, in April 1991 commented, "The treatment of Iraqi prisoners of war by U.S. forces was the best compliance with the Geneva Convention by any nation in any conflict in history."[20]

Iraqi treatment of Coalition POWs combined rough handling with inadequate treatment. In Baghdad, the mostly aircrew POWs were taken to a holding facility they referred to as the "Bunker" for interrogation. With that phase completed, the Iraqis incarcerated them in the "Biltmore," the Iraqi Intelligence Service Regional Headquarters, which unfortunately remained a military target and was bombed on 23 February 1991. There, in violation of the Geneva Convention, the Coalition POWs experienced food deprivation and inadequate protection from the cold.[21] After the bombing the POWs were sent to Abu Ghraib prison, dubbed "Joliet Prison," and Al-Rashid military prison, called the "Halfway House," until repatriation. The Iraqis denied the ICRC visitation rights in Baghdad up to repatriation, and the POWs, subjected to torture and intimidation, were forced to make propaganda statements on television. All this constituted a serious breach of international law.[22] Other Iraqi war crimes such as the taking of hostages, the use of human shields, rape and plunder in Kuwait, pillage, theft of property, igniting Kuwaiti oil fields, and attacks against Israel all went unpunished.

After the cease-fire the repatriation of large numbers of EPWs became a high priority. Iraq was anxious to return Coalition POWs but remained unwilling to accept large numbers of its own soldiers in return, saying it was not prepared to receive them. On 4 March 1991 Iraq released the first group of ten Coalition POWs, six of whom were Americans. Two days later the United States reciprocated by releasing 294 EPWs for repatriation to Iraq. This was the only repatriation the United States sponsored; the rest were accomplished by the Saudi Arabian government at a rate of 5,000 a day.[23] No Iraqi was ever forced to return home against his will by the Saudis, and those who wanted resettlement returned to Saudi Arabian custody.

Following the Gulf War in 1991, captured Iraqi soldiers fell into two categories: those who had participated in a failed rebellion against Saddam Hussein before the war, and those who had actively repressed their country's minorities. With the forced repatriations after World War II, the Korean prison revolts, and the South Vietnamese mistreatment of civilian detainees still in mind, American military authorities conducted rigorous screening of Iraqi EPWs to determine which ones were likely to suffer political retribution and imprisonment following repatriation. Many of these prisoners were granted political asylum. Of the 4,600 Iraqi refugees permitted entry into the United States in 1993, 453 were former soldiers who had deserted prior to the invasion of Kuwait.[24] According to Lieutenant Colonel Bilbo:

> The Gulf War was a spectacular show of the will of the American people to rally behind their president to support a just and worthwhile cause, the political power of a coalition force acting under the auspices of the United Nations, and the special and unique characteristics and challenges of fighting with coalition forces. It also demonstrated the sophistication and awesome power of the highly trained, well motivated and professionally led US Armed Forces.[25]

There can be little doubt that Operation Desert Storm stripped Saddam Hussein of most of his military capability.

Optimism over the Coalition victory and the insistence on a U.S.-enforced embargo and a no-fly zone over Iraqi airspace later gave the illusion of control over Saddam Hussein's ambitions. However, Saddam waged a vicious campaign against his internal enemies, the Shia Muslims in southern Iraq and the Kurds in the north. Commenting on the Gulf War, Alvin and Heidi Toffler reminded readers of the *World Monitor* that the "allied force was not a *machine* but a *system* with far greater internal feedback, communication, and self-regulatory adjustment capability"; it was what Alvin Toffler called a "Third Wave 'thinking system' right down to the lowest-ranked soldiers in the field."[26] Perhaps Toffler was correct in his assessment, but would a systems approach be sufficient to confront a wholly different paradigm, one that employed terrorism as a tool of war on a grand, unimaginable scale?

During the 1990s President Bill Clinton became fully aware of the dangers imposed on the West by Osama bin Laden and his international al-Qaeda terrorist organization. *Time* reported in 1998 that Clinton had signed a top-secret order, approved by the congressional intelligence committees, that authorized the CIA to begin covert operations to break up bin Laden's terror network. The agency's counterterrorism center had set up a special bin Laden task force, and analysts were assigned to read every word he had spoken or written. The CIA also developed plans to capture bin Laden if possible. More important, if the CIA spotted al-Qaeda operatives in foreign countries, it could quietly enlist local security services to arrest or deport them. The CIA would then move in and sift through materials in their abandoned apartments.[27] As a result of these cloak-and-dagger operations, the intelligence community gained some knowledge of bin Laden's reach, but there was little understanding of how powerful he truly was.

By 2000 Iraqi and Afghan politics heated up again. In Afghanistan the Islamic fundamentalist Taliban controlled the country. After its victory (with American help) over the Soviet Union in the 1980s, the Taliban imposed severe medieval Islamist laws on the population while providing training camps for al-Qaeda operatives to launch attacks against the West. According to David Brooks's probing article in the *Weekly Standard*, Saddam Hussein was busy too. After killing large numbers of Shiites who opposed him in the south and dropping lethal biological weapons on the Kurds in the north, he defied United Nations inspectors looking for his biological and possibly nuclear weapons facilities. Despite his loss to the Coalition in 1991, Saddam was determined to take on everyone who opposed him. Brooks notes accurately:

> Human beings are not all rational actors carefully calculating their interests. Certain people—many people, in fact—are driven by goals, ideals, and beliefs. Saddam Hussein has taken such awful risks throughout his career not because he "miscalculated," as the game theorists assert, but because he was chasing his vision. He was following the dictates of the Baathist ideology, which calls for warfare, bloodshed, revolution, and conflict, on and on, against one and all, until the end of time.[28]

Then 11 September 2001 arrived and changed everything.

In the northeastern United States, the morning of Tuesday, 11 September 2001, dawned sunny, clear, warm, and beautiful—a nearly perfect day. Then disaster struck. Writing for the *New York Times* on 12 September, Serge Schmemann reported:

Aftermath of 9/11 at the Pentagon. U.S. Department of Defense photograph.

Hijackers rammed jetliners into each of New York's World Trade Center towers yesterday, toppling both in a hellish storm of ash, glass, smoke and leaping victims, while a third jetliner crashed into the Pentagon in Virginia. There was no official count, but President Bush said thousands had perished, and in the immediate aftermath the calamity was already being ranked the worst and most audacious terror attack in American History.[29]

An attack like the one on Pearl Harbor on 7 December 1941 had happened again, this time with even more dead and inside the continental United States. And this time the targets were not battleships or military bases but primarily American icons and innocent civilians. To the perpetrators, every American became a target. Schmemann continued:

The attacks seemed carefully coordinated. The hijacked planes were all en route to California, and therefore gorged with fuel, and their departures were spaced within an hour and forty minutes. The first, out of Boston for Los Angeles, crashed into the north tower at 8:48 A.M. Eighteen minutes later, United Airline Flight 175, also headed from Boston to Los Angeles, plowed into the south tower. Then an American Airlines Boeing 757, Flight 77, left Washington's Dulles

International Airport bound for Los Angeles, but instead hit the western part of the Pentagon, the military headquarters where 24,000 people work, at 9:40 A.M. Finally, United Airlines Flight 93, a Boeing 757 flying from Newark to San Francisco, crashed near Pittsburgh, raising the possibility that its hijackers had failed in whatever their mission was.[30]

The country froze in shock as it watched the Twin Towers of the World Trade Center in New York City come crashing down, spewing debris, including human remains, throughout the immediate area. One observer recalled her personal experience:

I saw the whole thing from my office window. The first plane hit, and one of my coworkers came rushing down to my office because he heard about the hit on the radio. In about two minutes there were twenty people in my office watching the smoke. Our view is from the south, so all we saw from the first crash was smoke coming out of the far side (i.e., the north side) of Tower One.

People were shaken up seeing the fire and smoke (two employees had kids working in the World Trade Center), but we all thought it was just a tragic accident of some sort. I was in my office alone when I watched the second plane come right over my head really low. My jaw dropped because the plane was just so huge, and then it went straight up to the World Trade Center and turned into Tower Two. It was unbelievable. The plane went through the building like it was made out of butter. I know that everyone has seen the image a million times on TV, but when I saw it right in front of my face as it was happening, it made my blood run cold. It really did. Two other employees saw it from the office next to mine and within about ten seconds people were shouting and running down the hall.

People totally freaked. Men and women were diving under the conference table and diving out of the room into the hallway. My heart totally stopped. I thought that this was it. Then the whole building shook like we were in an earthquake. When we realized that we weren't being incinerated, we ran down the hall to the windows that looked out onto World Trade. We thought another plane must have hit the WTC, but we were completely engulfed in smoke and couldn't see a thing except ash, half burned papers and ceiling tiles falling right in front of our windows. Now people were really freaked out, yours truly included. The air outside was horrible. It was like trying to breathe when you're sucking on the exhaust pipe of a car. I don't have any idea what junk I was breathing in through my wet paper towel. Cars were abandoned in the streets, covered with several inches of gray dust, most of the windows were blown out. Very creepy.[31]

No one knew how many dead there were; only guesses and speculation filled the airwaves, as did the last cell phone messages from many victims just before the towers collapsed. Many people recalled the 1993 attempt to blow up the towers but believed the threat had passed. Historian Geoffrey Megargee wrote: "I'm very much afraid this will dwarf the original Day of Infamy (2,403 dead at Pearl Harbor on 7 December 1941). Hell, it could well dwarf Antietam (1862) as the costliest day in U.S. history. Another difference from Pearl Harbor just entered my mind—then, we knew whom to hit."[32] In the end, just under 3,300 people died at the World Trade Center, at the Pentagon, and in the hijacked airliners. For the Americans and for millions of people around the world, it was truly another Day of Infamy. President George W. Bush, facing his first major crisis in office, vowed that the United States would hunt down and punish those responsible for the "evil, despicable acts of terror" that took thousands of American lives. Bush attempted to rally the American people and said the United States would make no distinction between those who had carried out the hijackings and those who harbored and supported them.[33] The global war on terror had begun.

The perpetrators of the attack were members of Osama bin Laden's al-Qaeda, one of many Islamist fundamentalist organizations that had attempted to harm the United States, Israel, and the West for decades after World War II. Al-Qaeda, meaning "the base" in Arabic, formed in 1988 around the leadership a wealthy Saudi, Osama bin Laden, during the Afghan-mujahideen war against the Soviet Union's invasion. Osama bin Laden had led the Arab fighters in that war but refused to mix with the Afghans or the American advisors in the field. According to the American *National Intelligence Estimate* in 2007, al-Qaeda remains the single most dangerous enemy of the United States and, for that matter, of Western civilization in general.[34] It was responsible for the 11 September 2001 attacks in New York and Washington, as well as earlier attacks against American, Saudi, and other targets, including the 1993 World Trade Center bombing; the 1998 bombings of the American embassies in Nairobi, Kenya, and Dar es Salaam, Tanzania; the October 2000 attack against the USS *Cole* in Yemen; several spring 2002 bombings in Pakistan; a November 2002 car-bomb attack and a failed attempt to destroy an Israeli airliner in Kenya; the March 2004 train-bomb attacks in Madrid, Spain, that killed nearly 200 people; and the July 2005 bombings in the London underground. Representing no nation-state, al-Qaeda's agents of terror regularly use assassination, bombing, hijacking, kidnapping, and suicide attacks against innocent civilians. Many countries, both Christian and Muslim, are unsure how to deal with men who fight and die to establish a pan-Islamic caliphate throughout the world.

In a 2004 interview with Javier Jordán, a Spanish specialist on terrorism and defense and a recipient of a NATO fellowship to collaborate with Spain's National Defense Center of Higher Studies, the Vatican news service posed the question: what is radical Islamism, secular fundamentalism, and the clash between them? Jordán responded, "Radical Islamism wants all of society to be governed by the parameters of its religion, and secular fundamentalism tries to erase all traces of God in the public sphere."[35] Looking back to the writing of Hugo Grotius (1583–1645), one finds a positive way of thinking about religious war. Grotius, a Dutch Protestant lawyer and himself a former political prisoner (and escapee) during the Thirty Years' War, wrote *De Jure Belli ac Pacis* (On the Law of War and Peace) as a response to the religious nature of that war. It is divided into three books: the first book addresses the nature of *jus belli,* the law of war, as a conventional concept among nations and treats different kinds of wars; the second book addresses the causes of war, or the violation of public or private rights that justifies the taking up of arms; and the third book deals with the course of war, in which he considers what is permissible behavior in war and the conventions or treaties that end it. Grotius was the first statesman to advocate an end to chemical warfare, which at the time took the form of venom on arrows and poisoned wells. He pleaded that for the benefit of nations, armies, and soldiers, there should be a recognized common law of war.

The Thirty Years' War (1618–1648) in Europe seemed to force both divine and human law to disappear behind the clash of this hellish war, which permitted men to commit all sorts of unspeakable acts in the name of duty or religion or orders given by superiors. Grotius attempted to find a compromise position between the extremes of the military commander, who wants to use only the force of arms to settle a dispute, and the lawyer, who rejects the force of arms completely. Simply stated, Grotius attempted to devise a set of rules that combatant nations could follow to their mutual advantage to wage war and establish peace. He

Hugo Grotius (1583–1645), a Dutch lawyer and the "Father of International Law." Painting by Michiel Jansz von Mierevelt, 1631.

suggested that nations establish sets of international laws and an international forum to put them in place. Neither solution was successful in itself, but Grotius at least publicized the problem and was responsible for the provisions in the Treaty of Westphalia (1648) that negated the idea that POWs should be treated as criminals. He also categorically denied that religion, any religion, could ever be the basis of a legal, just, or moral war.

A different approach to religious war took root in the United States, articulated by a group of defense intellectuals called the neoconservatives, or "neocons," under the leadership of Secretary of Defense Donald Rumsfeld; Richard Perle, a member of the Defense Policy Board; Deputy Secretary of Defense Paul Wolfowitz; and Douglas J. Feith, the third ranking official at the Department of Defense, all prominent members of President George W. Bush's administration in 2001. At the end of the Cold War, the last thing on anyone's mind was a global war on terror.[36] Taking advantage of the 9/11 attacks to advance their ideas to the president, this group, who called themselves the Vulcans, formulated the policies designed not only to drive the United States to oust the Taliban from Afghanistan in 2001 but also to attack Iraq in 2003 as a preemptive war with the goal of a total regime change. Critics on the American Right accused this group of hijacking the conservative movement in the United States; liberal critics accused them of being nothing short of sinister.[37]

By 1989 the mujahideen fighters, with American and Arab help, had driven the Soviets from Afghanistan, and three years later they managed to wrest control of the government in Kabul from Marxist President Muhammad Najibullah. Severe infighting among the mujahideen factions continued, however, under the presidency of Burhanuddin Rabbani. Their internal war devastated Kabul; tens of thousands of civilians lost their lives, and the Afghan infrastructure was destroyed by rocket fire. This chaos, and the Afghans' exhaustion, permitted the radical Islamist Taliban to gain power. Cultivated in Pakistan, especially in the radical Islamic schools, or madrassas, the Taliban emerged first in Kandahar, gained control of Kabul in 1996, and controlled most of the country by 1998. The Taliban imposed an extremely severe kind of Islamist Sharia based on retrograde interpretations of the Quran and an absolute disregard for human rights, repugnant to the world community.[38]

Shortly after the 9/11 attacks, President George W. Bush announced to the people of the world that the United States had had enough. On 20 September 2001 Bush addressed a joint session of Congress and stated the American position on Afghanistan's Taliban very clearly. He issued the following ultimatum:

> Tonight the United States of America makes the following demands on the Taliban: Deliver to the United States authorities all the leaders of al-Qaeda who hide in your land.
>
> Release all foreign nationals, including American citizens you have unjustly imprisoned. Protect foreign journalists, diplomats, and aid workers in your country.
>
> Close immediately and permanently every terrorist training camp in Afghanistan, and hand over every terrorist, and every person in their support structure, to appropriate authorities. Give the United States full access to terrorist training camps, so we can make sure they are no longer operating.
>
> These demands are not open to negotiation or discussion. The Taliban must act, and act immediately. They will hand over the terrorists, or they will share their fate.[39]

The result was silence. The Bush Doctrine took hold: the United States would attack al-Qaeda terrorists where they lived, regardless of the address.

Because Osama bin Laden had used Taliban-ruled Afghanistan as a base of operations, Operation Enduring Freedom–Afghanistan began on the night of 7 October 2001 with powerful air attacks against al-Qaeda and Taliban camps and bases.[40] The president announced to the nation: "On my orders, the United States military has begun strikes against al-Qaeda terrorist training camps and military installations of the Taliban regime in Afghanistan. These carefully targeted actions are designed to disrupt the use of Afghanistan as a terrorist base of operations, and to attack the military capability of the Taliban regime."[41] The goals were the destabilization of the Taliban regime in Kabul, the defeat of the Taliban's fighters in the field, and the capture or death of Osama bin Laden.[42]

The Americans understood that putting a large army into Afghanistan was perilous. Part of the danger involved the mountainous terrain, which is always favorable to guerrillas. But they also knew that the mujahideen had all but defeated a powerful 100,000-man force fielded by the Soviet Union in 1979. For hundreds of years, Afghanistan had been the graveyard of armies, and the American command, short on available troops, looked to the 15,000-man Northern Alliance consisting of Uzbeks and Tajiks, already at war with the Pashtun Taliban, to link with U.S. Special Forces. Lots of American cash greased the wheels of action and loyalty.[43] On 19 October a Special Forces A Team infiltrated twelve men into the Bagram Air Base outside of Kabul, and on 20 October about 100 men of the Seventy-fifth Ranger Regiment and some Special Forces personnel dropped on an airstrip at Kandahar. As a raiding operation, they attacked some Taliban facilities and set the tone for Operation Enduring Freedom: airpower plus indigenous ground forces plus American Special Forces operations in small numbers. From 16 November to 16 December, with Special Forces personnel on the ground directing air strikes, aircraft pounded the Tora Bora mountains attempting to interdict bin Laden, but airpower was not enough. Finally, about 500 members of the Fifteenth Marine Expeditionary Unit arrived at Kandahar on 25 November and set up Camp Rhino, from which they conducted offensive operations.[44] Also on 25 November, captured Taliban revolted at the Qala Jangi Fortress Prison, where sixteen Special Forces troops fought 500 Taliban prisoners for seventy-two hours; by 27 November most of the Taliban in the prison had been killed in action by air strikes. The disadvantage of this tactic was that although the Taliban suffered defeat, Osama bin Laden evaded the American attempt to kill or capture him and simply crossed the mountain border into Pakistan.[45] By 2002 more conventional American troops arrived in Afghanistan, and Operation Anaconda, with units of the Tenth Mountain Division and the 101st Airborne Division, patrolled the Shahi-Kot Valley near Gardez and faced Arabs and the Taliban with full fury from 1 to 16 March. Part of this operation was the Battle of Takur Ghar, a seventeen-hour firefight against Taliban soldiers resulting in the loss of seven U.S. Special Forces personnel.

From 2002 to 2006 the fighting in Afghanistan was mostly low-intensity combat, resulting in enemy ambushes of American patrols and a steady rise in airplane crashes, friendly-fire deaths, and the taking of detainees. During this time the United States lost 255 dead and 685 wounded. Even more troubling in Afghanistan was that some of the prisoners the Americans took were not Middle Eastern at all. Two examples were David Hicks and Mahmoud Habib, both Australians, who were apprehended in Pakistan as terrorists and shipped to the American detention facility at Guantánamo Naval Base in Cuba, where they stayed for years confined as "unlawful combatants"—a new designation for a new war.

Could one imagine an American citizen fighting with the Taliban? Hardly, but when John Walker Lindh was taken into custody in November 2001 and discovered to be an American, the country convulsed. After his capture Lindh was taken to an American warship in the Arabian Sea and questioned by marines. Once he revealed to them that he was an American from California, he was immediately transferred to the United States, where he stood trial on ten charges, including conspiracy against U.S. nationals. Facing a possible ninety-year sentence if convicted on all counts, Lindh bargained a guilty plea to serving the Taliban and carrying weapons. For his treasonous actions, he received a twenty-year sentence. Lindh told the judge that he had made a mistake by joining the Taliban. The judge responded, "Life is making choices and living with the consequences. You made a bad choice to join the Taliban."[46] Arnold Krammer notes that in earlier centuries, any prisoner who turned renegade would have been shot as a turncoat. Barring any parole, "Jihad Johnny" Lindh will remain in federal custody until 2019.[47]

The year 2002 became pivotal. The Bush Doctrine prevailed, and as the nation recovered from the 9/11 attack, the Pentagon went into action in Afghanistan seeking to overthrow the Taliban government in Kabul and doing battle with Osama bin Laden's al-Qaeda. In a Pentagon briefing from the Office of Public Affairs on 17 January 2002, the highest level of the American military let the world know that it considered captured fighters to be "detainees"—captives held without clearly defined international rules—rather than traditional prisoners of war. Because they were considered very dangerous, they would be transported from battlefields around the world to the detention center at the Guantánamo Bay Naval Base, Cuba, for their own safety and the nation's as well. The Pentagon also stated that military commissions were needed to bring these foreign terrorists to justice, noting that they had been used effectively since the American Revolution. Last, the briefing revealed something unique: "We are battling an enemy that has flagrantly violated the rules of war. They do not wear uniforms. They hide in caves abroad and among us here at home. They target civilians and intend to attack us again."[48]

The United States declared that the enemy in this fight consisted of terrorists suspected of being war criminals, and they would certainly not be considered legitimate EPWs as in past wars. It was intent on prosecuting as many as possible, especially those who had solid connections to al-Qaeda and the 9/11 holocaust. For Afghanistan and soon Iraq, a wholly new paradigm emerged. Gone was the era of reciprocity, the Golden Rule, and strict adherence to both the rules of war and the Geneva Conventions. Gone were advantageous legal restraints on both sides. Arrived was a period of excess, hard words, hard fighting, and ill treatment of detainees at Bagram in Afghanistan and Abu Ghraib in Iraq, the rendition of prisoners to foreign prisons where torture was common and to the prison facility at Guantánamo Bay, which would nearly shatter the cohesion, to say nothing of the reputation, of the American military establishment. None of these issues was resolved by 2003; instead, they intensified as the United States set its sights on removing Saddam Hussein from power in Iraq.

FIFTEEN

Iraqi Freedom, Abu Ghraib, and Guantánamo

The Problem of the Moral High Ground

The events occurred on my watch. As Secretary of Defense, I am accountable for them. I take full responsibility.
—Donald H. Rumsfeld

The war against Saddam Hussein began in 2003. It had little to do with the 9/11 attacks or even al-Qaeda's intention to damage the United States, but more to do with the overthrow of Hussein's Hitlerian Baath Party dictatorship and a show of force against al-Qaeda. By 2003 fissures began to appear at the highest level in the Pentagon between Donald H. Rumsfeld, the new secretary of defense, and his senior management. In 1999 then-candidate George W. Bush delivered a speech at the Citadel in South Carolina that addressed the heart of the American army's capability to wage war. Bush reminded his audience that Desert Storm had been an impressive victory, but it had taken six months to plan and amass all the Coalition assets for the attack. That was just too much time, so the United States needed to develop a lighter, more mobile, and more lethal force.[1] His appointment of Rumsfeld—one of the most senior of the Vulcans, the neoconservative group that dominated the Department of Defense in 2001—made certain that a reformation of the American military services would take place whether the generals and the Joint Chiefs of Staff approved or not. Any senior officer not in full agreement with the Rumsfeld team either conformed or was forced to retire.[2]

The Pentagon strategy developed in 2001 was based on the probability of a two-front war for the U.S. Army: one front aimed to be a decisive win, and the other a solid hold until assets could be diverted from the first to the second. Rumsfeld and the Vulcans also advocated a smaller, more mobile, and more lethal ground force than the army had used in Desert Storm. In 2000 the age of the massive assault force came to an end; Rumsfeld's Pentagon planners began the process of change they called "Transformation."[3] Meanwhile, the Rumsfeld team had

Secretary of Defense Donald H. Rumsfeld led the Vulcans, the neoconservative group that dominated the Department of Defense in 2001. U.S. Department of Defense photograph.

tired of the Clinton policy of containment against Saddam and sought a real regime change. At the State Department, retired General Colin L. Powell, the new secretary of state, was alarmed by the talk of war at the Pentagon and urged the Bush administration to act with restraint, implying that Saddam's containment was working reasonably well. Powell saw no need to go to war. Despite all of Saddam's bluster, the only terrorism he supported was his own against the Iraqi people—namely, the Shiites in the south, Kurds in the north, and anyone else who opposed him. As the world discovered, violence was a political tool for Saddam, but chances were slim that he had been directly involved in al-Qaeda's attack against the United States.

The Rumsfeld team began the process of formulating preemptive war plans, that is, launching an offensive war to prevent a larger defensive one. The mission to prepare plans for the invasion of southern Iraq went to V Corps, the army's main fighting force in Europe.[4] Still reeling from the 9/11 attacks, President Bush issued an executive order on 13 November 2001 that defined international terrorists everywhere as enemies of the United States who, if captured, were to be detained outside the United States and tried by military commissions for war crimes.[5]

Despite being outside the civilian judicial system, military commissions had been used as early as the Revolutionary War to try Major John André for espionage; in the Civil War to incarcerate Copperhead Democrats, Southern sympathizers, and the Lincoln conspirators; during the Indian wars to incarcerate tribal leaders and Geronimo's Chiricahua Apaches; and most recently in both Germany and Japan following World War II. Thus, there were ample precedents for President Bush's decision to use such tribunals for those terrorists captured in Afghanistan and Iraq. Most judicial scholars accepted the fact in 2001 that al-Qaeda terrorists stood outside the American judicial system.

Writing for the Department of Justice on 9 January 2002, Robert J. Dalhunty argued that by using the U.S. Naval Base at Guantánamo Bay, Cuba, as a long-term detention facility for terrorists captured in military or civilian operations or by allies in Afghanistan, no enemy alien prisoner could file a writ of habeas corpus because, as leased territory, the naval base was located outside federal court jurisdiction. Further, the government maintained that no Taliban prisoner captured in Afghanistan could be regarded as an EPW. The Taliban militia did not represent the government of Afghanistan, and its fighters were virtually the same as al-Qaeda—terrorists and war criminals. Because Afghanistan was a failed state, the protective provisions of the 1949 Geneva Convention did not apply.[6] In a 25 January 2002 memorandum, Alberto R. Gonzalez in the Department of Justice (later to become attorney general) opined that the president could indeed bypass the Geneva Convention legally. On 7 February 2002 the Bush administration responded to the Gonzalez memo and changed the rule book completely. President Bush issued his memorandum on the humane treatment of al-Qaeda and Taliban fighters, which stated the case clearly:

> I accept the legal conclusion of the Department of Justice and determine that none of the provisions of Geneva apply to our conflict with al-Qaeda in Afghanistan or elsewhere throughout the world because, among other reasons, al-Qaeda is not a High Contracting Party to Geneva. I determine that the Taliban detainees are unlawful combatants and, therefore, do not qualify as prisoners of war under Article 4 of Geneva 1949. I note that, because Geneva does not apply to our conflict with al-Qaeda, al-Qaeda detainees also do not qualify as prisoners of war. As a matter of policy, the United States Armed Forces shall continue to treat detainees humanely and, to the extent

appropriate and consistent with military necessity, in a manner consistent with the principles of Geneva.[7]

Those taken captive by the Americans in the Iraq and Afghanistan theaters became new and different kinds of prisoners—unlawful combatants—in wars far distant from anything the United States had fought in recent memory, with the possible exception of the counterguerrilla war in the Philippines.

Secretary of State Powell disagreed with the new policy and urged President Bush to accord these captives the protections of the Geneva Convention, offering some very powerful arguments. He wrote:

- It will reverse over a century of U.S. policy and practice in supporting the Geneva Convention and undermine the protections of the law of war for our troops, both in this specific conflict and in general.
- It has a high cost in terms of negative international reaction, with immediate adverse consequences for our conduct of foreign policy.
- It will undermine public support among critical allies, making military cooperation more difficult to sustain.
- Europeans and others will likely have legal problems with extradition or other forms of cooperation in law enforcement, including bringing terrorists to justice.
- It may provoke some individual foreign prosecutors to investigate and prosecute our officials and troops.
- It will make us more vulnerable to domestic and international legal challenge and deprive us of important legal options.[8]

The secretary of state, a man of remarkable military and diplomatic credentials, made the point that not honoring the Geneva Convention for any reason would put the United States in a terribly vulnerable position, right or wrong, in the international community. If the United States eliminated any possibility of using the Golden Rule of reciprocity in dealing with enemy prisoners, what might be done to American prisoners in enemy hands remained dangerously in doubt. Last, the United States risked losing the moral high ground when it pursued the abrogation of international law, regardless of the expediency or, perhaps, the justice of doing so. In the global war on terror, no Taliban or al-Qaeda prisoner would be considered an EPW by the detaining power—this time, the United States. The 1949 Geneva Convention was indeed suspended, and the Bush administration believed it had all been done legally, morally, and properly. Unfortunately, the policy opened a Pandora's box of opposition to American foreign policy. The policy also created an opportunity for interrogators and untrained military police (MPs) to commit war crimes against prisoners in American hands.

On 19 March 2003 Operation Iraqi Freedom, the invasion of Iraq, commenced with five teams of twenty navy SEALs inserted into off-shore oil refineries to prevent their destruction.[9] The drive to Baghdad, dubbed Cobra II by General David McKiernan—in honor of General George S. Patton's Operation Cobra, the breakout from Normandy to liberate France in 1944—lasted until 2 April, when Baghdad fell. It was a near-perfect military campaign. Iraq was liberated from the dictator Saddam Hussein in short order. Maybe the war, like Desert Storm, was over too quickly. Maybe not.

In the beginning, about 8,000 Iraqi EPWs were diverted to a new American-built and -staffed POW camp for interrogation, Camp Bucca in southern Iraq.[10] Medical treatment was provided to Iraqi EPWs immediately by U.S. and allied medical staffs, and the seriously injured were sent immediately to Kuwait.[11] Although most Iraqi enlisted soldiers were released, Iraqi officers were retained for any political and tactical information they might be privy to. But what should be done with foreign fighters and nonuniformed Iraqis who carried weapons against the Americans and other Coalition partners? The new Department of Defense Directive 2310.1 instructed the MPs to call nonuniformed partisans "detainees" and to withhold protections of the Geneva Convention. Held for twenty to seventy-two hours at initial collecting points for evaluation and classification, the detainees were then sent to division-level and then theater-level detention facilities. As a result, the Iraqis and foreign fighters were sent to prisons in Saddam's extensive prison system, now used by the Americans as interrogation centers. On 22 April 2003 American forces took over Abu Ghraib prison and on 4 August 2003 renamed it the Baghdad Detention Center. If a detainee was considered especially dangerous, he could be sent to the strategic internment facility at Guantánamo Bay, Cuba. Yet in spite of command directions, things went wrong.

On 12 May 2003 four soldiers from the 320th Military Police Battalion abused detainees at Camp Bucca, and the army's Criminal Investigation Division (CID) immediately looked into the incident. On 9 June a riot broke out at another prison facility, Camp Cropper, where

Camp Bucca in southern Iraq was a staffed POW camp for interrogations and held about 8,000 Iraqi EPWs in 2003. U.S. Department of Defense photograph.

five detainees were shot. On 1 July Amnesty International criticized the U.S. Army for subjecting Iraqi detainees to degrading conditions. At this time, the army command clearly understood that it was involved in an insurgency rather than a traditional war and wanted to extract usable tactical intelligence from its prisoners.

From 31 August to 9 September 2003 numerous photographs showing American guards performing sadistic acts against detainees at Abu Ghraib became public. Command oversight of the guards failed completely. Army leadership and discipline broke down, and more riots and shootings took place at various prison facilities in November. Based on tactical intelligence gathered by interrogations, on 13 December American troops captured Saddam Hussein in a hole in Adwar, about ten miles south of his hometown of Tikrit.[12]

On 13 January 2004 Specialist Joseph M. Darby with the 800th Military Police Brigade reported that significant detainee abuse was taking place at Abu Ghraib, and the army's CID began an investigation. At this time, command at the highest level intervened, and Lieutenant General Ricardo Sanchez requested that U.S. Central Command launch an investigation into the 800th Military Police Brigade's detention and internment operations, given all the reports of detainee mistreatment and abuse.[13] Events then proceeded quickly. In February 2004 General

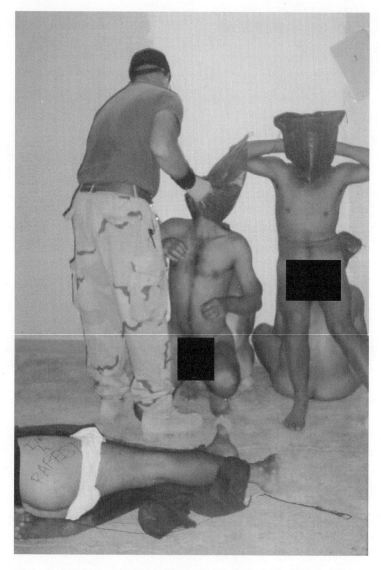

Abu Ghraib prisoners being abused. U.S. Army photograph.

McKiernan appointed Major General Antonio M. Taguba to conduct an investigation. By the end of the month the command suspended seventeen American soldiers from duty while Taguba conducted interviews, collected documents, compiled references, and analyzed the data.

Major General Antonio M. Taguba conducted an investigation that resulted in the suspension of seventeen American soldiers. U.S. Army photograph.

In late February the International Committee of the Red Cross (ICRC) provided the Coalition Authority with a confidential report on prison abuse throughout Iraq, and on 3 March the Taguba team presented its initial report to McKiernan. Charges were then lodged against six noncommissioned officers, and the story was about to go public on CBS's *60 Minutes II*. Air force General Richard Myers, head of the Joint Chiefs of Staff, the most senior military officer in the United States, asked CBS to delay its report on Abu Ghraib, which it did for two weeks. On 1 May 2004 Seymour Hersh, the journalist who had broken the My Lai story in 1969, used the Taguba report to publish his own exposé, "Torture at Abu Ghraib," followed by two other articles, "Chain of Command" and "The Gray Zone." When CBS learned that Hersh and the *New Yorker* planned to publish the stories, it presented its own report on 28 April 2003. The country was shocked as the army feebly updated the public on its investigation. Three days later, on 1 May 2004, President Bush declared that hostilities in Iraq were over. How could hostilities be over when American MPs were torturing Iraqi prisoners in Baghdad?

Congress demanded answers. How could America soldiers, who had always maintained the moral high ground in POW issues since the time of the Revolutionary War, be guilty of such deplorable behavior in Iraq? Rumsfeld went to Capitol Hill to talk to Congress on 7 May and again on 11 May, telling senators that hard interrogation procedures had indeed been authorized, but Pentagon lawyers had confirmed their compliance with the Geneva Convention. Even President Bush attempted to downplay the importance of the incidents, but the Senate refused to accept either Bush's or Rumsfeld's rationales. Finally Rumsfeld apologized before the Senate Armed Services Committee:

> The events occurred on my watch. As Secretary of Defense, I am accountable for them. I take full responsibility. It is my obligation to evaluate what happened, to make sure those who have committed wrongdoing are brought to justice, and to make changes as needed to see that it doesn't happen again. I feel terrible about what happened to these Iraqi detainees. They are human beings. They were in U.S. custody. Our country had an obligation to treat them right. We didn't do that. That was wrong. To those Iraqis who were mistreated by members of the U.S. armed forces, I offer my deepest apology. It was un-American. And it was inconsistent with the values of our nation.[14]

Apparently, the secretary of defense had been caught off guard, but the Taguba report plus all the media attention made the mistreatment and torture of detainees a national event.

The Taguba report was damning. It found MP training prior to deployment inadequate, saying:

> The 800th MP units did not receive Internment/Resettlement (I/R) and corrections specific training during their mobilization period. Corrections training is only on the METL [Mission Essential Task List] of two MP (I/R) Confinement Battalions throughout the Army, one currently serving in Afghanistan, and elements of the other are at Camp Arifjan, Kuwait. MP units supporting JTF-GTMO received ten days of training in detention facility operations, to include two days of unarmed self-defense, training in interpersonal communication skills, forced cell moves, and correctional officer safety.[15]

There was no doubt that heads would roll over the Abu Ghraib scandal, but whose heads?

That the secretary of defense had interfered with the planning process and forced the army to activate untrained reservists for MP duty in

Iraq and Afghanistan was nearly unthinkable. Michael R. Gordon and General Bernard Trainor state the case in *Cobra II:*

> In the field, the second guessing in Washington was enormously disruptive. The decision to delay activation of many of the reservists delayed the establishment of the Theater Support Command, which was to manage the logistics for the ground forces and played havoc with the deployments. The reservists who would run the port and airfield were not fully in place as the troops and equipment started to flow in, nor were many of the military police.[16]

An independent commission, chaired by former Secretary of Defense James R. Schlesinger, concluded that the Abu Ghraib scandal took place in part because many MP units had been deployed pell-mell. The Schlesinger report noted, "The unit could neither train at its stateside mobilization site without its equipment nor upon arrival overseas, as two or three weeks could go by before joining with its equipment. The MP brigade commander did not know who would be deployed next."[17] So, one must conclude that the MPs in charge of handling detainees in all the prisons were not adequately prepared for their mission.

Additionally, the prison itself was in the combat zone and received a considerable number of mortar attacks. Not only were the Iraqi prisoners in danger; so too were the guards and the military intelligence forces.[18] The ICRC reported in February 2004 that in July 2003 the prison received twenty-five such attacks: "On 16 August, three mortar rounds landed in the prison compound, killing at least five and injuring sixty-seven persons deprived of their liberty."[19] At the time, many of the prisoners lived in tents, while the guard force lived in concrete bunkers. Danger was everywhere, inside and outside Abu Ghraib.

General Taguba then visited Abu Ghraib and began his work. In the "Findings and Recommendations" section of his report, he noted:

> The US Army Criminal Investigation Command (CID), led by Col. Jerry Mocello, and a team of highly trained professional agents have done a superb job of investigating several complex and extremely disturbing incidents of detainee abuse at the Abu Ghraib Prison. They conducted over fifty interviews of witnesses, potential criminal suspects, and detainees. They also uncovered numerous photos and videos portraying in graphic detail detainee abuse by Military Police personnel on numerous occasions from October to December 2003.

Several potential suspects rendered full and complete confessions regarding their personal involvement and the involvement of fellow soldiers in this abuse. Several potential suspects invoked their rights under Article 31 of the Uniform Code of Military Justice (UCMJ) and the 5th Amendment of the U.S. Constitution.[20]

On 13 May 2004 Secretary of Defense Rumsfeld actually visited Abu Ghraib. The next day the army announced that Specialist Charles Graner would be court-martialed, and more were coming. What had occurred? According to Taguba, between October and December 2003 numerous sadistic, blatant, and wanton criminal abuses had been inflicted on several detainees at Abu Ghraib. This systemic and illegal abuse of detainees was intentionally perpetrated by several members of the MP guard force consisting of members of the 372nd Military Police Company, 320th Military Police Battalion, and 800th Military Police Brigade in Tier 1-A of the Abu Ghraib prison. These allegations of abuse were substantiated by detailed witness statements and the discovery of extremely graphic photographic evidence.[21] The Taguba team found evidence of the following misconduct by MP personnel:

1. Punching, slapping, and kicking detainees; jumping on their naked feet;
2. Videotaping and photographing naked male and female detainees;
3. Forcibly arranging detainees in various sexually explicit positions for photographing;
4. Forcing detainees to remove their clothing and keeping them naked for several days at a time;
5. Forcing naked male detainees to wear women's underwear;
6. Forcing groups of male detainees to masturbate themselves while being photographed and videotaped;
7. Arranging naked male detainees in a pile and then jumping on them;
8. Positioning a naked detainee on a[n] MRE [meal ready to eat] Box, with a sandbag on his head, and attaching wires to his fingers, toes, and penis to simulate electric torture;
9. Writing "I am a Rapest" [sic] on the leg of a detainee alleged to have forcibly raped a 15-year old fellow detainee, and then photographing him naked;
10. Placing a dog chain or strap around a naked detainee's neck and having a female Soldier pose for a picture;

11. A male MP guard having sex with a female detainee;
12. Using military working dogs (without muzzles) to intimidate and frighten detainees, and in at least one case biting and severely injuring a detainee;
13. Taking photographs of dead Iraqi detainees.[22]

None of this constituted authorized interrogation techniques; rather, it reflected the meanest kind of prison harassment found in the worst American jails many decades ago when guards could do anything they wanted just for the primal fun of it. Indicted were the following MP and intelligence personnel: Specialist Jeremy Sivits, Specialist Sabrina Harman, Sergeant Jarval S. Davis, Private First Class Lynndie R. England, Specialist Joseph M. Darby, Corporal Matthew Scott Bolanger, and Specialist Matthew C. Wisdom, all of the 372nd Military Police Company; Adel Nakhla, civilian translator, and Torin S. Nelson, contractor, Titan Corporation, assigned to the 205th Military Intelligence Brigade; Sergeant Neil A. Wallin, 109th Area Support Medical Battalion; Sergeant Samuel Jefferson Provance, 302nd Military Intelligence Battalion; Staff Sergeant Reuben R. Layton, medic, 109th Medical Detachment; and Specialist John V. Polak, 229th Military Police Company.

General Taguba reported additional abuses after interviewing several detainees and wrote:

In addition, several detainees also described the following acts of abuse, which under the circumstances, I find credible based on the clarity of their statements and supporting evidence provided by other witnesses:

1. Breaking chemical lights and pouring the phosphoric liquid on detainees;
2. Threatening detainees with a charged 9 mm pistol;
3. Pouring cold water on naked detainees;
4. Beating detainees with a broom handle and a chair;
5. Threatening male detainees with rape;
6. Allowing a military police guard to stitch the wound of a detainee who was injured after being slammed against the wall in his cell;
7. Sodomizing a detainee with a chemical light and perhaps a broom stick.
8. Using military working dogs to frighten and intimidate detainees with threats of attack, and in one instance actually biting a detainee.[23]

Never in U.S. history has the treatment of prisoners or detainees been worse than this, not even in the Philippine-American War at the turn of the twentieth century. It was no wonder that Americans were shocked and dismayed that their troops could behave more like thugs than soldiers.[24]

Was Abu Ghraib an American concentration camp with virtually no command oversight of the guard force? It seemed to be, especially after the Taguba report published some of the prisoners' statements. On 18 January 2004 one prisoner, identified as Detainee 151108 (name redacted), reported:

> They stripped me of all my clothes, even my underwear. They gave me woman's underwear that was rose color with flowers in it and they put the bag over my face. One of them whispered in my ear, "Today I am going to fuck you," and he said this in Arabic. Whoever was with me experienced the same thing. That's what the American soldiers did. And they forced me to wear this underwear all the time, for 51 days. And most of the days I was wearing nothing else.
>
> I faced more harsh punishment from Grainer [sic]. He cuffed my hands with irons behind my back to the metal of the window, to the point my feet were off the ground and I was hanging there, for about five hours just because I asked about the time, because I wanted to pray. After he released me from the window, he tied me to my bed until before dawn. Grainer [sic] and the other two soldiers were taking pictures of everything they did to me. I don't know if they took a picture of me because they beat me so bad I lost consciousness after an hour or so.[25]

Detainee 19446 responded in a question-and-answer format:

> Q: How did you feel when the guards were treating you this way?
> A: I was trying to kill myself, but I didn't have any way of doing it.
> Q: Did the guards force you to crawl on your hands and knees on the ground?
> A: Yes, They forced us to do this thing.
> Q: What were the guards doing while you were crawling on your hands and knees?
> A: They were sitting on our backs like riding animals.[26]

The detainee statements continued in this vein and helped convict eleven American soldiers of breaking military laws; five others were disciplined. General Taguba concluded that several soldiers had committed terrible acts and breached international law at Abu Ghraib and Camp Bucca in Iraq, although the ICRC reported in February 2004 that no prisoners at Camp Bucca or Um Qasr spoke of physical ill treatment during interrogation. What abuse they encountered took place during their arrest, initial internment at collection points and holding areas, and "tactical questioning" by military intelligence officers attached to battle groups units.[27] Even worse, the key leadership of the 800th Military Police Brigade and the 205th Military Intelligence Brigade failed to comply with established regulations, policies, and command directives to prevent detainee abuse from August 2003 to February 2004.[28]

On 18 May 2004 Specialist Charles Graner, Staff Sergeant Ivan L. Frederick, and Sergeant Jarval Davis were arraigned on charges of abusing the detainees at Abu Ghraib.[29] Two days later the army released 454 detainees from Abu Ghraib. On 23 May the army suspended Brigadier General Janis L. Karpinski from her command of the 800th Military Police Brigade; she was formally relieved her of command on 8 April 2005 and reduced to the rank of colonel. On 11 September, after Specialist Armin J. Cruiz pleaded guilty of conspiracy to maltreat and actual maltreatment of detainees at Abu Ghraib, he was sentenced to a reduction in rank to private, eight months' confinement, and a bad-conduct discharge. Staff Sergeant Ivan L. Frederick was convicted of detainee maltreatment and dereliction of duty; the court-martial reduced his rank to private and sentenced him to confinement for eight years, forfeiture of all pay and allowances, and a dishonorable discharge. Specialist Charles Graner was found guilty of physically and sexually abusing detainees at Abu Ghraib and was sentenced to ten years' imprisonment and a dishonorable discharge. The others received similar sentences but received bad-conduct discharges rather than dishonorable discharges. One significant consequence of these kinds of discharges is the government's refusal to grant veterans' benefits to these former soldiers. On 26 September 2005, 1,000 detainees were released from Abu Ghraib after the Iraqi government asked the Multinational Forces to set up a special release board.[30]

After the abuse of prisoners in Iraq, the *Army Times* reported that the Pentagon issued a broad new directive mandating that detainees be treated humanely and banning the use of dogs to intimidate or harass suspects. The directive consolidated all the Defense Department's existing policies and memos covering the interrogation of detainees captured in the war against terrorism. Although the policy mapped out broad requirements for humane treatment and for the reporting of violations, it was just the first step in the development of a new army manual that detailed more precisely which interrogation techniques are acceptable and which are not.[31] Congress acted too. In 2005 it passed and the president signed the Detainee Treatment Act, which provided uniform standards for the treatment and interrogation of detainees. According to Major James F. Gebhardt, U.S. Army detention doctrine was not broken so much as disjointed. MP guards and military intelligence interrogators, if they are trained according to current branch doctrinal manuals and competently led and supervised, will treat detainees and sources with due respect as required by the Geneva Convention. It should be noted, however, that an inherent conflict exists between guarding and protecting the rights of detainees (the MP mission) and extracting the maximum intelligence from a source under the law (the military intelligence mission). Those who seek to repair the damage done by the Abu Ghraib prison scandal must resolve this conflict.[32]

In 2006 Abu Ghraib prison, Saddam Hussein's torture central and the center of the American abuse and mistreatment cases, closed; however, more prison space was needed. According to an Associated Press report, the facility received a facelift and a new name, Baghdad Central Prison, and reopened in 2009 under the control of the new Iraqi government with the capacity for about 15,000 inmates. The announcement came as the U.S. military began to transfer about 15,000 detainees to the Iraqis under a new security agreement, prompting concern about Iraq's beleaguered judicial system. The United Nations warned in a recent human rights report about overcrowding and "grave human rights violations of detainees in Iraqi custody."[33] In Iraq, as long as insurgents wage war, the prisoner problem will linger, regardless of who the jailers are.

In December 1903 the United States leased the Guantánamo Bay Naval Base from Cuba as a naval coaling station. During the early part of the twentieth century, American sailors often sang the "GTMO Song" with gusto, grit, and bawdy humor to the tune of "The Irish Washerwoman":

> At Guantánamo Bay, call her GTMO for short,
> Not much of a base, much less of a port,
> One look at the docks, and you know what you're seein'
> The goddamnest hole in the whole Caribbean
> So hurrah for old GTMO on Cuba's fair shore,
> The home of the cockroach, the flea, and the whore,

We'll sing of her praises and pray for the day,
We'll get the hell out of Guantánamo Bay.[34]

Most naval personnel who have ever visited the Atlantic Fleet Training Center at Guantánamo Bay at the far end of Cuba have no good memories of it. Every warship stationed on the East Coast that experienced a shipyard refit went to GTMO for six weeks of shakedown and refresher training. It was an extremely difficult training cycle, and crews quickly tired of the fast pace, extreme heat, and generally unpleasant nature of GTMO. In a way, it was a busy but sleepy place, and for Atlantic Fleet sailors, it was a jail before it became a prison.[35]

In 1934 the Americans agreed to pay Cuba $2,000 in gold each year for the rights to use the land. Since 1960 the Cuban government has refused to cash the check.[36] There are two distinct sides to the base, separated by a wide bay. Visitors land on the smaller leeward side to the west, and because the Cubans guard the waist of the bay, they take a boat to the windward, larger side. The base is self-contained, makes all its own water, and imports all the food and other necessities required by base personnel. Before Fidel Castro came to power, GTMO was a hustle-bustle kind of place; then, during the Cold War, activities subsided nearly to a stand-still except for the Fleet Training Center. By the fall of 2001 GTMO had become active in the Caribbean antidrug effort but still hosted only about 2,000 personnel.[37] The 9/11 debacle changed everything, and the base has played a significant role in the global war on terror.

In 2002 the Department of Justice suggested that GTMO might be a good choice for a secure prison compound for high-value al-Qaeda and Taliban prisoners from the Afghanistan operation. According to Gordon Cucullu, "After extensive interagency staffing, the U.S. Naval Base at Guantánamo Bay was ultimately selected as a holding site for captured enemy combatants."[38] It is not a prison in the civilian sense, with a rehabilitation mission; rather, it is a military detention facility designed to keep dangerous enemy combatants from returning to the battlefield. Essentially, as far as the Pentagon and the Department of Justice were concerned, GTMO became a matter of military necessity during wartime, vital to the security interests of the United States.

Initially, the process of sorting the prisoners taken in Afghanistan presented some unique difficulties. Great numbers of Afghan Taliban and foreign al-Qaeda fighters from many countries were taken prisoner mostly by Northern Alliance and American Special Forces troops. Critics have observed with accuracy that this combined force was too small, with the result that high-ranking al-Qaeda members, including Osama bin Laden, escaped from Afghanistan and fled to the friendly tribal border area of Pakistan, where they continued their planning to devastate the West whenever and wherever possible.[39] With only small numbers of interrogators available in country at the time, the Americans were interested primarily in high-ranking individuals and others who could provide operational or tactical intelligence for the forces in the field. In all cases, the prisoners needed to be removed from the battlefield, held securely, and interrogated.

It was a standing intelligence requirement in 2002 to find out whether al-Qaeda planned another attack on the American mainland or against Americans anywhere else. There is no doubt that the interrogations got rough. Nearly everyone alive in 2002 remembered and remained embittered by the Iran hostage fiasco in 1979 and all the hostage taking in Beirut in the 1980s. It seemed clear that radical Islamists were marching in a holy war, or jihad, against all the American people—civilian and military, men, women, and children. Who could deny that the United States had been aggressively attacked worldwide prior to 9/11? The attack against the marines in Beirut in 1983, the 1993 World Trade Center bombing, the 1998 bombings of the American embassies in Nairobi and Dar es Salaam, and the October 2000 attack against the USS *Cole* in Yemen all shocked and angered Americans to the bone. There were also the near misses, such as al-Qaeda's attempt to blow up the Los Angeles airport, and the possible use of "dirty bombs"—explosives containing nuclear materials to provide extra killing power from radiation poisoning. All seemed possible, if not probable. In Afghanistan the Americans apprehended terrorists from all over the Muslim world under arms in killer groups, and it was no wonder that interrogators sincerely believed they needed to work fast. What the interrogators faced, however, became the challenge of our age.

Before Americans are sent into a combat environment where capture is possible, they receive specialized POW training—called SERE, for Survival, Escape, Resistance, Evasion—that teaches them how to behave as a prisoner or war. Each military service operates its own schools, but the curricula are similar. Students undergo capture and initial hard interrogations, often with a brief but scary water-board experience. Then students undergo a series of interrogations with the objective of showing them how each technique can be used against them. Along with the

1949 Geneva Convention, Americans have the Code of Conduct, first developed and issued after the Korean War in 1954 (see appendix 12). Updated and degendered in 1988, the code provides moral and ethical guidelines and gives substance to the act of resistance, support for other prisoners, and even escape when and where possible.[40]

What the American interrogators never expected in Afghanistan, Iraq, or Guantánamo was a jihadist resistance manual designed to accomplish much the same objectives as SERE, but in jihadist terms. Known as the *Manchester Manual,* because British police seized and translated a copy in Manchester during an antiterrorist raid, it provided guidelines for behavior in religious terms, with little left to the imagination: "Islamic governments have never and will never be established through peaceful solutions and cooperative councils. They are established as they [always] have been by pen and gun, by word and bullet, by tongue and teeth."[41] Given that al-Qaeda came out of the deep recesses of the Islamic world, it seems clear that the agenda was set: the overthrow of what jihadists call "godless regimes" and their replacement by Islamic ones. To do that, the jihadist leadership ordered its followers to gather information about their enemies; kidnap enemy personnel; acquire documents, secrets, and arms; assassinate enemy personnel as well as foreign tourists; free captured jihadists; spread rumors that instigated problems for the enemy; and blow up and destroy places of amusement, the enemy's embassies, and its vital economic centers.[42] Lesson 18 spells out what a prisoner must do when brought before a trial:

1. At the beginning of the trial, once more the brothers must insist on proving that torture was inflicted on them by State Security [investigators] before the judge.
2. Complain to the court of mistreatment while in prison.
3. Make arrangements for the brother's defense with an attorney, whether he was retained by the brother's family or court-appointed.
4. The brother has to do his best to know the names of the state security officers who participated in his torture and mention their names to the judge.
5. Some brothers may tell and may be lured by the state security investigators to testify against the brothers i.e. affirmation witness, either by not keeping them together in the same prison during the trials, or by letting them talk to the media. In this case, they have to be treated gently, and should be offered good advice, good treatment, and pray that God may guide them.

6. During the trial, the judge has to be notified of any mistreatment of the brothers inside the prison.
7. It is possible to resort to a hunger strike, but it is a tactic that can either succeed or fail.
8. Take advantage of visits to communicate with brothers outside prison and exchange information that may be helpful to them in their work outside prison according to what occurred during the investigations. The importance of mastering the art of hiding messages is self-evident here.[43]

If one recalls the North Korean resistance organization at Koje-do and the other Korean POW camps in 1952, the jihadist movement's resistance orders are nearly a mirror image. One must be impressed by such a clearly written set of instructions and specific guidelines for its membership.

It is reasonably safe to conclude that detainee misbehavior in the GTMO detention facilities was organized by prisoners behind the wire. Detainees often attacked one another, and it became apparent that a racial hierarchy existed among the prisoners as well. Fights, stabbings, and beatings often took place. Well-traveled, highly educated Saudi and Yemeni prisoners looked down on Afghans and Africans, often referring to the Africans in English as "stupid niggers."[44] In June 2006 three detainees hanged themselves in their cells. According to a BBC News report, the camp commandant, Rear Admiral Harry Harris, said they had died as an "act of asymmetric warfare against us"; lawyers said the men who hanged themselves had been driven by despair.[45] Clearly, the suicides were acts of resistance, and just as clearly, the lawyers had little understanding of the intense jihadist commitment to the Islamist cause. Uprisings were planned, and weapons were discovered made from anything that could strangle, puncture, cut, tear, or bludgeon—what inmates in U.S. prisons call "shanks." Confiscating these materials became a major mission for the GTMO staff. In addition to weapons making, the detainees were busy learning basic bomb making, small-unit tactics, and, as always, the tenets of Islamic jihad. As explained by one officer assigned to GTMO, "Experts in certain areas would present instruction to the others. We were actually empowering these guys to work against us."[46]

Probably the most imposing resistance behavior in GTMO was the nearly constant attacks on the guards. In his study of the Guantánamo facility, Lieutenant Colonel Gordon Cucullu reports the worst detainee behavior:

> They throw spit, urine, feces, vomit, and semen at guards at every opportunity. They curse, threaten, and tell guards that they will have their al-Qaeda friends rape and murder their families. They refuse to obey instructions, leaping from bunks onto guards when they need to be moved, or wedging themselves under bunks so that the guards have to pry them out. They claw under guards' protective masks, trying to gouge eyes and to rip and tear lips and ears. They are the organizers and the motivators. When mixed with a more benign population, they may be enforcers—intimidating, attacking, and beating other detainees in order to bend them to their will.[47]

It is clear that some of the detainees resisted strenuously and demanded resistance from the other prisoners as well, much as the Nazi sergeants did in the American camps during World War II. Then there were the hunger strikes.

The first hunger strike came in GTMO's first year, beginning with a small number of detainees but eventually growing to 131 participants. Given that the average detainee ate about 4,200 calories a day, they had been getting fat. The Americans found themselves having to force-feed these men just to keep them alive. By fall 2005 another hunger strike was launched, and again 131 detainees participated. After force-feeding, some vomited all the liquid nourishment given to them. In time, the hunger strikes subsided, but they became a media circus. Knowing how vulnerable Western armies are to the power of the media in general and to cries of torture or depravation in particular, the *Manchester Manual* required captives to make extravagant claims that they were being tortured. The indiscretions at Abu Ghraib clearly helped write the script for all this, and they gave credibility to any jihadist accusations of torture made to British or American reporters, human rights activists, or courts. Although trying jihadist detainees for war crimes should have been an easy matter, the process began to turn on its head when American civil rights interests clashed with the perceived needs of homeland security. Neither side would ever be satisfied.[48]

On 1 September 2005 Neil A. Lewis of the *New York Times* reported that Pentagon officials had announced procedural changes to the military commissions created by the Bush administration to try suspected terrorists on war crimes charges at Guantánamo Bay. Criticism mounted about the unfair nature of these trials, similar to the criticisms of the Lincoln military tribunals after the Civil War, the military commissions in the Philippines, and the Dachau trials in Germany after World War II. John B. Bellinger III, the legal advisor at the State Department who worked on the changes, said, "We want the terrorists to be on trial, not the fairness of the U.S. military commissions." The issues of fairness were pale in comparison to what human rights organizations would put forth in American courts on behalf of their detainee clients, whether the clients agreed to their representation or not. Activist organizations such as the American Civil Liberties Union (ACLU), Center for Constitutional Rights, and National Lawyers Guild, as well as various prestigious law firms and academics, all jumped into the arena.[49]

On 28 June 2004 the U.S. Supreme Court ruled in *Rasul v. Bush* that detainees at Guantánamo Bay could file habeas corpus writs to appeal their detention, but the Court also maintained that they could be held without charges or trial. The war crimes proceedings were abruptly halted in November 2004 when a federal district judge ruled that they violated both domestic law and the nation's international treaty obligations. Under those obligations, the court held that the United States must treat the Guantánamo detainees as prisoners of war unless a special tribunal, as described by the Geneva Convention, determines that they are not. In a confusing turnabout of military tradition, as an EPW, a detainee charged with war crimes could be tried by court-martial—where the rules protecting defendants are closer to those of civilian courts—but not by a military commission.

In March 2005 all the prisoners at GTMO received hearings before Combatant Review Tribunals, which released 38 and confirmed the "enemy combatant" status of 520.[50] Committed jihadist Salim Ahmed Hamdan, a Yemeni driver for Osama bin Laden and a GTMO detainee, petitioned the Supreme Court for review of his status. The Bush administration asserted that the Military Commissions Act of 2006, which denied habeas corpus in favor of the military commissions and authorized trial for violations of the law of war, applied. The Department of Defense "Fact Sheet" described that act as providing for a "fair trial in accordance with the applicable laws of war; all the necessary judicial guarantees which are recognized as indispensable by civilized peoples for the purpose of common Article 3 of the Geneva Conventions; appropriate protection of national security interests, and the protection and safety for all personnel participating in the process including the accused."[51] The opposition's "Fact Sheet," published by the ACLU, attacked the Military Commissions Act vigorously, saying that it "eliminates due process, rejects core American values, permits coerced evidence, turns a blind eye to past abuses, and makes the president his own judge and jury."[52]

On 29 June 2006 the Supreme Court agreed with the ACLU and ruled in *Hamdan v. Rumsfeld* that the United States is bound by common Article 3 of the Geneva Convention regarding the treatment of detainees, especially those captured in the global war on terror. It also noted that conspiracy, a common charge against detainees, is not a war crime, especially if it was committed before the war started. The Court ruled that a military commission lacked the authority to try Hamdan. The Court did not dispute the fact that Hamdan was a dangerous person who would inflict great harm on innocent people if given the chance, but the government was obligated to try him as a criminal in a court that had jurisdiction. Then came *Al Odah v. United States,* first filed by the Center for Constitutional Rights in 2002 and heard by the Supreme Court in December 2007. On 12 June 2008 the Military Commissions Act was struck down as unconstitutional, and on 21 January 2009 President Barack Obama ordered the Guantánamo detention facility closed down. What the nation will do with these detainees remains to be seen.

The Central Intelligence Agency—also known as the "Company"—remains a secretive civilian organization within the U.S. government. As observers of the CIA, the National Security Agency, the Defense Intelligence Agency, and other intelligence organizations have learned, people who know something say nothing, whereas people who know nothing say a lot. Under the Bush administration, the CIA was allowed to conduct harsh interrogations that went well beyond military methods, but no one except for freed detainees had anything to say about it. On 6 September 2006 President Bush defended the coercive methods used by CIA interrogators, saying that, under duress, top al-Qaeda operative Abu Zubaydah provided information that led to the apprehension of Khalid Sheikh Mohammed, the 9/11 mastermind, and his colleague Ramzi bin al Shibh. Further interrogations led to other captures and to the uncovering of post-9/11 bomb plots inside the United States, a plan to bomb high-rise buildings, and a mission to launch a truck bomb against a U.S. marine base in Djibouti in East Africa.[53]

In Guantánamo Bay the CIA ran its own detention center separate from those operated by the military command. Called "Secret Squirrel" at GTMO, the camp became the last stop for those prisoners subjected to the rendition process, which had housed them in secret facilities around the world. Everything near the compound was off-limits to the rest of the camp, and it was certain that the CIA kept the most high profile al-Qaeda detainees there.[54] Rendition itself is a questionable practice, always done in secret, and always overseas. *Extraordinary rendition* refers to transferring detainees from U.S. custody to a foreign state known to use harsher interrogation methods than those permitted by American law and practice. According to Amnesty International, extraordinary rendition has been practiced since 1995.[55] The U.S. government maintains that the practice is legal and in accordance with conventions against torture and other international laws, but Amnesty International takes the opposite view. Outside of close CIA circles, no one knows for certain how many individuals have suffered extraordinary rendition, but the government admits to about thirty high-value al-Qaeda detainees. The actual number, who they were, and where they went remain a mystery.

According to Amnesty International, the CIA reportedly runs "black sites"—that is, covert prison facilities—in approximately eight countries.[56] Secret Squirrel at GTMO is just one of them. High-value detainees are rotated through these prisons, and no one but former detainees has ever discussed them.[57] Whether one accepts the government's justification for this harsh treatment or opposes it for humanitarian or legal reasons, there is little doubt that the CIA's use of extraordinary rendition, regardless of its effectiveness, is a severe point of contention in the global war on terror.[58]

In a war like no other before it, Iraq and Afghanistan act as two fronts in the same war. The enemies, for the most part, belong to or are associated with al-Qaeda, with no nation-state affiliation and no inclination to adhere to any law but their own. True, al-Qaeda has failed to generate a religious uprising anywhere in the Middle East. Likewise, it seems clear that al-Qaeda terrorists are war criminals in every sense, but there is no agreement about how to treat them. This confusion has evolved into a period of excess, hard words, hard fighting, and illegal mistreatment of detainees and the rendition of prisoners to foreign prisons where torture is apparently common. The secrecy surrounding the prison facility at Guantánamo Bay has generated deep uncertainties and suspicions among many Americans who are concerned about an assault on the moral high ground, which has been treasured since

George Washington's letters to British General William Howe during the Revolutionary War. Even worse, these suspicions might shatter the cohesion, to say nothing of the reputation, of the American civilian and military establishments at war and split the citizenry right down the middle.

SIXTEEN

The Evolution of New Paradigms

Reflections on the Past, Present, and Future

Remember those in prison as if you were there with them.
—Hebrews 13:3

One always has to ask, does the end justify the means? Nicoló Machiavelli stated as much in *The Prince,* published in 1532, but it is a difficult question to pose, especially in terms of the treatment of EPWs. The temptation is to oppose Machiavelli and assert that the end never justifies the means. But the devil lies in the details. Civilized peoples and nations claim that there are ethics germane to war—the Geneva Convention, for example—as well as other treaties and conventions dealing with the treatment of war prisoners. W. L. La Croix reminds us in *War and International Ethics* that there must be certain values and standards that act as moral bases for actions. Likewise, there must be an appeal to virtuous motives, even if some acts seem heinous on the surface. He asserts correctly that values of prudence and contributive justice are at stake and notes that a virtuous person must always be a moral realist who chooses the principle of the double effect—that is, one must choose the lesser of two evils to achieve a contributively just effect.[1] By so doing, one must ascertain that the good one achieves far outweighs the evil one commits.

This simple dichotomy has both defined and muddled the nature of the moral high ground relative to EPWs in American hands. There exists a perpetual philosophical problem: do ethics have a role in international politics or not? Can the art of diplomacy or, for that matter, military science be thought of as existing without ethical boundaries? If international politics consists of a constant forum for intersocietal competition, can one take a realist's position and assert that the end justifies any means that are expedient?[2] Do goals alone function as the ethical standards in international relations? If so, expediency becomes the sole measure for the actions that become the means to those goals. There are no easy answers here; thus it is necessary to look at each American war's major EPW issues that conflicted presidents, generals, and soldiers and often created precedents for future policies or, in some cases, cause for rejecting history and sometimes good sense in favor of new policies. At stake is the moral high ground, something that Americans value and in which they sincerely believe.

It has often been stated in the literature of war that the American Revolution was fought without real rules of conduct. This is only partially true; there was no signatory-based international law at the time, but General George Washington and the British Generals Gage, Howe, Burgoyne, Clinton, and Cornwallis all had precedents and traditions as guidelines for the treatment of prisoners of war in their charge. By 1748 the spirit of Hugo Grotius could be found in the French Enlightenment philosophers Montesquieu and Rousseau. Montesquieu claimed that the only right the captor held over the captive was prevention from harm. Rousseau urged captors to remove captives from the battlefield immediately following surrender.[3] More important than Montesquieu or Rousseau was Emmerich de Vattel's *The Law of Nations or the Principles of Natural Law* (1758), the most important legal and philosophical treatise about war of the era. In the chapter titled "Civil War," de Vattel notes that "rebel is the name given to all subjects who unjustly take up arms against the ruler of the society, whether their view be to deprive him of the supreme authority, or to resist his commands in some particular instance, and to impose conditions on him." He further notes, "It is a question very much debated, whether a sovereign is bound to observe the common laws of war toward rebellious subjects who have openly taken up arms against him."[4]

Because the issue at hand was the status of prisoners, the British declared the Americans to be rebels in the legal sense and refused to accord them the rights of prisoners of war. Early in the war the Americans believed they had just cause to resist British rule in the colonies, and later in the war the colonies evolved into a sovereign nation after the Declaration of Independence in 1776. Ethical conflicts arose when the Americans believed they were fighting for national existence, whereas Britain believed not only in its own sovereignty but also that it should punish its citizens in rebellion. Caught in the middle were POWs on both sides. Based on the North Act of 1777, the British government intended to reserve and exercise all its sovereign judicial powers to punish the American colonials for treason if they were captured on land and for piracy at sea, at the pleasure of the Crown.[5] In effect, the British believed the Americans were criminals, not POWs, and a mutual, reasonable understanding eluded both the principal combatant nations. As a result, thousands of Americans suffered a punitive, criminal captivity rather than receiving the treatment commonly given to POWs at the time. Both British and Hessian prisoners received proper treatment in American captivity, and their writings indicate that they suffered few real hardships. If any conclusion can be drawn, it is that the precedent of reciprocity in the treatment of EPWs was set during the American Revolution: it is in everyone's best interest to obey the Golden Rule and to treat EPWs fairly and humanely, hoping that the enemy will do the same.

Another, more subtle precedent was set during the Revolution: use of the military tribunal to establish status and try prisoners for crimes committed before capture. George Washington convened a military tribunal to try British Major John André. Found guilty of espionage, André went to the gallows with dignity on 2 October 1780. Military commissions and tribunals were used extensively, perhaps questionably at times, in subsequent wars. Heavily used during and after the Civil War, military tribunals tried Copperheads such as Clement L. Vallandigham of Toledo, Ohio.[6] With habeas corpus flaunted, as it was with the Quakers during the Revolution, the U.S. Supreme Court declared in 1866 in *Ex parte Milligan* that civilians could not be held as prisoners of war and that no president, Congress, or judiciary could disturb any civil liberties incorporated into the American Constitution. But civil war has a way of skirting constitutional rights. The trials and executions of Captain Henry Wirtz, the Confederate commandant of Andersonville prison in Georgia, and the Lincoln conspirators after the Civil War both bypassed the civil courts and raised questions of legal and moral clarity.

Military commissions and tribunals were brought to bear against the Santee Sioux in 1862; the Arapaho, Comanche, Kiowa, and southern Cheyenne tribes in 1875; and again against the Chiricahua Apaches in 1886. During the Philippine war (1899–1905), military tribunals enforced the laws of war and tried hundreds of cases, both against American soldiers who transgressed orders or misbehaved in the field and against Filipino *insurrectos*. Rightly or wrongly, the commissions served as powerful tools that helped end the fighting and make the establishment of civil government possible. Yet some ambiguity arises when one examines the moral ground on which they were based. Used during World War II against German saboteurs in the United States, military commissions served when no other court could, including at the Dachau trials after the war. Finally, military commissions were called against the 9/11 al-Qaeda conspirators in Guantánamo Bay, Cuba. Although the Supreme Court halted their use in 2008, they were reestablished in 2009, and their ultimate usefulness remains in question.

During the Revolution the Americans were openly hostile toward a group of their own countrymen they viewed as traitors: the Loyalists in general and the small number of Quakers imprisoned for suspicion of sedition. As de Vattel noted in 1758, civil war breaks the bonds between society and government and gives rise to two independent parties with no common judge or common superior.[7] The American Revolution was surely an international war against Great Britain, but it was also a civil war pitting American against American. Rather than creating large field armies, the Loyalists operated as freebooting partisan raiders against their neighbors, which generated extreme savagery on and off the battlefield. Confiscating Loyalist property, trying these men for treason, and executing them after capture were extreme forms of retribution and created lasting hatred that refused to heal. For the Americans, it was a case of retributive justice, that is, setting right the wrongs already suffered and punishing those who had caused the wrongs.[8] However justified the Loyalists' persecution may have seemed at the time, the United States paid a high price not only for the executions but also for the states' Test Acts and the Loyalists' eventual expulsion to Great Britain, Ontario, and Nova Scotia, as evidenced by the Canadian United Empire Loyalists' readiness for war and revenge against the United States in 1812.

When the United States and Britain found themselves at war again, the former colonies were no longer subject to the internal laws of Britain. In 1812 they were the United States of America, a sovereign nation. As sovereign nations at public war against each other, their military captives were legal POWs. No longer would Americans in British hands be considered either rebels or political criminals. After the battles ended, the traditional courtesies were extended, particularly at sea. Most important, however, was the cartel arrangement beginning in 1812, when British and American representatives met in Halifax, Nova Scotia (see appendix 2). The cartel worked for the most part, and prisoners were exchanged regularly or returned on parole until exchanged. Better yet, few prisoners on either side died in captivity or were terribly mistreated. The Golden Rule of reciprocity worked well among the Americans, Canadians, and British from 1812 to 1815.

During the Mexican-American War (1846–1848) another new precedent was established—namely, the mass parole of captured soldiers who promised not to fight against the Americans for the duration of the war. It evolved mostly because of the problems of cost and supply in holding captured enemy soldiers behind friendly lines or even sending them back to the United States for internment. Major General Zachary Taylor understood where he was—on a campaign in the middle of a hostile country—and how thin his force really was. Advocating release on parole for as many Mexican EPWs as possible made perfect sense. No doubt exists that returning captured Mexican soldiers to their homes and trusting them not to reengage the American army was a huge risk for Taylor and later for General Winfield Scott, but it worked.

Dealing with the men of the San Patricio Battalion, however, involved a military court-martial that found them all guilty of desertion and, worse, of being renegades who fought their former comrades in bloody combat. True, there were serious incidents of religious oppression in the immigrant American army in 1846. True too, there were about 3,000 Catholics in General Winfield Scott's army, mostly illiterate Irish and German immigrants who suffered terribly from anti-Catholic rhetoric, prejudice, and hostility from those native-born American troops who believed the Catholic Church meant to destroy the United States as they knew it. Understanding this problem, General Santa Anna seized the initiative and attempted to recruit these immigrants, hoping they might be unhappy enough with the Americans to join the Catholic Mexicans. Called the "Irish deserters" by the Americans, fifty men were condemned to death by hanging. Those who had deserted before war was declared received severe whippings, branding, and dishonorable dismissal from the American army at war's end. It was an ugly affair that is not well remembered in American history, but it was legal and ethical in accordance with the articles of war at the time. Although the soldiers are still honored in Mexico today as national heroes, the San Patricio executions became a stern warning to immigrant soldiers that an oath of enlistment meant something in the American army, then as now.

Treatment of enemy prisoners of war during the Civil War (1861–1865) was a work in progress from start to finish. In the beginning, Abraham Lincoln refused to recognize the Confederate government as a legitimate, sovereign regime. Thus, those Confederate prisoners taken early in the war could not legally be held as prisoners of war. When hostilities between the Union and Confederate armies escalated to a war of conquest, committing huge numbers of soldiers on both sides to massive battles without proper POW guidelines for field commanders, the captivity experience became a chaotic mess. At the whim of field commanders, there were acts of reprisal (hangings) against prisoners who had participated in guerrilla warfare (raids), and both sides provided totally inadequate facilities for the prisoners taken on the battlefield. Recalling the successful cartel established during the War of 1812, the officers of the Civil War attempted to replicate it with the Dix-Hill Cartel, concluded on 22 July 1862. Prior to the agreement, field commanders often exchanged or paroled their prisoners on an informal basis for humanitarian reasons—what had been done during the Revolution and the Mexican War, for the most part. Yet the Dix-Hill Cartel broke down quickly. Something had to be done fast, before what had evolved from a rebellion between states to a full-blown civil war likewise devolved into the catastrophe of uncontrolled, retributive bloodletting. The solution was Francis Lieber's General Order 207, issued on 3 July 1863. It not only changed the rule book for the Civil War but also initiated a worldwide change in the treatment of prisoners of war. Later known as General Order 100, this document became one of the true innovations of the nineteenth century, setting the stage for the international community to follow suit (see appendix 4). The Hague Conventions of 1899 and 1907, as well as the Geneva Conventions of 1929 and 1949, reflected Lieber's fundamental thinking: the moral precept formulated by Hugo Grotius, which recognized the enemy as a fellow human being with lawful rights. If these rights were violated, the offender could be brought to trial.[9] Modified and updated over time, General Order 100 remains in force today and serves as the major guideline for the American army's humane behavior toward EPWs and lies at the heart of the Army's Field Manual 19–40, *Enemy Prisoners of War, Civilian Internees, and Detained Persons* (1976). Intelligence collection procedures were outlined in Field Manual 34–52 (1992), replaced and updated by Field Manual 2–22.3, *Human Intelligence Collector Operations* (2006).

Internally, Abraham Lincoln changed the rules in a less than humane way. Beginning on 27 April 1862, Lincoln first suspended the writ of habeas corpus because he believed the Confederates threatened the rail line from Philadelphia to Washington. On 24 September 1862 Lincoln suspended habeas corpus throughout the Union for all cases of disloyalty and ordered the arbitrary arrest of anyone guilty of disloyal speech or practice. A deep chill descended on anyone in the Union who openly opposed the war or Republican political policies. Enforcing Lincoln's executive orders, the Union Army used military commissions and tribunals to try supposedly disloyal civilians and often incarcerated them in POW camps along with Confederate prisoners. Lincoln believed that the Union itself was under attack from Northern war resisters who, in his mind, functioned as a fifth column for the Confederates. Only the final Union victory settled this issue, but military tribunals continued to hear both civilian and military cases outside normal civilian courts.

The Spanish-American War in 1898 became a perfect example of the United States taking the moral high ground relative to EPWs, but for Americans, fighting guerrilla wars has always presented moral and ethical difficulties. In the Philippines, General Order 100 acted as the rule book for the treatment of enemy soldiers captured in battle, but dealing with partisans was another matter. They were considered "war rebels" at the time, and General Order 100 excluded them from POW status. The war against the Filipino *insurrectos* resembled the Indian wars from 1865 to 1890 more than anything else, in part because the American army had no other model to use as a precedent. The Filipino leader, Emilio Aguinaldo, called for a guerrilla war against the invading Americans on 13 November 1899, at which time he had more than 40,000 troops under arms. When captured, Filipino partisans experienced trial by American military tribunals that attempted to determine a captive's status and, if necessary, inflict punishment, including execution.

What seemed to be the moral high ground to soldiers on the ground facing nonuniformed Filipino guerrillas received severe condemnation at home, chiefly from newspapers charging cruelty, torture by the "water cure," and other mischief. Rightly or wrongly, senior officers found no way to achieve a moral high ground that was accepted by everyone. It was difficult to defend hard interrogations to achieve tactical intelligence about immediate enemy attacks. Officers preferred to look the other way when told about these desperate interrogation methods, while at the same time issuing general orders against the physical abuse of prisoners. Thus, they found themselves in a classic double bind: they were damned by the law if they treated prisoners roughly, and damned by the failure to obtain hard field intelligence if they refrained. Thus the Spanish-American War and the Philippine-American War became one war with two very different kinds of theaters. In the former, Americans and Spaniards understood the international rules of warfare and behaved accordingly; in the latter, Aguinaldo and his colleagues made the conscious decision to wage guerrilla war throughout the Philippines, leaving the rule book behind and leading to the inhumane treatment of captives by determined American soldiers who, in their view, acted out of military necessity.

The issue remains: one must choose the lesser of two evils, and the historical record indicates that many soldiers failed to do that in the Philippines. The problem of dealing with partisans in a guerrilla war plagued the American sense of the moral high ground well into the future. Partisan or guerrilla war is war on the cheap, and over time, a small force can defeat or at least demoralize a larger one. But despite the clear American victory in 1902 and the end of hostilities in most of the Philippine Islands, the soldiers who fought there returned to the United States unwelcomed and feared as torturers. So did many Vietnam, Iraq, and Afghanistan veterans, for much the same reason. The Hague Convention that governed conduct in World War I had no provisions for dealing with partisans; neither did the 1929 or 1949 Geneva Conventions. It remains a major issue on the world stage, a problem yet to be solved not just by the United States but by all nations in the twenty-first century.

Luckily for the Americans, the fighting in France during World War I never devolved into any sort of partisan or guerrilla warfare. After 1917, when the United States finally entered the war, the Hague Convention and the International Committee of the Red Cross (ICRC) were firmly in place to deal with the POWs held by all the belligerents. There were virtually no hard interrogations in the field, and principles of humanity, restraint, and honor remained the guidelines for nearly everyone involved. In their narratives, American officer POWs such as Edouard Isaacs and James Hall tell of dining with their captors before their removal to prison camps.[10] The problem for the Americans in France was the actual taking of prisoners, which was discouraged by their British and French trainers. Regardless of their precombat training, the armed forces of the United States had long upheld the tradition of taking prisoners in battle and took more than 48,000 German soldiers as EPWs (see appendix 7). Thus, in Europe it is reasonable to conclude that the Americans upheld the moral high ground, at least in their treatment of enemy prisoners who surrendered in large groups after battle. In American stockades, General John Pershing, commanding officer of the American Expeditionary Force, made certain that all the provisions of the Hague Convention were upheld. The Germans certainly upheld the Hague Convention for 4,000-plus Americans in their prison camps. Where the United States fell short in World War I was at home, not in France. Journalist George Creel, head of the Committee on Public Information, Woodrow Wilson's anti-German propaganda machine, did his work very well.

Congress passed two contentious laws during World War I: the Espionage Act, passed on 15 June 1917, criminalized any act that conveyed information intended to interfere with successful military operations or that promoted the success of America's enemies; the Sedition Act of 1918 made it illegal to speak out against the government. The Wilson administration, like the Lincoln administration before it, created the category of political prisoner in the United States for those men and women who publicly opposed Wilson's war policies. They suffered shame and imprisonment by the federal government, much as antiwar dissenters had suffered in wars past. Both laws were repealed in 1921, and anyone found guilty and imprisoned under them was set free.

World War II was, without a doubt, America's finest hour in terms of its treatment of EPWs. Between 1942 and 1946 the U.S. Army held more than 425,000 German, 50,000 Italian, and 5,000 Japanese EPWs in some 500 prison camps throughout the United States. Hardly anyone died in captivity, and both the popular and historical literature makes it clear that the United States strained to uphold all the provisions of the Geneva Convention of 1929, hoping that the enemy would do the same. If the Americans failed to attain the moral high ground during this era, it was through sins of omission rather than commission. Because camp commandants wanted quiet, organized, and disciplined camps, they allowed the Germans to govern themselves. Controlling the camps for enlisted men were some hard-bitten, tough Afrika Korps sergeants who remained faithful to their belief in a German victory. They insisted that their men display minimal cooperation with their captors, and anyone showing overt collaboration might well be visited by squads of fellow prisoners who inflicted severe beatings or even death. That the Americans responded by bringing charges against those Germans who murdered their own men set the ethical and legal bar very high. In this sense, the American authorities cannot be charged with revenge or inhumane behavior. They observed the Geneva Convention and the laws of war, and the fourteen executions of German EPWs were both legal and proper.

After the Americans de-Nazified their POW camps in 1944, many German EPWs enjoyed their captivity experience in the United States. They worked hard, learned trades, read books forbidden in Nazi Germany, wrote to their families often, gained weight, and eventually returned home with a positive attitude toward Americans and the United States. The Italian EPWs also enjoyed their captivity experience. In the end, captivity in the United States posed few serious problems for German, Italian, or Japanese prisoners of war, who thrived behind the wire until repatriation in 1945–1946.

Real problems arose when more than 7.6 million German soldiers surrendered to the Americans before and just after 8 May 1945. Because the war was over, these troops could no longer be classified as EPWs, and the problem of status became complex when the German ex-soldiers became "disarmed enemy forces" (DEFs). With that status change, the protection of the Geneva Convention disappeared, as did Red Cross rations and camp inspections by the ICRC. The Supreme Headquarters, Allied Expeditionary Force no longer took responsibility for providing these men with rations equal to those received by the American army. As a result of these policy changes, more than 50,000 men died in the Rhine Meadow Camps, a series of simple enclosures built in the vast, empty fields along the Rhine River near Remagen.

The American army wanted to clear these camps as quickly as possible and released more than 1 million former German soldiers immediately.However, the Americans sought members of the SS, SD, and Gestapo for war crimes, knowing full well that many had been hiding among the surrendered Wehrmacht soldiers. Instead of sending vast amounts of rations to these camps, the rations went to displaced persons (DPs), and none went to the German civilian population in 1945 and 1946. One must judge the withholding of rations from starving men, many held too long behind the wire, very harshly. There may have been good reasons for it at the time, but the chaos of war is no excuse, and it is safe to assert that the United States lost the moral high ground at this point and only regained it when the commitments of the Cold War redefined the American relationship as one of goodwill toward the people in West Germany.

European DEF imprisonment and DP problems at the end of World War II were unforeseen difficulties for the Americans, especially in defeated Germany. After 8 May 1945 the United Nations Relief and Rehabilitation Administration (UNRRA) took responsibility for all the DP camps in the American, British, and French Zones of Occupation. Dominating the chaos was the forced repatriation of former citizens and soldiers of the USSR who were taken prisoner by the Nazis and then decided to become turncoats and fight with the Germans against their communist oppressors. For them, political asylum became an impossibility, and the Allies agreed to return them against their will to certain execution or probable incarceration in the feared Soviet Gulag system. By 1947 those under American care in the UNRRA camps enjoyed political asylum, and forced repatriation was no longer acceptable.

In Korea the issue of forced repatriation became the sticking point between the warring parties, and President Harry S. Truman refused to change his decision to provide political asylum to both communist Chinese and North Korean soldiers if requested. After Joseph Stalin died on 5 March 1953, the communists contacted the UN Command and indicated there might be grounds to conduct serious armistice negotiations. This was welcome news indeed, because the cost of the American decision to prohibit forced repatriation was high: two more years of war and numerous violent uprisings in the United Nations POW camps. Yet the moral high ground was achieved for 83,000 EPWs who received a lifeline to a noncommunist future in either South Korea or Taiwan.

The Vietnam War presented an entirely new set of problems for the Americans in terms of the treatment of EPWs, especially after 1964, when American participation in the war expanded. The battlefield was everywhere, with no actual front lines and a mix of guerrilla and uniformed warfare. Because of the agreement that established South Vietnam as the detaining power, General William C. Westmoreland faced an unenviable quandary. The South Vietnamese government declared indigenous South Vietnamese who joined and fought for the communists to be Vietcong (Vietnamese communist) outlaws and criminals. That decision put any Vietcong prisoners outside the parameters of international law, allowing the South Vietnamese to mistreat them as they wished. General Westmoreland realized that he had to intervene to create an EPW environment that was acceptable to the international community—specifically, the ICRC, which demanded visitation and inspection rights. For Vietnamese communist soldiers, the Americans and the South Vietnamese made more than reasonable accommodations, but for captured communist cadres—active members of the Communist Party—there were no protections.

From 1961 to 1964 the Vietcong kidnapped 28,504 South Vietnamese and assassinated 6,587 civilians. Reports of Vietcong cadres marching through villages with severed heads on sticks to terrify the locals were commonplace. During the Tet Offensive of 1968, the U.S. Marine Corps discovered thousands of South Vietnamese civilians murdered execution style, with their hands tied behind their backs, outside the city of Hue. None of this boded well for the treatment of Vietcong cadres captured by the allies, in part because these kinds of war crimes, rightly or wrongly, screamed for retribution. The Phoenix program became the answer. After William E. Colby's reforms in 1968, the program was purely political and aimed at the destruction of the Communist Party. To this day, the jury remains out about its moral efficacy, yet there was one distinct high point—the *Chieu Hoi* (Open Arms) program. The Americans and South Vietnamese invited any member of the Communist Party—that is, any level of military or political cadre, main force (North Vietnamese), local force, or guerrilla soldier—to change sides. Unfortunately, those who participated became victims of the retributive wrath of the victorious communists in 1975 and 1976. Returned to their original combat units, they were often executed as deserters.

During Operation Desert Storm in 1991 the Coalition took more than 69,822 Iraqi EPWs in 100 hours of combat, an astounding number for such a short period. In this fight the United States decided to conclude an agreement with Saudi Arabia to hold all the Iraqi EPWs, and as in Vietnam, the Americans provided liaison teams for management and administrative assistance. In the end, Desert Storm, perhaps because of its short duration, but more likely because of its superb organization, never challenged the moral high ground in terms of American treatment of EPWs. The Americans, however, had another date with Saddam Hussein in 2003. Before that, the people of the United States met the Taliban in Afghanistan and Osama bin Laden's nineteen stealthy al-Qaeda hijackers in New York City, Washington, D.C., and a deserted field in southwestern Pennsylvania.

Representing no nation-state, al-Qaeda's agents of terror regularly used assassination, bombing, hijacking, kidnapping, and suicide attacks against innocent civilians. The al-Qaeda hijackers certainly wore no uniforms on 11 September 2001 and could never have been accorded POW rights under the Geneva Convention if captured. Were they enigmas to the intelligence community? No, according to Richard A. Clarke, a ranking member of the Senior Executive Service who, prior to 9/11, constantly warned the Bush administration about Osama bin Laden and al-Qaeda.[11] Clarke appeared before the National Commission on Terrorist Attacks upon the United States, popularly known as the 9/11 Commission, on 24 March 2004 and severely criticized the Bush administration's operatives from the CIA and the FBI for not doing their jobs in preventing the attacks. In particular, Clarke faulted these agencies for not sharing their intelligence concerning the presence of the hijackers, most of whom were in the United States illegally. When examining Clarke's highly critical assertions, one should be mindful that charges of neglect and dereliction of duty are not new. They were also made after the Pearl Harbor attack in 1941 and the German attack in the Ardennes in 1944. Someone had to be asleep at the wheel for such major disasters to take place. Yet no one wanted to say publicly what the real situation was. There are no crystal balls or silver bullets in the world of intelligence.

Unlike with the Japanese in 1941,[12] and nearly unknown to the Western world since the Thirty Years' War ended in 1648, the United States faced religious fanatics intent on destroying the Western Enlightenment concept of democracy and replacing it with a medieval Islamist theocracy. In Afghanistan, the intelligence community knew, the Taliban was allied with al-Qaeda and permitted it to establish training facilities for fighters sent to attack the United States in 2001. When President George W. Bush demanded that the Kabul Taliban government close these camps permanently, the Taliban failed to respond. Operation Enduring Freedom–Afghanistan began on the night of 7 October 2001 with powerful air attacks against al-Qaeda and Taliban training camps. On 17 January 2002 the Pentagon announced that Taliban prisoners would not receive the protection of POW status under the Geneva Convention. Because they were "unlawful combatants," they were considered "detainees" and would be taken to the new detention facility at Guantánamo Bay, Cuba. Gone were the traditional notions of the Golden Rule, and a new paradigm emerged, one that not only fit cold and hardened military necessity but also disturbed the ideas of reciprocity and the moral high ground.

Critics charge that Iraq was an unnecessary war, yet its final results remain uncertain. It is difficult to tell American combat veterans who fought valiantly for many years and on repeated tours of duty that they fought an unnecessary war. That was done to the Vietnam veterans, leaving an ugly legacy for those men and women who went into harm's way in service to their country. The war against a resurgent Taliban in Afghanistan is America's battleground in 2009, and bloody hostilities there may continue well into the future. Technology is changing rapidly with the introduction of Predators and Reapers, U.S. Air Force and CIA drones that seek out and destroy the enemy behind its own lines. Yet the hard soldiering in the Middle East and South Asia will continue until it somehow ends, perhaps in a negotiated armistice, perhaps in a Taliban victory, perhaps in a Coalition victory. No one knows yet.

There is little doubt that the rule book for EPWs will change, especially with regard to interrogation techniques. What critics call torture may not be torture at all. Moderate physical pressure to gather technical or tactical intelligence has been acceptable in the modern era, but extreme measures that inflict a great deal of pain have not.[13] Solitary confinement might be terrible, but it is clearly not torture. Techniques such as sleep deprivation, loud music, intense interviewing, light punching and slapping, and screaming are not torture. Use of the water board probably is torture because it produces the sensation of drowning. Excruciating stress positions, mock executions, and severe beatings can be torture, depending on the degree of pain they inflict. Real torture, such as the "ropes," the bastinado (beating of the feet), and the strapado (hanging by the arms), which the North Vietnamese inflicted on American POWs from 1965 to 1973, are all intrinsically immoral. This was especially true because the North Vietnamese used them to derive sadistic pleasure.[14] Senator John McCain understands the Hanoi experience very well. He was there and wrote in his memoir that he would sit in his cell, "sometimes listening to the screams of a tortured friend fill the air."[15] One of his POW friends, Jeremiah A. Denton Jr., a senior naval officer in Hanoi, recalled the "ropes" in his captivity memoir:

> Pigeye began roping one arm from shoulder to elbow. With each loop, one guard would put his foot on my arm and pull, another guard joining him in the effort to draw the rope as tightly as their combined strengths would permit. The other arm was then bound, and both were tied together so closely that the elbows touched. The first pains were from the terrible pinching of the flesh. After about ten minutes, an agonizing pain began to flow through the arms and shoulders as my heart struggled to pump blood through the strangled veins. The weight of my body spread my fingers so grotesquely that two of them were dislocated.[16]

Denton finally signed a meaningless confession about aggression and bombing. Real torture did its work well: the American prisoners would say or sign just about anything to stop the pain.

The Detainee Treatment Act of 2005 incorporated an amendment sponsored by Senator McCain that prohibits the infliction of cruel, inhumane, or degrading treatment by American soldiers anywhere in the world.[17] The CIA lies outside this legislation, and it seems certain that its secret policies, at least some of them, will remain in place in the future.

In dealing with resistance to interrogation, American intelligence personnel need to be smarter than their enemies rather than depending on a heavy hand; it is all too easy to inflict excruciating pain on a prisoner who refuses to communicate. Arnold Krammer comments on this issue in *Prisoners of War: A Reference Handbook*: "The treatment of war prisoners is now an issue of expediency—whatever is required to extract critical information, immobilize enemy fighters, or break the nationalist spirit or religious devotion of opponents. Whether necessary or not in the face of a new type of warfare, this change signals a sad turn to earlier and more barbaric times."[18] The charge of barbarity is correct, but a larger question looms just below the surface: how much and to what degree might national vulnerability be enhanced if one side uses the World War II EPW model based on reciprocity and good treatment and the other side does not? What is the lesser of two evils here? Where is the elusive moral high ground? Few people on either side of the issue seem to agree.

On orders from President Barack Obama, the Guantánamo Bay facility will be closed, and there is no more conversation in Washington about the global war on terror.[19] From a peak population of about 700, only about 200 remained there in August 2009, and depending on the hazy legal positions being argued in the courts, between 60 and 80 of these men may face war crimes trials in some form. On 28 February 2009 the Associated Press reported that in Afghanistan there may be between 10,000 and 15,000 Taliban partisans fighting inside the country, and the insurgent group is operating across about seventeen provinces.[20] On a positive note, as of February 2009, Abu Ghraib prison belongs again to the Iraqi government. The Associated Press reported on 2 March 2009 that in Iraq, the number of detainees held by the American command had dropped to 13,832 from a peak of 26,000 in 2007. In effect, the prisoners are being released or transferred to Iraqi custody to meet the requirements of a security agreement that took effect on 1 January 2009.[21]

Perhaps pragmatism trumps idealism, but it never trumps the law. In the end, Congress, not the president, is sovereign over international treaties and customs, even though they are considered the law of the land.[22] Former President George W. Bush will probably face harsh criticism well into the future concerning his administration's legal memos and policy changes regarding EPWs, detainees, and interrogation techniques promulgated from 2002 to 2004. That the CIA destroyed a large number of interrogation tapes in Thailand offers little to bolster American hopes for reconciliation anytime soon.[23] Although the difficult relationship between intelligence and security will continue, finding just and lawful solutions will become the new challenge of the present era.[24] Nonvengeance neither requires nor implies nondefense.[25]

Critics also charge that both the Iraq and Afghanistan wars have trampled civil liberties over there and over here. No one can deny that civil liberties have been curtailed in nearly every war the United States has ever fought. Whether because of questions of loyalty (Revolution, Mexico, Civil War, World War I), national security (World War II, Korea, Afghanistan, Iraq), military necessity (Philippines, World War II, Korea, Vietnam), or population control (Indian wars, Japanese American internment), individual and collective civil liberties have indeed been victims in America's wars. The record is clear, and the challenge is ongoing.

How we as Americans treat enemy prisoners who wage war against us speaks volumes about who and what we are. Although there is always hope that the reciprocity-based Golden Rule will reemerge as a guideline for the wars of the twenty-first century, perhaps the nations of the world should gather again to devise a more flexible international convention that addresses the new paradigms of war and captivity. If we abandon the hope for reciprocity, and if we reject the humane treatment of enemy prisoners of war in favor of *lex talionis,* an eye for an eye and a tooth for a tooth, there is a good chance that in a heightened state of fear, we will all become blind and toothless. Recall the prophet Jeremiah's words in the Book of Lamentations: "For men are not cast off by the Lord forever. Though He brings grief, He will show compassion, so great is His unfailing love. For He does not willingly bring affliction or grief to the children of men." The choice is ours.

Appendixes

Appendix One

Loyalist Units Organized in the American Revolution

Loyal New Englanders
New York Volunteers
New York Rangers
New Jersey Volunteers
New York Highlanders
Pennsylvania Loyalists
Maryland Loyalists
South Carolina Loyalists
South Carolina Volunteers
Georgia Light Dragoons
Georgia Loyalists
Loyal Virginia Regiment

Westchester Refugees
Buck's County Dragoons
General Wentworth's Volunteers
King's American Regiment
King's Orange Rangers
Prince of Wales Regiment
General Delancy's Brigade
Volunteers of Ireland
British Legion
Royal Fensible Americans
Skinner's Volunteers
Rogers' Rangers

Appendix Two

Cartel for the Exchange of POWS in the War of 1812

The Provisional agreement for the exchange of naval prisoners of war, made and concluded at Halifax in the province of Nova Scotia on the 28th day of November 1812 between the Honourable Richard John Uniacke His Britannic Majestys attorney and advocate General for the province of Nova Scotia and William Miller Esquire Lieutenant in the Royal navy and agent for Prisoners of War at Halifax; and John Mitchell Esquire late consul of the united states at St Jago de Cuba, american agent for Prisoners of war at Halifax, having been transmitted to the Department of state of the United States for approval and John Mason Esquire Commissary General for Prisoners for the United States having been duely authorised to meet Thomas Barclay Esquire his Britanic Majestys agent for Prisoners of war and for carrying on an exchange of Prisoners for the purpose of considering and revising the said provisional agreement and the articles of the said agreement having been by them considered and discussed—it has been agreed by the said Thomas Barclay and John Mason subject to the ratification of both their governments that the said provisional agreement shall be so altered and revised as to stand expressed in the following words.

Article First

The Prisoners taken at sea or on land on both sides shall be treated with humanity conformable to the usage and practice of the most civilized nations during war; and such prisoners shall without delay, and as speedily as circumstances will admit, be exchanged on the following terms and conditions. That is to say—An admiral or a General commanding in chief shall be exchanged for officers of equal rank or for sixty men each: a vice admiral or a Lieutenant General for officers of equal rank or for forty men each, a Rear Admiral or a Major General, for officers of equal rank, or for thirty men each; a Commodore with a broad pendant and a Captain under him or a Brigadier General for officers of equal rank or for twenty men each; a Captain of a line of Battle ship or a Colonel for officers of equal rank or for fifteen men each; a Captain of a frigate, or Lieutenant Colonel for officers of equal rank or for ten men each; Commanders of sloops of war, Bomb Catches, fire ships, and Packets or a Major for officers of equal rank, or for eight men each; Lieutenants or masters in the navy, or Captains in the army, for officers of equal rank, or for six men each; Masters-Mates, or Lieutenants in the army for officers of equal rank, or for four men each; Midshipmen, warrant officers, Masters of merchant vessels, and Captains of private armed vessels, or sub Lieutenants and Ensigns for officers of equal rank, or for three Men each: Lieutenants and mates of private armed vessels Mates of merchant vessels and all petty officers of ships of war, or all non commissioned officers of the army, for officers of equal rank, or for two men each; seamen and private soldiers one for the other.

Article Second

All non combatants that is to say, surgeons and surgeons mates, Pursers, secretaries Chaplains and Schoolmasters, belonging to the army or men of war; surgeons and surgeons mates of merchant vessels, or Privateers; passengers, and all other men who are not engaged in the naval or Military service of the enemy, not being sea faring persons; all women and girls, and all Boys under twelve years of age; every person of the foregoing description, or of whatever description exempt from capture by the usage and practice of the most civilized nations when at war—if taken shall be immediately released without exchange and shall take their departure at their own charge, agreeably to passports to be granted them, or otherwise shall be put on board the next cartel which sails; persons found on board recaptured ships, whatever situation they may have held in the Capturing ship, shall not be considered as non combatants—non combatants are not to be imprisoned except for improper conduct, and if poor or unprovided with means to support themselves, the government of each nation will allow them a reasonable subsistence, having respect to their rank and situation in life.

Article Third

American prisoners taken and brought within any of the dominions of his Brittanick majesty shall be stationed for exchange at Halifax in Nova Scotia—Quebec, Bridgetown in Barbadoes, Kingstown in Jamaica—Falmouth and Liverpool in England and at no other posts or places—and British prisoners taken and brought into the United States shall be stationed at Salem in Massachusets—Schnecteday in the state of New York—Providence in Rhode Island—Wilmington in Deleware, Annapolis in Maryland—Savannah in Georgia—New Orleans in Louisiana and at no other ports or places in the United States. The Government of Great Brittain will receive and protect an agent to be appointed by the Government of the United States, to reside at or near each of the before mentioned places in the British Dominions for the purpose of inspecting the management and care which is taken of the american prisoners of war at each station: and the Government of the United States will in like manner receive and protect an agent, to be appointed by the British Government to reside at or near each of the stations before mentioned within the dominions of the United States for the like purpose of inspecting the management and care taken of the British prisoners of war at each of the stations—and each Government shall be at liberty to appoint an agent to reside at or near any Depot established for prisoners by the other nation, for the purpose of taking care and inspecting the state and situation of such prisoners—and such agents shall be protected respectively in the same manner as the agents at the stations for exchange.

Article Fourth

Whenever a Prisoner is admitted to parole the form of such parole shall be as follows—

Whereas the agent appointed for the care and custody of prisoners of war at _____ in _____ has been pleased to grant leave to the undersigned Prisoner of war as described on the back hereof to reside in __ _____ upon condition that give parole of honor not to withdraw from the bounds prescribed there without leave for that purpose from the said agent. That _____ will behave decently and with due respect to the laws of this country and also that _____ will not during continuance in either directly or indirectly carry on a correspondence with any of the enemies of or receive or write any letter or letters whatever, but through the hands of said agent, in order that they may be read and approved by him do hereby declare _____ have given parole of honor accordingly, and that will keep it inviolably, dated at _____ .

Signature
Quality
Ships or Corps
Men of War Privateer or Mercht in which taken

And the agent who shall take such parole shall grant a certificate to each prisoner so paroled, certyfying the limits to which his parole extends, the hours and other rules, to be observed, and granting permission to such person to remain unmolested within such limits and every commissioned officer in the navy or army, when so paroled, if in health shall be paid by the agent that has granted such parole to him during the continuance thereof the sum of three shillings sterling per day each, for subsistence; and all other prisoners so paroled shall be paid each person at the rate of one shilling and six pence per day sterling, at the rate of four shillings and six pence sterling per American milled dollar; which pay in case of actual sickness shall be doubled to each so long as the surgeon shall certify the continuance of such sickness; and each sick prisoner shall also be allowed the attendance of a nurse, in case the surgeon shall certify the person to be so ill as to require such help; all which subsistence and pay is to be paid in advance twice in every week. and prisoners who shall wilfully disobey the rules and regulations established for Prisoners on parole, may be sent to Prison. and all rules and regulations to be observed by prisoners on parole, are to be published and made known to each prisoner—and when any prisoner shall be allowed to depart at his own expence if he has not a sufficiency of money for that purpose he shall be allowed necessary money not to exceed the parole subsistence, to which he would have been entitled for one month, if he had remained.

Article Fifth

And in case any prisoner be permitted to return to his own country on parole, on condition of not serving untill duly exchanged such prisoner shall sign an engagement in the following form—

Whereas Agent for the care and custody of Prisoners of War at _____ _____ has granted me the undersigned prisoner, described on the back hereof, permission to return to _____ upon condition that I give my parole of honor that I will not enter into any naval military or other service whatever against the _____ or any of the dominions thereunto belonging; or against any powers at peace with _____ until I shall have been regularly exchanged, and that I will surrender myself, if required by the agent of the government at such place and at such time as may be appointed, in case my exchange, shall not be effected;

and I will until exchanged, give notice from time to time of my place of residence. Now in consideration of my enlargement I do hereby declare, that I have given my parole of honour accordingly and that I will keep it inviolably—given under my hand at this day in the year of our Lord.

and to the Prisoner so granted his enlargement on parole, shall be given a certificate and passport specifying the terms and conditions of his enlargement, and a description of his person, & notice of such parole agreement shall be sent to the agent for prisoners of war at the nearest station to the place where such parole shall be granted.

Article Sixth

In case any prisoner of war shall become unmindfull of the honourable obligation he lies under, to the nation which shall have granted him his parole, and shall violate the same, he shall be liable to be dealt with according to the usages and customs observed in such cases, by the most civilized nations, when at war; and either nation shall have a right to demand from the other, the surrender and restoration of any prisoner of war who shall violate his parole, and every just & reasonable satisfaction shall be given to the nation demanding the same, to shew that if such prisoner be not returned, it is by reason of its not being in the power of the nation to which he originally belonged.

Article Seventh

NO prisoner shall be struck with the hand, whip, stick or any other weapon whatever, the complaints of the prisoners shall be attended to, and real grievances redressed; and if they behave disorderly, they may be closely confined, and Kept on two thirds allowance for a reasonable time not exceeding ten days. They are to be furnished by the government in whose possession they may be, with a subsistence of sound and wholesome provisions, consisting of, one pound of Beef, or twelve ounces of pork; one pound of wheaten bread, and a quarter of a pint of pease, or six ounces of rice, or a pound of potatoes, per day to each man; and of salt and vinegar in the proportion of two quarts of salt and four quarts of vinegar to every hundred days subsistence. Or the ration shall consist of such other meats and vegetables (not changeing the proportion of meat to the vegetables, and the quantity of bread salt and vinegar always remaining the same) as may from time to time be agreed on, at the several stations, by the respective agents of the two governments, as of equal nutriment with the ration first described—Both Governments shall be at liberty, by means of their respective agents to supply their prisoners with clothing, and such other small allowances, as may be deemed reasonable, and to inspect at all times the quality and quantity of subsistence provided for the prisoners of their nations respectively as stipulated in this article.

Article Eighth

Every facility shall be given, as far as circumstances will permit, to the exchange of prisoners; and they shall be selected for exchange according to the scale hereby established on both sides, by the respective agents of the country to which they may belong, without any interference whatever of the government in whose possession they may be—and if any prisoner is kept back, when his exchange shall be applied for, good and sufficient cause shall be assigned for such detention.

Article Ninth

To carry on a regular exchange of prisoners between the two countries, four vessels shall be employed, two of which shall be provided by the British government and two by the government of the United States; and the two vessels of each government shall be as near as possible, of the burthen of five hundred tons together and neither of them less than two hundred tons; and shall be manned, victualled and provided with every necessary and convenience for the safe transportation of prisoners, The expence of the two british vessels is to be defrayed by the British government and of the two american vessels, by the government of the United States; when these vessels are provided, surveyed and approved of, by the proper officers of both governments, they shall be furnished with passports from each government, as flags of truce, and shall carry arms and ammunition sufficient with a guard not exceeding a non commissioned officer and six men, to guard the Prisoners, and keep them in subjection; and shall each carry one signal gun with a few charges of powder, and shall carry a white flag constantly at the fore top-mast head; the British Cartel ships shall carry a British ensign at the gaff end, or ensign staff, and the american ensign at the main top-mast head and the american cartel ships shall carry the american ensign at the gaff end or ensign staff, and the British ensign at the main topmast head. No cartel shall be suffered to proceed to sea with less than 30 days full allowance of water and provisions for the ships company, and the number of Prisoners embarked on board; and when such cartels shall be established, they shall be kept at all times, constantly well provided with sails rigging and every thing proper and necessary to make them staunch, safe and sea worthy; and shall be constantly employed in carrying prisoners to and from the different stations herein before named and appointed for the exchange of prisoners; and when carrying american prisoners from a British port to an american port the american agent at the port of embarkation shall direct the station at which such prisoners shall be delivered: and when carrying British prisoners from an american port the British agent shall direct at which of the british stations such prisoners shall be delivered—and the agents for prisoners of war on both sides, shall by agreement settle and fix the several species of provisions which shall constitute the daily ration to be served out to prisoners while on board cartels, with the value thereof: and a regular account shall be kept of the number of days each prisoner shall have been victualled on board each cartel, and the British government shall pay at that rate the expence and cost of victualling the British prisoners delivered at a British station; and so the american government shall in like manner pay at the same rate the daily charge for victualling the american Prisoners, delivered at an american station; but no charge is to be introduced for the transportation or carriage of Prisoners as each nation is to furnish for that service an equal number of tons of shipping—no cartel shall be permitted to remain in port more than ten days after her arrival, unless delayed by winds or weather, or the order of the Commanding officer of the station at which she may be, whether british or american. And in future cartels shall on no account unless driven by stress of weather or some other unavoidable necessity, put into any british or american port—save the ports herein before appointed for the exchange of Prisoners, unless specially agreed upon by the principal agents of the two governments—and in case the number of vessels now agreed on, to be provided as cartels, shall be found insufficient the number may be encreased, and so in like manner diminished, by agreement, as the occasion may require—each nation always furnishing an equal share of the tonnage necessary.

Article Tenth

Untill regular Cartels shall be provided as stipulated in the foregoing article, the transportation of prisoners is to be conducted and paid for by each nation, according to the method hitherto observed in the present war; and after regular cartels are established in case a number of prisoners, not less than one hundred may be collected at any British or american port, different from the ports before named a temporary cartel may be fitted out by order of the Commanding officer at such post or Ports, for the purpose of carrying such prisoners, if British to one of the British stations before named, and if american to one of the american stations before named—and to no other port or place, provided always that such cartel shall bring at least one hundred prisoners, and shall receive an equal number in exchange with liberty to return with them to any port of the nation to which she belongs; and the prisoners so delivered in exchange on board such temporary cartel, shall be certified to one of the regular stations of exchange, where they shall be credited to the nation so delivering them in exchange, whether they arrive at the port of destination or not—But should there not be an equal number at such station to exchange for the number brought, the transportation in such temporary Cartel, must be paid for so many prisoners as shall not be exchanged.

Article Eleventh

Commanders of all public ships of war of either of the two nations shall be permitted to send flags of truce into any of the established stations for exchange of prisoners of the other nation, with prisoners to be delivered to the agent for prisoners of war of the nation to which such port belongs, and the agent receiving them, shall give a receipt for them, specifying their names, quality, when and in what ship taken, and the prisoners so delivered shall be placed to the credit of the nation sending them.

Article Twelfth

Commanders of ships of war Captains of Privateers and letters of marque of either of the two nations shall be permitted to send prisoners belonging to the other nation, in neutral vessels to any of the stations for exchange aforementioned of the nation to which the prisoners belong: and they shall be delivered to the agent and receipted for in the same manner as is directed and expressed in the eleventh article; and the prisoners when delivered shall be placed to the credit of the nation sending them in the neutral vessel—The expences incurred under this and the eleventh article are to be paid by the nation sending the prisoners—and the prisoners so embarked in neutral vessels shall be permitted to proceed to the port of destination without molestation or other interruption by the subjects or citizens of either of the nations.

Article Thirteenth

Lists shall be exchanged by the agents on both sides, of the prisoners hitherto delivered and after such lists are adjusted and signed agreeably to the rule of exchange hereby established, the persons named therein shall be considered as liberated and free to serve again, as well as those heretofore exchanged, notwithstanding any parole or engagement they may have previously entered into; and in future prisoners embarked in a cartel—belonging to the nation sending such prisoners, shall not be credited to the nation so sending them untill they are delivered at one of the stations of the nation to which such prisoners belong, and a receipt is obtained from the proper agent of such delivery—But where the Prisoners and Cartel both belong to the same nation the delivery shall take place and receipts be given at the port of embarkation; provided that the delivery shall not be considered compleat, untill the cartel is in the act of departing the port, and the nation delivering the prisoners, shall retain the custody of them by maintaining a sufficient guard on board the Cartel untill she is actually under way—when the receipt shall be duely executed and delivered. and when special exchanges are negotiated in discharge of special paroles, a certificate of such exchange must be forwarded to the station where the parole was granted.

Article Fourteenth

If either nation shall at any time have delivered more prisoners than it has received, it is optional with such nation to stop sending any more prisoners on credit, untill a return shall be made equal in number to the balance so in advance.

Article Fifteenth

This cartel is to be submitted for ratification to the secretary of State for and in behalf of the government of the United States and to the Right Honourable the Lords Commissioners of the Admiralty for and in behalf of the Government of Great Britain, and if approved by the Secretary of state of the United States—shall be provisionally executed untill the assent or dissent of the Lords Commissioners of the admiralty of Great Britain be known—and it is further agreed that after the mutual ratification of this cartel, either of the parties on six months notice to the other may declare and render the same null and no longer binding.

In witness whereof, we the undersigned, have hereunto set our hands and Seals, at Washington this twelfth day of May in the Year of our Lord one thousand eight hundred and thirteen.

[Seal] J. Mason
[Seal] Tho Barclay

Source: Hunter Miller, ed., *Treaties and Other International Acts of the United States of America,* vol. 2, *Documents 1–40: 1776–1818* (Washington, DC: U.S. Government Printing Office, 1931), Avalon Project, Yale Law School, http://www.yale.edu/lawweb/avalon/diplomacy/britain/cart1812.htm.

Appendix Three

Confederate and Union POW Camps

Major Confederate POW Camps, 1861–1865

Name	Town	State	Population
Americus	Americus	Georgia	Enlisted
Belle Island	Richmond	Virginia	Enlisted
Blackshear Prison	Blackshear	Georgia	Officers
Cahaba (Castle Morgan)	Cahaba	Alabama	Enlisted
Camp Asylum	Columbia	South Carolina	Enlisted
Camp Davidson	Savannah	Georgia	Enlisted
Camp Florence	Florence	South Carolina	Enlisted
Camp Ford	Tyler	Texas	Enlisted
Camp Groce	Hemstead	Texas	Enlisted
Camp Lawton	Millen	Georgia	Enlisted
Camp Oglethorpe	Macon	Georgia	Officers
Camp Sorghum	Columbia	South Carolina	Officers
Camp Sumter	Andersonville	Georgia	Enlisted
Castle Goodwin	Richmond	Virginia	Enlisted

Major Confederate POW Camps, 1861–1865 (cont'd)

Name	*Town*	*State*	*Population*
Castle Pinckney	Charleston	South Carolina	Officers
Castle Thunder	Petersburg	Virginia	Enlisted
Charleston Jail	Charleston	South Carolina	Enlisted
City Jail	Savannah	Georgia	Enlisted
Crews Prison	Richmond	Virginia	Enlisted
Danville Prison	Danville	Virginia	Enlisted
Fort Norfolk	Norfolk	Virginia	Enlisted
Grant's Factory	Richmond	Virginia	Enlisted
Libby Prison	Richmond	Virginia	Officers
Liggons Prison	Richmond	Virginia	Enlisted
Marine Hospital	Savannah	Georgia	Officers
Military Prison Camp	Lynchburg	Virginia	Enlisted
Old Cotton Factory	Salisbury	North Carolina	Enlisted
Old Hospital	Charleston	South Carolina	Enlisted
Paper Mill/Cotton Shed	Tuscaloosa	Alabama	Enlisted
Parrish Prison	New Orleans	Louisiana	Enlisted
Pemberton Prison	Richmond	Virginia	Enlisted
Salisbury Prison	Salisbury	North Carolina	Officers
Scott's Prison	Richmond	Virginia	Enlisted
Ship Island	Gulfport	Mississippi	Enlisted
Smith Factory	Richmond	Virginia	Enlisted
Southern Prison	Tupelo	Mississippi	Enlisted
Stockade Prison	Thomasville	Georgia	Enlisted
Tobacco Warehouses	Danville	Virginia	Enlisted

Major Union POW Camps, 1861–1865

Name	*Town*	*State*	*Population*
Beaufort Hospital	Beaufort	South Carolina	Officers/Enlisted
Belle Plain Encampment	Fredericksburg	Virginia	Enlisted
Benton Barracks	St. Louis	Missouri	Enlisted
Camp Butler	Springfield	Illinois	Enlisted
Camp Chase	Columbus	Ohio	Enlisted
Camp Douglas	Chicago	Illinois	Enlisted
Camp Morton	Indianapolis	Indiana	Enlisted
Camp Parole	Annapolis	Maryland	Officers/Enlisted
Carroll Hall Prison	Fort Monroe	Virginia	Officers
David's Island	New York	New York	Enlisted
Elmira	Elmira	New York	Enlisted
Forest Hall Military Prison	Georgetown	DC	Officers/Enlisted

Major Union POW Camps, 1861–1865 (cont'd)

Name	Town	State	Population
Fort Columbus	Governor's Island	New York	Enlisted
Fort Delaware	Pea Patch Island	Delaware	Officers/Enlisted
Fort Lafayette	New York	New York	Enlisted
Fort Leavenworth	Leavenworth	Kansas	Officers/Enlisted
Fort McHenry	Baltimore	Maryland	Enlisted
Fort Mifflin	Philadelphia	Pennsylvania	Enlisted
Fort Pickens	Pensacola	Florida	Enlisted
Fort Warren	Boston	Massachusetts	Officers
Fort Wood	New York Harbor	New York	Enlisted
Gratiot Street Prison	St. Louis	Missouri	Enlisted
Hart's Island	New York Harbor	New York	Enlisted
Illinois State Prison	Alton	Illinois	Officers/Enlisted
Johnson's Island	Sandusky	Ohio	Officers
Lincoln General Hospital	Washington, DC	—	Officers/Enlisted
Louisville Prison	Louisville	Kentucky	Enlisted
Mackinac Island	Mackinac	Michigan	Enlisted
McClean Barracks	Cincinnati	Ohio	Enlisted
Morris Island	Charleston	South Carolina	Enlisted
Ohio State Penitentiary	Columbus	Ohio	Officers
Old Capitol Prison	Washington, DC	—	Political
Point Lookout	Baltimore	Maryland	Enlisted
Rock Island	Rock Island	Illinois	Enlisted
St. Helena's Episcopal Church	Beaufort	South Carolina	Enlisted
St. Joseph Prison	St. Joseph	Missouri	Enlisted
Western Pennsylvania	Allegheny City	Pennsylvania	Enlisted

APPENDIX FOUR

General Order 207: Instructions for the Government of Armies of the United States

The first comprehensive codification of international law used by any government was based on moral precepts that recognized the enemy as a fellow human being with lawful rights. It was issued 3 July 1863 by President Abraham Lincoln as General Order 207, and the principles in this first document remain the heart of General Order 100: Rules of Land Warfare. Some of the provisions in Francis Lieber's original work include the following:

1. No belligerent has the right to declare he will treat every captured man at arms . . . as a brigand or a bandit.
2. A POW is subject to no punishment for being a public enemy, nor is any revenge wreaked upon him by the intentional infliction of any suffering, or disgrace, by cruel imprisonment, want of food, by malnutrition, death or by any other barbarity.
3. A POW remains amenable for his crimes committed before the captor's army or people, [for crimes] committed before he was captured, and for which he has not been punished by his own authorities.
4. A POW . . . is the prisoner of the government and not of the captor.
5. POWs are subject to confinement or imprisonment such as may be deemed necessary on account of safety, but they are to be subjected to no other intentional suffering or indignity.
6. A POW who escapes may be shot, or otherwise killed in flight; but neither death nor any other punishment shall be inflicted on him for his attempt to escape, which the law of order does not consider a crime. Stricter means of security shall be used after an unsuccessful attempt at escape.
7. Every captured wounded man shall be medically treated according to the ability of the medical staff.
8. POWs will receive the same rations as the captors.
9. Honorable men, when captured, will abstain from giving to the enemy information concerning their own army, and the modern law of war permits no longer the use of any violence against prisoners, in order to extort the desired information, or to punish them for having given false information.

Source: A. J. Barker, *Prisoners of War* (New York: Universe, 1975), 13.

APPENDIX FIVE

Andersonville Deaths, 1864–1865

Of the 45,000 men imprisoned at Andersonville, almost 13,000 died.

Year	Month	Number Held	Deaths
1864	February	1,600	Unknown
	March	7,500	283
	April	10,000	576
1864	May	15,000	708
	June	22,291	1,201
	July	29,030	1,817
	August	32,193	2,993

Andersonville Deaths, 1864–1865

Year	Month	Number Held	Deaths
1864	September	17,733	2,677
	October	5,885	1,595
	November	2,024	499
	December	2,218	165
1865	January	4,931	197
	February	5,195	147
	March	4,800	108
	April	unknown	28
	Total dead		12,994

Source: Leon Basile, *The Civil War Diary of Amos E. Stearns, a Prisoner at Andersonville* (Rutherford, NJ: Fairleigh Dickinson University Press, 1981), 117.

APPENDIX SIX

Hague Convention Ratified by the United States, 3 December 1909

Section I, On Belligerents: Chapter II, Articles 4–20, Prisoners of War

Article 4

Prisoners of war are in the power of the hostile Government, but not of the individuals or corps who capture them. They must be humanely treated. All their personal belongings, except arms, horses, and military papers, remain their property.

Article 5

Prisoners of war may be interned in a town, fortress, camp, or other place, and bound not to go beyond certain fixed limits; but they can not be confined except as an indispensable measure of safety and only while the circumstances which necessitate the measure continue to exist.

Article 6

Prisoners may be authorized to work for the public service, for private persons, or on their own account. Work done for the State is paid for at the rates in force for work of a similar kind done by soldiers of the national army, or, if there none in force, at a rate according to the work executed. When the work is for other branches of the public service or for private persons the conditions are settled in agreement with the military authorities. The wages of the prisoners shall go towards improving their position, and the balance shall be paid them on their release, after deducting the cost of their maintenance.

Article 7

The Government into whose hands prisoners of war have fallen is charged with their maintenance. In the absence of a special agreement between the belligerents, prisoners of war shall be treated as regards board, lodging and clothing on the same footing as the troops of the Government who captured them.

Article 8
Prisoners of war shall be subject to the laws, regulations and orders in force in the army of the State in whose power they are. Any act of insubordination justifies the adoption towards them of such measures of severity as may be considered necessary. Escaped prisoners who are retaken before rejoining their own army or before leaving the territory occupied by the army which captured them are liable to disciplinary punishment.

Article 9
Every prisoner of war is bound to give, if he is questioned on the subject, his true name and rank, and if he infringes this rule, he is liable to have the advantages given to prisoners of his class curtailed.

Article 10
Prisoners of war may be set at liberty on parole if the laws of their country allow, and, in such cases, they are bound, on their personal honor, scrupulously to fulfill, both towards their own Government and the Government by whom they were made prisoners, the engagements they contracted. In such cases their own Government is bound neither to require of nor accept from them any service incompatible with the parole given.

Article 11
A prisoner of war can not be compelled to accept his liberty on parole; similarly the hostile Government is not obliged to accede to the request of the prisoner to be set at liberty on parole.

Article 12
Prisoners of war liberated on parole and recaptured bearing arms against the Government to whom they had pledged their honor, or against the allies of that Government, forfeit their right to be treated as prisoners of war, and can be brought before the courts.

Article 13
Individuals who follow an army directly belonging to it, such as newspaper correspondents and reporters, sutlers and contractors, who fall into the enemy's hands and whom the latter thinks expedient to detain, are entitled to be treated as prisoners of war, provided they are in possession of a certificate from the military authorities of the army which they were accompanying.

Article 14
An inquiry office for prisoners of war is instituted on the commencement of hostilities in each of the belligerent States, and, when necessary, in neutral countries which have received belligerents in their territory. It is the function of this office to reply to all inquiries about the prisoners. It receives from the various services concerned full information respecting internments and trans-

fers, releases on parole, exchanges, escapes, admissions into hospital, deaths, as well as other information necessary to enable it to make out and keep up to date an individual return for each prisoner of war. The office must state in this return the regimental number, name, and surname, age, place of origin, rank, unit, wounds, date and place of capture, internment, wounding, and death, as well as any observations of a special character. The individual return shall be sent to the Government of the other belligerent after the conclusion of peace. It is likewise the function of the inquiry office to receive and collect all objects of personal use, valuables, letters, etc., found on the field of battle or left by prisoners who have been released on parole, or exchanged, or who have escaped or died in hospital or ambulances, and to forward them to those concerned.

Article 15
Relief societies for prisoners of war, which are properly constituted in accordance with the laws of their country and with the object of serving as a channel for charitable effort shall receive from the belligerents, for themselves and their duly accredited agents every facility for the efficient performance of their humane task within the bounds imposed by military necessities and administrative regulations. Agents of these societies may be admitted to the places of internment for the purpose of distributing relief, as also to the halting places of repatriated prisoners, if furnished with a personal permit by the military authorities, and on giving an undertaking in writing to comply with all measures of order and police which the latter may issue.

Article 16
Inquiry offices enjoy the privilege of free postage. Letters, money orders, and valuables, as well as parcels by post, intended for prisoners of war, or dispatched by them, shall be exempt from all postal duties in the countries of origin and destination, as well as in the countries they pass through. Presents and relief in kind for prisoners of war shall be admitted free of all import or other duties, as well as of payments for cartage by the State railways.

Article 17
Officers taken prisoners shall receive the same rate of pay as officers of corresponding rank in the country where they are detained, the amount to be ultimately refunded by their own Government.

Article 18
Prisoners of war shall enjoy complete liberty in the exercise of their religion, including attendance at the services of whatever church they may belong to, on the sole condition that they comply with the measures of order and police issued by the military authorities.

Article 19
The wills of prisoners of war are received or drawn up in the same way as for soldiers of the national army. The same rules shall be observed regarding death

certificates as well as for the burial of prisoners of war, due regard being paid to their grade and rank.

Article 20
After the conclusion of peace, the repatriation of prisoners of war shall be carried out as quickly as possible.

APPENDIX SEVEN

German Prisoners Captured by U.S. Divisions, 1917–1918

Division	Captures	Division	Captures
2nd	12,026	80th	1,813
1st	6,409	37th	1,495
89th	5,061	42nd	1,317
33rd	3,987	79th	1,077
30th	3,848	28th	921
26th	3,148	82nd	845
4th	2,756	35th	781
91st	2,412	77th	750
5th	2,358	36th	549
27th	2,357	78th	432
3rd	2,240	81st	101
29th	2,187	92nd	38
32nd	2,153	6th	12
90th	1,876	88th	3

Total captures   62,952

Sources: Harvey A. DeWeerd, *President Wilson Fights His War: World War I and the American Intervention* (New York: Macmillan, 1968), 391; Leonard P. Ayres, *The War with Germany: A Statistical Summary* (Washington, DC: U.S. Government Printing Office, 1919), 116.

APPENDIX EIGHT

Executive Order 9066

Whereas the successful prosecution of the war requires every possible protection against espionage and against sabotage to national-defense material, national-defense premises, and national-defense utilities as defined in Section 4, Act of April 20, 1918, 40 Stat. 533, as amended by the Act of November 30, 1940, 54 Stat. 1220, and the Act of August 21, 1941, 55 Stat. 655 (U.S.C., Title 50, Sec. 104),

Now, therefore, by virtue of the authority vested in me as President of the United States, and Commander in Chief of the Army and Navy, I hereby authorize and direct the Secretary of War, and the Military Commanders whom he may from time to time designate, whenever he or any designated Commander deems such action necessary or desirable, to prescribe military areas in such places and of such extent as he or the appropriate Military Commander may determine, from which any or all persons may be excluded, and with respect to which, the right of any person to enter, remain in, or leave shall be subject to whatever restrictions the Secretary of War or the appropriate Military Commander may impose in his discretion. The Secretary of War is hereby authorized to provide for residents of any such area who are excluded therefrom, such transportation, food, shelter, and other accommodations as may be necessary, in the judgment of the Secretary of War or the said Military Commander, and until other arrangements are made, to accomplish the purpose of this order. The designation of military areas in any region or locality shall supersede designations of prohibited and restricted areas by the Attorney General under the Proclamations of December 7 and 8, 1941, and shall supersede the responsibility and authority of the Attorney General under the said Proclamations in respect of such prohibited and restricted areas.

I hereby further authorize and direct the Secretary of War and the said Military Commanders to take such other steps as he or the appropriate Military Commander may deem advisable to enforce compliance with the restrictions applicable to each Military area hereinabove authorized to be designated, including the use of Federal troops and other Federal Agencies, with authority to accept assistance of state and local agencies.

I hereby further authorize and direct all Executive Departments, independent establishments and other Federal Agencies, to assist the Secretary of War or the said Military Commanders in carrying out this Executive Order, including the furnishing of medical aid, hospitalization, food, clothing, transportation, use of land, shelter, and other supplies, equipment, utilities, facilities, and services.

This order shall not be construed as modifying or limiting in any way the authority heretofore granted under Executive Order No. 8972, dated December 12, 1941, nor shall it be construed as limiting or modifying the duty and responsibility of the Federal Bureau of Investigation, with respect to the investigation of alleged acts of sabotage or the duty and responsibility of the Attorney General and the Department of Justice under the Proclamations of December 7 and 8, 1941, prescribing regulations for the conduct and control of alien enemies, except as such duty and responsibility is superseded by the designation of military areas hereunder.

Franklin D. Roosevelt
The White House
February 19, 1942

Sources: http://usgovinfo.about.com/od/rightsandfreedoms/a/e09066.htm; Roger Daniels, *Concentration Camps: North America: Japanese in the United States and Canada During World War II* (Malabar, FL: Krieger, 1993), 208.

APPENDIX NINE

World War II Trials of U.S. Personnel

10,110,113	Number of men inducted
1,532,500	Number excused from military service as unstable, maladjusted, or overly nervous
2,670,000	Number trained for combat
40,000	Number of soldiers charged with desertion before the enemy
2,864	Number of soldiers tried by general courts-martial for crimes
49	Number of soldiers found guilty and given death sentences by the general courts and confirmed by the convening authority
48	Number of death sentences commuted
1	Number of soldiers executed (Private Eddie D. Slovik)
95	Number of men hanged as war criminals for crimes of violence against unarmed civilians

Source: William Bradford Huie, *The Execution of Private Slovik* (1954; New York: Dell, 1970), 4, 8–9.

APPENDIX TEN

Nuremberg Principles, 1946

The Nuremberg Principles are those "principles of international law recognized by the Charter of the Nuremberg Tribunal and the Judgment of the Tribunal" (United States, France, United Kingdom, and Union of Soviet Socialist Republics), 11 December 1946.

I   Any person who commits an act which constitutes a crime under international law is responsible therefore and liable to punishment.

II   The fact that internal law does not impose a penalty for an act which constitutes a crime under international law does not relieve the person who committed an act from responsibility under international law.

III The fact that a person who committed an act which constitutes a crime under international law acted as a Head of State or a responsible government official does not relieve him from responsibility under international law.

IV   The fact that a person acted pursuant to an order of his government or of a superior does not relieve him from responsibility under international law, provided a moral choice was in fact possible to him.

V   Any person charged with a crime under international law has the right to a fair trial on the facts and law.

VI   The crimes hereinafter set out are punishable as crimes under international law.

a. Crimes against the Peace:
   (i) Planning, preparation, initiation or waging a war of aggression or a war in violation of international treaties, agreements or assurances;
   (ii) Participation in a common plan or conspiracy for the accompliment of any of the acts mentioned under (i).
b. War Crimes:
   Violations of the laws or customs of war which include, but are not limited to, murder, ill-treatment or deportation to slave-labor or for any other purpose of the civilian population in an occupied territory, murder or ill-treatment of prisoners of war or persons on the seas, killing of hostages, plunder of public or private property, wanton destruction of cities, towns or villages, or devastation not justified by military necessity.
c. Crimes against Humanity:
   Murder, extermination, enslavement, deportation and other inhuman acts done against any civilian population, or persecution on political, racial, or religious grounds, when such acts are done or such persecution are carried on in execution of or in connection with any crime against peace or any war crime.
VII Complicity in the commission of a crime against peace, a war crime, or a crime against humanity as set forth in Principle VI is a crime under international law.

APPENDIX ELEVEN
Geneva Convention, 1949

Under Article 4, a prisoner of war is a person belonging to one of the following categories who has fallen into the power of the enemy:

1. Members of the armed forces of a Party to the conflict, as well as members of militias or volunteer corps forming part of such armed forces.
2. Members of other militias and members of other volunteer corps, including those of organized resistance movements, belonging to a Party to the conflict and operating inside or outside their own territory . . . provided that such militias or volunteer corps . . . fulfill the following conditions:
   a. that of being commanded by a person responsible for his subordinates;
   b. that of having a fixed distinctive sign recognizable at a distance;
   c. that of carrying arms openly;
   d. that of conducting their operations in accordance with the laws and customs of war.
3. Members of regular armed forces who profess allegiance to a government or an authority not recognized by the Detaining Power.
4. Persons who accompany the armed forces without actually being members thereof, such as civilian members of military aircraft crews, war

correspondents, supply contractors, members of labor units or of services responsible for the welfare of the armed forces, provided that they have received authorized from the armed forces which they accompany, who shall provide them for that purpose with an identity card.

5. Members of crews . . . of the merchant marine . . . and civil aircraft of the Parties to the conflict, who do not benefit by more favorable treatment under any other provision of international law.

6. Inhabitants of a nonoccupied territory, who on the approach of the enemy spontaneously take up arms to resist the invading forces, without having had time to form themselves into regular armed units, provided they carry arms openly and respect the laws and customs of war.

Article 12 clarified the matter even further: "Prisoners of war are in the hands of the enemy Power, but not of the individuals or military units who have captured them. Irrespective of the individual responsibilities that may exist, the Detaining Power is responsible for the treatment given them."

Source: Sydney Axinn, *A Moral Military* (Philadelphia: Temple University Press, 1989), 87f.

Appendix Twelve

U.S. Code of Conduct, 1954

1. I am an American fighting man. I serve in the forces which guard my country and our way of life. I am prepared to give my life in their defense.

2. I will never surrender of my own free will. If in command I will never surrender my men while they still have the means to resist.

3. If I am captured I will continue to resist by all means available. I will make every effort to escape and aid others to escape. I will not accept parole nor special favors from the enemy.

4. If I become a prisoner or war, I will keep faith with my fellow prisoners. I will give no information or take part in any action which might be harmful to my comrades. If I am senior, I will take command. If not, I will obey the lawful orders of those appointed over me and will back them up in every way.

5. When questioned, should I become a prisoner of war, I am bound to give only name, rank and service number and date of birth. I will evade answering further questions to the utmost of my ability. I will make no oral or written statements disloyal to my country and its allies or harmful to their cause.

6. I will never forget that I am an American fighting man, responsible for my actions, and dedicated to the principles which make my country free. I will trust in my God and the United States of America.

Notes

Preface

1. Interview with Carl Nash, November 1990, transcribed by Lois Seitz and Robert C. Doyle, May 1991.

2. Captain Giles R. Norrington, USN (Ret.), foreword in Robert C. Doyle, *Voices from Captivity: Interpreting the American POW Narrative* (Lawrence: University Press of Kansas, 1994), ix.

3. Arthur M. Schlesinger Jr., *The Disuniting of America: Reflections on a Multicultural Society* (New York: Norton, 1992), 45.

4. "Narrative of Marie LeRoy and Barbara Leininger," *Pennsylvania German Society Proceedings* 15 (1906): 113. See also Robert C. Doyle, *A Prisoner's Duty: Great Escapes in U.S. Military History* (Annapolis, MD: Naval Institute Press, 1997), 20–21.

5. Narrative of Robert Blakeney, Needham, Massachusetts, transcribed by Robert C. Doyle, 19 May 1993. Blakeney received the Silver Star, Air Medal, POW Medal, three Combat Stars, Good Conduct Medal, Victory Medal, and Presidential Unit Citation.

6. Personal correspondence from Markus Spiecker, 24 November 1998.

Introduction

1. J. Glen Gray, *The Warriors: Reflections on Men in Battle* (New York: Harcourt Brace, 1959), 132.

2. See John Dower, *War without Mercy: Race and Power in the Pacific War* (New York: Pantheon, 1986).

3. Gray, *Warriors,* 135.

4. Ibid., 139.

5. Marcus Cunliffe, *George Washington: Man and Monument* (New York: New American Library, 1982), 154–55.

6. The literature of dispossession is extensive. See Richard Slotkin, *Regeneration through Violence: The Mythology of the American Frontier, 1600–1860* (Middletown, CT: Wesleyan University Press, 1973). See also Wilbur R. Jacobs, *Dispossessing the American Indian: Indians and Whites on the Colonial Frontier* (Norman: University of Oklahoma Press, 1985).

7. Henry R. Luce, "The American Century," *Life,* February 17, 1941.

Chapter One. Prisoners of Independence

1. Washington to Howe, in *The Writings of George Washington from the Original Manuscript Sources, 1745–1799,* 25 vols., ed. John C. Fitzpatrick (Washington, DC: U.S. Government Printing Office, 1932–1938), 6:101.

2. Ibid., 100.

3. Washington to the President of Congress, ibid., 117.

4. For American complaints about British treatment of American prisoners, see U.S. Congress, House, *Report on the Spirit and Manner in Which the War Has Been Waged by the Enemy* (New York: Garland, 1813; reprint, 1978). On the incident involving the British treatment of Irish American prisoners at sea and the American response, see Ralph Robinson, "Retaliation for the Treatment of Prisoners in the War of 1812," *American Historical Review* 49, no. 1 (October 1943): 65–70.

5. Douglas Southall Freeman, *George Washington, A Biography*, 5 vols. (New York: Scribner's, 1951–1952); James Kirby Martin and Mark Edward Lender, *A Respectable Army: The Military Origins of the Republic, 1763–1789* (Wheeling, IL: Harlan Davidson, 1982), 58.

6. See Freeman, *George Washington*, 4:322–24, for a brief summary of the battle and aftermath.

7. Washington to Colonel John Cadwalader, in *Writings of George Washington*, 6: 447.

8. See Christopher Hibbert, *Redcoats and Rebels: The American Revolution through British Eyes* (New York: Avon, 1991), 183ff.

9. Ibid., 183.

10. Ibid., 190.

11. Roger Lamb, *An Original and Authentic Journal of Occurrences during the Late American War*. 1809; reprint, New York: Arno, 1968), 170. Lamb had escaped his Convention captivity in 1778 and returned to New York, where he was reassigned to General Cornwallis's army. He escaped again in 1782 after the Yorktown surrender and took seven men back to New York. His narrative is highly respected. For a brief biography, see http://famousamericans.net/rogerlamb (accessed 12 August 2008).

12. Susan Burnham Greeley, "Sketches of the Past," in *Loyalist Narratives from Upper Canada*, ed. James J. Talman (Toronto: Champlain Society, 1946), 83.

13. See "The Real Story of the American Revolution: The Convention Army's Six-Year Imprisonment," http://www.rsar.org/military/convarmy.htm (accessed 1 August 2008) and www.nps.gov/archive/thst/battle.htm/.

14. Edwin G. Burrows, *Forgotten Patriots: The Untold Story of American Prisoners during the Revolutionary War* (New York: Basic Books, 2008), 189–90.

15. See Robert C. Doyle, *Voices from Captivity: Interpreting the American POW Narrative* (Lawrence: University Press of Kansas, 1994) and *A Prisoner's Duty: Great Escapes in U.S. Military History* (Annapolis, MD: Naval Institute Press, 1997), for extensive discussions of the British prison ship system, especially in Brooklyn during the Revolutionary War. See also Burrows, *Forgotten Patriots*, 201. Burrows argues convincingly that approximately 35,800 patriots died in the war and roughly half died as POWs, effectively doubling the number traditionally accepted by historians.

16. "The Battle of Waxhaws/Buford's Massacre, May 29, 1780, Waxhaws, South Carolina," http://www.myrevolutionarywar.com/battles/800529.htm (accessed 1 August 2008).

17. Hibbert, *Redcoats and Rebels*, 281–82. See also Woodrow Wilson,

A History of the American People, 10 vols. (New York: Harper and Brothers, 1901–1918), 4:304–10. Although somewhat dated, Wilson presents a fine history of the Saratoga surrender.

18. Hibbert, *Redcoats and Rebels,* 282.

19. See C. Hammett, "King's Mountain Prisoners of War," http//www.tngenweb.org/revwar/kingsmountain/prisoners.html, 1–11 (accessed 1 August 2008), for a brief synopsis of the battle and the EPW aftermath.

20. George Washington Papers, 1741–1799, Series 4, General Correspondence, 1697–1799, American Memories Collection, Library of Congress, quoted ibid.

21. Christopher Andrew, *For the President's Eyes Only: Secret Intelligence and the American Presidency from Washington to Bush* (New York: HarperCollins, 1995), 8–9. See also "Stories of Spies and Letters," in *Spy Letters of the American Revolution,* Collections of the Clements Library, University of Michigan, Ann Arbor, at http://si.umich.edu/spies/stories-networks-3.html (accessed 17 May 2009).

22. Joseph Plumb Martin, *Private Yankee Doodle: Being a Narrative of Some of the Adventures and Sufferings of a Revolutionary Soldier* (1830; reprint, Harrisburg, PA: Eastern Acorn Press, 1997), 204–5.

23. Andrew, *For the President's Eyes Only,* 9.

24. Hibbert, *Redcoats and Rebels,* 330.

25. Charles H. Metzger, S.J., *The Prisoner in the American Revolution* (Chicago: Loyola University Press, 1971), 26. See also Richard M. Dorson, *America Rebels: Narratives of the Patriots* (Greenwich, CT: Fawcett, 1966), 133–66, for several revealing narratives written by American Loyalists. For departmental and state papers concerning British troops captured in America during the Revolution, see Charles M. Andrews, *Guide to the Materials for American History, to 1783, in the Public Record Office of Great Britain,* 2 vols. (Washington, DC: U.S. Government Printing Office, 1912–1914). See also "Prisoners of War 1660–1919: Documents in the PRO," *Public Record Office Information Bulletin* 72 (London, 1987), 1–7.

26. William S. Stryker, *The Battles of Trenton and Princeton* (Boston: Houghton, Mifflin, 1898), 207.

27. Ibid., 208.

28. Lamb, *Original and Authentic Journal,* 171.

29. Thomas Anburey, *Travels through the Interior Parts of America* (1789; reprint, New York: Arno, 1969), 1:466–67.

30. Ibid., 2:65.

31. See Proceedings, Court Martial, Held at Cambridge, by Order of Major General Heath, Commanding the American Troops for the Northern District, for the Trial of Colonel David Henley, Accused by General Burgoyne, of Ill-Treatment of the British Soldiers, etc. Taken in Short Hand by an Officer, Who Was Present, Library of Thomas Jefferson (London: Printed for J. Almon, 1778; Washington, DC: Microcard Editions, 1973).

32. Anburey, *Travels,* 2:191.

33. Ibid., 442.

34. Ibid., 452–53.

35. Ibid., 509.

36. Herman S. Frey, ed. and comp., *Foundations of the Republic: Select Im-*

portant United States Historical Documents (Murfreesboro, TN: Published by the editor, 1993), n.p.

37. See Lucy Leigh Bowie, "German Prisoners in the American Revolution," *Maryland Historical Magazine,* September 1945, 185–200.

38. Heide Buhmann and Hanspeter Haeseler, *Das kleine dicke Liederbuch: Lieder und Tänze bis unsere Zeit* (Darmstadt: Hollman, 1994), 418–19.

39. Translation by Beate T. Engel-Doyle.

40. Ludwig Erk and Franz Magnus Böhme, *Deutsche Liedenhort,* 3 vols. (Leipzig, 1893), 144.

41. Edward J. Lowell, *The Hessians and Other German Auxiliaries of Great Britain in the Revolutionary War* (1884; reprint, Gansevoort, NY: Corner House, 1997), 20–21; Bowie, "German Prisoners in the American Revolution," 196.

42. See Laura L Becker, "Prisoners of War in the American Revolution: A Community Perspective," *Military Affairs* 46, no. 4 (December 1982): 169–73.

43. Joseph G. Rosengarten, "A Defense of the Hessians," *Pennsylvania Magazine of History and Biography* 23 (1899): 157.

44. Lowell, *Hessians,* 8.

45. One of the most engaging narratives in the Hessian collection is Baroness Friederike Charlotte Luise von Massow Riedesel's *Letters and Journals Related to the War of the American Revolution and the Capture of the German Troops at Saratoga,* trans. William L. Stone (Albany, NY: Joel Munsel, 1867), 113–35, where she describes her near-death experiences in the cannonade and her revulsion at the cordial relationship between Gates and Burgoyne after the surrender; quoted in Dorson, *America Rebels,* 210–31.

46. See Johann Conrad Döhla, *A Hessian Diary of the American Revolution,* trans. and ed. Bruce E. Burgoyne (Norman: University of Oklahoma Press, 1990), ix–x. Other translations by Bruce E. Burgoyne are located in the Library of Congress and the Johannes Schwalm Historical Association in the Lancaster County Historical Society, Lancaster, Pennsylvania.

47. Döhla, *Hessian Diary,* 210–11.

48. Ibid., 222.

49. For Revolutionary War travelers, Trenton holds Patriot Week from 26 to 31 December each year and features a re-creation of the Battle of Trenton. See http://www.patriotsweek.com for details.

50. *The Historical Management of POWs: A Synopsis of the 1968 US Army Provost Marshal General's Study Entitled "A Review of United States Policy on Treatment of Prisoners of War"* (San Diego, CA: Naval Health Research Center, 1970), 21–22.

Chapter Two. Habeas Corpus

1. William H. Nelson, *The American Tory* (Boston: Beacon, 1961), 3. See Michael S. Adelberg, "An Evenly Balanced County: The Scope and Severity of Civil Warfare in Revolutionary Monmouth County, New Jersey," *Journal of Military History* 73 (January 2009): 19, for a description of a third category, "Trimmers," who, in a desire to be neutral, drifted from one side to the other.

2. Claude Halstead Van Tyne, *The Loyalists in the American Revolution* (1902; reprint, Bowie, MD: Heritage Facsimile, 1989), 8f.

3. Nelson, *American Tory*, 5.

4. Van Tyne, *Loyalists*, 8.

5. Ibid., 23.

6. Quebec Act, http://www.yale.edu/lawweb/avalon/amerrev/parliament/quebec_act_1774.htm (accessed 29 August 2008).

7. Francis D. Cogliano, *No King, No Popery: Anti-Catholicism in Revolutionary New England* (Westport, CT: Greenwood, 1995), 49.

8. Donald Barr Chidsey, *The Loyalists: The Story of Those Americans Who Fought against Independence* (New York: Crown, 1973), 118.

9. James Kirby Martin and Mark Edward Lender, *A Respectable Army: The Military Origins of the Republic, 1763–1789* (Wheeling, IL: Harlan Davidson, 1982), 28.

10. "Proclamation by the King for Suppressing Rebellion and Sedition," 23 August 1775, in *The Documents of American History*, 10th ed., ed. Henry Steele Commager and Milton Cantor (Englewood Cliffs, NJ: Prentice Hall, 1988), 1:96.

11. "First Edition of the American Prohibitory Act of 1775," Manhattan Rare Book Company, http://www.manhattanrarebooks-history.com/prohibitory-act.htm (accessed 28 August 2008).

12. See Richard L. Blanco and Paul J. Sanborn, eds., *The American Revolution, 1775–1783: An Encyclopedia* (New York: Garland, 1993), 2:1337–45, for a discussion of propaganda during the entire war.

13. Van Tyne, *Loyalists*, 318–26.

14. Robert A. East and Jacob Judd, eds., *The Loyalist Americans: A Focus on Greater New York* (Tarrytown, NY: Sleepy Hollow Restorations, 1975), 9.

15. *The Historical Management of POWs: A Synopsis of the 1968 US Army Provost Marshal General's Study Entitled "A Review of United States Policy on Treatment of Prisoners of War"* (San Diego, CA: Naval Health Research Center, 1970), 20.

16. Martin and Lender, *Respectable Army*, 140.

17. Ibid., 141–42.

18. East and Judd, *Loyalist Americans*, 16.

19. Van Tyne, *Loyalists*, 182–83. See also Chidsey, *Loyalists*, 101.

20. *Historical Management of POWs*, 20.

21. Charles H. Metzger, S.J., *The Prisoner in the American Revolution* (Chicago: Loyola University Press, 1971), 26. See also Richard M. Dorson, *America Rebels: Narratives of the Patriots* (Greenwich, CT: Fawcett, 1966), 133–66, for several revealing narratives written by American Loyalists. For departmental and state papers concerning British troops captured in America during the Revolution, see Charles M. Andrews, *Guide to the Materials for American History, to 1783, in the Public Record Office of Great Britain*, 2 vols. (Washington, DC: U.S. Government Printing Office, 1912–1914). See also "Prisoners of War 1660–1919: Documents in the PRO," *Public Record Office Information Bulletin* 72 (London, 1987), 1–7.

22. Johann Conrad Döhla, *A Hessian Diary of the American Revolution*, trans. and ed. Bruce E. Burgoyne (Norman: University of Oklahoma Press, 1990), 101.

23. See East and Judd, *Loyalist Americans*, 56–73, for a short biography of William Franklin, son of Benjamin Franklin.

24. James Moody, *Lieut. James Moody's Narrative of His Exertions and Sufferings in the Cause of Government, since the Year 1776* (1783; reprint, New York: New York Times and Arno, 1968), 3.

25. Ibid., 31.

26. See Arthur J. Mekeel, "Suspicion of Quaker Treachery and the Virginia Exiles," in *The Relation of the Quakers to the American Revolution* (Lanham, MD: University Press of America, 1979), 173–88, and "The Relation of the Quakers to the American Revolution," *Quaker History* 65 (1976): 3–18.

27. Mekeel, "Relation of the Quakers to the American Revolution," 14.

28. Lorette Treese, *The Storm Gathering: The Penn Family and the American Revolution* (University Park: Penn State University Press, 1992), 175.

29. Major General John Sullivan to Congress, in *Exiles in Virginia: With Observations on the Conduct of the Society of Friends during the Revolutionary War, 1777–1778* (Philadelphia: Published for the Subscribers, 1848), 61–62.

30. Robert F. Oaks, "Philadelphians in Exile: The Problem of Loyalty during the American Revolution," *Pennsylvania Magazine of History and Biography* 9 (1972): 306.

31. Ibid., 316.

32. Mekeel, "Relation of the Quakers to the American Revolution," 18.

33. Oaks, "Philadelphians in Exile," 325.

Chapter Three. The Second American Revolution

1. The Alien and Sedition Acts of 1798 were passed by Congress and signed by President John Adams.

2. According to Ernest Dupuy and William Baumer, *The Little Wars of the United States* (New York: Hawthorne, 1968), 11, American prisoners taken at sea were interned at Brasseterre on Saint Kitts during the 1797 undeclared war with France.

3. See H. M. Barnby, "Palaces and Prisons," in *The Prisoners of Algiers* (New York: Oxford University Press, 1966), 39–57, for a full description of the prisons of Algiers from 1785 to 1787.

4. Herbert C. Fooks, *Prisoners of War* (Federalsburg, MD: J. W. Stowell, 1924), 13. See also Article 16 of the Treaty of Peace and Amity between the United States and Tripoli, concluded 4 June 1805.

5. Leland D. Baldwin, *The Adult American History* (Rindge, NH: Richard R. Smith, 1955), 169.

6. John K. Mahon, *The War of 1812* (Gainesville: University of Florida Press, 1972), 17.

7. Baldwin, *Adult American History,* 171.

8. Stephen Jarvis, "The Narrative of Colonel Stephen Jarvis," in *Loyalist Narratives from Upper Canada,* ed. James J. Talman (Toronto: Champlain Society, 1946), 254.

9. Mahon, *War of 1812,* 9.

10. Ibid., 8.

11. Ibid., 9.

12. H. H. Brinkley, "The Loss of the *Lapwing,* Post Office Packet," *Mariner's Mirror* 16 (January 1930): 25.

13. Ibid., 27.

14. Captain James R. Dacres, RN, to Vice Admiral Herbert Sawyer, RN, 7 September 1812, in *The Naval War of 1812: A Documentary History*, 3 vols., ed. William S. Dudley (Washington, DC: Naval Historical Center, 1985), 1:244.

15. Captain James Lawrence to Secretary of the Navy Jones, 19 March 1813, ibid., 71.

16. See also John Brannon, ed., *Official Letters of the Military and Naval Officers of the United States, during the War with Great Britain in the Years 1812, 13, 14 & 15* (1823; reprint, New York: Arno Press and New York Times, 1971), 279, for an affidavit by Abraham Walter, who testifies about the British illegally removing American citizens from ships and impressing them into the Royal Navy.

17. "USS *Hornet* Sinks HMS *Peacock,* 24 February 1813," http://www.history .navy.mil/photos/events/war1812/atsea/hnt-peck.htm (accessed 6 November 2008). This is the U.S. Navy Historical Center's official Web site.

18. H. Craig, "Notes on the Action between the *Hornet* and *Peacock,*" *American Neptune* 11, no. 1 (January 1951): 75.

19. Baldwin, *Adult American History,* 170.

20. Donald R. Hickey, *The War of 1812* (Urbana: University of Illinois Press, 1989), 182.

21. Andrew Jackson started his career as a lawyer after being a POW in the Revolution. He was Tennessee's first senator and representative in Congress and Florida's first territorial governor. He died in 1845 at the age of seventy-eight.

22. Hickey, *War of 1812,* 182.

23. Baldwin, *Adult American History,* 177.

24. George Lockhart Rives, *Selections from the Correspondence of Thomas Barclay, Formerly British Consul General at New York* (New York: Harper and Brothers, 1894), 313.

25. "Cartel for the Exchange of Prisoners of War between Great Britain and the United States of America May 12, 1813," in *Treaties and Other International Acts of the United States of America,* vol. 2, *Documents 1–40 : 1776–1818,* ed. Hunter Miller (Washington, DC: U.S. Government Printing Office, 1931), Avalon Project, Yale Law School, http://www.yale.edu/lawweb/avalon/diplomacy/britain/ cart1812.htm (accessed 5 September 2006). All quotes from this document come from this source.

26. See *The Historical Management of POWs: A Synopsis of the 1968 US Army Provost Marshal General's Study Entitled "A Review of United States Policy on Treatment of Prisoners of War"* (San Diego, CA: Naval Health Research Center, 1970), 23. The 1813 cartel was based on the 1785 treaty with Great Britain, which provided for prisoner exchanges during wartime. Both sides agreed that humane treatment and preservation of POW rights were vital to both countries' best interests.

27. Ralph Robinson, "Retaliation for the Treatment of Prisoners in the War of 1812," *American Historical Review* 49, no. 1 (October 1943): 65.

28. Barclay to Lord Castlereagh, in *Selections from the Correspondence of Thomas Barclay,* 337.

29. Henry Kelly to Secretary of State, quoted in Robinson, "Retaliation," 66.

30. Robinson, "Retaliation," 66.

31. Ibid., 67.

32. Correspondence from the House of Representatives, Commonwealth of Pennsylvania, to the author, 27 January 1992.

33. James Madison to John Mason, quoted in Robinson, "Retaliation," 67.

34. Michael J. Crawford, ed., *The Naval War of 1812: A Documentary History* (Washington, DC: Naval Historical Center, 2002), 3:223–25.

35. Hickey, *War of 1812,* 305.

36. See Mahon, *War of 1812,* 382–83.

37. Ibid., 384–85.

38. Gerard T. Altoff, *Amongst My Best Men: African Americans and the War of 1812* (Put-in-Bay, Ohio: Perry Group, 1996), 162.

Chapter Four. Manifest Destiny versus Nativism

1. See *United States Democratic Review,* July–August 1845, 5–6, 9–10.

2. President James K. Polk, War Message to Congress, 11 May 1846, in *A Complication of the Messages and Papers of the Presidents of the United States, 1789–1897,* 8 vols., ed. James Richardson (Washington, DC: U.S. Government Printing Office, 1897), 4:442, quoted in Ernesto Chávez, *The U.S. War with Mexico: A Brief History with Documents* (Boston: Bedford/St. Martin's, 2008), 75.

3. Executive Document 60, 30th Congress, 1st Session, "Mexican War Correspondence," VII, 297, 348–49, in George G. Lewis and John Mewha, *History of Prisoner of War Utilization by the United States Army, 1776–1945,* Department of the Army Pamphlet No. 20–213 (Washington, DC: Department of the Army, 1955), 25. See also William E. S. Flory, *Prisoners of War: A Study in the Development of International Law* (Washington, DC: American Council on Public Affairs, 1942), 18.

4. Steven R. Butler, ed. *A Documentary History of the Mexican War* (Richardson, TX: Descendants of Mexican War Veterans, 1995), 77–78.

5. John S. D. Eisenhower, *So Far from God: The U.S. War with Mexico, 1846–1848* (Norman: University of Oklahoma Press, 2000), 84.

6. Butler, *Documentary History of the Mexican War,* 79–81.

7. Ibid., 96.

8. See Eisenhower, *So Far from God,* 146–48, for a detailed description of the Battle of Monterrey.

9. Ibid., 164. See also John L. O'Sullivan, "Annexation," *United States Democratic Review,* July–August 1845, 5, in Chávez, *U.S. War with Mexico,* 37.

10. Eisenhower, *So Far from God,* 170.

11. Ibid., 173.

12. Butler, *Documentary History of the Mexican War,* 108.

13. Eisenhower, *So Far from God,* 244.

14. Butler, *Documentary History of the Mexican War,* 105–7.

15. Eisenhower, *So Far from God,* 250.

16. Ibid., 263.

17. Ibid., 282.

18. Butler, *Documentary History of the Mexican War,* 207–8.

19. See Irving W. Levinson, "A New Paradigm for an Old Conflict: The Mex-

ico–United States War," *Journal of Military History* 73 (April 2009): 407. Scott negotiated with church officials in Mexico City to release these men and freed them on 16 December 1847.

20. Lewis and Mewha, *History of Prisoner of War Utilization,* 26.

21. Eisenhower, *So Far from God,* 318.

22. Ibid., 327.

23. Butler, *Documentary History of the Mexican War,* 219–25.

24. Ibid., 228–29.

25. Ibid., 231–37.

26. General Antonio Lopez de Santa Anna, *New York Herald,* 17 October 1847, quoted in Edward S. Wallace, "Deserters in the Mexican War," *Hispanic American Historical Review* (August 1935): 379.

27. Dennis J. Wynn, *The San Patricio Soldiers: Mexico's Foreign Legion,* Southwestern Studies Monograph No. 74 (El Paso: University of Texas at El Paso, 1984), 40.

28. Kevin Kenny, *The American Irish: A History* (London: Longman, 2000), 89.

29. Ibid., 90.

30. Ibid., 121.

31. Wallace, "Deserters in the Mexican War," 375.

32. For a complete study of Reilly and the San Patricio Battalion, see Peter F. Stevens, *The Rogue March: John Riley and the St. Patrick's Battalion, 1846–48* (Washington, DC: Potomac Books, 1999). Stevens shows just how idealistic and religious these immigrant soldiers were.

33. G. T. Hopkins, "The San Patricio Battalion in the Mexican War," *Cavalry Journal* (September 1913), quoted in Wallace, "Deserters in the Mexican War," 379.

34. Edward S. Wallace, "The Battalion of Saint Patrick in the Mexican War," *Military Affairs* 14, no. 2 (July 1950): 84. See also Robert Ryal Miller, *Shamrock and Sword: The Saint Patrick's Battalion in the U.S.-Mexican War* (Norman: University of Oklahoma Press, 1989), for an insightful study of the San Patricios.

35. Wallace, "Battalion of Saint Patrick," 90. The *American Star* was a Spanish- and English-language newspaper edited and published in Mexico City from September 1847 to May 1848 during the American occupation.

36. *One Man's Hero* (Arco Films, 1999). See also the documentary directed by Ginny Martin, *The U.S. Mexican War, 1846–1848* (KERA, Dallas, TX, 1998), for a fair treatment of the war from both the American and Mexican historical perspectives, and Jason Dominick Hool's documentary *St. Patrick's Battalion* (Set Productions, 1998).

37. Elizabeth D. Schaefer, "Mexican-American War," *Encyclopedia of Prisoners of War and Internment,* ed. Jonathan F. Vance (Santa Barbara, CA: ABC-CLIO, 2000), 187.

38. See Gorton Carruth, *The Encyclopedia of American Facts and Dates,* 10th ed. (New York: HarperCollins, 1997), for more data on the Mexican-American War.

39. Schaefer, "Mexican-American War," 187.

40. Jim Marks, "Looking Back," *Sabre News,* January–February 1992, 13.

Chapter Five. Prisoners of Politics

1. William Best Hesseltine, *Civil War Prisons: A Study in Prison Psychology* (Columbus: Ohio State University Press, 1930), 256.

2. Alexander H. Stephens, "The Treatment of Prisoners during the War Between the States," *Southern Historical Society Papers* 1, no. 3 (March 1876): 507–10.

3. Drew Gilpin Faust, "'Numbers on Top of Numbers': Counting the Civil War Dead," 2006 George C. Marshall Lecture in Military History, *Journal of Military History* 70 (October 2006): 995.

4. One book in particular is useful in this regard: Ovid L. Futch, *History of Andersonville Prison* (Gainesville: University of Florida Press, 1968). Futch fully departs from the validity of prisoners' narratives in his analysis of the Andersonville experience in his bibliographical essay (135–42). So too does William Marvel, *Andersonville: The Last Depot* (Chapel Hill: University of North Carolina Press, 1994).

5. See Brian Temple, *The Union Prison at Fort Delaware: A Perfect Hell on Earth* (Jefferson, NC: McFarland, 2003). Fort Delaware was constructed as part of American coastal defenses between 1813 and 1860. It was built at the mouth of the Delaware River on Pea Patch Island near Delaware City to protect the seaborne entry to Philadelphia. Although somewhat biased in favor of those POWs held at Fort Delaware, Temple's book presents an interesting regional history.

6. See Charles W. Sanders Jr., *While in the Hands of the Enemy: Military Prisons of the Civil War* (Baton Rouge: Louisiana State University Press, 2005).

7. Robert C. Doyle, *Voices from Captivity: Interpreting the American POW Narrative* (Lawrence: University Press of Kansas, 1994), 47–49.

8. See Sanders, *While in the Hands of the Enemy*.

9. James M. Gillispie, *Andersonvilles of the North: The Myths and Realities of Northern Treatment of Civil War Confederate Prisoners* (Denton: University of North Texas Press, 2008). See also Philip Burnham, "Andersonvilles of the North," *Military History Quarterly* (Autumn 1997): 48–55, for an interesting study of Northern prisons.

10. Gillispie, *Andersonvilles of the North*. See Walter L. Williams, "Again in Chains: Black Soldiers Suffering in Captivity," *Civil War Times Illustrated,* May 1981, 36–43, for a summary of the Confederate treatment of black Union troops.

11. Alexander D. Brown, *The Galvanized Yankees* (Urbana: University of Illinois Press, 1963), 1, 9.

12. Sir Henry Morton Stanley, *The Autobiography of Sir Henry Morton Stanley* (Boston: Houghton Mifflin, 1909), 214. Stanley was a member of the Arkansas Grays captured at Shiloh in 1862.

13. See Doyle, *Voices from Captivity,* 18, 124–25, 130, 203–4, 239, for commentary about Henry Morton Stanley's captivity experience.

14. Buehring H. Jones, *The Sunny Land; or, Prison Prose and Poetry* (Baltimore: Innes, 1868), 338.

15. Christopher Andrew, *For the President's Eyes Only: Secret Intelligence and the American Presidency from Washington to Bush* (New York: HarperCollins, 1995), 16.

16. James D. Richardson, ed., *A Compilation of the Messages and Papers of the Presidents, 1789–1897,* 8 vols. (Washington, DC: U.S. Government Printing Office, 1897), 6:17.

17. Ibid., 102–4.

18. William E. Gienapp, *Abraham Lincoln and Civil War* (New York: Oxford University Press, 2002), 299.

19. Ibid., 83.

20. David H. Donald, *Lincoln* (New York: Simon and Schuster, 1995), 437.

21. John A. Marshall, *American Bastile,* 8th ed. (Philadelphia: Thomas Hartley, 1871), 668–69.

22. Ibid., 358–59.

23. Ibid., 127.

24. Ibid., 71–91. See also *Ex parte Milligan* (1866), www.tourolaw.edu/patch/Milligan, for complete details of this case.

25. William H. Rehnquist, "The Milligan Decision," *Military History Quarterly* (Winter 1999): 49.

26. See *Ex parte Vallandigham* (1863), http://caselaw.lp.findlaw.com.

27. Alissa Dackaert-Skovira, "The Copperhead's Venom," *Journal of Unconventional History* 11, no. 3 (2000): 71.

28. Stanley F. Horn, *The Army of Tennessee* (New York: Bobbs-Merrill, 1941), 467.

29. Doyle, *Voices from Captivity,* 178–79.

30. Donald E. Markle, *Spies & Spymasters of the Civil War* (New York: Hippocrene, 2000), 157–58. See Belle Boyd, *Belle Boyd, Confederate Spy* (Baton Rouge: Louisiana State University Press, 1998).

31. The Rose O'Neal Greenhow Papers are located in the Special Collections Library, Duke University, Durham, North Carolina; see http://scrptorium.lib .duke/greenhow. See also Markle, *Spies & Spymasters,* 159–64, and 91–94 for lists of spies executed on each side.

32. See Rose O'Neal Greenhow, "In Prison for My Country," in *The War the Women Lived: Female Voices from the Confederate South,* ed. Walter Sullivan (Nashville, TN: J. S. Sanders, 1995), 37–53.

33. See the docudrama *Andersonville Trial,* directed by George C. Scott (KCET Los Angeles, 1970).

34. Futch, *History of Andersonville Prison,* 120.

35. See R. Fred Ruhlman, *Captain Henry Wirtz and Andersonville Prison: A Reappraisal* (Knoxville: University of Tennessee Press, 2006), 208–13, for an excellent description of Wirtz's execution. See also 183–204 for an evaluation of his trial.

36. Ibid., 222.

37. See *Chronicle of Higher Education,* 31 January 1987, A6. Alexander H. Stephens was the only Confederate official to whom Abraham Lincoln ever sent a personal letter. In 1865 Lincoln informed Stephens that he had arranged to exchange his nephew, Lieutenant John Stephens, for a captured Union officer. The letter resides in Special Collections, University of Georgia, Athens.

38. Bruce Chadwick, *The Two American Presidents: A Dual Biography of Abraham Lincoln and Jefferson Davis* (New York: Birch Lane, 1998), 552.

39. Ibid., 555.

40. Ibid., 556.

41. See "The Prison Life of Jefferson Davis: The Trying Experience of the Ex-President at Fort Monroe, Prevarication of General Miles," *Southern Historical Society Papers* 32 (January–December 1904), www.civilwarhome.com/davisinprision.htm (accessed 6 October 2008).

42. Chadwick, *Two American Presidents,* 556.

43. See David J. Eicher, *The Longest Night: A Military History of the Civil War* (New York: Simon and Schuster, 2001), 629.

44. Doyle, *Voices from Captivity,* 49.

Chapter Six. Indians as POWs in America

1. Amerigo Vespucci, "The Fullest Extent of Hospitality," in *Amerigo Vespucci: Letter to Piero Soderini, Gonfaloniere,* trans. and ed. George Tyler Northup (Princeton, NJ: Princeton University Press, 1916), 7–10, quoted in Wilcomb E. Washburn, ed., *The Indian and the White Man* (Garden City, NY: Doubleday, 1964), 6–8.

2. Bartolomé de las Casas, *The Devastation of the Indies: A Brief Account,* trans. Herma Briaffault (Baltimore: Johns Hopkins University Press, 1992), 28.

3. Susan Howe, *The Birth-Mark: Unsettling the Wilderness in American Literary History* (Hanover, NH: Wesleyan University Press, 1993), 127.

4. Robert M. Utley and Wilcomb E. Washburn, *Indian Wars* (New York: American Heritage, 1977), 43. See also John S. C. Abbot, *American Pioneers and Patriots: Miles Standish, the Puritan Captain* (New York: Doss and Mead, 1872), for an interesting but dated discussion of the Pequot War.

5. See Keith Johnson, "An Indian Tribe's Promised Land," *New York Times,* reprinted in *Vocable,* 1 February 1995, 4–7.

6. Ray Allen Billington, *The Westward Movement in the United States* (New York: D. Van Nostrand, 1959), 16–78; see also Robert F. Berkhofer Jr., *The White Man's Indian: Images of the American Indian from Columbus to the Present* (New York: Vintage, 1979).

7. Kenneth Carley, *The Sioux Uprising of 1862* (St. Paul: Minnesota Historical Society, 1976), 4.

8. Dee Brown, *Bury My Heart at Wounded Knee* (New York: Holt, Rinehart and Winston, 1971), 32.

9. See Gary C. Anderson, and Alan R. Woolworth, eds., *Through Dakota Eyes: Narrative Accounts of the Minnesota Indian War of 1862* (St. Paul: Minnesota Historical Society Press, 1988), 26–27.

10. Gary C. Anderson, *Little Crow: Spokesman for the Sioux* (St. Paul: Minnesota Historical Society Press, 1986), 116.

11. William E. Loas, *Minnesota* (New York: Norton, 1977), 105.

12. Robert H. Jones, *The Civil War in the Northwest* (Norman: University of Oklahoma Press, 1960), 39–40.

13. Robert M. Utley, *Frontiersmen in Blue* (New York: Macmillan, 1967), 266.

14. See Anderson and Woolworth, *Through Dakota Eyes,* 163–65.

15. Colonel Sibley, excerpts from speeches and letters concerning the Dakota conflict in 1862, http://www.law.umkc.edu (accessed 8 October 2008).

16. Utley, *Frontiersmen in Blue,* 268.

17. Anderson, *Little Crow,* 160.

18. Carley, *Sioux Uprising of 1862,* 68–69.

19. Fairfax Downey, *Indian Wars of the U.S. Army, 1776–1865* (Garden City, NY: Doubleday, 1963), 207.

20. Anderson and Woolworth, *Through Dakota Eyes,* 221.

21. See Charles S. Bryant and Abel B. Murch, *A History of the Great Massacre by the Sioux Indians in Minnesota* (Cincinnati, OH: Rickey and Carrol, 1864), 479.

22. William Brandon, *Indians* (Boston: Houghton Mifflin, 1961), 387.

23. Brad D. Lookingbill, *War Dance at Fort Marion: Plains Indian War Prisoners* (Norman: University of Oklahoma Press, 2006), 22.

24. Ibid., 23.

25. Ibid., 24.

26. Ibid., 25.

27. Ibid., 38.

28. Ibid., 52–53.

29. Ibid., 171.

30. W. David Edmunds, "The Nez Perce Fight for Justice," *American Heritage* 58, no. 5 (Fall 2008): 39.

31. George Crook died on 21 March 1890 at Chicago, while in command of the Department of the West. Crook Walk in Arlington National Cemetery is named for him. He was originally buried in Oakland, Maryland, but was moved to Section 2 of Arlington National Cemetery on 11 November 1898. See http://www.arlingtoncemetery.net/gcrook.htm (accessed 10 October 2008).

32. H. Henrietta Stockel, *Survival of the Spirit: Chiricahua Apaches in Captivity* (Reno, NV: University of Las Vegas Press, 1993), 67.

33. Ibid., 75.

34. See Robert M. Utley, *The Indian Frontier of the American West 1846–1890* (Albuquerque: University of New Mexico Press, 1984); Utley and Washburn, *Indian Wars.*

35. S. M. Barrett, ed., *Geronimo: My Life* (1906; reprint, Mineola, NY: Dover, 2005), 94.

36. S. M. Barrett, ed., *Geronimo: His Own Story* (New York: Ballantine, 1974), 103.

37. Stockel, *Survival of the Spirit,* 107.

38. Ibid., 108.

39. Ibid., 137.

40. Ibid., 149.

41. Barrett, *Geronimo: His Own Story,* 104.

42. See Jon Brudvig, "The Apache Wars (1861–1886)," in *Encyclopedia of Prisoners of War and Internment,* ed. Jonathan F. Vance (Santa Barbara, CA: ABC-CLIO, 2000), 10–12. See also Colin G. Calloway, *First Peoples: A Documentary History of American Indian Peoples* (Boston: Bedford/St. Martin's, 1999), 290–92.

43. Geronimo at http://www.americanindians.com (accessed 10 October 2008).

44. Barrett, *Geronimo: His Own Story,* 115.

45. Utley, *Indian Frontier,* 210; see also chapter 7, "The Reformers," for a thorough history of the Indian reform movement of the late nineteenth century.

46. Ibid., 4, 12.

47. U.S. Adjutant General, "Chronological List," in Joseph P. Peters, comp., *Indian Battles and Skirmishes on the American Frontier* (New York, 1966), cited in Robert M. Utley, *Frontier Regulars: The United States Army and the Indian, 1866–1891* (1973; reprint, Lincoln: University of Nebraska Press, Bison Books, 1984), 412n19.

48. See Barrett, "A Prisoner of War," in *Geronimo: His Own Story,* 156–60. See also Berkhofer, *White Man's Indian,* for a critical analysis of American treatment of its aboriginal peoples. In February 2009 Harlyn Geronimo, great-grandson of Geronimo, filed suit against Yale's Skull and Bones Society for the return of Geronimo's skull, which was allegedly stolen from the grave at Fort Sill in 1918. See "Verbatim," *Time,* 9 March 2009, 14.

49. See Fergus Bordewich, *Killing the White Man's Indian: Reinventing Native Americans at the End of the Twentieth Century* (New York: Doubleday, 1996), for a thorough description of contemporary life in Indian country. Bordewich tells his readers in this eloquent book that modern American Indians are anything but "savage" or "noble" or "pathetic" in the way they conduct business (324). Tribal concerns with education, wealth creation, water rights, and political sovereignty remain haunting nonetheless and go well beyond the old clarion call for mere survival.

Chapter Seven. Spaniards and *Insurrectos*

1. Hawaii became a territory in 1900 and a state in 1959.

2. Cuba had conducted the Ten Years' War against Spain from 1868 to 1878, the precursor of the 1895 insurrection.

3. Walter Millis, *The Martial Spirit: A Study of the War with Spain* (New York: Viking, 1965), 42–43.

4. Ibid., 25.

5. Cuban-Spanish-American War, 1898—Historical Text Archive, http://historicalarchive.com (accessed 15 October 2008).

6. The USS *Maine* was refloated in 1912, removed from Havana Harbor, and sunk four miles out at sea with honors. Sixty-two years later, Admiral Hyman Rickover conducted a scientific inquiry that revealed the ship had exploded from an accidental overheating and ignition of its coal bunkers, which sat next to the ammunition magazines. This is what destroyed the ship, not a Spanish mine. See Michael D. Haydock, "Sinking of *Maine* Brings War with Spain," *VFW Magazine,* February 1998, 12–14. See also Edward Marolda, *Theodore Roosevelt, the U. S. Navy, and the Spanish-American War* (New York: Palgrave, 2001); John Walsh, *The Sinking of the USS* Maine (New York: Franklin Watts, 1969).

7. Philip Jenkins, *A History of the United States,* 3rd ed. (London: Palgrave Macmillan, 2007), 165.

8. "America's War Dead, 1775–2008: A Memorial Listing by the Numbers," *VFW Magazine,* May 2008, 25.

9. "The World of 1898: The Spanish American War," Hispanic Division,

Library of Congress, http://www.loc.gov/rr/hispanic/1898/chronspain.html (accessed 15 October 2008).

10. Christopher Andrew, *For the President's Eyes Only: Secret Intelligence and the American Presidency from Washington to Bush* (New York: HarperCollins, 1995), 26.

11. See David E. Trask, "Spanish-American War," in *The Oxford Companion to American Military History*, ed. John Whiteclay Chambers II (New York: Oxford University Press, 1999), 667–68.

12. Lori Bogle, "Spanish-American War (1898)," in *Encyclopedia of Prisoners of War and Internment*, ed. Jonathan F. Vance (Santa Barbara, CA: ABC-CLIO, 2000), 279.

13. Jeffrey C. Livingston, "Spanish American War (1898)," in *The War of 1898 and U.S. Interventions, 1898–1934: An Encyclopedia,* ed. Benjamin R. Beede (New York: Garland, 1994), 438.

14. W. D. Howells, "Our Spanish Prisoners at Portsmouth," *Harper's Weekly* 42, no. 2174 (1898): 826.

15. P. H. Magruder, "The Spanish Naval Prisoners of War at Annapolis, 1898," *U.S. Naval Institute Proceedings* 56, no. 6 (June 1930): 490.

16. Ibid., 489.

17. Ibid., 491. See also Patrick McSherry, "The *Harvard* Incident," http://www.spanamwar.com/harvardincident.htm (accessed 15 October 2008).

18. Magruder, "Spanish Naval Prisoners," 495.

19. Treaty of Peace between the United States and Spain, 10 December 1898, http://www.msc.edu.ph/centennial/tr981210.html (accessed 15 October 2008).

20. The Platt Amendment lasted from 1901 to 1934 and permitted the United States to exert rights in Cuba. See the Platt Amendment, 1901, http://www.fordham.edu/halsall/mod/1901platt.html (accessed 15 October 2008).

21. "The Spanish American War and the Philippine American War," http://www.spanamwar.com/genealogy6.html (accessed 17 October 2008).

22. "The Philippine Insurrection: The Consequence of Imperialism," http://military.com (accessed 17 October 2008).

23. *The Statutes at Large of the United States of America from March 1897 to March 1899 and Recent Treaties, Conventions, Executive Proclamations, and the Concurrent Resolutions of the Two Houses of Congress,* vol. 30 (Washington, DC: U.S. Government Printing Office, 1899), http://www.msc.edu.ph/centennial/mc981221.html (accessed 16 October 2008).

24. Ibid.

25. John M. Gates, "The Philippines and Vietnam: Another False Analogy," *Asian Studies* 10 (1972): 65.

26. *Statutes at Large.*

27. Richard E. Welch Jr., *Response to Imperialism: The United States and the Philippine-American War, 1899–1902* (Chapel Hill: University of North Carolina Press, 1979), 42.

28. Ibid. Other historians raise that figure to 500,000. Perhaps no one knows how many Filipinos actually died of war-related causes. For the argument in rich detail, see John M. Gates, "War-Related Deaths in the Philippines, 1898–1902," *Pacific Historical Review* 53 (November 1983): 367–78. Gates points out that

anti-imperialist members of Congress accepted the anti-imperialist press without question; thus the huge numbers of dead are questionable at best.

29. Gates, "War-Related Deaths," 376.

30. H. C. Thompson, "War without Medals," *Oregon Historical Quarterly* 59 (December 1958): 317.

31. Willard B. Gatewood Jr., *Smoked Yankees and the Struggle for Empire* (Urbana: University of Illinois Press, 1971), 15.

32. Michael C. Robinson and Frank N. Schubert, "David Fagan: An Afro-American Rebel in the Philippines, 1899–1901," *Pacific Historical Review* 44, no. 1 (February 1975): 78.

33. Ibid., 81. Noted too were two African American deserters who were apprehended and executed by the American command.

34. General Order 100, Partisans, http://avalon.law.yale.edu/19th_century/lieber.asp#sec4 (accessed 20 October 2008).

35. D. H. Boughton, "How Soldiers Have Ruled in the Philippines," *International Quarterly* (December–March 1902): 227.

36. Richard K. Kolb, "Bamboo Vets Waged Philippines War," *VFW Magazine*, May 1990, 19.

37. For a short outline of battles, see "Philippines War: A Combat Chronology, 1899–1902," *VFW Magazine*, February 1999, 32–35.

38. See First Lieutenant Elam L. Stewart, "The Massacre of Balangiga," *Infantry Journal* 30 (April 1927): 407–14, for a riveting narration of the fight between General Vincente Lukban's guerrillas and the American troops.

39. Welch, *Response to Imperialism*, 40–41.

40. Major C. J. Crane, "Paragraphs 93, 97 and 88, of General Orders 100," *Journal of the Military Service Institution of the United States* 32 (March–April 1903): 255.

41. Kolb, "Bamboo Vets," 20.

42. Melvin G. Holli, "A View of the American Campaign against 'Filipino Insurgents': 1900," *Philippine Studies* 17 (1969): 101.

43. Ibid., 105.

44. Ibid., 100.

45. Ibid., 105.

46. Matthew E. Pearson, "Philippine-American War," in Vance, *Encyclopedia of Prisoners of War and Internment*, 221.

47. Glenn A. May, "Why the United States Won the Philippine-American War, 1899–1902," *Pacific Historical Review* 52, no. 4 (November 1983): 374.

48. Mark Twain, *New York Herald*, 15 October 1900, http://www.loc/rr/hispanic/1898/twain.html (accessed 21 October 2008).

49. See Richard E. Welch, Jr. "'The Philippine Insurrection' and the American Press," *Historian, A Journal of History* 36 (November 1973): 34–51, for a comparison of American newspapers for and against the war. Beyond a doubt, most American newspapers supported the annexation of the Philippines.

50. Frederick Palmer, "White Man and Brown Man in the Philippines," *Scribner's Magazine*, January–June 1900, 85.

51. Ibid. See also C. Crane, "The Fighting Tactics of Filipinos," *Journal of the Military Service Institution of the United States* 30 (July 1902): 507.

52. Major General Oliver O. Howard, "Is Cruelty Inseparable from War?" *Independent*, May 1902, 162.

53. Todd D. Wagoner, "Fighting Aguinaldo's Insurgents in the Philippines," *Kansas Historical Quarterly* 18 (May 1951): 160.

54. Brian McAllister Linn, *The Philippine War, 1899–1902* (Lawrence: University Press of Kansas, 2000), 223. Edward Peters, *Torture* (New York: Basil Blackwell, 1985), 107, discusses the military use of torture to extract immediate information from prisoners. See also George Riley Scott, *A History of Torture* (1940; reprint, London: Senate, 1977).

55. Clarence H. Bowers, "Builders of an Island Empire," *Bulletin of the American Historical Collection* 23 (July–September 1995): 20.

56. Ibid., 21.

57. J. A. Ryan, "The Defense of Captain J. A. Ryan," *Journal of the United States Cavalry Association* 13 (October 1902): 188, 190.

58. Brian M. Linn, "Guerrilla Fighter: Frederick Funston in the Philippines, 1900–1901," *Kansas History* 10 (1987): 2.

59. Shortly before the U.S. entry into World War I, President Woodrow Wilson favored Funston to head an American Expeditionary Force in France. Funston's intense focus on work would lead to health problems in January 1917, followed by a fatal heart attack at age fifty-one in San Antonio, Texas.

60. For a close evaluation of General Elwell S. Otis, especially his dealings with Major General Henry W. Lawton, see Thomas F. Burdett, "A New Evaluation of General Otis' Leadership in the Philippines," *Military Review* 55 (January 1955): 79–87.

61. Linn, "Guerrilla Fighter," 3.

62. This group of soldiers had been loyal to Spain and despised what the Filipino revolutionaries were doing. By war's end the Macabebe Scouts totaled approximately 15,000 men. See Linn, *Philippine War,* 128.

63. Welch, *Response to Imperialism,* 38.

64. Aguinaldo's Proclamation of Formal Surrender to the United States, 19 April 1901, in *Statutes at Large.*

65. Stuart Creighton Miller, "Empire in the Philippines: America's Forgotten War of Colonial Conquest," in William Graebner, *True Stories from the American Past* (New York: McGraw Hill, 2003), 89. Miller is one of the most critical of the modern historians dealing with the Philippine war.

66. Linn, "Guerrilla Fighter," 13.

67. Ibid., 14–15.

68. Ibid., 16.

69. President Theodore Roosevelt's Proclamation Formally Ending the Philippine Insurrection and Granting of Pardon and Amnesty, 4 July 1902, in *Statutes at Large.*

70. Ibid.

71. Kolb, "Bamboo Vets," 21.

72. Ibid.

73. See Miller, "Empire in the Philippines," 78–97.

74. Donald Chaput, "Private William W. Grayson's War in the Philippines, 1899," *Nebraska History* 61 (Fall 1980): 364.

Chapter Eight. Over There and Over Here

1. See Walter Höbling, *Fiktionen vom Krieg in Neueren amerikanischen Roman* (Tübingen: Gunter Narr Verlag, 1987), 297–98.

2. David M. Kennedy, *Over Here: The First World War and American Society* (New York: Oxford University Press, 2004), 38.

3. This position is amplified in John Mosier, *The Myth of the Great War: A New Military History of World War I* (New York: Perennial, 2002).

4. General John J. Pershing, *Final Report of General John J. Pershing, Commander-in-Chief, American Expeditionary Forces* (Washington, DC: U.S. Government Printing Office, 1920), 85. Numbers are a problem in POW studies. Most historians use 48,000 as the number of German EPWs taken by the AEF; however, Harvey A. DeWeerd, *President Wilson Fights His War: World War I and the American Intervention* (New York: Macmillan, 1968), 391, offers 63,079, based on details and figures from Leonard P. Ayres, *The War with Germany: A Statistical Summary* (Washington, DC: U.S. Government Printing Office, 1919).

5. Thomas Fleming, *The Illusion of Victory: America in World War* (New York: Basic Books, 2003), 246–47. See also William H. Thomas Jr., *Unsafe for Democracy: World War I and the U.S. Justice Department's Covert Campaign to Suppress Dissent* (Madison: University of Wisconsin Press, 2008), for a remarkable study of the effects of the Espionage Act of 1917 and Sedition Act of 1918 to empower the Department of Justice's Bureau of Investigation to squash dissent against America's participation in World War I. Managing the clergy was vital in German areas such as Wisconsin, Minnesota, and Illinois.

6. Niall Ferguson, *The Pity of War* (London: Allen Lane, Penguin, 1998), 368–69.

7. Ibid., 368–71.

8. See Tim Cook, "The Politics of Surrender: Canadian Soldiers and the Killing of Prisoners in the Great War," *Journal of Military History* 70 (July 2006): 637–66, for an analysis of the Canadian approach to taking and sometimes killing German EPWs on the Western Front from 1915 to 1918.

9. See http://www.answers.com/topic/prisoner-of-war (accessed 16 October 2008).

10. Meirion Harries and Susie Harries, *The Last Days of Innocence: America at War, 1917–1918* (New York: Random House, 1997), 143.

11. Ferguson, *Pity of War*, 387. See also Elton E. Mackin, *Suddenly We Didn't Want to Die: Memoirs of a World War I Marine* (Novato, CA: Presidio, 1993).

12. Harries and Harries, *Last Days of Innocence*, 360.

13. Mackin, *Suddenly We Didn't Want to Die*, 92, 94.

14. Hector Macquarrie, *How to Live at the Front: Tips for American Soldiers* (Philadelphia: Lippincott, 1917), 248, 250, 251.

15. Harries and Harries, *Last Days of Innocence*, 360.

16. John S. D. Eisenhower, *Yanks: The Epic Story of the American Army in World War I* (New York: Simon and Schuster, 2002), 132.

17. See http://www.nationmaster.com/encyclopedia/Dan-Daly for a summary of the battle and aftermath of Belleau Wood. Daly is one of two U.S. marines who won two Medals of Honor in two different engagements (accessed 27 October 2008).

18. Linda D. Kozaryn, "Belleau Wood: Marines' Mecca," *American Forces Press Service News Articles,* 18 June 1998, 1.

19. Eisenhower, *Yanks,* 150.

20. Edwin L. James, "Our Men Gain Near Fismes," *New York Times,* 24 August 1918.

21. Eisenhower, *Yanks,* 173.

22. Vincent J. Esposito, *The West Point Atlas of War: World War I* (New York: Tess, 1995), 120.

23. Medal of Honor Citation, Corporal Alvin C. York, http://www.homeofheroes .com/moh/citations_1918_wwi/york_alvin.htm (accessed 27 October 2008).

24. John Perry, "Just Ordinary Boys," *American Legion Magazine,* November 1998, 25.

25. Ayres, *War with Germany,* 114–15.

26. Peter T. Scott, "Captive Labour: The German Companies of the British Expeditionary Force (BEF) 1916–1920," *Army Quarterly and Defence Journal* 110, no. 3 (July 1980).

27. John J. Pershing, *My Experiences in the World War,* 2 vols. (New York: Frederick A. Stokes, 1931), 2:201.

28. Robert C. Doyle, *Voices from Captivity: Interpreting the American POW Narrative* (Lawrence: University Press of Kansas, 1994), 44.

29. Jonathan F. Vance, "Central POW Agency," in *Encyclopedia of Prisoners of War and Internment,* ed. Jonathan F. Vance (Santa Barbara, CA: ABC-CLIO, 2000), 43.

30. Doyle, *Voices from Captivity,* 49, 52.

31. George G. Lewis and John Mewha, *History of Prisoner of War Utilization by the United States Army, 1776–1945,* Department of the Army Pamphlet No. 20–213 (Washington, DC: Department of the Army, 1955), 52–53, quoted in Allan Kent Powell, *Splinters of a Nation: German Prisoners of War in Utah* (Salt Lake City: University of Utah Press, 1989), 14.

32. Powell, *Splinters of a Nation,* 14–15.

33. John Rieken, "Fort McPherson: World War I," http://www.georgiaencyclo-pedia.org (accessed 13 October 2008).

34. Susan Copeland Henry, "Foreign Prisoners of War: World War I," http://www.georgiaencyclopedia.org (accessed 10 October 2008).

35. Jim Clifford, "Fort McPherson, Georgia," *On Point* 12, no. 3 (Winter 2006): 28.

36. Karl P. Huebecher and Charles Vuillenmeier, "Inspection Report of Fort Douglas," 20 and 21 November 1917, Record Group 407, Box 76, Folder 6, 1, "Report of the Inspection by the Swiss Commission, Ft. Oglethorpe, Ft. McPherson, and Ft. Douglas," National Archives, Washington, DC, quoted in Powell, *Splinters of a Nation,* 24.

37. The "PW" became a source of humor for the German POWs during World War II. They translated it as *Pensionierte Wehrmacht,* or "Retired Armed Forces," much to the amusement of everyone except the Americans, who had no idea what they were chuckling about.

38. Huebecher and Vuillenmeier, "Fort Douglas," 7, quoted in Powell, *Splinters of a Nation,* 29.

39. *The Historical Management of POWs: A Synopsis of the 1968 US Army Provost Marshal General's Study Entitled "A Review of United States Policy on Treatment of Prisoners of War"* (San Diego, CA: Naval Health Research Center, 1970), 33.

40. Powell, *Splinters of a Nation,* 30–31.

41. Ferguson, *Pity of War,* 388.

42. Records of the Adjutant General's Office (Record Group 407) and War Department General and Special Staffs (Record Group 165), National Archives, provide the documents related to German internment in the United States during World War I.

43. Proclamation 1364—Declaring that a State of War Exists between the United States and Germany, 6 April 1917, Papers of Woodrow Wilson, http://www.presidency.ucsb.edu/ws/index.php?pid=598 (accessed 27 October 2008).

44. Arnold Krammer, *Undue Process: The Untold Story of America's German Alien Internees* (Lanham, MD: Rowman and Littlefield, 1997), 14.

45. Mitchel Yockelson, "The War Department: Keeper of Our Nation's Enemy Aliens," paper presented to the Society for Military History, April 1998, http://www.net.lib.byu.edu/estu/wwi/comment/yockel.htm (accessed 26 October 2008).

46. See Krammer, *Undue Process,* 13–15.

47. Yockelson, "War Department," 2.

48. Letter dated 1 February 1919, Fort Oglethorpe Correspondence, Records of the Adjutant General's Office, Record Group 407, quoted in Yockelson, "War Department," 5.

49. Robert H. Zieger, *America's Great War: World War I and the American Experience* (Lanham, MD: Rowman and Littlefield, 2000), 79.

50. Ibid., 79–80.

51. Espionage Act of 15 June 1917 in *Statutes at Large,* vol. 40 (Washington, DC: U.S. Government Printing Office, 1918), 553ff. See also http://wwi.lib.byu.edu/index.php/The_U.S._Sedition_Act (accessed 31 October 2008).

52. See Eugene V. Debs at http://www.marxists.org/archive/debs/ (accessed 2 November 2008).

53. Max Eastman, "The Trial of Eugene Debs," *Liberator* 1, no. 9 (November 1918): 6.

54. Eugene V. Debs http://www.marxists.org/archive/debs/works/1918/court.htm (accessed 2 November 2008).

55. See Jim Robbins, "Pardons Granted 88 Years after Crimes of Sedition," *New York Times,* 3 May 2006, http://www.nytimes.com (accessed 3 May 2006). See also Clemens P. Work, *Darkest before Dawn: Sedition and Free Speech in the American West* (Albuquerque: University of New Mexico Press, 2005), for a history of the war against the IWW.

56. Harries and Harries, *Last Days of Innocence,* 53.

57. Ibid.,72.

58. Charles D. Ameringer, *U.S. Foreign Intelligence: The Secret Side of American History* (Lexington, MA: D. C. Heath, 2000), 113.

59. "Conditions of an Armistice with Germany," in DeWeerd, *President Wilson Fights His War,* 407.

60. *Historical Management of POWs,* 37.

61. Ibid.

62. Harries and Harries, *Last Days of Innocence,* 446.

Chapter Nine. *Pensionierte Wehrmacht*

1. See Erich Maschke, *Zur Geschichte der deutschen Kriegsgefangenen des 2. Weltkrieges: Eine Zuzammenfassung* (Munich: Gieseking, 1974), 3.

2. Helmut Hörner, *A German Odyssey: The Journal of a German Prisoner of War,* trans. and ed. Allan Kent Powell (Golden, CO: Fulcrum, 1991), 159.

3. Ibid., 261.

4. Ibid., 264.

5. Ibid., 268.

6. Hans Werner Richter, *Die Geschlagenen* (Munich, 1949), 330.

7. Letter from POW Private Leo Korcz to his sister, Viktoria Gatz, who lived in Berlin-Charlottenburg, 10 September 1944, courtesy of Joachim S. Heise, Hannover, Germany; translation by the author. Although Private Korcz mentions picking cotton, that probably took place in the Deep South before his transfer to New York. German prisoners transferred regularly from one work region to another.

8. S. P. MacKenzie, "The Treatment of Prisoners of War in World War II," *Journal of Modern History* 66 (September 1994): 491.

9. International Committee of the Red Cross, *Reports of the International Committee of the Red Cross on Its Activities during the Second World War (September 1, 1939–June 30, 1947),* vol. 1, *General Activities* (Geneva, 1948), quoted in MacKenzie, "Treatment of Prisoners of War," 491.

10. For an excellent analysis of Soviet troops in German hands, see Geoffrey P. Megargee, *War of Annihilation: Combat and Genocide on the Eastern Front, 1941* (Lanham, MD: Rowman and Littlefield, 2006), 141–42.

11. See Jonathan F. Vance, "Geneva Convention of 1929," in *Encyclopedia of Prisoners of War and Internment,* ed. Jonathan F. Vance (Santa Barbara, CA: ABC-CLIO, 2000), 107–8.

12. Arnold Krammer, *Nazi Prisoners of War in America* (New York: Stein and Day, 1979), viii; Jake W. Spidle Jr., "Axis Prisoners of War in the United States, 1942–1946: A Bibliographical Essay," *Military Affairs* 39, no. 2 (April 1975): 60–63.

13. Krammer, *Nazi Prisoners of War in America,* 7.

14. See Spidle, "Axis Prisoners of War," 63.

15. For a discussion of the categories of escapes and escapers, see Robert C. Doyle, *A Prisoner's Duty: Great Escapes in U.S. Military History* (Annapolis, MD: Naval Institute Press, 1997), 1–13.

16. John Hammond Moore, *The Faustball Tunnel: German POWs and Their Great Escape* (New York: Random House, 1978), 70–71.

17. See William H. Rehnquist, "The Milligan Decision," *Military History Quarterly* (Winter 1999): 49.

18. W. A. Swanberg, "The Spies Who Came in from the Sea," *American Heritage,* April 1970, 66–69, 87–91.

19. John Brown Mason, "German Prisoners of War in the United States," *American Journal of International Law* 24 (April 1945): 207.

20. Ibid., 212.

21. Arnold Krammer, "American Treatment of German Generals during World War II," *Journal of Military History* 54 (January 1990): 27.

22. Ibid.

23. Ibid., 33. Krammer noted in a History Channel documentary, *Nazi Prisoners in America* (2002), produced and written by Sharon Young, that the Americans called it "The Fritz Ritz." In a personal communication to the author on 21 May 2009, Krammer wrote, "The phrase was used by locals who resented the POWs' ability to eat food which was otherwise rationed, wine and beer sold in camp canteens regardless of local 'dry county laws' (since Federal law superseded county laws), and the stories about German officers, sometimes with valets, who pranced around the camps, ordered flowers for their dinner tables, and weren't required to do physical labor."

24. Ibid., 35

25. Ibid., 42.

26. Curt Vinz, "Das freie Buch," *Der Ruf* 26 (1 April 1946), privately reprinted by his wife on his eightieth birthday as a *Festschrift;* copy courtesy of Matthias Steiner, University of Regensburg, September 1994. *Der Ruf* was a prison camp anti-Nazi newspaper-journal produced in 1944–1946 by the Prisoner of War Special Projects Division, Fort Phil Kearney, Rhode Island. Copies can be found in the Wisconsin State Library.

27. Gerald H. Davis, "Biographical Essay on Re-Education of Prisoners of War in Two World Wars," unpublished paper given to the author at a conference at the Australian Defense Force Academy, Canberra, Australia, 12 May 1994. *Der Ruf* followed in the tradition of the *Orgelsdorfer Eulenspiegel,* a camp literary and satiric newspaper published by German internees during World War I. See Gerald H. Davis, "'Orgelsdorf': A World War I Internment Camp in America," *Yearbook of German-American Studies* 26 (1991): 249–65. See also "Prisoners and Prisons," File O 68, Hoover Institution on War, Revolution, and Peace, Stanford University, California.

28. See John Melady, *Escape from Canada: The Untold Story of German Prisoners of War in Canada, 1939–1945* (Toronto: Macmillan, 1981).

29. Kendal Burt and James Leasor, *The One that Got Away* (New York: Ballantine, 1957), reprinted in Charles S. Verral, ed., *True Stories of Great Escapes* (Pleasantville, NY: Reader's Digest Association, 1977), 416; Melady, *Escape from Canada,* 98.

30. See Philip Flammer, "Dulag Luft: The Third Reich's Prison Camp for Airmen," *Aerospace Historian* 19, no. 2 (1972): 58–62.

31. *The One that Got Away,* directed by Roy Baker, with Hardy Krüger, Alec McCowen, Michael Goodleffe, and Colin Gordon (Rank, 1957). The German-language version is *Einer Kam Durch* (1957).

32. See David Fairbank White, *Bitter Ocean: The Battle of the Atlantic, 1939–1945* (New York: Simon and Schuster, 2006), 250.

33. Moore, *Faustball Tunnel,* 64–65. During World War II the FBI was responsible for recapturing escaped EPWs and others in federal custody.

34. See "Kriegsmarine Escape," *Newsweek,* 8 January 1945, 33–34.

35. See Krammer, *Nazi Prisoners of War in America,* 146.

36. Hörner, *German Odyssey,* 299.

37. See Kurt W. Böhme, *Die deutschen Kriegsgefangenen in amerikanischer Hand—Europa*, vol. 10.2 (Munich: Gieseking, 1973), for an analysis of the postwar problem. See also James Bacque, *Other Losses: An Investigation into the Mass Deaths of German Prisoners in the Hands of the French and Americans after World War II* (Toronto: Stoddart, 1989). Although about 50,000 German soldiers died in American postwar captivity, Bacque's claim of millions deliberately killed by General Dwight D. Eisenhower's policies cannot be proved by hard evidence.

38. See Agostino von Hassel and Sigrid MacRae, with Simone Ameskamp, *Alliance of Enemies: The Untold Story of the Secret American and German Collaboration to End World War II* (New York: Thomas Dunne/St. Martin's, 2006), 239–40.

39. Frank Biess, *Homecomings: Returning POWs and the Legacies of Defeat in Postwar Germany* (Princeton, NJ: Princeton University Press, 2006), 131.

40. See ibid., 44–45, for a discussion of the several stages of German POW repatriation from the Soviet Union.

41. Curt Bondy, "Observation and Reeducation of German Prisoners of War," *Harvard Educational Review* 14 (January 1944): 16–17.

42. Henry R. Luce, "The American Century," *Life*, 17 February 1941.

43. Ron Robin, *The Barbed-Wire College: Reeducating German POWs in the United States during World War II* (Princeton, NJ: Princeton University Press, 1995), 41.

44. See Jack Fincher, "By Convention, the Enemy within Never Did Without," *Smithsonian* 26, no. 3 (June 1995): 132.

45. Robin, *Barbed-Wire College*, 87.

46. Hörner, *German Odyssey*, 287.

47. See ibid., 376–77; Krammer, *Nazi Prisoners of War in America*, 248–50.

48. The author attended a reunion of these men as their guest at the Foreign Legion Barracks in Strasbourg, France, in 1998. Many of the former Wehrmacht soldiers who attended had been EPWs in the United States, returned to Le Havre in 1946, and joined the Foreign Legion. They were all old men, but their toughness never left them.

49. See J. Edgar Hoover, "Enemies at Large," *American Magazine*, April 1944, 29–30.

50. Reinhold Pabel, *Enemies Are Human* (Philadelphia: John C. Winston, 1955), 165. See also Hermann Jung, *Die deutschen Kriegsgefangenen in amerikanischer Hand—USA* (Munich: Gieseking, 1972), for a historical analysis of American captivity practices from a German point of view. Pabel was born on 4 May 1914 in Oran, Algeria, and died on 22 February 1995 in Boulogne, France (information courtesy of Arnold Krammer).

51. Georg Gaertner, with Arnold Krammer, *Hitler's Last Soldier in America* (New York: Stein and Day, 1985), 33.

52. Krammer, *Nazi Prisoners of War in America*, 266.

53. Louis E. Keefer, *Italian Prisoners of War in America, 1942–1946: Captives or Allies?* (New York: Praeger, 1992), xv.

54. Ibid., 15. See also Susan Badger Doyle, "German and Italian Prisoners of War in Albuquerque, 1943–1946," *New Mexico Historical Review* 66, no. 3 (July 1991): 327–40, for a solid regional study.

55. Keefer, *Italian Prisoners of War,* 51.

56. Ibid., 56–57.

57. See Allen V. Koop, *Stark Decency: German Prisoners of War in a New England Village* (Hanover, NH: University Press of New England, 1988), for the story of the anti-Nazi woodcutters' camp near Berlin, New Hampshire. See also http://home.arcor.de/kriegsgefangene/ (accessed 11 March 2009), a massive German POW site that offers a German interpretation of Allied imprisonment.

58. See David Westheimer, *Sitting It Out: A World War II POW Memoir* (Houston, TX: Rice University Press, 1992), for his POW story and movement from Italy to Germany (Stalag Luft III) in 1943. His novel *Von Ryan's Express* (New York: Doubleday, 1964) fictionalizes a plan to steal a train and escape into Switzerland; it was made into a film of the same title starring Frank Sinatra and Trevor Howard in 1965. Westheimer died in 2005.

59. See MacKenzie, "Treatment of Prisoners of War," 502.

60. John Hammond Moore, "Italian POWs in America: War Is Not Always Hell," *Prologue: The Journal of the National Archives* 8, no. 3 (Fall 1976): 144.

61. Keefer, *Italian Prisoners of War in America,* 78.

62. Moore, "Italian POWs in America," 144.

63. Ibid., 146; Keefer, *Italian Prisoners of War in America,* 129. See also Jack Harmann, *On American Soil: How Justice Became a Casualty of World War II* (Seattle: University of Washington Press, 2005), for a detailed analysis of this terrible incident. Three American soldiers were tried and found guilty on questionable evidence.

64. See James Brooke, "After Silence, Italians Recall the Internment," *New York Times International,* 11 August 1997, A 10.

65. See Lisa Scottoline, "About Italian Americans," http://scottoline.com/Site/Italians/internment.aspx (accessed 16 November 2008). Myriad Web sites address the Italian alien problem during World War II.

66. Arnold Krammer, *Undue Process: The Untold Story of America's German Alien Internees* (Lanham, MD: Rowman and Littlefield, 1997), 3.

67. See ibid., 6, for a list of Nazi sympathetic newsletters that circulated in the United States prior to December 1941.

68. Ibid., 25.

69. Ibid., 53.

70. Ibid., 164.

71. Ibid., 171.

72. See Guido Knopp, "Heimkehr, Flüchtlinge und Vertriebene," *Damals,* December 1994, 8–11.

73. See James Brooke, "Germans Back on U.S. Base, Now as Tenants," *New York Times,* 14 August 1996, A1, B6.

Chapter Ten. The Reborn

1. E. Bartlett Kerr, *Surrender and Survival: The Experience of American POWs in the Pacific 1941–1945* (New York: William Morrow, 1985), 335.

2. MacDonald to the Foreign Office, 15 May 1905, Foreign Office Papers, Public Record Office, London, FO-46-596, quoted in Philip A. Towle, "Japanese

Treatment of Prisoners in 1904–1905—Foreign Officers' Reports," *Military Affairs* 39, no. 3 (October 1975): 116.

3. FO-181-847, quoted ibid.

4. See Charles Burdick and Ursula Moessner, *The German Prisoners of War in Japan, 1914–1920* (Lanham, MD: University Press of America, 1984), for a study that shows how well the Japanese treated German prisoners during World War I.

5. See Charlotte Carr-Gregg, "Japanese Personality and Value Orientation," in *Japanese Prisoners of War in Revolt: The Outbreaks at Featherston and Cowra during World War II* (Brisbane, Australia: University of Queensland Press, 1978), 128–68. Carr-Gregg discusses the complicated Japanese attitude toward death (129).

6. Towle, "Japanese Treatment of Prisoners," 117.

7. Elizabeth Head Vaughn, *Community under Stress: An Internment Camp Culture* (Princeton, NJ: Princeton University Press, 1949), 74.

8. Carr-Gregg, *Japanese Prisoners of War in Revolt*, 104–5. See also John Keegan, *A History of Warfare* (New York: Vintage, 1993), 40–46, for a discussion of the samurai's role in Japanese military culture.

9. See Hillis Lory, *Japan's Military Masters* (New York: Viking, 1943), 123, quoted in Carr-Gregg, *Japanese Prisoners of War in Revolt*, 106.

10. See Richard Story, *History of Modern Japan* (Hammondsworth, UK: Penguin, 1960), 162, quoted in Lory, *Japan's Military Masters*, 106.

11. Robert B. Edgerton, *Warriors of the Rising Sun: A History of the Japanese Military* (Boulder, CO: Westview, 1997), 324.

12. Story, *History of Modern Japan*, 115–16.

13. Saburo Ienaga, *The Pacific War, 1931–1945* (New York: Pantheon, 1978), 45.

14. Ulrich Straus, *The Anguish of Surrender: Japanese POWs of World War II* (Seattle: University of Washington Press, 2003), 39.

15. Robert C. Doyle, *A Prisoner's Duty: Great Escapes in U.S. Military History* (Annapolis, MD: Naval Institute Press, 1997), 150–51.

16. Edgerton, *Warriors of the Rising Sun*, 324.

17. See Charles G. Roland, "Allied POWs, Japanese Captors and the Geneva Convention," *War and Society* 9, no. 2 (October 1991): 83–101.

18. S. P. MacKenzie, "The Treatment of Prisoners of War in World War II," *Journal of Modern History* 66 (September 1994): 513.

19. Tamura Yoshio quoted in Haruko Taya Cook and Theodore F. Cook, *Japan at War: An Oral History* (New York: New Press, 1992), 164.

20. Ienaga, *The Pacific War*, 189.

21. Personal letter from James Clavell to the author, 22 February 1993. See James Clavell, *King Rat* (1962; reprint, New York: Dell, 1980). See also the film made from the novel, *King Rat*, directed by Bryan Forbes, with George Segal and Tom Courtenay (Columbia, 1965). Clavell joined the Royal Artillery in 1940 and was sent to Malaya to fight the Japanese. Wounded by machine gun fire, he was eventually captured and sent to a Japanese POW camp on Java. Later he was transferred to Changi prison in Singapore, notorious for its poor living conditions.

22. The number of books and articles concerning the Bataan Death March

is enormous, including analytical histories, personal narratives, and government documents. The same is true of the British and Australian experience on the Death Railway in Thailand and Burma.

23. Edgerton, *Warriors of the Rising Sun*, 15.

24. See Marc Landas, *The Fallen: A True Story of American and Japanese Wartime Atrocities* (Hoboken, NJ: John Wiley and Sons, 2004), for a very sad story about the murder of American POWs late in the war by order of the Japanese Western Army Headquarters in Kyushu.

25. MacKenzie, "Treatment of Prisoners of War," 516.

26. See Stanley Weintraub, *Long Day's Journey into War: December 7, 1941* (New York: Dutton, 1991), 612; Straus, *Anguish of Surrender*, 1–16.

27. Straus, *Anguish of Surrender*, 11.

28. Arnold Krammer, "Japanese Prisoners of War in America," *Pacific Historical Review* 52, no. 1 (February 1983): 79.

29. Kazuo Sakamaki, *I Attacked Pearl Harbor*, trans. Toru Matsumoto (New York: Association, 1949), 98.

30. Ibid., 129.

31. Straus, *Anguish of Surrender*, 48.

32. Yamauchi Takeo quoted in Cook and Cook, *Japan at War*, 291.

33. Ibid.

34. Miyagi Kikuko quoted ibid., 360.

35. Ooka Shohei, *Taken Captive: A Japanese POW's Story*, trans. and ed. Wayne P. Lammers (1952; reprint, New York: John Wiley and Sons, 1996), 6.

36. Ibid., 29.

37. Ibid., 68.

38. Kojima Kiofumi quoted in Cook and Cook, *Japan at War*, 377.

39. See Allied Translator and Intelligence Section of the Southwest Pacific Area, Maxwell Air Force Base Archives.

40. Report 595, Serial 752, Allied Translator and Intelligence Section of the Southwest Pacific Area, 3–4; Serial 756, 23 January 1945, Interrogation Report 599, 6.

41. Allison B. Gilmore, "'We Have Been Reborn': Japanese Prisoners and the Allied Propaganda War in the Southwest Pacific," *Pacific Historical Review* 64, no. 2 (May 1995): 201. See also her remarkable book-length examination of this topic: *You Can't Fight Tanks with Bayonets: Psychological Warfare against the Japanese Army in the Southwest Pacific* (Lincoln: University of Nebraska Press, 1998).

42. Gilmore, "We Have Been Reborn," 211.

43. Straus, *Anguish of Surrender*, 92.

44. See Paul F. Boller Jr., *Memoirs of an Obscure Professor and Other Essays* (Fort Worth: Texas Christian University Press, 1992), 35–41.

45. Ibid., 46–49.

46. Krammer, "Japanese Prisoners of War in America," 67.

47. Straus, *Anguish of Surrender*, 171–72.

48. Ibid., 174–75.

49. See Krammer, "Japanese Prisoners of War in America," 85–87.

50. See Straus, *Anguish of Surrender*, 177–78; see also Jonathan F. Vance,

"Featherston Incident," in *Encyclopedia of Prisoners of War and Internment*, ed. Jonathan F. Vance (Santa Barbara, CA: ABC-CLIO, 2000), 97.

51. See Harry Gordon, *Die Like a Carp: The Story of the Greatest Prison Escape Ever* (Stanmore: Cassell Australia, 1978), for a journalistic and heavily opinionated version of the Cowra incident.

52. Straus, *Anguish of Surrender*, 186–91. See also Anthony Staunton, "Cowra Incident," in Vance, "Featherston Incident," 64–65; Kenneth Seaforth Mackenzie, *Dead Men Rising* (Sydney, Australia: Pacific Books, 1969); Carr-Gregg, *Japanese Prisoners of War in Revolt*.

53. John Toland, *Captured by History* (New York: St. Martin's, 1997), 163.

54. Lillian Baker, *American and Japanese Relocation in World War II: Fact, Fiction, and Fallacy* (Medford, OR: Webb Research Group, 1990), 56.

55. John Tateishi, *And Justice for All: An Oral History of Japanese-American Detention Camps* (New York: Random House, 1984), xv.

56. Baker, *American and Japanese Relocation*, 56.

57. Tateishi, *And Justice for All*, xv.

58. Mark Weber, "The Japanese Camps in California," *Journal for Historical Review* 2, no. 1 (Spring 1980): 54.

59. See Arnold Krammer, *Undue Process: The Untold Story of America's German Alien Internees* (Lanham, MD: Rowman and Littlefield, 1997), 51.

60. "Relocation of Japanese Americans" (Washington, DC: War Relocation Authority, 1943), www.sfmuseum.org/hist10/relocbook.html (accessed 3 December 2008).

61. See Roger Daniels, "American Historians and East Asian Immigrants," *Pacific Historical Review* 53, no. 4 (November 1974): 449–72, for a comprehensive examination of Asian immigration and renewed nativism.

62. Tateishi, *And Justice for All*, xv.

63. Robert Harvey, *Amache: The Story of Japanese Internment in Colorado during World War II* (Lanham, MD: Taylor Trade Publishing, 2004), 3.

64. Tateishi, *And Justice for All*, xiii. .

65. Baker, *American and Japanese Relocation*, 52.

66. Tateishi, *And Justice for All*, xxi.

67. Jeanne Wakatsuki Houston and James Houston, *Farewell to Manzanar* (New York: Bantam, 1973), 20–21.

68. Daniel Davis, *Behind Barbed Wire* (New York: Dutton, 1982), 98.

69. Ibid., 99.

70. Roger Daniels, *Concentration Camps: North America: Japanese in the United States and Canada during World War II* (Malabar, FL: Krieger, 1993), 112.

71. See Susan D. Moeller, "The Pictures of the Enemy: Fifty Years of Images of Japan in the American Press, 1941–1992," *Journal of American Culture* 19, no. 1 (Spring 1996): 29–42, for an analysis of the press's treatment of the Japanese at home and at war during World War II.

72. George Sullivan, *Strange but True Stories of World War II* (New York: Walker, 1983), 84.

73. Ibid., 92.

74. Daniels, *Concentration Camps: North America*, 131.

75. Sarah L. Brew, "Making Amends for History: Legislative Reparations for Japanese Americans and other Minority Groups," *Law and Inequality* 8 (1989): 183.

76. Daniels, *Concentration Camps: North America*, 132. In 1984 a federal district court issued a writ of *error corum nobis*, which set aside the 1942 Hirabayashi conviction.

77. See ibid., 137–39, for a full description of this case.

78. See George Miller, *Personal Justice Denied*, in U.S. Congress, Commission on Wartime Relocation and Internment of Civilians, 102rd Cong., 2nd sess., Committee Print No. 6 (Washington, DC: U.S. Government Printing Office, 1982), 118.

79. Daniels, *Concentration Camps: North America*, 219.

Chapter Eleven. After the Victory

1. See http://users.erols.com/mwhite28/warstat1.htm#Second (accessed 4 December 2008). These composite figures are approximations at best and agree generally with those published by the U.S. Holocaust Museum.

2. For an excellent summary of German POW discipline in the American camps, see Lewis H. Carlson, *We Were Each Other's Prisoners: An Oral History of World War II American and German Prisoners of War* (New York: Basic Books, 1997), 155–60.

3. Richard Whittingham, *Martial Justice: The Last Mass Execution in the United States* (1971; reprint, Annapolis, MD: Naval Institute Press, 1997), 107.

4. See ibid., 249–51.

5. Ibid., 281.

6. See Benedict B. Kimmelman, "The Example of Private Slovik," *American Heritage* 38, no. 6 (September–October 1987), www.americanheritage.com/articles/magazine/ah/1987/6/1987_6_97.shtml (accessed 6 December 2008); see also William Bradford Huie, *The Execution of Private Slovik* (1954; reprint, New York: Dell, 1970), 4, 8–9. There are competing figures regarding this issue. Manfred Messerschmidt and Fritz Wüllner, *Die Wehrmachtjustiz im Dienste des Nationalsozialismus. Zerstörung einer Legende* (Baden-Baden: Nomos, 1987), 29, note that according to the Office of the Judge Advocate General on 2 June 1987, U.S. courts-martial sentenced 763 American servicemen to death between 8 December 1941 and 15 March 1946; 146 were actually executed. The breakdown they provide is as follows: fifty-two for rape, eighteen for rape and murder, seventy-five for murder, and one (Slovik) for desertion with intent to avoid hazardous duty.

7. Mark Wyman, *DP: Europe's Displaced Persons, 1945–1951* (Philadelphia; Balch Institute, 1989), 17.

8. Ibid., 25.

9. Ibid., 46.

10. For prewar American efforts to rescue Jewish refugees, see Peter Eisner, "Bingham's List," *Smithsonian*, March 2009, 50–57.

11. Wyman, *DP*, 47.

12. Ibid., 63.

13. David Dallin and Boris Nikolaevsky, *Forced Labor in Soviet Russia* (New Haven, CT: Yale University Press, 1947), 282, 283, quoted in Mark Elliott, "The

United States and Forced Repatriation of Soviet Citizens, 1944–47," *Political Science Quarterly* 88, no. 2 (June 1973): 259n.

14. See Julius Epstein, *Operation Keelhaul: The Story of Forced Repatriation from 1944 to the Present* (Old Greenwich, CT: Devin-Adair, 1973), for a history and analysis of the American cooperation with the Soviets.

15. Elliott, "The United States and Forced Repatriation of Soviet Citizens," 253–54.

16. Ibid., 273.

17. Author's personal conversation with the late Sergeant George Zong in State College, Pennsylvania, in the late 1980s. Many American soldiers were utterly speechless and for decades found it difficult to speak of it.

18. Wyman, *DP,* 132. The bibliography of the Holocaust is enormous and growing. The Holocaust Museum of the United States in Washington, D.C., is creating a massive work tentatively called *The Encyclopedia of the Holocaust.*

19. Wyman, *DP,* 135.

20. Ibid., 132.

21. Kurt Böhme, *Die deutschen Kriegsgefangenen in amerikanischer Hand—Europa,* vol. 10.2 (Munich: Gieseking, 1973), cited in Edward N. Peterson, *The Many Faces of Defeat: The German People's Experience in 1945* (New York: Peter Lang, 1990), 27.

22. James Bacque, *Other Losses: An Investigation into the Mass Deaths of German Prisoners in the Hands of the French and Americans after World War II* (Toronto: Stoddart, 1989). See Günter Bischof and Stephen E. Ambrose, eds., *Eisenhower and the German POWs: Facts against Falsehood* (Baton Rouge: Louisiana State University Press, 1992). The Maschke Commission published twenty-two volumes on German POWs in Yugoslavian, Russian, Polish, Czechoslovakian, American (in Europe and in the United States), British, Belgian, and French hands. It was a massive, comprehensive effort with definitive scholarship deemed vital today for the study of German POWs in enemy hands.

23. The author taught at the Westfäliche Wilhelms Universität, Münster, on a Fulbright grant in 1994–1995 and guided several graduate students in research projects on German POW issues. The students' experience with families taught them about the guilt factor, which they found very difficult to penetrate.

24. Helmut Hörner, *A German Odyssey: The Journal of a German Prisoner of War,* trans. and ed. Allan Kent Powell (Golden, CO: Fulcrum, 1991). See "Ike's Revenge," *Time,* 2 October 1989, 19. See also John Keegan, "James Bacque and the 'Missing Million,'" *Times Literary Supplement,* 23 July 1993, 13.

25. Walter F. Greiner, "Other Losses," Letter to the Editor, *Times Literary Supplement,* 23–29 November 1990.

26. Peterson, *Many Faces of Defeat,* 33.

27. W. L. White, *Report on the Germans* (New York: Harcourt, Brace, 1947), 141–42.

28. The British and French occupation authorities established different rules, and some prisoners remained in captivity for years.

29. Robert Shnayerson, "Judgment at Nuremberg," *Smithsonian* 27, no. 7 (1996): 130.

30. Telford Taylor, *The Anatomy of Nuremberg: A Personal Memoir* (New York: Alfred A. Knopf, 1992), 269.

31. See Alice Kaplan, "War on Trial," *Civilization* 4, no. 5 (1997): 63.

32. Roger Manvell, *SS and Gestapo: Rule by Terror* (New York: Ballantine, 1969), 9.

33. See Kazuko Tsurumi, *Social Change and the Individual: Japan before and after Defeat in World War II* (Princeton, NJ: Princeton University Press, 1970), 138. Although this author examined the Far East trials, the categories were the same as at Nuremberg.

34. The bibliography concerning the Nuremberg trials is enormous. The *New York Times* and all the other national newspapers reported on the trials daily. See, for example, Kathleen McLaughlin, "Allies Open Trial of 20 Top Germans for Crimes of War," *New York Times*, 20 November 1945, http://www.nytimes.com/learning/general/onthisday/big/1120.html (accessed 10 December 2008).

35. See Robert W. Kesting, "Forgotten Victims: Blacks in the Holocaust," *Journal of Negro History* 77, no. 1 (Winter 1992): 30–36. Kesting points to a number of cases of black American soldiers allegedly murdered by Nazi soldiers or civilians. Sadly, these cases were dismissed for lack of evidence.

36. See "The Dachau Trials by U.S. Army Courts in Europe 1945–1948," http://www.jewishvirtuallibrary.org/jsource/Holocaust/DachauTrials.html (accessed 10 December 2008).

37. Letter from Robert H. Jackson to Harry S. Truman, Avalon Project, Yale Law School, www.yale.edu/lawweb/avalon/imt/Jackson/jack63.htm (accessed 10 December 2008).

38. See Kaplan, "War on Trial," 63.

39. Matt Rojansky, "Tribunal Tribulations," *Harvard International Review* 22, no. 2 (2000): 13; Shnayerson, "Judgment at Nuremberg," 125.

40. For biographies of these Nazi broadcasters and some others, see John Carver Edwards, *Berlin Calling: American Broadcasters in Service to the Third Reich* (New York: Praeger, 1991).

41. For a comprehensive description of Koischwitz and Gillers, see ibid., 57–98.

42. On 26 July 1943 a grand jury in Washington, D.C., indicted Max Koischwitz, Robert H. Best, Jane Anderson, Douglas Chandler, Edward Delaney, Constance Drexel, Fred W. Kaltenbach, and Ezra Pound in absentia for treason.

43. Edwards, *Berlin Calling*, 93.

44. Ibid., 98.

45. Mildred Gillers, "Axis Sally," http://www.findagrave.com/cgi-bin/fg.cgi?page=gr&GRid=23000 (accessed 12 December 2008).

46. Potsdam Declaration, 1945, quoted in Tsurumi, *Social Change and the Individual*, 138.

47. Jonathan F. Vance, "Tokyo War Crimes Trials," in *Encyclopedia of Prisoners of War and Internment*, ed. Jonathan F. Vance (Santa Barbara, CA: ABC-CLIO, 2000), 291.

48. Douglas MacArthur, *Reminiscences* (1964; reprint, Annapolis, MD: Naval Institute Press, 2001), 318.

49. Tsurumi, *Social Change and the Individual*, 139.

50. See Arnold C. Brackman, *The Other Nuremberg: The Untold Story of the Tokyo War Crimes Trials* (New York: William Morrow, 1987), 369.

51. Ibid., 383.

52. Ibid., 399.

53. Richard H. Minear, *Victors Justice: The Tokyo War Crimes Trial* (1971; reprint, Ann Arbor: University of Michigan Center for Japanese Studies, 2001), 169.

54. MacArthur, *Reminiscences*, 319.

55. Saburo Ienaga, *The Pacific War, 1931–1945* (New York: Pantheon, 1978), 238.

56. Keiichi Sakuda, "Rapprochement with Death—The Logic of Responsibility of the Japanese as It Appeared in the Messages of the War Criminals Convicted to Death," *Tenbo* 72 (December 1964): 64, quoted in Tsurumi, *Social Change and the Individual*, 161.

57. Tsurumi, *Social Change and the Individual*, 162.

58. Haruko Taya Cook and Theodore F. Cook, *Japan at War: An Oral History* (New York: New Press, 1992), 405.

59. Frank Fugita, *Foo: A Japanese-American Prisoner of the Rising Sun, The Secret Prison Diary of Frank "Foo" Fugita* (Denton: University of North Texas Press, 1993), 207n. The author's father, a navy chief petty officer in the Pacific from 1943 to 1945, often related how much he and his shipmates enjoyed listening to the Tokyo Rose broadcasts.

60. Ibid., 196.

61. Stanley I. Kutler, *The American Inquisition: Justice and Injustice in the Cold War* (New York: Hill and Wang, 1982), 4.

62. For a short version of the Tokyo Rose–Iva Toguri d'Aquino story, see the FBI's historical site, http://www.fbi.gov/libref/historic/famcases/rose/rose.htm (accessed 12 December 2008).

63. Kutler, *American Inquisition*, 12.

64. Ibid., 31. See also Russell Warren Howe, *The Hunt for "Tokyo Rose"* (Lanham, MD: Madison Books, 1990), for a comprehensive, personal, and sympathetic analysis of Iva Toguri d'Aquino's activities in Tokyo during the war, her trial, and her incarceration.

65. "Obituary, Iva Toguri," *Economist*, 7 October 2006, 93.

66. For the trials of the British traitors and renegades, see Adrian Weale, *Renegades: Hitler's Englishmen* (London: Warner, 1995), 194–95.

67. See Nicholas Bethell, *The Last Secret: Forcible Repatriation to Russia, 1944–7* (London: Andre Deutsch, 1974), 204–11.

Chapter Twelve. Prisoners at War

1. Robert C. Doyle, *A Prisoner's Duty: Great Escapes in U.S. Military History* (Annapolis, MD: Naval Institute Press, 1997), 184.

2. Sven Steenburg, *Vlasov* (New York: Knopf, 1970), 5.

3. Nikolai Tolstoy, *Stalin's Secret War* (New York: Holt, Rinehart, and Winston, 1982), 143.

4. Nikolai Tolstoy, *Victims of Yalta* (London: Hodder and Stoughton, 1977), 97.

5. Steenburg, *Vlasov*, 219.

6. Tolstoy, *Victims of Yalta*, 87.

7. The Soviets detained millions of German POWs, thus making a huge forced labor force available for reconstruction following World War II. See Stefan Karner, *Im Archipel GUPVI: Kriegsgefangenshaft und Internierung in der Sowjetunion, 1941–1956* (Vienna: Oldenbourg, 1995), for a critical study of Germans and Austrians in postwar Soviet captivity. Although the Maschke Commission examined this problem in the 1960s, Karner, a professor of modern history at the University of Graz, was the first Western scholar to receive permission to search the Russian archives in Moscow for records kept by the Soviets.

8. Paul Gregory and Valery Lazarev, eds., *The Economics of Forced Labor: The Soviet Gulag* (Stanford, CA: Hoover Institution, 2003), 2.

9. According to the U.S. Department of Defense, *Selected Manpower Statistics FY 1994*, Table 2-23 (Principal Wars), 112, cited in *VFW Magazine*, February 1996, 8, combat losses amounted to 33,652 killed in action and noncombat losses reached 3,262, for a total of 36,914 American dead in Korea.

10. Hyo-Soon Song, *The Fight for Freedom: The Untold Story of the Korean War Prisoners* (Seoul: Korean Library Association, 1980), 36.

11. Robert Cowley and Geoffrey Parker, eds., *The Readers Companion to Military History* (Boston: Houghton Mifflin, 1996), 370.

12. Captain Francis "Ike" Fenton Jr., quoted in Donald Knox, *The Korean War, Pusan to Chosin: An Oral History* (New York: Harcourt Brace, 1986), 253.

13. Keyes Beech, *Tokyo and Points East* (Garden City, NY: Doubleday, 1954), 180.

14. Ibid.

15. Ibid., 181.

16. William T. Bowers, William M. Hammond, and George L. MacGarrigle, *Black Soldier White Army: The 24th Infantry Regiment in Korea* (Washington, DC: U.S. Army Center of Military History, 1996), 140. In 1951 President Truman ordered the U.S. Army to integrate all its units, and the existence of the all-black infantry regiments came to an end.

17. Alexander L. George, *The Chinese Communist Army in Action: The Korean War and Its Aftermath* (New York: Columbia University Press, 1967), 9. See also Samuel M. Meyers and William C. Bradbury, *The Political Behavior of Korean and Chinese Prisoners of War in the Korean Conflict: A Historical Analysis*, Human Resources Research Office Technical Report 50, Psychological Warfare Division (Washington, DC: George Washington University, Human Resources Research Office for the Department of the Army, August 1958).

18. Ed Evanhoe, *Dark Moon: Eighth Army Special Operations in the Korean War* (Annapolis, MD: Naval Institute Press, 1995), 90–91.

19. Ibid., 91.

20. See William Lindsey White, *An Unofficial White Paper on the Treatment of War Prisoners* (New York: Charles Scribner's Sons, 1957), 105.

21. Stan Summers, *The Korea Story* (Marshfield MN: American Ex–Prisoners of War National Medical Research Committee, 1981), 27.

22. Quoted in Robert C. Doyle, *Voices from Captivity: Interpreting the American POW Narrative* (Lawrence: University Press of Kansas, 1994), 186; see also

William F. Dean and William Warden, *General Dean's Story* (New York: Harper and Brothers, 1956), 107–8.

23. Quoted in Doyle, *Voices from Captivity,* 187; see also Lloyd W. Pate and B. J. Cutler, *Reactionary* (New York: Harper and Brothers, 1956), 69.

24. Lewis H. Carlson, *Remembered Prisoners of a Forgotten War: An Oral History of Korean War POWs* (New York: St. Martin's, 2002), 193. See also Henry A. Segal, "Initial Psychiatric Findings of Recently Repatriated Prisoners of War," *American Journal of Psychiatry* 3 (1954): 358–63, to get a feel for the spirit of the times.

25. See Virginia Pasley, *22 Stayed* (London: W. H. Allen, 1955), for a critical examination of each of the Americans and the one British soldier who refused repatriation in 1953. See also Albert D. Biderman, *March to Calumny: The Story of American POW's in the Korean War* (New York: Macmillan, 1963), and Eugene Kincaid, *In Every War But One* (New York: Norton, 1959), for the postwar battle of theories about why these soldiers defected to the communists in 1953.

26. 29th Report of the UN Command for the period 1–15 September 1951, UN Document No. S/2400, 25, Department of State Bulletin 1034 (1951), quoted in George S. Prugh, "Prisoners at War: The POW Battleground," *Dickinson Law Review* 60, no. 2 (January 1956): 129.

27. Nicholas Bethell, *The Last Secret: Forcible Repatriation to Russia, 1944–7* (London: Andre Deutsch, 1974), 211.

28. Kenneth K. Hansen, *Heroes behind Barbed Wire* (Princeton, NJ: D. von Nostrand, 1957), 17.

29. Ibid., 19.

30. Matthew B. Ridgway, *The Korean War* (Garden City, NY: Doubleday, 1967), 206.

31. Ibid.

32. Hansen, *Heroes behind Barbed Wire,* 21.

33. See Anthony Farrar-Hockley, *The British Past in the Korean War: An Honourable Discharge* (London: HMSO, 1995), 2:380. See also *The Communist War in POW Camps,* Headquarters, United Nations and Far East Command, Military Intelligence Section, General Staff, 28 January 1953.

34. Ridgway, *Korean War,* 207. See also Mark W. Clark, *From the Danube to the Yalu* (New York: Harper and Brothers, 1954), 55.

35. Personal correspondence from Stanley Weintraub to the author, 24 December 2008.

36. Song, *Fight for Freedom,* 66. Song reports that Colonel Pak was returned to North Korea after the armistice, even though the UN Command knew he had ordered the murder of other Korean EPWs in the Koje-do prison camp.

37. Hansen, *Heroes behind Barbed Wire,* 23.

38. William Roskey, "Koje Island: The 1952 Korean Hostage Crisis," *Land Warfare Papers* 19 (September 1994): 1.

39. Ibid., 2.

40. Ibid., 6.

41. Joseph C. Goulden, *The Untold Story of the War* (New York: McGraw-Hill, 1983), 596, quoted in Roskey, "Koje Island," 7.

42. See Roskey, "Koje Island," 8.

43. Clark, *From the Danube to the Yalu,* 41, quoted in ibid., 16.

44. Ridgway, *Korean War,* 213.

45. See Haydon L. Boatner, "POW's for Sale," *American Legion,* August 1962, 14.

46. Song, *Fight for Freedom,* 70.

47. 47th Report of the UN Command for the period 1–15 June 1952, UN Document No. S/2774, 27, Department of State Bulletin 669 (1952), quoted in Prugh, "Prisoners at War," 129f.

48. Song, *Fight for Freedom,* 96.

49. Ibid., 73. See also Harry G. Summers Jr., *Korean War Almanac* (New York: Facts on File, 1990), 213.

50. 54th Report of the UN Command for the period 16–30 September 1952, UN Document No. S/2897, 28, Department of State Bulletin (1953), 224, 226, quoted in Prugh, "Prisoners at War," 130.

51. Clark, *From the Danube to the Yalu,* 33.

52. Ibid., 51.

53. Based on several conversations with Stanley Weintraub, who participated in the program. See Stanley Weintraub, *War in the Wards: Korea's Unknown Battle in a Prisoner-of-War Hospital Camp,* 2nd ed. (San Rafael, CA: Presidio, 1976).

54. Personal correspondence from Stanley Weintraub to the author, 24 December 2008.

55. Weintraub, *War in the Wards,* 17. Weintraub makes it clear that the First POW Field Hospital served friend and foe alike.

56. Song, *Fight for Freedom,* 158.

57. Quoted in ibid., 159.

58. Ibid., 155–56.

59. Ibid., 221.

60. Ibid., 223.

61. Charles H. Murphy, "Prisoners of War: Repatriation or Internment in Wartime—American and Allied Experiences, 1775 to Present," in U.S. House Committee on Foreign Affairs, *American Prisoners of War in Southeast Asia, 1971* (Washington, DC: U.S. Government Printing Office, 1971), 484.

62. See Clark, *From the Danube to the Yalu,* 63–67.

Chapter Thirteen. Vietnam Quagmire

1. George S. Prugh, *Law at War: Vietnam, 1964–1973* (Washington, DC: Department of the Army, Center of Military History, 1975), 62.

2. General William C. Westmoreland, *A Soldier Reports* (Garden City, NY: Doubleday, 1976), 297.

3. See ibid., 298.

4. Prugh, *Law at War,* 68.

5. Personal conversation with Colonel Barry Wallace, U.S. Army (Ret.), 3 August 2009. Colonel Wallace served as senior advisor at the Phu Quoc POW camp in 1968.

6. Ibid.

7. Prugh, *Law at War,* 68.

8. George E. Smith, *POW: Two Years with the Vietcong* (Berkeley, CA: Ramparts, 1971), 298.

9. Ibid.

10. Article 85 refers to the treatment of war criminals. It stipulates that POWs prosecuted under the laws of the detaining power for actions committed prior to capture retain the benefits of the convention. Article 108 empowers punishment and defines how detaining powers may carry out sentences. The Soviet Union and its satellite states rejected these concepts. See A. J. Barker, *Behind Barbed Wire* (London: Purnell Book Services, 1974), 216–18, for a discussion of this problem in international law. See also Walter J. Landon, "Geneva Conventions—The Broken Rules," *Naval Institute Proceedings* 99, no. 2 (February 1973): 34–39; Howard S. Levie, "Maltreatment of Prisoners of War in Vietnam," *Boston University Law Review* 48, no. 3 (Summer 1968): 323–59.

11. Prugh, *Law at War*, 77.

12. Joseph Califano Jr., *Governing America: An Insider's Report from the White House and the Cabinet* (New York: Simon and Schuster, 1981), 221.

13. Thomas Patrick Melady, "Background to US-Vatican Relations," *New Catholic World* 209 (1969): 109; Wilton Wynn, *Keepers of the Keys: John XXIII, Paul VI and John Paul II: Three Who Changed the Church* (New York: Random House, 1988), 196.

14. "Trial and Error," *Newsweek*, 1 August 1966, 35–36.

15. Peter C. Rollins, "Television's Vietnam: The Visual Language of Television News," *Journal of American Culture* 4 (1981): 132.

16. Peter C. Rollins, "The Vietnam War: Perceptions through Literature, Film, and Television," *American Quarterly* 36 (1984): 420.

17. Roger Hilsman, *To Move a Nation* (New York: Doubleday, 1967), 525. At the same time, the Americans lost 267 advisors killed in action.

18. Personal correspondence with Blaise Hogan, 30 January 2009.

19. Quoted in Keith Walker, *A Piece of My Heart: The Stories of Twenty-six American Women Who Served in Vietnam* (New York: Ballantine, 1985), 99.

20. The Americans called the People's Army of Vietnam the North Vietnamese Army or NVA. In a show of respect, Americans called the NVA soldiers "Mr. Charles," as opposed to the Vietcong guerrillas, who were called "Victor Charlie." Other epithets, such as "Chuck," were often heard in the field too.

21. Quoted in Walker, *Piece of My Heart*, 100.

22. Ibid., 173.

23. Personal correspondence with Robert Senior, 19 January 1990.

24. W. D. Ehrhart, *Vietnam-Perkesie: A Combat Marine Memoir* (Jefferson, NC: McFarland, 1983), 264–65.

25. A unique personal wartime memoir in this regard is Sedgwick D. Tourison Jr., *Talking with Victor Charlie: An Interrogator's Story* (New York: Ballantine/ Ivy, 1991).

26. Michael Lee Lanning and Dan Cragg, *Inside the VC and NVA: The Real Story of North Vietnam's Armed Forces* (1992; reprint, New York: Ivy, 1994), 82.

27. See Konrad Kellen, *Conversations with Enemy Soldiers in Late 1968/Early 1969: A Study of Motivation and Morale* (Santa Monica, CA: RAND, 1970), for a

comprehensive study based on EPW interviews. Like veterans' personal interviews and correspondence, it shows that these soldiers were dedicated to the reunification of Vietnam as their first cause. Communist political philosophy played virtually no role.

28. See Eric M. Smith, "Combat Intelligence," *Vietnam Magazine,* June 1995, 44.

29. Ibid.

30. Personal correspondence with Larry Serra, Naval Intelligence liaison officer, Ha Tien Province, 1969–1970, 7 January 2009.

31. Personal correspondence with Peter Decker, Naval Intelligence liaison ifficer, Duc Hoa, Hau Nghia Province, 1969–1970, 6 January 2009.

32. Ibid.

33. Donald E. Bordenkircher, *Tiger Cage: An Untold Story* (Cameron, WV: Abby Publishing, 1998), 48.

34. Ibid., 50.

35. Ibid.

36. Prugh, *Law at War,* 65.

37. Bordenkircher, *Tiger Cage,* 51.

38. Ibid., 73–74.

39. Prugh, *Law at War,* 65.

40. See Douglas Valentine, *The Phoenix Program* (New York: William Morrow, 1990), for an extremely critical treatment of Phoenix in South Vietnam.

41. Nathan Miller, *Spying for America: The Hidden History of U.S. Intelligence* (New York: Dell, 1989), 439.

42. Bordenkircher, *Tiger Cage,* 31.

43. Ibid.

44. Charles D. Ameringer, *U.S. Foreign Intelligence: The Secret Side of American History* (Lexington, MA: D. C. Heath, 2000), 313.

45. See William E. Colby with James McCargar, *Lost Victory: A Firsthand Account of America's Sixteen-Year Involvement in Vietnam* (Chicago: Contemporary Books, 1989). Colby, an OSS and CIA man and director of the Civilian Operations Revolutionary Development Staff in Saigon from 1969 to 1971, wrote this book as a defense of the pacification policies developed by the CIA and State Department in Vietnam. He especially defends the Phoenix program against its critics who damned it as an assassination effort only.

46. The provincial Kit Carson Scouts came under the operational control of the province U.S. Army intelligence officer, the Sector S-2. This force captured hundreds of kilos of documents and any number of prisoners during the author's 1970 tour in Vietnam. Because the scouts were all former Vietcong, the command was considered very sensitive at the time.

47. Debrief, Lieutenant Robert C. Doyle, U.S. Navy , Naval Historical Center, Washington Navy Yard, Washington, DC, 19 September 1978.

48. Prugh, *Law at War,* appendix H.

49. See Edward S. Herman, *Atrocities in Vietnam: Myths and Realities* (Philadelphia; Pilgrim Press, 1970), 30–33, for grizzly summations of supposed U.S. and ARVN torture.

50. "Inspections and Investigations of War Crimes," MACV Directive 20-41, 18 May 1968, in Prugh, *Law at War,* 137–38.

51. For a counterargument against supposed American blood lust, see A. Francis Hatch, "One Despicable Part of the Vietnam War Is the False Portrayal of American Soldiers as Bloodthirsty Barbarians," *Vietnam Magazine,* August 1995, 58, 60–62. It should also be noted that the courts-martial of these soldiers and marines were based on various offenses, not just prisoner abuse.

52. "U.S. Army Disciplinary Actions, Republic of Vietnam, 1965–1972," appendix K, in Prugh, *Law at War,* 154.

53. Prugh, *Law at War,* 71.

54. Ibid.

55. Edith K. Roosevelt, "How They Treat Red POWs in S. Vietnam," *Connecticut Sunday Herald,* 25 June 1972.

56. Prugh, *Law at War,* 72.

57. For a South Vietnamese evaluation of the suffering endured by members of special units after hostilities ended in April 1975, see Nguyen Van Canh and Earle Cooper, *Vietnam under Communism, 1975–1982* (Stanford, CA: Hoover Institution Press, 1983).

58. See Zalin Grant, *Survivors: American POW's in Vietnam* (1975; reprint, New York: Berkley, 1985), and Monika Schwinn and Bernhard Diehl, *We Came to Help* (New York: Harcourt Brace Jovanovich, 1976), for one side of the Garwood story. See Winston Groom and Duncan Spencer, *Conversations with the Enemy: The Story of PFC Robert Garwood* (New York: Putnam, 1983) for Garwood's side. See also Charles L. Nichols, "Article 105: Misconduct as a Prisoner," *Air Force JAG Law Review* 11 (Fall 1969): 393–98, for a legal perspective on Vietnam POW behavior.

59. Groom and Spencer, *Conversations with the Enemy,* 344.

60. Ibid.

61. In the film, Garwood received more positive treatment than he did from the U.S. Marine Corps. See *The Last P.O.W.? Bobby Garwood Story,* directed by George Stafford Brown, with Ralph Macchio and Martin Sheen (1990). It was a British production, not shown in the United States until 1993.

62. Prugh, *Law at War,* 78.

63. See Engineer Studies Group, *U.S. Preparedness for Future Enemy Prisoner of War/Detainee Operations* (Washington, DC: Department of the Army, Office, Chief of Engineers, January 1977), C-11–D-35.

64. See Jeffrey J. Clarke, *United States Army in Vietnam, Advice and Support: The Final Years, 1965–1973* (Washington, DC: U.S. Army, Center of Military History, 1988), 170. See also *The Historical Management of POWs: A Synopsis of the 1968 US Army Provost Marshal General's Study Entitled "A Review of United States Policy on Treatment of Prisoners of War"* (San Diego, CA: Naval Health Research Center, 1970), 49–59, for a review of the problematic history of EPW policies developed during the Vietnam War.

65. Clarke, *United States Army in Vietnam,* 377.

Chapter Fourteen. To Desert Storm and Beyond

1. Alan Axelrod, *America's Wars* (New York: John Wiley and Sons, 2002), 499.

2. Quoted in ibid., 500.

3. Ronald H. Cole, *Operation Urgent Fury: The Planning and Execution of Joint Operations in Grenada 12 October–21 November 1983* (Washington, DC: Joint History Office of the Chairman of the Joint Chiefs of Staff, 1997), 62, http://www.dtic.mil/doctrine/jel/history/urgfury.pdf (accessed 12 January 2009). See also General H. Norman Schwarzkopf, with Peter Petre, *The Autobiography: It Doesn't Take a Hero* (New York: Bantam,1993), 276–308, for a personal narrative and analysis of the Granada operation.

4. See James R. Locher III, "Taking Stock of Goldwater-Nichols," *JFQ* (Autumn 1999): 10–16; Ronald H. Cole, "Grenada, Panama, and Haiti: Joint Operational Reform," *JFQ* (Autumn–Winter 1998–1999): 57–64; William A Owens, "Making the Joint Journey," *JFQ* (Spring 1999): 92–95, for expert explanations of the development of joint commands that dominate military operations today.

5. Michael R. Gordon, "U.S. Troops Move in Panama in Effort to Seize Noriega; Gunfire Is Heard in Capital," *New York Times,* 20 December 1990, A1.

6. See Axelrod, *America's Wars,* 502–3.

7. David Brooks, "Saddam's Brain: The Ideology behind the Thuggery," *Weekly Standard,* 11 November 2002, 24.

8. Axelrod, *America's Wars,* 503.

9. Ibid., 504.

10. Andrew Rosenthal, "No Ground Fighting Yet; Call to Arms by Hussein," *New York Times,* 17 January 1991, A1.

11. President George H. W. Bush, televised address to the nation, 16 January 1991, quoted in Axelrod, *America's Wars,* 506.

12. See Axelrod, *America's Wars,* 505.

13. John R. Brinkerhoff, Ted Silva, and John Seitz, *United States Army Reserve in Operation Desert Storm, Enemy Prisoner of War Operations: The 800th Military Police Brigade* (Washington, DC: Department of the Army, 1992), 1.

14. Lieutenant Colonel Jon Bilbo, *Enemy Prisoners of War (EPW) Operations during Operation Desert Storm,* Individual Study Project (Carlisle, PA: U.S. Army War College, 15 April 1992), 65–66.

15. U.S. forces took 63,948, the British took 5,005, the French 869, and Arab forces took 16,921. The U.S. numbers include 1,492 displaced civilians. See *Conduct of the Persian Gulf War* (Washington, DC: Department of Defense, 1992), 578.

16. Ibid., 577.

17. Brinkerhoff et al., *United States Army Reserve in Operation Desert Storm,* 7.

18. Lieutenant Colonel Dario T. Cappucci Jr., VC, USAR, and Lieutenant Colonel Stanley L. K. Flemming, MC, USAR, "Medical Observations of Malingering in Iraqi Enemy Prisoners of War during Operation Desert Storm," *Military Medicine* 159 (June 1994): 462–63.

19. Shortly after the conclusion of the Persian Gulf War, the author informally interviewed two U.S. Marine Corps reservists who believed that the Coalition and the Marine Corps went to extremes to render humane treatment strictly in accordance with the Geneva Convention on Prisoners of War. One reservist was an enlisted woman who, on orders from her sergeant, hid her gender from the EPWs as well as she could. The other informant was her sergeant, who expressed

his concern that the Iraqi EPWs might riot if they thought a woman was guarding them. Nothing of substance took place in their holding area, except that the marines removed a sizable number of teenage boys from the compound. Rightly or wrongly, the young marines believed that these boys did not belong in a compound with mature enemy soldiers.

20. *Conduct of the Persian Gulf War,* 577.

21. Ibid., 619.

22. U.S. POWs of the Gulf War attempted to bring a suit against Iraq in April 2002. Although they won the suit initially, the U.S. government opposed it and argued the case in the Supreme Court. The government won; the POWs never received any compensation for their injuries. See Adam Liptak, "U.S. Fights Verdict Backing Ex-P.O.W.'s," *New York Times,* 29 July 2003, http://www.nytimes.com/2003/07/29/politics/29POW.html?ei=1&en=d82fec656bca6f3e&ex=1060507680&pagewanted=print&position= (accessed 23 January 2009).

23. *Conduct of the Persian Gulf War,* 586–87.

24. Steve van Buskirk, "Enemy Ex-POWs in Our Midst?" *VFW Magazine,* January 1994, 36.

25. Bilbo, *Enemy Prisoners of War Operations,* 99–100.

26. Alvin Toffler and Heidi Toffler, "War, Wealth, and a New Era in History," *World Monitor* 4, no. 5 (May 1991): 51. See also Alvin Toffler, *The Third Wave* (New York: Bantam, 1980), for a futuristic explanation of the 1980s and 1990s.

27. See "The Hunt for Osama," *Time,* 17 May 2004, 19.

28. Brooks, "Saddam's Brain," 26.

29. Serge Schmemann, "U.S. Attacked; Hijacked Jets Destroy Twin Towers and Hit Pentagon in Day of Terror: President Vows to Exact Punishment for 'Evil,'" *New York Times,* 12 September 2001, A1.

30. Ibid.

31. Personal correspondence with Kelly Hackett, 14 October 2001.

32. Personal correspondence with Dr. Geoffrey Megargee, 14 October 2001.

33. Schmemann, "U.S. Attacked," A1.

34. See Jayshree Bajoria, "Backgrounder," Council of Foreign Relations (updated 18 April 2008), 3, http://cfr.org/publications/9126/ (accessed 23 January 2009).

35. Interview with Javier Jordán, "Radical Islamism, Secular Fundamentalism and the Clash," ZENIT, the Vatican News Service, 18 May 2004.

36. See George Friedman, *America's Secret War: Inside the Hidden Worldwide Struggle between the United States and Its Enemies* (New York: Broadway Books, 2004), 79.

37. See Robert J. Lieber, "The Neoconservative-Conspiracy Theory: Pure Myth," *Chronicle Review* 49, no. 34 (2003): B14.

38. "1996: Taliban Take over Kabul, and End Mujahideen Rule," http://terrorism.about.com/od/warinafghanistan/ss/AfghanistanWar_5.htm (accessed 23 January 2009).

39. Quoted in Axelrod, *America's Wars,* 519.

40. See "Afghanistan: A U.S. Combat Chronology, 2001–2006," *VFW Magazine,* March 2006, 16.

41. Quoted in Amy Zalman, "War in Afghanistan—the History behind the U.S. War in Afghanistan," http://terrorism.about.com/od/warinafghanistan/ss/AfghanistanWar_6.htm (accessed 24 January 2009).

42. Axelrod, *America's Wars*, 520.

43. See Friedman, *America's Secret War*, 151–89, for a strategic analysis of the Afghanistan war and the Special Forces' relationship with the Northern Alliance forces.

44. "Afghanistan: A U.S. Combat Chronology," 17.

45. Adrian Lewis, *The American Culture of War: The History of U.S. Military Force from World War II to Operation Iraqi Freedom* (New York: Routledge, 2007), 399.

46. Susan Candiotti, "Walker Lindh Sentenced to 20 Years," CNN.com/Law Center, 4 October 2002, http://archives.cnn.com/2002/LAW/10/04/lindh.staterment (accessed 25 January 2009).

47. See Arnold Krammer, *Prisoners of War: A Reference Handbook* (Westport, CT: Praeger, 2008), 66–67.

48. Pentagon briefing, "The War on Terrorism," Office of Public Affairs, Department of Defense, 17 January 2002, 1–2.

Chapter Fifteen. Iraqi Freedom, Abu Ghraib, and Guantánamo

1. Michael R. Gordon and General Bernard E. Trainor, *Cobra II: The Inside Story of the Invasion and Occupation of Iraq* (New York: Pantheon, 2006), 5.

2. See Richard A. Clarke, *Your Government Failed You: Breaking the Cycle of National Security Disasters* (New York: HarperCollins, 2008), 52. Clarke discusses the fate of General Eric Shinseki, army chief of staff before the Iraq war began. When Shinseki came to the conclusion that a huge troop strength was needed for both combat and postcombat operations in Iraq, he was forced to leave his post and retire.

3. Gordon and Trainor, *Cobra II*, 8.

4. Ibid., 19.

5. George W. Bush, "Detention, Treatment, and Trial of Certain Non-Citizens in the War Against Terror," *Federal Register* 66, no. 2 (16 November 2001): 57831–36, quoted in Karen J. Greenberg and Joshua L. Dratel, eds., *The Torture Papers: The Road to Abu Ghraib* (New York: Cambridge University Press, 2005), 25–28.

6. John Yoo, deputy assistant attorney general, and Robert J. Dalhunty, special counsel, "Memorandum for William J. Haynes II, General Counsel, Department of Defense, U.S. Department of Justice, Office of Legal Counsel, Office of the Deputy Assistant Attorney General," 9 January 2002, quoted in Greenberg and Dratel, *Torture Papers*, 38–79. For a legal criticism of this position, see George H. Aldrich, "The Taliban, al-Qaeda, and the Determination of Illegal Combatants," *American Journal of International Law* 96 (2002): 891–98, http:www.lexisnexis.com (accessed 6 February 2009). Aldrich contends that the Taliban should be accorded EPW status; al-Qaeda fighters and operatives, however, are criminals and lie outside the Geneva Convention.

7. George W. Bush, "Humane Treatment of al-Qaeda and Taliban Detainees," Memorandum for the Vice President, Secretary of State, Secretary of Defense, At-

torney General, Chief of Staff to the President, Director of Central Intelligence, Assistant to the President for National Security Affairs, and Chairman of the Joint Chiefs of Staff, 7 February 2002, quoted in Mark Danner, *Torture and Truth: America, Abu Ghraib, and the War on Terror* (New York: New York Review of Books, 2004), 105–6.

8. Secretary of State Colin L. Powell to George W. Bush, "Draft Decision Memorandum for the President on the Applicability of the Geneva Convention to the Conflict in Afghanistan," quoted in Greenberg and Dratel, *Torture Papers,* 123.

9. See "Iraq: A U.S. Combat Chronology, 2003–2006," *VFW Magazine,* March 2005, 22–23.

10. Camp Bucca was named after Ronald Bucca, one of the firefighters who died at the World Trade Center in New York on 9/11. See Arnold Krammer, *Prisoners of War: A Reference Handbook* (Westport, CT: Praeger, 2008), 67.

11. Lieutenant Colonel Jeremy John Hobart Tuck, "Medical Management of Iraqi Enemy Prisoners of War during Operation Telic," *Military Medicine* 170, no. 3 (March 2005): 178.

12. Saddam Hussein was known as "Black List #1" by U.S. Army interrogators in Iraq. The intricate and highly professional search for him has been chronicled in Eric Maddox with Davin Seay, *Mission: Black List #1: The Inside Story of the Search for Saddam Hussein as Told by the Soldier Who Mastermided His Capture* (New York: HarperCollins, 2008). The search for al-Qaeda chieftain Abu Musab al Zarqawi in 2007 was similar and can be found in Matthew Alexander with John R. Bruning, *How to Break a Terrorist: The U.S. Interrogators Who Used Brains, Not Brutality, to Take Down the Deadliest Man in Iraq* (New York: Free Press, 2008).

13. "Abu Ghraib Prison Prisoner Abuse: A Chronology," http://globalsecurity. org/intell/world/iraq/abu-ghurayb-chronology, 4 (accessed 2 February 2009).

14. "Iraqi Prisoner Abuse 'Un-American,' Says Rumsfeld," *Washington Times,* http://www.washtimes.com/national/20040507–115901–6736r.htm (accessed 2 February 2009).

15. "Report on Detention and Correction in Iraq," Article 15–6 Investigation of the 800th Military Police Brigade, also known as the Taguba report, http://news .findlaw.com/hdocs/docs/iraq/tagubarpt.html (accessed 3 February 2009).

16. Gordon and Trainor, *Cobra II,* 99.

17. "Final Report of the Independent Panel to Review DOD Detention Operations," August 2004, 54, quoted in Gordon and Trainor, *Cobra II,* 100.

18. See Alex Kingsbury, "Q&A: Philip Gourevitch: Recalling the Shame of Abu Ghraib," *U.S. News & World Report,* 9 June 2008, 14.

19. "The ICRC Report: Report of the International Committee of the Red Cross (ICRC) on the Treatment by the Coalition Forces of Prisoners of War and Other Protected Persons by the Geneva Convention in Iraq during Arrest, Internment and Interrogation," February 2004, in Greenberg and Dratel, *Torture Papers,* 403. See also Danner, *Torture and Truth,* 251–75, for the ICRC report. This book is a compilation of Danner's essays and original report documents and is similar to Greenberg and Dratel, *Torture Papers.*

20. Taguba report, "Findings and Recommendations" (part 1).

21. Taguba report, "Specific Findings of Facts." See also Michelle Brown, "'Setting the Conditions' for Abu Ghraib: The Prison Nation Abroad," *American Quarterly* 57, no. 3 (September 2005): 973–97, for an extremely harsh criticism of the Abu Ghraib scandal and the implication that the terrible events at Abu Ghraib were really just "terror as usual" in the American penal system.

22. Taguba report, "Specific Findings of Facts."

23. Ibid.

24. See George Friedman, *America's Secret War: Inside the Hidden Worldwide Struggle between the United States and its Enemies* (New York: Broadway Books, 2004), 326. Friedman argues that the Iraqis were not shocked or surprised by the Abu Ghraib events. Saddam Hussein's torturers behaved far more violently.

25. Translation of statement by Detainee 151108, 18 January 2004, in Greenberg and Dratel, *Torture Papers,* 503.

26. Translation of statement by Detainee 19446, 18 January 2004, in ibid., 501.

27. "ICRC Report," February 2004, in ibid., 395.

28. Taguba report, in ibid., 444.

29. "Abu Ghraib Prison Prisoner Abuse: A Chronology," 5.

30. Ibid., 1.

31. Lolita C. Baldor, "Pentagon Issues Guidelines for Detainee Treatment," *Army Times,* 9 November 2005, http://www.armytimes.com/story.php?f=1–292925–1231770.php (accessed 6 February 2009).

32. Major James F. Gebhardt, "The Road to Abu Ghraib: U.S. Army Detainee Doctrine and Experience," *Military Review* (January–February 2005): 50.

33. "Iraq to Reopen Abu Ghraib Prison," Associated Press, 26 January 2009, http://military.com (accessed 6 February 2009).

34. This version of the "GTMO Song" comes from a traditional version recorded by Oscar Brand, a popular folksinger of the 1950s and 1960s.

35. The author was the damage control assistant aboard the USS *Steinaker* and experienced refresher training at GTMO firsthand in 1969. Never were the officers and crew so glad to leave a port, saying, "anywhere but GTMO," as the ship steamed back to its home port of Norfolk, Virginia.

36. See Lieutenant Colonel Gordon Cucullu, *Inside Gitmo: The True Story behind the Myths of Guantánamo Bay* (New York: HarperCollins, 2009), 3.

37. Ibid., 4.

38. Ibid., 6.

39. See Adrian R. Lewis, *The American Culture of War: The History of U.S. Military Force from World War II to Operation Iraqi Freedom* (New York: Routledge, 2007), 399. Lewis suggests that the United States needed a much larger force in Afghanistan in 2001.

40. The author attended the navy's SERE school in 1970 before deployment to Vietnam. The present curriculum differs considerably from the one used in 1970, but the principles remain intact.

41. *Manchester Manual,* British translation, 19, http://www.usdoj.gov/ag/manual (accessed 9 February 2009).

42. Ibid., 12.

43. Ibid., 176.

44. Cucullu, *Inside Gitmo,* 135.

45. "Guantánamo Suicides 'Acts of War,'" BBC News, 6 November 2006, http://news.bbc.uk/go/pr/fr/-/2hi/americas/5068606.stm (accessed 10 February 1009).

46. Cucullu, *Inside Gitmo,* 117.

47. Ibid., 121.

48. See Friedman, *America's Secret War,* 119–23. Friedman argues that the American legal system was not equipped to deal with al-Qaeda then or now.

49. Neil A. Lewis, "U.S. Alters Rules for War Crime Trials," *New York Times,* 1 September 2005, http://www.nytimes.com/2005/09/01/politics/01detain.html (accessed 1 September 2005).

50. The Obama administration revoked the "enemy combatant" status on 13 March 2009, but nothing replaced it.

51. "Fact Sheet: Military Commissions," U.S. Department of Defense, 8 February 2007, http://www.defenselink.mil/news/commissionacts.html (accessed 11 February 2009).

52. "Fact Sheet: Military Commissions," American Civil Liberties Union, n.d., http://aclu.org/safefree/detention/29145res20070322.html (accessed 11 February 2009).

53. See Robert J. Caldwell, "Bush, McCain and 'Torture,'" *San Diego Union Tribune,* 24 September 2006, http://signonsandiego.com/uniontrib/20060924/news_mz1e24caldwe.htm (accessed 11 February 2009).

54. See Cucullu, *Inside Gitmo,* 145–46.

55. "'Rendition' and Secret Detention: A Global System of Human Rights Violations, Questions and Answers," *Amnesty International,* n.d., 1, http://www.amnesty.org (accessed 11 February 2009).

56. Ibid., 3–4.

57. See ibid., 6–7, for abbreviated testimonies by former detainees.

58. See Friedman, *America's Secret War,* 256–57, for a discussion of the arbitrary but effective nature of rendition.

Chapter Sixteen. The Evolution of New Paradigms

1. W. L. La Croix, S. J., *War and International Ethics: Tradition and Today* (Lanham, MD: University Press of America, 1988), 19.

2. See ibid., 21.

3. Richard Garrett, *P.O.W.: The Uncivil Face of War* (Devon: David and Charles, 1981), 28.

4. Quoted in Richard A Falk, *The Vietnam War and International Law* (Princeton, NJ: Princeton University Press, 1968), 17–23.

5. Herbert C. Fooks, *Prisoners of War* (Federalsburg, MD: J. W. Stowell, 1924), 272.

6. Vallandigham appealed to the Supreme Court and won; thus he never served the two-year sentence imposed by the military commission.

7. Quoted in Falk, *Vietnam War and International Law,* 20.

8. See La Croix, *War and International Ethics,* 142.

9. See Robert C. Doyle, *Voices from Captivity: Interpreting the American Captivity Narrative* (Lawrence: University Press of Kansas, 1994), 47–49.

10. See Edouard Victor Isaacs, *Prisoner of the U-90* (New York: Houghton Mifflin, 1919); James Norman Hall, *My Island Home: An Autobiography* (Boston: Little, Brown, 1952).

11. See Stephen F. Hayes, "On Richard Clarke," *Weekly Standard,* 22 March 2004.

12. See Michael Bess, *Choices under Fire: Moral Dimensions of World War II* (New York: Vintage, 2008), 142.

13. See Patrick Lee, "Interrogational Torture," *American Journal of Jurisprudence* 51 (2006): 131–47, for a philosophical discussion of torture. He concludes that torture is intrinsically immoral, especially if it is inflicted for sadistic pleasure.

14. Ibid., 132.

15. John McCain, with Mark Salter, *Faith of My Fathers: A Family Memoir* (New York: Random House, 1999), 225.

16. Jeremiah A. Denton Jr., with Ed Brandt Jr., *When Hell Was in Session* (Washington, DC: Morely Books, 1997), 88–91.

17. See "Is Torture Ever Justified," *Economist,* 22 September 2007, 72.

18. Arnold Krammer, *Prisoners of War: A Reference Handbook* (Westport, CT: Praeger, 2008), 77.

19. See "Promises to Keep," *Economist,* 31 January 2009, 38.

20. See Associated Press, "Taliban Fighters Have up to 15,000 Fighters," http://www.military.com/news/article/taliban-may-have-up-to-15000-fighters .html?wh=news (accessed 3 March 2009).

21. See Associated Press, "US Military Says Number of Iraq Detainees Falling," http://news.yahoo.com/s/ap/20090303/ap_on_re_mi_ea/ml_iraq (accessed 3 March 2009).

22. La Croix, *War and International Ethics,* 126.

23. See "U.S. Says C.I.A. Destroyed 92 Tapes of Interrogations," *New York Times,* 3 March 2009, http://www.nytimes.com/2009/03/03/washington/03web -intel.html (accessed 3 March 2009).

24. Robert Guest, "Goodbye Guantánamo," *Economist: The World in 2009,* January 2009, 36.

25. La Croix, *War and International Ethics,* 93.

Bibliography

Books and Articles

Abbot, John S. C. *American Pioneers and Patriots: Miles Standish, the Puritan Captain.* New York: Doss and Mead, 1872.

Adelberg, Michael S. "An Evenly Balanced County: The Scope and Severity of Civil Warfare in Revolutionary Monmouth County, New Jersey." *Journal of Military History* 73 (January 2009): 9–47.

"Afghanistan: A U.S. Combat Chronology, 2001–2006." *VFW Magazine*, March 2006, 16–19, 20.

Aldrich, George H. "The Taliban, al-Qaeda, and the Determination of Illegal Combatants." *American Journal of International Law* 96 (2002): 891–98.

Alexander, Matthew, with John R. Bruning. *How to Break a Terrorist: The U.S. Interrogators Who Used Brains, Not Brutality, to Take Down the Deadliest Man in Iraq.* New York: Free Press, 2008.

Altoff, Gerard T. *Amongst My Best Men: African Americans and the War of 1812.* Put-in-Bay, OH: Perry Group, 1996.

"America's War Dead, 1775–2008: A Memorial Listing by the Numbers." *VFW Magazine*, May 2008, 24–26.

Ameringer, Charles D. *U.S. Foreign Intelligence: The Secret Side of American History.* Lexington, MA: D. C. Heath, 2000.

Anburey, Thomas. *Travels through the Interior Parts of America.* 1789. Reprint, New York: Arno, 1969.

Anderson, Gary C. *Little Crow: Spokesman for the Sioux.* St. Paul: Minnesota Historical Society Press, 1986.

Anderson, Gary C., and Alan R. Woolworth, eds. *Through Dakota Eyes: Narrative Accounts of the Minnesota Indian War of 1862.* St. Paul: Minnesota Historical Society Press, 1988.

Andrew, Christopher. *For the President's Eyes Only: Secret Intelligence and the American Presidency from Washington to Bush.* New York: HarperCollins, 1995.

Andrews, Charles M. *Guide to the Materials for American History, to 1783, in the Public Record Office of Great Britain.* 2 vols. Washington, DC: U.S. Government Printing Office, 1912–1914.

Axelrod, Alan. *America's Wars.* New York: John Wiley and Sons, 2002.

Axinn, Sydney. *A Moral Military.* Philadelphia: Temple University Press, 1989.

Ayres, Leonard P. *The War with Germany: A Statistical Summary.* Washington, DC: U.S. Government Printing Office, 1919.

Bacque, James. *Other Losses: An Investigation into the Mass Deaths of German Prisoners in the Hands of the French and Americans after World War II.* Toronto: Stoddart, 1989.

Baker, Lillian. *American and Japanese Relocation in World War II: Fact, Fiction, and Fallacy.* Medford, OR: Webb Research Group, 1990.

Baldwin, Leland D. *The Adult American History.* Rindge, NH: Richard R. Smith, 1955.

Barker, A. J. *Behind Barbed Wire.* London: Purnell Book Services, 1974.

———. *Prisoners of War.* New York: Universe, 1975.

Barnby, H. M. *The Prisoners of Algiers.* New York: Oxford University Press, 1966.

Barrett, S. M. ed. *Geronimo: His Own Story.* New York: Ballantine, 1974.

———. *Geronimo: My Life.* 1906. Reprint, Mineola, NY: Dover, 2005.

Basile, Leon. *The Civil War Diary of Amos E. Stearns, a Prisoner at Andersonville.* Rutherford, NJ: Fairleigh Dickinson University Press, 1981.

Becker, Laura L. "Prisoners of War in the American Revolution: A Community Perspective." *Military Affairs* 46, no. 4 (December 1982): 169–73.

Beech, Keyes. *Tokyo and Points East.* Garden City, NY: Doubleday, 1954.

Beede, Benjamin R., ed. *The War of 1898 and U.S. Interventions, 1898–1934: An Encyclopedia.* New York: Garland, 1994.

Berkhofer, Robert F. Jr. *The White Man's Indian: Images of the American Indian from Columbus to the Present.* New York: Vintage, 1979.

Bess, Michael. *Choices under Fire: Moral Dimensions of World War II.* New York: Vintage, 2008.

Bethell, Nicholas. *The Last Secret: Forcible Repatriation to Russia, 1944–7.* London: Andre Deutsch, 1974.

Biderman, Albert D. *March to Calumny: The Story of American POW's in the Korean War.* New York: Macmillan, 1963.

Biess, Frank. *Homecomings: Returning POWs and the Legacies of Defeat in Postwar Germany.* Princeton, NJ: Princeton University Press, 2006.

Bilbo, Lieutenant Colonel Jon. *Enemy Prisoners of War (EPW) Operations during Operation Desert Storm.* Individual Study Project. Carlisle, PA: U.S. Army War College, 15 April 1992.

Billington, Ray Allen. *The Westward Movement in the United States.* New York: D. Van Nostrand, 1959.

Bischof, Günter, and Stephen E. Ambrose, eds. *Eisenhower and the German POWs: Facts against Falsehood.* Baton Rouge: Louisiana State University Press, 1992.

Blanco, Richard L., and Paul J. Sanborn, eds. *The American Revolution, 1775–1783: An Encyclopedia.* New York: Garland, 1993.

Boatner, Haydon L. "POW's for Sale." *American Legion,* August 1962, 14.

Böhme, Kurt W. *Die deutschen Kriegsgefangenen in amerikanischer Hand—Europa.* Vol. 10.2. Munich: Gieseking, 1973.

Boller, Paul F. Jr. *Memoirs of an Obscure Professor and Other Essays.* Fort Worth: Texas Christian University Press, 1992.

Bondy, Curt. "Observation and Reeducation of German Prisoners of War." *Harvard Educational Review* 14 (January 1944): 12–19.

Bordenkircher, Donald E. *Tiger Cage: An Untold Story*. Cameron, WV: Abby Publishing, 1998.

Bordewich, Fergus. *Killing the White Man's Indian: Reinventing Native Americans at the End of the Twentieth Century*. New York: Doubleday, 1996.

Boughton, D. H. "How Soldiers Have Ruled in the Philippines." *International Quarterly* (December–March 1902): 215–28.

Bowers, Clarence H. "Builders of an Island Empire." *Bulletin of the American Historical Collection* 23 (July–September 1995): 7–28.

Bowers, William T., William M. Hammond, and George L. MacGarrigle. *Black Soldier White Army: The 24th Infantry Regiment in Korea*. Washington, DC: U.S. Army Center of Military History, 1996.

Bowie, Lucy Leigh. "German Prisoners in the American Revolution." *Maryland Historical Magazine*, September 1945, 185–200.

Boyd, Belle. *Belle Boyd, Confederate Spy*. Baton Rouge: Louisiana State University Press, 1998.

Brackman, Arnold C. *The Other Nuremberg: The Untold Story of the Tokyo War Crimes Trials*. New York: William Morrow, 1987.

Brandon, William. *Indians*. Boston: Houghton Mifflin, 1961.

Brannon, John, ed. *Official Letters of the Military and Naval Officers of the United States, during the War with Great Britain in the Years 1812, 13, 14 & 15*. 1823. Reprint, New York: Arno Press and New York Times, 1971.

Brew, Sarah L. "Making Amends for History: Legislative Reparations for Japanese Americans and Other Minority Groups." *Law and Inequality* 8 (1989): 179–201.

Brinkerhoff, John R., Ted Silva, and John Seitz. *United States Army Reserve in Operation Desert Storm, Enemy Prisoner of War Operations: The 800th Military Police Brigade*. Washington, DC: Department of the Army, 1992.

Brinkley, H. H. "The Loss of the *Lapwing*, Post Office Packet." *Mariner's Mirror* 16 (January 1930): 18–47.

Brooke, James. "After Silence, Italians Recall the Internment." *New York Times International*, 11 August 1997.

———. "Germans Back on U.S. Base, Now as Tenants." *New York Times*, 14 August 1996.

Brooks, David. "Saddam's Brain: The Ideology behind the Thuggery." *Weekly Standard*, 11 November 2002, 22–26.

Brown, Alexander D. *The Galvanized Yankees*. Urbana: University of Illinois Press, 1963.

Brown, Dee. *Bury My Heart at Wounded Knee*. New York: Holt, Rinehart and Winston, 1971.

Brown, Michelle. "'Setting the Conditions' for Abu Ghraib: The Prison Nation Abroad." *American Quarterly* 57, no. 3 (September 2005): 973–97.

Bryant, Charles S., and Abel B. Murch. *A History of the Great Massacre by the Sioux Indians in Minnesota*. Cincinnati, OH: Rickey and Carrol, 1864.

Buhmann, Heide, and Hanspeter Haeseler. *Das kleine dicke Liederbuch: Lieder und Tänze bis unsere Zeit*. Darmstadt: Hollman, 1994.

Burdett, Thomas F. "A New Evaluation of General Otis' Leadership in the Philippines." *Military Review* 55 (January 1955): 79–87.

Burdick, Charles, and Ursula Moessner. *The German Prisoners of War in Japan, 1914–1920*. Lanham, MD: University Press of America, 1984.

Burnham, Philip. "Andersonvilles of the North." *Military History Quarterly* (Autumn 1997): 48–55.

Burrows, Edwin G. *Forgotten Patriots: The Untold Story of American Prisoners during the Revolutionary War*. New York: Basic Books, 2008.

Burt, Kendal, and James Leasor. *The One that Got Away*. New York: Ballantine, 1957.

Bush, George W. "Detention, Treatment, and Trial of Certain Non-Citizens in the War against Terror." *Federal Register* 66, no. 2 (16 November 2001): 57831–36.

Butler, Steven R., ed. *A Documentary History of the Mexican War*. Richardson, TX: Descendants of Mexican War Veterans, 1995.

Califano, Joseph Jr. *Governing America: An Insider's Report from the White House and the Cabinet*. New York: Simon and Schuster, 1981.

Calloway, Colin G. *First Peoples: A Documentary History of American Indian Peoples*. Boston: Bedford/St. Martin's, 1999.

Canh, Nguyen Van, and Earle Cooper. *Vietnam under Communism, 1975–1982*. Stanford, CA: Hoover Institution Press, 1983.

Cappucci, Lieutenant Colonel Dario T. Jr., and Lieutenant Colonel Stanley L. K. Flemming. "Medical Observations of Malingering in Iraqi Enemy Prisoners of War during Operation Desert Storm." *Military Medicine* 159 (June 1994): 462–64.

Carley, Kenneth. *The Sioux Uprising of 1862*. St. Paul: Minnesota Historical Society, 1976.

Carlson, Lewis H. *Remembered Prisoners of a Forgotten War: An Oral History of Korean War POWs*. New York: St. Martin's, 2002.

———. *We Were Each Other's Prisoners: An Oral History of World War II American and German Prisoners of War*. New York: Basic Books, 1997.

Carr-Gregg, Charlotte. *Japanese Prisoners of War in Revolt: The Outbreaks at Featherston and Cowra during World War II*. Brisbane, Australia: University of Queensland Press, 1978.

Carruth, Gorton. *The Encyclopedia of American Facts and Dates*. 10th ed. New York: HarperCollins, 1997.

Chadwick, Bruce. *The Two American Presidents: A Dual Biography of Abraham Lincoln and Jefferson Davis*. New York: Birch Lane, 1998.

Chambers, John Whiteclay II, ed. *The Oxford Companion to American Military History*. New York: Oxford University Press, 1999.

Chaput, Donald. "Private William W. Grayson's War in the Philippines, 1899." *Nebraska History* 61 (Fall 1980): 355–66.

Chávez, Ernesto. *The U.S. War with Mexico: A Brief History with Documents*. Boston: Bedford/St. Martin's, 2008.

Chidsey, Donald Barr. *The Loyalists: The Story of Those Americans Who Fought against Independence*. New York: Crown, 1973.

Clark, Mark W. *From the Danube to the Yalu*. New York: Harper and Brothers, 1954.

Clarke, Jeffrey J. *United States Army in Vietnam, Advice and Support: The Final

Years, 1965–1973. Washington, DC: U.S. Army, Center of Military History, 1988.

Clarke, Richard A. *Your Government Failed You: Breaking the Cycle of National Security Disasters.* New York: HarperCollins, 2008.

Clavell, James. *King Rat.* 1962. Reprint, New York: Dell, 1980.

Clifford, Jim. "Fort McPherson, Georgia." *On Point* 12, no. 3 (Winter 2006): 27–29.

Cogliano, Francis D. *No King, No Popery: Anti-Catholicism in Revolutionary New England.* Westport, CT: Greenwood, 1995.

Colby, William E., with James McCargar. *Lost Victory: A Firsthand Account of America's Sixteen-Year Involvement in Vietnam.* Chicago: Contemporary Books, 1989.

Cole, Ronald H. "Grenada, Panama, and Haiti: Joint Operational Reform." *JFQ* (Autumn–Winter 1998–1999): 57–64.

———. *Operation Urgent Fury: The Planning and Execution of Joint Operations in Grenada 12 October–21 November 1983.* Washington, DC: Joint History Office of the Chairman of the Joint Chiefs of Staff, 1997.

Commager, Henry Steele, and Milton Cantor, eds. *The Documents of American History.* 10th ed. Englewood Cliffs, NJ: Prentice Hall, 1988.

Conduct of the Persian Gulf War. Washington, DC: Department of Defense, 1992.

Connolly, John. *A Narrative of the Transactions, Imprisonment, and Sufferings of John Connolly.* 1783. Reprint, New York: Charles L. Woodward, 1889.

Cook, Haruko Taya, and Theodore F. Cook. *Japan at War: An Oral History.* New York: New Press, 1992.

Cook, Tim. "The Politics of Surrender: Canadian Soldiers and the Killing of Prisoners in the Great War." *Journal of Military History* 70 (July 2006): 637–66.

Cowley, Robert, and Geoffrey Parker, eds. *The Readers Companion to Military History.* Boston: Houghton Mifflin, 1996.

Craig, H. "Notes on the Action between the *Hornet* and *Peacock*." *American Neptune* 11, no. 1 (January 1951): 73–76.

Crane, C. "The Fighting Tactics of Filipinos." *Journal of the Military Service Institution of the United States* 30 (July 1902): 499–507.

Crane, Major C. J. "Paragraphs 93, 97 and 88, of General Orders 100." *Journal of the Military Service Institution of the United States* 32 (March–April 1903): 254–56.

Crawford, Michael J., ed. *The Naval War of 1812: A Documentary History.* Vol. 3. Washington, DC: Naval Historical Center, 2002.

Cucullu, Lieutenant Colonel Gordon. *Inside Gitmo: The True Story behind the Myths of Guantánamo Bay.* New York: HarperCollins, 2009.

Cunliffe, Marcus. *George Washington: Man and Monument.* New York: New American Library, 1982.

Dackaert-Skovira, Alissa. "The Copperhead's Venom." *Journal of Unconventional History* 11, no. 3 (2000): 63–76.

Dallin, David, and Boris Nikolaevsky. *Forced Labor in Soviet Russia.* New Haven, CT: Yale University Press, 1947.

Daniels, Roger. "American Historians and East Asian Immigrants." *Pacific Historical Review* 53, no. 4 (November 1974): 449–72.

————. *Concentration Camps: North America: Japanese in the United States and Canada during World War II*. Malabar, FL: Krieger, 1993.

Danner, Mark. *Torture and Truth: America, Abu Ghraib, and the War on Terror*. New York: New York Review of Books, 2004.

Davis, Daniel. *Behind Barbed Wire*. New York: Dutton, 1982.

Davis, Gerald H. "'Orgelsdorf': A World War I Internment Camp in America." *Yearbook of German-American Studies* 26 (1991): 249–65.

Dean, William F., and William Warden. *General Dean's Story*. New York: Harper and Brothers, 1956.

de las Casas, Bartolomé. *The Devastation of the Indies: A Brief Account*. Trans. Herma Briaffault. Baltimore: Johns Hopkins University Press, 1992.

Denton, Jeremiah A. Jr., with Ed Brandt Jr. *When Hell Was in Session*. Washington, DC: Morely Books, 1997.

DeWeerd, Harvey A. *President Wilson Fights His War: World War I and the American Intervention*. New York: Macmillan, 1968.

Dictionary of American History. Rev. ed. New York: Scribner's Sons, 1976.

Döhla, Johann Conrad. *A Hessian Diary of the American Revolution*. Trans. and ed. Bruce E. Burgoyne. Norman: University of Oklahoma Press, 1990.

Donald, David H. *Lincoln*. New York: Simon and Schuster, 1995.

Dorson, Richard M. *America Rebels: Narratives of the Patriots*. Greenwich, CT: Fawcett, 1966.

Dower, John W. *War without Mercy: Race and Power in the Pacific War*. New York: Pantheon, 1986.

Downey, Fairfax. *Indian Wars of the U.S. Army, 1776–1865*. Garden City, NY: Doubleday, 1963.

Doyle, Robert C. *A Prisoner's Duty: Great Escapes in U.S. Military History*. Annapolis, MD: Naval Institute Press, 1997.

————. *Voices from Captivity: Interpreting the American POW Narrative*. Lawrence: University Press of Kansas, 1994.

Doyle, Susan Badger. "German and Italian Prisoners of War in Albuquerque, 1943–1946." *New Mexico Historical Review* 66, no. 3 (July 1991): 327–40.

Dudley, William S., ed. *The Naval War of 1812: A Documentary History*. 3 vols. Washington, DC: Naval Historical Center, 1985.

Dupuy, Ernest, and William Baumer. *The Little Wars of the United States*. New York: Hawthorne, 1968.

East, Robert A., and Jacob Judd, eds. *The Loyalist Americans: A Focus on Greater New York*. Tarrytown, NY: Sleepy Hollow Restorations, 1975.

Eastman, Max. "The Trial of Eugene Debs." *Liberator* 1, no. 9 (November 1918): 5–12.

Edgerton, Robert B. *Warriors of the Rising Sun: A History of the Japanese Military*. Boulder, CO: Westview, 1997.

Edmunds, W. David. "The Nez Perce Fight for Justice." *American Heritage* 58, no. 5 (Fall 2008): 36–39.

Edwards, John Carver. *Berlin Calling: American Broadcasters in Service to the Third Reich*. New York: Praeger, 1991.

Ehrhart, W. D. *Vietnam-Perkesie: A Combat Marine Memoir*. Jefferson, NC: McFarland, 1983.

Eicher, David J. *The Longest Night: A Military History of the Civil War.* New York: Simon and Schuster, 2001.

Eisenhower, John S. D. *So Far from God: The U.S. War with Mexico, 1846–1848.* Norman: University of Oklahoma Press, 2000.

———. *Yanks: The Epic Story of the American Army in World War I.* New York: Simon and Schuster, 2002.

Eisner, Peter. "Bingham's List." *Smithsonian,* March 2009, 50–57.

Elliott, Mark. "The United States and Forced Repatriation of Soviet Citizens, 1944–47." *Political Science Quarterly* 88, no. 2 (June 1973): 253–75.

Enemy Prisoners of War, Civilian Internees, and Detained Persons. Field Manual 19–40. Washington, DC: Headquarters, Department of the Army, 27 February 1976.

Engineer Studies Group. *U.S. Preparedness for Future Enemy Prisoner of War/Detainee Operations.* Washington, DC: Department of the Army, Office, Chief of Engineers, January 1977.

Epstein, Julius. *Operation Keelhaul: The Story of Forced Repatriation from 1944 to the Present.* Old Greenwich, CT: Devin-Adair, 1973.

Erk, Ludwig, and Franz Magnus Böhme. *Deutsche Liedenhort.* 3 vols. Leipzig, 1893.

Esposito, Vincent J. *The West Point Atlas of War: World War I.* New York: Tess, 1995.

Evanhoe, Ed. *Dark Moon: Eighth Army Special Operations in the Korean War.* Annapolis, MD: Naval Institute Press, 1995.

Exiles in Virginia: With Observations on the Conduct of the Society of Friends during the Revolutionary War, 1777–1778. Philadelphia: Published for the Subscribers, 1848.

Falk, Richard A. *The Vietnam War and International Law.* Princeton, NJ: Princeton University Press, 1968.

Farrar-Hockley, Anthony. *The British Past in the Korean War: An Honourable Discharge.* Vol. 2. London: HMSO, 1995.

Faust, Drew Gilpin. "'Numbers on Top of Numbers': Counting the Civil War Dead." 2006 George C. Marshall Lecture in Military History. *Journal of Military History* 70 (October 2006): 995–1010.

Ferguson, Niall. *The Pity of War.* London: Allen Lane, Penguin, 1998.

Fincher, Jack. "By Convention, the Enemy within Never Did Without." *Smithsonian* 26, no. 3 (June 1995): 126–34.

Fitzpatrick, John C., ed. *The Writings of George Washington from the Original Manuscript Sources, 1745–1799.* 25 vols. Washington, DC: U.S. Government Printing Office, 1932–1938.

Flammer, Philip. "Dulag Luft: The Third Reich's Prison Camp for Airmen." *Aerospace Historian* 19, no. 2 (1972): 58–62.

Fleming, Thomas. *The Illusion of Victory: America in World War.* New York: Basic Books, 2003.

Flory, William E. S. *Prisoners of War: A Study in the Development of International Law.* Washington, DC: American Council on Public Affairs, 1942.

Fooks, Herbert C. *Prisoners of War.* Federalsburg, MD: J. W. Stowell, 1924.

Freeman, Douglas Southall. *George Washington, A Biography.* 5 vols. New York: Scribners, 1951–1952.

Frey, Herman S., ed. and comp. *Foundations of the Republic: Select Important United States Historical Documents*. Murfreesboro, TN: Published by the Editor, 1993.

Friedman, George. *America's Secret War: Inside the Hidden Worldwide Struggle between the United States and Its Enemies*. New York: Broadway Books, 2004.

Fugita, Frank. *Foo: A Japanese-American Prisoner of the Rising Sun, The Secret Prison Diary of Frank "Foo" Fugita*. Denton: University of North Texas Press, 1993.

Futch, Ovid L. *History of Andersonville Prison*. Gainesville: University of Florida Press, 1968.

Gaertner, Georg, with Arnold Krammer. *Hitler's Last Soldier in America*. New York: Stein and Day, 1985.

Garrett, Richard. *P.O.W.: The Uncivil Face of War*. Devon: David and Charles, 1981.

Gates, John M. "The Philippines and Vietnam: Another False Analogy." *Asian Studies* 10 (1972): 64–76.

———. "War-Related Deaths in the Philippines, 1898–1902." *Pacific Historical Review* 53 (November 1983): 367–78.

Gatewood, Willard B. Jr. *Smoked Yankees and the Struggle for Empire*. Urbana: University of Illinois Press, 1971.

Gebhardt, Major James F. "The Road to Abu Ghraib: U.S. Army Detainee Doctrine and Experience." *Military Review* (January–February 2005): 44–50.

George, Alexander L. *The Chinese Communist Army in Action: The Korean War and Its Aftermath*. New York: Columbia University Press, 1967.

Gienapp, William E. *Abraham Lincoln and Civil War*. New York: Oxford University Press, 2002.

Gillispie, James M. *Andersonvilles of the North: The Myths and Realities of Northern Treatment of Civil War Confederate Prisoners*. Denton: University of North Texas Press, 2008.

Gilmore, Allison B. "'We Have Been Reborn': Japanese Prisoners and the Allied Propaganda War in the Southwest Pacific." *Pacific Historical Review* 64, no. 2 (May 1995): 195–215.

———. *You Can't Fight Tanks with Bayonets: Psychological Warfare against the Japanese Army in the Southwest Pacific*. Lincoln: University of Nebraska Press, 1998.

Gordon, Harry. *Die Like a Carp: The Story of the Greatest Prison Escape Ever*. Stanmore: Cassell Australia, 1978.

Gordon, Michael R. "U.S. Troops Move in Panama in Effort to Seize Noriega; Gunfire Is Heard in Capital." *New York Times,* 20 December 1990.

Gordon, Michael R., and General Bernard E. Trainor. *Cobra II: The Inside Story of the Invasion and Occupation of Iraq*. New York: Pantheon, 2006.

Goulden, Joseph C. *The Untold Story of the War*. New York: McGraw-Hill, 1983.

Graebner, William. *True Stories from the American Past*. New York: McGraw-Hill, 2003.

Grant, Zalin. *Survivors: American POW's in Vietnam.* 1975. Reprint, New York: Berkley, 1985.

Gray, J. Glen. *The Warriors: Reflections on Men in Battle.* New York: Harcourt Brace, 1959.

Greenberg, Karen J., and Joshua L Dratel, eds. *The Torture Papers: The Road to Abu Ghraib.* New York: Cambridge University Press, 2005.

Greenhow, Rose O'Neal. *My Imprisonment and the First Year of Abolition Rule at Washington.* London: Richard Bentley, 1863.

Gregory, Paul, and Valery Lazarev, eds. *The Economics of Forced Labor: The Soviet Gulag.* Stanford, CA: Hoover Institution, 2003.

Greiner, Walter F. "Other Losses." Letter to the editor. *Times Literary Supplement,* 23–29 November 1990.

Groom, Winston, and Duncan Spencer. *Conversations with the Enemy: The Story of PFC Robert Garwood.* New York: Putnam, 1983.

Grotius, Hugo. *On the Rights of War and Peace.* Abridged translation by William Whewell. Cambridge: Cambridge University Press, 1853.

Guest, Robert. "Goodbye Guantánamo." *Economist: The World in 2009,* January 2009, 36.

Hall, James Norman. *My Island Home: An Autobiography.* Boston: Little, Brown, 1952.

Hansen, Kenneth K. *Heroes behind Barbed Wire.* Princeton, NJ: D. von Nostrand, 1957.

Harmann, Jack. *On American Soil: How Justice Became a Casualty of World War II.* Seattle: University of Washington Press, 2005.

Harries, Meirion, and Susie Harries. *The Last Days of Innocence: America at War, 1917–1918.* New York: Random House, 1997.

Harvey, Robert. *Amache: The Story of Japanese Internment in Colorado during World War II.* Lanham, MD: Taylor Trade Publishing, 2004.

Hatch, A. Francis. "One Despicable Part of the Vietnam War Is the False Portrayal of American Soldiers as Bloodthirsty Barbarians." *Vietnam Magazine,* August 1995, 58, 60–62.

Haydock, Michael D. "Sinking of *Maine* Brings War with Spain." *VFW Magazine,* February 1998, 12–14.

Hayes, Stephen F. "On Richard Clarke." *Weekly Standard,* 22 March 2004.

Herman, Edward S. *Atrocities in Vietnam: Myths and Realities.* Philadelphia: Pilgrim Press, 1970.

Hesseltine, William Best. *Civil War Prisons: A Study in Prison Psychology.* Columbus: Ohio State University Press, 1930.

Hibbert, Christopher. *Redcoats and Rebels: The American Revolution through British Eyes.* New York: Avon, 1991.

Hickey, Donald R. *The War of 1812.* Urbana: University of Illinois Press, 1989.

Hilsman, Roger. *To Move a Nation.* New York: Doubleday, 1967.

The Historical Management of POWs: A Synopsis of the 1968 US Army Provost Marshal General's Study Entitled "A Review of United States Policy on Treatment of Prisoners of War." San Diego, CA: Naval Health Research Center, 1970.

"Hitler's Last Soldier in America Gives Up." *Newsweek,* 23 September 1955.

Höbling, Walter. *Fiktionen vom Krieg in Neueren amerikanischen Roman.* Tübingen: Gunter Narr Verlag, 1987.

Holli, Melvin G. "A View of the American Campaign against 'Filipino Insurgents': 1900." *Philippine Studies* 17 (1969): 97–111.

Hoover, J. Edgar. "Enemies at Large." *American Magazine,* April 1944, 29–30.

Horn, Stanley F. *The Army of Tennessee.* New York: Bobbs-Merrill, 1941.

Hörner, Helmut. *A German Odyssey: The Journal of a German Prisoner of War.* Trans. and ed. Allan Kent Powell. Golden, CO: Fulcrum, 1991.

Houston, Jeanne Wakatsuki, and James Houston. *Farewell to Manzanar.* New York: Bantam, 1973.

Howard, Major General Oliver O. "Is Cruelty Inseparable from War?" *Independent,* May 1902, 161–62.

Howe, Russell Warren. *The Hunt for "Tokyo Rose."* Lanham, MD: Madison Books, 1990.

Howe, Susan. *The Birth-Mark: Unsettling the Wilderness in American Literary History.* Hanover, NH: Wesleyan University Press, 1993.

Howells, W. D. "Our Spanish Prisoners at Portsmouth." *Harper's Weekly* 42, no. 2174 (1898): 826–27.

Huie, William Bradford. *The Execution of Private Slovik.* 1954. Reprint, New York: Dell, 1970.

"The Hunt for Osama." *Time,* 17 May 2004, 19.

Ienaga, Saburo. *The Pacific War, 1931–1945.* New York: Pantheon, 1978.

"Ike's Revenge." *Time,* 2 October 1989, 19.

"Iraq: A U.S. Combat Chronology, 2003–2006." *VFW Magazine,* March 2005, 22–24, 26.

"Is Torture Ever Justified." *Economist,* 22 September 2007, 71–72.

Isaacs, Edouard Victor. *Prisoner of the U-90.* New York: Houghton Mifflin, 1919.

Jacobs, Wilbur R. *Dispossessing the American Indian: Indians and Whites on the Colonial Frontier.* Norman: University of Oklahoma Press, 1985.

James, Edwin L. "Our Men Gain Near Fismes." *New York Times,* 24 August 1918.

Jenkins, Philip. *A History of the United States.* 3rd ed. London: Palgrave Macmillan, 2007.

Johnson, Keith. "An Indian Tribe's Promised Land." *New York Times,* reprinted in *Vocable,* 1 February 1995, 4–7.

Jones, Buehring H. *The Sunny Land; or, Prison Prose and Poetry.* Baltimore: Innes, 1868.

Jones, Robert H. *The Civil War in the Northwest.* Norman: University of Oklahoma Press, 1960.

Jordán, Javier. "Radical Islamism, Secular Fundamentalism and the Clash." Interview. ZENIT, Vatican News Service, 18 May 2004.

Jung, Hermann. *Die deutschen Kriegsgefangenen in amerikanischer Hand—USA.* Munich: Gieseking, 1972.

Kaplan, Alice. "War on Trial." *Civilization* 4, no. 5 (1997): 60–66.

Karner, Stefan. *Im Archipel GUPVI: Kriegsgefangenshaft und Internierung in der Sowjetunion, 1941–1956.* Vienna: Oldenbourg, 1995.

Keefer, Louis E. *Italian Prisoners of War in America, 1942–1946: Captives or Allies?* New York: Praeger, 1992.

Keegan, John. *A History of Warfare.* New York: Vintage, 1993.

———. "James Bacque and the 'Missing Million.'" *Times Literary Supplement,* 23 July 1993, 13.

Kellen, Konrad. *Conversations with Enemy Soldiers in Late 1968/Early 1969: A Study of Motivation and Morale.* Santa Monica, CA: RAND, 1970.

Kennedy, David M. *Over Here: The First World War and American Society.* New York: Oxford University Press, 2004.

Kenny, Kevin. *The American Irish: A History.* London: Longman, 2000.

Kerr, E. Bartlett. *Surrender and Survival: The Experience of American POWs in the Pacific 1941–1945.* New York: William Morrow, 1985.

Kesting, Robert W. "Forgotten Victims: Blacks in the Holocaust." *Journal of Negro History* 77, no. 1 (Winter 1992): 30–36.

Kincaid, Eugene. *In Every War But One.* New York: Norton, 1959.

Kingsbury, Alex. "Q&A: Philip Gourevitch: Recalling the Shame of Abu Ghraib." *U.S. News & World Report,* 9 June 2008, 14.

Knopp, Guido. "Heimkehr, Flüchtlinge und Vertriebene." *Damals,* December 1994, 8–11.

Knox, Donald. *The Korean War, Pusan to Chosin: An Oral History.* New York: Harcourt Brace, 1986.

Kolb, Richard K. "Bamboo Vets Waged Philippines War." *VFW Magazine,* May 1990, 18–21.

Koop, Allen V. *Stark Decency: German Prisoners of War in a New England Village.* Hanover, NH: University Press of New England, 1988.

Kozaryn, Linda D. "Belleau Wood: Marines' Mecca." *American Forces Press Service News Articles,* 18 June 1998.

Krammer, Arnold. "American Treatment of German Generals during World War II." *Journal of Military History* 54 (January 1990): 27–46.

———. "Japanese Prisoners of War in America. *Pacific Historical Review* 52, no. 1 (February 1983): 67–91.

———. *Nazi Prisoners of War in America.* New York: Stein and Day, 1979.

———. *Prisoners of War: A Reference Handbook.* Westport, CT: Praeger, 2008.

———. *Undue Process: The Untold Story of America's German Alien Internees.* Lanham, MD: Rowman and Littlefield, 1997.

"Kriegsmarine Escape." *Newsweek,* 8 January 1945, 33–34.

Kutler, Stanley I. *The American Inquisition: Justice and Injustice in the Cold War.* New York: Hill and Wang, 1982.

La Croix, W. L., S. J. *War and International Ethics: Tradition and Today.* Lanham, MD: University Press of America, 1988.

Lamb, Sergeant Roger. *An Original and Authentic Journal of Occurrences during the Late American War from Its Commencement to the Year 1783.* 1809. Reprint, New York: Arno, 1968.

Landas, Marc. *The Fallen: A True Story of American and Japanese Wartime Atrocities.* Hoboken, NJ: John Wiley and Sons, 2004.

Landon, Walter J. "Geneva Conventions—The Broken Rules." *Naval Institute Proceedings* 99, no. 2 (February 1973): 34–39.

Lanning, Michael Lee, and Dan Cragg. *Inside the VC and NVA: The Real Story of North Vietnam's Armed Forces.* 1992. Reprint, New York: Ivy, 1994.

Lee, Patrick. "Interrogational Torture." *American Journal of Jurisprudence* 51 (2006): 131–47.

Levie, Howard S. "Maltreatment of Prisoners of War in Vietnam." *Boston University Law Review* 48, no. 3 (Summer 1968): 323–59.

Levinson, Irving W. "A New Paradigm for an Old Conflict: The Mexico–United States War." *Journal of Military History* 73 (April 2009): 393–416.

Lewis, Adrian. *The American Culture of War: The History of U.S. Military Force from World War II to Operation Iraqi Freedom.* New York: Routledge, 2007.

Lewis, George G., and John Mewha. *History of Prisoner of War Utilization by the United States Army, 1776–1945.* Department of the Army Pamphlet No. 20–213. Washington, DC: Department of the Army, 1955.

Lieber, Robert J. "The Neoconservative-Conspiracy Theory: Pure Myth." *Chronicle Review* 49, no. 34 (2003): B14.

Linn, Brian M. "Guerrilla Fighter: Frederick Funston in the Philippines, 1900–1901." *Kansas History* 10 (1987): 2–16.

———. *The Philippine War, 1899–1902.* Lawrence: University Press of Kansas, 2000.

Liptak, Adam. "U.S. Fights Verdict Backing Ex-P.O.W.'s." *New York Times,* 29 July 2003.

Loas, William E. *Minnesota.* New York: Norton, 1977.

Locher, James R. III. "Taking Stock of Goldwater-Nichols." *JFQ* (Autumn 1999): 10–16.

Lookingbill, Brad D. *War Dance at Fort Marion: Plains Indian War Prisoners.* Norman: University of Oklahoma Press, 2006.

Lory, Hillis. *Japan's Military Masters.* New York: Viking, 1943.

Lowell, Edward J. *The Hessians and Other German Auxiliaries of Great Britain in the Revolutionary War.* 1884. Reprint, Gansevoort, NY: Corner House, 1997.

Luce, Henry R. "The American Century." *Life,* 17 February 1941.

MacArthur, Douglas. *Reminiscences.* 1964. Reprint, Annapolis, MD: Naval Institute Press, 2001.

Mackenzie, Kenneth Seaforth. *Dead Men Rising.* Sydney, Australia: Pacific Books, 1969.

MacKenzie, S. P. "The Treatment of Prisoners of War in World War II." *Journal of Modern History* 66 (September 1994): 487–520.

Mackin, Elton E. *Suddenly We Didn't Want to Die: Memoirs of a World War I Marine.* Novato, CA: Presidio, 1993.

Macquarrie, Hector. *How to Live at the Front: Tips for American Soldiers.* Philadelphia: Lippincott, 1917.

Maddox, Eric, with Davin Seay. *Mission: Black List #1: The Inside Story of the Search for Saddam Hussein as Told by the Soldier Who Mastermided His Capture.* New York: HarperCollins, 2008.

Magruder, P. H. "The Spanish Naval Prisoners of War at Annapolis, 1898." *U.S. Naval Institute Proceedings* 56, no. 6 (June 1930): 489–95.

Mahan, Alfred Thayer. *The Influence of Sea Power upon History, 1660–1783.* Cambridge, MA: John Wilson and Son, 1890.

Mahon, John K. *The War of 1812.* Gainesville: University of Florida Press 1972.

Manvell, Roger. *SS and Gestapo: Rule by Terror.* New York: Ballantine, 1969.

Markle, Donald E. *Spies & Spymasters of the Civil War.* New York: Hippocrene, 2000.

Marks, Jim. "Looking Back." *Sabre News,* January–February 1992, 13.

Marolda, Edward. *Theodore Roosevelt, the U.S. Navy, and the Spanish-American War.* New York: Palgrave, 2001.

Marshall, John A. *American Bastile.* 8th ed. Philadelphia: Thomas Hartley, 1871.

Martin, James Kirby, and Mark Edward Lender. *A Respectable Army: The Military Origins of the Republic, 1763–1789.* Wheeling, IL: Harlan Davidson, 1982.

Martin, Joseph Plumb. *Private Yankee Doodle: Being a Narrative of Some of the Adventures and Sufferings of a Revolutionary Soldier.* 1830. Reprint, Harrisburg, PA: Eastern Acorn Press, 1997.

Marvel, William. *Andersonville: The Last Depot.* Chapel Hill: University of North Carolina Press, 1994.

Maschke, Erich. *Zur Geschichte der deutschen Kriegsgefangenen des 2. Weltkrieges: Eine Zuzammenfassung.* Munich: Gieseking, 1974.

Mason, John Brown. "German Prisoners of War in the United States." *American Journal of International Law* 24 (April 1945): 198–215.

May, Glenn A. "Why the United States Won the Philippine-American War, 1899–1902." *Pacific Historical Review* 52, no. 4 (November 1983): 353–77.

McCain, John, with Mark Salter. *Faith of My Fathers: A Family Memoir.* New York: Random House, 1999.

McLaughlin, Kathleen. "Allies Open Trial of 20 Top Germans for Crimes of War." *New York Times,* 20 November 1945.

Megargee, Geoffrey P. *War of Annihilation: Combat and Genocide on the Eastern Front, 1941.* Lanham, MD: Rowman and Littlefield, 2006.

Mekeel, Arthur J. *The Relation of the Quakers to the American Revolution.* Lanham, MD: University Press of America, 1979.

———. "The Relation of the Quakers to the American Revolution." *Quaker History* 65 (1976): 3–18.

Melady, John. *Escape from Canada: The Untold Story of German Prisoners of War in Canada, 1939–1945.* Toronto: Macmillan, 1981.

Melady, Thomas Patrick. "Background to US-Vatican Relations." *New Catholic World* 209 (1969): 107–11.

Messerschmidt, Manfred, and Fritz Wüllner. *Die Wehrmachtjustiz im Dienste des Nationalsozialismus. Zerstörung einer Legende.* Baden-Baden: Nomos, 1987.

Metzger, Charles H., S. J. *The Prisoner in the American Revolution.* Chicago: Loyola University Press, 1971.

Meyers, Samuel M., and William C. Bradbury. *The Political Behavior of Korean and Chinese Prisoners of War in the Korean Conflict: A Historical Analysis.* Human Resources Research Office Technical Report 50. Psychological Warfare Division. Washington, DC: George Washington University, Human Resources Research Office for the Department of the Army, August 1958.

Miller, Nathan. *Spying for America: The Hidden History of U.S. Intelligence.* New York: Dell, 1989.

Miller, Robert Ryal. *Shamrock and Sword: The Saint Patrick's Battalion in the U.S.-Mexican War.* Norman: University of Oklahoma Press, 1989.

Millis, Walter. *The Martial Spirit: A Study of the War with Spain.* New York: Viking, 1965.

Minear, Richard H. *Victors Justice: The Tokyo War Crimes Trial.* 1971. Reprint, Ann Arbor: University of Michigan Center for Japanese Studies, 2001.

Moeller, Susan D. "The Pictures of the Enemy: Fifty Years of Images of Japan in the American Press, 1941–1992." *Journal of American Culture* 19, no. 1 (Spring 1996): 29–42.

Moody, James. *Lieut. James Moody's Narrative of His Exertions and Sufferings in the Cause of Government, since the Year 1776.* 1783. Reprint, New York: New York Times and Arno, 1968.

Moore, John Hammond. *The Faustball Tunnel: German POWs and Their Great Escape.* New York: Random House, 1978.

———. "Italian POWs in America: War Is Not Always Hell." *Prologue: The Journal of the National Archives* 8, no. 3 (Fall 1976): 140–51.

Mosier, John. *The Myth of the Great War: A New Military History of World War I.* New York: Perennial, 2002.

Murphy, Charles H. "Prisoners of War: Repatriation or Internment in Wartime—American and Allied Experiences, 1775 to Present." In U.S. Congress, House Committee on Foreign Affairs. *American Prisoners of War in Southeast Asia, 1971.* Washington, DC: U.S. Government Printing Office, 1971.

"Narrative of Marie LeRoy and Barbara Leininger." *Pennsylvania German Society Proceedings* 15 (1906): 112–22.

Nelson, William H. *The American Tory.* Boston: Beacon, 1961.

Nichols, Charles L. "Article 105: Misconduct as a Prisoner." *Air Force JAG Law Review* 11 (Fall 1969): 393–98.

Oaks, Robert F. "Philadelphians in Exile: The Problem of Loyalty during the American Revolution." *Pennsylvania Magazine of History and Biography* 9 (1972): 298–325.

"Obituary, Iva Toguri." *Economist,* 7 October 2006, 93.

O'Sullivan, John L. "Annexation." *United States Democratic Review,* July–August 1845, 5.

Owens, William A. "Making the Joint Journey." *JFQ* (Spring 1999): 92–95.

Pabel, Reinhold. *Enemies Are Human.* Philadelphia: John C. Winston, 1955.

———. "It's Easy to Bluff Americans." *Colliers,* December 1994, 8–11.

Palmer, Frederick. "White Man and Brown Man in the Philippines." *Scribner's Magazine,* January–June 1900, 73–86.

Pasley, Virginia. *22 Stayed.* London: W. H. Allen, 1955.

Pate, Lloyd W., and B. J. Cutler. *Reactionary.* New York: Harper and Brothers, 1956.

Pentagon briefing. "The War on Terrorism." Washington, DC: Office of Public Affairs, Department of Defense, 17 January 2002.

Perry, John. "Just Ordinary Boys." *American Legion Magazine,* November 1998, 24, 25–27.

Pershing, General John J. *Final Report of General John J. Pershing, Commander-in-Chief, American Expeditionary Forces.* Washington, DC: U.S. Government Printing Office, 1920.

———. *My Experiences in the World War.* 2 vols. New York: Frederick A. Stokes, 1931.

Peters, Edward. *Torture.* New York: Basil Blackwell, 1985.

Peterson, Edward N. *The Many Faces of Defeat: The German People's Experience in 1945.* New York: Peter Lang, 1990.

Phelps, Richard H. *A History of Newgate of Connecticut.* 1860. Reprint, New York: Arno Press and New York Times, 1969.

"Philippines War: A Combat Chronology, 1899–1902." *VFW Magazine,* February 1999, 32–35.

Powell, Allan Kent. *Splinters of a Nation: German Prisoners of War in Utah.* Salt Lake City: University of Utah Press, 1989.

Proceedings, Court Martial Held at Cambridge, by Order of Major General Heath, Commanding the American Troops for the Northern District, for the Trial of Colonel David Henley, Accused by General Burgoyne, of Ill-Treatment of the British Soldiers, etc. Taken in Short Hand by an Officer, Who Was Present. Library of Thomas Jefferson. London: Printed for J. Almon, 1778. Washington, DC: Microcard Editions, 1973.

"Promises to Keep." *Economist,* 31 January 2009, 38.

Prugh, George S. *Law at War: Vietnam, 1964–1973.* Washington, DC: Department of the Army, Center of Military History, 1975.

———. "Prisoners at War: The POW Battleground." *Dickinson Law Review* 60, no. 2 (January 1956): 123–38.

Rehnquist, William H. "The Milligan Decision." *Military History Quarterly* (Winter 1999): 44–49.

Richardson, James, ed. *A Compilation of the Messages and Papers of the Presidents of the United States, 1789–1897.* 8 vols. Washington, DC: U.S. Government Printing Office, 1897.

Richter, Hans Werner. *Die Geschlagenen.* Munich, 1949.

Ridgway, Matthew B. *The Korean War.* Garden City, NY: Doubleday, 1967.

Riedesel, Baroness Friederike Charlotte Luise von Massow. *Letters and Journals Related to the War of the American Revolution and the Capture of the German Troops at Saratoga.* Trans. William L. Stone. Albany, NY: Joel Munsel, 1867.

Rives, George Lockhart. *Selections from the Correspondence of Thomas Barclay, Formerly British Consul General at New York.* New York: Harper and Brothers, 1894.

Robbins, Jim. "Pardons Granted 88 Years after Crimes of Sedition." *New York Times,* 3 May 2006.

Robin, Ron. *The Barbed-Wire College: Reeducating German POWs in the United States during World War II.* Princeton, NJ: Princeton University Press, 1995.

Robinson, Michael C., and Frank N. Schubert. "David Fagan: An Afro-American Rebel in the Philippines, 1899–1901." *Pacific Historical Review* 44, no. 1 (February 1975): 68–83.

Robinson, Ralph. "Retaliation for the Treatment of Prisoners in the War of 1812." *American Historical Review* 49, no. 1 (October 1943): 65–70.

Rojansky, Matt. "Tribunal Tribulations." *Harvard International Review* 22, no. 2 (2000): 13–14.

Roland, Charles G. "Allied POWs, Japanese Captors and the Geneva Convention." *War and Society* 9, no. 2 (October 1991): 83–101.

Rollins, Peter C. "Television's Vietnam: The Visual Language of Television News." *Journal of American Culture* 4 (1981): 114–35.

———. "The Vietnam War: Perceptions through Literature, Film, and Television." *American Quarterly* 36 (1984): 419–32.

Roosevelt, Edith K. "How They Treat Red POWs in S. Vietnam." *Connecticut Sunday Herald,* 25 June 1972.

Rosengarten, Joseph G. "A Defense of the Hessians." *Pennsylvania Magazine of History and Biography* 23 (1899): 157–83.

Rosenthal, Andrew. "No Ground Fighting Yet; Call to Arms by Hussein." *New York Times,* 17 January 1991.

Roskey, William. "Koje Island: The 1952 Korean Hostage Crisis." *Land Warfare Papers* 19 (September 1994): 1–21.

Ruhlman, R. Fred. *Captain Henry Wirtz and Andersonville Prison: A Reappraisal.* Knoxville: University of Tennessee Press, 2006.

Ryan, J. A. "The Defense of Captain J. A. Ryan." *Journal of the United States Cavalry Association* 13 (October 1902): 185–93.

Sakamaki, Kazuo. *I Attacked Pearl Harbor.* Trans. Toru Matsumoto. New York: Association, 1949.

Sakuda, Keiichi. "Rapprochement with Death—The Logic of Responsibility of the Japanese as It Appeared in the Messages of the War Criminals Convicted to Death," *Tenbo* 72 (December 1964).

Sanders, Charles W. Jr. *While in the Hands of the Enemy: Military Prisons of the Civil War.* Baton Rouge: Louisiana State University Press, 2005.

Schlesinger, Arthur M. Jr. *The Disuniting of America: Reflections on a Multicultural Society.* New York: Norton, 1992.

Schmemann, Serge. "U.S. Attacked; Hijacked Jets Destroy Twin Towers and Hit Pentagon in Day of Terror: President Vows to Exact Punishment for 'Evil.'" *New York Times,* 12 September 2001.

Schwarzkopf, General H. Norman, with Peter Petre. *The Autobiography: It Doesn't Take a Hero.* New York: Bantam, 1993.

Schwinn, Monika, and Bernhard Diehl. *We Came to Help.* New York: Harcourt Brace Jovanovich, 1976.

Scott, George Riley. *A History of Torture.* 1940. Reprint, London: Senate, 1977.

Scott, Peter T. "Captive Labour: The German Companies of the British Expeditionary Force (BEF) 1916–1920." *Army Quarterly and Defence Journal* 110, no. 3 (July 1980).

Segal, Henry A. "Initial Psychiatric Findings of Recently Repatriated Prisoners of War." *American Journal of Psychiatry* 3 (1954): 358–63.

Shnayerson, Robert. "Judgment at Nuremberg." *Smithsonian* 27, no. 7 (1996): 124–40.

Shohei, Ooka. *Taken Captive: A Japanese POW's Story.* Trans. and ed. Wayne P. Lammers. 1952. Reprint, New York: John Wiley and Sons, 1996.

Slotkin, Richard. *Regeneration through Violence: The Mythology of the American Frontier, 1600–1860*. Middletown, CT: Wesleyan University Press, 1973.

Smith, Eric M. "Combat Intelligence." *Vietnam Magazine*, June 1995, 42–48.

Smith, George E. *POW: Two Years with the Vietcong*. Berkeley, CA: Ramparts, 1971.

Song, Hyo-Soon. *The Fight for Freedom: The Untold Story of the Korean War Prisoners*. Seoul: Korean Library Association, 1980.

Spidle, Jake W. Jr. "Axis Prisoners of War in the United States, 1942–1946: A Bibliographical Essay." *Military Affairs* 39, no. 2 (April 1975): 61–66.

Stanley, Henry Morton. *The Autobiography of Sir Henry Morton Stanley*. Boston: Houghton Mifflin, 1909.

The Statutes at Large of the United State of American from March 1887 to March 1899 and Recent Treaties, Conventions, Executive Proclamations, and the Concurrent Resolutions of the Two Houses of Congress. Vol. 30. Washington, DC: U.S. Government Printing Office, 1899.

Steenburg, Sven. *Vlasov*. New York: Knopf, 1970.

Stephens, Alexander H. "The Treatment of Prisoners during the War Between the States." *Southern Historical Society Papers* 1, no. 3 (March 1876): 507–10

Stevens, Peter F. *The Rogue March: John Riley and the St. Patrick's Battalion, 1846–48*. Washington, DC: Potomac Books, 1999.

Stewart, First Lieutenant Elam L. "The Massacre of Balangiga." *Infantry Journal* 30 (April 1927): 407–14.

Stockel, H. Henrietta. *Survival of the Spirit: Chiricahua Apaches in Captivity*. Reno, NV: University of Las Vegas Press, 1993.

Story, Richard. *History of Modern Japan*. Hammondsworth, U.K.: Penguin, 1960.

Straus, Ulrich. *The Anguish of Surrender: Japanese POWs of World War II*. Seattle: University of Washington Press, 2003.

Stryker, William S. *The Battles of Trenton and Princeton*. Boston: Houghton Mifflin, 1898.

Sullivan, George. *Strange But True Stories of World War II*. New York: Walker, 1983.

Sullivan, Walter, ed. *The War the Women Lived: Female Voices from the Confederate South*. Nashville, TN: J. S. Sanders, 1995.

Summers, Harry G. Jr. *Korean War Almanac*. New York: Facts on File, 1990.

Summers, Stan. *The Korea Story*. Marshfield, MN: American Ex–Prisoners of War National Medical Research Committee, 1981.

Swanberg, W. A. "The Spies Who Came in from the Sea." *American Heritage*, April 1970, 66–69, 87–91.

Talman, James J., ed. *Loyalist Narratives from Upper Canada*. Toronto: Champlain Society, 1946.

Tateishi, John. *And Justice for All: An Oral History of Japanese American Detention Camps*. New York: Random House, 1984.

Taylor, Telford. *The Anatomy of Nuremberg: A Personal Memoir*. New York: Knopf, 1992.

Temple, Brian. *The Union Prison at Fort Delaware: A Perfect Hell on Earth*. Jefferson, NC: McFarland, 2003.

Thomas, William H. Jr. *Unsafe for Democracy: World War I and the U.S. Justice Department's Covert Campaign to Suppress Dissent.* Madison: University of Wisconsin Press, 2008.

Thompson, H. C. "War without Medals." *Oregon Historical Quarterly* 59 (December 1958): 293–325.

Toffler, Alvin. *The Third Wave.* New York: Bantam, 1980.

Toffler, Alvin, and Heidi Toffler. "War, Wealth, and a New Era in History." *World Monitor* 4, no. 5 (May 1991): 46–52.

Toland, John. *Captured by History.* New York: St. Martin's, 1997.

Tolstoy, Nikolai. *Stalin's Secret War.* New York: Holt, Rinehart and Winston, 1982.

———. *Victims of Yalta.* London: Hodder and Stoughton, 1977.

Tourison, Sedgwick D. Jr. *Talking with Victor Charlie: An Interrogator's Story.* New York: Ballantine/Ivy, 1991.

Towle, Philip A. "Japanese Treatment of Prisoners in 1904–1905—Foreign Officers' Reports." *Military Affairs* 39, no. 3 (October 1975): 115–17.

Treese, Lorette. *The Storm Gathering: The Penn Family and the American Revolution.* University Park, PA: Penn State University Press, 1992.

"Trial and Error." *Newsweek,* 1 August 1966, 35–36.

Tsurumi, Kazuko. *Social Change and the Individual: Japan before and after Defeat in World War II.* Princeton, NJ: Princeton University Press, 1970.

Tuck, Lieutenant Colonel Jeremy John Hobart. "Medical Management of Iraqi Enemy Prisoners of War during Operation Telic." *Military Medicine* 170, no. 3 (March 2005): 177–82.

U.S. Congress. House. Commission on Wartime Relocation and Internment of Civilians. 102nd Cong., 2nd sess. *Personal Justice Denied* by George Miller. Committee Print no. 6. Washington, DC: U.S. Government Printing Office, 1982.

———. *Report on the Spirit and Manner in Which the War Has Been Waged by the Enemy.* New York: Garland, 1813; reprint, 1978.

U.S. Department of Defense. *Selected Manpower Statistics FY 1994,* Table 2–23 (Principal Wars), 112, *VFW Magazine,* February 1996, 8.

Utley, Robert M. *Frontier Regulars: The United States Army and the Indian, 1866–1891.* 1973. Reprint, Lincoln: University of Nebraska Press, Bison Book Reprint, 1984.

———. *Frontiersmen in Blue.* New York: Macmillan, 1967.

———. *The Indian Frontier of the American West, 1846–1890.* Albuquerque: University of New Mexico Press, 1984.

Utley, Robert M., and Wilcomb E. Washburn. *Indian Wars.* New York: American Heritage, 1977.

Valentine, Douglas. *The Phoenix Program.* New York: William Morrow, 1990.

van Buskirk, Steve. "Enemy Ex-POWs in Our Midst?" *VFW Magazine,* January 1994, 36.

Vance, Jonathan F., ed. *Encyclopedia of Prisoners of War and Internment.* Santa Barbara, CA: ABC-CLIO, 2000.

Van Doren, Carl Clinton. *Secret History of the American Revolution: An Account of the Conspiracies of Benedict Arnold and Numerous Others, Drawn from the Secret Service Papers of the British Headquarters in North America.* 1941. Reprint, Clifton, NJ: A. M. Kelley, 1973.

Van Tyne, Claude Halstead. *The Loyalists in the American Revolution.* 1902. Reprint, Bowie, MD: Heritage Facsimile, 1989.

Vaughn, Elizabeth Head. *Community under Stress: An Internment Camp Culture.* Princeton, NJ: Princeton University Press, 1949.

"Verbatim." *Time,* 9 March 2009, 14.

Verral, Charles S., ed. *True Stories of Great Escapes.* Pleasantville, NY: Reader's Digest Association, 1977.

Vespucci, Amerigo. "The Fullest Extent of Hospitality." *Amerigo Vespucci: Letter to Piero Soderini, Gonfaloniere.* Trans. and ed. George Tyler Northup. Princeton, NJ: Princeton University Press, 1916.

Vinz, Curt. "Das freie Buch." *Der Ruf* 26 (1 April 1946).

von Hassel, Agostino, and Sigrid MacRae, with Simone Ameskamp. *Alliance of Enemies: The Untold Story of the Secret American and German Collaboration to End World War II.* New York: Thomas Dunne/St. Martin's, 2006.

Wagoner, Todd D. "Fighting Aguinaldo's Insurgents in the Philippines." *Kansas Historical Quarterly* 18 (May 1951): 145–73.

Walker, Keith. *A Piece of My Heart: The Stories of Twenty-six American Women Who Served in Vietnam.* New York: Ballantine, 1985.

Wallace, Edward S. "The Battalion of Saint Patrick in the Mexican War." *Military Affairs* 14, no. 2 (July 1950): 84–91.

———. "Deserters in the Mexican War." *Hispanic American Historical Review* (August 1935), 374–83.

Walsh, John. *The Sinking of the USS* Maine. New York: Franklin Watts, 1969.

Washburn, Wilcomb E., ed. *The Indian and the White Man.* Garden City, NY: Doubleday, 1964.

Weale, Adrian. *Renegades: Hitler's Englishmen.* London: Warner, 1995.

Weber, Mark. "The Japanese Camps in California." *Journal for Historical Review* 2, no. 1 (Spring 1980): 45–59.

Weintraub, Stanley. *Long Day's Journey into War: December 7, 1941.* New York: Dutton, 1991.

———. *War in the Wards: Korea's Unknown Battle in a Prisoner-of-War Hospital Camp.* 2nd ed. San Rafael, CA: Presidio, 1976.

Welch, Richard E. Jr. "'The Philippine Insurrection' and the American Press." *Historian, A Journal of History* 36 (November 1973): 34–51.

———. *Response to Imperialism: The United States and the Philippine-American War, 1899–1902.* Chapel Hill: University of North Carolina Press, 1979.

Westheimer, David. *Sitting It Out: A World War II POW Memoir.* Houston, TX: Rice University Press, 1992.

———. *Von Ryan's Express.* New York: Doubleday, 1964.

Westmoreland, General William C. *A Soldier Reports.* Garden City, NY: Doubleday, 1976.

White, David Fairbank. *Bitter Ocean: The Battle of the Atlantic, 1939–1945.* New York: Simon and Schuster, 2006.

White, W. L. *Report on the Germans*. New York: Harcourt, Brace, 1947.

White, William Lindsey. *An Unofficial White Paper on the Treatment of War Prisoners*. New York: Charles Scribner's Sons, 1957.

Whittingham, Richard. *Martial Justice: The Last Mass Execution in the United States*. 1971, Reprint, Annapolis, MD: Naval Institute Press, 1997.

Wilkinson, Rupert. *American Tough: The Tough-Guy Tradition and American Character*. New York: Harper and Row, 1986.

Williams, Walter L. "Again in Chains: Black Soldiers Suffering in Captivity." *Civil War Times Illustrated*, May 1981, 36–43.

Wilson, Woodrow. *A History of the American People*. 10 vols. New York: Harper and Brothers, 1901–1918.

Work, Clemens P. *Darkest before Dawn: Sedition and Free Speech in the American West*. Albuquerque: University of New Mexico Press, 2005.

Wyman, Mark. *DP: Europe's Displaced Persons, 1945–1951*. Philadelphia: Balch Institute, 1989.

Wynn, Dennis J. *The San Patricio Soldiers: Mexico's Foreign Legion*. Southwestern Studies Monograph No. 74. El Paso: University of Texas at El Paso, 1984.

Wynn, Wilton. *Keepers of the Keys: John XXIII, Paul VI and John Paul II: Three Who Changed the Church*. New York: Random House, 1988.

Zieger, Robert H. *America's Great War: World War I and the American Experience*. Lanham, MD: Rowman and Littlefield, 2000.

Archival Sources

Allied Translator and Intelligence Section of the Southwest Pacific Area. Maxwell Air Force Base Archives.

The Communist War in POW Camps, Headquarters, United Nations and Far East Command. Military Intelligence Section, General Staff. 28 January 1953. G2 Section Report January 1953. NARA, Suitland, MD.

Debrief, Robert C. Doyle, Lt. USN. Naval Historical Center, Washington Navy Yard, Washington, DC, 19 September 1978.

Foreign Morale Analysis Division, Bureau of Overseas Intelligence, Office of War Information. Record Group 208, National Archives, Bibliography of Articles and Books Relating to Japanese Psychology, Report no. 24, 25 August 1945; The Attitudes of Japanese Prisoners of War: An Overall View. Report no. 31, 29 December 1945.

George Washington Papers. 1741–1799: Series 4, General Correspondence, 1697–1799, American Memories. Library of Congress.

Huebecher, Karl P., and Charles Vuillenmeier. "Inspection Report of Fort Douglas." 20 and 21 November 1917. Record Group 407, Box 76, Folder 6, 1. "Report of the Inspection by the Swiss Commission, Ft. Oglethorpe, Ft. McPherson, and Ft. Douglas." National Archives, Washington, DC.

International Committee of the Red Cross. Reports of the International Committee of the Red Cross on Its Activities during the Second World War (1 September 1939–30 June 1947). Vol. 1. General Activities. Geneva, Switzerland, 1948.

International Military Tribunal for the Far East. Judgment. November 1948, Annex-1.

Bibliography

29th Report of the UN Command for the Period 1–15 September 1951, UN Document No. S/2400, 25, *Department of State Bulletin* 1034 (1951).

U.S. National Archives. World War I: Prisons and Prisoners—Prisoners of War and Allied Enemies in the United States. Subject File NA RG 407/23.

Web Sites

"Abu Ghraib Prison Prisoner Abuse: A Chronology." http://globalsecurity.org/intell/world/iraq/abu-ghurayb-chronology.htm, 1–5.

American Civil Liberties Union. "Fact Sheet: Military Commissions." http://aclu.org/safefree/detention/29145res20070322.html.

Amnesty International. "'Rendition' and Secret Detention: A Global System of Human Rights Violations, Questions and Answers." http:www.amnesty.org.

Articles of War, 1776. http://www.yale.edu/lawweb/avalon/contcong/09–20–76.htm.

Associated Press. "Iraq to Reopen Abu Ghraib Prison." 26 January 2009. http://military.com.

———. "Taliban Fighters Have up to 15,000 Fighters." 28 February 2009. http://www.military.com/news/article/taliban-may-have-up-to-15000-fighters.html.

———. "US Military Says Number of Iraq Detainees Falling." 3 March 2009. http://news.yahoo.com/s/ap/20090303/ap_on_re_mi_ea/ml_iraq.

Bajoria, Jayshree. "Backgrounder." Council of Foreign Relations. Updated 18 April 2008, 1. http://cfr.org/publications/9126/.

Baldor, Lolita C. "Pentagon Issues Guidelines for Detainee Treatment." *Army Times,* 9 November 2005. http://www.armytimes.com/story.php?f=1–292925–1231770.php.

"The Battle of Waxhaws/Buford's Massacre, May 29, 1780, Waxhaws, South Carolina." http://www.myrevolutionarywar.com/battles/800529.htm.

Caldwell, Robert J. "Bush, McCain and 'Torture.'" *San Diego Union Tribune,* 24 September 2006. http://signonsandiego.com/uniontrib/20060924/news_mz1e24caldwe.htm.

Candiotti, Susan. "Walker Lindh Sentenced to 20 Years." CNN.com/Law Center, 4 October 2002. http://archives.cnn.com/2002/LAW/10/04/lindh.statement.

Cuban-Spanish-American War, 1898—Historical Text Archive. http://historicalarchive.com.

"The Dachau Trials by U.S. Army Courts in Europe 1945–1948." http://www.jewishvirtuallibrary.org/jsource/Holocaust/DachauTrials.html.

Debs, Eugene V. http://www.marxists.org/archive/debs/.

Espionage Act of 15 June 1917, http://wwi.lib.byu.edu/index.php/The_U.S._Sedition_Act.

Ex parte Milligan (1866). www.tourolaw.edu/patch/Milligan.

Ex parte Vallandigham (1863). http://caselaw.lp.findlaw.com.

Executive Order 9066, 19 February 1942. http://usgovinfo.about.com/od/rightsandfreedoms/a/e09066.htm.

General Order 100, Partisans. http://avalon.law.yale.edu/19th_century/lieber.asp#sec4.

"George Crook." http://www.arlingtoncemetery.net/gcrook.htm.

German Prisoners of War. World War II. http://home.arcor.de/kriegsgefangene/.

"Geronimo." http://www.americanindians.com.

Gillers, Mildred. "Axis Sally." http://www.findagrave.com/cgi-bin/fg.cgi?page=gr&GRid=23000.

"Guantanamo Suicides 'Acts of War.'" BBC News, 6 November 2006. http://news.bbc.uk/go/pr/fr/-/2hi/americas/5068606.stm.

"Gunnery Sergeant Dan Daly at the Battle of Belleau Wood." http://www.nationmaster.com/encyclopedia/Dan-Daly.

Hammett, C. "King's Mountain Prisoners of War," 1–11. http//www.tngenweb.org/revwar/kingsmountain/prisoners.html.

Henry, Susan Copeland. "Foreign Prisoners of War: World War I." http://www.georgiaencyclopedia.org.

"Iraqi Prisoner Abuse 'Un-American,' Says Rumsfeld." *Washington Times.* http://www.washtimes.com/national/20040507-115901-6736r.htm.

Kimmelman, Benedict B. "The Example of Private Slovik." *American Heritage* 38, no. 6 (September–October 1987). www.americanheritage.com/articles/magazine/ah/1987/6/1987_6_97.shtml.

Letter from Robert H. Jackson to Harry S. Truman. Avalon Project, Yale Law School. www.yale.edu/lawweb/avalon/imt/Jackson/jack63.htm.

Lewis, Neil A. "U.S. Alters Rules for War Crime Trials." *New York Times,* 1 September 2005. http://www.nytimes.com/2005/09/01/politics/01detain.html.

McSherry, Patrick. "The Harvard Incident." http://www.spanamwar.com/harvardincident.htm.

Medal of Honor Citation, Corporal Alvin C. York. http://www.homeofheroes.com/moh/citations_1918_wwi/york_alvin.htm.

Miller, Hunter, ed. *Treaties and Other International Acts of the United States of America,* vol. 2, *Documents 1–40: 1776–1818.* Washington, DC: U.S. Government Printing Office, 1931. Avalon Project, Yale Law School, http://www.yale.edu/lawweb/avalon/diplomacy/britain/cart1812.htm.

"1996: Taliban Take over Kabul, and End Mujahideen Rule." http://terrorism.about.com/od/warinafghanistan/ss/AfghanistanWar_5.htm.

Papers of Woodrow Wilson, Proclamation 1364—Declaring that a State of War Exists between the United States and Germany, 6 April 1917. http://www.presidency.ucsb.edu/ws/index.php?pid=598.

Platt Amendment, 1901. http://www.fordham.edu/halsall/mod/1901platt.html.

"The Philippine Insurrection: The Consequence of Imperialism." http://military.com.

President Theodore Roosevelt's Proclamation Formally Ending the Philippine Insurrection and Granting of Pardon and Amnesty, 4 July 1902. In *Statutes at Large.* http://www.msc.ph/centennial/tr020704.html.

"The Prison Life of Jefferson Davis: The Trying Experience of the Ex-President at Fort Monroe, Prevarication of General Miles." *Southern Historical Society Papers* 32 (January–December 1904). www.civilwarhome.com/davisinprision.htm.

Quebec Act. http://www.yale.edu/lawweb/avalon/amerrev/parliament/quebec_act_1774.htm.

"The Real Story of the American Revolution: The Convention Army's Six-Year Imprisonment." http://www.rsar.org/military/convarmy.htm and www.nps .gov/archive/thst/battle.html.

"Relocation of Japanese Americans." Washington, DC: War Relocation Authority, 1943. www.sfmuseum.org/hist10/relocbook.html.

"Report on Detention and Correction in Iraq." Article 15–6 Investigation of the 800th Military Police Brigade. http://news.findlaw.com/hdocs/docs/iraq /tagubarpt.html.

Rieken, John. "Fort McPherson: World War I." http://www.georgiaencyclopedia .org.

Rose O'Neal Greenhow Papers. Special Collections Library, Duke University, Durham, NC. http://scrptorium.lib.duke/greenhow.

Sibley, Colonel. Excerpts from speeches and letters concerning the Dakota conflict, 1862. http://www.law.umkc.edu.

"The Spanish American War and the Philippine American War." http://www .spanamwar.com/genealogy6.html.

The Statutes at Large of the United State of American from March 1887 to March 1899 and Recent Treaties, Conventions, Executive Proclamations, and the Concurrent Resolutions of the Two Houses of Congress. Vol. 30. Washington, DC: U.S. Government Printing Office, 1899. http://www.msc.edu.ph/centen nial/mc981221.html.

"Stories of Spies and Letters." *Spy Letters of the American Revolution.* Collections of the Clements Library, University of Michigan, Ann Arbor. http://si.umich .edu/spies/stories-networks-3.html.

Tokyo Rose/Iva Toguri d'Aquino. http://www.fbi.gov/libref/historic/famcases /rose/rose.htm.

Treaty of Peace between the United States and Spain, 10 December 1898. http:// www.msc.edu.ph/centennial/tr981210.html.

Twain, Mark. *New York Herald,* 15 October 1900. http://www.loc/rr/hispanic /1898/twain.html.

U.S. Department of Defense. "Fact Sheet: Military Commissions." 8 February 2007. http://www.defenselink.mil/news/commissionacts.html.

"U.S. Says C.I.A. Destroyed 92 Tapes of Interrogations." *New York Times,* 3 March 2009. http://www.nytimes.com/2009/03/03/washington/03web-intel .html.

"USS *Hornet* Sinks HMS *Peacock,* 24 February 1813." http://www.history.navy .mil/photos/events/war1812/atsea/hnt-peck.htm.

"The World of 1898: The Spanish American War." Hispanic Division, Library of Congress. http://www.loc.gov/rr/hispanic/1898/chronspain.html.

Yockelson, Mitchell. "The War Department: Keeper of Our Nation's Enemy Aliens." Presented to the Society for Military History, April 1998. http://www .net.lib.byu.edu/estu/wwi/comment/yockel.htm.

Zalman, Amy. "War in Afghanistan—the History behind the U.S. War in Afghanistan." http://terrorism.about.com/od/warinafghanistan/ss/AfghanistanWar _6.htm.

Index

Abu Ghraib prison, 10
American takeover of, 314
   closing of, 324
   Coalition POWs sent to, 298
   prisoner abuse scandal, 314, 315–24
   renamed Baghdad Central Prison,
      324
   return to the Iraqi government, 348
Adams, Sgt. Harry J., 163
Adams, John, 34, 51
   Declaration of Independence, 38
   Declaration of Rights and
      Grievances, 36
   Franco-American relations and, 49,
      50
   Sedition Act of 1798, 174
Adams, Samuel, 34
Adenauer, Konrad, 201
Adolph, Maj. Gen. Friedrich, 13
Afghanistan, 300
   the Taliban and, 346
Afghanistan War
   Bush Doctrine and, 306
   legal handling of terrorist captives,
      312–14
   number of Taliban partisans, 348
   overview, 307–8, 346
   treatment of Taliban prisoners, 10,
      346
Afrika Korps, 185, 186, 194, 195
Afrikaners, 180
agents provocateur, in Korean POW
   camps, 256–57
Aguinaldo, Emilio, 6, 145, 146,
   153–55, 340
Alexandra Hospital (Singapore), 207
Algeria, 51

Alien and Sedition Act, 198
Alien Enemies Act of 1792, 198
Alien Registration Act, 199
All-American Division (AEF), 165
Allen, Ethan, 2
Al Odah v. United States, 331
al-Qaeda
   attacks by, 10, 303–4
   the Bush Doctrine and, 306
   CIA probing of, 300
   intelligence community knowledge
      of, 345–46
   origin of, 303
   prisoners at Guantánamo Bay
      detention facility, 325–26, 327–31
   tactics of, 304
   U.S. legal handling of, 312–14
Al-Rashid military prison, 298
Altoff, Gerard T., 68
Ambrose, Stephen E., 230
"American Century, The" (Luce), 7
American Civil Liberties Union
   (ACLU), 221, 330, 331
American colonies
   anti-Loyalist statutes, 38–40
   Forest Wars, 114–15
   relationship to Great Britain, 32,
      33–36
   Tories and Whigs, 32–33
American Expeditionary Force (AEF),
   160
American Historical Division, 186
American Legion, 178
American Red Cross, 168
American Revolution
   American treatment of POWs, 336
   Benedict Arnold, 20–22

American Revolution (*continued*)
British declaration of war, 37–38
British legal handling of POWs
during, 11–12, 335–36
Camden, 19
Charleston, siege of, 16
commissaries of prisoners, 12
Convention of Saratoga, 15–16
Convention prisoners, 25–27
Cowpens, 22
Declaration of Independence, 38
espionage in, 20
exchange of POWs, 12, 13
French entry into, 22
great escapers, xv
guerrilla warfare, 41–42
Guilford Courthouse, 22
Hessian EPWs, 23–25, 27–30
Iroquois and, 116
King's Mountain, 17–19
large group captures in, 13
Lexington and Concord, 33–36
Loyalists (*see* Loyalists)
military tribunals and, 336
origins of, 33–36
partisan groups in, 19
POW exchanges, 30–31
prison hulks, 16
Saratoga, 14–15
treatment of POWs, 11, 12, 16,
23–27, 30–31 (*see also* British
POWs; Hessian POWs)
Trenton, 13–14
Wyoming Valley, 40–41
Yorktown, 16, 22–23
Yorktown prisoners, 27
American Special Forces, 307
Amery, John, 246, 248
Amish, 226
Amity, Treaty of, 167
Amnesty International, 315, 332
Ampudia, Gen. Pedro de, 72, 73
Anburey, Lt. Thomas, 25–27
Anderson, Jane, 400n42
Andersonville, 93, 107–8, 362–63
Andersonvilles of the North (Gillispie),
94

André, Maj. John, 20–21, 336
Angel Island, 209
Anglicans, 36
AntiFa, 190
Anti-Imperialist League, 151
anti-imperialists, 151
anti-Semitism, 229
Apache. *See* Chiricahua Apache
Arapaho, 5, 119, 123, 124, 125, 128
Argonne offensive, 165–66
Arista, Mariano, 71
Armstrong, John, 63–64
Armstrong, Samuel Chapman, 127
Army Intelligence Service, 219–20
Army of Vietnam (ARVN), 270
Arnim, Gen. Jürgen von, 185
Arnold, Benedict, 12, 15, 20–22, 43
Article I (U.S. Constitution), 45, 99
ARVN. *See* Army of Vietnam
Association Test Acts, 38–39
atomic bombs, 213
Atwater, Dorrance, 108
Auger, Anne Simon, 276–77
Australia, Japanese POWs and, 214–15
Ayres, Col. Leonard P., 166
Azerodt, George, 108
Azia, Tariq, 294

Baath Party, 294
Bacque, James, 8, 190, 230
Bad Kreuznach, 232
Badoglio, Gen. Pietro, 195
Baghdad Central Prison, 324
Baghdad Detention Center, 314. *See*
also Abu Ghraib prison
bagnio, 50–51
Bagram, 309
Bagram Air Base, 307
Baker, James, 294
Balangiga, 149–50
Baldwin, Leland D., 53, 57
Baltimore, War of 1812, 58–59
Bamboo War. *See* Philippine-American
War
Barbary Wars, 50–52
Barclay, Thomas, 60, 63
Barnby, H. M., 50

Bartoloméo, Anastasio, 147
Barton, Clara, 108, 168
bastinado, 51, 347
Bataan Death March, 207
Bathurst, Lord, 64
Battalion of Saint Patrick, 3, 84,
    85–86, 338
Battle Lake, 121
Beauregard, Gen. P. T. G., 83, 107
Beaver Dams, battle of, 65
Beech, Keyes, 250–51
Beirut bombing, 292
Bella Vista, 197
Belleau Wood, 164
Bellinger, John, III, 330
Benedict XV, 268
Benevolent Assimilation Proclamation,
    145
Bennett, Sgt. Harold C., 272
Berger, Ernest Peter, 183, 184
Bermann-Fischer, 186, 187
Best, Robert H., 236, 400n42
Biddle, Francis, 216–17
Bien Hoa camp, 271
Biess, Frank, 191
Big Eagle, 119, 121
Bilbo, Lt. Col. Jon, 296, 299
"Biltmore," 298
bin Laden, Osama, 10, 299–300, 303,
    307–8, 326, 345
Birch Coulee, battle of, 121
Bischof, Günter, 230
Black, Hugo, 221
Black Hawk's War, 117–18
Black Kettle, 119, 123
"Black List #1," 411n12
"black sites," 332
black soldiers
    Loyalists in the American
        Revolution, 44
    race relations with Italian POWs,
        197
    Union troops in the Civil War, 94,
        96
Bladensburg, battle of, 65
Bladensburg Races, 65
Blakeney, Robert, xiv–xv

bloodlust, 2
Blood Thirsters, 119
boarding schools
    Carlisle Indian School, 128
    Hampton Institute, 127
Boatner, Gen. Haydon L., 261, 262,
    268
Böhme, Franz Magnus, 28
Böhme, Kurt W., 190, 230, 393n37
Bolanger, Matthew Scott, 321
Boller, Paul F., Jr., 213
Bondy, Curt, 191
"bone films," 189
Book of Chronicles, 349
Booth, John Wilkes, 102
Bordenkircher, Donald E., 281, 282
Boston Massacre, 33
Boston Tea Party, 35
Boudinot, Elias, 12
Boughton, Capt. D. H., 149
Bowers, Brig. Gen. Clarence H., 153
Bowie, Lucy Leigh, 27
Bowmansville prison camp, 188
Boyd, Belle, 105–7
Bradley, Gen. Omar, 259
Bragg, Gen. Braxton, 75, 104, 105
Brand, Oscar, 412n34
Brandon, William, 123
Brant, Chief Joseph, 40, 41
Brasseterre, 376n2
Bricha, 229
Brinkley, H. H., 55
British Expeditionary Force (BEF), 166
British Legion, 17
British POWs
    from the American Revolution, 12,
        15–16, 25–27
    Convention Army, 15–16
    treatment by Japan during World
        War II, 206–8
broadcasters, treason during World
        War II, 236–39
"Bronx" camp, 298
"Brooklyn" camp, 298
Brooks, David, 294–95, 300
Brown, Dee, 119
Brown, Maj. Gen. Preston, 186

Brundidge, Henry, 243
Brussels Code, 111, 168
Bucca, Ronald, 411n10
Buddhism, 212
Buena Vista, battle of, 75–76
Buffalo Soldiers, 147
Buford, Col. Abraham, 17
Bullard, Maj. Gen. Robert Lee, 163–64
"Bunker," 298
Bunker, Elsworth, 284
Bureau of Indian Affairs, 118
Burgoyne, Maj. Gen. John, 13, 14, 15, 16, 25, 26
Burma-Thailand Railway, 206
Burnside, Gen. Ambrose, 103–4
Burt, Kendal, 187
Burton, Colonel H. S., 109, 110
Bush, George H. W., 294, 295
Bush, George W., 310
    Abu Ghraib scandal and, 318
    Afghanistan War and, 306, 346
    Bush Doctrine, 306
    declares hostilities in Iraq over, 317
    executive order on the legal handling of international terrorists, 311–12
    global war on terror, 10, 303
    memorandum on the humane treatment of international terrorists, 312–13
Bush Doctrine, 306, 308
Bushido warrior code, 203, 205–6
Butler, Gen. Benjamin, 97
Butler, Gen. William O., 88
Byron Hot Springs, 186

Camden, battle of, 19
Campbell, Col. William, 18
Camp Bucca, 314, 315, 323, 411n10
Camp Chase, 95
Camp Clinton, 186
Camp Cropper, 314–15
Camp Ellis, 193
Camp Elmira, 95
Camp Featherston, 214
Camp George Johnson, 197

Camp Hot Springs, 169
Camp Jessup, 169
Camp Joseph T. Robinson, 180–81
Camp McCoy, 208, 209, 213
Camp Mexia, 186
Camp Papago Park, 189
Camp Rhino, 307
Camp Savage, 213
Camp Sumter, 108
Camp Topaz, 221
Camp Upton, 192
Canada
    POWs in the Convention Army, 16
    treatment of World War II German POWs, 187
    War of 1812 and, 67
Can Tho camp, 271
Cantigny, 163–64
Cao Dai, 282
Carleton, Gen. Sir Guy, 30
Carlisle, Abraham, 46
Carlisle Indian School, 128
Carlson, Lewis H., 253
cartels
    of 1813, 377n26
    Dix-Hill cartel, 4, 92, 96, 110–11, 339
    War of 1812, 60–62, 337, 351–59
Carter, Jimmy, 222
Catholics and the Catholic Church
    American nativism and, 84, 85, 87
    Mexican War and, 84, 85, 86–87, 338
    in Mexico, 73–74, 78
    the Quebec Act and, 35
Caudle, Theron L., 244
Cavite, battle of, 140
CBS, 317
Center for Constitutional Rights, 330, 331
Central Intelligence Agency (CIA)
    "black sites," 332
    destruction of interrogation tapes in Thailand, 349
    detention centers, 331–32
    interrogations and, 331

operations against al-Qaeda, 300
torture and, 347–48
Vietnam War and, 282–83
Cerro Gordo, battle of, 78–79
Cervera, Adm. Pascual, 140, 142, 143, 144
Chaffee, Gen. Adna, 154, 155
Chandler, Douglas, 236, 400n42
Chapultepec, battle of, 83–84
Charleston, siege of, 16
"Charlie," 270. *See also* Vietcong
Chase, Salmon P., 110
Chateau-Thierry, battle of, 164
Chatto, 129–30
Cheju-do, 255–56
Cherokees, 115, 118
Chesapeake (USS), 52
Chesney, Capt. Alexander, 18
Cheyenne Indians, 119, 123, 124, 125, 128
Chickasaw, 118
Chief Joseph, 128
Chieu Hoi (Open Arms) program, 284, 288, 345
Chihuahua, 77
Chimborazo Hospital, 95
Chinese POWs of the Korean War, 250. *See also* Korean War POWs
Chiricahua Apache, 5, 128–34
Chivington, Col. John M., 119
Choctaw, 118
Chou En-lai, 265
Christian slaves, during the Barbary Wars, 50–51
Chronicles, Book of, 349
Churchill, Winston, 227, 248, ix
Churubusco, battle of, 80–81, 86
City of Rome (USS), 144
Civilian Irregular Defense Forces (South Vietnam), 270
Civil Liberties Act, 222
Civil War
  beginning of, 89
  Confederate spies, 104–7
  Dix-Hill cartel, 4, 92, 96, 110–11, 339

great escapers, xv
habeas corpus suspended, 99–104, 339
intelligence in, 98
military commissions and tribunals, 336, 339–40
parole system and, 89
political prisoners, 5, 99–104, 111
post-war trial of Henry Wirtz, 93–94
POW camps and prisons, 90–92, 96–97, 101, 108, 110, 359–61
POW exchanges, 4, 110–11
precedents set by, 111
spies, 112
Union General Order 207, 92–93
Union halt to POW exchanges, 92, 94, 96
war criminals, 107–10
Civil War POWs
  black Union troops, 94, 96
  captivity narratives, 94–95
  Confederate spies, 104–7
  conversion of, 97–98
  disease and, 96–97
  exchanges, 4, 110–11
  experiences in captivity, 89–90, 110
  General Order 100 and, 93
  General Order 207 and, 92–93
  memoir writers, 90
  numbers of, 90
  political prisoners, 99–104
  starvation and, 96
  treatment of, 4–5, 92, 94–96, 338–40
Clark, Gen. Mark W., 229, 259, 260, 262–63, 267
Clarke, Richard A., 345, 346
class A criminals, 234, 235, 239, 240
class B criminals, 234, 239, 240
class C criminals, 234, 239, 240
class II labor, 184
Clavell, James, 206–7, 395n21
Cleveland, Grover, 138
Clinton, Bill, 198, 289, 299–300
Clinton, Henry, 13, 14, 16, 17, 20, 29

Coalition (Persian Gulf War), 9, 294
Cobra II, 314
Cobra II (Gordon & Trainor), 319
Code of Conduct of 1954, 327, 370
Cogliano, Francis D., 35
Colby, William E., 284, 345, 406n45
Cole, Ronald H., 293
Collins, Wayne, 244
colonialism, American, 136–37
Colson, Brig. Gen. Charles F., 259–60, 261
Columbus, Christopher, 113
Columbus (SS), 199
Colville Reservation, 128
Comanches, 5, 123, 124, 125, 128
Combatant Review Tribunals, 330
commissaries of prisoners, 12
Committee for the Liberation of the Peoples of Russia, 249
Committee on Public Information, 173, 342
Committees of Correspondence, 33
Committees of Safety, 3
Common Sense (Paine), 38
Communist Party, in Germany, 178
concentration camps, 228
Concord, 36
Condé, Brig. Gen. Garcia, 76
Condor (British blockade runner), 107
Congregationalists, 25
Connecticut, Test Act of, 39
Connor, Commodore David E, 77
Con Son Island, 285
Constellation (USS), 50
Constitution (USS), 56, 57
Contereas, battle of, 80–81
Continental Association, 36
Continental Congress
    First, 35–36
    Quaker political prisoners and, 44–45
    Second, 37
Convention Army, 15–16
Convention of 1800, 50
Convention of Saratoga, 15–16
Convention prisoners, 25–27
Cook, Haruko Taya, 241
Cook, Theodore F., 241

Cook, Tim, 161
Copperheads, 99, 100, 103–4
Cornwallis, Gen. Charles Lord, 13, 17, 22
corpus delicti, 45
Cousens, Maj. Charles W., 242
cowardice, 226
Cowpens, battle of, 22
Cowra, 214–15
Cragg, Dan, 278
Crane, Maj. C. J., 150
Craven, John, 109
Creek, 117, 118
Creel, George, 173, 342
Crook, Gen. George, 128, 129, 383n31
Cruiz, Armin J., 323
Cuba, 6
    American expansionism and, 137
    American "yellow" journalism and, 137
    Guantánamo Bay Naval Base and, 325
    insurrection against Spain, 138
    Ten Years' War, 384n2
    terms of the treaty ending the Spanish-American War and, 144
    USS *Maine* incident, 138–39
Cucullo, Lt. Col. Gordon, 329
Culper Spy Ring, 20
Cunningham, Owen, 240
Currency Act, 33
Custodial Detention Index, 199

Dachau concentration camp, 235
Dacres, James R., 56
Daehne, Wilhelm, 199
Dalhunty, Robert J., 312
Daly, Sgt. Dan, 164, 388n17
Damangus, 149
Da Nang camp, 271
d'Aquino, Felipe, 242
d'Aquino, Iva Toguri. *See* Toguri, Iva
Darby, Joseph M., 315, 321
Darkest before Dawn (Work), 176
Dartmoor military prison, 60, 67
Dasch, Georg, 183–84
Daughters of Liberty, 33

Davie, William, 42
Davis, David, 103
Davis, Sgt. Jarval S., 321, 323
Davis, Jefferson, 72, 104, 107, 108–10
Davis, Sam, 104–5
Davis, Varina, 109
Davison, Edward, 191
Dean, Gen. William F., 253
Dearborn, Maj. Gen. John, 64
death camps, 189, 228
"Death" Railway, 206
Debs, Eugene V., 160, 174–76
Declaration of Independence, 38
Declaratory Act, 33
Defense Directive 2310.1, 314
Defense of the Realm Act, 172–73
Defense Reorganization Act of 1986,
    293
De Jur Belli ac Pacis (Grotius), 304
DeLancey, James, 41–42
DeLancey's Cowboys, 41–42
Delaney, Edward, 400n42
de las Casas, Bartolomé, 113, 114
Delaware, Test Act of, 39
Demilitarized Zone (Korea), 265
Democratic Republic of Vietnam. See
    North Vietnam
Denton, Jeremiah A., Jr., 347
Der Ruf, 187, 191–92, 392nn26–27
deserters
    Americans during World War II, 226
    San Patricios, 3, 84, 85–86, 338
    treatment during the Mexican War,
        3–4
"detainees"
    Abu Ghraib prison scandal, 314,
        315–24
    German, 199–200
    in the Iraq War, 314
    Taliban prisoners as, 346
    in the Vietnam War, 285
    in the war on terror, 309
Detainee Treatment Act, 324, 347
detention centers, CIA-run, 331–32
Devastation of the Indies (de las
    Casas), 113
Dewey, Adm. George, 145

Dewey, Commodore George, 140, 141
DeWitt, Gen. John L., 216, 219
DeWolfe, Thomas, 244
Die Geschlagenen (Richter), 180
diplomatic codes, World War I and,
    159–60
diplomats, 199
Directive 20-41 (MACV), 287
disarmed enemy forces (DEFs),
    German, 190, 230–33, 343
"disarmed enemy personnel," 190
displaced person camps, 226
displaced persons
    administration of, 226
    admitted to the U.S., 229–30
    categories of, 226
    Jews, 228–29
    repatriation problem following
        World War II, 8, 226–28, 245–46
Displaced Persons Act, 229
dissenters, treatment during World
    War I, 173–76
Dix, John A., 110
Dix-Hill cartel, 4, 92, 96, 110–11, 339
Dodd, Brig. Gen. Francis, 258–60, 261
Döhla, Johann Conrad, 29, 30, 42–43
domestic subversion, American fears of
    during World War I, 160
Dominguez, Manuel, 84
Dominguez's Scouts, 84
Dominicans, 114
Doniphan, Alexander, 76–77
Dower, John, 1
Dreschler, Werner, 224, 225
Drexel, Constance, 400n42
Drinker, Henry, 47
Drottningholm (SS), 200
Dummer's War, 115
Dunant, Henri, 111, 167–68
Durchgagslager Luftwaffe, 188
dysentery, 232

Eager, John B., 195
East, Robert A., 40
East Germany, 190–91
East India Tea Company, 35
Eastman, Max, 176

Eden, Anthony, 254
Ehrhart, W. D., 277–78
Eighteenth U.S. Infantry, 153
800th Military Police Brigade, 315, 318, 320, 323
Eighty-Second Division (All American Division), 165
Eisenhower, Dwight D., 226, 229
Eisenhower, John S. D., 72
El Caney, 140
Elliff, Nathan T., 244
Elliott, Andrew, 40
Ellis Island, 199
Elmira prison, 131
Emergency Detention Program, 198–99
Emory, Maj. C. D., 124–25
emperor death cult, 7
encomienda system, 114
Endicott, William C., 129
Endo, Mitsuye, 221
"Enemies at Large" (Hoover), 193
enemy aliens
  German, 198
  Italian, 197–98
  treatment in America during World War I, 171–72
Enemy Prisoners of War, Civilian Internees, and Detained Persons, 339
England, Lynndie R., 321
English common law, habeas corpus and personal freedom in, 45
Erk, Ludwig, 28
escapers
  of intolerable cruelty, xiv
  by opportunity, xiv–xv
  See also great escapes
Esopus War, 115
espionage
  in the American Revolution, 20, 43
  See also spies
Espionage Act, 160, 174, 176, 342
Ethiopian Regiment, 44
Eulate, Capt. Antonio, 143
event scenarios, of POWs, xiii–xiv
exchange cartels. *See* cartels

exchanges. *See* POW exchanges
Executive Order 9066, 215, 216, 221, 366–67
Executive Order 1 (Lincoln), 99
expansionism, American, 136–37
Ex parte Endo, 221
Ex parte Merryman, 99
Ex parte Milligan, 103, 172, 184, 336
extraordinary rendition, 332

Factory, 191
Fagan, David, 147
Fairfield Camp, 195
Fallen Timbers, battle of, 52, 117
famines, 85
Faust, Drew Gilpin, 90
"Faustball Tunnel," 189
Federal Bureau of Investigation (FBI)
  arrests of Germans in America, 200
  Custodial Detention Index, 199
  recapture of escape POWs, 392n33
  rounding up of Japanese Americans, 215
Federalists, 67
Feith, Douglas J., 305
Ferguson, Niall, 161, 170–71
Ferguson, Lt. Col. Patrick, 17–18
Fifteenth Marine Expeditionary Unit, 307
Fifteenth U.S. Cavalry, 153
Fifth Infantry, 124
Filipino EPWs
  Emilio Aguinaldo, 153–55
  torture of, 152–53
  treatment of, 6, 340
Filipino insurrection, 340–41
Filipinos, Bataan Death March and, 207
First Continental Congress, 35–36
First Division (AEF), 163–64
First Missouri Mounted Infantry, 76, 77
First POW Field Hospital (Korea), 263–64
First Tidewater War, 114
Fischer Verlag, 187
Fleming, Thomas, 160

"Flying Artillery," 72
forced repatriation
  following World War II, 8, 227, 246,
    343–44
  Korean War and, 8, 230, 254, 344
  Yalta agreement and, 248–49
Ford, Antonia, 105
Ford, Gerald R., 245
Forest Wars, 114–15
Fort Dearborn, 53
Fort Delaware, 90–92, 108, 380n5
Fort Douglas, 169, 170
Fort George Meade, 186
Fort Henry, 59
Fort Lafayette, 101
Fort Leavenworth, 130, 224
Fort Marion, 126, 127, 128, 129, 130,
    132
Fort McPherson, 169
Fort Missoula, 197
Fort Monroe, 109
Fort Oglethorpe, 169, 172
Fort Pickens, 130, 131, 132
Fort Ridgely, 120–21
Fort Sill, 132–33, 134
Fort Snelling, 213
Fort Stanton, 199
Forty-second Division, 162
442nd Regimental Combat Team,
    220–21
"Four-Minute Men," 173
Fox (American privateer), 55–56
Fox Indians, 118
France
  the American Revolution and, 22
  employment of German POWs in the
    Foreign Legion, 193
  relations with America following the
    Revolution, 49–50
Frank, Hans, 235
Franklin, Benjamin, 38
Franzozen, 180
Fraser, Brig. Gen. Simon, 15
Frederick, Sgt. Ivan L., 323
"Freedom Village," 267
Freeman, Douglas Southall, 13
Freikorps, 178

French and Indian War, 115
French Foreign Legion, 193
Frick, William, 235
frigates, 56
"Fritz Ritz, The," 392n23
From the Danube to the Yalu (Clark),
    262–63
Fugita, Sgt. Frank, 242
Funston, Brig. Gen. Fred, 153–56,
    387n59
Furutaka (Japanese heavy cruiser), 214
Furze, John, 55
Futch, Ovid L., 107

Gaertner, Georg, 194
Gage, Gen. Thomas, 35, 36
"galvanized" Yankees, 97–98, 119, 121
Gardner, Alexander, 108
Gardner, Col. Cornelius, 150
Garroway, Dave, 194
Garwood, Robert, 289
Gates, Gen. Horatio ("Granny Gates"),
    13, 15, 16, 18–19, 25
Gates, John M., 147
Gatewood, Lt. Charles, 128, 130
Gatewood, Willard B., Jr., 147
Gebhardt, Maj. James F., 324
General H. F. Hodges (USS), 244
General Order 100, 167, 168
  the Civil War and, 4
  origin of, 93
  the Philippine-American War and,
    148, 157
  treatment of POWs and, 93
  during World War I, 6
  See also General Order 207
General Order 207
  origin and significance of, 92–93, 339
  text of, 361–62
  See also General Order 100
General Order 38 (Ambrose Burnside),
    103
General Order 54 (War Department),
    169
General Order 116 (William Butler), 88
General Order 296 (Winfield Scott),
    86–87

General Order 340 (Winfield Scott), 86
Geneva Accords of 1954, Vietnam and, 269
Geneva Convention of 1864, 143
Geneva Convention of 1925, 181
Geneva Convention of 1929, 7, 181, 182, 342
Geneva Convention of 1949, 245
  Articles 85 and 108, 405n10
  North Vietnam and, 269
  text of, 369–70
  U.S. legal handling of international terrorists and, 10, 312, 313, 314
  Vietnam War and, 290
Geneva Conventions, General Order 100 and, 339
George, Alexander L., 252
George III, 37, 38
Georgia
  forced removal of the Cherokees, 118
  Test Act of, 39
German, John and Lydia, 123
German, Julia and Adelaide, 124
German American Bund, 198
German American community, during World War II, 198
German Democratic Republic, 190–91
German "detainees," 199–200
German enemy aliens, 198
German immigrants, 173
German Odyssey, A (Hörner), 179, 180
German POWs of World War I
  American attitude toward, 167
  British utilization of, 166–67
  held in America, 169–70
  number of, 340, 388n4
  treatment of, 170, 176–77, 203
German POWs of World War II
  Afrikaners and *Franzozen,* 180
  conditions in Canada, 187
  detained by the Soviet Union, 402n7
  as "disarmed enemy forces," 190, 230–33, 343
  escapes, 182, 187–89, 193–94
  executed for murder, 223–24
  experiences and treatment of, 8, 179–81, 184–85, 342–43
  in the French Foreign Legion, 193
  generals, 185–86
  the Holocaust and, 189–90
  interrogations, 186, 188
  labor and, 184
  numbers of, 179, 366
  post-war treatment, 230–33, 343
  prison camps, 186–87
  propagandizing of, 190–92
  reception at home, 201
  return from Russia, 201
  return to Europe, 192–93
  saboteurs, 182–84
  submarine crews, 188
Germany
  Italian POWs in, 194
  military intelligence during World War II, 188
  reception of World War II POWs, 201
Geronimo, Harlyn, 384n48
Geronimo (Goyathlay), 128–29, 130–31, 132–33, 134, 384n48
Ghent, Treaty of, 59
Gillers, Mildred ("Axis Sally"), 190, 237–39, 248
Gillispie, James M., 94, 95, 96
Gilmore, Allison B., 212
Gilpin, Thomas, 47
Girth, Harry, 194
Goering, Hermann, 235
Goldwater-Nichols Act, 293
Gonard, Samuel A., 273
Gonfaloniere, Pedro Soderini, 113
Gonzalez, Alberto R., 312
Gordon, Michael R., 319
Gordon Highlanders, 59
Gottlieb, Col. Johann, 13
Government of Vietnam. *See* South Vietnam
Granada, 292–93
Graner, Charles, 320, 323
Grant, Ulysses S., 4, 122–23, 125
Grasse, Comte de, 22
Gray, J. Glen, 1–2
Gray Beard, 126
Grayson, William W., 157

Great Britain
  declares war on the American
    colonies, 37–38
  Defense of the Realm Act, 172–73
  execution of traitors following World
    War II, 246
  German POWs of senior rank and,
    185–86
  legal handling of POWs during the
    American Revolution, 335–36
  relationship of American colonies to,
    32, 33–36
Greater East Asia Co-Prosperity
  Sphere, 205
great escapes
  examples, xv
  of World War II German POWs, 189
Great Plains Wars, 119
Great War. See World War I
Greeley, Susan Burnham, 15
Greene, Nathanael, 22
Greenhow, Rose O'Neal, 107
Greenville, Treaty of, 52, 117
Gripsholm (SS), 200
Grotius, Hugo, 93, 304–5, 339
"GTMO" song, 324–25
Guadalupe-Hidalgo, Treaty of, 87
Guam, 137, 144
Guantánamo Bay detention facility
  American uncertainty about, 332–33
  CIA-run center within, 331–32
  closing of, 331, 348
  interrogations at, 326
  Iraqi "detainees" sent to, 314
  prisoner resistance behavior at,
    327–29
  purpose of, 325
  Taliban prisoners sent to, 312, 346
  "unlawful combatants" detained at,
    308
  U.S. legal handling of prisoners,
    329–31
  war on terror "detainees" held at,
    309
Guantánamo Bay Naval Base, 324–25
Guerriere (HMS), 56, 57
guerrillas, in General Order 100, 148

guerrilla warfare
  in the American Revolution, 41–42
  Filipino insurrection, 340–41
  impact on the Philippine-American
    War, 152–53
Guilford Courthouse, battle of, 22
Gulags, 249

habeas corpus
  in English and American law, 45
  Guantánamo Bay prisoners and, 330
  Japanese American internees and,
    217
  suspended during the Civil War,
    99–104, 339
Habeas Corpus Act, 45
Habib, Mahmoud, 308
Hague Convention of 1899, 6, 168
Hague Convention of 1907, 6
Hague Convention of 1909, 363–66
Hague Conventions, 167, 168
  General Order 100 and, 339
  Japan and, 202, 203
  World War I and, 160, 340
Hale, Capt. Nathan, 20
"Halfway House," 298. See also Al-
  Rashid military prison
Hall, James, 340
Halleck, Henry W., 92
Halpine, Charles, 109
Hamdan, Salim Ahmed, 330, 331
Hamdan v. Rumsfeld, 331
Hampton Institute, 127
Harbord, James, 164
Hardinge, Samuel, 106
Harman, Sabrina, 321
Harmar, Josiah, 117
Harris, Adm. Harry, 328
Harrison, Earl G., 229
Harrison, William Henry, 57, 65, 117
Hartford, Treaty of, 116
Hartford Convention, 66–67
Harvard incident, 143–44
Harworth, James M., 124
Hawaii, 217–18, 384n1
Hay, John, 142
Hearst, William Randolph, 137

Index

Heister, Gen. von, 23
Hellfirtsch, Capt. Wolfgang Hermann, 188–89
Helms, Richard, 283
Henley, Col. David, 11, 26
Herald, David, 108
Hersh, Seymour, 317
Hess, John M., xv
Hess, Rudolf, 235
Hesse, 29
Hessian (derogatory term), 28
Hessian POWs
   from the battle of Trenton, 23–25
   Convention Army, 16
   treatment of, 27, 30
Hessians
   battle of Trenton, 13–14
   folksongs, 27–28
   history of, 28–29
Hezbollah, 292
Hickey, Donald R., 58
Hicks, David, 308
Higgins, Marguerite, 250–51
Hill, D. H., 111
Hilsman, Roger, 275
Hirabayashi, Gordon, 221
Hirabayashi v. United States, 221
Hiroshima, 213
Hispaniola, 114
Hitler, Adolf, 178
Hitler's Last Soldier in America (Gaertner), 194
Hoa Hao, 282
Hobbs bill, 198
Ho Chi Minh, 273, 274
Hoffman, Col. William, 95
Hoi Chanh, 284, 285, 289
Holocaust, 189–90, 228
Holoman Air Force Base, 201
"Home Sweet Home" (propaganda radio program), 238
Hool, Lance, 87
Hoover, J. Edgar, 183, 193, 199, 216–17
Hörner, Helmut, 179, 180, 189, 192, 231
Hornet (USS), 56–57

Horseshoe Bend, battle of, 58
House Resolution 2442, 198
Houston, Jeanne Wakatsuki, 219
Houston, Sam, 69
Howard, Gen. Oliver O., 151–52
Howe, Gen. Lord William, 11, 13
Howells, W. D., 142
How to Live at the Front (Macquarrie), 163
Hudnut, S. B., 101–2
Hue, battle of, 277–78, 344
Huebecher, Karl, 170
Hull, Gen. William, 53
Human Intelligence Collector Operations, 339
hunger strikes, 329
Hunt, John, 47
Hunter College, 238, 239
Hurons, 115
Hussein, Saddam
   Baathist ideology and, 294–295, 300
   capture of, 315
   Persian Gulf War and, 294, 295, 296
   referred to as "Black List #1," 411n12
   violence against Kurds and Shiites, 9, 299, 300, 311
Hutchinson, Thomas, 34
Hyo-Soon Song, 250

I Attacked Pearl Harbor (Sakamaki), 209
Ienaga, Saburo, 205, 206, 240
immigrants
   World War I and, 173
   See also Irish immigrants
immigrant soldiers, treatment in the Mexican War, 3
Immigration and Naturalization Service, 199
imperialism, American, 136–37
Imperial Rescript to Soldiers and Sailors (Japan), 203
impressment, 52, 59, 62–63
Inchon, 250
Indian POWs
   Carlisle Indian School, 128
   Chiricahua Apaches, 128–34

experiences of, 135
treatment of, 5, 124–27
Indian reservations
forced concentration on, 118–19
railroad right-of-ways and, 123
Indians
assimilation policy, 127–28, 134–35
federal government assumes
stewardship of, 117
forced concentration on reservations,
118–19
nineteenth century demographics,
135
post-Revolution attitudes toward,
116–17
Spanish treatment of, 113–14
treated as POWs, 5, 124–27
War of 1812 and, 67
Indian schools
Carlisle Indian School, 128
residential, 5
Indian Territory, 117, 118, 123
Indian Wars
casualties from the Plains wars, 135
Forest Wars, 114–15
military commissions and tribunals,
336
Santee war, 119–22
treatment of Indian POWs, 5,
124–27
wars of annihilation, 123–24
wars of westward expansion, 117–18
Industrial Workers of the World
(IWW), 160, 177
*Influence of Sea Power upon History,
The* (Mahan), 136–37
Intelligence Coordination and
Exploitation of the Enemy (ICES),
283–84. *See also* Phoenix program
International Committee of the Red
Cross (ICRC), 111, 168, 273, 317,
319, 340
international law, Hugo Grotius and,
304–5
International Military Tribunal,
233–35, 239
International POW Agency, 168

international terrorists
American legal handling of, 10,
311–14
See also al-Qaeda
internment, of Japanese Americans
during World War II, 215–19
internment camps
Germans in, 199–200
for Japanese Americans, 216, 217,
218–19
interrogation
the CIA and, 331
at Guantánamo Bay detention
facility, 326
of Japanese POWs, 211
techniques, 347
of Vietnam War EPWs, 278–80
of World War II POWs, 181, 188
World War I rules on, 177–78
Intolerable Acts, 35
intolerable cruelty, xiv
Iraq
number of American-held detainees,
348
Saddam Hussein's violent repression
in, 300
weapons of mass destruction and,
300
Iraqi EPWs
Geneva Convention of 1949 and, 297
number of, 297
political asylum and, 299
POW camps, 298
repatriation, 298–99
Saudi Arabia and, 297–98
treatment in the Persian Gulf War, 9,
297, 298, 314, 345, 408–9n19
Iraq War
Abu Ghraib prison scandal, 314,
315–24
background to, 310–14
"detainees," 314
military actions in, 314
treatment of non-uniform wearing
captives, 10
U.S. legal handling of terrorist
captives, 311–14

Iraq War (*continued*)
  U.S. plans for, 311
"Irish Deserters," 338. *See also*
    Battalion of Saint Patrick
Irish immigrants, 173
  the Saint Patrick's Battalion, 3, 84,
    85–86, 338
Irish potato famine, 85
Irish problem, 85
"Iron Mike," 164
Iroquois, 40–41
Iroquois Six Nation Confederacy, 116
Isaacs, Edouard, 340
Issei, 216
Italian enemy aliens, 197–98
Italian POWs of World War II
  changing status of, 195
  conditions and treatment of, 194–95,
    343
  held by Germany, 194
  held by Great Britain, 194
  Italian Service Units, 195–97
  marriages while in the U.S. and, 197
  numbers in the U.S., 194, 195
  race relations and, 197
  repatriation, 197
  stereotyping of, 195
Italian Service Units, 195–97

Jackson, Andrew, 58, 59, 377n21
Jackson, Robert H., 236
Jackson, Gen. Thomas "Stonewall,"
    106
James, Edwin L., 164
Jamestown, 114
Japan
  attitudes toward surrender, 206
  Bushido warrior code and, 203,
    205–6
  development into a quasi-military
    state, 203–5
  emperor death cult during World
    War II, 7
  failure to ratify the Geneva
    Convention, 181
  Greater East Asia Co-Prosperity
    Sphere, 205

Hague Conventions and, 202, 203
  number of casualties in the
    Philippines, 210
  Russian POWs and, 202–3
  treatment of World War II POWs, 7,
    206–8
  treatment of World War I POWs,
    203
  U.S. psychological warfare against,
    212–13
Japan at War: An Oral History (Cook
    & Cook), 241
Japanese-American Citizen's League,
    220, 222
Japanese-American Evacuation Claims
    Act, 222
Japanese American internment
  apology and restitution for, 222
  legal challenges to, 221
  overview, 215–19
Japanese Americans
  internment during World War II (*see*
    Japanese American internment)
  racism against, 215–16
  soldiers during World War II,
    219–21
  See also Nisei
*Japanese Army Regulations for
    Handling Prisoners of War,* 202,
    205
Japanese POWs
  attitudes toward surrender, 208
  at Camp Featherston in New
    Zealand, 214
  at Cowra in Australia, 214–15
  escapes, 214
  executed as war criminals, 239–40
  experiences of, 208–10
  interrogation, 211
  Kojima Kiofumi, 211
  numbers of, 209
  prison camps, 213–14
  Kazuo Sakamaki, 208–9
  Ooka Shohei, 210
  Yamauchi Takeo, 209–10
  treatment of, 7, 211
  types of, 214

Jarvis, Stephen, 54
Jay's Treaty, 117
Jefferson, Thomas, 38, 51, 52
Jeremiah, 349
Jewish refugees, 200
Jews
    following World War II and the
        Holocaust, 228–29
    Zionist, 246
Jodl, Alfred, 235
Johnson, Andrew, 108–9
Johnson, Lyndon B., 273, 274, 275,
    282–83, 286
Johnston, Joseph E., 77
Joint Intelligence Center, Pacific Ocean
    Area (JOICPOA), 213
"Joliet Prison," 298. See also Abu
    Ghraib prison
Jones, Col. Buehring H., 98
Jones, Robert H., 121
Jones Act, 158
Jordán, Javier, 304
Joyce, William ("Lord Haw Haw"),
    246, 248
"Juchheiße nach Amerika," 27–28
Judd, Jacob, 40
Jünger, Ernst, ix
jurisdiction, Civil War political
    prisoners and, 102–3
Justice Act, 35

Kabul, 306
Kaltenbach, Frederick W., 236, 400n42
Kaltenbrunner, Ernst, 235
kamikaze missions, 208
Kandahar, 306
Karpinski, Brig. Gen. Janis, L., 323
Kaunas, 161
Keefer, Louis, 194–95
Keift's War, 114–15
Kennan, George, 248–49
Kenny, Kevin, 85
Kent, Gen. Jacob, 140
Kettle Hills, 140
Key, Francis Scott, 59
Khalid Sheikh Mohammed, 331
Kibata, Terumasa, 214

Kikuko, Miyagi, 210
Kimball Plan, 140
King Philip, 115
King Philip's War, 115
King Rat (Clavell), 206, 395n21
King's Mountain, battle of, 13, 17–19
Kiofumi, Kojima, 211
Kiowa, 5, 123–24, 125, 128
Kiowa-Apache, 123
Kit Carson Scouts, 284, 285, 406n46
Knockenfilmen, 189
Knox, Henry, 116, 117
Knyphausen, Gen. Wilhelm von, 29
Koischwitz, Emma, 238
Koischwitz, Max Otto, 236, 237–38,
    400n42
Koje-do prison camp, 267
    screening of EPWs, 255–56, 257
    uprising at, 258–62
Komer, Robert W. ("Blowtorch"), 283
Korcz, Leo, 180–81, 391n7
Korean People's Army, 249
Korean War
    beginning of, 249–50
    conclusion of, 268
    cost of, 250
    forced repatriation and, 8, 230, 254,
        344
    Koje-do prison camp uprising, 258–62
    Operation Big Switch, 267
    Operation Little Switch, 265–66
    Pongam-do camp uprising, 262
    surrender of North Korean and
        Chinese soldiers, 250–51
    taking of prisoners in, 251
    treatment of UN POWs in, 252–53
    UN forces in, 250
    UN troops refusing repatriation, 253
Korean War POWs
    agents provocateur, 256–57
    exchange of, 265–266, 267
    forced repatriation issue, 8, 230,
        254, 344
    insurrection and continuing the war
        within the camps, 258–64
    Koje-do prison camp uprising,
        258–62

Korean War POWs (*continued*)
  numbers of, 250, 251
  repatriation issue, 265
  screening of, 254–56, 257
  South Korean release of
    noncommunist POWs, 266–67
  treatment of, 253–54
  use of noncommunist POWs for
    intelligence operations, 252
Korematsu, Fred, 221
Kozur, Walter, 189
Krammer, Arnold, 182, 186, 194, 198,
  214, 308, 348, 392n23
Kretschmer, Otto, 188
Kugler, Joseph, 101–2
Kuhn, Fritz, 198
Kumagi, Naoshige, 211
Kurds, 9, 299, 300
Kutler, Stanley I., 245
Kuwait, 294

La Croix, W. L., 334
Laden, Osama bin. *See* bin Laden,
  Osama
Lafayette, Marquis de, 23
Lake Champlain, battle of, 58
Lake Erie, 57
Lake Mohonk Conference, 134
Lakota. *See* Sioux
Lamar, L. Q. C., 129
Lamb, Roger, 15, 25, 372n11
Landero, Gen. J. J., 78
Langdon, Col. Loomis L., 129
Lanning, Michael Lee, 278
Lapwing (British ship), 55–56
Las Guasimas, 140
Laurens, Henry, 46
*Law of Nations or the Principles of
  Natural Law, The* (Vattel), 335
law of war
  Hugo Grotius and, 304–5
  See also General Order 100; General
    Order 207
Lawrence, Frederick, 137
Lawrence, Capt. James, 56–57
Layton, Sgt. Reuben R., 321
League of German Officers, 190

League of Nations, Japan and, 204
Lean Bear, 126
Leasor, James, 187
Lee, Clark, 243
Lee, Patrick, 414n13
Lee, Richard Henry, 38
Lee, Robert E., 111
  Mexican War, 77, 78, 79, 80, 83
  Union General Order 207 and, 93
Lee Hak-loo, 261
"legality Tories," 36
Leininger, Barbara, xiv
Leipzig trials, 233
Lender, Mark Edward, 36
Leopard (HMS), 52
Lewis, Neil A., 329
Lexington, 36
Libby officer's prison, xv
liberalism, 159
libraries, 186–87
Lieber, Francis, 4, 92, 111
Lieut. James Moody's Narrative
  (Moody), 43
Lincoln, Abraham
  assassination, 102
  attitude toward Northern war
    resisters, 340
  Civil War and, 89
  election of 1864, 104
  POW issues and, 4, 92, 338, 339
  the Santee Sioux and, 122
  Alexander Stephens and, 381n37
  treatment of political prisoners and, 5
  Clement Vallandigham and, 104
  wartime suspension of habeas
    corpus, 99
Lincoln, Gen. Benjamin, 16
Lincoln conspirators, 108
Lindh, John Walker, 308
Lindsey, Gen. Julian R., 165
Linn, Brian McAllister, 152, 155, 156
l'Insurgente (French ship), 50
Little Crow, 120, 121–22
Livingston, Robert, 38
Lôme, Enrique Dupuy de, 139
Long Binh Jail, 287
Long Island, battle of, 12

Lord Dunmore's War, 115
Loring, Joshua, 12
"Lost Battalion," 220–21
Louisiana purchase, 51
Lovell, Edward J., 27
Lovell, James, 46
Loyalist captives
  battle of King's Mountain and, 13
  treatment of, 42–43
Loyalists
  alliance with the Iroquois, 40–41
  black, 44
  in the British army, 42
  emigrants following the Revolution,
   48
  failure to stop the Patriots, 38
  legal harassment of, 38–40
  loyalty oaths required of, 38–39
  military units, 40, 44
  organized units of, 351
  prior to the Revolution, 36
  privateers, 42
  Quaker, 44–48
  treatment during the Revolutionary
   War, 3, 337
Loyalty Acts, 3
loyalty oaths, 38–39
Luce, Henry R., 7, 191
Lukban, Gen. Vincente, 148, 149
Luzon Island, 155, 156

Macabebe Scouts, 154, 387n62
MacArthur, Gen. Arthur, 154, 155
MacArthur, Gen. Douglas, 239, 240
MacDonough, Lt. Thomas, 58
Machiavelli, Nicoló, 334
Mackenzie, Col. Ranald, 124–25
MacKenzie, S. P., 181, 206
Mackin, Elton E., 162–63
Macquarrie, Hector, 163
Madison, Dolley, 58
Madison, James, 52, 53, 57, 58, 63, 64
Mahan, Alfred Thayer, 136–37
Mahon, John K., 55
Maine (USS), 138–39, 384n6
"Major Evils of the Tokyo Trial, The"
  (Cunningham), 240

Manchester Manual, 327–28, 329
Manifest Destiny, 5, 69
Mankato, 121
Manzanar relocation center, 217, 219
March, Gen. Peyton C., 169
Marcy, William L., 71
Marechaussee Corps, 16
Mariana Island, 144
Marion, Francis, 42, 126
marriages, 197
Marshall, John A., 102
Marshall, John (Chief Justice), 118
Martial Justice (Whittingham), 224
Martin, James Kirby, 36
Martin, Joseph Plumb, 2, 21–22
Maryland, Test Act of, 39
Maschke, Erich, 230
Maschke Commission, 230, 399n22
Maschke series, 230
Mason, John, 60, 64
Massachusetts, Test Act of, 39
Massachusetts Government Act, 35
mass executions, of the Santee Sioux,
  122
Massow Riedesel, Friederike, 374n45
May, Glenn A., 151
McCain, John, 347
McClellan, George, 104
McCloy, John, 220
McIlhenny, Col. James, 186
McKiernan, Gen. David, 314, 316, 317
McKinley, William, 137, 139, 144, 145
McWhorter, Dean F., 183
Meade, George, 77
Medicine Lodge Treaty, 123
Megargee, Geoffrey, 303
Meiji era, 204
Meiji (Japanese emperor), 204, 205
Mein Flucht aus England (Werra), 188
Mekeel, Arthur J., 47
Menschner, Edgar, 224
Merryman, John, 99–100
Mescalero Apache reservation, 134
Metacom, 115
Meuse-Argonne campaign, 164–66
Mexican War
  American deserters, 84, 85–86

Mexican War (*continued*)
American recruitment of Mexicans,
· 84
end of, 87
EPW policy, 71, 79–80
immigrant soldiers in, 85
major battles of, 71–84
origins of, 69–70
parole of EPWs, 78, 79, 337–38
return of battle flags to Mexico, 88
San Patricio Battalion, 3, 84, 85–86,
338
terms of surrender in, 87
treatment of EPWs, 3, 87–88
treatment of immigrant deserters,
3–4
Mexico, 160, 189
Mexico City, 81, 83
Miles, Gen. Nelson A., 109, 129, 130
Military Assistance Command
Vietnam (MACV), 9, 271
Military Commission Act, 331
military commissions
Civil War, 339–40
the Dachau trials and, 235
Indian Wars, 336
Philippine-American War, 148–49
trying of "detainees" from the war
on terror, 309
trying of the Santee Sioux, 122
in U.S. legal handling of
international terrorists, 311–12
World War II, 336–37
Military Field Code (Japan), 205–6
military intelligence
Civil War, 98
German, during World War II, 188
Vietnam War, 282–83
Military Intelligence Service Language
School, 213
military tribunals
American Revolution, 336
Civil War, 336
Indian Wars, 336
Philippine-American War, 336
"militia myth," 67
Millbay Naval Prison, xv

Milligan, Lamdin P., 102–3
Mindanao Island, 156, 157
Minear, Richard H., 240
Minnesota Volunteers, 121
Mississippi Rifles, 75
Mohammed, Khalid Sheikh, 331
Mohegans, 116
Molino del Rey, battle of, 82
Monroe, James, 65, 66
Monroe Doctrine, 66
Montenegro, 168
Monterrey, battle of, 72–73
Montesquieu, 335
Montfauçon, 165
Montgomery, Gen. Bernard, 185
Montojo, Adm. Patricio, 140
Montreal, battle of, 53
Moody, James, 43
Moore, John Hammond, 196
Morales, Gen. Juan, 78
Morgan, Col. Albert C., 258
Morgan, Daniel "Big Dan," 14, 22
Morocco, 51
Mount Vernon Barracks, 132
"Mr. Charles," 405n20
Mudd, Samuel, 108
mujahideen, 307
Murray, John, 44
Myers, Gen. Richard, 317
My Lai, 2, 275
Myrick, Andrew, 120

Nagasaki, 213
Najibullah, Muhammad, 306
Nakhla, Adel, 321
Nam Il, 257
Napoleon Bonaparte, 51, 58, 199
Narragansetts, 116
*Narrative of a Revolutionary Soldier,
A* (Martin), 2
Narrative of Ethan Allen, The (Allen),
2
Nash, Carl, xii
National Commission on Terrorist
Attacks upon the United States
(9/11 Commission), 345
National Lawyers Guild, 330

National Liberation Front (Vietnam), 272–73. *See also* Vietminh
National Prisoner of War Memorial, 108
National Socialist German Workers Party. *See* Nazis
nativists, 198
naturalization, 52, 59, 62–63
Nazi British Free Corps, 248
Nazis, rise of, 178
Nelson, Torin S., 321
Nelson, William H., 33, 34
neoconservatives ("neocons"), 305–6
Neutral Nations Repatriation Commission, 265, 267
New Jersey, Test Act of, 39
New Orleans, battle of, 59
Newtown, battle of, 41
New Ulm, 120, 121
New York, Test Act of, 39
New Yorker, 317
New York Herald, 151
New Zealand, 214
Nez Perce, 128
Ngo Dinh Diem, 270
Nguyen Van Troi, 272
Niantics, 116
Nicholas II, 168
9/11 Commission, 345
Ninth Infantry Regiment, 149–50
Ninth Massachusetts Regiment, 143–44
Nisei
  internment during World War II, 215–19
  interrogation of Japanese POWs, 211
  psychological warfare and, 213
  soldiers during World War II, 219–21
Nixon, Richard M., 275
NKVD, 246, 249
noncombatants, treated in the exchange cartel of 1812, 61–62
Noriega, Manuel Antonio, 293–94
Norrington, Giles, xiii
Norris, George, 177
North Act, 60, 335

North Carolina, Test Act of, 39
North Korean POWs
  number of, 250
  See also Korean War POWs
North Vietnam
  sovereignty issue, 269–70
  torture of American POWs, 347
North Vietnamese Army (NVA), 405n20
North Vietnamese EPWs
  interrogation of, 278–80
  treatment of, 269
  See also Vietnam War EPWs
Northwest Ordinances, 116
Northwest Territory, 35
Nuremberg Principles, 8, 234, 245, 368–69
Nuremberg trials, 233–36

Oaks, Robert F., 46
oaths of allegiance, 156–57
Obama, Barack, 331, 348
O'Brien, Grace Barolet, 277
"Office of the Special Ambassador" (OSA), 281
Ohio Invasions, 117
Okinawa, 210
Old Capitol Prison, 105, 106, 107, 112
"Olive Branch Petition," 37
Olivotto, Guglielmo, 197
Olympia (USS), 140
101st Airborne Division, 308
109th Area Support Medical Battalion, 321
141st Infantry, Thirty-Sixth Division, 220
187th Airborne Regimental Combat Team, 261
109th Medical Detachment, 321
One Man's Hero (film), 87
One that Got Away, The (Burt & Leasor), 187
On the Law of War and Peace (Grotius), 304
Open Arms program. *See Chieu Hoi* (Open Arms) program
Operation Anaconda, 308

Operation Aviary, 252
Operation Big Switch, 267
Operation Bobcat, 252
Operation Desert Shield. *See* Persian
  Gulf War
Operation Desert Storm, 9, 345. *See
  also* Persian Gulf War
Operation Enduring Freedom, 307
Operation Iraqi Freedom, 314
Operation Just Cause, 293–94
Operation Keelhaul, 227
Operation Little Switch, 265–66
Operation Pastorius, 182–84
Operation Sauerkraut, 190
Operation Turncoat, 252
Operation Urgent Fury, 292–93
Operation Vapor, 193
Oregon Campaigns, 118
Osama bin Laden. *See* bin Laden,
  Osama
Osceola, 117, 126
O'Sullivan, John L., 69
Other Losses (Bacque), 8
Otis, Gen. Elwell S., 145–46, 154
Ottawa tribes, 115

Pabel, Sgt. Reinhold, 193–94, 393n50
Packard, J. W., 100–101
Packingham, Gen. Edward M., 59
Paine, Thomas, 38
Pak Sang-hyon, 256–57, 258, 403n36
Palestine, 229
Palmer, Frederick, 151
Palo Alto, battle of, 71–72
Palo Duro Canyon, 124
Panama, 293–94
Panama Canal, 294
Panay Island, 149
Papago Park, 224
Paredes, Mariano, 70
Paris, Treaty of, 6
Paris Peace Accords, 289
paroles
  Civil War, 89
  Mexican-American War, 78, 79,
    337–38

partisans
  in the American Revolution, 19
  in General Order 100, 148
partisan warfare, Filipino insurrection,
    340–41
Pashtun Taliban, 307
Pate, Lloyd, 253
Paul III, 114
Paul VI, 273–74
Peacock (HMS), 56–57
Pearl Harbor, 208
Pennsylvania
  holding of British prisoners during
    the War of 1812, 64
  Quakers and, 44–48
  Test Act of, 39
Pequot War, 114, 116
Perle, Richard, 305
Perry, Commodore Matthew G., 78
Perry, Commodore Oliver Hazard, 57
Pershing, Gen. John J., 160, 162, 167,
    340
Persian Gulf War
  air campaign, 295–96
  background to, 294–95
  Coalition losses, 296
  Coalition troop buildup, 295
  freezing of Iraqi assets, 295
  ground offensive, 296
  Iraqi losses, 296–97
  Iraqi treatment of Coalition POWs,
    298
  naval blockade of Iraq, 295
  U.S. POWs, 409n22
  See also Iraqi EPWs
personal freedom, English common
    law and, 45
Philippine-American War
  American soldiers' letters home,
    150–51
  anti-imperialists and, 151
  capture of Emilio Aguinaldo,
    153–55
  casualties, 146–47, 385n28
  conclusion of, 155–57
  conversion of American soldiers, 147

impact of guerrilla warfare in,
152–53
military commissions and tribunals,
148–49, 336
the nature of fighting in, 147, 149–50
number of soldiers in, 146
oath of allegiance, 156–57
origins of, 145–46
overview, 145
reception and treatment of American
veterans, 157
treatment of Filipino guerrillas, 6,
152–53, 340
unpopularity in America, 157
See also Filipino EPWs
Philippine Cavalry, 154
Philippine Insurrection. *See* Philippine-
American War
Philippines
American expansionism and, 137
independence, 158
Japanese casualties during World
War II, 210
World War II and, 158
Phillips, Maj. Gen. William, 16
Phoenix program, 9, 283–85, 291,
345, 406n45
Phu Quoc Island camp, 271, 272
Phytophthora infestans, 85
Pierrepoint, Albert, 246
Pike, Gen. Zebulon, 54
Pingree, H. S., 150
Pinkerton, Allan, 98
Plains Indians, 5
Platt Amendment, 144, 385n20
Playboy technique, 279–80
Pleiku camp, 271
Point Lookout, 108
Polak, John V., 321
Poland, 229
political asylum
Iraqi EPWs and, 299
Korean War POWs and, 344
World War II POWs and, 343–44
political prisoners
Civil War, 5, 99–104, 111

Quakers in the American
Revolution, 44–48
World War I, 174–76, 177
Polk, James K., 69–70, 71, 73, 74
Pongam-do camp, 262
Pontiac, Chief, 115
Pope, Gen. John, 121, 124
Port Act, 35
potato famine, 85
Potsdam Declaration, 213
Pound, Ezra, 400n42
POW camps and prisons
Civil War, 90–92, 96–97, 101, 108,
110, 359–61
German POWs of World War II,
186–87
Iraqi EPWs, 298
Japanese POWs of World War II,
213–14
Vietnam War EPWs, 271
Powell, Allan Kent, 176
Powell, Gen. Colin L., 311, 313
Powell, Lewis, 108
POW exchanges
American Revolution, 13, 30–31
Civil War, 4, 92, 94, 110–11
War of 1812, 60–62
World War II, 181
See also cartels
Powhatan Feedfights, 114
Pratt, Richard Henry, 124, 125–26,
126–27, 128, 134–35
press gang, 63
Prevost, George, 58, 64, 65
Prince, The (Machiavelli), 334
prison camps. *See* POW camps and
prisons
prisoners of state
Emergency Detention Program and,
198–99
German "detainees," 199–200
German enemy aliens, 198
internment camps, 199–200
Italian enemy aliens, 197–98
number of during World War II, 200
Prisoners of War (Kramer), 348

prisoners of war (POWs)
  event scenarios experienced by,
    xiii–xiv
  Geneva Convention of 1929 and,
    181
  as a humanitarian issue, 167–68
  "pure cussedness," 247
prisoner uprisings
  Koje-do prison camp, 258–62
  Pongam-do camp, 262
prison hulks, 16, 60
privateers, 42, 55–56
Proclamation 1364, 171
"Proclamation by the King for
    Suppressing Rebellion and
    Sedition," 37–38
Proctor, Gen. Henry, 58
Prohibitory Act, 38
propaganda
  treatment of Korean POWs and,
    252–53
  treatment of World War II POWs
    and, 190–92
  U.S use of against Japan in World
    War II, 212–13
Provance, Sgt. Samuel Jefferson, 321
Province Reconnaissance Units, 284,
  285
Prugh, George S., 270
Prussia, 167
psychological warfare, by the U.S.
    against Japan, 212–13
psychosis, in war, 2
Puebla, 84
Puerto Rico, 140, 144, 145
Pulitzer, Joseph, 137
"pure cussedness," 247
Puritans, 114
"PW," 183, 184, 389n37

Qala Jangi Fortress Prison, 307
Quakers, 44–48, 337
Quartering Act, 33, 35
Quebec Act, 35
Queenston, battle of, 53, 63
Quentz Lake spy school, 182

Quezon, Manuel, 158
Qui Nhon camp, 271

Rabbani, Burhanuddin, 306
race relations, between black soldiers
    and Italian POWs, 197
racism, Japanese attitudes toward
    POWs and, 206
radical Islamism, 304
Railroad Enabling Act of 1866, 123
ralliers, 284, 289
"rallying," 284
Rangers, 40
Rasul v. Bush, 330
Raven, Lt. Col. Wilbur R., 258–59
Reagan, Ronald, 222, 293
Red army purges, 248
Red Cloud, 122–23
Red Scare, 160
Red Stick Creeks, 58
Reed, Walter, 132
Rehnquist, William, 103
Reilly, Sgt. John, 85
"relocation center." See internment
    camps
Remembered Prisoners of a Forgotten
    War (Carlson), 253
rendition, 332
Renville Rangers, 120, 121
repatriation
  following World War II, 8, 226–28,
    245–46
  of World War I POWs, 177
  See also forced repatriation
Republican Guard, 297
Resaca de la Palma, battle of, 72
Rescript to Soldiers and Sailors
    (Japan), 205
Research and Development (RAND)
    Corporation, 251–52
reservations, forced removal to, 118–19
retaliation, 2
revenge, 2
Rhee, Syngman, 266–67
Rhine Meadows Camps, 230, 231, 343
Ribbentrop, Joachim von, 235

Richter, Hans Werner, 180, 192
Rickover, Adm. Hyman, 384n6
Ridgway, Gen. Matthew B., 256, 257, 259, 261
Riedesel, Friederike von, 15
Ringgold, Maj. Samuel, 72
River Raisin, battle of, 57
Roberts, John, 46
Robin, Ron, 192
Robinson, Michael C., 147
Robinson, Ralph, 62
Roche, Michael J., 244
"Rock of the Marne Division," 164
Rollins, Peter C., 275
Room 40, 159–60
Roosevelt, Edith K., 288
Roosevelt, Franklin Delano
    declares martial law in Hawaii, 217–18
    Executive Order 9066, 215, 216
    German saboteurs and, 183, 184
    Italian Americans and, 198
    use of Japanese American troops in World War II, 220
    Yalta agreement and, 227, 248
Roosevelt, Theodore, 136, 140, 155, 156, 159
Roosevelt, Theodore, Jr., 178
"ropes," 347
Roraback, Sgt. Kenneth, 273
Rosenberg, Alfred, 235
Rosengarten, Joseph G., 29
Ross, Maj. Gen. Robert, 65–66
Rossmeisl, Kurt, 194
Rousseau, Jean-Jacques, 335
Roxas, Manuel, 158
Rules of Land Warfare. See General Order 100
Rumsfeld, Donald H., 305, 310, 311, 318, 320
Russian POWs
    Russo-Japanese War, 202–3
    World War I, 161
    World War II, 246, 248–49
Russians, propagandizing of German POWs, 190–91

Russo-Japanese War, 202–3
Rutledge, John, 17
Ryan, Capt. J. A., 153

saboteurs, 182–84
Sacramento, battle of, 76–77
Saigo, 204
Sainte-Maire-au-Mines, 226
Saint-Mihiel, battle of, 164
Saint Patrick's Battalion, 3, 84, 85–86
Sakamaki, Kazuo, 208–9, 215
Samar Island, 149–50, 156
Samoa, 137
Sampson, Adm. William, 141
San Carlos Reservation, 128, 129
Sanchez, Lt. Gen. Ricardo, 315
Sand Creek massacre, 119
San Geronimo, 81
San Juan, 140
San Patricio Battalion, 3, 84, 85–86, 338
Santa Anna, Gen. Antonio Lopez de, 73–74, 75, 78–79, 81–82, 84, 338
Santee war, 119–22
Santiago de Cuba, 140
Santo Domingo, 51
Saratoga, battle of, 13, 14–15
Saudi Arabia, 9, 297–98, 345
Sauk Indians, 118
Schlesinger, Arthur M., Jr., xiii
Schlesinger, James R., 319
Schmemann, Serge, 300–302
Schubert, Frank N., 147
Schutzstaffel (SS), 178
Schwartzkopf, Maj. Gen. Norman, 293
Scott, Peter T., 166–67
Scott, Gen. Winfield
    forced removal of Cherokees and, 118
    Mexican War, 3–4, 74–87 passim
    War of 1812, 63
Scribner's Magazine, 151
Scud missiles, 296
SEALs, 283, 314
Seaveys Island, 142–43
Second Continental Congress, 37

Second Division (AEF), 164
Second Oregon Volunteer Infantry, 147
Second Tidewater War, 115
Second Virginia Regiment, 17
Second Würtemberg Landwehr
    Division, 166
"Secret Squirrel," 332
secular fundamentalism, 304
Seddon, James A., 96
Sedition Act of 1798, 174
Sedition Act of 1918, 160, 174, 342
Seminoles, 117, 118
Senate Armed Services Committee, 318
Senior, Col. Henry, 55–56
Senior Executive Service, 345
September 11 terrorist attacks, 300–303
Serbia, 168
SERE, 326–27, 412n40
Seventh Virginia Regiment, 17
Seventy-fifth Ranger Regiment, 307
Seven Year's War, 115
Seyss-Inquart, Arthur, 235
Shahi-Kot Valley, 308
"shanks," 328
Sharia, 306
Shawnees, 52, 53, 115
Sheridan, Gen. Philip, 124, 129
Sherman, Roger, 38
Sherman, Gen. William T., 123
Shibh, Ramzi bin al, 331
Shiites, 9, 299, 300
Shinseki, Gen. Eric, 410n2
Shohei, Ooka, 210
"shoot and scoot," 22, 72
Sibley, Henry H., 121
Sigsbee, Capt. Charles D., 139
Singapore, 207
Sioux Indians, Santee war, 119–22
Sisk, Mildred Elizabeth. See Gillers,
    Mildred
Sivits, Jeremy, 321
Sixth Cavalry, 124
Sixty Fourth Field Hospital (Korea),
    255
Skeleton Canyon, 130
slave prisons, 50
slaves, during the Barbary Wars, 50–51

Slovik, Eddie, 226
Smith, Eric M., 278
Smith, Jake, 150
Smith, William Drewet, 47
Smoked Yankees and the Struggle for
    Empire (Gatewood), 147
snapping, during war, 2
Social Democratic Party, 175, 177
socialism, American fears of during
    World War I, 160
Socialist Party, 160
Socialist Republic of Vietnam, 289
So Far from God (Eisenhower), 72
Soissons, battle of, 164
Soldier Reports, A (Westmoreland),
    271
Sons of Liberty, 3, 34, 35
South Carolina, Test Act of, 39
Southeast Asia Treaty Organization,
    274
South Vietnam
    ARVN treatment of EPWs, 286
    civilian prisons, 281
    political prisoners, 281–82
    sovereignty issue, 269–70
    treatment of Vietcong captives, 282,
        344–45
    Vietcong attacks on civilian prisons,
        282
Soviet Union
    detainment of German POWs, 402n7
    failure to sign the Geneva
        Convention, 181
    forced repatriation following World
        War II and, 227
    Red army purges, 248
    treatment of returning POWs from
        World War II, 246
Spain, 6, 208
    the Cuban insurrection and, 138
    terms of the treaty ending the
        Spanish-American War and, 144
    treatment of American Indians,
        113–14
Spandau prison, 235
Spanish-American War
    casualties in, 140

final peace treaty, 144–45
land engagements, 140
origins of, 136–39
Spanish EPWs, 142–44
treatment of EPWs, 340
U.S. Army in, 139–40
U.S. Navy and naval engagements,
140–42
Spanish flu epidemic, 172
Spanktown Yearly Meeting hoax,
45–46
Special Forces, 307
Special Operations Command, 293
Special Projects Division (U.S. Army),
191–92
Spidle, Jake W., 182
spies
American Revolution, 20, 43
Civil War, 112
Confederate, 104–7
James Moody, 43
Splinters of a Nation (Powell), 176
St. Clair, Arthur, 117
Stalag Luft III, xv
Stalin, Joseph, 227, 248
Stamp Act, 33
Stanley, Henry Morton, 97–98
Stanton, Edwin, 102, 108, 109, 110,
121
"Star-Spangled Banner," 59
Steinaker (USS), 412n35
Stephens, Alexander H., 90, 91, 109,
381n37
Stephens, Lt. John, 381n37
Steuben, Friedrich von, 40
Stirling, Gen. Lord, 12, 23
Stockel, H. Henrietta, 129
strapado, 347
Streicher, Julius, 235
Stuart, J. E. B., 105
Sturmabteilung (SA), 178
Sublimus Dei, 114
submarine crews, 188
Suddenly We Didn't Want to Die
(Mackin), 162–63
Suffolk County Resolves, 36
Sugamo prison, 239

Sugar Act, 33
Sullivan, Gen. John, 41, 45
Sumter, Thomas, 42
Supreme Headquarters, Allied
Expeditionary Force (SHAEF),
226, 227, 230
surface-to-air missiles, 296
Surrat, Mary, 108
surrender, Japanese attitude toward,
206
Sweitzer, Brian, 176
Switzerland, 168
Sword's Farm, 14

Taft, William Howard, 155
Taguba, Maj. Gen. Antonio M., 316,
317, 319–20
Taguba report, 317, 318, 319–23
Tajiks, 307
Taken Captive (Shohei), 210
Takeo, Yamauchi, 209–10
Takur Ghar, battle of, 308
Taliban, 10, 300, 306, 307, 348
Taliban captives, legal handling of,
312–14, 346
Talleyrand-Périgord, Charles-Maurice
de, 49, 50
Tallmadge, Maj. Benjamin, 20
Tampico, battle of, 74
Taney, Roger, 99–100
Tannenberg, 161
Tarleton, Lt. Col. Banastre, 17, 18, 42
"Tarleton's Quarter," 18
Taylor, Daniel, 14
Taylor, Gen. Zachary, 3, 338
Mexican War, 70–76 *passim*, 85, 87
tea, 33–34
Tea Act, 33
Tecumseh, 52, 53, 58, 117
Teller Amendment, 139
Temple, Brian, 90–91
Tenskwatawa, 52
Tenth Cavalry, 124
Tenth Mountain Division, 308
Ten Years' War, 384n2
terrorist attacks
by al-Qaeda, 303–4

terrorist attacks (*continued*)
Beirut bombing, 292
September 11, 2001, 300–303
terrorists. *See* al-Qaeda; international
terrorists
Test Acts, 3, 44, 48
Tet Offensive, 344
Teton Sioux, 122–23
Teufelhunde ("Devil Dogs"), 164
Texas, 69, 87
Thames, battle of the, 58, 117
Third Colorado Calvary, 119
Third Indiana Infantry, 75
Third Infantry Division (AEF), 164
Thirty-first Michigan Volunteers, 150
Thirty Year's War, 304
Thoma, Lt. Gen. Ritter von, 185
Thompson, H. C., 147
302nd Military Intelligence Battalion,
321
372nd Military Police Company, 320,
321
320th Military Police Battalion, 314,
320
Tibbitts, Craig, 166
Tiger Cage (Bordenkircher), 281
Tippecanoe, battle of, 117
Toffler, Alvin and Heidi, 299
Toguri, Ikuko. *See* Toguri, Iva
Toguri, Iva ("Tokyo Rose"), 190, 237,
241–45
Tokyo War Crimes Tribunal, 239–40
Toland, John, 215
Tolstoy, Nikolai, 248
Tonkin Gulf Declaration, 290
Tories, 32–33, 36
torture
the CIA and, 347–48
of Filipino EPWs, 6, 152–53
techniques, 347
"water board," 152
"water cure," 6, 152, 153
Towle, Philip A., 203
Townsend, Gen. E. D., 124
Townsend Acts, 34
Trail of Tears, 118
Trainor, Gen. Bernard, 319

traitors
treatment following World War II,
246
See also treason
"Transformation," 310
Traynor, Duane L., 183
treason
American's indicted for during
World War II, 400n42
broadcasters during World War II,
236–39
See also traitors
Treaty of Alliance of 1778, 49, 50
Treaty of Amity, 167
Treaty of Westphalia, 305
Trenton, battle of, 13–14
Tripoli, 51, 52
Trist, Nicholas, 82
Truman, Harry S., 220, 224, 229, 249,
344, 402n16
Truxton, Capt. Thomas "Terrible
Tom," 50
Tsurumi, Kazuko, 241
Tule Lake internment camp, 218–19
Tunis, 51
Turnbull, Maj. William, 80
Turner, Frederick Jackson, 136
Tuscarora War, 115
Tuskegee Institute, 127
Twain, Mark, 151
Twentieth Kansas Volunteer Infantry,
152, 153–54
Twenty-eighth Infantry Division (AEF),
164
Twenty-fourth Infantry Regiment, 147,
251
Twiggs, Brig. Gen. David E., 79
205th Military Intelligence Brigade,
321, 323
229th Military Police Company, 321
Tydings-McDuffie Act, 158

U-99, 188
U-202, 182
Um Qasr, 323
Undue Process (Krammer), 198
United Empire Loyalists, 53, 337

United Nations POWs, treatment
during the Korean War, 252–53
United Nations Relief and
Rehabilitation Administration
(UNRRA), 343
U.S. Army
Field Manual 2-22.3, 339
Field Manual 19-40, 339
integration of, 402n16
U.S. Code of Conduct of 1954, 327,
370
U.S. Constitution, on habeas corpus
and corpus delicti, 45
U.S. Displaced Persons Commission,
229
U.S. Marine Corps, Belleau Wood, 164
U.S. Navy
birth of, 50
SEALs, 283, 314
War of 1812, 54–55, 56–57
U.S. Supreme Court, Tokyo trials and,
240
United States Democratic Review, 69
"unlawful combatants," 308, 346
Un Souvenir de Solferino (Dunant),
111, 167–68
uprisings. *See* prisoner uprisings
Utley, Robert M., 135
Uzbeks, 307

Valencia, Gen. Gabriel, 80, 81
Vallandigham, Clement L., 103–4,
413n6
Van Fleet, Gen. James, 258, 259
Van Tyne, Claude Halstead, 42
Vattel, Emmerich de, 335
Vaux, battle of, 164
V Corps, 311
Velasco, Don Luis de, 113
Ventura, Mary Asaba, 221
Vera Cruz, battle of, 77–78
Versace, Capt. Humbert, 273
Versailles Treaty, 172, 204
*Very Brief Relation of the Destruction
of the Indies* (de las Casas), 114
Vespucci, Amerigo, 113
"Victor Charlie," 405n20

Vietcong
attacks on civilian prisons, 282
called "Victor Charlie," 405n20
kidnappings and assassinations by,
344
origin of, 270
reprisal executions, 272–73
treatment of American POWs,
272–73
Vietcong EPWs
South Vietnamese handling of, 282
status and treatment of, 270–71,
344–45
See also Vietnam War EPWs
Vietcong infrastructure, 281
Vietminh, 272–73
Vietnamese communists. *See* Vietcong
Vietnam Independence League. *See*
Vietminh
Vietnam-Perkesie (Ehrhart), 277–78
Vietnam War
American intelligence and, 282–83
Americans punished for war crimes,
287
background to, 269–70
"credibility gap," 274
"detainees," 285
Geneva Convention and, 271, 290
lack of a declaration of war in, 290
My Lai, 275
North Vietnamese Army, 405n20
Paris Peace Accords, 289
peace efforts through Pope Paul VI,
273–74
Phoenix program, 9, 283–85, 291,
345, 406n45
political prisoners, 285–86
the press and, 275
repatriation of EPWs, 287–89
reprisal executions, 272–73
treatment of American POWs,
272–73, 274, 347
Vietnam War EPWs
ARVN treatment of, 286
camps for, 271
Geneva Convention of 1949 and,
290

Vietnam War EPWs (*continued*)
interrogation, 278–80
medical care and, 276–77
North Vietnamese and Vietcong
housed together, 271–72
number of, 272
repatriation, 287–89, 291
status and treatment of, 8–9,
275–76, 286, 287, 290
See also Vietcong EPWs
Villingen breakout, xv
Vinz, Curt, 187
Virginia, Test Act of, 39
Virginia Massacre, 114
Virgin Islands, 158
Viriginia War, 114
Vison of an Invasion (Koischwitz), 239
Vlasov, Gen. Andrei, 249
Von Ryan's Express (Westheimer),
394n58
von Werra, Franz, 187–88
Vuillenmeier, Charles, 170
Vulcans, 10, 305–6, 310

Wabasha, 121
Wagoner, Todd D., 152
Walker (HMS), 188
Waller, Maj. Littleton W. T., 150
Walling, Sgt. Neil A., 321
Walter, Abraham, 377n16
Wampanoag, 115
War and International Ethics (La
Croix), 334
war crimes trials
following World War II, 8
Leipzig trials, 233
Nuremberg trials, 233–36
war criminals
in the Civil War, 107–10
Japanese, 239–40
War Hawks, 52–53
War of 1812
burning of Washington, 58, 65–66
cartel for the exchange of prisoners,
337, 351–59
causes of, 52
conclusion of, 59

consequences of, 66–67, 68
cost of, 68
engagements at sea, 54–57
exchange cartel, 60–62
issues of naturalization and
impressment, 52, 59, 62–63
on Lake Erie, 57
land engagements, 53–54, 57–59
POW reprisal crisis, 63–65
treatment of POWs, 59–60, 67
War Hawks, 52–53
War of 1812, The (Mahon), 55
war on terror
in Afghanistan, 306–8
"detainees," 309
neoconservatives and, 305–6
treatment of captives, 10, 309
"war rebels," 148. *See also* guerrillas
War Relocation Administration, 216,
218
Warren, Earl, 216
Warriors, The (Gray), 1–2
Washington, Booker T., 127
Washington, DC, burned in the War of
1812, 58, 65–66
Washington, George
battle of Trenton, 13
British surrender at Yorktown and,
23
chosen to lead the Continental
Army, 37
espionage and, 20
exchange of prisoners and, 12
Gilbert Stewart portrait of, 58
James Moody and, 43
Pennsylvania Quakers and, 46, 47
on POWs from King's Mountain, 19
treatment of British and Hessian
POWs, 11, 12
use of military tribunals, 336
Washita Massacre, 123
"water board," 152
"water cure," 6, 152, 153
Wattenberg, Capt. Jürgen, 189
Wayne, Gen. Anthony, 117
Weimar Republic, 178
Weintraub, Stanley, 257, 263–64

Welch, Richard E., Jr., 146
Wellington, Lord, 59
Westchester Refugees, 41–42
Westheimer, David, 394n58
Westmoreland, Gen. William C., 271, 284, 290, 344
Westphalia, Treaty of, 305
Weyler, Gen. Valeriano, 138
Wheeler, Gen. Joe, 140
Whigs, 32–33, 36
White. W. L., 232
"whitewashed" rebels, 97–98
Whittingham, Richard, 224
Wilhelm IX, 29
Wilkinson, Maj. Gen. James, 64
Willard, Maj. Joseph, 105
Wilson, Woodrow
    Committee on Public Information and, 173
    enemy aliens and, 171, 198
    Espionage Act and, 174
    Frederick Funston and, 387n59
    "peace without victory," 268
    Treaty of Versailles and, 177
    World War I and, 159, 160
Wilton Park, 185
Winchell, Walter, 244
Winder, Gen. William H., 58, 65
Wirtz, Capt. Henry, 93–94, 107–8, 336
Wisdom, Matthew C., 321
Wobblies, 160
Wolfowitz, Paul, 305
women spies, in the Civil War, 105–7, 112
Woods, John C., 235
Wool, Gen. John E., 75
Wootonokanuske, 115
Work, Clemens P., 176
World Court, 168
World Jewish Congress, 228
World War I
    American battles of 1918, 163–66
    American disillusionment with, 177
    American domestic fears during, 160
    American entry, 160
    American immigrant community and, 173

Americans indicted for treason, 400n42
American treatment of dissenters, 173–76
America prior to, 159
battlefield training, 161–62
dangers of surrender on the western Front, 161
end of, 177
German saboteurs, 182–83
great escapers, xv
the Hague Convention and, 160
Japanese treatment of German POWs, 203
legacy of, 178
political prisoners, 174–76, 177
taking prisoners, 162–63
treaties concerning the treatment of POWs, 168–69
treatment of enemy aliens in America, 171–72
See also World War I POWs
World War I POWs
    American attitude toward, 167
    British utilization of, 166–67
    dangers during the act of surrender, 161
    held in America, 169–70
    number of, 160, 161, 166, 169
    repatriation at war's end, 177
    rule on the questioning of, 177–78
    treaties concerning the treatment of, 168–69
    treatment of, 6, 169, 170, 176–77, 340
World War II
    Allied POWs sent from Italy to Germany, 195
    American desertions, 226
    Americans executed as war criminals, 225, 398n6
    American treatment of POWs, 7
    "disarmed enemy forces," 343
    forced repatriation and, 248–49, 343–44
    Geneva Conventions and, 181
    German DEFs, 230–33

World War II (*continued*)
  German saboteurs, 182–84
  great escapers, xv
  internment of Japanese Americans,
    215–19
  Japanese American troops, 219–21
  Japanese treatment of POWs, 7,
    206–8
  military commissions, 336–37
  the Philippines and, 158
  repatriation problem, 8, 226–28,
    245–46
  Eddie Slovik executed for cowardice,
    226
  total civilian and military deaths
    from, 223
  trials of U.S. personnel, 368
  U.S. psychological warfare against
    Japan, 212–13
World War II POWs
  exchanges, 181
  experiences of, 179–81
  Geneva Conventions and, 181, 182
  interrogation and, 181
  kinds of, 182
  labor and, 182
  numbers of, 179
  propagandizing of, 190–92
  treatment of, 8, 182, 342

See also German POWs of World
  War II
Worth, Brig. Gen. William J., 72, 73,
  80, 82
Wyman, Mark, 226
Wyoming Valley, 40–41

XYZ Affair, 49, 174

Yalta agreement, 227, 246, 248–49
Yamasee War, 115
Yankee Tunnel, xv
"yellow" journalism, 137
Yockelson, Mitchel, 172
York, Alvin C., 165
York, battle of, 54
Yorktown, 22–23
Yorktown, battle of, 13, 16
Yoshio, Tamura, 206
Yount, Brig. Gen. Paul F., 259, 260

zeks, 249
"Zero Hour" radio program, 242
Zimmermann, Arthur, 160
Zimmermann telegram, 160
Zionism, 229
Zionist Jews, 246
Zubaydah, Abu, 331